THE PSYCHOLOGY BOOK

BIG IDEAS

THE ARCHITECTURE BOOK
THE ART BOOK
THE ASTRONOMY BOOK
THE BIBLE BOOK
THE BIOLOGY BOOK
THE BLACK HISTORY BOOK
THE BUSINESS BOOK
THE CHEMISTRY BOOK
THE CLASSICAL MUSIC BOOK
THE CRIME BOOK
THE DESIGN BOOK
THE ECOLOGY BOOK
THE ECONOMICS BOOK
THE FEMINISM BOOK
THE HISTORY BOOK
THE ISLAM BOOK
THE LAW BOOK
THE LGBTQ+ HISTORY BOOK
THE LITERATURE BOOK
THE MATH BOOK
THE MEDICINE BOOK
THE MOVIE BOOK
THE MYTHOLOGY BOOK
THE PHILOSOPHY BOOK
THE PHYSICS BOOK
THE POETRY BOOK
THE POLITICS BOOK
THE PSYCHOLOGY BOOK
THE RELIGIONS BOOK
THE SCIENCE BOOK
THE SHAKESPEARE BOOK
THE SHERLOCK HOLMES BOOK
THE SOCIOLOGY BOOK
THE WORLD WAR I BOOK
THE WORLD WAR II BOOK

SIMPLY EXPLAINED

THE PSYCHOLOGY BOOK

DK LONDON

SECOND EDITION

SENIOR EDITOR
Stephanie Farrow

SENIOR ART EDITOR
Nicola Rodway

MANAGING EDITOR
Gareth Jones

SENIOR MANAGING ART EDITOR
Lee Griffiths

SENIOR US EDITOR
Kayla Dugger

EXECUTIVE US EDITOR
Lori Cates Hand

JACKET DESIGNER
Stephanie Cheng Hui Tan

JACKET DESIGN DEVELOPMENT MANAGER
Sophia MTT

SENIOR PRODUCTION CONTROLLER
Rachel Ng

FIRST EDITION

PROJECT ART EDITOR
Amy Orsborne

SENIOR EDITORS
Sam Atkinson, Sarah Tomley

EDITORS
Cecile Landau, Scarlett O'Hara

JACKET DESIGNER
Stephanie Cheng Hui Tan

MANAGING ART EDITOR
Karen Self

MANAGING EDITORS
Esther Ripley, Camilla Hallinan

ART DIRECTOR
Philip Ormerod

ASSOCIATE
PUBLISHING DIRECTOR
Liz Wheeler

PUBLISHING DIRECTOR
Jonathan Metcalf

ILLUSTRATIONS
James Graham

PICTURE RESEARCH
Myriam Megharbi

PRODUCTION EDITOR
Tony Phipps

PRODUCTION CONTROLLER
Angela Graef

DK DELHI

SECOND EDITION

SENIOR ART EDITOR
Chhaya Sajwan

PROJECT EDITOR
Abhijit Dutta

ART EDITOR
Aanchal Singal

ASSISTANT ART EDITOR
Sulagna Das

ASSISTANT PICTURE RESEARCHER
Shubhdeep Kaur

DTP DESIGNERS
Bimlesh Tiwary, Rakesh Kumar

PRODUCTION EDITOR
Umesh Singh Rawat

SENIOR JACKETS COORDINATOR
Priyanka Sharma Saddi

MANAGING EDITOR
Soma B. Chowdhury

SENIOR MANAGING ART EDITOR
Arunesh Talapatra

FIRST EDITION

PROJECT ART EDITOR
Shruti Soharia Singh

SENIOR ART EDITOR
Chhaya Sajwan

ART EDITOR
Priyanka Singh

ASSISTANT ART EDITORS
Niyati Gosain, Nidhi Mehra, Jomin Johny,
Vidit Vashisht

DEPUTY MANAGING ART EDITOR
Priyabrata Roy Chowdhury

MANAGING ART EDITOR
Arunesh Talapatra

SENIOR EDITOR
Monica Saigal

EDITORIAL TEAM
Sreshtha Bhattacharya, Gaurav Joshi

DEPUTY MANAGING EDITOR
Pakshalika Jayaprakash

PRODUCTION MANAGER
Pankaj Sharma

DTP MANAGER/CTS
Balwant Singh

DTP DESIGNERS
Arvind Kumar, Rajesh Singh Adhikari

DTP OPERATOR
Vishal Bhatia

styling by
STUDIO8 DESIGN

This American Edition, 2024
First American Edition, 2011
Published in the United States by
DK Publishing, a division of
Penguin Random House LLC
1745 Broadway, 20th Floor, New York,
NY 10019

24 25 26 27 28 10 9 8 7 6 5 4 3 2 1
001–337262–Jun/2024

Published in Great Britain by Dorling Kindersley Limited

A catalog record for this book
is available from the Library of Congress.

ISBN 978-0-5938-4706-0

Printed and bound in China

www.dk.com

This book was made with Forest Stewardship Council™ certified paper—one small step in DK's commitment to a sustainable future.
Learn more at
www.dk.com/uk/information/sustainability

CONTRIBUTORS

CATHERINE COLLIN

A clinical psychologist, our consultant Catherine Collin is an Associate Professor (Senior Lecturer in Psychological Therapies) at the University of Plymouth. Catherine's interests lie in primary care mental health and cognitive behavior therapy.

NIGEL BENSON

A lecturer in philosophy and psychology, Nigel Benson has written several bestselling books on the subject of psychology, including *Psychology for Beginners* and *Introducing Psychiatry*.

JOANNAH GINSBURG

A clinical psychologist and journalist, Joannah Ginsburg works in community treatment centers in New York City, Boston, Philadelphia, and Dallas and regularly contributes to psychology publications. She is joint author of *This Book has Issues: Adventures in Popular Psychology*.

VOULA GRAND

As a business psychologist, Voula Grand consults to international corporations on leadership and executive performance. Her first novel, *Honor's Shadow* (2011), is about the psychology of secrets, betrayal, and revenge. She is currently writing the sequel, *Honor's Ghost*.

MERRIN LAZYAN

A writer, editor, and classical singer, Merrin Lazyan studied psychology at Harvard University and has worked on several fiction and nonfiction books spanning a broad range of topics.

MARCUS WEEKS

A writer and musician, Marcus Weeks studied philosophy and worked as a teacher before embarking on a career as an author. He has contributed to many books on the arts and popular sciences.

CONTENTS

PSYCHOTHERAPY
THE UNCONSCIOUS DETERMINES BEHAVIOR

COGNITIVE PSYCHOLOGY
THE CALCULATING BRAIN

SOCIAL PSYCHOLOGY
BEING IN A WORLD OF OTHERS

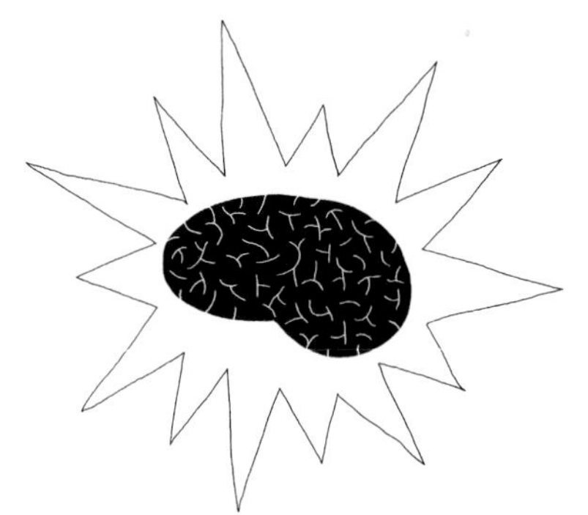

Among all the sciences, psychology is perhaps the most mysterious to the general public and the most prone to misconceptions. Even though its language and ideas have infiltrated everyday culture, most people have only a hazy idea of what the subject is about and what psychologists actually do. For some, psychology conjures up images of people in white coats either staffing an institution for mental disorders or conducting laboratory experiments on rats. Others may imagine a man with a Middle European accent psychoanalyzing a patient on a couch or, if movie scripts are to be believed, plotting to exercise some form of mind control.

Although these stereotypes are an exaggeration, some truth lies beneath them. It is perhaps the huge range of subjects that fall under the umbrella of psychology (and the bewildering array of terms beginning with the prefix "psych-") that creates confusion over what psychology entails; psychologists themselves are unlikely to agree on a single definition of the word. "Psychology" comes from the ancient Greek *psyche*, meaning "soul" or "mind," and *logia*, a "study" or "account," which seems to sum up the broad scope of the subject. Today, the word most accurately describes "the science of mind and behavior."

The new science

Psychology can also be seen as a bridge between philosophy and physiology. Where physiology describes and explains the physical make-up of the brain and nervous system, psychology examines the mental processes that take place within them and how these are manifested in our thoughts, speech, and behavior. Where philosophy is concerned with thoughts and ideas, psychology studies how we come to have them and what they tell us about the workings of our minds.

Like all sciences and all valuations, the psychology of women has hitherto been considered only from the point of view of men.
Karen Horney

All sciences evolved from philosophy, by applying scientific methods to philosophical questions, but the intangible nature of subjects such as consciousness, perception, and memory meant that psychology was slow to transition from philosophical speculation to scientific practice. In some universities, particularly in the US, psychology faculties started out as branches of the philosophy department, while in others, notably in Germany, they were established in the science faculties. Only in the late 19th century did psychology become established as a scientific discipline in its own right.

The founding of the world's first laboratory of experimental psychology by Wilhelm Wundt at the University of Leipzig in 1879 marked the recognition of psychology as a truly scientific subject—one that was venturing into previously unexplored areas of research. During the 20th century, psychology blossomed; all of its major branches and movements evolved. From the start, the agenda was set by the major players in the US and Germany, which led to an inevitable Eurocentric cultural bias and largely precluded the participation of women. As with all sciences, its history is built upon the theories and discoveries of successive generations, with many of the older

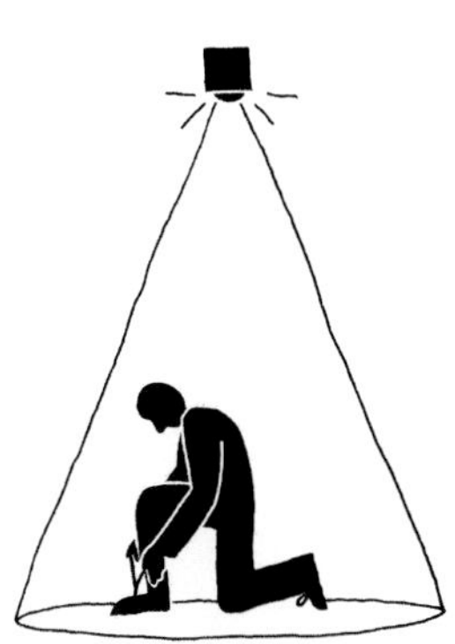

theories remaining relevant to contemporary psychologists. Some areas have been the subject of study from psychology's earliest days, undergoing different interpretations by the various schools of thought, while others have fallen in and out of favor. However, each time they have exerted a significant influence on subsequent thinking and have occasionally spawned completely new fields for exploration.

The simplest way to approach this vast subject for the first time is to look, as we do in this book, at some of its main movements in roughly chronological order: from its roots in philosophical thought; through behaviorism, psychotherapy, and the study of cognitive, social, and developmental psychology; to the psychology of difference.

Two approaches

Even in its earliest days, psychology meant different things to different people. In the US, its roots lay in philosophy, so the approach taken was speculative and theoretical, dealing with concepts such as consciousness and the self. In Europe, the study was rooted in the sciences, so the emphasis was on examining mental processes such as sensory perception and memory under controlled laboratory conditions. However, even the research of these more scientifically oriented psychologists was limited by the introspective nature of their methods: pioneers such as Hermann Ebbinghaus became the subject of their own investigations, effectively restricting the range of topics to those that could be observed in themselves. Although they used scientific methods and their theories laid the foundations for the new science, many in the next generation of psychologists found their processes too subjective and began to look for a more objective methodology.

The experiments of Russian physiologist Ivan Pavlov in the 1890s were key to the development of psychology in both Europe and the US. He proved that animals could be conditioned to produce a response, an idea that developed into a new movement: behaviorism. While behaviorists felt that it was not possible to study mental processes objectively, they found it relatively easy to measure behavior—the manifestation of those processes. They designed experiments that could be conducted under controlled conditions, at first on animals, to gain an insight into human psychology, and later on humans. Their studies concentrated almost exclusively on how behavior is shaped by interaction with the environment; this "stimulus–response" theory became well known through the work of John B. Watson. New learning theories began to spring up in Europe and the US and attracted the interest of the general public.

However, at much the same time as behaviorism began to emerge in the US, a young neurologist in Vienna started to develop a theory of mind that was to overturn contemporary thinking and inspire a very different approach. Based on observation of patients and case histories rather than laboratory experiments, Sigmund Freud's psychoanalytic theory marked a return to the study of subjective experience. Although his ideas seemed shocking at the time, they »

The first fact for us then, as psychologists, is that thinking of some sort goes on.
William James

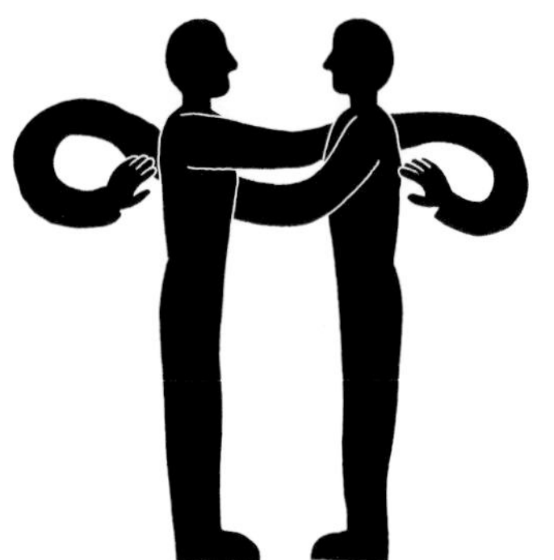

were quickly and widely adopted, and the notion of a "talking cure" continues within the various forms of psychotherapy today.

New fields of study

In the mid-20th century, both behaviorism and psychoanalysis fell out of favor, with a return to the scientific study of mental processes. This marked the beginning of cognitive psychology, a movement with its roots in the holistic approach of Gestalt psychologists, who were interested in studying perception. Their work began to emerge in the US in the years following World War II; by the late 1950s, cognitive psychology had become the predominant approach. The rapidly growing fields of communications and computer science provided psychologists with a useful analogy; they used the model of information processing to develop theories in areas such as attention, perception, memory and forgetting, language and language acquisition, problem-solving and decision-making, and motivation. The converse also soon became the case; the study of mental processes in psychology and neuroscience provided a model for the emerging subject of artificial intelligence and led to fruitful interdisciplinary cross-fertilization. Even psychotherapy, which grew in myriad forms from the original "talking cure," was influenced by the cognitive approach. The emergence of cognitive therapy and cognitive behavioral therapy as alternatives to psychoanalysis led to movements such as humanist psychology, which focused on the qualities unique to human life. These therapists turned their attention from healing the sick to guiding healthy people toward living more meaningful lives and on changing negative attitudes to mental health issues. This has also been partly achieved by a reappraisal of the classification of mental disorders, noting the distinction between psychological health issues and mental illnesses resulting from neurological conditions.

While psychology in its infancy focused mainly on the individual mind and behavior, there was now growing interest in how we interact with others and with our environment: social psychology, as it became known. Like cognitive psychology, it owed much to Gestalt psychologists, especially Kurt Lewin, who had fled from Nazi Germany to the US in the 1930s. Social psychology gathered pace from the mid-20th century, when research revealed intriguing new facts about our attitudes and prejudices, our tendencies toward obedience and conformity, and our reasons for aggression or altruism—all of which were increasingly relevant in a modern world of urban life, ever-faster communications, and the unprecedented influences of the internet and social media.

Freud's continuing influence was felt mainly through the new field of developmental psychology. Initially concerned only with childhood development, study in this area expanded to include change throughout life, from infancy to old age. Researchers charted methods of social, cultural, and moral learning and the ways in which we form attachments. Developmental psychology has had a significant impact on education and training

If the 19th century was the age of the editorial chair, ours is the century of the psychiatrist's couch.
Marshall McLuhan

and has also influenced thinking about the relationship between childhood development and attitudes toward race and gender, especially in an age of changing cultural norms, as well as the ways that the media, computer games, videos, and social media affect development.

Almost every psychological school has touched upon the subject of human uniqueness, but in the late 20th century, this area was recognized as a field in its own right in the psychology of difference. As well as attempting to identify and measure personality traits and the various factors that make up intelligence, psychologists in this growing field examine definitions and measures of normality and abnormality and look at how much our individual differences are a product of our environment or the result of genetic inheritance.

An influential science

The many branches of psychology that exist today cover the whole spectrum of mental life and human and animal behavior. The overall scope has extended to overlap with many other disciplines, including medicine, physiology, neuroscience, computer science, education, sociology, anthropology, and even politics, economics, and the law. Psychology has become perhaps the most diverse of sciences. It continues to influence and be influenced by the other sciences, especially in areas such as neuroscience and genetics. In particular, neuroscience and the technology of brain imaging has enhanced our understanding of the nature of consciousness, sleep, and dreaming and has reopened exploration of the psychology of these phenomena.

Psychology is a huge subject, and its findings concern every one of us. In one form or another, it informs many decisions made in government, business and industry, advertising, and the mass media. It affects us as groups and as individuals, contributing as much to public debate about the ways our societies are or might be structured as it does to diagnosing and treating mental disorders.

The purpose of psychology is to give us a completely different idea of the things we know best.

Paul Valéry

New applications for the ideas and theories of psychology are being found all the time. They have helped provide insights into many aspects of the modern world, not least the vastly increased speed and ubiquity of mass communication; the manipulation of our attitudes and prejudices by governments and media; and the use of misinformation as a propaganda tool by social media "influencers," populist politicians, and even malign foreign powers.

In its short history, psychology has given us many ideas that have changed our ways of thinking and helped us understand ourselves, other people, and the world we live in. It has questioned deeply held beliefs, unearthed unsettling truths, and provided startling insights and solutions to complex questions. Its increasing popularity as a college course is a sign not only of psychology's relevance in the modern world, but also of the enjoyment and stimulation that can be had from exploring the richness and diversity of a subject that continues to examine the mysterious world of the human mind. ■

PHILOSO
ROOTS
PSYCHOLOGY IN THE MAKING

PHICAL

1649

René Descartes publishes *The Passions of the Soul*, claiming that **the body and soul are separate**.

1816

Johann Friedrich Herbart describes a dynamic mind with **a conscious and an unconscious** in *A Text-book in Psychology*.

1819

Abbé Faria investigates **hypnosis** in his book *On the Cause of Lucid Sleep*.

1849

Søren Kierkegaard's book *The Sickness Unto Death* marks the beginning of **existentialism**.

1859

Charles Darwin publishes *On the Origin of the Species*, proposing that all our traits are inherited.

1861

Neurosurgeon **Pierre Paul Broca** discovers that the left and right hemispheres of the brain have separate functions.

1869

Francis Galton's research suggests that **nature is more important than nurture** in *Hereditary Genius*, although his work is subsequently discredited.

1874

Carl Wernicke provides evidence that damage to a specific area of the brain causes the loss of specific skills.

Many of the issues that are examined in modern psychology had been the subject of philosophical debate long before the development of science as we know it today. The very earliest philosophers of ancient Greece sought answers to questions about the world around us, and the way we think and behave. Since then, we have wrestled with ideas of consciousness and self, mind and body, knowledge and perception, how to structure society, and how to live a "good life."

The various branches of science evolved from philosophy, gaining momentum from the 16th century onward, until finally exploding into a "scientific revolution" that ushered in the "Age of Reason" in the 18th century. While these advances in scientific knowledge answered many of the questions about the world we live in, they were still not capable of explaining the workings of our minds. Science and technology did, however, provide models from which we could start asking the right questions, and begin to test theories through the collection of relevant data.

Separating mind and body

One of the key figures in the scientific revolution of the 17th century, the philosopher and mathematician René Descartes, outlined a distinction between mind and body that was to prove critical to the development of psychology. He claimed that all human beings have a dualistic existence—with a separate machinelike body and a nonmaterial, thinking mind, or soul. Later psychological thinkers, among them Johann Friedrich Herbart, were to extend the machine analogy to include the brain as well, describing the processes of the mind as the working of the brain-machine.

The degree to which mind and body are separate became a topic for debate. Scientists wondered how much the mind is formed by physical factors, and how much is shaped by our environment. The "nature versus nurture" debate, fueled by British naturalist Charles Darwin's evolutionary theory and taken up by Francis Galton, brought subjects such as free will, personality, development, and learning to the fore. These areas had not yet been fully described by philosophical inquiry, and were now ripe for scientific study. Meanwhile,

1877
Jean-Martin Charcot produces *Lectures on the Diseases of the Nervous System.*

1879
Wilhelm Wundt founds the **first laboratory** of experimental psychology in Leipzig, Germany.

1883
Emil Kraepelin publishes the *Textbook of Psychiatry.*

1885
Hermann Ebbinghaus details his experiments learning nonsense syllables in his book *Memory.*

1887
G. Stanley Hall publishes the first edition of the *American Journal of Psychology.*

1889
Pierre Janet suggests that **hysteria** involves dissociation and splitting of the personality.

1890
William James, the "father of psychology" publishes *Principles of Psychology.*

1895
Alfred Binet opens the first laboratory of **psychodiagnosis**.

the mysterious nature of the mind was popularized by the discovery of hypnosis, prompting more serious scientists to consider that there was more to the mental life than immediately apparent conscious thought. These scientists set out to examine the nature of the "unconscious," and its influence on our thinking and behavior.

The birth of psychology

Against this background, the modern science of psychology emerged. In 1879, Wilhelm Wundt founded the very first laboratory of experimental psychology at Leipzig University in Germany, and departments of psychology also began to appear in universities across Europe and the US. Just as philosophy had taken on certain regional characteristics, psychology developed in distinct ways in the different centers: in Germany, psychologists such as Wundt, Hermann Ebbinghaus, and Emil Kraepelin took a strictly scientific and experimental approach to the subject; while in the US, William James and his followers at Harvard adopted a more theoretical and philosophical approach. Alongside these areas of study, an influential school of thought was growing in Paris around the work of neurologist Jean-Martin Charcot, who had used hypnosis on sufferers of hysteria. The school attracted psychologists such as Pierre Janet, whose ideas of the unconscious anticipated Freud's psychoanalytic theories.

The final two decades of the 19th century saw a rapid rise in the importance of the new science of psychology, as well as the establishment of a scientific methodology for studying the mind, in much the same way that physiology and related disciplines studied the body. For the first time, the scientific method was applied to questions concerning perception, consciousness, memory, learning, and intelligence, and its practices of observation and experimentation produced a wealth of new theories.

Although these ideas often came from the introspective study of the mind by the researcher or from highly subjective accounts by the subjects of their studies, the foundations were laid for the next generation of psychologists at the turn of the century to develop a truly objective study of mind and behavior and to apply their own new theories to the treatment of mental disorders. ■

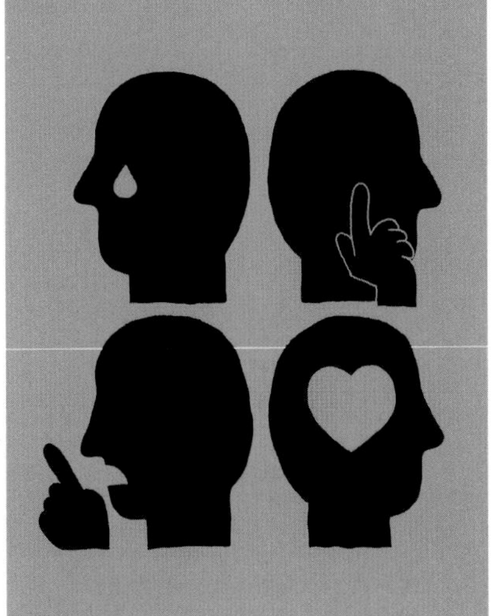

THE FOUR TEMPERAMENTS OF PERSONALITY

GALEN (c.129–c.201 CE)

IN CONTEXT

APPROACH
Humorism

BEFORE
c.400 BCE Greek physician Hippocrates says that the qualities of the four elements are reflected in body fluids.

c.325 BCE Greek philosopher Aristotle names four sources of happiness: sensual (*hedone*), material (*propraietari*), ethical (*ethikos*), and logical (*dialogike*).

AFTER
1543 Anatomist Andreas Vesalius publishes *On the Fabric of the Human Body* in Italy. It illustrates Galen's errors and he is accused of heresy.

1879 Wilhelm Wundt says that temperaments develop in different proportions along two axes: "changeability" and "emotionality."

1947 In *Dimensions of Personality*, Hans Eysenck suggests personality is based on two dimensions.

All things are combinations of **four basic elements**: earth, air, fire, and water.

↓

The **qualities** of these elements can be found in **four corresponding humors** (fluids) that affect the functioning of our bodies.

↓

These humors also affect our emotions and behavior—our **"temperaments."**

↓

Temperamental problems are caused by an **imbalance** in our humors …

↓

… so by **restoring the balance** of our humors, a physician can cure our emotional and behavioral problems.

The Roman philosopher and physician Claudius Galen formulated a concept of personality types based on the ancient Greek theory of humorism, which attempted to explain the workings of the human body.

The roots of humorism go back to Empedocles (c.495–435 BCE), a Greek philosopher who suggested that different qualities of the four basic elements—earth (cold and dry), air (warm and wet), fire (warm and dry), and water (cold and wet)—could explain the existence of all known substances. Hippocrates (460–370 BCE), the "Father of Medicine," developed a medical model based on these elements, attributing their qualities to four fluids within the body. These fluids were called "humors" (from the Latin *umor*, meaning body fluid).

Five hundred years later, Galen expanded the theory of humorism into one of personality; he saw a direct connection between the levels of the humors in the body and emotional and behavioral inclinations—or "temperaments."

Galen's four temperaments—sanguine, phlegmatic, choleric, and melancholic—are based on the balance of humors in the body.

See also: René Descartes 20–21 ▪ Gordon Allport 312–319 ▪ Hans J. Eysenck 322–327 ▪ Walter Mischel 332–333

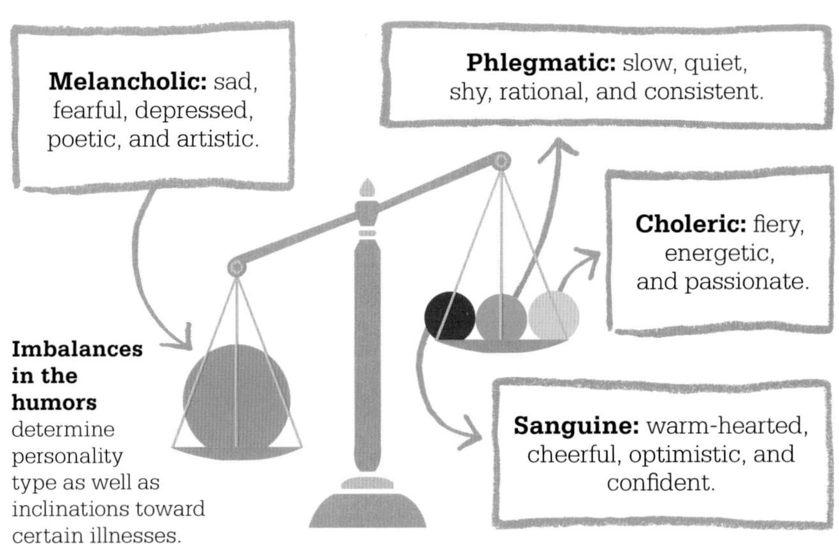

Melancholic: sad, fearful, depressed, poetic, and artistic.
Phlegmatic: slow, quiet, shy, rational, and consistent.
Choleric: fiery, energetic, and passionate.
Imbalances in the humors determine personality type as well as inclinations toward certain illnesses.
Sanguine: warm-hearted, cheerful, optimistic, and confident.

If one of the humors develops excessively, the corresponding personality type begins to dominate. A sanguine person has too much blood (*sanguis* in Latin) and is warm-hearted, cheerful, optimistic, and confident, but can be selfish. A phlegmatic person, suffering from excess phlegm (*phlegmatikós* in Greek), is quiet, kind, cool, rational, and consistent, but can be slow and shy. The choleric (from the Greek *kholé*, meaning bile) personality is fiery, suffering from excess yellow bile. Lastly, the melancholic (from the Greek *melas kholé*), who suffers from an excess of black bile, is recognized by poetic and artistic leanings, which are often also accompanied by sadness and fear.

Imbalance in the humors

According to Galen, some people are born predisposed to certain temperaments. However, since temperamental problems are caused by imbalances of the humors, he claimed they can be cured by diet and exercise. In more extreme cases, cures may include purging and blood-letting. For example, a person acting selfishly is overly sanguine, and has too much blood; this is remedied by cutting down on meat, or by making small cuts into the veins to release blood.

Galen's doctrines dominated medicine until the Renaissance, when they began to decline in the light of better research. In 1543, the physician Andreas Vesalius (1514–1564), practicing in Italy, found more than 200 errors in Galen's descriptions of anatomy, but although Galen's medical ideas were discredited, he later influenced 20th-century psychologists. In 1947, Hans Eysenck concluded that temperament is biologically based, and noted that the two personality traits he identified—neuroticism and extraversion—echoed the ancient temperaments.

Although humorism is no longer part of psychology, Galen's idea that many physical and mental illnesses are connected forms the basis of some modern therapies. ■

Galen

Claudius Galenus, better known as "Galen of Pergamon" (now Bergama in Türkiye) was a Roman physician, surgeon, and philosopher. His father, Aelius Nicon, was a wealthy Greek architect who provided him with a good education and opportunities to travel. Galen settled in Rome and served emperors, including Marcus Aurelius, as principal physician. He learned about trauma care while treating professional gladiators, and wrote more than 500 books on medicine. He believed the best way to learn was through dissecting animals and studying anatomy. However, although Galen discovered the functions of many internal organs, he made mistakes because he assumed that the bodies of animals (such as monkeys and pigs) were exactly like those of humans. There is debate over the date of his death, but Galen was at least 70 when he died.

Key works

c.190 CE *The Temperaments*
c.190 CE *The Natural Faculties*
c.190 CE *Three Treatises on the Nature of Science*

THERE IS A REASONING SOUL IN THIS MACHINE

RENÉ DESCARTES (1596–1650)

IN CONTEXT

APPROACH
Mind/body dualism

BEFORE
4th century BCE Greek philosopher Plato claims that the body is from the material world, but the soul, or mind, is from the immortal world of ideas.

4th century BCE Greek philosopher Aristotle says that the soul and body are inseparable: the soul is the actuality of the body.

AFTER
1710 In *A Treatise Concerning the Principles of Human Knowledge*, Anglo-Irish philosopher George Berkeley claims that the body is merely the perception of the mind.

1904 In *Does Consciousness Exist?* William James asserts that consciousness is not a separate entity but a function of particular experiences.

The mind and the body are **separate**.

The mind (or "soul") is **immaterial**, but seated in the pineal gland of the **brain**.

The body is a **material**, **mechanical machine**.

The mind can **control** the physical body by causing **"animal spirits"** to flow through the nervous system.

The idea that the mind and body are separate and different dates back, in Europe, to Plato and the ancient Greeks, but it was the 17th-century philosopher René Descartes who first described in detail the mind-body relationship. In *De Homine* ("*Man*"), his first philosophical book, written in 1633, he describes the dualism of mind and body: the nonmaterial mind, or "soul," Descartes says, is seated in the brain's pineal gland doing the thinking, while the body is like a machine that operates by "animal spirits," or fluids, flowing through the nervous system to cause movement. This idea had been popularized in the 2nd century by Galen, who attached it to his theory of the humors; but Descartes was the first to describe it in detail, and to emphasize the separation of mind

See also: Galen 18–19 ▪ William James 38–45 ▪ Sigmund Freud 92–99

and body. In a letter to the French philosopher Marin Mersenne, Descartes explains that the pineal gland is the "seat of thought," and so must be the home of the soul, "because the one cannot be separated from the other." This was important, because otherwise the soul would not be connected to any solid part of the body, he said, but only to the psychic spirits.

Descartes imagined the mind and body interacting through an awareness of the animal spirits that were said to flow through the body. The mind, or soul, residing in the pineal gland, located deep within the brain, was thought to sometimes become aware of the moving spirits, which then caused conscious sensation. In this way, the body could affect the mind. Likewise, the mind could affect the body by causing an outflow of animal spirits to a particular region of the body, initiating action.

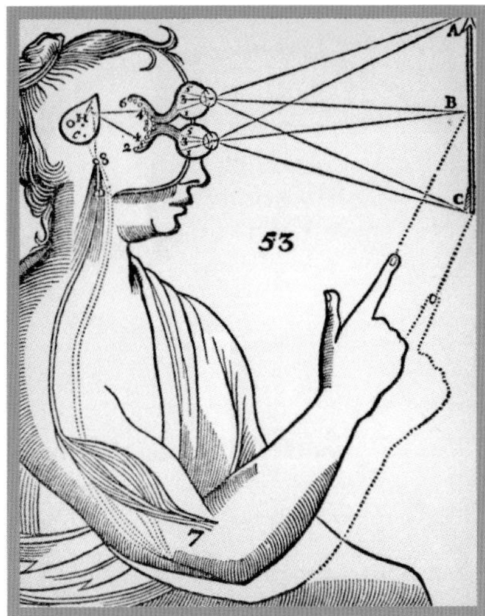

Descartes illustrated the pineal gland, a single organ in the brain ideally placed to unite the sights and sounds of the two eyes and the two ears into one impression.

There is a great difference between mind and body.
René Descartes

An analogy for the mind

Taking his inspiration from the French formal gardens of Versailles, with their hydraulic systems that supply water to the gardens and their elaborate fountains, Descartes describes the spirits of the body operating the nerves and muscles like the force of water, and "by this means to cause motion in all the parts." The fountains were controlled by a fountaineer, and here Descartes found an analogy for the mind. He explained: "There is a reasoning soul in this machine; it has its principal site in the brain, where it is like the fountaineer who must be at the reservoir, whither all the pipes of the machine are extended, when he wishes to start, stop, or in some way alter their actions."

While philosophers still argue as to whether the mind and brain are somehow different entities, most psychologists equate the mind with the workings of the brain. However, in practical terms, the distinction between mental and physical health is a complex one: the two being closely linked when mental stress is said to cause physical illness, or when chemical imbalances affect the brain. ■

René Descartes

René Descartes was born in La Haye en Touraine (now called Descartes), France. He contracted tuberculosis from his mother, who died a few days after he was born, and remained weak his entire life. From the age of eight, he was educated at the Jesuit college of La Flèche, Anjou, where he began the habit of spending each morning in bed, due to his poor health, doing "systematic meditation"—about philosophy, science, and mathematics. From 1612 to 1628, he contemplated, traveled, and wrote. In 1649, he was invited to teach Queen Christina of Sweden, but her early-morning demands on his time, combined with a harsh climate, worsened his health; he died on February 11, 1650. Officially, the cause of death was pneumonia, but some historians believe that he was poisoned to stop the Protestant Christina from converting to Catholicism.

Key works

1637 *Discourse on the Method*
1662 *De Homine* (written 1633)
1647 *The Description of the Human Body*
1649 *The Passions of the Soul*

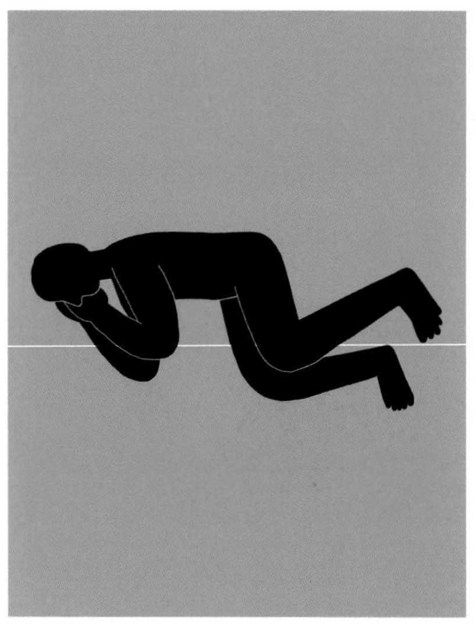

DORMEZ!

ABBE FARIA (1756–1819)

IN CONTEXT

APPROACH
Hypnosis

BEFORE
1027 Persian philosopher and physician Ibn Sînâ (Avicenna) writes about trances in *The Book of Healing.*

1779 German physician Franz Mesmer publishes *A Memoir on the Discovery of Animal Magnetism.*

AFTER
1843 Scottish surgeon James Braid coins the term "neuro-hypnotism" in *Neurypnology.*

1880s French psychologist Emile Coué discovers the placebo effect and publishes *Self-Mastery Through Conscious Autosuggestion.*

1880s Sigmund Freud investigates hypnosis and its apparent power to control unconscious symptoms.

The practice of inducing trance states to promote healing is not new. Several ancient cultures, including those of Egypt and Greece, saw nothing strange about taking their sick to "sleep temples" so they could be cured, while in a sleeplike state, by suggestions from specially trained priests. In 1027, the Persian physician Ibn Sînâ documented the characteristics of the trance state, but its use as a healing therapy was largely abandoned until the German doctor Franz Mesmer reintroduced it in the 18th century. Mesmer's treatment involved manipulating the body's natural, or "animal," magnetism, through the use of magnets and suggestion. After being "mesmerized," or "magnetized," some people suffered a convulsion, after which they claimed to feel better.

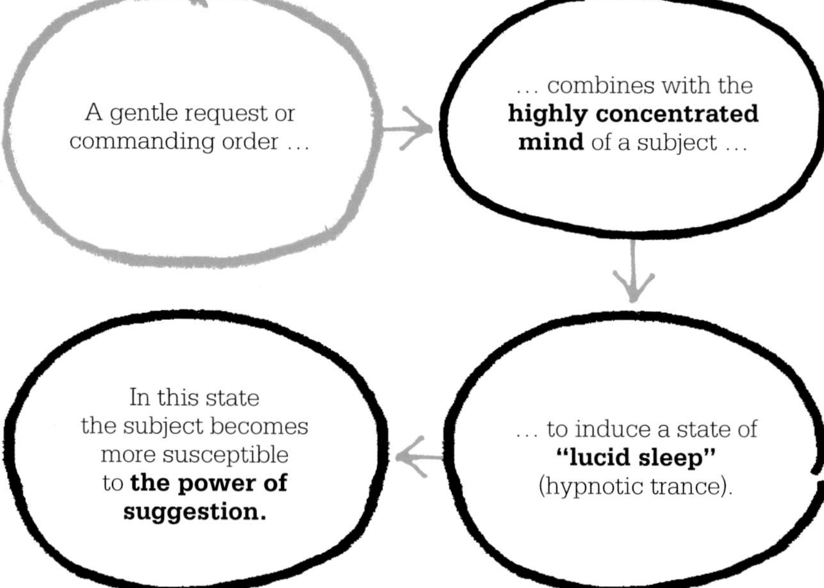

A gentle request or commanding order …
… combines with the **highly concentrated mind** of a subject …
… to induce a state of **"lucid sleep"** (hypnotic trance).
In this state the subject becomes more susceptible to **the power of suggestion.**

See also: Jean-Martin Charcot 30 ▪ Sigmund Freud 92–99 ▪ Carl Jung 102–107 ▪ Milton Erickson 343

A few years later, Abbé Faria, a Portuguese-Goan monk, studied Mesmer's work and concluded that it was "entirely absurd" to think that magnets were a vital part of the process. The truth was even more extraordinary: the power to fall into trance or "lucid sleep" lay entirely with the individuals concerned. No special forces were necessary, because the phenomena relied only upon the power of suggestion.

Lucid sleep

Faria saw his role as a "concentrator," helping his subject get into the right state of mind. In *On The Cause of Lucid Sleep*, he describes his method: "After selecting subjects with the right aptitude, I ask them to relax in a chair, shut their eyes, concentrate their attention, and think about sleep. As they quietly await further instructions, I gently or commandingly say: '*Dormez*!' (Sleep!) and they fall into lucid sleep."

It was from Faria's lucid sleep that the term "hypnosis" was coined in 1843 by the Scottish surgeon James Braid, from the Greek *hypnos*, meaning "sleep" and *osis* meaning "condition." Braid concluded that hypnosis is not a type of sleep but a concentration on a single idea, resulting in heightened suggestibility. After his death, interest in hypnosis largely waned until the French neurologist Jean-Martin Charcot began to use hypnotism systematically in the treatment of traumatic hysteria. This brought hypnosis to the attention of Josef Breuer and Sigmund Freud, who were to question the drive behind the hypnotic self, and discover the power of the unconscious. ■

Franz Mesmer induced trance through the application of magnets, often to the stomach. These were said to bring the body's "animal" magnetism back into a harmonious state.

Nothing comes from the magnetizer; everything comes from the subject and takes place in his imagination.
Abbé Faria

Abbé Faria

Born in Portuguese Goa, José Custódio de Faria was the son of a wealthy heiress, but his parents separated when he was 15. Armed with introductions to the Portuguese court, Faria and his father traveled to Portugal where both trained as priests. On one occasion, the young Faria was asked by the queen to preach in her private chapel. During the sermon, he panicked, but his father whispered, "They are all men of straw—cut the straw!" Faria immediately lost his fear and preached fluently; he later wondered how a simple phrase could so quickly alter his state of mind. He moved to France, where he played a prominent part in the French Revolution and refined his techniques of self-suggestion while imprisoned. Faria became a professor of philosophy, but his theater shows demonstrating "lucid sleep" undercut his reputation; when he died of a stroke in 1819 he was buried in an unmarked grave in Montmartre, Paris.

Key work

1819 *On the Cause of Lucid Sleep*

CONCEPTS BECOME FORCES WHEN THEY RESIST ONE ANOTHER

JOHANN FRIEDRICH HERBART (1776–1841)

IN CONTEXT

APPROACH
Structuralism

BEFORE
1704 German philosopher Gottfried Leibniz discusses *petites perceptions* (perceptions without consciousness) in his *New Essays on Human Understanding*.

1869 German philosopher Eduard von Hartmann publishes his widely read *Philosophy of the Unconscious*.

AFTER
1895 Sigmund Freud and Josef Breuer publish *Studies on Hysteria*, introducing psychoanalysis and its theories of the unconscious.

1912 Carl Jung writes *The Psychology of the Unconscious*, suggesting that all people have a culturally specific collective unconscious.

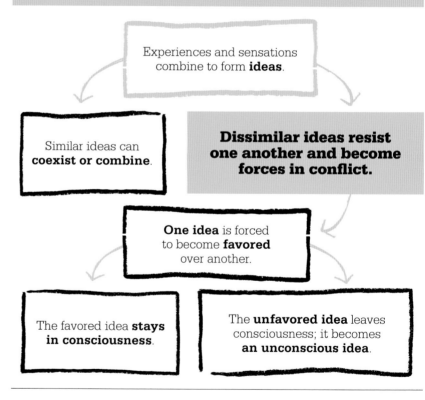

Experiences and sensations combine to form **ideas**.

Similar ideas can **coexist or combine**.

Dissimilar ideas resist one another and become forces in conflict.

One idea is forced to become **favored** over another.

The favored idea **stays in consciousness**.

The **unfavored idea** leaves consciousness; it becomes **an unconscious idea**.

Johann Herbart was a German philosopher who wanted to investigate how the mind works—in particular, how it manages ideas or concepts. Given that we each have a huge number of ideas over the course of our lifetime, how do we not become increasingly confused? It seemed to Herbart that the mind must use some kind of system for differentiating and storing ideas. He also wanted to account for the fact that although ideas exist forever (Herbart thought them incapable of being destroyed), some seem to exist beyond our conscious awareness. The 18th-century German philosopher

See also: Wilhelm Wundt 32–37 ▪ Sigmund Freud 92–99 ▪ Carl Jung 102–107 ▪ Anna Freud 111 ▪ Leon Festinger 166–169

Thoughts and feelings contain energy, according to Herbart, acting on each other like magnets to attract or repel like or unlike ideas.

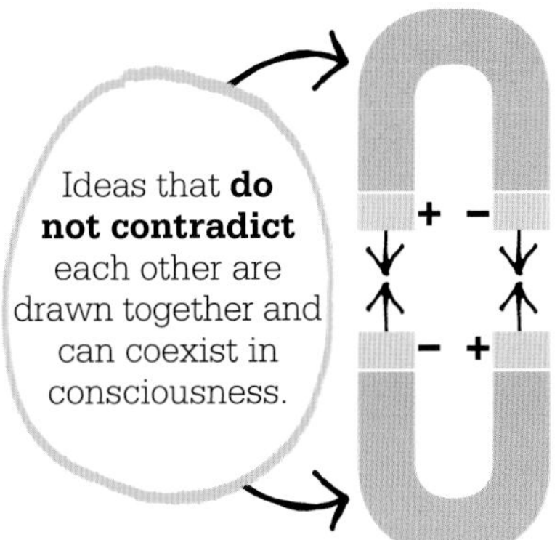

Ideas that **do not contradict** each other are drawn together and can coexist in consciousness.

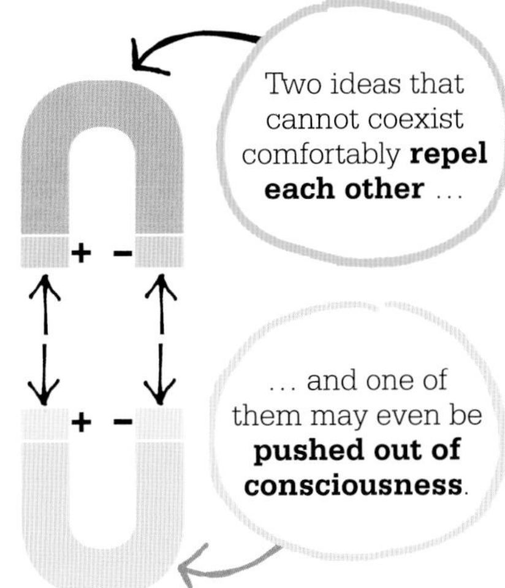

Two ideas that cannot coexist comfortably **repel each other** ...

Gottfried Leibniz was the first to explore the existence of ideas beyond awareness, calling them *petite* ("small") perceptions. As an example, he pointed out that we often recall having perceived something—such as the detail in a scene—even though we are not aware of noticing it at the time. This means that we perceive things and store a memory of them despite the fact that we are unaware of doing so.

Dynamic ideas

According to Herbart, ideas form as information from the senses combines. The term he used for ideas—*Vorstellung*—encompasses thoughts, mental images, and even emotional states. These make up the entire content of the mind, and Herbart saw them not as static but dynamic elements, able to move and interact with one another. Ideas, he said, can attract and combine with other ideas or feelings, or repulse them, rather like magnets. Similar ideas, such as a color and tone, attract each other and combine to form a more complex idea. However, if two ideas are unalike, they may continue to exist without association. This causes them to weaken over time, so that they eventually sink below the "threshold of consciousness." Should two ideas directly contradict one another, "resistance occurs" and "concepts become forces when they resist one another." They repel one another with an energy that propels one of them beyond consciousness, into a place that Herbart referred to as "a state of tendency"; and we now know as "the unconscious."

Herbart saw the unconscious as simply a kind of storage place for weak or opposed ideas. In positing a two-part consciousness, split by a distinct threshold, he was attempting to deliver a structural solution for the management of ideas in a healthy mind. But Sigmund Freud was to see it as a much more complex and revealing mechanism. He combined Herbart's concepts with his own theories of unconscious drives to form the basis of the 20th-century's most important therapeutic approach: psychoanalysis. ■

Johann Friedrich Herbart

Johann Herbart was born in Oldenburg, Germany. He was tutored at home by his mother until he was 12, after which he attended the local school before entering the University of Jena to study philosophy. He spent three years as a private tutor before gaining a doctorate at Göttingen University, where he lectured in philosophy. In 1806, Napoleon defeated Prussia, and in 1809, Herbart was offered Immanuel Kant's chair of philosophy at Königsberg, where the Prussian king and his court were exiled. While moving within these aristocratic circles, Herbart met and married Mary Drake, an English woman half his age. In 1833, he returned to Göttingen University, following disputes with the Prussian government, and remained there as Professor of Philosophy until his death from a stroke, aged 65.

Key works

1808 *General Practical Philosophy*
1816 *A Text-book in Psychology*
1824 *Psychology as Science*

BE THAT SELF WHICH ONE TRULY IS

SØREN KIERKEGAARD (1813–1855)

IN CONTEXT

APPROACH
Existentialism

BEFORE
5th century BCE Socrates states the key to happiness is discovering the "true self."

AFTER
1879 Wilhelm Wundt uses self-analysis as an approach to psychological research.

1913 John B. Watson denounces self-analysis in psychology, stating that "introspection forms no essential part of its methods."

1951 Carl Rogers publishes *Client-centered Therapy*, and in 1961 *On Becoming a Person*.

1960 R. D. Laing's *The Divided Self* redefines "madness," offering existential analysis of inner conflict as therapy.

1996 Rollo May bases his book, *The Meaning of Anxiety*, on Kierkegaard's *The Concept of Anxiety*.

The fundamental question, "Who am I?," has been studied in Europe since the time of the ancient Greeks. Socrates (470–399 BCE) believed the main purpose of philosophy is to increase happiness through analyzing and understanding oneself, famously saying: "The unexamined life is not worth living." Søren Kierkegaard's book *The Sickness Unto Death* (1849) offers self-analysis as a means to understanding the problem of "despair," which he

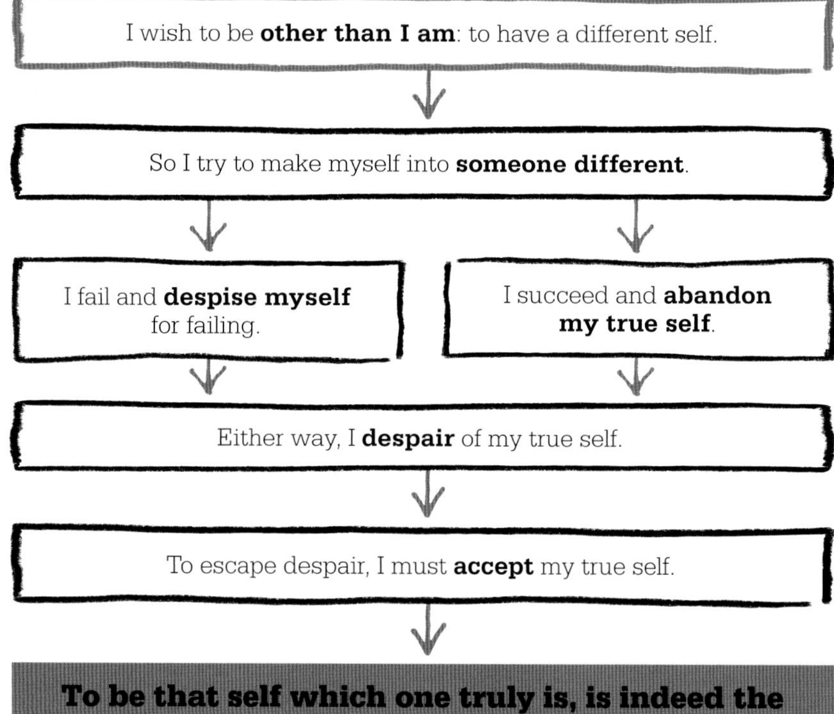

I wish to be **other than I am**: to have a different self.
So I try to make myself into **someone different**.
I fail and **despise myself** for failing.
I succeed and **abandon my true self**.
Either way, I **despair** of my true self.
To escape despair, I must **accept** my true self.
To be that self which one truly is, is indeed the opposite of despair.

See also: Wilhelm Wundt 32–37 ▪ William James 38–45 ▪ Carl Rogers 130–137 ▪ Rollo May 141 ▪ R. D. Laing 150–151

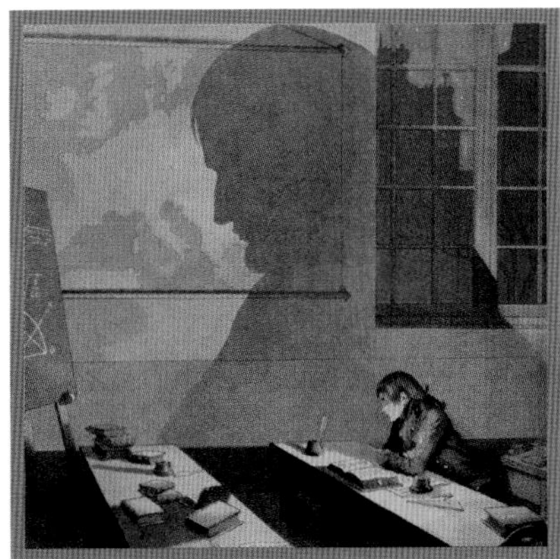

Napoleon's overreaching ambition for power, as depicted in this painting of him as a student, led him to lose sight of his true self and all-too-human limitations, and ultimately to despair.

considered to stem not from depression, but rather from the alienation of the self.

Kierkegaard described several levels of despair. The lowest, and most common, stems from ignorance: people who have the wrong idea about what "self" is and are unaware of the existence or nature of their potential self. Such ignorance is close to bliss, and so inconsequential that Kierkegaard was not even sure it could be counted as despair. Real desperation arises, he suggested, with growing self-awareness, and the deeper levels of despair stem from an acute consciousness of the self, coupled with a profound dislike of it. When something goes wrong, such as failing an exam to qualify as a doctor, a person may seem to be despairing over something that has been lost. But on closer inspection, Kierkegaard argues, it becomes obvious that they are not really despairing of the thing (failing an exam) but of themselves. The self that failed to achieve a goal has become intolerable. The person wanted to become a different self (a doctor), but is now stuck with a failed self and in despair.

Abandoning the real self

Kierkegaard took the example of a man who wanted to become an emperor, and pointed out that ironically, even if this man did somehow achieve his aim, he would have effectively abandoned his old self. In both his desire and accomplishment, he wants to "be rid of" his self. This disavowal of the self is painful: despair is overwhelming when a man wants to shun himself—when he "does not possess himself; he is not himself."

However, Kierkegaard did offer a solution. He concluded that people can find peace and inner harmony by finding the courage to be their true selves rather than wanting to be someone else. "To will to be that self which one truly is, is indeed the opposite of despair," he said. He believed that despair evaporates when we stop denying who we really are and attempt to uncover and accept our true nature.

Kierkegaard's emphasis on individual responsibility, and the need to find one's true essence and purpose in life, is frequently regarded as the beginning of existentialist philosophy. His ideas led directly to R. D. Laing's use of existential therapy, and have influenced the humanistic therapies practiced by clinical psychologists such as Carl Rogers. ■

Søren Kierkegaard

Søren Kierkegaard was born to an affluent Danish family and raised as a strict Lutheran. He studied theology and philosophy at Copenhagen University. When he came into a sizable inheritance, he decided to devote his life to philosophy, but ultimately this left him dissatisfied. "What I really need to do," he said, "is to get clear about what I am to do, not what I must know." In 1840, he became engaged to Regine Olsen, but broke off the engagement, saying that he was unsuited to marriage. His general state of melancholy had a profound effect on his life. A solitary figure, his main recreational activities included walking the streets to chat with strangers and taking long carriage rides alone into the countryside.

Kierkegaard collapsed in the street on October 2, 1855, and died on November 11 in Friedrich's Hospital, Copenhagen.

Key works

1843 *Fear and Trembling*
1843 *Either/Or*
1844 *The Concept of Anxiety*
1849 *The Sickness Unto Death*

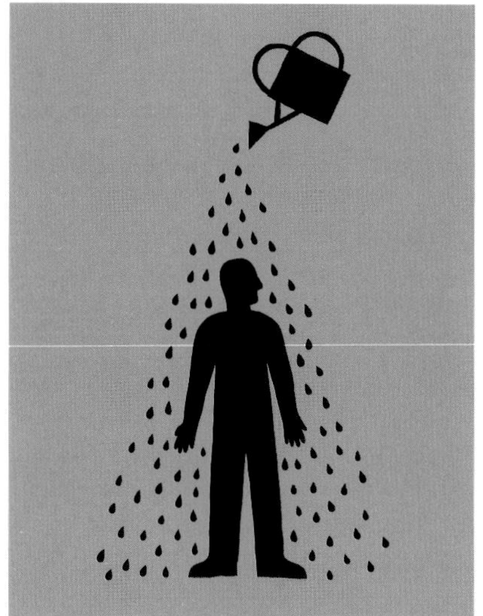

PERSONALITY IS COMPOSED OF NATURE AND NURTURE

FRANCIS GALTON (1822–1911)

IN CONTEXT

APPROACH
Bio-psychology

BEFORE
1690 British philosopher John Locke proposes that the mind of every child is a tabula rasa, or blank slate, and hence we are all born equal.

1859 Biologist Charles Darwin suggests that all human development is the result of adaptation to the environment.

1890 William James claims that people have genetically inherited individual tendencies, or "instincts."

AFTER
1925 Behaviorist John B. Watson says there is "no such thing as inheritance of capacity, talent, temperament, or mental constitution."

1940s Nazi Germany seeks to create a "master Aryan race" through eugenics.

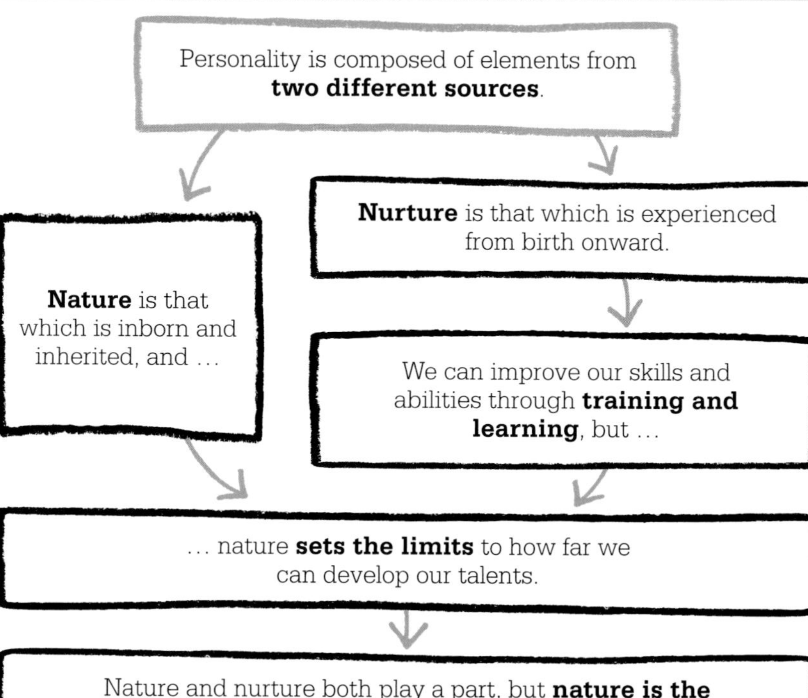

Personality is composed of elements from **two different sources**.
Nature is that which is inborn and inherited, and …
Nurture is that which is experienced from birth onward.
We can improve our skills and abilities through **training and learning**, but …
… nature **sets the limits** to how far we can develop our talents.
Nature and nurture both play a part, but **nature is the determining factor**.

Francis Galton counted many gifted individuals among his relatives, including the evolutionary biologist Charles Darwin. So it's not surprising that Galton was interested in the extent to which abilities are either inborn or learned. He was the first person to identify "nature" and "nurture" as two separate influences whose effects could be measured and compared, maintaining that these two elements alone were responsible for determining personality. In 1869, he used his own family tree, as well as those of "judges, statesmen,

See also: G. Stanley Hall 46–47 ▪ John B. Watson 66–71 ▪ Zing-Yang Kuo 75 ▪ Eleanor E. Maccoby 292–293 ▪ Raymond Cattell 320–321

Characteristics cling to families.
Francis Galton

commanders, scientists, literary men … diviners, oarsmen, and wrestlers," to research inherited traits for his book *Hereditary Genius*. As predicted, he found more talented individuals in certain families than in the general population. However, he could not safely attribute this to nature alone, as there were also conferred benefits from growing up in a privileged home environment. Galton himself grew up in a wealthy household with access to unusually good educational resources.

A necessary balance

Galton proposed a number of other studies, including the first large survey by questionnaire, which was sent out to members of the Royal Society to inquire about their interests and affiliations. Publishing his results in *English Men of Science*, he claimed that where nature and nurture are forced to compete, nature triumphs. External influences can make an impression, he says, but nothing can "efface the deeper marks of individual character." However, he insists that both nature and nurture are essential in forming personality, since even the highest natural talents may be "starved by defective nurture." Intelligence, he says, is inherited but must be fostered through education. In 1875, Galton undertook a study of 159 pairs of twins. He found that they did not follow the "normal" distribution of similarity between siblings, in which they are moderately alike, but were always extremely similar or extremely dissimilar. What really surprised him was that the degree of similarity never changed over time. He had expected a shared upbringing to lessen dissimilarity between twins as they grew up, but found that this was not the case. Nurture seemed to play no role at all.

The "nature–nurture debate" continues to this day. Some of Galton's theories, including his controversial notion—now known as eugenics—that people could be "bred" like horses to promote certain characteristics have become linked with and used to promote racist and ableist views. Many psychologists prefer to believe that every baby is a tabula rasa, or blank slate, and that we are all born equal, recognizing that nature and nurture are both crucially important in human development and interact in complex ways. ■

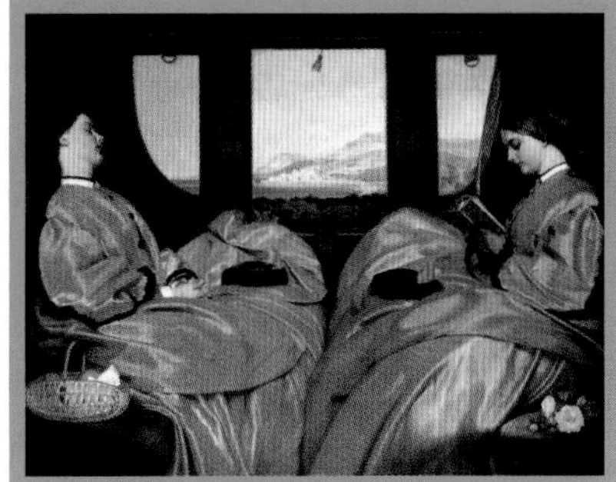

Galton's study of twins looked for resemblances in many ways, including height, weight, hair and eye color, and disposition. Handwriting was the only aspect in which twins always differed.

Francis Galton

Sir Francis Galton was a polymath who wrote prolifically on many subjects, including anthropology, criminology (classifying fingerprints), geography, meteorology, biology, and psychology. Born in Birmingham, England, into a wealthy Quaker family, he was a child prodigy. He studied medicine in London and Birmingham, then mathematics at Cambridge, but his study was cut short by a mental breakdown, worsened by his father's death in 1844.

Galton turned to traveling and inventing. His marriage in 1853 to Louisa Jane Butler lasted 43 years, but was childless. He devoted his life to measuring physical and psychological characteristics, devising mental tests, and writing. He received many honors, including several honorary degrees and a knighthood, but his work was subsequently overshadowed by association with racist and ableist views.

Key works

1869 *Hereditary Genius*
1874 *English Men of Science: Their Nature and Nurture*
1875 *The History of Twins*

THE LAWS OF HYSTERIA ARE UNIVERSAL

JEAN-MARTIN CHARCOT (1825–1893)

IN CONTEXT

APPROACH
Neurological science

BEFORE
1900 BCE The Egyptian Kahun Papyrus recounts behavioral disturbances in women caused by a "wandering uterus."

c.400 BCE Greek physician Hippocrates invents the term "hysteria" for certain women's illnesses in his book, *On the Diseases of Women.*

1662 English physician Thomas Willis performs autopsies on "hysterical" women, and finds no sign of uterine pathology.

AFTER
1883 Alfred Binet joins Charcot at the Salpêtrière Hospital in Paris, and later writes about Charcot's use of hypnotism to treat hysteria.

1895 Sigmund Freud, a former student of Charcot, publishes *Studies on Hysteria.*

Known as the founder of modern neurology, French physician Jean-Martin Charcot was interested in the relationship between psychology and physiology. During the 1860s and 1870s, he studied "hysteria," a term then used to describe extreme emotional behavior in women, thought to be caused by problems with the uterus (*hystera* in Greek). Symptoms included excessive laughing or crying, wild bodily movements and contortions, fainting, paralysis, convulsions, and temporary blindness and deafness.

From observing thousands of cases of hysteria at the Salpêtrière Hospital in Paris, Charcot defined "The Laws of Hysteria," believing that he understood the disease completely. He claimed that hysteria was a lifelong, inherited condition and its symptoms were triggered by shock. In 1882, Charcot stated: "In the [hysterical] fit … everything unfolds according to the rules, which are always the same; they are valid for all countries, for all epochs, for all races, and are, in short, universal."

Charcot suggested that hysteria's similarity to a physical disease warranted a search for a biological cause, but his contemporaries dismissed his ideas. Some even believed that Charcot's "hysterics" were merely acting out behavior that Charcot had suggested to them. But one student of Charcot, Sigmund Freud, was convinced of hysteria's status as a physical illness, and was intrigued by it. It is the first disease Freud describes in his theory of psychoanalysis. ■

Charcot gave lectures on hysteria at the Salpêtrière Hospital in Paris. He believed hysteria always followed ordered, clearly structured phases, and could be cured by hypnotism.

See also: Alfred Binet 50–53 ▪ Pierre Janet 54–55 ▪ Sigmund Freud 92–99

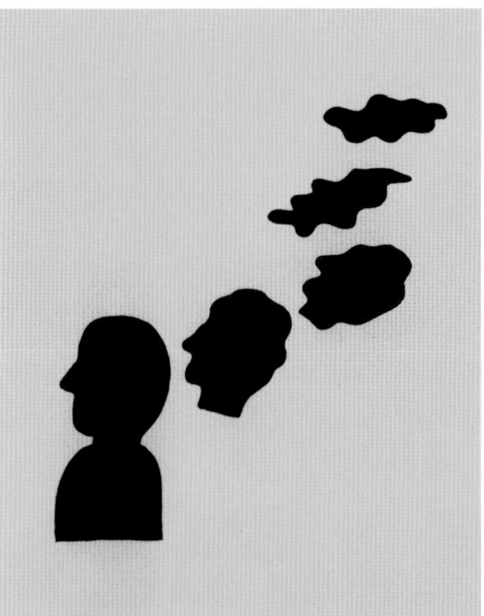

A PECULIAR DESTRUCTION OF THE INTERNAL CONNECTIONS OF THE PSYCHE

EMIL KRAEPELIN (1856–1926)

IN CONTEXT

APPROACH
Medical psychiatry

BEFORE
c.50 BCE Roman poet and philosopher Lucretius uses the term "dementia" to mean "being out of one's mind."

1874 Wilhelm Wundt, Kraepelin's tutor, publishes *Principles of Physiological Psychology.*

AFTER
1908 Swiss psychiatrist Eugen Bleuler coins the term "schizophrenia," from the Greek words *skhizein* (to split) and *phren* (the mind).

1948 The World Health Authority (WHO) includes Kraepelin's classifications of mental illnesses in its International Classification of Diseases (ICD).

1950s Chlorpromazine, the first antipsychotic drug, is used to treat schizophrenia.

German physician Emil Kraepelin believed that the origins of most mental illnesses are biological, and he is often regarded as the founder of modern medical psychiatry. In his *Textbook of Psychiatry*, published in 1883, Kraepelin offered a detailed classification of mental illnesses, including "dementia praecox," meaning "early dementia," to distinguish it from late-onset dementia, such as Alzheimer's.

Schizophrenia

In 1893, Kraepelin described dementia praecox, now called schizophrenia, as consisting "of a series of clinical states which hold as their common a peculiar destruction of the internal connections of the psychic personality." He observed that the illness, characterized by confusion and antisocial behavior, often starts in the late teens or early adulthood. Kraepelin later divided it into four subcategories. The first, "simple" dementia, is marked by slow decline and withdrawal. The second, paranoia, manifests in patients as a state of fear and persecution; they report being "spied upon" or "talked about." The third, hebephrenia, is marked by incoherent speech, and often by inappropriate emotional reactions and behavior, such as laughing loudly at a sad situation. The fourth category, catatonia, is marked by extremely limited movement and expression, often in the form of either rigidness, such as sitting in the same position for hours, or excessive activity, such as rocking backward and forward repeatedly.

Kraepelin's classification still forms the basis of schizophrenia diagnosis. In addition, postmortem investigations have shown that there are biochemical and structural brain abnormalities, as well as impairments of brain function, in schizophrenia sufferers. Kraepelin's belief that a great number of mental illnesses are strictly biological in origin exerted a lasting influence on the field of psychiatry, and many mental disorders are still managed with medication today. ■

See also: Wilhelm Wundt 32–37 ▪ Sigmund Freud 92–99 ▪ Carl Jung 102–107 ▪ R. D. Laing 150–151

THE BEGINNINGS OF THE MENTAL LIFE DATE FROM THE BEGINNINGS OF LIFE

WILHELM WUNDT (1832–1920)

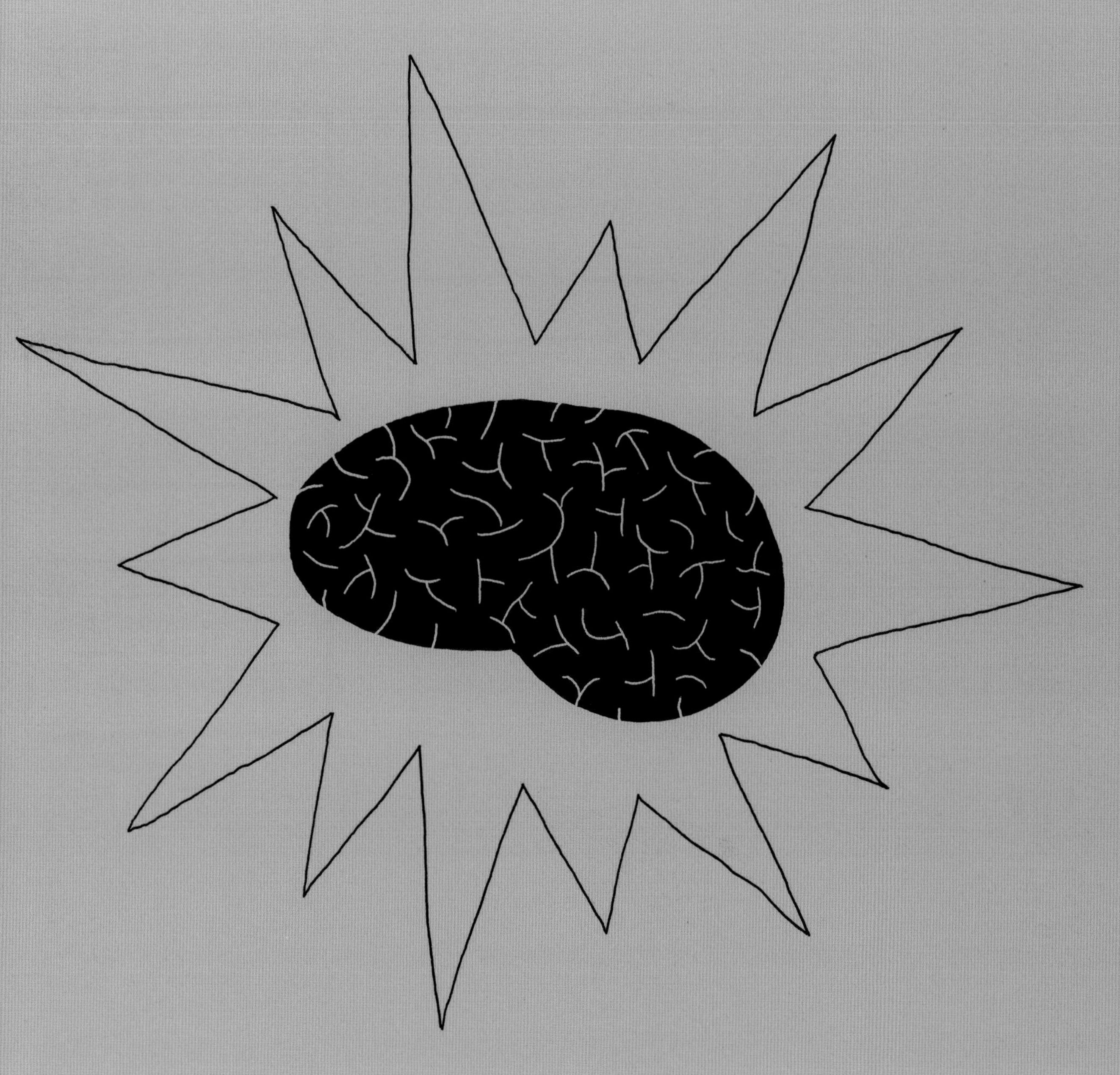

IN CONTEXT

APPROACH
Experimental psychology

BEFORE
5th century BCE Ancient Greek philosophers Aristotle and Plato claim that animals have a low-level, distinctly nonhuman consciousness.

1630s René Descartes says that animals are automata without feeling.

1859 British biologist Charles Darwin links humans to animal ancestors.

AFTER
1949 Konrad Lorenz changes the way people see animals by showing their similarities to humans in *King Solomon's Ring*.

2001 American zoologist Donald Griffin argues in *Animal Minds* that animals have a sense of the future, complex memory, and perhaps consciousness itself.

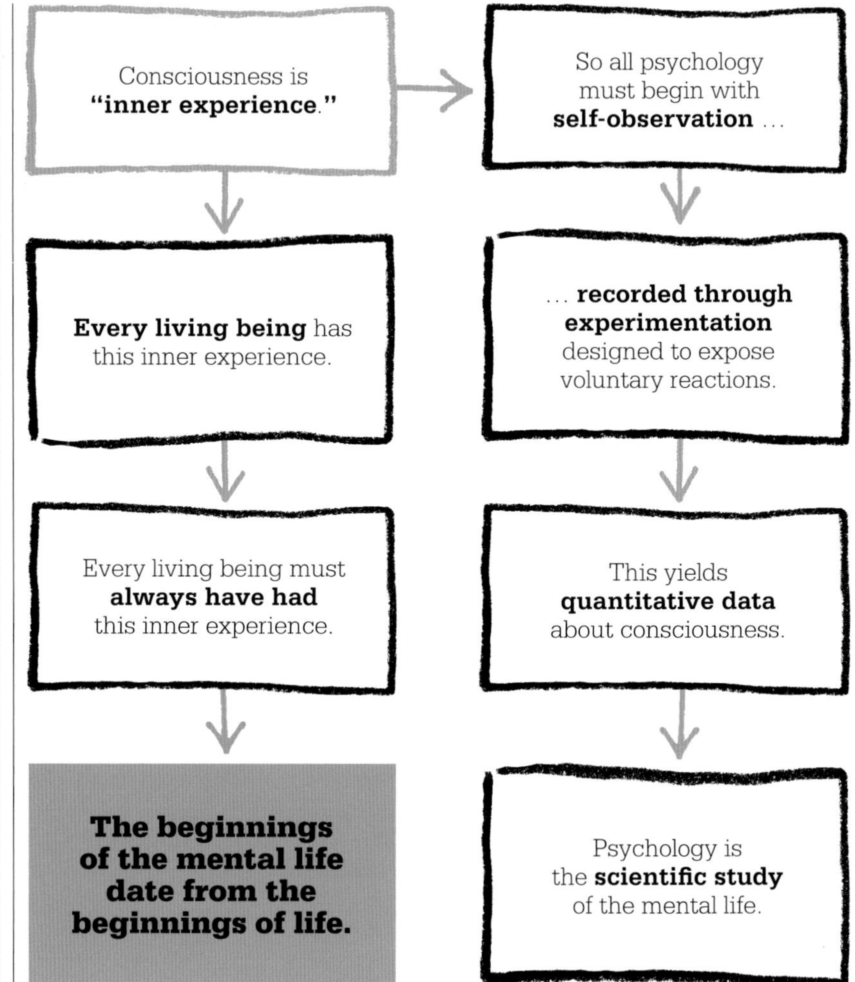

Consciousness is "inner experience."
So all psychology must begin with self-observation ...
Every living being has this inner experience.
... recorded through experimentation designed to expose voluntary reactions.
Every living being must always have had this inner experience.
This yields quantitative data about consciousness.
The beginnings of the mental life date from the beginnings of life.
Psychology is the scientific study of the mental life.

The idea that nonhuman animals have minds and are capable of some form of thought dates back, in Europe, to the ancient Greek philosophers. Aristotle believed that there are three kinds of mind: plant, animal, and human. The plant mind is concerned only with nutrition and growth. The animal mind has these functions, but can also experience sensations, such as pain and desire, as well as initiating motion. The human mind can do all this and reason; Aristotle claims that only humans have self-awareness and are capable of higher-level cognition. The similarity of humans to animals was a critical issue for philosophers, but even more so for psychologists. In the 17th century, the French philosopher René Descartes claimed that animals are no more than reflex-driven, complex machines. If Descartes was correct, observing animals could tell us nothing about our own behavior. However, when Charles Darwin asserted some 200 years later that humans are linked to other animals genetically and that consciousness operates from the creatures at the very lowest end of the evolutionary scale to ourselves, it became clear that experiments on animals might be revealing. This was the position held by the German physician, philosopher, and psychologist Wilhelm Wundt, who described a continuum of life from even the smallest animals to ourselves. In his book *Principles of Physiological Psychology*, he claimed that consciousness is a universal possession of all living organisms, and has been since the evolutionary process began.

To Wundt, the very definition of life includes having some kind of mind. He declared: "From the standpoint of observation, then, we must regard it as a highly probable

See also: René Descartes 20–21 ▪ William James 38–45 ▪ Edward Thorndike 62–65 ▪ John B. Watson 66–71 ▪ B. F. Skinner 78–85

The beginnings of a differentiation of mental function can be found even in the protozoa.
Wilhelm Wundt

hypothesis that the beginnings of the mental life date from as far back as the beginnings of life at large. The question of the origin of mental development thus resolves itself into the question of the origin of life." Wundt went on to say that even simple organisms such as protozoa have some form of mind. This last claim is surprising today, when few people would expect a single-celled animal to demonstrate even simple mental abilities, but it was even more surprising when first stated more than 100 years ago.

Wundt was eager to test out his theories, and he is often called "the father of experimental psychology" because he set up the world's first formal laboratory of experimental psychology in Leipzig University, Germany, in 1879. He wanted to carry out systematic research on the mind and behavior of humans, initially through subjecting the basic sensory processes to close examination. His laboratory inspired other universities in the US and Europe to set up psychology departments, many of which were modeled on his original laboratory and were led by pupils such as Edward Titchener and James Cattell.

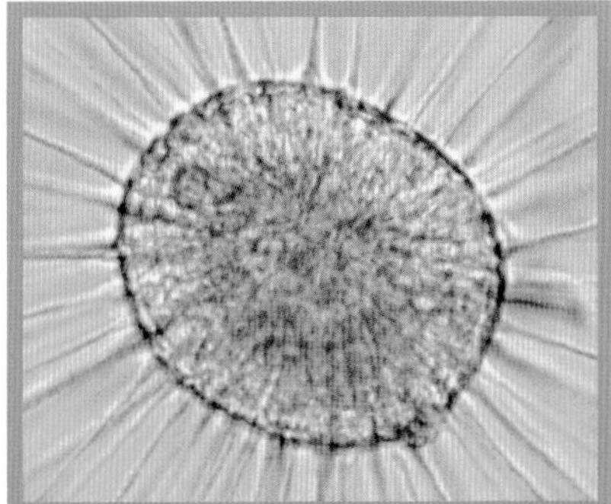

Even single-celled organisms have some form of consciousness, according to Wundt. He suggested the amoeba's ability to devour food items indicates a continuity of mental processes.

Observing behavior

Wundt believed that "the exact description of consciousness is the sole aim of experimental psychology." Although he understood consciousness as an "inner experience," he was only interested in the "immediately real" or apparent form of this experience. This ultimately led him to the study of behavior, which could be studied and quantified by "direct observation."

Wundt said that there are two types of observation: external and internal. External observation is used to record events that are visible in the external world and is useful in assessing relationships such as cause and effect on physical bodies—for example, in stimulus and response experiments. If a nerve fiber in a dead frog is given a small electric shock, the connecting muscles twitch, causing the legs to move. The fact that this happens even in a dead animal illustrates that such movements can occur without any consciousness. In living creatures, such actions are the basis of the automatic behavior that we call "reflexes," such as immediately moving your hand when you touch something hot.

Wundt's second type of observation, termed "introspection" or "self-observation," is internal observation. This involves noticing and recording internal events such as thoughts and feelings. It is crucial in research because it provides information about how the mind is working. Wundt was interested in the relationship between the inner and outer worlds, which he did not see as mutually exclusive, but as interactive, describing it as »

Wundt's laboratory set the style for psychology departments around the world. His experiments moved psychology out of the domain of philosophy and into science.

"physical and psychical." He began to concentrate on the study of human sensations, such as the visual sensation of light, because these are the agencies that link the external physical world and the internal mental world.

In one experiment, Wundt asked individuals to report on their sensations when shown a light signal—which was standardized to a specific color and a certain level of brightness, and shone for a fixed length of time. This ensured that each participant experienced exactly the same stimulus, enabling responses of different participants to be compared and the experiment to be repeated at a later date, if required. In insisting upon this possibility for replication, Wundt set the standard for all future psychological experiments.

In his sensory experiments, Wundt set out to explore human consciousness in a measurable way. He refused to see it as an unknowable, subjective experience that is unique to each individual. In the light-response experiments, he was particularly interested in the amount of time between a person receiving some form of stimulus and making a voluntary reaction to it (rather than an involuntary one), and he used various instruments to measure this response exactly. He was also just as interested to hear what his participants reported in common as he was in apparent individual differences.

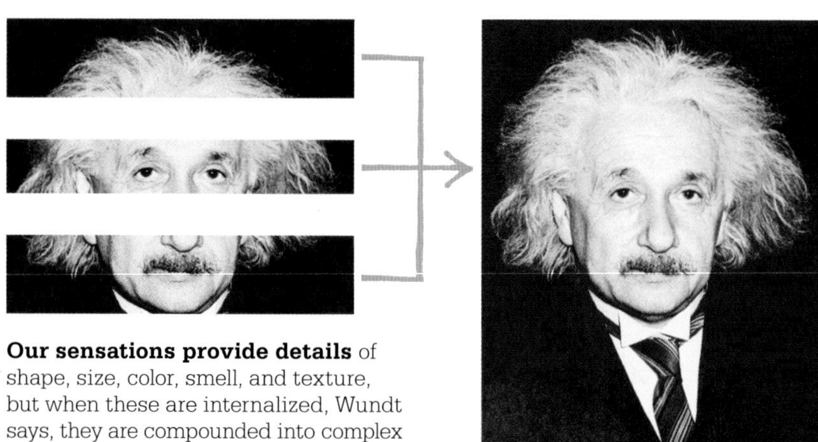

Our sensations provide details of shape, size, color, smell, and texture, but when these are internalized, Wundt says, they are compounded into complex representations, such as a face.

The exact description of consciousness is the sole aim of experimental psychology.
Wilhelm Wundt

Pure sensations, Wundt suggested, have three components: quality, intensity, and "feeling-tone." For example, a certain perfume may have a sweet odor (quality) that is distinct but faint (intensity) and is pleasant to smell (feeling-tone), while a dead rat might give off a nauseating (quality), strong (intensity) stench (feeling-tone). All consciousness originates in sensations, he said, but these are not internalized as "pure" sensory data; they are perceived as already collected or compounded into representations, such as a dead rat. Wundt called these "images of an object or of a process in the external world." So, for example, if we see a face with certain features—mouth shape, eye color, nose size, and so on—we may recognize the face as a person we know.

Categories of consciousness

Based on his sensory experiments, Wundt claimed that consciousness consists of three major categories of actions—representation, willing, and feeling—which together form an impression of a unitary flow of events. Representations are either "perceptions," if they represent an image in the mind of an object perceived in the external world (such as a tree within eyesight), or "intuitions" if they represent a subjective activity (such as remembering a tree, or imagining a unicorn). He named the process through which a perception or intuition becomes clear in consciousness "apperception." So, for example, you may perceive a sudden loud noise and then apperceive that it is a warning sign, meaning that you are about to be hit by a car if you don't get out of the way quickly enough.

The willing category of consciousness is characterized by the way it intervenes in the external world; it expresses our volition, or "will," from raising an arm to choosing to wear red. This form of consciousness is beyond experimental control or measurement. However, Wundt found that the third category of consciousness, feeling, could be measured through subjective reports from experimental participants, or through measuring levels of behavior such as tension and relaxation or excitement.

Cultural psychology

For Wundt, the psychological development of a person is determined not only by sensations but also by complex social and cultural influences, which cannot be replicated or controlled in an experimental situation. He included religion, language, myths, history, art, laws, and customs among these influences, discussing them in a 10-volume work, *Cultural Psychology*, which he wrote during the last 20 years of his life.

Wundt saw language as an especially important part of culture's contribution to consciousness. Any verbal communication begins with a "general impression," or unified idea of something we wish to say. Having "apperceived" this general starting point, we then choose words and sentences to express it. While speaking, we monitor the accuracy of the intended meaning. We might say, "No, that's not right, I mean ...," and then choose a different word or phrase to express ourselves better. Whoever is listening has to understand the meaning that the speaker is trying to convey, but the actual words may not be as important as the general impression, especially if strong emotions are involved. As evidence of the fact that we use this process, Wundt points out that we often remember the general meaning of what a person has said long after we've forgotten the specific words that were used.

In the course of normal speaking ... the will is continuously directed to bringing the course of ideas and the articulatory movements into harmony with each other.
Wilhelm Wundt

The ability to use true language, as opposed to just exchanging limited signs and signals, is today considered by many psychologists to be a key difference between human beings and the rest of the animal kingdom. There may be a few exceptions, including nonhuman primates such as chimpanzees, but language is generally considered to be a human ability that is very important in consciousness.

Consciousness and species

The definition of consciousness continues to be debated, but it has not fundamentally changed since Wundt. The level of consciousness within animals has not yet been established, and this has led to the formation of special Codes of Ethics for animal experiments, intensive farming, and blood sports such as fox hunting and bull fighting. Of particular concern is whether animals experience discomfort, fear, and pain in ways that resemble the form in which we feel them ourselves. The fundamental question of which animals have self-awareness or consciousness remains unanswered, although few psychologists today would assume, as Wundt did, that it applies even to the microscopic protozoa. ■

Wilhelm Wundt

Born in Baden (now Mannheim), Germany, Wilhelm Wundt was the fourth child in a family with a long history of intellectual achievement. His father was a Lutheran minister. The young Wundt was allowed little time for play, as he was pushed through a rigorous educational regime, attending a strict Catholic school from the age of 13. He went on to study at the universities of Berlin, Tübingen, and Heidelberg, graduating in medicine in 1856.

Two years later, Wundt became assistant to the physician Hermann von Helmholtz, who was famous for his work on visual perception. While at Heidelberg, Wundt started teaching the world's first course in experimental psychology, and in 1879 opened the first psychology laboratory. Wundt wrote over 490 works and was probably the world's most prolific scientific writer.

Key works

1863 *Lectures on the Mind of Humans and Animals*
1896 *Outline of Psychology*
1873 *Principles of Physiological Psychology*

WE KNOW THE MEANING OF "CONSCIOUSNESS" SO LONG AS NO ONE ASKS US TO DEFINE IT

WILLIAM JAMES (1842–1910)

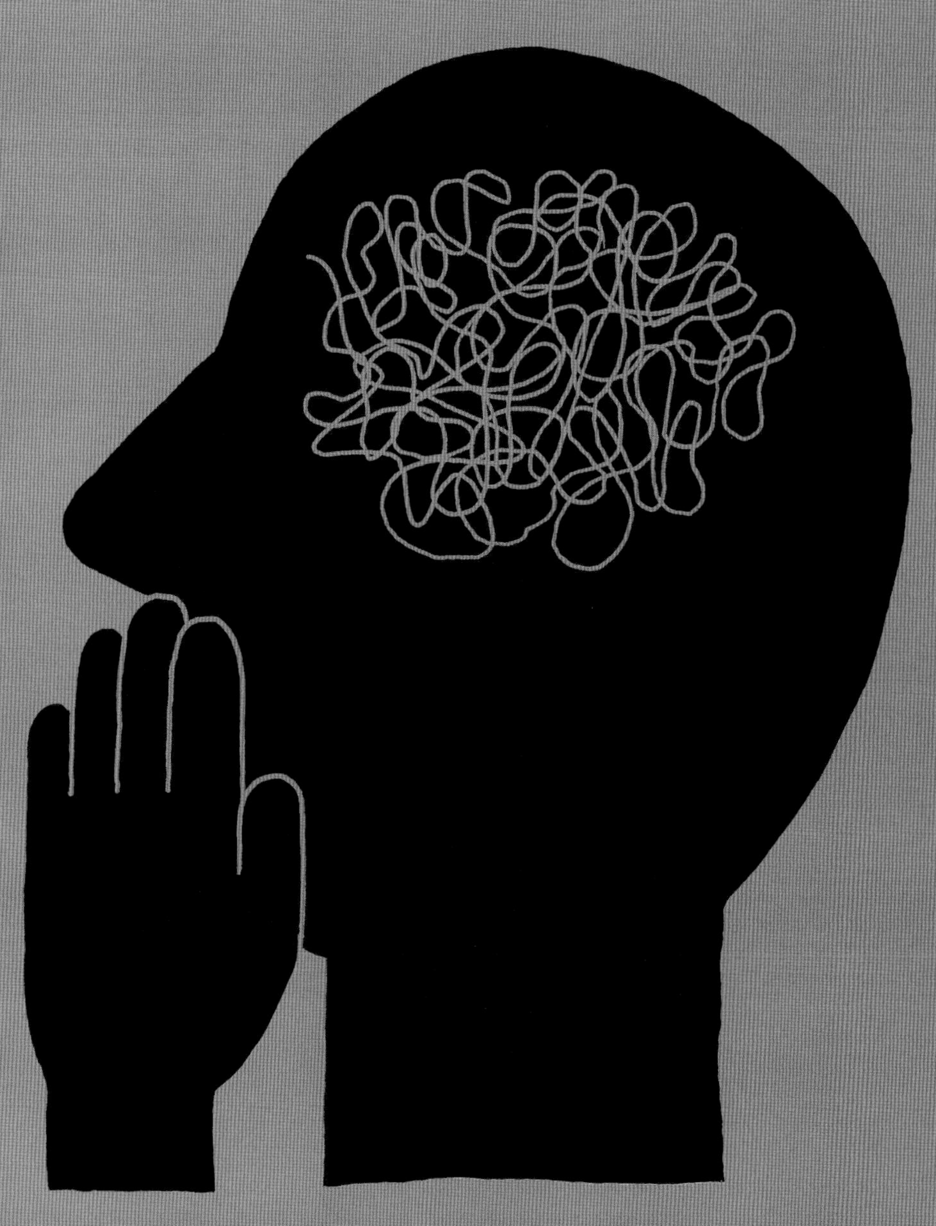

IN CONTEXT

APPROACH
Analysis of consciousness

BEFORE
1641 René Descartes defines consciousness of self in terms of the ability to think.

1690 English philosopher and physician John Locke defines consciousness as "the perception of what passes in a man's own mind."

1781 German philosopher Immanuel Kant states that simultaneous events are experienced as a "unity of consciousness."

AFTER
1923 Max Wertheimer in *Laws of Organization in Perceptual Forms* shows how the mind actively interprets images.

1925 John B. Watson dismisses consciousness as "neither a definite nor a usable concept."

The term "consciousness" is generally used to refer to individuals' awareness of their own thoughts, including sensations, feelings, and memories. We usually take this awareness for granted, except when we are having difficulties—such as trying to do something when we are very tired. But if you focus your thoughts on your consciousness, you soon become aware that your conscious experiences are constantly changing. While reading this book, for example, you may be reminded of past experiences or present discomforts that interrupt your concentration; plans for the future may spontaneously spring to mind. Thinking about your conscious experiences makes you realize just how much your thoughts are changing, and yet they seem to come together, merging and carrying on smoothly as a whole.

American psychologist William James compared these everyday experiences of consciousness to a stream that continuously flows, despite the odd interruption and change of direction. He declared: "A 'river' or a 'stream' are the metaphors by which it is most naturally described. In talking of it hereafter, let us call it the stream of thought, of consciousness …."

Consciousness … does not appear to itself chopped up in bits … It is nothing jointed; it flows.
William James

James's famous description of the "stream … of consciousness" is one that almost everyone can identify with, because we all experience it. Yet, at the same time, James points out that it is very hard to actually define: "When I say every thought is part of a personal consciousness, 'personal consciousness' is one of the terms in question … to give an accurate account of it is the most difficult of philosophic tasks."

William James

William James was born in 1842 to a wealthy and influential New York family and traveled widely as a child, attending schools in both Europe and the US. James showed early artistic ability and initially pursued a career as a painter, but his growing interest in science eventually led him to enrol at Harvard University in 1861. By 1864, he had moved to Harvard Medical School, although his studies were interrupted by bouts of physical illness and depression. He finally qualified as a physician in 1869, but never practiced medicine.

In 1873, James returned to Harvard, where he became a professor of both philosophy and psychology. He set up the first experimental psychology courses in the US, playing a key role in establishing psychology as a truly scientific discipline. He retired in 1907, and died peacefully at his home in New Hampshire in 1910.

Key works

1890 *The Principles of Psychology*
1892 *Psychology*
1897 *The Will to Believe*

See also: René Descartes 20–21 ▪ Wilhelm Wundt 32–37 ▪ John B. Watson 66–71 ▪ Sigmund Freud 92–99 ▪ Fritz Perls 112–117 ▪ Wolfgang Köhler 160–161 ▪ Max Wertheimer 341

This "most difficult of philosophic tasks" has a long history. The ancient Greeks discussed the mind but did not use the term "consciousness" or any equivalent. However, there was debate as to whether something separate from the body exists at all. In the 4th century BCE, Plato made a distinction between the soul and body, but Aristotle argued that even if there is a distinction, the two cannot be separated.

Early definitions

René Descartes, in the mid-17th century, was one of the first philosophers to attempt to describe consciousness, proposing that it resides in an immaterial domain he called "the realm of thought," in contrast to the physical domain of material things, which he called "the realm of extension." However, the first person accredited with the modern concept of consciousness as an ongoing passage of individual perceptions is the 17th-century English philosopher John Locke. James was drawn to Locke's idea of passing perceptions and also to the work of the 18th-century German philosopher Immanuel Kant. Kant was impressed by the way our experiences come together, noting that if we hear a noise and feel pain at the same time, we typically experience these as one event. He called this the "unity of consciousness," a concept that influenced many later philosophers, including William James.

James felt the most important point about consciousness is that it is not a "thing" but a process—it is what the brain does to "steer a nervous system grown too complex to regulate itself." It allows us to »

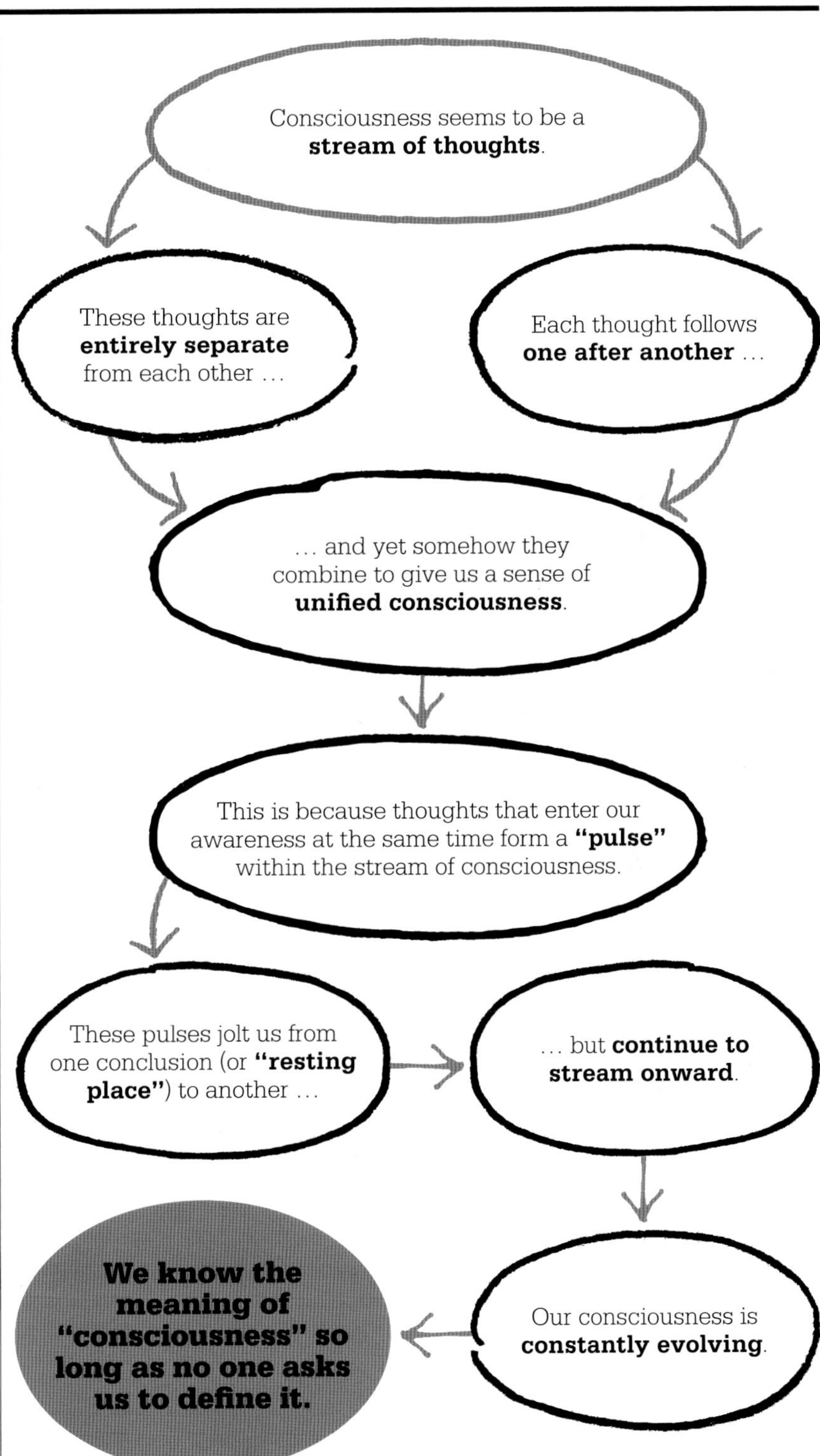

Consciousness seems to be a **stream of thoughts**.
These thoughts are **entirely separate** from each other …
Each thought follows **one after another** …
… and yet somehow they combine to give us a sense of **unified consciousness**.
This is because thoughts that enter our awareness at the same time form a **"pulse"** within the stream of consciousness.
These pulses jolt us from one conclusion (or **"resting place"**) to another …
… but **continue to stream onward**.
Our consciousness is **constantly evolving**.
We know the meaning of "consciousness" so long as no one asks us to define it.

No-one ever had a simple sensation by itself: consciousness … is of a teeming multiplicity of objects and relations.
William James

reflect upon the past, present, and future, to plan and adapt to circumstances and so fulfill what he believed was the prime purpose of consciousness—to stay alive.

But James found it hard to imagine the structure of a unified consciousness. He likened it to a group of 12 men: "Take a dozen words, take twelve men, and to each give one word. Then stand the men in a row or jam, and let each think of his word as intently as he will; nowhere will there be a consciousness of the whole sentence." If consciousness is a stream of distinct thoughts, James struggled to see how these combine. As he said, "The idea of *a* plus the idea of *b* is not identical with the idea of (*a* + *b*)." Two thoughts added together cannot be made into one idea. They are more likely to form an entirely new idea. For example, if thought *a* is "it's nine o'clock" and thought *b* is "the train leaves at 9:02," thought *c*—"I'm going to miss my train!"—might follow.

Combining thoughts

James concluded that the simplest way to understand how thoughts within the stream of consciousness might combine to make sense is to suppose "that things that are known together are known in single pulses of that stream." Some thoughts, or sensations, he believed, are unavoidably connected, like Kant's example of hearing a noise and feeling pain at precisely the same time, because any thoughts that enter our awareness during the same moment of time combine to form a pulse, or current, within the stream. We may have many of these currents flowing through our consciousness, some fast and some slow. James stated that there are even resting points, where we pause to form pictures in our minds, which can be held and contemplated at length. He called the resting places "substantive parts," and the moving currents the "transitive parts," claiming that our thinking is constantly being dislodged from one substantive part toward another, propelled by the transitive parts, or current. We are, therefore, effectively "bumped" from one conclusion to another by the constant stream of thoughts, whose purpose is to pull us ever forward in this way. There is no

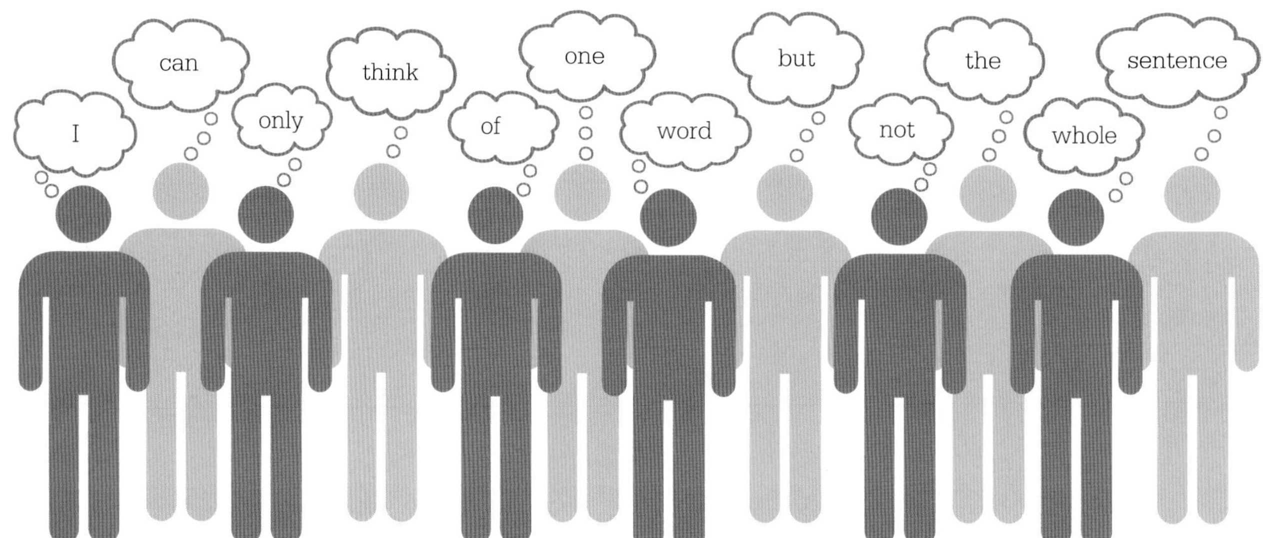

The 12-word sentence problem was used by James to illustrate his difficulty in grasping how a unified consciousness stems from separate thoughts. If each man is aware of just one word, how can there be a consciousness of the whole sentence?

Dots of pure color make up this work by the French Post-Impressionist painter Georges Seurat. Yet our brain combines these separate elements, so what we see is a human figure.

final conclusion; consciousness is not a thing but a process, which is constantly evolving.

James also drew attention to the personal nature of consciousness, stating that thoughts do not exist independently of a thinker—they are your thoughts or mine. Each one is "owned" by someone, and never "comes into direct sight of a thought in another personal consciousness than its own." And it is these thoughts "connected as we feel them to be connected" that form the self. As thoughts cannot be divided from the self, James said that investigating this self should be the starting point of psychology. Experimental psychologists did not agree, because "the self" cannot be offered up for experimentation, but James thought it was enough to work with our understanding of a self that does certain things and feels in certain ways. He called this the "empirical self," which manifests itself through its behavior, and suggested that it consists of several parts—the material self, spiritual self, and social self—each of which can be studied through introspection.

Theory of emotion

In the early stages of his research into consciousness, James realized that the emotions play an important role in our daily lives, and went on to develop, with his colleague Carl Lange, a theory about how they relate to our actions and behavior. What was to become known as the James–Lange Theory of Emotion states that emotions arise from your conscious mind's perception of your physiological condition. To illustrate this theory, James used the example of seeing a bear, then running away. It is not the case that you see the bear, feel afraid, and then run away because of the fear. What is really happening is that you see the bear and run away, and the conscious feeling of fear is caused by the action of running. This contradicts what most people might think, but James's view was that the mind's perception of the physical effects of running—rapid breathing, increased heartbeat, and perspiring heavily—is translated into the emotion of fear. Another example, according to his theory, would be that you feel happy because you are conscious that you are smiling; it is not that you feel happy first, and then smile.

Pragmatism

Related to James's theories about consciousness is his approach to the way we believe things to be true or not. He stated that "truths emerge from facts … but … the 'facts' themselves are not true; they simply are. Truth is the function of the beliefs that start and terminate among them." »

There is but one indefectibly certain truth … the truth that the present phenomenon of consciousness exists.
William James

James defined "true beliefs" as those that the believer finds useful. This emphasis on the usefulness of beliefs lies at the heart of the American philosophical tradition of pragmatism, which was central to James's thinking.

In the course of our lives, James claimed that we are continually testing "truths" against each other, and our conscious beliefs keep changing as "old truths" are modified and sometimes replaced by "new truths." This theory is particularly relevant to the way that all scientific research, including psychology, progresses. James cited the discovery of the radioactive element radium by Pierre and Marie Curie in 1902 as an example. In the course of their investigations, the Curies found that radium appeared to give off unlimited amounts of energy, which "seemed for a moment to contradict our ideas of the whole order of nature." However, after conscious consideration of this revelation, they concluded that "although it extends our old ideas of energy, it causes a minimum of alteration in their nature." In this instance, the Curies' scientific knowledge had been questioned and modified, but its core truths remained intact.

Further studies

The period following James's death saw the rise of the behaviorist movement, and a decline of interest in consciousness. Consequently, little theorizing on the subject happened from around the start of the 1920s up until the 1950s. One important exception was the German-based Gestalt movement, which emphasized that the brain operates in a holistic way, taking account of whole conscious experiences, rather than separate events—just as when we look at a picture, we see not just separate dots, lines, and shapes, but a meaningful whole. This concept is behind the now famous Gestalt phrase: "The whole is greater than the sum of the parts."

Since the 1980s, however, psychologists and neuroscientists have developed a new field of research called "consciousness studies," focusing on two main areas of interest: the content of consciousness, as reported by people who are considered to be normal and healthy; and the consciousness of people whose state of awareness has been impaired in some way. The latter group includes cases, such as when the subject is in a "persistent vegetative state" (PVS)—in which patients in a coma are awake and breathing independently, but have apparently lost all higher brain functions. The goal with both paths of research is to try to find ways of assessing consciousness as objectively as possible and to understand its underlying mechanisms—both physical and psychological.

Modern neuroscience has demonstrated that there are mechanisms of consciousness. By the closing years of the 20th century, the British molecular biologist and biophysicist Francis Crick was claiming that consciousness is related to a specific part of the brain—the prefrontal cortex area, which is involved in thought processes such as planning, problem-solving, and the control of behavior.

Research carried out by the Colombian neuroscientist Rodolfo Llinas links consciousness to the activities of the thalamus in conjunction with the cerebral cortex. The thalamus, a structure embedded deep in the center of the brain, is responsible for regulating vibrations inside the brain at certain frequencies; if these regular rhythms are disrupted—by an infection or genetic causes—then an individual may experience neurological disorders, such as epilepsy and Parkinson's disease, as well as psychological conditions, such as depression.

Pierre and Marie Curie's research, like most scientific work, modified, rather than totally contradicted, earlier theories. New "truths," James claimed, constantly modify our basic beliefs in a similar way.

MRI scans of the brain have helped identify structures such as the thalamus, seen in the center of this scan, that appear to have links to consciousness.

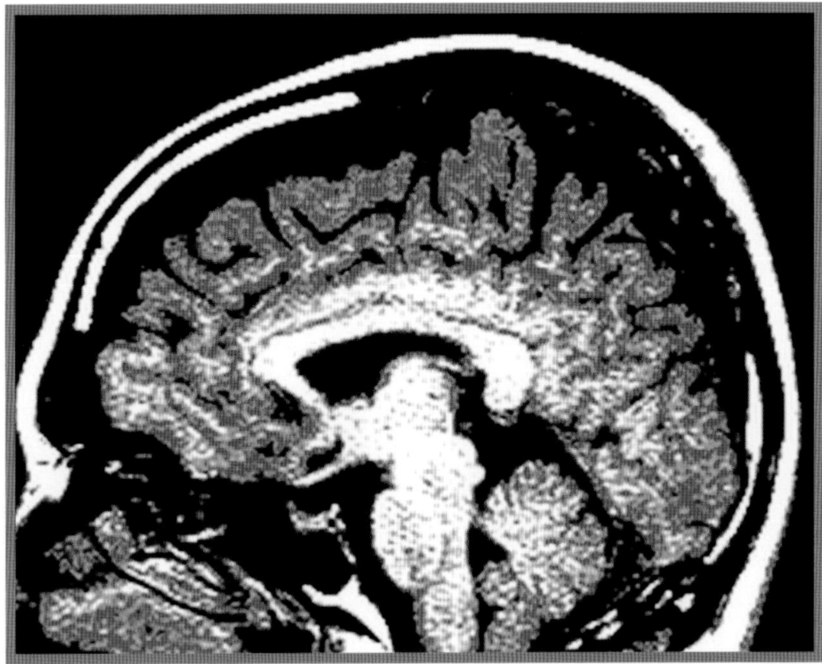

But when it comes to definitions of consciousness, modern attempts still remain vague and difficult to apply. For example, the American neuroscientist Antonio Damasio calls consciousness "the feeling of what happens," and defines it as "an organism's awareness of its own self and its surroundings." As William James suggested more than 100 years earlier, consciousness is hard to define.

Lasting legacy

An edited version of James's 1890 book, *The Principles of Psychology*, is still in print, and his ideas have been a major influence on many psychologists, as well as other scientists and thinkers. The application of his pragmatic philosophy to facts—concentrating not on what is "true" but on what it is "useful to believe"—has helped psychology move on from the question of whether the mind and body are separate or not to a more useful study of mental processes, such as attention, memory, reasoning, imagination, and intention. James claimed his approach helped move philosophers and psychologists "away from abstraction, fixed principles, closed systems, and pretended absolutes and origins, towards facts, action, and power." His insistence on focusing on the wholeness of events, including the effects of different environments on our actions—in contrast to the introspective, structuralist approach of breaking down our experiences into small details—has also shaped our understanding of behavior.

Before James started teaching the subject at Harvard in 1875, there were no independent psychology courses available in any American university. But within 20 years, around 24 colleges and universities in the US had recognized psychology as a distinct academic discipline and were offering degrees in the subject. Three specialist psychology journals were also founded in that time, and a professional organization—the American Psychological Association—was formed.

James introduced experimental psychology to America, despite claiming to "hate experimental work." He did so because he had come to realize that it was the best way to prove or disprove a theory. But he continued to value the use of introspection as a tool of discovery, especially of mental processes.

The shift in the perception of psychology and its concerns from being considered "a nasty little subject" (in James's words) into a vastly beneficial discipline owes much to his work. In 1977, in a speech celebrating the 75th anniversary of the formation of the American Psychological Association, David Krech, then Professor Emeritus in psychology at the University of California at Berkeley, referred to James as the "father of psychology." ■

All these consciousnesses melt into each other like dissolving views. Properly they are but one protracted consciousness, one unbroken stream.
William James

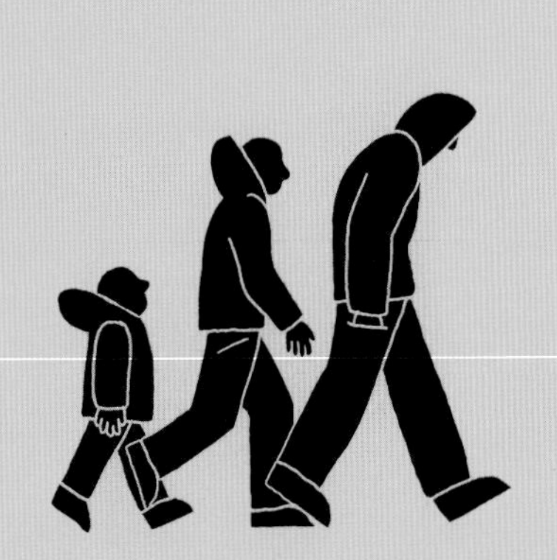

ADOLESCENCE IS A NEW BIRTH

G. STANLEY HALL (1844–1924)

IN CONTEXT

APPROACH
Human development

BEFORE
1905 Sigmund Freud, in *Three Essays on the Theory of Sexuality*, claims the teenage years are the "genital stage."

AFTER
1928 American anthropologist Margaret Mead, in *Coming of Age in Samoa*, declares that adolescence is only recognized as a distinct stage of human development in Western society.

1950 Erik Erikson, in *Childhood and Society*, describes adolescence as the stage of "Identity vs. Role Confusion," coining the term "identity crisis."

1983 In *Margaret Mead and Samoa*, New Zealand anthropologist Derek Freeman disputes Mead's claim that adolescence is merely a socially constructed concept.

Human development is determined by **nature**: it is a repetition of our **"ancestral record."**

↓

A child has **animallike dispositions** and goes through **several growth stages**.

↓

At **adolescence**, the evolutionary momentum subsides; this is a time for **individual change**.

↓

During this wild, lawless time, teenagers are increasingly **sensitive**, **reckless**, **self-conscious**, and prone to depression.

↓

The child then emerges as an adult: a more **civilized**, **"higher-order" being**.

↓

Adolescence is a new birth.

See also: Francis Galton 28–29 ▪ Wilhelm Wundt 32–37 ▪ Sigmund Freud 92–99 ▪ Erik Erikson 280–281

The word "adolescence" literally means "growing up" (from the Latin *adolescere*). In theory, it describes a distinct stage between childhood and adulthood, but in practice often simply defines the "teenage" years. In most Western societies, the idea of adolescence was not recognized until the 20th century; childhood ended and adulthood began at a certain age—typically at 18.

Pioneering psychologist and educator, G. Stanley Hall, in his 1904 book *Adolescence*, was the first academic to explore the subject. Hall was influenced by Darwin's theory of evolution, believing that all childhoods, especially with regard to behavior and early physical development, reflect the course of evolutionary change, and that we each develop in accordance with our "ancestral record."

One key influence on Hall was the 18th-century *Sturm und Drang* ("Storm and Stress") movement of German writers and musicians, which promoted total freedom of expression. Hall referred to adolescence as "Sturm und Drang"; he considered it a stage of emotional turmoil and rebellion, with behavior ranging from quiet moodiness to wild risk-taking. Adolescence, he stated, "craves strong feelings and new sensations ... monotony, routine, and detail are intolerable." Awareness of self and the environment greatly increases; everything is more keenly felt, and sensation is sought for its own sake.

Modern echoes

Many of Hall's findings are echoed in research today. Hall believed that adolescents are highly susceptible to depression, and described a "curve of despondency" that starts at the age of 11, peaks at 15, then falls steadily until the age of 23. Modern research acknowledges a similar pattern. The causes of depression that Hall identified are startlingly familiar: suspicion of being disliked and having seemingly insuperable character faults, and "the fancy of hopeless love." He believed the self-consciousness of adolescence leads to self-criticism and censoriousness of self and others. This view mirrors later studies, which argue that teenagers' advanced reasoning skills allow them to "read between the lines," while also magnifying their sensitivity to situations. Even Hall's claim that criminal activity is more prevalent in the teenage years, peaking around 18, still holds true.

But Hall was not totally negative about adolescence. As he wrote in *Youth: Its Education, Regiment, and Hygiene*, "Adolescence is a new birth, for the higher and more completely human traits are now born." So, for Hall, adolescence was in fact a necessary beginning of something much better. ■

Adolescence is when the very worst and best impulses in the human soul struggle against each other for possession.
G. Stanley Hall

G. Stanley Hall

Born into a farming family in Ashfield, Massachusetts, Granville Stanley Hall graduated from Williams College, Massachusetts in 1867. His plans to travel were thwarted through lack of funds, so he followed his mother's wish and studied theology for a year in New York, before moving to Germany. On Hall's return to America in 1870, he studied with William James for four years at Harvard, gaining the first psychology PhD in the US. He then returned to Germany for two years to work with Wilhelm Wundt in his Leipzig laboratory.

In 1882, Hall became a professor at Johns Hopkins University, Baltimore, where he set up the first US laboratory specifically for psychology. He also launched the *American Journal of Psychology* in 1887, and became the first president of the American Psychological Association in 1892.

Key works

1904 *Adolescence*
1906 *Youth: Its Education, Regiment, and Hygiene*
1911 *Educational Problems*
1922 *Senescence*

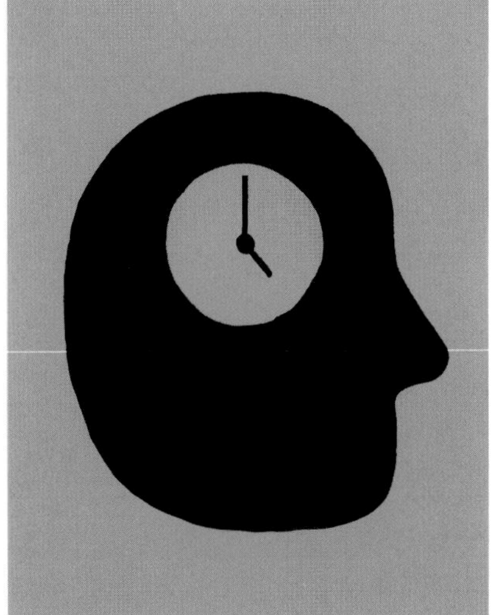

24 HOURS AFTER LEARNING SOMETHING, WE FORGET TWO-THIRDS OF IT

HERMANN EBBINGHAUS (1850–1909)

IN CONTEXT

APPROACH
Memory studies

BEFORE
5th century BCE The ancient Greeks make use of "mnemonics"—techniques, such as key words or rhymes, that aid memory.

1582 Italian philosopher Giordano Bruno in *The Art of Memory* gives methods for memorizing, using diagrams of knowledge and experience.

AFTER
1932 Frederick Bartlett says that every memory is a blend of knowledge and inference.

1949 Donald Hebb, in *The Organization of Behavior,* describes how learning results from stimulated brain cells linking up into "assemblies."

1960 US psychologist Leo Postman finds that new learning can interfere with previous learning, causing "retroactive interference."

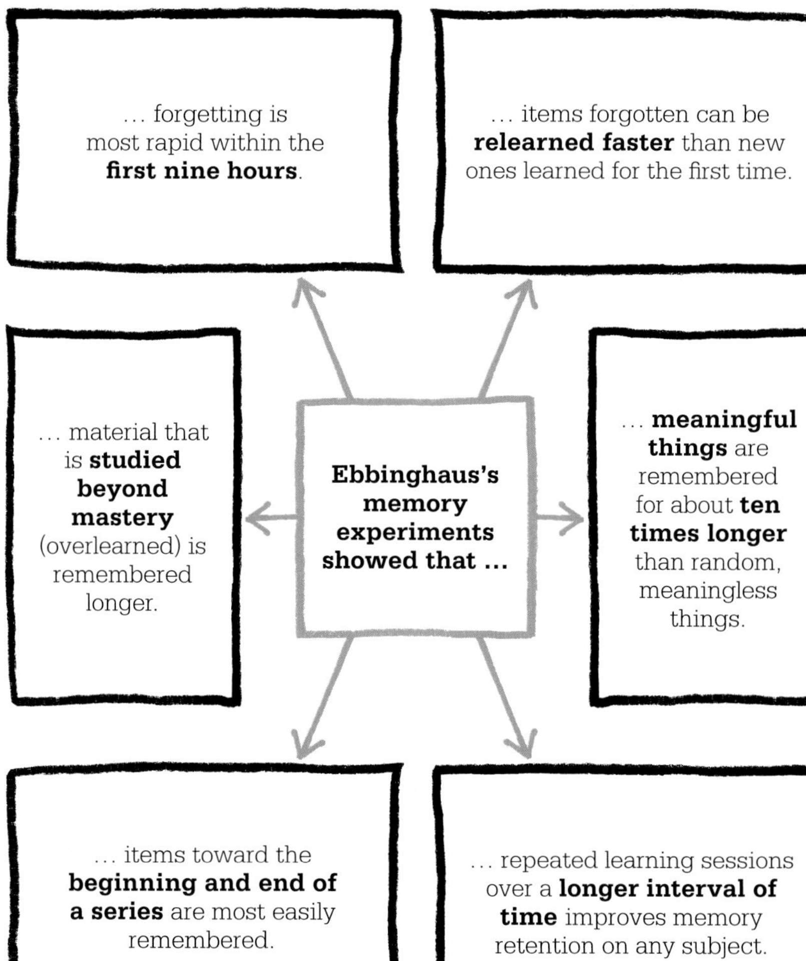

Ebbinghaus's memory experiments showed that ...
... forgetting is most rapid within the first nine hours.
... items forgotten can be relearned faster than new ones learned for the first time.
... material that is studied beyond mastery (overlearned) is remembered longer.
... meaningful things are remembered for about ten times longer than random, meaningless things.
... items toward the beginning and end of a series are most easily remembered.
... repeated learning sessions over a longer interval of time improves memory retention on any subject.

See also: Bluma Zeigarnik 162 ▪ Donald Hebb 163 ▪ George Armitage Miller 170–173 ▪ Endel Tulving 186–191 ▪ Gordon H. Bower 194–195 ▪ Daniel Schacter 208–209 ▪ Frederic Bartlett 342

In 1885, Hermann Ebbinghaus became the first psychologist to systematically study learning and memory by carrying out a long, exhausting experiment on himself. Philosophers such as John Locke and David Hume had argued that remembering involves association—linking things or ideas by shared characteristics, such as time, place, cause, or effect. Ebbinghaus tested the effect of association on memory, recording the results mathematically to see if memory follows verifiable patterns.

Memory experiments

Ebbinghaus started by memorizing lists of words and testing how many he could recall. To avoid the use of association, he then created 2,300 "nonsense syllables," all three letters long and using the standard word format of consonant–vowel–consonant: for example, "ZUC" and "QAX." Grouping these into lists, he looked at each syllable for a fraction of a second, pausing for 15 seconds before going through a list again. He did this until he could recite a series correctly at speed. He tested different list lengths and different learning intervals, noting the speed of learning and forgetting.

Ebbinghaus found that he could remember meaningful material, such as a poem, ten times more easily than his nonsense lists. He also noted that the more times the stimuli (the nonsense syllables) were repeated, the less time was needed to reproduce the memorized information. Also, the first few repetitions proved the most effective in memorizing a list.

When looking at his results for evidence of forgetting, Ebbinghaus found, unsurprisingly, that he tended to forget less quickly the lists that he had spent the most time memorizing, and that recall is best performed immediately after learning. Ebbinghaus also uncovered an unexpected pattern in memory retention. He found that there is typically a very rapid loss of recall in the first hour, followed by a slightly slower loss, so that after nine hours, about 60 percent is forgotten. After 24 hours, about two-thirds of anything memorized is forgotten. Plotted on a graph, this shows a distinct "forgetting curve" that starts with a sharp drop, followed by a shallow slope.

Learning material and committing it to memory within an hour of hearing it, Ebbinghaus showed, will mean that we remember it for longer and can recall it more easily.

Ebbinghaus's research launched a new field of enquiry, and helped establish psychology as a scientific discipline. His meticulous methods remain the basis of all psychological experimentation to this day. ■

Hermann Ebbinghaus

Hermann Ebbinghaus was born in Barmen, Germany, to a family of Lutheran merchants. At 17, he began to study philosophy at Bonn University, but his academic career was disrupted in 1870 by the Franco-Prussian War. In 1873, he completed his studies and moved to Berlin, later traveling to France and England, where he carried out research on the power of his own memory, starting in 1879. He published *Memory* in 1885, detailing the "nonsense syllable" research, and in the same year became a professor at Berlin University, where he set up two psychology laboratories and founded an academic journal. Ebbinghaus later moved to Breslau University, where he also established a laboratory, and finally to Halle, where he taught until his death from pneumonia at the age of 59.

Key works

1885 *Memory: A Contribution to Experimental Psychology*
1897–1908 *Fundamentals of Psychology* (2 volumes)
1908 *Psychology: An Elementary Textbook*

THE INTELLIGENCE OF AN INDIVIDUAL IS NOT A FIXED QUANTITY

ALFRED BINET (1857–1911)

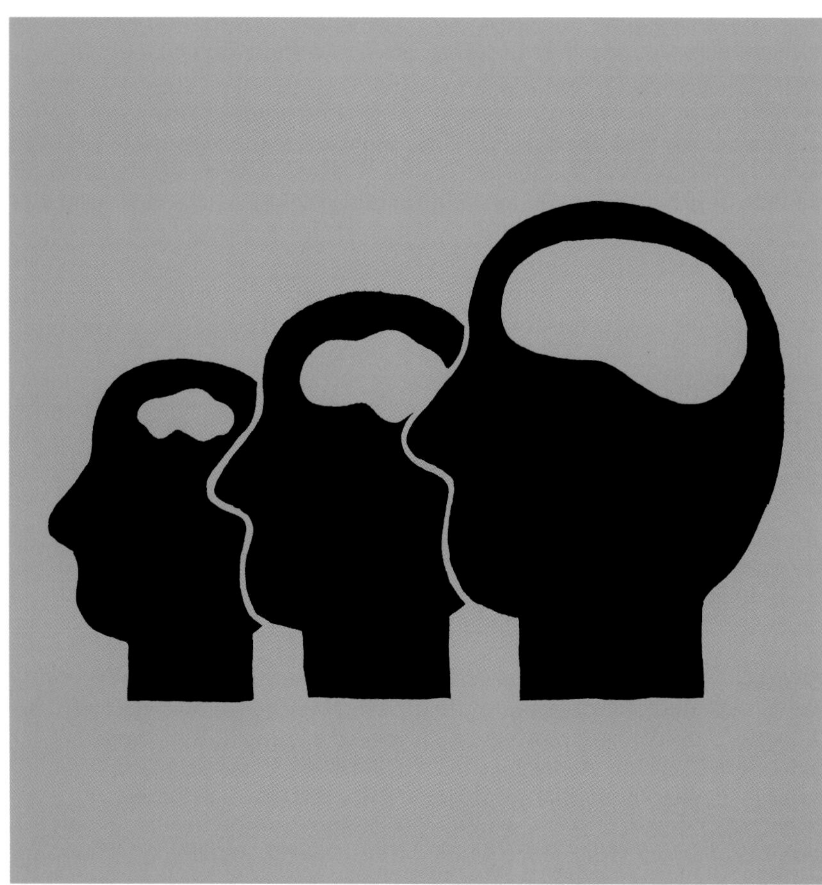

IN CONTEXT

APPROACH
Intelligence theory

BEFORE
1859 English naturalist Charles Darwin proposes that intelligence is inherited in *On the Origin of Species.*

From 1879 Wilhelm Wundt applies scientific methods to psychology, seeking objective ways of measuring mental abilities such as intelligence.

1890 US psychologist James Cattell devises tests to measure differences in individual mental abilities.

AFTER
1920s English educational psychologist Cyril Burt claims intelligence is mainly genetic.

1940s Raymond Cattell defines two types of intelligence: fluid (inborn) and crystallized (shaped by experience).

In 1859, Charles Darwin set out his theory of evolution in *On the Origin of Species*, providing a framework for the debate over whether intelligence was fixed by genetic inheritance, or could be modified by circumstances. His cousin, Francis Galton, tested cognitive ability in 9,000 people in London in the early 1880s, concluding that basic intelligence was fixed at birth, but his work was later tainted by controversy. Around the same time, Wilhelm Wundt proposed the idea of an intelligence quotient (IQ), and made attempts to measure it. Wundt's work inspired studies into the measurement of mental abilities by the American

See also: Francis Galton 28–29 ▪ Jean-Martin Charcot 30 ▪ Wilhelm Wundt 32–37 ▪ Raymond Cattell 320–321

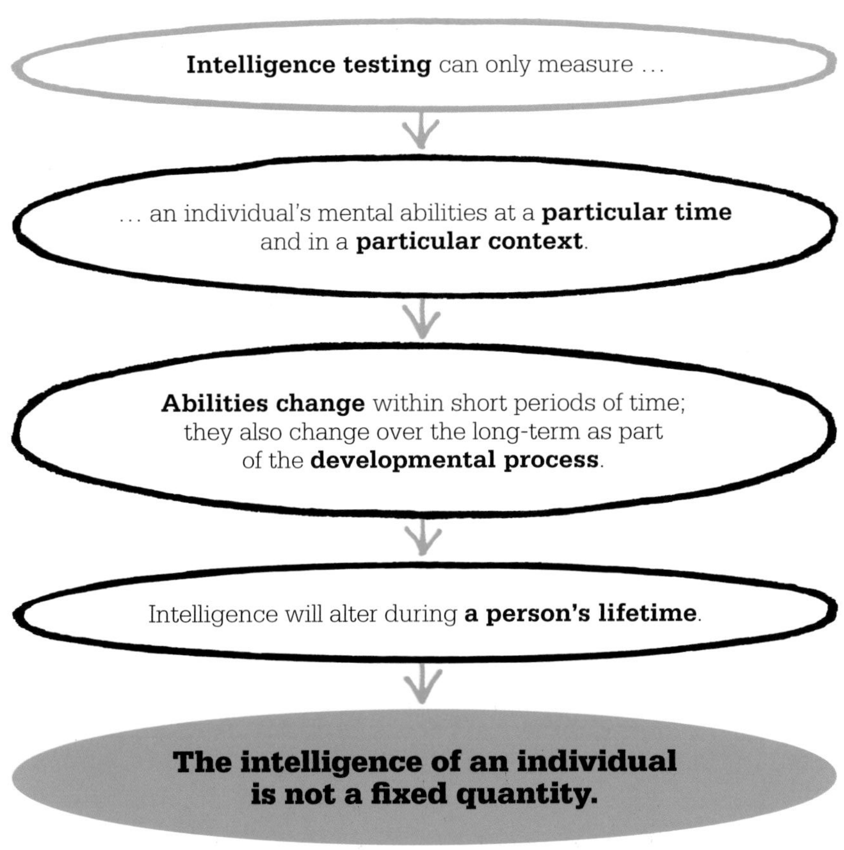

psychologist James Cattell, and were also to form the basis of Alfred Binet's research into human intelligence.

Intelligence testing can only measure ...
... an individual's mental abilities at a **particular time** and in a **particular context**.
Abilities change within short periods of time; they also change over the long-term as part of the **developmental process**.
Intelligence will alter during **a person's lifetime**.
The intelligence of an individual is not a fixed quantity.

Fascination with learning

Binet studied law and natural science before psychology captured his interest. He was largely self-taught, although working with Jean-Martin Charcot at Paris's Salpêtrière Hospital for more than seven years gave him a firm grasp of experimental procedures, with their need for precision and careful planning. His desire to study human intelligence grew out of his fascination with the development of his own two daughters. He noted that the speed and ease with which his children absorbed new information varied according to how much they were paying attention. Context, and the child's frame of mind, seemed critical to learning.

On hearing of Francis Galton's testing in London, Binet decided to carry out his own large-scale research on assessing differences in individual abilities between various special-interest groups, such as mathematicians, chess players, writers, and artists. At the same time, he continued his study of the functional intelligence of children, noting that they became capable of certain skills at specific ages. For example, very young »

Alfred Binet

Alfred Binet was born in Nice, France, but moved to Paris at a young age after his parents separated. He gained a law degree in 1878, then studied sciences at the Sorbonne, in preparation for taking up medicine. But Binet decided that his real interest lay in psychology, and although he was largely self-taught, in 1883, he was offered a post at Paris's Salpêtrière Hospital by Jean-Martin Charcot. After his marriage the following year, and the birth of two daughters, he began to take an interest in intelligence and learning. In 1891, Binet was appointed associate director of the Sorbonne's Laboratory of Experimental Psychology, becoming director in 1894.

Many honors have been heaped upon Binet since his untimely death in 1911. These include changing the name of La Société Libre pour l'Etude Psychologique de l'Enfant to La Société Alfred Binet in 1917.

Key works

1903 *Experimental Study of Intelligence*
1905 *The Mind and Brain*
1911 *A Method of Measuring the Development of Intelligence*

children were not capable of abstract thought—this seemed to be a hallmark of an increased level of intelligence that was directly attributable to age.

In 1899, Binet was invited to join a new organization dedicated to educational research, La Société Libre pour L'Etude Psychologique de l'Enfant (The Free Society for the Psychological Study of the Child). Within a short time, he became the group's leader, and began to publish articles and information useful to teachers and education officials. Around the same time, it became mandatory for all children in France to attend school between the ages of six and 12, and Binet was asked to consider how to develop a test that would identify children who might have specific learning difficulties so that they could receive schooling that was appropriate to their needs. In 1904, this work led to Binet being asked to join a government commission to devise a method of assessing learning potential in infants, and he made it his mission to establish the differences between normal and intellectually challenged children, and to find a way of measuring these differences.

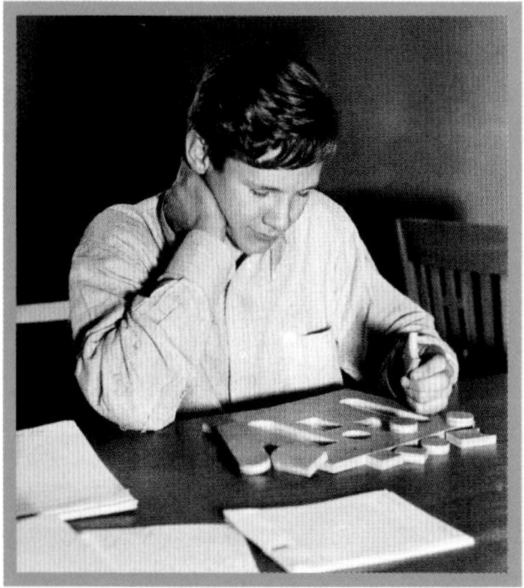

Taking intelligence tests, which are still largely based on the Binet–Simon Scale, has become an almost standard way of predicting a child's potential to be successful at school.

The Binet–Simon Scale

Binet was joined in his task by Théodore Simon, a research scientist at the Sorbonne's Laboratory of Experimental Psychology, where Binet had been director since 1894. It was to be the beginning of a long and fruitful collaboration between the two scientists.

By 1905, Binet and Simon had created their first test, labeled (in language now outdated) "New Methods for Diagnosing Idiocy, Imbecility, and Moron Status." Soon after, they introduced a revised version, for children aged three to 13, called simply the Binet–Simon Scale. It was revised once more in 1908, and then again in 1911.

Based on their many years of observing children, Binet and Simon put together 30 tests of increasing difficulty, using a range of tasks that reflected the average abilities of children at different ages. The easiest tasks included following a beam of light or engaging in basic conversation with the person who was testing them. Slightly more difficult tasks included pointing to various named body parts, repeating a series of two digits, repeating simple sentences, and defining basic words such as "house" or "fork." In the more difficult tests, children were asked to describe the difference between pairs of similar objects, to reproduce drawings from memory, and to construct sentences around three given words. The very hardest tasks included repeating seven random digits, finding three rhymes for the French word "obéisance," and answering questions such as

There is in intelligence … a fundamental agency, the lack or alteration of which has the greatest importance for practical life: that is judgment.
Alfred Binet

"My neighbor has been receiving strange visitors. He has received in turn a doctor, a lawyer, and then a priest. What is taking place?"

Binet and Simon tested their Scale on a sample of 50 children, divided equally between five age groups. These children had been selected by their school teachers as being average for their age, providing a baseline measure of normality against which children of all abilities could be measured.

Binet and Simon's 30 tasks, arranged in order of difficulty, were to be carried out under carefully controlled conditions. Binet had learned from observing his daughters that children are easily distracted and that their level of attention plays a critical role in their ability to perform. He saw intelligence as a mixture of multifaceted mental faculties that operate within a real world of ever-changing circumstances and are controlled by practical judgment.

Intelligence is not fixed

Binet was always frank about the limitations of the Binet–Simon Scale. He was eager to point out that the scale simply ordered children from their performance of intellectual tasks in relation to other children of a similar age. The tests of 1908 and 1911 placed greater emphasis on tests for different age groups, and it was this that eventually led to the concept of "mental age."

Binet also stressed that mental development progressed at different rates and could be influenced by environmental factors. He preferred to think of his tests as a way of assessing mental level at a particular point in time, because this allowed for an individual's level to change as their circumstances changed. This was in opposition to the views of the influential English psychologist Charles Spearman, who later proposed that intelligence was based on biological factors alone.

Binet maintained that a child's "intelligence is not a fixed quantity," but grows just as the child does, and that even though he had devised a way of quantifying it, no number could ever give an accurate measure of a person's intelligence. A complete picture, Binet thought, could only be formed from an accompanying case study. Ultimately, Binet did not believe that it was possible to measure intellectual aptitude as if it were a length or a capacity; it was only possible to classify it.

Binet–Simon tests generate an IQ (intelligence quotient) number, representing an overall level of performance. This can be plotted on a graph to reveal IQ variations across groups or populations.

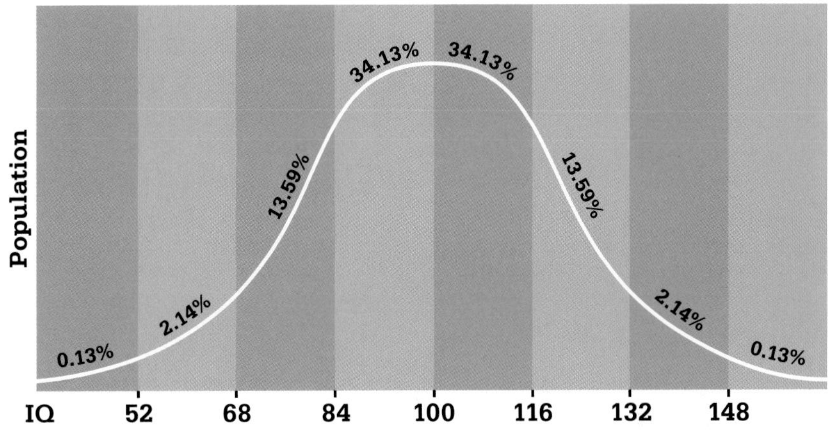

Uses and abuses

In 1908, the American psychologist Henry H. Goddard traveled to Europe, where he discovered the Binet–Simon tests. He translated them, distributing around 22,000 copies across the US to be used for testing in schools. Unfortunately, while Binet had been careful not to attribute intelligence to hereditary factors, Goddard thought that it was genetically determined. He saw the Binet–Simon Scale as a way of rooting out "feeble-minded people" for compulsory sterilization.

In 1916, yet another American psychologist, Lewis Terman, modified the Binet–Simon Scale. Using test results from a large sample of American children, he renamed it the Stanford–Binet Scale. It was no longer used solely to identify children with specific learning difficulties, but to pick out those who might be suitable for streaming off into more vocational, or job-oriented, education, effectively condemning them to a lifetime of menial work. Terman, like Goddard, believed that intelligence was inherited and unchangeable, so no amount of schooling could alter it.

Binet was probably unaware of these uses of his work for quite some time. He was an isolated figure, who rarely concerned himself with professional developments outside his immediate sphere. He never traveled outside France, where the Binet–Simon Scale was not adopted during his lifetime, so he was never confronted by any modifications of his work. When he eventually became aware of the "foreign ideas being grafted on his instrument," he strongly condemned those who with "brutal pessimism" and "deplorable verdicts" promoted the concept of intelligence as a single constant.

Binet's concept of the "IQ test" remains the basis of intelligence testing today. Despite its shortcomings, it has generated research that has advanced our knowledge of human intelligence. ■

I have not sought to sketch a method of measuring … but only a method of classification of individuals.
Alfred Binet

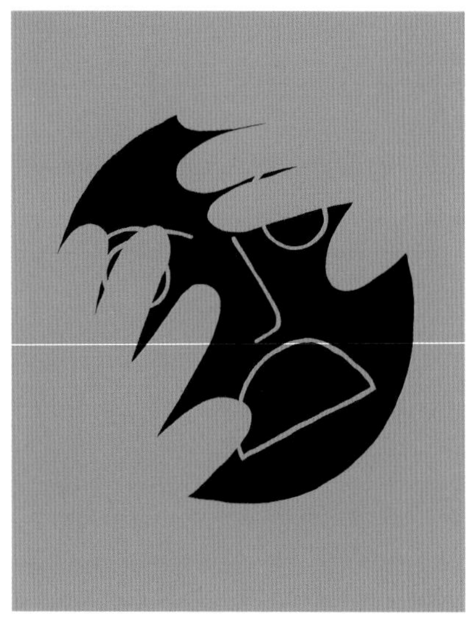

THE UNCONSCIOUS SEES THE MEN BEHIND THE CURTAINS

PIERRE JANET (1859–1947)

IN CONTEXT

APPROACH
Neurological science

BEFORE
1878 Jean-Martin Charcot in *Diseases of the Nervous System* describes the symptoms of hysteria, then considered to be a distinct, biological illness.

AFTER
1895 Sigmund Freud suggests that dissociation is one of the mind's defense mechanisms.

1900s American neurologist Morton Prince suggests that there is a spectrum of dissociative disorders.

1913 French naturalist J. P. F. Deleuze describes dissociation as being like the formation of two distinct people—one of them fully awake, and the other in a trancelike state.

1977 Ernest R. Hilgard's *Divided Consciousness* discusses the splitting up of consciousness by hypnosis.

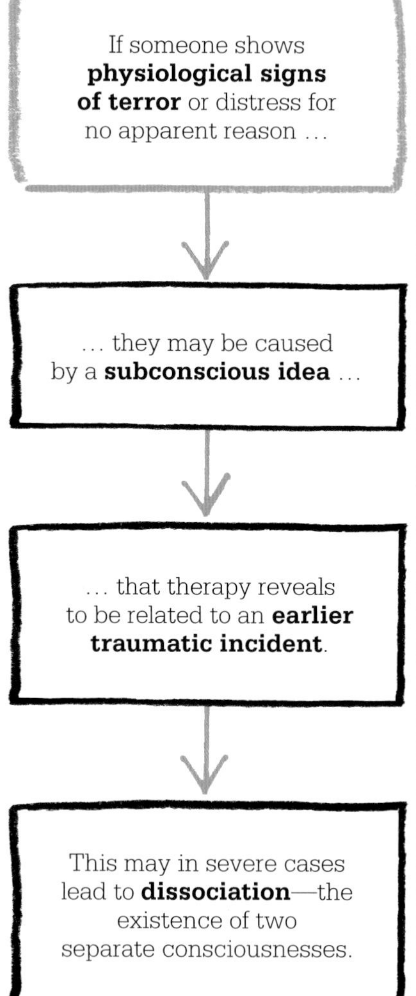

If someone shows **physiological signs of terror** or distress for no apparent reason …
… they may be caused by a **subconscious idea** …
… that therapy reveals to be related to an **earlier traumatic incident**.
This may in severe cases lead to **dissociation**—the existence of two separate consciousnesses.

Between around 1880 and 1910, there was a great deal of interest in the condition of "dissociation"—the separation of some mental processes from a person's conscious mind, or normal everyday personality. Mild dissociation, in which the world seems "dreamlike" and "unreal," is common, and affects most people at some time or other. It is often caused by illnesses, such as flu, or drugs, including alcohol, and may lead to a partial or complete loss of memory during and after the period of dissociation. In rare cases of what was then described as multiple personality disorder, a person appears to have two or more distinct personalities. Such extreme examples are now classified as "dissociative identity disorder."

The French philosopher and physician Pierre Janet is credited with being the first person to study and describe dissociation as a psychiatric condition. In the late 1880s and early 1890s, he worked at the Salpêtrière hospital in Paris, where he treated patients who were suffering from "hysteria." He published case studies of several women who showed extreme symptoms. A patient called

See also: Jean-Martin Charcot 30 ▪ Alfred Binet 50–53 ▪ Sigmund Freud 92–99 ▪ Thigpen & Cleckley 336–337 ▪ Ernest R. Hilgard 343

These people are persecuted by something, and you must investigate carefully to get to the root.
Pierre Janet

"Lucie," for example, would usually be calm, but then suddenly became agitated, crying and looking terrified for no apparent reason. She seemed to have three distinct personalities, which Janet named "Lucie 1," "Lucie 2," and "Lucie 3," and would change between them unexpectedly, especially when hypnotized. Lucie 1 had only "her own" memories, as did Lucie 2, but Lucie 3 could remember events relating to all three personalities. Significantly, Lucie 3 could recall a traumatic experience, while on vacation at the age of 7, when she was terrified by two men who were hiding behind a curtain.

Subconscious trauma

Lucie's childhood trauma, Janet concluded, was the cause of her dissociation. As he wrote in *Psychological Automatism*: "To have one's body in the posture of terror is to feel the emotion of terror; and if this posture is determined by a subconscious idea, the patient will have the emotion alone in his consciousness without knowing why he feels this way." As her terror took hold, Lucie would say, "I'm afraid and I don't know why." "The unconscious," said Janet, "is having its dream; it sees the men behind the curtains, and puts the body in a posture of terror." Janet added that he believed traumatic events and stress could cause dissociation in anyone with that predisposition.

Janet described the part of the mind that he believed was behind uncharacteristic and disturbed behavior as "the subconscious." But Sigmund Freud thought this term was too vague, and instead labeled the source of his patients' mental traumas as the "unconscious." Freud also developed Janet's ideas, stating that dissociation was a universal "defense mechanism."

Janet's work was neglected for decades, as the use of hypnotism to investigate and treat mental illness was discredited. However, since the late 20th century, it has again attracted interest from psychologists studying dissociative disorders. ■

Childhood traumas may appear to be forgotten, but according to Pierre Janet, they can often remain in the "subconscious" part of the mind, giving rise to mental problems in later life.

Pierre Janet

Pierre Janet was born into a cultured, middle-class family in Paris, France. As a child he loved the natural sciences, and began collecting and cataloging plants. His philosopher uncle, Paul Janet, encouraged him to study both medicine and philosophy, and after attending the elite École Normale Supérieure in Paris, he went on to receive a master's degree in philosophy from the Sorbonne. Aged just 22, Janet was appointed Professor of Philosophy at the Lycée in Le Havre, where he launched his research into hypnotically induced states.

Influenced by Jean-Martin Charcot, Janet extended his studies to include "hysteria," becoming director of Charcot's laboratory at Paris's Salpêtrière Hospital in 1898. He also taught at the Sorbonne, and was made Professor of Psychology at the Collège de France in 1902.

Key works

1893 *The Mental State of Hystericals*
1902 *Neuroses*
1907 *The Major Symptoms of Hysteria*

BEHAVIO

RESPONDING TO OUR ENVIRONMENT

RISM

Charles Darwin publishes *The Expression of the Emotions in Men and Animals* arguing that behaviors are evolutionary adaptations.

1872

1898

Edward Thorndike's **Law of Effect** states that responses which produce satisfying effects are more likely to be repeated.

John B. Watson publishes *Psychology As The Behaviorist Views It*, which becomes the unofficial **behaviorist manifesto**.

1913

1920

John B. Watson experiments on "Little Albert," teaching the baby a **conditioned emotional response**.

Ivan Pavlov demonstrates **classical conditioning** in his experiments on dogs.

1927

1929

Karl Lashley's experiments in brain dissection show that **the whole brain is involved in learning**.

Zing-Yang Kuo's experiments with cats and rats attempt to show that **there is no such thing as instinct**.

1930

1930

B. F. Skinner demonstrates the effects of **"operant conditioning"** in experiments on rats.

By the 1890s, psychology was accepted as a scientific subject separate from its philosophical origins. Laboratories and university departments had been established in Europe and the US, and a second generation of psychologists was emerging.

In the US, psychologists anxious to put the new discipline on an objective, scientific footing reacted against the introspective, philosophical approach taken by William James and others. Introspection, they felt, was by definition subjective, and theories based on it could be neither proved nor disproved; if psychology was to be treated as a science, it would have to be based on observable and measurable phenomena. Their solution was to study the manifestation of the workings of the mind—behavior—under strictly controlled laboratory conditions. As John B. Watson put it, psychology is "that division of Natural Science which takes human behavior—the doings and sayings, both learned and unlearned—as its subject matter." Early "behaviorists," including Edward Thorndike, Edward Tolman, and Edwin Guthrie, designed experiments to observe the behavior of animals in carefully devised situations, and from these tests inferred theories about how humans interact with their environment, as well as about learning, memory, and conditioning.

Conditioning responses

Behaviorist experiments were influenced by similar experiments devised by physiologists studying physical processes, and it was a Russian physiologist, Ivan Pavlov, who unwittingly provided a basis for the emergent behaviorist psychology. In his now famous study of salivation in dogs, Pavlov described how an animal responds to a stimulus in the process of conditioning, and gave psychologists the foundation on which to build the central idea of behaviorism. The notion of conditioning, often referred to as "stimulus–response" (S–R) psychology, shaped the form behaviorism was to take.

The behaviorist approach concentrated on observing responses to external stimuli, ignoring inner mental states and processes, which were thought to be impossible to examine scientifically and therefore could not be included in any analysis of

Konrad Lorenz discovers the phenomenon of **imprinting**, where baby animals assume a parent because of sensory information received at a critical time.

1935

Clark L. Hull states that **drive reduction** (satisfying our basic human needs) is the only true basis of reinforcement.

1943

B. F. Skinner publishes *Verbal Behavior,* in which he claims that speech is a product of past

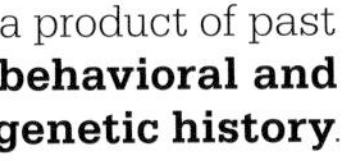

behavioral and genetic history.

1957

Noam Chomsky writes a critical review of *Verbal Behavior* that helps spark the **cognitive revolution**.

1959

1938

Edwin Guthrie suggests that **"single-trial learning"** is adequate; conditioning need not rely on repetition.

1948

Cognitive Maps in Rats and Men by Edward Tolman suggests that we develop **cognitive maps** while we go about our daily lives.

1958

Joseph Wolpe conducts **desensitization techniques** on war veterans suffering from "war neurosis."

1960s

Neal Miller's experiments lead to the discovery of **biofeedback** techniques.

behavior. The shift from "mind" to "behavior" as a basis for the study of psychology was revolutionary, and was even accompanied by a "behaviorist manifesto"—the paper *Psychology as the Behaviorist Views It,* delivered in 1913 by Watson.

In the US, which was leading the field in psychology, behaviorism became the dominant approach for the next 40 years. Evolving from the idea of Pavlovian or classical conditioning came Watson's assertion that environmental stimuli alone shape behavior; innate or inherited factors are not involved. The next generation included the "radical behaviorist" B. F. Skinner, who proposed a rethink of the stimulus–response notion in his theory of "operant conditioning"—which stated that behavior was shaped by consequences, not by a preceding stimulus. Although the concept was similar to ideas proposed by William James, it radically altered the course of behaviorism, taking into account genetic factors and explaining mental states as a result (rather than as a cause) of behavior.

The cognitive revolution

By the mid-20th century, however, psychologists were questioning the behaviorist approach. Ethology, the study of animal behavior, showed the importance of instinctive as well as learned behavior—a finding that sat uncomfortably with strict ideas of conditioning. A reaction to Skinner's ideas also sparked the "cognitive revolution," which turned attention once again from behavior back to the mind and mental processes. A key figure at this time was Edward Tolman, a behaviorist whose theories had not dismissed the importance of perception and cognition, due to his interest in German-based Gestalt psychology. Advances in neuroscience, explored by another behaviorist, Karl Lashley, also played a part in shifting the emphasis from behavior to the brain and its workings.

Behaviorism had now run its course, and was superseded by the various branches of cognitive psychology. However, its legacy, particularly in establishing a scientific methodology for the subject, and in providing models that could be used in psychological experimentation, was a lasting one. Behavioral therapy is also still in use today, as an essential part of cognitive-behavioral therapy. ■

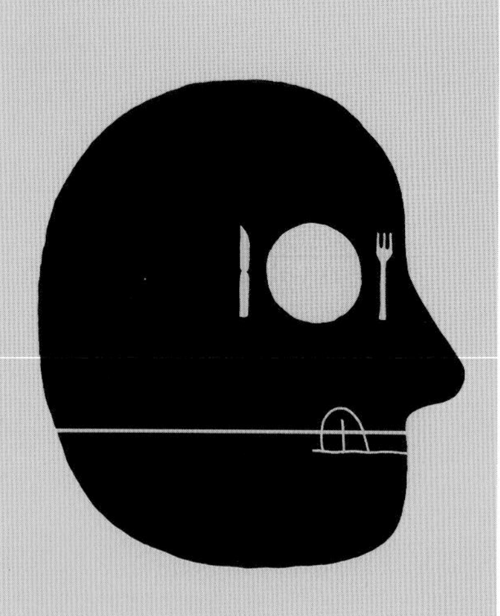

THE SIGHT OF TASTY FOOD MAKES A HUNGRY MAN'S MOUTH WATER

IVAN PAVLOV (1849–1936)

IN CONTEXT

APPROACH
Classical conditioning

BEFORE
Early 12th century Arab physician Avenzoar (Ibn Zuhr) performs experiments on animals in order to test surgical procedures.

1890 In *Principles of Psychology,* William James states that in animals "the feeling of having executed one impulsive step is an indispensable part of the stimulus of the next one."

AFTER
1920 John B. Watson's "Little Albert" experiment demonstrates classical conditioning in humans.

1930s B. F. Skinner shows that rats can be "conditioned" to behave in a specific way.

1950s Psychotherapists employ "conditioning" as part of behavior therapy.

An **unconditioned stimulus** (such as being presented with food) …

… can provoke an **unconditioned response** (such as beginning to salivate).

If an unconditioned stimulus is accompanied by a **neutral stimulus** (such as a ringing bell) …

… a **conditioned response** begins to develop.

After repeated episodes, the **conditioned stimulus** alone (the ringing bell) …

… will **provoke** a **conditioned response** (beginning to salivate).

Many of the key discoveries made when modern psychology was still in its infancy were the result of research by scientists working in other fields. Ivan Pavlov, a Russian physiologist, is one of the best known of these early pioneers, whose investigations into the secretion of saliva during digestion in dogs led him to some unexpected conclusions.

During the 1890s, Pavlov carried out a series of experiments on dogs, using various surgically implanted devices to measure the flow of saliva when these animals were being fed. He noted that the dogs salivated not only when they were actually eating, but also whenever they could just smell or see some appetizing food. The dogs would even salivate, in anticipation of food being produced, when they were simply being approached by one of their keepers.

Pavlov's observations led him to investigate the links between various stimuli and the responses they elicited. In one experiment, he set off a clicking metronome just before offering food to the dogs, repeating this process until the animals always associated the sound with a good meal. This

See also: William James 38–45 ▪ John B. Watson 66–71 ▪ B. F. Skinner 78–85 ▪ Stanley Schachter 345

Pavlov's dogs would salivate simply at the sight of someone in a white lab coat. They had become "conditioned" to associate the coat with eating, as whoever fed them always wore one.

"conditioning" eventually resulted in the dogs salivating in response to the click of the metronome alone.

In further experiments, Pavlov replaced the metronome with a bell or buzzer, a flashing light, and whistles of different pitches. However, regardless of the nature of the stimulus used, the result was always the same: once an association between the neutral stimulus (bell, buzzer, or light) and food had been established, the dogs would respond to the stimulus by salivating.

Conditioned response

Pavlov concluded that the food offered to the dogs was an "unconditioned stimulus" (US), because it led to an unlearned, or "unconditioned" response (UR)—in this case, salivation. The click of the metronome, however, only became a stimulus to salivation after its association with food had been learned. Pavlov then called this a "conditioned stimulus" (CS). The salivation in response to the metronome was also learned, so was a "conditioned response" (CR).

In later experiments, Pavlov showed that conditioned responses could be repressed, or "unlearned," if the conditioned stimulus was given repeatedly without being followed by food. He also demonstrated that a conditioned response could be mental as well as physical, by carrying out experiments in which various stimuli were associated with pain or some form of threat and began to elicit a conditioned response of fear or anxiety.

The principle of what is now known as classical or Pavlovian conditioning, as well as Pavlov's experimental method, marked a groundbreaking step in the emergence of psychology as a truly scientific, rather than philosophical, discipline. Pavlov's work was to be hugely influential, particularly on US behaviorist psychologists, such as John B. Watson and B. F. Skinner. ■

Facts are the air of science. Without them a man of science can never rise.
Ivan Pavlov

Ivan Pavlov

Ivan Pavlov, the eldest son of a village priest in Ryazan, Russia, was initially destined to follow in his father's footsteps. However, he quickly abandoned his training at a local seminary, transferring to the University of St. Petersburg to study natural science. After graduation in 1875, he enrolled at the Academy of Medical Surgery, where he gained a doctorate and later a fellowship. In 1890, Pavlov became a professor at the Military Medical Academy, and was also made director of the physiology department at the Institute of Experimental Medicine. It was here that he carried out his famous research into the digestive secretions of dogs, which won him the Nobel Prize in 1904. Pavlov retired officially in 1925, but continued his experiments until his death from pneumonia in February 1936.

Key works

1897 *Lectures on the Work of the Principal Digestive Glands*
1928 *Lectures on Conditioned Reflexes*
1941 *Conditioned Reflexes and Psychiatry*

PROFITLESS ACTS ARE STAMPED OUT

EDWARD THORNDIKE (1874–1949)

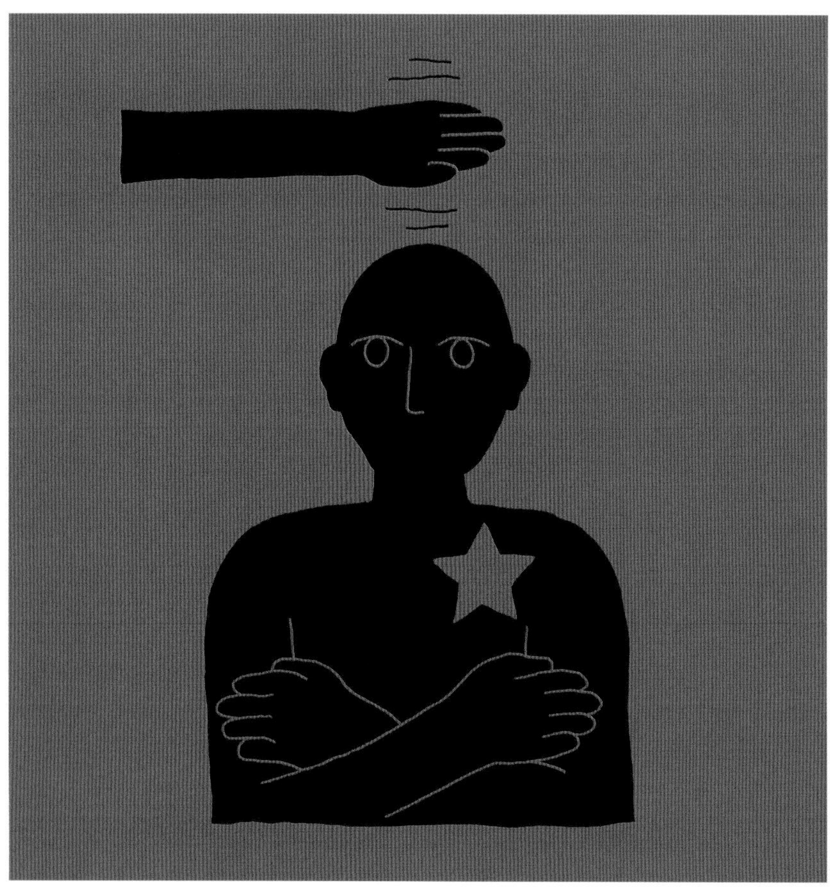

IN CONTEXT

APPROACH
Connectionism

BEFORE
1885 In his book *On Memory*, Hermann Ebbinghaus describes the "forgetting curve"—the rate at which human memories fade.

1890s Ivan Pavlov establishes the principle of classical conditioning.

AFTER
1918 John B. Watson's "Little Albert" experiments apply conditioning to a human baby.

1923 English psychologist Charles Spearman proposes a single general factor—the "g factor"—in measurements of human intelligence.

1930s B. F. Skinner develops a theory of conditioning from consequences—"operant conditioning."

At much the same time as Pavlov was conducting his experiments on dogs in Russia, Edward Thorndike began researching animal behavior for his doctoral thesis in the US. He was perhaps the first true "behaviorist" psychologist, although his research took place long before the term was adopted.

Scientific psychology was emerging as a fresh field of study in universities when Thorndike graduated in the 1890s, and he was attracted by the prospect of applying this new science to his interest in education and learning. Thorndike's original intention had been to study learning in humans,

See also: Hermann Ebbinghaus 48–49 ▪ Ivan Pavlov 60–61 ▪ John B. Watson 66–71 ▪ Edward Tolman 72–73 ▪ B. F. Skinner 78–85 ▪ Donald Hebb 163 ▪ Hans Eysenck 322–327

Psychology helps to measure the probability that an aim is attainable.
Edward Thorndike

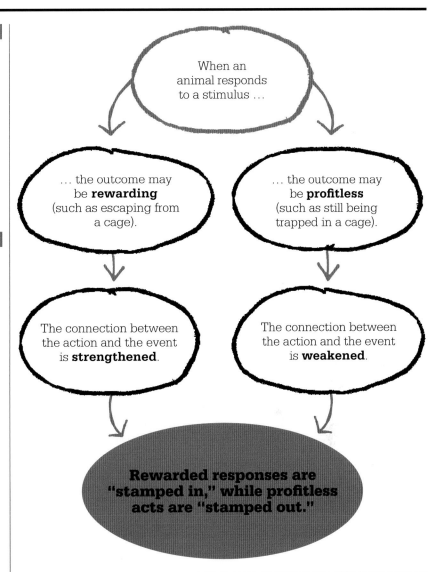

When an animal responds to a stimulus …

… the outcome may be **rewarding** (such as escaping from a cage).

… the outcome may be **profitless** (such as still being trapped in a cage).

The connection between the action and the event is **strengthened**.

The connection between the action and the event is **weakened**.

Rewarded responses are "stamped in," while profitless acts are "stamped out."

but when he was unable to obtain a suitable subject for his research, he turned his attention to animals, with the aim of examining the processes of intelligence and learning through observation in a series of controlled experiments. Thorndike's results went much further than this, however, laying down the foundations of behaviorist psychology.

Learning environments

Thorndike's first studies were of chicks learning to negotiate mazes that he designed and built specifically for his experiments. This later became a hallmark of behaviorist experimental technique—the use of a specially created environment in which a subject is given specific stimuli or tasks, now known as "instrumental conditioning" or "instrumental learning." As his research progressed, Thorndike turned his attention to cats, inventing "puzzle boxes" to observe their ability to learn mechanisms for escape.

A hungry cat was locked inside a puzzle box, and by exploring its environment would come across various devices, such as a loop of string, or a ring, or a button or panel to be pressed, only one of which would be connected to the latch that would open the door of the box. In time, the cat would discover the device, which would allow it to escape and receive a reward of food. The process was repeated and it was noted how long it took for the cat to open the puzzle box each time; this indicated how quickly the animal was learning about its environment.

The experiment was carried out using several different cats, placing each one in a series of puzzle boxes that were opened by different devices. What Thorndike noticed was that although the cats had all discovered the escape mechanism by trial and error in their first »

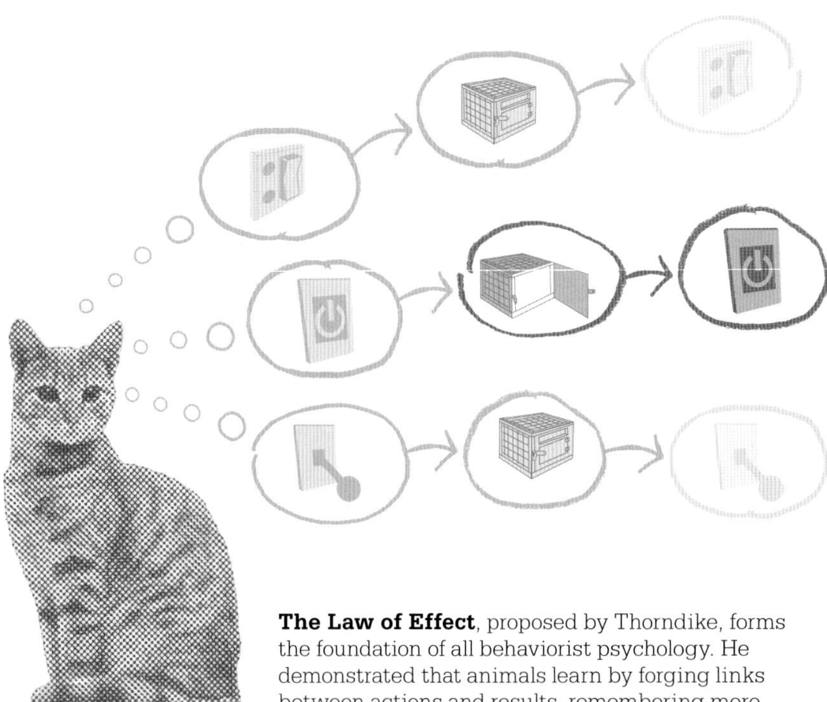

The Law of Effect, proposed by Thorndike, forms the foundation of all behaviorist psychology. He demonstrated that animals learn by forging links between actions and results, remembering more positive outcomes and forgetting negative ones.

attempt, on successive occasions the amount of trial and error gradually decreased as the cats learned which actions were going to be fruitless and which would lead to a reward.

The Law of Effect

As a result of these experiments Thorndike proposed his Law of Effect, which states that a response to a situation that results in a satisfying outcome is more likely to occur again in the future; and conversely, that a response to a situation that results in an unsatisfying outcome is less likely to occur again. This was the first formal statement of an idea that lies behind all behaviorist psychology, the connection between stimulus and response and its relevance to the process of learning and behavior. Thorndike proposed that when a connection is made between a stimulus (S) and a response (R), a corresponding neural connection is made in the brain. He referred to his brand of S-R learning as "connectionism," asserting that the connections made during learning are "stamped in" the circuitry of the brain.

What Thorndike proposed was that it is the outcome of an action that determines how strongly or weakly the stimulus-response connection is stamped in; in the case of the puzzle boxes, whether pulling a string or pushing a panel resulted in escape or frustration. In other words, when particular stimulus-response sequences are followed by a satisfying or pleasant state of affairs (such as escape or a reward), those responses tend to become "more firmly connected with the situation, so that, when it recurs, they will be more likely to recur." They become "stamped in" as a neural connection. When stimulus-response sequences are followed by an annoying or unpleasant state of affairs (such as continued imprisonment or punishment), the neural connections between the situation and response are weakened, until eventually "profitless acts are stamped out."

This focus on the outcome of a stimulus and its response, and the idea that the outcome could work back to strengthen the stimulus-response connection, is an example of what would later be called a reinforcement theory of learning. Reinforcement, and the importance of outcomes, was virtually ignored by psychologists in the next generation of behaviorists, such as John B. Watson, but the Law of Effect brilliantly anticipated the work of B. F. Skinner and his theory of "operant conditioning."

In later research, Thorndike refined the Law of Effect to take into account other variables, such as the delay between response and reward, the effect of repetition of a task, and how quickly a task was forgotten when it was not repeated. From this, he derived his Law of Exercise, which states that

The intellect, character, and skill possessed by any man are the product of certain original tendencies and the training which they have received.
Edward Thorndike

Adult learners were once thought to be less capable of retaining information than children. Thorndike showed that the only significant difference was in speed of learning, not memory.

stimulus-response connections that are repeated are strengthened, while those that are not used again are weakened. Moreover, the rate at which connections strengthen or weaken can vary. According to Thorndike, "the greater the satisfaction or discomfort, the greater the strengthening or weakening of the bond."

Interestingly, although Thorndike was studying animal behavior using what were to become standard behaviorist methods—and authoring a book, *Animal Intelligence* (1911), which was to become a classic of early behaviorism—he considered himself primarily an educational psychologist. He had originally intended to examine animal intelligence, not behavior. He wanted to show, for example, that animals learned by simple trial and error rather than by using a faculty of insight, an idea that was prevalent in psychology at the time: "In the first place, most of the books do not give us a psychology, but rather a eulogy of animals. They have all been about animal intelligence, never about animal stupidity," he wrote. The fact that his cats in puzzle boxes learned gradually, rather than suddenly gaining an insight into how to escape, confirmed his theories. The animals were forced to learn by trial and error, because they were unable to use reason to work out the link between the door and the operating handle.

Human intelligence

After the publication of *Animal Intelligence*, Thorndike turned his attention to human intelligence. In his opinion, the most basic intelligence is characterized by simple stimulus and response association, resulting in a neural connection. The more intelligent an animal, the more capable it will be of making such connections. Therefore, intelligence can be defined in terms of the ability to form neural bonds, which is dependent not only on genetic factors, but also on experience.

To find a measurement of human intelligence, Thorndike devised his CAVD (Completion, Arithmetic, Vocabulary, and Directions) test. It became the model for all modern intelligence tests, and assessed mechanical intelligence (understanding of how things work), as well as abstract intelligence (creative ability) and social intelligence (interpersonal skills). Thorndike was especially interested in how age might affect learning, and also proposed a theory of learning that remains at the heart of educational psychology to this day, a contribution that is perhaps what Thorndike would have wished more than anything else to be remembered for. However, it is for his enormous influence on the behaviorist movement that Thorndike is most often lauded. ■

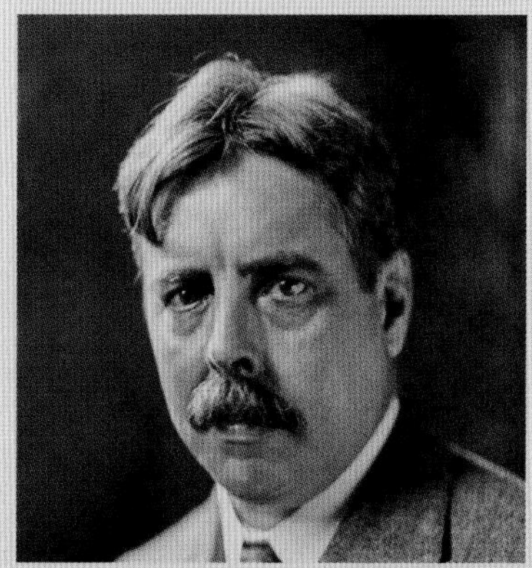

Edward Thorndike

The son of a Methodist minister, Edward Thorndike was born in Williamsburg, Massachusetts, in 1874. He graduated in sciences from Wesleyan University in 1895, proceeding to Harvard to study psychology under William James. In 1897, Thorndike moved to Columbia University in New York City, where he completed his doctorate thesis in 1898.

Thorndike's interest in educational psychology led to a teaching post at the College for Women of Case Western Reserve in Cleveland, Ohio, but he returned to Columbia just a year later, in 1899, teaching there until his retirement in 1939. In 1912, his peers elected him President of the American Psychological Association. Thorndike continued to research and write until his death, aged 74, in Montrose, New York.

Key works

1905 *The Elements of Psychology*
1910 *The Contribution of Psychology to Education*
1911 *Animal Intelligence*
1927 *The Measurement of Intelligence*

ANYONE REGARDLESS OF THEIR NATURE CAN BE TRAINED TO BE ANYTHING

JOHN B. WATSON (1878–1958)

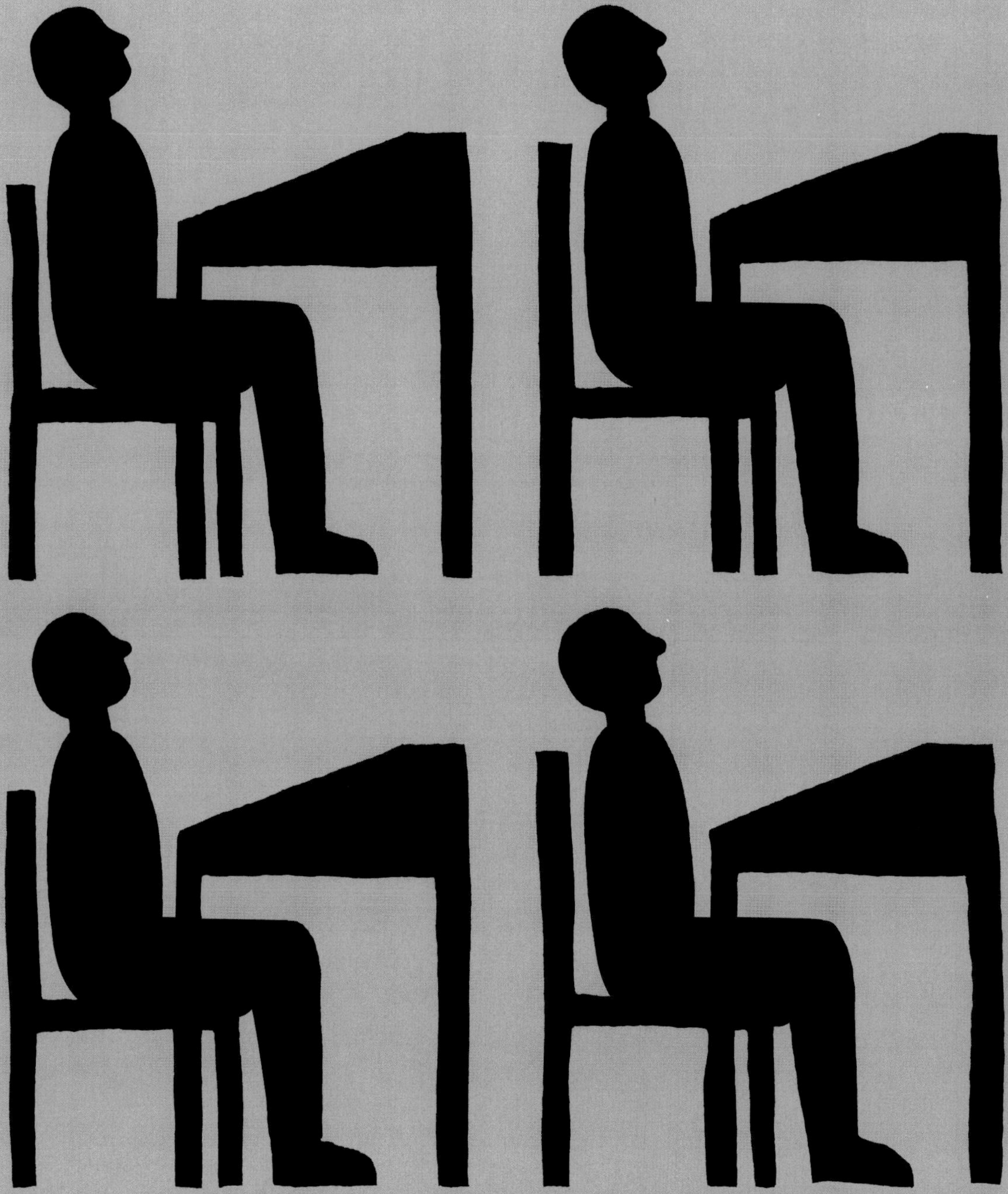

IN CONTEXT

APPROACH
Classical behaviorism

BEFORE
1890s German-born biologist Jacques Loeb (one of Watson's professors) explains animal behavior in purely physical-chemical terms.

1890s The principle of classical conditioning is established by Ivan Pavlov using experiments on dogs.

1905 Edward Thorndike shows that animals learn through achieving successful outcomes from their behavior.

AFTER
1932 Edward Tolman adds cognition into behaviorism in his theory of latent learning.

1950s Cognitive psychologists focus on understanding the mental processes that both lie behind and produce human behavior.

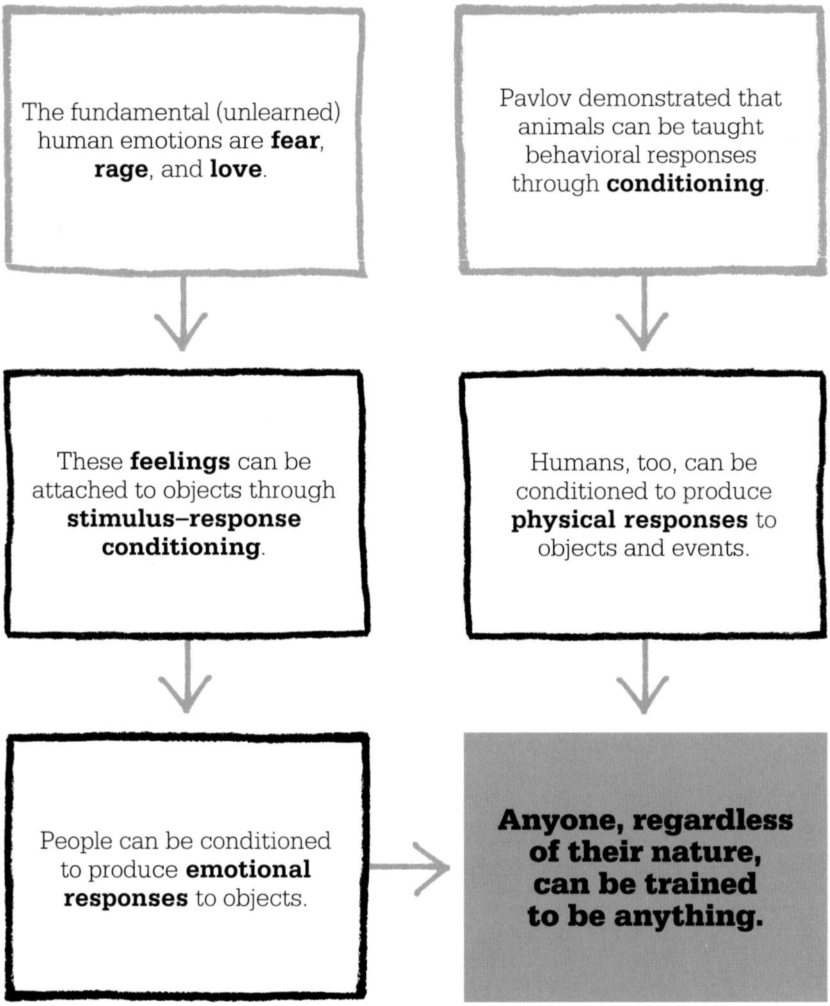

The fundamental (unlearned) human emotions are **fear**, **rage**, and **love**.

These **feelings** can be attached to objects through **stimulus–response conditioning**.

People can be conditioned to produce **emotional responses** to objects.

Pavlov demonstrated that animals can be taught behavioral responses through **conditioning**.

Humans, too, can be conditioned to produce **physical responses** to objects and events.

Anyone, regardless of their nature, can be trained to be anything.

By the beginning of the 20th century, many psychologists had concluded that the human mind could not be adequately studied through introspective methods, and were advocating a switch to the study of the mind through the evidence of behavior in controlled laboratory experiments.

John Watson was not the first advocate of this thoroughgoing behaviorist approach, but he was certainly the most conspicuous. In a career cut short by his marital infidelity, he became one of the most influential and controversial psychologists of the 20th century. Through his work on the stimulus–response learning theory that had been pioneered by Thorndike, he became regarded as the "founding father" of behaviorism, and he did much to popularize the use of the term. His 1913 lecture, *Psychology as the Behaviorist Views It*, put forward the revolutionary idea that "a truly scientific psychology would abandon talk of mental states … and instead focus on prediction and control of behavior." This lecture became known to later psychologists as the "behaviorist manifesto."

Before Watson's research at Johns Hopkins University, in Baltimore, Maryland, the majority of experiments on behavior had concentrated on animal behavior, with the results extrapolated to human behavior. Watson himself studied rats and monkeys for his doctorate but (perhaps influenced by his experience working with the military during World War I) was eager to conduct experiments using human subjects. He wanted to study the stimulus–response model of classical conditioning and how it applied to the prediction and

See also: Ivan Pavlov 60–61 ▪ Edward Thorndike 62–65 ▪ Edward Tolman 72–73 ▪ B. F. Skinner 78–85 ▪ Joseph Wolpe 86–87 ▪ Clark & Phipps Clark 290–291 ▪ Albert Bandura 294–299

Psychology, as the behaviorist views it, is a purely objective experimental branch of natural science.
John B. Watson

control of human behavior. He believed that people have three fundamental emotions—fear, rage, and love—and he wanted to find out whether a person could be conditioned into feeling these in response to a stimulus.

Little Albert

With his research assistant, Rosalie Rayner, Watson began a series of experiments involving "Albert B," a 9-month-old baby chosen from a local children's hospital. The tests were designed to see whether it is possible to teach an infant to fear an animal by repeatedly presenting it at the same time as a loud, frightening noise. Watson also wanted to find out whether such a fear would transfer to other animals or objects and how long this fear would persist. Today, his methods would be considered unethical and even cruel, but at the time they were seen as a logical and natural progression from previous animal studies.

In the now famous "Little Albert experiment," Watson placed the healthy but "on the whole stolid and unemotional" baby Albert on a mattress and then observed his reactions when introduced to a dog; a white rat; a rabbit; a monkey; and some inanimate objects, including human masks and burning paper. Albert showed no fear of any of these animals or objects and even reached out to touch them. In this way, Watson established a baseline from which he could measure any change in the child's behavior toward the objects.

On a separate occasion, while Albert was sitting on the mattress, Watson struck a metal bar with a hammer to make a sudden loud noise; unsurprisingly, Albert became frightened and distressed, bursting into tears. Watson now had an unconditioned stimulus (the loud noise) that he knew elicited a response of fear in the child. By pairing this with the sight of the rat, he hypothesized that he would be able to condition little Albert to become afraid of the animal.

When Albert was just over 11 months old, Watson carried out the experiment. The white rat was placed on the mattress with Albert, then Watson hit the hammer on the steel bar when the child touched the rat. The child burst into tears. This procedure was repeated seven times over two sessions, one week apart, after which Albert became distressed as soon as the rat was brought into the room, even when it was not accompanied by the noise.

By repeatedly pairing the rat with the loud noise, Watson was applying the same kind of classical »

John B. Watson

Born into a poor family in South Carolina, John Broadus Watson's childhood was unhappy; his father was an alcoholic womanizer who left when Watson was 13, and his mother was devoutly religious. Watson became a rebellious and violent teenager, but was a brilliant scholar, attending nearby Furman University at the age of 16. After gaining a PhD from the University of Chicago, he became associate professor at Johns Hopkins University, where his 1913 lecture became known as the "behaviorist manifesto." He worked briefly for the military during World War I, then returned to Johns Hopkins. Forced to resign after an affair with his research assistant, Rosalie Rayner, he turned to a career in advertising while still publishing books on psychology. After Rayner's death in 1935 aged 37, he became a recluse.

Key works

1913 *Psychology as the Behaviorist Views It*
1920 *Conditioned Emotional Reactions* (with Rosalie Rayner)
1924 *Behaviorism*

conditioning as Pavlov had in his experiments with dogs. The child's natural response to the noise—fear and distress—had now become associated with the rat. The child had become conditioned to respond to the rat with fear. In terms of classical conditioning, the rat was initially a neutral stimulus eliciting no particular response; the loud noise was an "unconditioned stimulus" (US) that elicited an "unconditioned response" (UR) of fear. After conditioning, the rat had become a "conditioned stimulus" (CS), eliciting the "conditioned response" (CR) of fear.

However, this conditioning seemed to go deeper than simply a fear of the white rat, and appeared to be far from temporary. In order to test whether Albert's fear had "generalized," or spread to other, similar objects, he was reintroduced to white furry things—including a rabbit, a dog, and a sheepskin coat—five days after the original conditioning. Albert showed the same distressed and fearful response to these as to the rat.

In these experiments, Watson demonstrated that human emotions are susceptible to classical conditioning. This was a new finding, because previous stimulus–response experiments had focused on testing the learning of physical behaviors. Watson had discovered that not only can human behavior be predicted—given certain stimuli and conditions—it can also be controlled and modified. A further check of Albert's reactions to the rat, rabbit, and dog one month later suggested that the effects of this conditioning were long-lasting, but this could not be proven, as Albert was soon after removed from the hospital by his mother. It has been suggested that this was a sign of the mother's distress, but according to Watson and Rayner's own account, it occurred on a prearranged date.

I shall never be satisfied until I have a laboratory in which I can bring up children … under constant observation.
John B. Watson

Infinitely malleable

Watson's career was abruptly brought to an end shortly after the Little Albert experiments when he was forced to resign his professorship amid the scandal of his affair with his researcher, Rosalie Rayner. Despite the incompleteness of his research, Watson felt vindicated in his belief in behaviorism, and more particularly the application of classical stimulus–response conditioning to humans. Perhaps

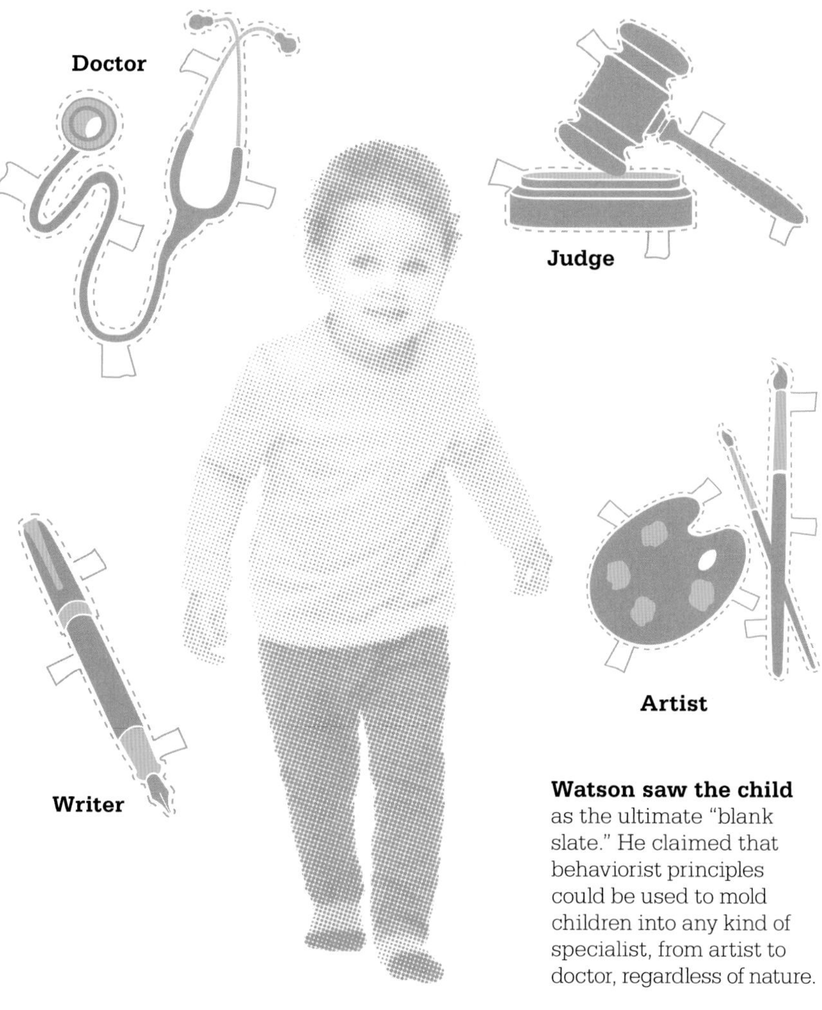

Watson saw the child as the ultimate "blank slate." He claimed that behaviorist principles could be used to mold children into any kind of specialist, from artist to doctor, regardless of nature.

because of his forced ejection from the academic world (into advertising, where he was hugely successful), he developed a tendency to overstate the scope of his findings, and with a natural gift for self-publicity continued to publish books on the subject of psychology.

Not content, for example, to claim that it is possible to condition emotional responses, he boasted that on the same principle it would be possible to control or modify almost any aspect of human behavior, no matter how complex. Just as Little Albert had been conditioned to fear certain white furry objects against his natural inclination, Watson believed that "Anyone, regardless of their nature, can be trained to be anything." He even boasted in his 1924 book *Behaviorism*: "Give me a dozen healthy infants, well-formed, and my own specified world to bring them up in and I'll guarantee to take any one at random and train him to become any type of specialist I might select—doctor, lawyer, artist, merchant-chief, and, yes, even beggar-man and thief, regardless of his talents, penchants, tendencies, abilities, vocations, and race of his ancestors." In the "nature versus nurture" debate, Watson was firmly on the side of nurture.

Watsonism has become gospel and catechism in the nurseries and drawing rooms of America.
Mortimer Adler

Unemotional parenting

Unable to continue his university research, Watson popularized his ideas on behaviorism by turning his attention to the business of childcare. It was in this that his views proved to be most publicly influential, and eventually most controversial. Predictably, he advocated a strictly behaviorist approach to bringing up children, and throughout the 1920s and '30s his many books on childcare became immensely popular. In retrospect, it is easy to see that his approach, based on extreme emotional detachment, was at best misguided and potentially damaging, but his methods were adopted by millions of parents, including Watson and Rosalie Rayner themselves.

The child, Watson believed, is shaped by its environment, and that environment is controlled by the parents. In essence, he saw child-raising as an objective exercise in behavior modification, especially of the emotions of fear, rage, and love. Perhaps understandably, given his own unhappy childhood, he dismissed affection as sentimental, leading to overdependence of the child on the parent. But he also advised against the opposite emotional extreme and was an opponent of physical punishment.

Watson's questionable application of stimulus–response conditioning to childcare eventually drew criticism. Later generations viewed the approach as manipulative and uncaring, with an emphasis on efficiency and results rather than on the well-being of the child. The long-term damage to children brought up according to Watson's behaviorist model became apparent only gradually but was significant. The popularity of his books as childcare "bibles" meant that a whole generation was affected by what can now be seen as a dysfunctional upbringing. Even Watson's own family suffered: Rosalie eventually saw the flaws in her husband's child-rearing theories and wrote a critical article for *Parents' Magazine* entitled "I Am the Mother of a Behaviorist's Sons," and Watson's granddaughter, the actor Mariette Hartley, gave an account of her disturbed family background in her autobiographical book *Breaking the Silence*.

Alternative approaches to childcare soon appeared, even among committed behaviorists. While accepting the basic principle of conditioning established by Watson (despite the dubious ethics of the Little Albert experiment) and using that as a starting point for his own "radical behaviorism," the psychologist B. F. Skinner was to apply behaviorism to the business of childcare in a much more benign (if eccentric) manner. ■

Watson applied his understanding of human behavior to advertising in the 1920s, demonstrating that people can be influenced into buying products through their image, not content.

THAT GREAT GOD-GIVEN MAZE WHICH IS OUR HUMAN WORLD

EDWARD TOLMAN (1886–1959)

IN CONTEXT

APPROACH
Cognitive ("purposive") behaviorism

BEFORE
1890s Ivan Pavlov's experiments with dogs establish the theory of classical conditioning.

1920 John B. Watson conducts behaviorist experiments on humans, notably "Little Albert."

AFTER
1938 B. F. Skinner's research into operant conditioning uses pigeons in place of rats, and becomes more sophisticated.

1950s Cognitive psychology replaces behaviorism as the dominant movement in psychology.

1980s Joseph Wolpe's behavioral therapy and Aaron Beck's cognitive therapy merge into cognitive behavioral therapy.

Although considered one of the leading figures of US behaviorist psychology, Edward Tolman took a very different approach from that of Thorndike and Watson. He agreed with the basic methodology of behaviorism—that psychology could only be studied by objective, scientific experiments—but was also interested in ideas about mental processes, including perception, cognition, and motivation, which he had encountered while studying Gestalt psychology in Germany. By bridging these two previously separate approaches, he developed a new theory about the role of conditioning, and created what he called "purposive behaviorism," now called cognitive behaviorism.

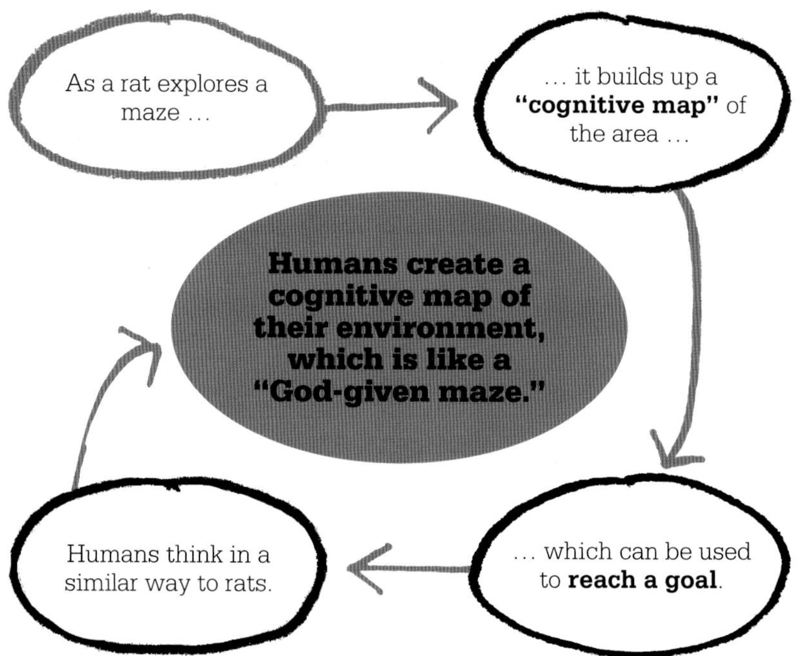
As a rat explores a maze …
… it builds up a **"cognitive map"** of the area …
… which can be used to **reach a goal**.
Humans think in a similar way to rats.
Humans create a cognitive map of their environment, which is like a "God-given maze."

See also: Ivan Pavlov 60–61 ▪ Edward Thorndike 62–65 ▪ John B. Watson 66–71 ▪ B. F. Skinner 78–85 ▪ Joseph Wolpe 86–87 ▪ Wolfgang Köhler 160–161 ▪ Daniel Kahneman 193

There is more than one kind of learning.
Edward Tolman

Tolman questioned the basic premise of conditioned learning—that behavior was learned simply by an automatic response to a stimulus. He believed that animals could learn about the world around them without the reinforcement of a reward, and later use that knowledge in decision-making.

He designed a series of experiments using rats in mazes to examine the role of reinforcement in learning. Comparing a group of rats that were rewarded with food daily for successfully negotiating the maze, with another group who were only rewarded after six days, and a third group rewarded after two days, Tolman's ideas were confirmed. The second and third groups made fewer errors when running the maze the day after they had been rewarded with food, demonstrating that they already "knew" their way around the maze, having learned it prior to receiving rewards. Once rewards were offered, they were able to use the "cognitive map" they had built in order to negotiate the maze faster.

Latent learning

Tolman referred to the rats' initial learning period, where there was no obvious reward, as "latent learning." He believed that as all animals, including humans, go about their daily lives, they build up a cognitive map of the world around them—the "God-given maze"—which they can apply to locate specific goals. He gave the example of how we learn the locations of various landmarks on our daily journeys, but only realize what we have learned when we need to find somewhere along the route. Further experiments showed that the rats learned a sense of location rather than merely the turns required to reach a particular place.

In *Purposive Behavior in Animals and Men*, Tolman outlined his theory of latent learning and cognitive maps, bringing together the methodology of behaviorism with Gestalt psychology, and introducing the element of cognition. ■

A cognitive map of our surroundings develops in the course of our daily lives. We may not be aware of this until we need to find somewhere that we have passed without noticing.

Edward Tolman

Edward Chace Tolman was born into a well-to-do family in West Newton, Massachusetts. He studied at the Massachusetts Institute of Technology, graduating in electrochemistry in 1911, but after reading works by William James opted for a postgraduate degree at Harvard in philosophy and psychology. While studying, he traveled to Germany and was introduced to Gestalt psychology. After gaining his doctorate, he taught at Northwestern University, but his pacifist views lost him his job, and he moved to the University of California at Berkeley. It was here that he experimented with rats in mazes. During the McCarthy period, he was threatened with dismissal for not signing a loyalty oath that he felt restricted academic freedom. The case was overturned in 1955. He died in Berkeley, aged 73, in 1959.

Key works

1932 *Purposive Behavior in Animals and Men*
1942 *Drives Toward War*
1948 *Cognitive Maps in Rats and Men*

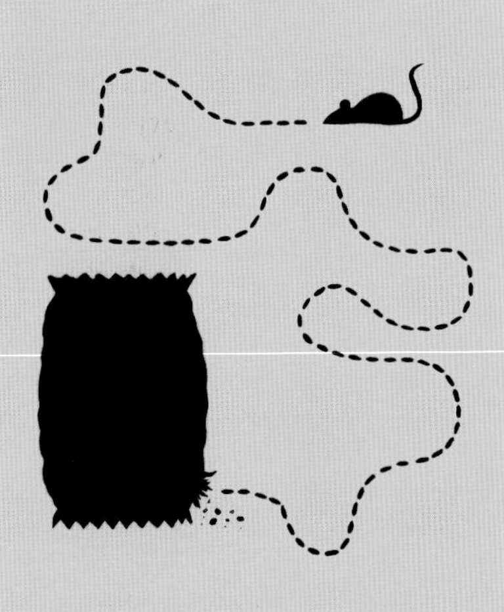

ONCE A RAT HAS VISITED OUR GRAIN SACK WE CAN PLAN ON ITS RETURN

EDWIN GUTHRIE (1886–1959)

IN CONTEXT

APPROACH
Learning theory

BEFORE
1890s Ivan Pavlov shows "classical conditioning" in dogs.

1890s Edward Thorndike designs the "puzzle box" for his experiments on cats.

1920s Edward Tolman queries the role of reinforcement in conditioning.

AFTER
1938 B. F. Skinner's *The Behavior of Organisms* presents the idea of operant conditioning, emphasizing the role of consequences in behavior.

1940s Jean Piaget develops a theory of learning that claims children are naturally driven to explore and acquire knowledge.

1977 Albert Bandura's *Social Learning Theory* states that behavior is learned from observing and copying the behavior of others.

By the 1920s, when American philosopher Edwin Guthrie turned his attention to psychology, the stimulus–response model of learning formed the basis of almost all behaviorist theories. Derived from Ivan Pavlov's idea of "classical conditioning," it claimed that repeatedly exposing subjects to particular stimuli combinations (such as being given food and ringing a bell) could eventually provoke conditioned responses (such as salivating when a bell is rung).

Although Guthrie was a strict behaviorist, he did not agree that conditioning needed reinforcement to be successful. He believed that a full association between a specific stimulus and response is made in their very first pairing. Guthrie's theory of one-trial learning was based on a study in which he observed cats trapped in "puzzle boxes." The cats, once they had discovered the mechanism for escape, made the association between escape and their action, which they would then repeat on subsequent occasions. In the same way, Guthrie said, once a rat has discovered a source of food, it knows where to come when it is hungry.

Guthrie expanded his idea into a theory of "contiguity," stating that "a combination of stimuli, which has accompanied a movement, will on its reoccurrence tend to be followed by that movement." A movement, not behavior, is learned from stimulus–response association. Related movements combine to form an act; repetition does not reinforce the association but leads to the formation of acts, which combine to form behavior. ■

We expect one quarrel to change attitudes.
Edwin Guthrie

See also: Ivan Pavlov 60–61 ▪ Edward Thorndike 62–65 ▪ Edward Tolman 72–73 ▪ B. F. Skinner 78–85 ▪ Jean Piaget 270–277 ▪ Albert Bandura 294–299

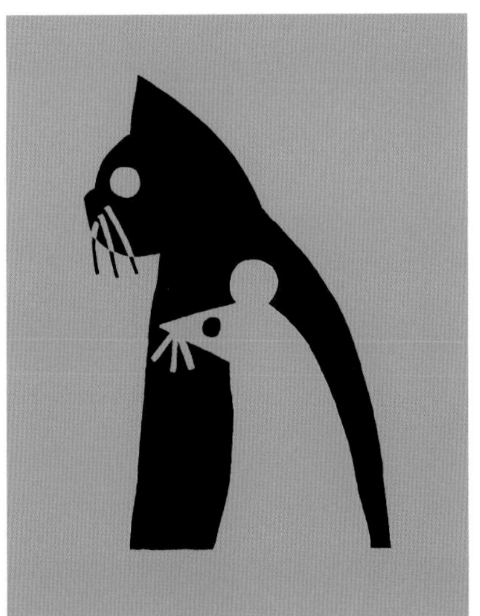

NOTHING IS MORE NATURAL THAN FOR THE CAT TO "LOVE" THE RAT

ZING-YANG KUO (1898–1970)

IN CONTEXT

APPROACH
Behavioral epigenetics

BEFORE
1874 Francis Galton addresses the nature–nurture controversy in *English Men of Science: Their Nature and Nurture.*

1924 John B. Watson makes his famous "dozen infants" boast that anyone, regardless of their basic nature, can be trained to be anything.

AFTER
1938 B. F. Skinner in *The Behavior of Organisms* explains his radical behaviorist ideas, claiming that circumstances, not instinct, govern behavior.

1942 Edward Tolman publishes *Drives Toward War,* which examines whether aggression is conditioned or instinctive.

1966 Konrad Lorenz publishes *On Aggression*, explaining aggressive behavior as an innate response.

In the 1920s, behaviorist John B. Watson was claiming that even innate behavior could be altered by conditioning. But it was the Chinese psychologist Zing-Yang Kuo who took the behaviorist idea to its extreme, denying the existence of instinct as an explanation for behavior.

Kuo felt that instinct was just a convenient way for psychologists to explain behavior that did not fit current theory: "Our behavior researches in the past have been in the wrong direction, because, instead of finding how we could build nature into the animal, we have tried to find nature in the animal." Kuo's most well-known experiments involved rearing kittens—some raised from birth in cages with rats, others introduced to rats at later stages. He found that "if a kitten was raised in the same cage with a rat since it was very young, it, when grown-up, became tolerant of rats: not only would it never attack a rat, but it adopted the rat as its 'mate,' played with it, and even became attached to it."

Harmonious relationships, Kuo proved, can exist between animals that are traditionally regarded as enemies. He concluded that there is no "innate mechanism" driving them to fight.

Kuo's work was cut short by political events in China, which forced him to flee the country. His ideas only became known in the West as behaviorism was beginning to wane and cognitive psychology was in the ascendant. However, his theory of ongoing development without innate mechanisms was influential as a counter to the instinct-based psychology of Konrad Lorenz. ■

See also: Francis Galton 28–29 ▪ John B. Watson 66–71 ▪ Edward Tolman 72–73 ▪ Konrad Lorenz 77 ▪ B. F. Skinner 78–85

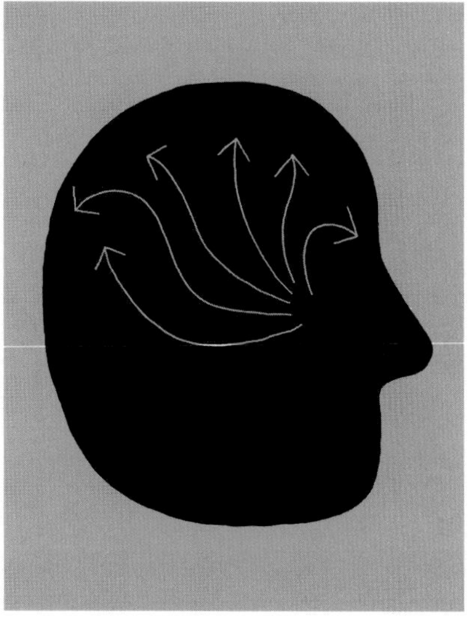

LEARNING IS JUST NOT POSSIBLE

KARL LASHLEY (1890–1958)

IN CONTEXT

APPROACH
Neuropsychology

BEFORE
1861 French anatomist Paul Broca locates the area of the brain responsible for speech.

1880s Spanish pathologist and neuroscientist Santiago Ramón y Cajal develops the theory that the body's nervous system is made up of cells, which German anatomist Heinrich Waldeyer-Hartz later calls "neurons."

AFTER
1949 Donald Hebb describes the formation of cell assemblies and phase sequences in the process of associative learning.

From 1980 Modern brain-imaging techniques such as CT, fMRI (functional magnetic resonance imaging) and PET (positron emission tomography) scanning allow neuroscientists to map specific brain functions.

American physiologist-turned-psychologist Karl Lashley was interested in what happens physically in the brain during the learning process. Pavlov and other behaviorists had suggested that conditioning causes chemical or electrical changes in the brain, and Lashley wanted to pinpoint exactly what these were.

In particular, Lashley wanted to locate the memory trace, or "engram," the specific place in the brain responsible for memory. Like many behaviorists, he used rats in mazes as the basis of a learning experiment. First, the rats learned to find their way through the maze to reach a food reward. Then, Lashley performed surgery on them to remove specific but different parts of the cerebral cortex from each one. After this, the rats were replaced in the maze to test their memory and learning abilities.

There is no great excess of cells which can be reserved as the seat of special memories.
Karl Lashley

No place for memory

What Lashley found was that no matter which part of the brain he removed, the rats' memory of the task remained. Their learning and retention of new tasks was impaired, but the amount of impairment depended on the extent, not the location, of the damage. He came to the conclusion that the memory trace is not localized in a particular place, but distributed evenly throughout the cerebral cortex; each part of the brain is therefore equally important, or equipotential. Decades later, he said that his experiment had led him to "sometimes feel … that the necessary conclusion is that learning is just not possible." ■

See also: John B. Watson 66–71 ▪ Donald Hebb 163 ▪ George Armitage Miller 170–173 ▪ Daniel Schachter 208–209 ▪ Roger Brown 243

IMPRINTING CANNOT BE FORGOTTEN!

KONRAD LORENZ (1903–1989)

IN CONTEXT

APPROACH
Ethology

BEFORE
1859 English biologist Charles Darwin publishes *On the Origin of Species*, describing the theory of natural selection.

1898 Lorenz's mentor, German biologist Oskar Heinroth, begins his study of duck and goose behavior, and describes the phenomenon of imprinting.

AFTER
1959 Experiments by the German psychologist Eckhard Hess show that in imprinting, what has been learned first is remembered best; whereas in association learning, recent learning is remembered best.

1969 John Bowlby argues that the attachment of newborn babies to their mothers is a genetic predisposition.

The Austrian zoologist and doctor Konrad Lorenz was one of the founding fathers of ethology—the comparative study of animal behavior in the natural environment. He began his work observing geese and ducks at his family's summer house in Altenberg, Austria. He noticed that the young birds rapidly made a bond with their mother after hatching, but could also form the same attachment to a foster parent if the mother was absent. This phenomenon, which Lorenz called "imprinting," had been observed before, but he was the first to study it systematically. Famously, he even persuaded young geese and ducks to accept him (by imprinting his Wellington boots) as a foster parent.

What distinguishes imprinting from learning, Lorenz discovered, is that it happens only at a specific stage in an animal's development, which he called the "critical period." Unlike learning, it is rapid, operates independently of behavior, and appears to be irreversible; imprinting cannot be forgotten.

Lorenz went on to observe many other stage-linked, instinctive behaviors, such as courtship behavior, and described them as "fixed-action patterns." These remain dormant until triggered by a specific stimulus at a particular critical period. Fixed-action patterns, he emphasized, are not learned but genetically programed, and as such have evolved through the process of natural selection. ■

Lorenz discovered that geese and other birds follow and become attached to the first moving object they encounter after emerging from their eggs—in this case, his boots.

See also: Francis Galton 28–29 ▪ Ivan Pavlov 60–61 ▪ Edward Thorndike 62–65 ▪ Karl Lashley 76 ▪ John Bowlby 282–285

BEHAVIOR IS SHAPED BY POSITIVE AND NEGATIVE REINFORCEMENT

B. F. SKINNER (1904–1990)

IN CONTEXT

APPROACH
Radical behaviorism

BEFORE
1890 William James outlines the theories of behaviorism in *The Principles of Psychology.*

1890s Ivan Pavlov develops the concept of conditioned stimulus and response.

1924 John B. Watson lays the foundations for the modern behaviorist movement.

1930s Zing-Yang Kuo claims that behavior is continually being modified throughout life, and that even so-called innate behavior is influenced by "experiences" as an embryo.

AFTER
1950s Joseph Wolpe pioneers systematic desensitization as part of behavior therapy.

1960s Albert Bandura's social learning theory is influenced by radical behaviorism.

Burrhus Frederic Skinner, better known as B. F. Skinner, is possibly the most widely known and influential behaviorist psychologist. He was not, however, a pioneer in the field, but developed the ideas of his predecessors, such as Ivan Pavlov and John B. Watson, by subjecting theories of behaviorism to rigorous experimental scrutiny in order to arrive at his controversial stance of "radical behaviorism."

Skinner proved to be an ideal advocate of behaviorism. Not only were his arguments based on the results of scrupulous scientific methodology (so they could be proved), but his experiments tended to involve the use of novel contraptions that the general public found fascinating. Skinner was an inveterate "gadget man" and a provocative self-publicist. But behind the showman image was a serious scientist, whose work helped to finally sever psychology from its introspective philosophical roots and establish it as a scientific discipline in its own right.

Skinner had once contemplated a career as an author, but he had little time for the philosophical theorizing of many of the early psychologists. Works by Pavlov and Watson were his main influence; he saw psychology as following in the scientific tradition, and anything that could not been seen, measured, and repeated in a rigorously controlled experiment was of no interest to him.

Processes purely of the mind, therefore, were outside Skinner's interest and scope. In fact, he reached the conclusion that they must be utterly subjective, and did not exist at all separately from the body. In Skinner's opinion,

The ideal of behaviorism is to eliminate coercion, to apply controls by changing the environment.
B. F. Skinner

B. F. Skinner

Burrhus Frederic Skinner was born in 1904 in Susquehanna, Pennsylvania. He studied English at Hamilton College, New York, intending to be a writer, but soon realized that the literary life was not for him. Influenced by the works of Ivan Pavlov and John B. Watson, he studied psychology at Harvard, gaining his doctorate in 1931 and becoming a junior fellow. He moved to the University of Minnesota in 1936, and from 1946 to 1947 ran the psychology department at Indiana University. In 1948, Skinner returned to Harvard, where he remained for the rest of his life. He was diagnosed with leukemia in the 1980s, but continued to work, finishing an article from his final lecture on the day he died, August 18, 1990.

Key works

1938 *The Behavior of Organisms: An Experimental Analysis*
1948 *Walden Two*
1953 *Science and Human Behavior*
1957 *Verbal Behavior*
1971 *Beyond Freedom and Dignity*

See also: William James 38–45 ▪ Ivan Pavlov 60–61 ▪ John B. Watson 66–71 ▪ Zing-Yang Kuo 75 ▪ Joseph Wolpe 86–87 ▪ Albert Bandura 294–299 ▪ Noam Chomsky 302–305

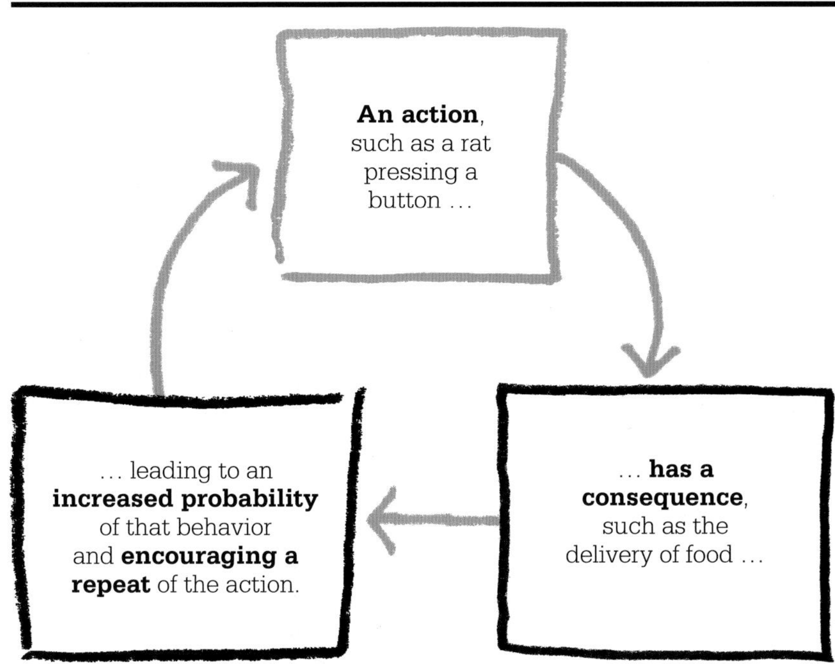

An action, such as a rat pressing a button …
… **has a consequence**, such as the delivery of food …
… leading to an **increased probability** of that behavior and **encouraging a repeat** of the action.

the way to carry out psychological research was through observable behavior, rather than through unobservable thoughts.

Although a strict behaviorist from the outset of his career, Skinner differed from earlier behaviorists in his interpretation of conditioning, in particular, the principle of "classical conditioning" as described by Pavlov. While not disagreeing that a conditioned response could be elicited by repeated training, Skinner felt that this was something of a special case, involving the deliberate, artificial introduction of a conditioning stimulus.

To Skinner, it seemed that the consequences of an action were more important in shaping behavior than any stimulus that had preceded or coincided with it. He concluded from his experiments that behavior is primarily learned from the results of actions. As with so many great insights, this may appear to be self-evident, but it marked a major turning point in behaviorist psychology.

Skinner boxes

While working as a research fellow at Harvard, Skinner carried out a series of experiments on rats, using an invention that later became known as a "Skinner box." A rat was placed in one of these boxes, which had a special bar fitted on the inside. Every time the rat pressed this bar, it was presented with a food pellet. The rate of bar-pressing was automatically recorded. Initially, the rat might press the bar accidentally, or simply out of curiosity, and as a consequence receive some food. Over time, the rat learned that food appeared whenever the bar was pressed, and began to press it purposefully in order to be fed. Comparing results from rats given the "positive reinforcement" of food for their bar-pressing behavior with those that were not, or were presented with food at different rates, it became clear that when food appeared as a consequence of the rat's actions, this influenced its future behavior.

Skinner concluded that animals are conditioned by the responses they receive from their actions and environment. As the rats explored the world around them, some of their actions had a positive consequence (Skinner was careful to avoid the word "reward" with its connotations of being given for "good" behavior), which in turn encouraged them to repeat that behavior. In Skinner's terms, an "organism" operates on its environment, and encounters a »

Skinner boxes were one of many ingenious devices that the psychologist created, giving him total control over the environment of the animals whose behavior he was observing.

Positive reinforcement can stimulate particular patterns of behavior, as Skinner demonstrated by placing a rat in one of his specially designed boxes, fitted with a lever or bar. Pellets of food appeared every time the animal pressed the bar, encouraging it to perform this action again and again.

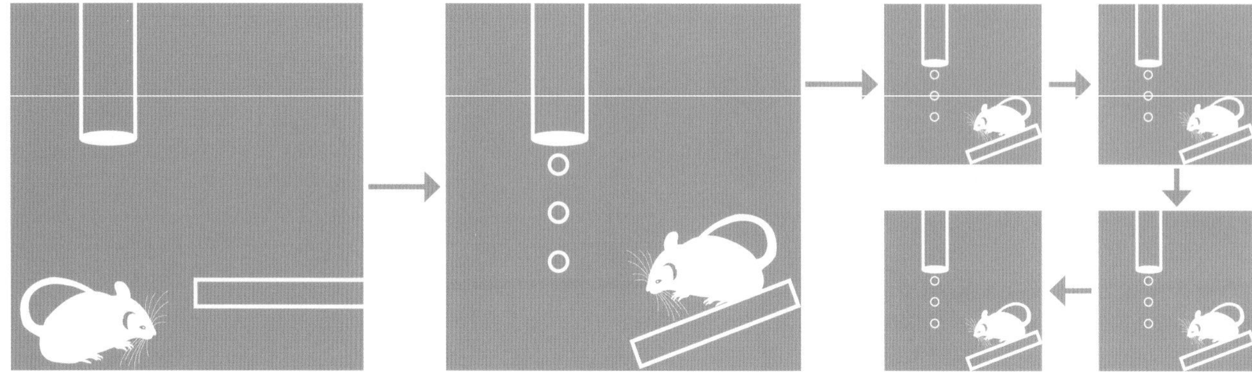

stimulus (a food pellet), which reinforces its operant behavior (pressing on the bar). In order to distinguish this from classical conditioning, he coined the term "operant conditioning;" the major distinction being that operant conditioning depends not on a preceding stimulus, but on what follows as a consequence of a particular type of behavior. It is also different in that it represents a two-way process, in which an action, or behavior, is operating on the environment just as much as the environment is shaping that behavior.

In the course of his experiments, Skinner began to run short of food pellets, forcing him to reschedule the rate at which they were being given to the rats. Some rats now received a food pellet only after they had pressed the bar a number of times repeatedly, either at fixed intervals or randomly. The results of this variation reinforced Skinner's original findings, but they also led to a further discovery: that while a reinforcing stimulus led to a greater probability of a behavior occurring, if the reinforcing stimulus was then stopped, there was a decrease in the likelihood of that behavior occurring.

Skinner continued making his experiments ever more varied and sophisticated, including changes of schedule to establish whether the rats could distinguish and respond to differences in the rate of delivery of food pellets. As he suspected, the rats adapted very quickly to the new schedules.

Negative reinforcement

In later experiments, the floors of the Skinner boxes were each fitted with an electric grid, which would give the rats an unpleasant shock whenever they were activated. This allowed for the investigation of the effect of negative reinforcement on behavior. Again, just as Skinner avoided the word "reward," he was careful not to describe the electric shock as "punishment," a distinction that became increasingly important as he examined the implications of his research.

Negative reinforcement was not a new concept in psychology. As early as 1890, William James had written in *Principles of Psychology*: "Animals, for example, awaken in a child the opposite impulses of fearing and fondling. But if a child, in his first attempts to pat a dog, gets snapped at or bitten, so that the impulse of fear is strongly aroused, it may be that for years to come no dog will excite in him the

Winning at gambling often boosts the compulsion to try again, while losing lessens it, just as changes in the rate at which Skinner's rats were fed made them modify their behavior.

impulse to fondle again." Skinner was to provide the experimental evidence for this idea.

Positive reinforcement

As expected, Skinner found that whenever a behavior resulted in the negative consequence of an electric shock, there was a decrease in that behavior. He went on to redesign the Skinner boxes used in the experiment, so that the rats inside were able to switch off the electrified grid by pressing a bar, which provided a form of positive reinforcement arising from the removal of a negative stimulus. The results that followed confirmed Skinner's theory—if a behavior leads to the removal of a negative stimulus, that behavior increases.

However, the results also revealed an interesting distinction between behavior learned by positive reinforcement and behavior elicited by negative stimuli. The rats responded better and more quickly to the positive stimuli (as well as the removal of negative stimuli), than when their behavior resulted in a negative response. While still careful to avoid the notions of "reward" and "punishment," Skinner concluded that behavior was shaped much more efficiently by a program of positive reinforcement. In fact, he came to believe that negative reinforcement could even be counter-productive, with the subject continuing to seek positive responses for a specific behavior, despite this leading to a negative response in the majority of cases.

This has implications in various areas of human behavior, too—for example, in the use of disciplinary measures to teach children. If a child is continually being punished for something they find enjoyable, such as picking their nose, they are likely to avoid doing so when adults are around. The child may modify their behavior, but only so far as it enables them to avoid punishment. Skinner himself believed that ultimately all forms of punishment were unsuitable for controlling children's behavior.

Skinner's pigeon experiments proved that the positive reinforcement of being fed on the achievement of a task helped to speed up and reinforce the learning of new behavior patterns.

Genetic predisposition

The "shaping" of behavior by operant conditioning has striking parallels with Charles Darwin's theory of natural selection—in essence, that only organisms suited by their genetic make-up to a particular environment will survive to reproduce, ensuring the "success" of their species. The likelihood of a rat behaving in a way that will result in a reinforcing stimulus, triggering the process of operant conditioning, is dependent on the level of its curiosity and intelligence, both of which are determined by genetic make-up. It was this combination of predisposition and conditioning that led Skinner to conclude that "a person's behavior is controlled by his genetic and environmental histories"—an idea that he explored further in his article *The Selection by Consequences,* written for the journal *Science* in 1981.

In 1936, Skinner took up a post at the University of Minnesota, where he continued to refine his experimental research in operant conditioning and to explore practical applications for his ideas, this time using pigeons instead of rats. With the pigeons, Skinner found that he was able to devise more subtle experiments. Using what he described as a "method of successive approximations," he could elicit and investigate more complex patterns of behavior.

Skinner gave the pigeons positive reinforcement for any behavior that was similar to that he was trying to elicit. For example, if he was trying to train a pigeon to fly in a circle clockwise, food would be given for any movement the pigeon made to the right, however small. Once this behavior had » been established, the food was only given for longer flights to the right, and the process was repeated until the pigeon had to fly a full circle in order to receive some food.

Teaching program

Skinner's research led him to question teaching methods used in schools. In the 1950s, when his own children were involved in formal education, students were often given long tasks that involved several stages, and usually had to wait until the teacher had graded work carried out over the entire project before finding out how well they had done. This approach ran contrary to Skinner's findings about the process of learning and, in his opinion, was holding back progress. In response, Skinner developed a teaching program that gave incremental feedback at every stage of a project—a process that was later incorporated into a number of educational systems. He also invented a "teaching machine" that gave a student encouraging feedback for correct answers given at every stage of a long series of test questions, rather than just at

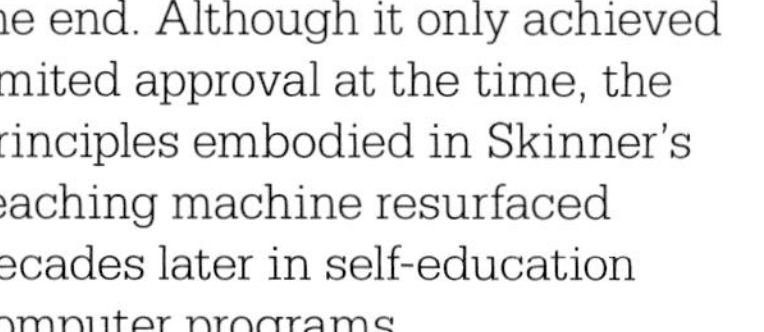

the end. Although it only achieved limited approval at the time, the principles embodied in Skinner's teaching machine resurfaced decades later in self-education computer programs.

It has to be said that many of Skinner's inventions were misunderstood at the time, and gained him a reputation as an eccentric. His "baby tender," for example, was designed as a crib alternative to keep his infant daughter in a controlled, warm, and draft-free environment. However, the public confused it with a Skinner box, and it was dubbed the "heir conditioner" by the press, amid rumors that Skinner was experimenting on his own children. Nevertheless, the baby tender attracted publicity, and Skinner was never shy of the limelight.

War effort

Yet another famous experiment called "Project Pigeon" was met with skepticism and some derision. This practical application of Skinner's work with pigeons was intended as a serious contribution to the war effort in 1944. Missile guidance systems were yet to be invented, so Skinner devised a nose cone that could be attached to a bomb and steered by three pigeons placed inside it. The birds had been trained, using operant conditioning, to peck at an image of the bomb's target, which was projected into the nose cone via a lens at the front. This pecking controlled the flight-path of the missile. The National Defense Research Committee helped fund the project, but it was never used in combat, because it was considered too eccentric and impractical. The suspicion was that Skinner, with his passion for gadgets, was more interested in the invention than in its application. When asked if he thought it right to involve animals in warfare, he replied that he thought it was wrong to involve humans.

In later life as an academic at Harvard, Skinner also expanded on the implications of his findings in numerous articles and books.

The objection to inner states is not that they do not exist, but that they are not relevant in a functional analysis.

B. F. Skinner

Praise or encouragement given at frequent intervals during the progress of a piece of work, rather than one large reward at the end, has been shown to boost the rate at which children learn.

Walden Two (1948) describes a utopian society based on behavior learned with operant conditioning. The book's vision of social control achieved by positive reinforcement caused controversy, and despite its benign intent was criticized by many as totalitarian. This was not a surprising reaction, given the political climate in the aftermath of World War II.

Radical behaviorism

Skinner remained true to his behaviorist approach, coining the term "radical behaviorism" for the branch of psychology he espoused. Although he did not deny the existence of thought processes and mental states, he believed that psychology should be concerned solely with the study of physical responses to prevailing conditions or situations.

In his book, *Beyond Freedom and Dignity*, Skinner took the concept of shaping behavior even further, resurrecting the philosophical debate between free will and determinism. For the radical behaviorist Skinner, free will is an illusion; selection by consequences controls all of our behavior, and hence our lives. Attempts to escape this notion are doomed to failure and chaos. As he put it: "When Milton's Satan falls from heaven, he ends in hell. And what does he say to reassure himself? 'Here, at least, we shall be free.' And that, I think, is the fate of the old-fashioned liberal. He's going to be free, but he's going to find himself in hell."

Views such as these gained him notoriety, and prompted some of his fiercest critics. In particular, the application of his behaviorist ideas to the learning of language in *Verbal Behavior* in 1957 received a scathing review from Noam Chomsky, which is often credited as launching the movement known as cognitive psychology.

Some criticism of Skinner's work, however, has been based on misunderstanding the principles of operant conditioning. Radical behaviorism has often been linked erroneously to the European philosophical movement of logical positivism, which holds the view that statements or ideas are only meaningful if they can be verified by actual experience. But it has in fact much more in common with American pragmatism, which measures the importance or value of actions according to their consequences. It has also been misinterpreted as presenting all living beings as the passive subjects of conditioning, whereas to Skinner operant conditioning was a two-way process, in which an organism operates on its environment and that environment responds, with the consequence often shaping future behavior.

In the 1960s, the focus in psychology swung away from the study of behavior to the study of mental processes, and for a time Skinner's ideas were discredited, or at least ignored. A reappraisal of behaviorism soon followed, however, and his work found an appreciative audience in many areas of applied psychology, especially among educationalists and clinical psychologists—the approach of cognitive behavioral therapy owes much to his ideas. ■

Skinner has an unbounded love for the idea that there are no individuals, no agents—there are only organisms.
Thomas Szasz

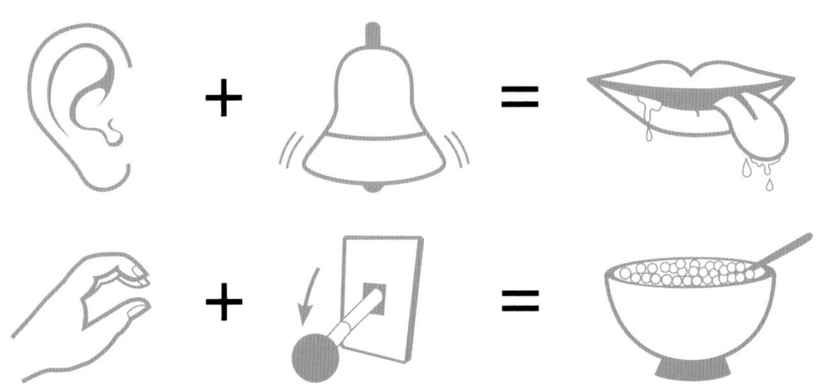

Classical conditioning creates an automatic behavioral response to a neutral stimulus, such as salivating in expectation of food when a bell is rung.

Operant conditioning creates a higher probability of repeated behavior through positive reinforcement, such as releasing food by pulling a lever.

STOP IMAGINING THE SCENE AND RELAX

JOSEPH WOLPE (1915–1997)

IN CONTEXT

APPROACH
Reciprocal inhibition

BEFORE
1906 Ivan Pavlov publishes the first studies on stimulus-response techniques, showing that behavior can be learned through conditioning.

1913 John B. Watson publishes *Psychology as a Behaviorist Views It*, establishing the basic tenets of behavioral psychology.

1920 John B. Watson's Little Albert experiments demonstrate that emotions can be classically conditioned.

1938 B. F. Skinner publishes *The Behavior of Organisms*, presenting his theories on how human behavior relates to biology and the environment.

AFTER
1961 Wolpe introduces the concept of systematic desensitization.

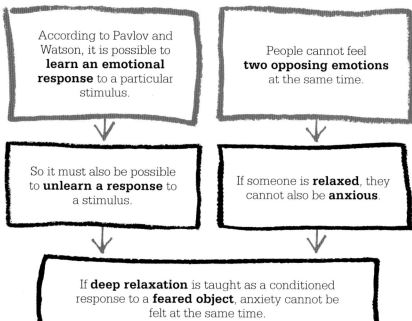

According to Pavlov and Watson, it is possible to **learn an emotional response** to a particular stimulus.

So it must also be possible to **unlearn a response** to a stimulus.

People cannot feel **two opposing emotions** at the same time.

If someone is **relaxed**, they cannot also be **anxious**.

If **deep relaxation** is taught as a conditioned response to a **feared object**, anxiety cannot be felt at the same time.

For most of the first half of the 20th century, psychotherapy was dominated by Freudian psychoanalysis, which assumes that anxiety results from conflicting forces deep within the psyche. This conflict can only be alleviated through a lengthy, introspective analysis of both the individual's conscious and subconscious thoughts, including their formative experiences. But South African-born psychiatrist Joseph Wolpe had treated soldiers for anxiety brought on by posttraumatic stress disorder (then known as "war neurosis") during World War II, and had found these psychotherapeutic practices ineffective in helping his patients. Talking to these men about their

See also: Ivan Pavlov 60–61 ▪ John B. Watson 66–71 ▪ B. F. Skinner 78–85 ▪ Aaron Beck 174–177 ▪ W. H. R. Rivers 340

Behavior depends upon the paths that neural excitation takes.
Joseph Wolpe

experiences did not stop their flashbacks to the original trauma, nor did it end their anxiety.

Unlearning fear

Wolpe believed that there must be a simpler and quicker way than psychoanalysis to address the problem of deep anxiety. He was aware of the work of behaviorists such as Ivan Pavlov and John Watson, who had successfully taught animals and children new behavioral patterns through stimulus-response training, or classical conditioning. They had been able to make a previously unfelt emotional response to an object or event become automatic. Wolpe reasoned that if behavior could be learned in this way, it could also be unlearned, and he proposed to find a method of using this to help disturbed war veterans.

Wolpe had discovered that a human being is not capable of experiencing two contradictory states of emotion at the same time. It is not possible, for example, to feel great anxiety of any kind, when you are feeling very relaxed. This inspired him to teach his patients deep-muscle relaxation techniques, which he went on to pair with simultaneous exposure to some form of anxiety-inducing stimuli—a technique that became known as reciprocal inhibition.

Wolpe's patients were asked to imagine the thing or event that they found disturbing. If they started to become anxious, they would be encouraged to "stop imagining the scene and relax." This approach gradually blocked out a patient's feelings of fear. Just as the patient had previously been conditioned by their experiences to become anxious when recalling certain particularly harrowing memories, they now became conditioned—within a very short time—to block out their anxiety response by focusing on the directly contradictory feeling of being totally relaxed.

Wolpe's reciprocal inhibition succeeded in reconditioning the brain by focusing solely on symptoms and current behavior, without any analysis of a patient's past. It was also effective and brought fast results, and led to many important new techniques in the field of behavioral therapy. Wolpe himself used it to develop a systematic desensitization program to cure phobias, such as fear of mice or flying, which is still widely used. ■

Phobias such as fear of flying have been treated successfully using methods developed from Wolpe's idea of reciprocal inhibition: the pairing of deep relaxation with exposure to the feared experience.

Joseph Wolpe

Joseph Wolpe was born in Johannesburg, South Africa. He studied medicine at the University of Witwatersrand, then served in the South African Army, where he treated people for "war neurosis." Returning to the university to develop his desensitization technique, he was ridiculed by the psychoanalytic establishment for attempting to treat neuroses without first identifying their cause. Wolpe relocated to the US in 1960, taking US citizenship. Initially, he taught at the University of Virginia, then became a professor of psychiatry at Temple University, Philadelphia, where he set up a respected behavioral therapy institute. Renowned as a brilliant teacher, Wolpe continued to teach until he died of lung cancer, aged 82.

Key works

1958 *Psychotherapy by Reciprocal Inhibition*
1969 *Practice of Behavioral Therapy*
1988 *Life Without Fear*

PSYCHOT

THE UNCONSCIOUS DETERMINES BEHAVIOR

HERAPY

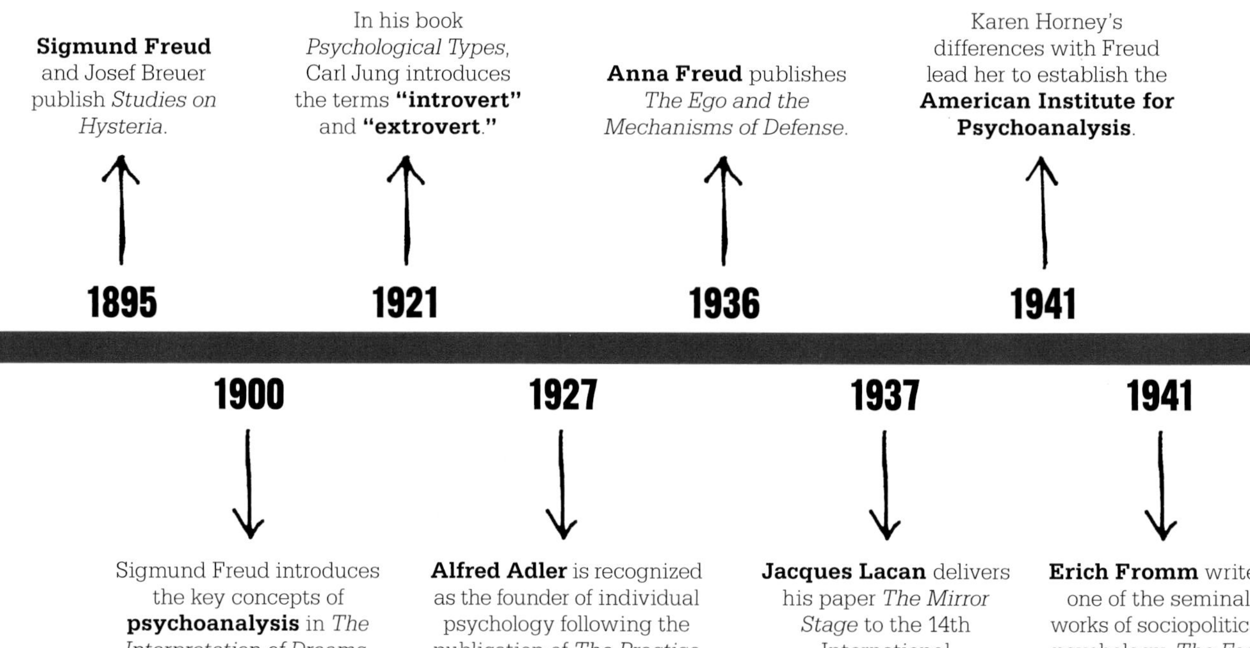

Sigmund Freud and Josef Breuer publish *Studies on Hysteria.*
1895
In his book *Psychological Types,* Carl Jung introduces the terms **"introvert"** and **"extrovert."**
1921
Anna Freud publishes *The Ego and the Mechanisms of Defense.*
1936
Karen Horney's differences with Freud lead her to establish the **American Institute for Psychoanalysis**.
1941
1900
Sigmund Freud introduces the key concepts of **psychoanalysis** in *The Interpretation of Dreams.*
1927
Alfred Adler is recognized as the founder of individual psychology following the publication of *The Practice and Theory of Individual Psychology.*
1937
Jacques Lacan delivers his paper *The Mirror Stage* to the 14th International Psychoanalytical Congress.
1941
Erich Fromm writes one of the seminal works of sociopolitical psychology, *The Fear of Freedom.*

At the turn of the 20th century, behaviorism was becoming the dominant approach to psychology in the US; psychologists in Europe, however, were taking a different direction. This was largely due to the work of Sigmund Freud, whose theories focused on psychopathology and treatment rather than the study of mental processes and behavior. Unlike behaviorism, his ideas were based on observation and case histories rather than experimental evidence.

Freud had worked with the French neurologist Jean Martin Charcot, and was much influenced by the latter's use of hypnosis for the treatment of hysteria. From his time with Charcot, Freud realized the importance of the unconscious, an area of nonconscious thought that he felt was key to our behavior. Freud believed that accessing the unconscious by talking to his patients would bring painful, hidden memories into conscious awareness where the patient could make sense of them, and so gain relief from their symptoms.

New psychotherapies

Freud's ideas spread across Europe and the US. He attracted a circle at his Vienna Psychoanalytic Society, which included Alfred Adler and Carl Jung. However, both these men came to disagree with elements of Freud's theories, going on to develop their own distinct psychodynamic approaches based on Freud's groundwork. Well-known therapists Melanie Klein and Karen Horney, and even Freud's daughter Anna, also broke away from Freud. Despite these differences of opinion, however, Freud's basic ideas were modified rather than rejected by the next generation of psychoanalysts, and subsequent theories place the emphasis on different areas. Erik Erikson, for example, took a more social and developmental approach, while Jung was to formulate the idea of a collective unconscious.

For the first half of the 20th century, psychoanalysis in its various forms remained the main alternative to behaviorism, and it faced no serious challenges until after World War II. In the 1950s, Freudian psychotherapy was still practiced by therapists, especially in France by Jacques Lacan and his followers, but new therapies appeared that sought to bring about genuine change in patients'

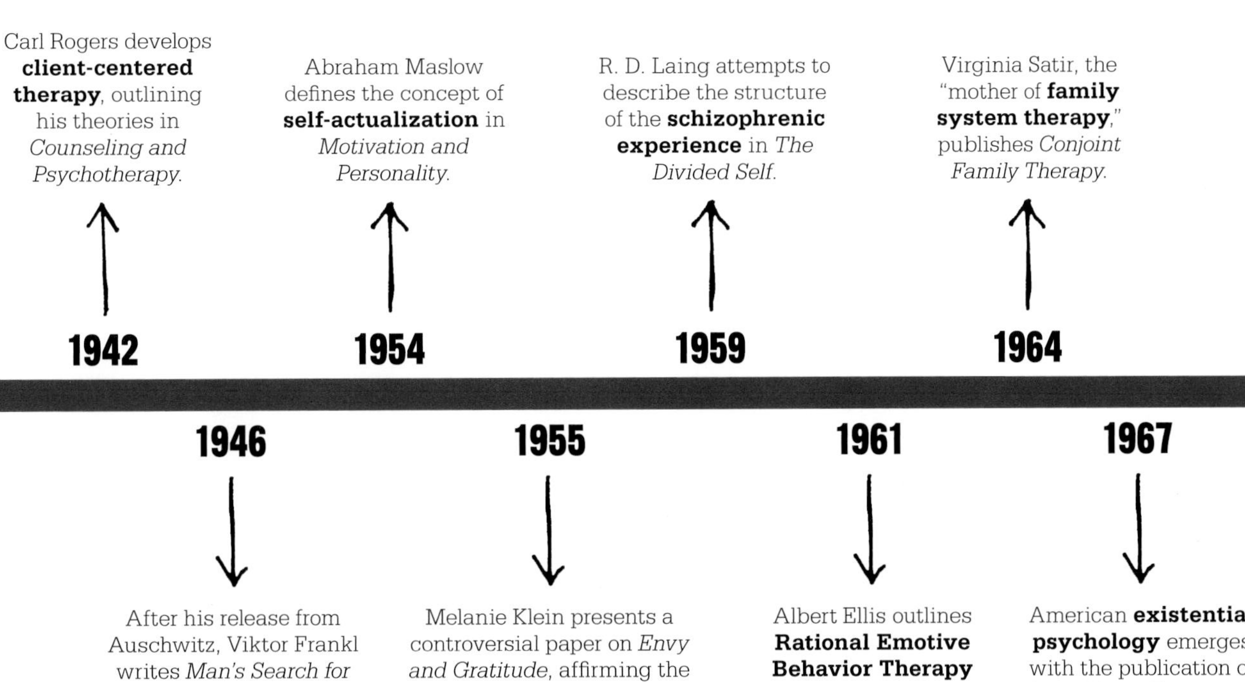

lives. The somewhat eclectic Gestalt therapy was developed by Fritz and Laura Perls and Paul Goodman, while existential philosophy inspired psychologists such as Viktor Frankl and Erich Fromm, who gave therapy a more sociopolitical agenda.

Carl Rogers develops **client-centered therapy**, outlining his theories in *Counseling and Psychotherapy*.
1942
Abraham Maslow defines the concept of **self-actualization** in *Motivation and Personality*.
1954
R. D. Laing attempts to describe the structure of the **schizophrenic experience** in *The Divided Self*.
1959
Virginia Satir, the "mother of **family system therapy**," publishes *Conjoint Family Therapy*.
1964
1946
After his release from Auschwitz, Viktor Frankl writes *Man's Search for Meaning*, outlining the necessity of **finding meaning in suffering**.
1955
Melanie Klein presents a controversial paper on *Envy and Gratitude*, affirming the innate presence of the **"death instinct."**
1961
Albert Ellis outlines **Rational Emotive Behavior Therapy** in *A Guide to Rational Living*.
1967
American **existential psychology** emerges with the publication of Rollo May's *Existence*.

Most importantly, a group of psychologists eager to explore a more humanistic approach held a series of meetings in the US in the late 1950s, setting out a framework for an association known as "the third force," which was dedicated to exploring themes such as self-actualization, creativity, and personal freedom. Its founders—including Abraham Maslow, Carl Rogers, and Rollo May—stressed the importance of mental health as much as the treatment of mental disorders and illnesses. Perhaps the most significant threat to psychoanalysis at this time came from cognitive psychology, which criticized psychoanalysis for its lack of objective evidence—either for its theories or its efficacy as treatment. In contrast, cognitive psychology provided scientifically proven theories and, later, clinically effective therapeutic practices.

Cognitive psychotherapy

Cognitive psychologists dismissed psychoanalysis as unscientific and its theories as unprovable. One of the key concepts of Freudian analysis—repressed memory—was questioned by Paul Watzlawick, and the validity of all forms of memory was shown to be unstable by Elizabeth Loftus. Cognitive psychology instead offered evidence-based psychotherapies such as Albert Ellis's Rational Emotive Behavior Therapy (REBT) and Aaron Beck's cognitive therapy. Freud's emphasis on childhood development and personal history inspired much developmental and social psychology, and in the late 20th century psychotherapists such as Guy Corneau, Virginia Satir, and Donald Winnicott turned their attention to the family environment; while others, including Timothy Leary and Dorothy Rowe, focused on social pressures.

Though Freud's original ideas have often been questioned over the years, the evolution from Freudian psychoanalysis to cognitive therapy and humanistic psychotherapy has led to huge improvements in mental health treatments; and has provided a model for the unconscious, our drives, and behavior. ■

THE UNCONSCIOUS IS THE TRUE PSYCHICAL REALITY

SIGMUND FREUD (1856–1939)

IN CONTEXT

APPROACH
Psychoanalysis

BEFORE
2500–600 BCE The Hindu Vedas describe consciousness as "an abstract, silent, completely unified field of consciousness."

1567 Swiss physician Paracelsus provides the first medical description of the unconscious.

1880s French neurologist Jean-Martin Charcot uses hypnotism to treat hysteria and other abnormal mental conditions.

AFTER
1913 John B. Watson criticizes Freud's ideas of the unconscious as unscientific and not provable.

1944 Carl Jung claims that the presence of universal archetypes proves the existence of the unconscious.

The unconscious is one of the most intriguing concepts in psychology. It seems to contain all of our experience of reality, although it appears to be beyond our awareness or control. It is the place where we retain all our memories, thoughts, and feelings. The notion fascinated Austrian neurologist and psychiatrist Sigmund Freud, who wanted to find out if it was possible to explain things that seemed to lie beyond the confines of psychology at the time. Those who had begun to examine the unconscious feared that it might be filled with psychic activity that was too powerful, too frightening, or too incomprehensible for our conscious mind to be able to incorporate. Freud's work on the subject was pioneering. He described the structure of the mind as formed of the conscious, the unconscious, and the preconscious, and he popularized the idea of the unconscious, introducing the notion that it is the part of the mind that defines and explains the workings behind our ability to think and experience.

Hypnosis and hysteria

Freud's introduction to the world of the unconscious came in 1885 when he came across the work of the French neurologist Jean-Martin Charcot, who seemed to be successfully treating patients for symptoms of mental illness using hypnosis. Charcot's view was that hysteria was a neurological disorder caused by abnormalities of the nervous system, and this idea provided important new possibilities for treatments. Freud returned to Vienna, eager to use this new knowledge, but struggled to find a workable technique.

He then encountered Joseph Breuer, a well-respected physician, who had found that he could greatly reduce the severity of one of his patient's symptoms of mental illness simply by asking her to describe her fantasies and hallucinations. Breuer began using hypnosis to facilitate her access to memories of a traumatic event, and after twice-weekly hypnosis sessions all her symptoms had been alleviated. Breuer concluded that her symptoms had been the result of disturbing memories buried in her unconscious mind, and that voicing the thoughts brought them to consciousness, allowing the symptoms to disappear. This is the case of Anna O, and is the first instance of intensive psychotherapy as a treatment for mental illness.

Anna O, actually Bertha Pappenheim, was diagnosed with paralysis and hysteria. She was treated successfully, with what she described as a "talking cure," by physician Josef Breuer.

Breuer became Freud's friend and colleague, and together the two developed and popularized a method of psychological treatment based on the idea that many forms of mental illness (irrational fears, anxiety, hysteria, imagined paralyses and pains, and certain types of paranoia) were the results of traumatic experiences that had occurred in the patient's past and were now hidden away from consciousness. Through Freud and Breuer's technique, outlined in the jointly published *Studies in Hysteria* (1895), they claimed to have found a way to release the repressed memory from the unconscious, allowing the patient to consciously recall the memory and confront the experience, both emotionally and intellectually. The process set free the trapped emotion, and the symptoms disappeared. Breuer disagreed with what he felt was Freud's eventual

See also: Johann Friedrich Herbart 24–25 ▪ Jean-Martin Charcot 30 ▪ Carl Jung 102–107 ▪ Melanie Klein 108–109 ▪ Anna Freud 111 ▪ Jacques Lacan 122–123 ▪ Paul Watzlawick 149 ▪ Aaron Beck 174–177 ▪ Elizabeth Loftus 202–207

overemphasis on the sexual origins and content of neuroses (problems caused by psychological conflicts), and the two parted; Freud to continue developing the ideas and techniques of psychoanalysis.

Our everyday mind

It is easy to take for granted the reality of the conscious, and naively believe that what we think, feel, remember, and experience make up the entirety of the human mind. But Freud says that the active state of consciousness—that is, the operational mind of which we are directly aware in our everyday experience—is just a fraction of the total psychological forces at work in our psychical reality. The conscious exists at the superficial level, to which we have easy and immediate access. Beneath the conscious lies the powerful dimensions of the unconscious, the warehouse from which our active cognitive state and behavior are dictated. The conscious is effectively the puppet in the hands of the unconscious. The conscious mind is merely the surface of a complex psychic realm.

Since the unconscious is all-encompassing, Freud says, it contains within it the smaller spheres of the conscious and an area called the "preconscious." Everything that is conscious—that we actively know—has at one time been unconscious before rising to consciousness. However, not everything becomes consciously known; much of what is unconscious remains there. Memories that are not in our everyday working memory, but which have not been repressed, reside in a part of the conscious mind that Freud called the preconscious. We are able to bring these memories into conscious awareness at any time. »

The poets and philosophers before me discovered the unconscious; what I discovered was the scientific method by which it could be studied.
Sigmund Freud

When ideas, memories, or impulses are **too overwhelming or inappropriate** for the conscious mind to withstand, they are **repressed** …

… and **stored in the unconscious** alongside our instinctual drives, where they are not accessible by immediate consciousness.

The unconscious silently **directs the thoughts and behavior** of the individual.

The difference between our unconscious and conscious thoughts creates **psychic tension** …

… that can only be released when repressed memories are **allowed into consciousness** through psychoanalysis.

The mind is like an iceberg; it floats with one-seventh of its bulk above water.
Sigmund Freud

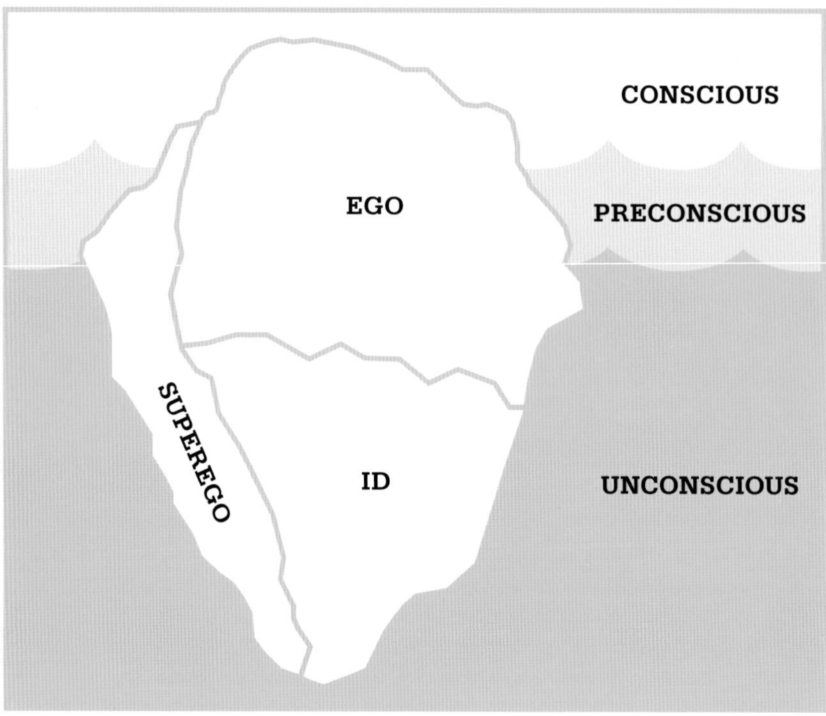

Our psyche, according to Freud, resembles an iceberg, with the area of primitive drives, the id, lying hidden in the unconscious. The ego deals with conscious thoughts and regulates both the id and the superego—our critical, judging voice.

The unconscious acts as a receptacle for ideas or memories that are too powerful, too painful, or otherwise too much for the conscious mind to process. Freud believed that when certain ideas or memories (and their associated emotions) threaten to overwhelm the psyche, they are split apart from a memory that can be accessed by the conscious mind, and stored in the unconscious instead.

Dynamic thought

Freud was also influenced by the physiologist Ernst Brücke, who was one of the founders of the 19th-century's "new physiology," which looked for mechanistic explanations for all organic phenomena. Brücke claimed that like every other living organism, the human being is essentially an energy system, and so must abide by the Principle of the Conservation of Energy. This law states that the total amount of energy in a system stays constant over time; it cannot be destroyed, only moved or transformed. Freud applied this thinking to mental processes, resulting in the idea of "psychic energy." This energy, he said, can undergo modification, transmission, and conversion, but cannot be destroyed. So if we have a thought that the conscious mind finds unacceptable, the mind redirects it away from conscious thought into the unconscious, in a process Freud called "repression." We may repress the memory of a childhood trauma (such as abuse or witnessing an accident), a desire we have judged as unacceptable (perhaps for your best friend's partner), or ideas that otherwise threaten our well-being or way of life.

Motivating drives

The unconscious is also the place where our instinctual biological drives reside. The drives govern our behavior, directing us toward choices that promise to satisfy our basic needs. The drives ensure our survival: the need for food and water; the desire for sex to ensure the continuation of our species; and the necessity to find warmth, shelter, and companionship. But Freud claims the unconscious also holds a contrasting drive, the death drive, which is present from birth. This drive is self-destructive and impels us forward, though as we do so we are moving closer to our death.

In his later works, Freud moved away from the idea that the mind was structured by the conscious, unconscious, and preconscious to propose a new controlling structure: the id, ego, and superego. The id (formed of primitive impulses) obeys the Pleasure Principle, which says that every wishful impulse must be immediately gratified: it wants everything now. However, another part of the mental structure, the ego, recognizes the Reality Principle, which says we can't have everything we desire, but must take account of the world we live in. The ego negotiates with the id, trying to find reasonable ways to help it get what it wants, without resulting in damage or other terrible consequences. The ego itself is controlled by the superego—the internalized voice of parents and society's moral codes. The superego is a judging force, and the source of our conscience, guilt, and shame.

In fact, Freud proposes, the unconscious holds a vast amount of conflicting forces. In addition to the drives of the life and death forces, it encompasses the intensity of repressed memories and emotions, as well as the contradictions inherent in our views of conscious reality alongside our repressed reality. According to Freud, the conflict that arises from these contrasting forces is the psychological conflict that underlies human suffering. Is it any wonder that humans exist in states of anxiety, depression, neurosis, and other forms of discontent?

Psychoanalytical treatment

Since the unconscious remains inaccessible, the only way the conflicts can be recognized is through the symptoms that are present in the conscious. Emotional suffering, Freud claims, is the result of unconscious conflict. We cannot continually fight against ourselves, against the uprising of repressed material, and against the force of death, without emotional turmoil.

Freud's unique approach to the treatment of psychological ailments involved working with the conflicts that existed in the unconscious. He sought to free the patient from repressed memories and so alleviate their mental pain. His approach to treatment is called psychoanalytic psychotherapy, or psychoanalysis. This process is not easy or quick. Psychoanalysis is only performed by a therapist trained in Freud's specific approach, and it is his therapy that encourages a patient to lie on a couch and talk. From Freud's first treatments, psychoanalysis has been practiced in sessions that can sometimes last for hours, take place several times per week, and continue for many years.

A man should not strive to eliminate his complexes, but to get into accord with them; they are legitimately what directs his conduct in the world.
Sigmund Freud

While unconscious thoughts cannot be retrieved through normal introspection, the unconscious can communicate with the conscious in some ways. It quietly communicates via our preferences, the frames of reference in which we tend to understand things, and the symbols that we are drawn to or create.

During analysis, the analyst acts as a mediator, trying to allow unspoken thoughts or unbearable feelings to come to light. Messages arising from a conflict between the conscious and the unconscious are likely to be disguised, or encoded, and it is the psychoanalyst's job to interpret the messages using the tools of psychoanalysis. »

Freud's patients would recline on this couch in his treatment room while they talked. Freud would sit out of sight while he listened for clues to the source of the patient's internal conflicts.

There are several techniques that allow the unconscious to emerge. One of the first to be discussed by Freud at length was dream analysis; he famously studied his own dreams in his book, *The Interpretation of Dreams*. He claimed that every dream enacts a wish fulfillment, and the more unpalatable the wish is to our conscious mind, the more hidden or distorted the desire becomes in our dreams. So the unconscious, he says, sends messages to our conscious mind in code. For instance, Freud discusses dreams where the dreamer is naked—the primary source for these dreams in most people is memories from early childhood, when nakedness was not frowned upon and there was no sense of shame. In dreams where the dreamer feels embarrassment, the other people in the dream generally seem oblivious, lending support to a wish-fulfillment interpretation where the dreamer wants to leave behind shame and restriction. Even buildings and structures have coded meanings; stairwells, mine shafts, locked doors, or a small building in a narrow recess all represent repressed sexual feelings, according to Freud.

Accessing the unconscious

Other well-known ways in which the unconscious reveals itself are through Freudian slips and the process of free association. A Freudian slip is a verbal error, or "slip of the tongue," and it is said to reveal a repressed belief, thought, or emotion. It is an involuntary substitution of a word or phrase for another that inadvertently reveals what is really on the speaker's mind. It is not uncommon, for example, for a married person to use the name of someone on whom they have a crush when they intended to refer

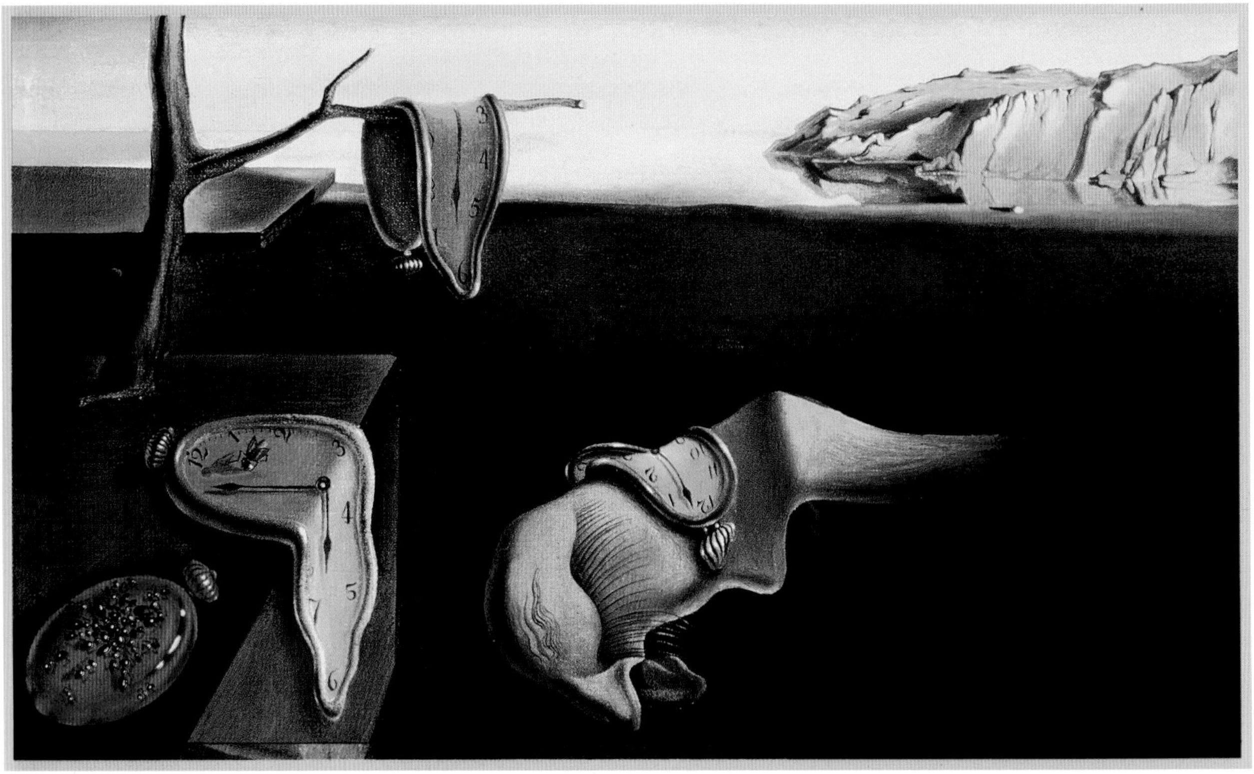

The interpretation of dreams is the royal road to knowledge of the unconscious activities of the mind.
Sigmund Freud

Salvador Dali's *The Persistence of Memory* (1931) is a surrealist vision of time passing, leading to decay and death. Its fantastical quality suggests the Freudian process of dream analysis.

to their spouse—the slip revealing their true feelings. Freud used the free-association technique (developed by Carl Jung), whereby patients heard a word and were then invited to say the first word that came into their mind. He believed that this process allowed the unconscious to break through because our mind uses automatic associations, so "hidden" thoughts are voiced before the conscious mind has a chance to interrupt.

In order to help individuals emerge from a repressed state and begin to consciously deal with the real issues that are affecting them, Freud believed that it is necessary to access repressed feelings. For example, if a person finds it difficult to confront others, they will choose to repress their feelings rather than deal with the confrontation. Over time, however, these repressed emotions build up and reveal themselves in other ways. Anger, anxiety, depression, drug and alcohol abuse, or eating disorders may all be the result of struggling to fend off feelings that have been repressed instead of being addressed. Unprocessed emotions, Freud asserts, are constantly threatening to break through, generating an increasingly uncomfortable tension and inciting more and more extreme measures to keep them down.

Analysis allows trapped memories and feelings to emerge, and the patient is often surprised to feel the emotion that has been buried. It is not uncommon for patients to find themselves moved to tears by an issue from many years ago that they felt they had long since "got over." This response demonstrates that the event and the emotion are still alive—still holding emotional energy—and have been repressed rather than dealt with. In Freudian terms, "catharsis" describes the act of releasing and feeling the deep emotions associated with repressed memories. If the significant event—such as the death of a parent—was not fully experienced at the time because it was too overwhelming, the difficulty and the energy remain, to be released at the moment of catharsis.

School of psychoanalysis

Freud founded the prominent Psychoanalytic Society in Vienna, from which he exerted his powerful influence on the mental health community of the time, training others in his methods and acting as the authority on what was acceptable practice. Over time, his students and other professionals modified his ideas, eventually splitting the Society into three: the Freudians (who remained true to Freud's original thoughts), the Kleinians (who followed the ideas of Melanie Klein), and the Neo-Freudians (a later group who incorporated Freud's ideas into their broader practice). Modern psychoanalysis encompasses at least 22 different schools of thought, though Freud's ideas continue to remain influential for all contemporary practitioners. ■

Like the physical, the psychical is not necessarily in reality what it appears to be.
Sigmund Freud

Sigmund Freud

Born Sigismund Schlomo Freud in Freiberg, Moravia, Freud was openly his mother's favorite child; she called him "Golden Siggie." When Freud was four years old, the family moved to Vienna and Sigismund became Sigmund. Sigmund completed a medical degree, and in 1886 he opened a medical practice specializing in neurology, and married Martha Bernays. Eventually, he developed the "talking cure" that was to become an entirely new psychological approach: psychoanalysis.

In 1908, Freud established the Psychoanalytic Society, which ensured the future of his school of thought. During World War II, the Nazis publicly burned his work, and Freud moved to London. He died by assisted suicide after enduring mouth cancer.

Key works

1900 *The Interpretation of Dreams*
1904 *The Psychopathology of Everyday Life*
1905 *Three Essays on the Theory of Sexuality*
1930 *Civilization and Its Discontents*

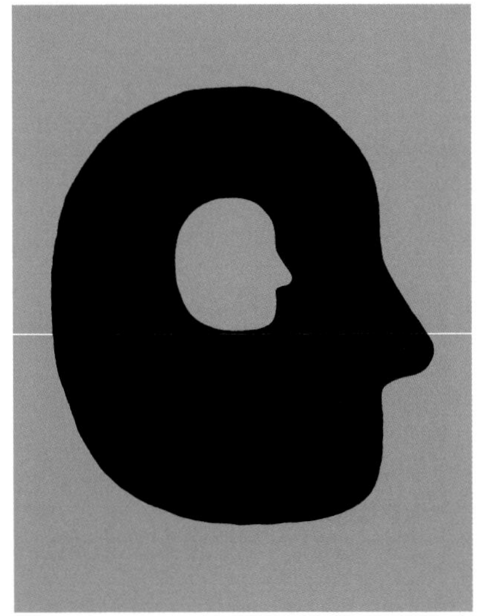

THE NEUROTIC CARRIES A FEELING OF INFERIORITY WITH HIM CONSTANTLY

ALFRED ADLER (1870–1937)

IN CONTEXT

APPROACH
Individual psychology

BEFORE
1896 William James says that self-esteem is about a ratio of "goals satisfied" to "goals unmet" and can be raised by lowering expectations as well as through achievements.

1902 Charles Horton Cooley describes the "looking glass self"; the way we view ourselves is based on how we imagine other people view us.

AFTER
1943 Abraham Maslow says that to feel both necessary and good about ourselves we need achievements as well as respect from others.

1960s British psychologist Michael Argyle states that comparison shapes self-esteem; we feel better when we feel more successful than others, and worse when we feel less successful than others.

Freudian thinking dominated psychotherapy in the late 19th century, but Freud's approach was limited to addressing unconscious drives and the legacy of an individual's past. Alfred Adler was the first psychoanalyst to expand psychological theory beyond the Freudian viewpoint, suggesting that a person's psychology was also influenced by present and conscious forces, and that the influence of the social realm and environment was equally vital. Adler founded his own approach, individual psychology, based on these ideas.

Adler's particular interest in inferiority and the positive and negative effects of self-esteem

Every child feels **inferior** because stronger, smarter people surround them.

Inferiority **motivates** them to try to do and achieve things.

In a **balanced psyche**, success relieves feelings of inferiority ...

... and **confidence** develops.

In an **imbalanced psyche**, success doesn't relieve feelings of inferiority ...

... and an **inferiority complex** develops.

See also: Karen Horney 110 ▪ Eric Fromm 124–129 ▪ Abraham Maslow 138–139 ▪ Rollo May 141 ▪ Albert Ellis 142–145

A paralympic athlete may be driven by a powerful desire to overcome her disabilities and reach greater levels of physical achievement. Adler described this trait as "compensation."

began early in his career, when he worked with physically disabled patients. Looking at the effects that disability had on achievement and sense of self, he found huge differences between his patients. Some disabled people were able to reach high levels of athletic success, and Adler noted that in these personalities, the disability served as a strong motivational force. At the other extreme, he witnessed patients who felt defeated by their disability and who made little effort to improve their situation. Adler realized that the differences came down to how these individuals viewed themselves: in other words, their self-esteem.

The inferiority complex

According to Adler, feeling inferior is a universal human experience that is rooted in childhood. Children naturally feel inferior because they are constantly surrounded by stronger, more powerful people with greater abilities. They will generally seek to emulate and achieve the abilities of their elders, motivated by the surrounding forces that propel them toward their own development and accomplishments.

Children and adults with a healthy and balanced personality gain confidence each time they realize that they are capable of meeting external goals. Feelings of inferiority dissipate until the next challenge presents itself and is overcome; this process of psychic growth is continual. However, an individual with a physical inferiority may develop more generalized feelings of inferiority—leading to an unbalanced personality and what Adler termed an "inferiority complex," where the feelings of inferiority are never relieved.

Adler also recognized the equally unbalanced "superiority complex," manifested in a constant need to strive toward goals. When attained, these goals do not instil confidence in the individual, but merely prompt him to continually seek further external recognition and achievements. ■

To be human is to feel inferior.
Alfred Adler

Alfred Adler

After coming close to death from pneumonia at the age of five, Alfred Adler expressed a wish to become a physician. Growing up in Vienna, he went on to study medicine, branching into ophthalmology before finally settling with psychology. In 1897, he married Raissa Epstein, a Russian intellectual and social activist, and they had four children.

Adler was one of the original members of the Freudian-based Vienna Psychoanalytical Society and the first to depart from it, asserting that individuals are affected by social factors as well as the unconscious drives that Freud identified. After this split in 1911, Adler flourished professionally, establishing his own school of psychotherapy and developing many of psychology's prominent concepts. He left Austria in 1932 for the US. He died of a heart attack while lecturing at Aberdeen University, Scotland.

Key works

1912 *The Neurotic Character*
1927 *The Practice and Theory of Individual Psychology*
1927 *Understanding Human Nature*

THE COLLECTIVE UNCONSCIOUS IS MADE UP OF ARCHETYPES

CARL JUNG (1875–1961)

IN CONTEXT

APPROACH
Psychoanalysis

BEFORE
1899 Sigmund Freud explores the nature of the unconscious and dream symbolism in *The Interpretation of Dreams*.

1903 Pierre Janet suggests that traumatic incidents generate emotionally charged beliefs, which influence an individual's emotions and behaviors for many years.

AFTER
1949 Jungian scholar Joseph Campbell publishes *Hero With a Thousand Faces,* detailing archetypal themes in literature from many different cultures throughout history.

1969 British psychologist John Bowlby states that human instinct is expressed as patterned action and thought in social exchanges.

Myths and symbols are strikingly similar in cultures around the world and across the centuries.

↓

Therefore, they must be a result of the **knowledge and experiences we share** as a species.

↓

The memory of this shared experience is held ...

↓

... in the **collective unconscious**, which is part of each and every person.

... in the form of **archetypes**—symbols that act as organizing forms for behavioral patterns.

↓

Each of us is born with the innate tendency to use these archetypes to **understand the world**.

Sigmund Freud introduced the idea that rather than being guided by forces outside ourselves, such as God or fate, we are motivated and controlled by the inner workings of our own minds, specifically, the unconscious. He claimed that our experiences are affected by primal drives contained in the unconscious. His protégé, the Swiss psychiatrist Carl Jung, took this idea further, delving into the elements that make up the unconscious and its workings.

Jung was fascinated by the way that societies around the world share certain striking similarities, despite being culturally very different. They share an uncanny commonality in their myths and symbols, and have for thousands of years. He thought that this must be due to something larger than a person's individual experience; the symbols, he decided, must exist as part of the human psyche.

It seemed to Jung that the existence of these shared myths proved that part of the human psyche contains ideas that are held in a timeless structure, which acts as a form of "collective memory." Jung introduced the notion that one distinct and separate part of the unconscious exists within each of us, which is not based on any of our own individual experiences—this is the "collective unconscious."

The commonly found myths and symbols are, for Jung, part of this universally shared collective unconscious. He believed that the symbols exist as part of hereditary memories that are passed on from generation to generation, changing only slightly in their attributes across different cultures and time periods. These inherited memories emerge within the psyche in the language of symbols, which Jung calls "archetypes."

See also: Pierre Janet 54–55 ▪ Sigmund Freud 92–99 ▪ Jacques Lacan 122–123 ▪ Steven Pinker 213

The personal unconscious rests upon a deeper layer … I call the collective unconscious.
Carl Jung

Ancient memories

Jung believes that the archetypes are layers of inherited memory, and they constitute the entirety of the human experience. The Latin word *archetypum* translates as "first-molded," and Jung believed that archetypes are memories from the experiences of our first ancestors. They act as templates within the psyche that we use unconsciously to organize and understand our own experience. We may fill out the gaps with details from our individual lives, but it is this preexisting substructure in the unconscious that is the framework that allows us to make sense of our experience.

Archetypes can be thought of as inherited emotional or behavioral patterns. They allow us to recognize a particular set of behaviors or emotional expressions as a unified pattern that has meaning. It seems that we do this instinctively, but Jung says that what seems to be instinct is actually the unconscious use of archetypes.

Jung suggests that the psyche is composed of three components: the ego, the personal unconscious, and the collective unconscious. The ego, he says, represents the conscious mind or self, while the personal unconscious contains the individual's own memories, including those that have been suppressed. The collective unconscious is the part of the psyche that houses the archetypes.

The archetypes

There are many archetypes, and though they can blend and mold into each other in different cultures, each of us contains within us the model of each archetype. Since we use these symbolic forms to make sense of the world and our experiences, they appear in all human forms of expression, such as art, literature, and drama.

The nature of an archetype is such that we recognize it instantly and are able to attach to it a specific, emotional meaning. Archetypes can be associated with many kinds of behavioral and emotional patterns, but there are certain prominent ones that are highly recognizable, such as The Wise Old Man, The Goddess, The Madonna, the Great Mother, and The Hero.

The Persona is one of the most important archetypes described by Jung. He recognized early in his own life that he had a tendency to share only a certain part of his personality with the outside world. He also recognized this trait in other people, and noted that human beings divide their personalities into components, selectively sharing only certain components of their selves according to the environment and situation. The self that we present to the world—our public image—is an archetype, which Jung calls the "Persona."

Jung's theories of gender take a binary perspective, and he believes that the self has both masculine and feminine parts and is molded into becoming fully male or female by society as much as biology. When we become wholly male or female we turn our backs on half of our potential, though we can still access this part of the self through an archetype. The Animus exists as the masculine component of the female personality, and the Anima as the feminine attributes of the male psyche. This is the "other half," the half that was taken from us as we grew into a girl or boy. These archetypes help us to understand the nature of the opposite sex, and because they contain "deposits of all the impressions ever made" by a man or woman, so they necessarily reflect the stereotyped ideas of masculine and feminine. »

Eve is one representation of the Anima, the female part of a man's unconscious. Jung says she is "full of snares and traps, in order that man should fall … and life should be lived."

All the most powerful ideas in history go back to archetypes.
Carl Jung

The Animus is represented in our culture as the "real man"; he is the muscle man, the commander of soldiers, the cool logician, and the romantic seducer. The Anima appears as a wood nymph, a virgin, a seductress. She can be close to nature, intuitive, and spontaneous. She appears in paintings and stories as Eve, or Helen of Troy, or a personality such as Marilyn Monroe, bewitching men or sucking the life from them. As these archetypes exist in our unconscious, they can affect our moods and reactions, and can manifest themselves as prophetic statements (Anima) or unbending rationality (Animus).

Jung defines one archetype as representing the part of ourselves we do not want the world to see. He calls it the Shadow, and it is the opposite of the Persona, representing all our secret or repressed thoughts and the shameful aspects of our character. It appears in the Bible as the devil, and in literature as Dr. Jekyll's Mr. Hyde. The Shadow is the "bad" side of ourselves that we project onto others, and yet it is not entirely negative; it may represent aspects that we choose to suppress only because they are unacceptable in a particular situation.

Of all the archetypes, the most important is the True Self. This is a central, organizing archetype that attempts to harmonize all other aspects into a unified, whole self. According to Jung, the real goal of human existence is to achieve an advanced, enlightened psychological state of being that he refers to as "self-realization," and the route to this lies in the archetype of the True Self. When fully realized, this archetype is the source of wisdom and truth, and is able to connect the self to the spiritual. Jung stressed that self-realization does not happen automatically, it must be consciously sought.

Dr. Jekyll transforms into the evil Mr. Hyde in a story by Robert Louis Stevenson that explores the idea of the "darker self," through a character that embodies Jung's Shadow archetype.

Archetypes in dreams

The archetypes are of significant importance in the interpretation of dreams. Jung believed that dreams are a dialogue between the conscious self and the eternal (the ego and the collective unconscious), and that the archetypes operate as symbols within the dream, facilitating the dialogue.

The archetypes have specific meanings in the context of dreams. For instance, the archetype of The Wise Old Man or Woman may be represented in a dream by a spiritual leader, parent, teacher, or doctor—it indicates those who offer guidance, direction, and wisdom. The Great Mother, an archetype who might appear as the dreamer's own mother or grandmother, represents the nurturer. She provides reassurance, comfort, and validation. The Divine Child, the archetype that represents your True Self in its purest form, symbolizing innocence or vulnerability, would appear as a baby or child in dreams, suggesting openness or potential. And lest the ego grow too large, it is kept in check by the appearance of the Trickster, a playful archetype that exposes the dreamer's vulnerabilities and plays jokes, preventing the individual from taking himself and his desires too seriously. The Trickster also

The tale of Snow White can be found all over the world with minor variations. Jung attributed the universal popularity of fairy tales and myths to their use of archetypal characters.

appears as the Norse half-god Loki, the Greek god Pan, the West African spider god Anansi, or simply a magician or clown.

Using the archetypes

The archetypes exist in our minds before conscious thought, and can therefore have an immensely powerful impact on our perception of experience. Whatever we may consciously think is happening, what we choose to perceive—and therefore experience—is governed by these preformed ideas within the unconscious. In this way, the collective unconscious and its contents affect the conscious state. According to Jung, much of what we generally attribute to deliberate, reasoned, conscious thinking is actually already being guided by unconscious activity, especially the organizing forms of the archetypes.

In addition to his ideas of the collective unconscious and the archetypes, Jung was the first to explore the practice of word association, and he also introduced the concepts of the "extrovert" and "introvert" personality types. These ultimately inspired widely used personality tests such as the Myers–Briggs Type Indicator (MBTI). Jung's work was influential in the fields of psychology, anthropology, and spirituality, and his archetypes are so widespread that they can easily be identified in film, literature, and other cultural forms that attempt to portray universal characters. ■

By understanding the unconscious we free ourselves from its domination.
Carl Jung

Carl Jung

Carl Gustav Jung was born in a small Swiss village to an educated family with a fair share of eccentrics. He was close to his mother, though she suffered from bouts of depression. A talented linguist, Jung mastered many European languages as well as several ancient ones, including Sanskrit. He married Emma Rauschenbach in 1903 and they had five children.

Jung trained in psychiatry, but after meeting Sigmund Freud in 1907, he became a psychoanalyst and Freud's heir apparent. However, the pair grew estranged over theoretical differences and never met again. In the years following World War I, Jung traveled widely through Africa, America, and India, studying native people and taking part in anthropological and archaeological expeditions. He became a professor at the University of Zurich in 1935, but gave up teaching to concentrate on research.

Key works

1912 *Symbols of Transformation*
1934 *The Archetypes and the Collective Unconscious*
1945 *On the Nature of Dreams*

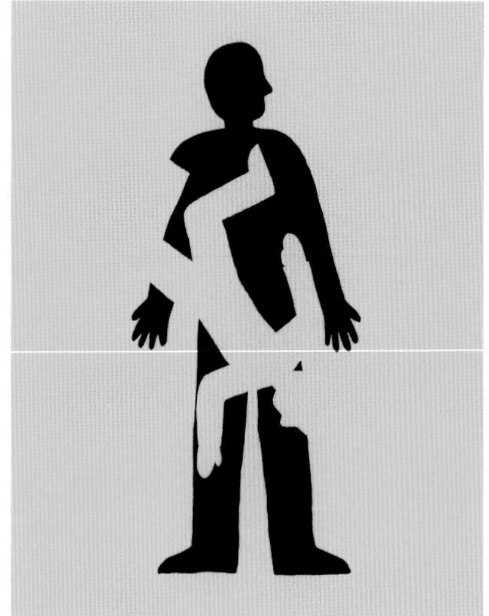

THE STRUGGLE BETWEEN THE LIFE AND DEATH INSTINCTS PERSISTS THROUGHOUT LIFE

MELANIE KLEIN (1882–1960)

IN CONTEXT

APPROACH
Psychoanalysis

BEFORE
1818 German philosopher Arthur Schopenhauer states that existence is driven by the will to live, which is constantly being opposed by an equally forceful death drive.

1910 Psychoanalyst Wilhelm Stekel suggests that social suppression of the sexual instinct is paralleled by the growth of a death instinct.

1932 Sigmund Freud claims that the most basic drive for satisfaction is in fact a striving toward death.

AFTER
2002 American psychologist Julie K. Norem introduces the idea of "defensive pessimism," suggesting that being pessimistic may in fact better prepare people to cope with the demands and stresses of modern life.

The theme of opposing forces has always intrigued writers, philosophers, and scientists. Literature, religion, and art are filled with tales of good and evil, of friend and foe. Newtonian physics states that stability or balance is achieved through one force being countered by an equal and opposite force. Such opposing forces appear to be an essential part of existence, and perhaps the most powerful of them are the instinctive drives we have for life and death.

To avoid being destroyed by our own death instinct, Sigmund Freud said, we employ our narcissistic or self-regarding life instinct (libido) to force the death instinct outward, directing it against other objects. Melanie Klein expanded on this, saying that even as we redirect the death force outward, we still sense the danger of being destroyed by "this instinct of aggression;" we acknowledge the huge task of "mobilizing the libido" against it. Living with these opposing forces is an inherent psychological conflict that is central to human experience. Klein claimed that our tendencies toward growth and creation—from procreation to creativity—are forced to run constantly against an equally powerful and destructive force, and that this ongoing psychic tension underlies all suffering.

Great drama reflects real emotions and feelings. Films such as *West Side Story* (both the original, shown, and the 2021 remake) portray love's life-affirming force and its toxic aspects.

Klein also stated that this psychic tension explains our innate tendency toward aggression and violence. It creates a related struggle between love and hate, present even in a newborn baby. This constant battle between our life and death instincts—between pleasure and pain, renewal and destruction—results in confusion within our psyches. Anger or

See also: Sigmund Freud 92–99 ▪ Anna Freud 111 ▪ Jacques Lacan 122–123

"bad" feelings may then become directed toward every situation, whether they are good or bad.

Constant conflict

Klein believed that we never shed these primitive impulses. We maintain them throughout life, never reaching a safe, mature state, but living with an unconscious that simmers with "primitive fantasies" of violence. Given the permeating influence of such a psychic conflict, Klein thought that traditional notions of happiness are impossible to attain, and that living is about finding a way to tolerate the conflict; it is not about achieving nirvana.

As this state of tolerance is the best that we can hope for, Klein found it unsurprising that life falls short of what people desire or believe they deserve, resulting in depression and disappointment. Human experience, to Klein, is inevitably filled with anxiety, pain, loss, and destruction. People must, therefore, learn to work within the extremes of life and death. ■

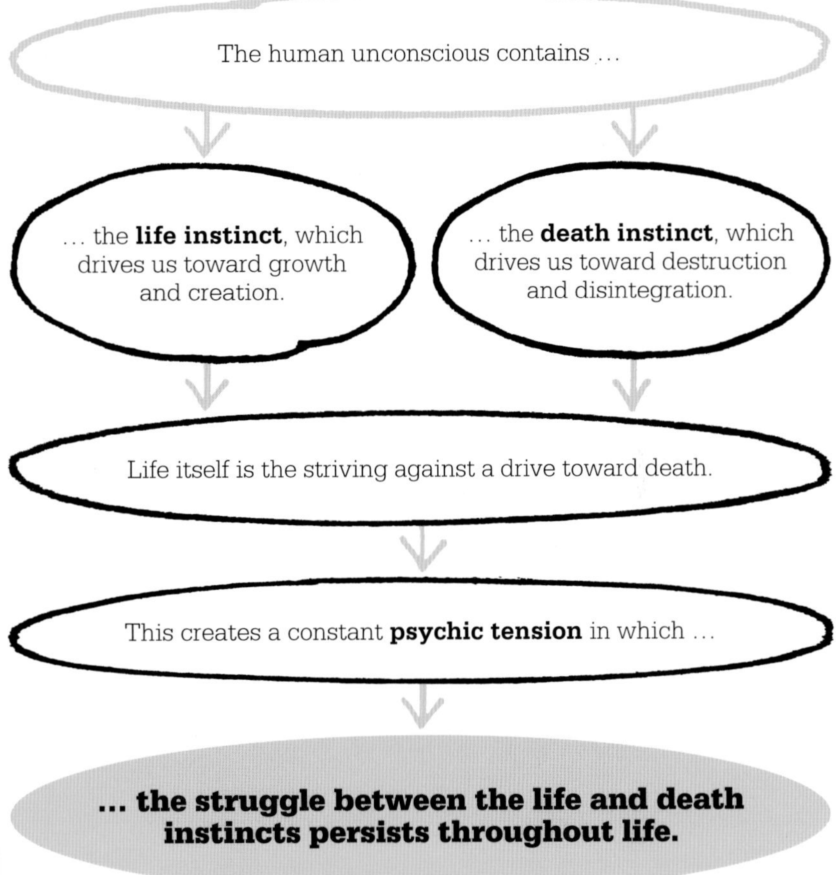

The human unconscious contains ...
... the **life instinct**, which drives us toward growth and creation.
... the **death instinct**, which drives us toward destruction and disintegration.
Life itself is the striving against a drive toward death.
This creates a constant **psychic tension** in which ...
... the struggle between the life and death instincts persists throughout life.

Melanie Klein

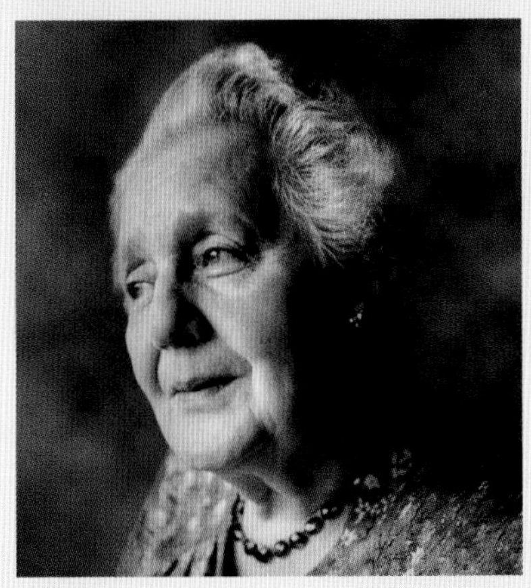

One of four children, Melanie Klein was born in Austria. Her parents, who later divorced, were cold and unaffectionate. At 17, she became engaged to Arthur Klein, an industrial chemist, casting aside her plans to study medicine.

Klein decided to become a psychoanalyst after reading a book by Sigmund Freud in 1910. She suffered from depression herself, and was haunted by death: her adored elder sister died when Klein was four; her older brother died in a suspected suicide; and her son was killed in a climbing accident in 1933.

Although Klein did not have any formal academic qualifications, she was a major influence in the field of psychoanalysis, and is particularly revered for her work with children, and for her use of play as a form of therapy.

Key works

1932 *The Psychoanalysis of Children*
1935 *A Contribution to The Psychogenesis of Manic Depressive States*
1961 *Narrative of a Child Analysis*

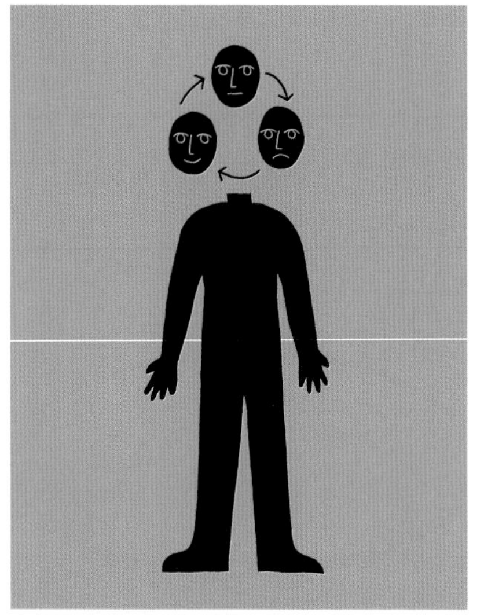

THE TYRANNY OF THE "SHOULDS"

KAREN HORNEY (1885–1952)

IN CONTEXT

APPROACH
Psychoanalysis

BEFORE
1889 In *L'Automatism Psychologique*, Pierre Janet describes "splitting," where a personality branches into distinct, separate parts.

AFTER
1950s Melanie Klein says that people split off parts of their personalities to cope with otherwise unmanageable, conflicting feelings.

1970s Austrian psychoanalyst Heinz Kohut claims that when a child's needs are not met, a fragmented self emerges, consisting of the narcissistic self and the grandiose self.

1970s Albert Ellis develops Rational Emotive Behavioral Therapy to free people from internalized "musts."

Social environments—from the family to schools, workplaces, and the wider community—develop cultural "norms" upheld by certain beliefs. The German-born psychoanalyst Karen Horney said that unhealthy, or "toxic," social environments are likely to create unhealthy belief systems in individuals, hindering people from realizing their highest potential.

Horney said that it is essential to recognize when we are not operating from self-determined beliefs, but from those internalized from a toxic environment. These play out as internalized messages, especially in the form of "shoulds," such as "I should be recognized and powerful" or "I should be thin." She taught her patients to become aware of two influences in their psyche: the "real self" with authentic desires, and the "ideal self" that strives to fulfill all the demands of the "shoulds." The ideal self fills the mind with ideas that are unrealistic and inappropriate to the journey of the real self, and generates negative feedback based on the "failures" of the real self to achieve the expectations of the ideal self. This leads to the development of a third, unhappy self—the "despised self."

Horney says the "shoulds" are the basis of our "bargain with fate"; if we obey them, we believe we can magically control external realities, though in reality they lead to deep unhappiness and neurosis. Horney's views were particularly relevant in her own social environment, early 20th-century Germany, which leaned heavily toward conformity. ■

Forget about the disgraceful creature you actually *are*; this is how you *should be*.
Karen Horney

See also: Pierre Janet 54–55 ▪ Sigmund Freud 92–99 ▪ Melanie Klein 108–109 ▪ Carl Rogers 130–137 ▪ Abraham Maslow 138–139 ▪ Albert Ellis 142–145

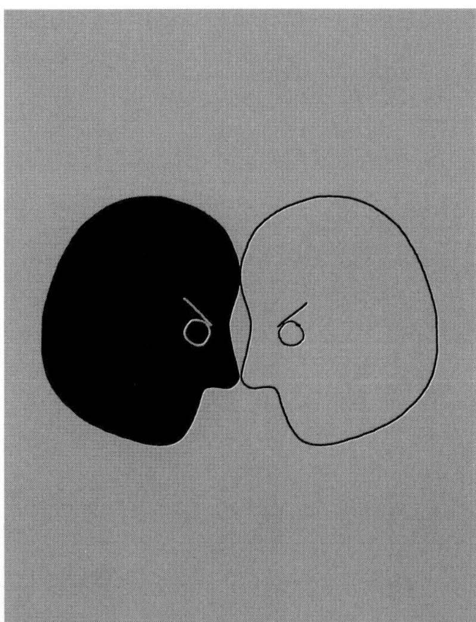

THE SUPEREGO BECOMES CLEAR ONLY WHEN IT CONFRONTS THE EGO WITH HOSTILITY
ANNA FREUD (1895–1982)

IN CONTEXT

APPROACH
Psychoanalysis

BEFORE
1920 Sigmund Freud first uses the concepts of the ego, id, and superego in his essay *Beyond the Pleasure Principle.*

AFTER
1950s Melanie Klein disagrees that actual parental influence is involved in the formation of the superego.

1961 Eric Berne presents the idea that we retain child, adult, and parental ego states throughout our lives, and says that these can be explored through analysis.

1976 American psychologist Jane Loevinger says that the ego develops in stages throughout a person's life, as a result of an interaction between the inner self and the outer environment.

According to the Bible, Adam and Eve in the Garden of Eden are decision-makers, faced with the choice between temptation and righteousness. In his structural model of the psyche, Sigmund Freud describes a similar model within the human unconscious, proposing a psychic apparatus of three parts: the id, the superego, and the ego.

The id, like a sneaky serpent, whispers to us to do what feels good. It is driven entirely by desire, seeking pleasure and the fulfilment of basic drives (such as food, comfort, warmth, and sex). The superego, like a righteous presence, calls us to follow the higher path. It imposes parental and societal values and tells us what we should and should not do. Lastly, the ego—like a decision-making adult—controls impulses and forms judgments on how to act; it is the moderator, suspended between the id and the superego.

Austrian psychoanalyst Anna Freud expanded upon her father's ideas, drawing attention to the formation of the superego and its effects upon the ego. The ego takes account of the realities of the world, and is also simultaneously engaged with the id and relegated to an inferior position by the superego. The superego speaks through the language of guilt and shame, like a kind of internalized critical parent. We hear the superego when we berate ourselves for thinking or acting a certain way; the superego becomes clear (or "speaks out") only when it confronts the ego with hostility.

Ego defense mechanisms

The critical voice of the superego leads to anxiety, and this is when, according to Anna Freud, we bring ego defenses into play. These are the myriad methods that the mind uses to prevent anxiety from becoming overwhelming. Freud described the many and creative defense mechanisms we employ, from humor and sublimation to denial and displacement. Her theory of ego defenses was to prove a rich seam of thought within the humanist therapies of the 20th century. ■

See also: Sigmund Freud 92–99 ▪ Melanie Klein 108–109 ▪ Eric Berne 344

TRUTH CAN BE TOLERATED ONLY IF YOU DISCOVER IT YOURSELF

FRITZ PERLS (1893–1970)

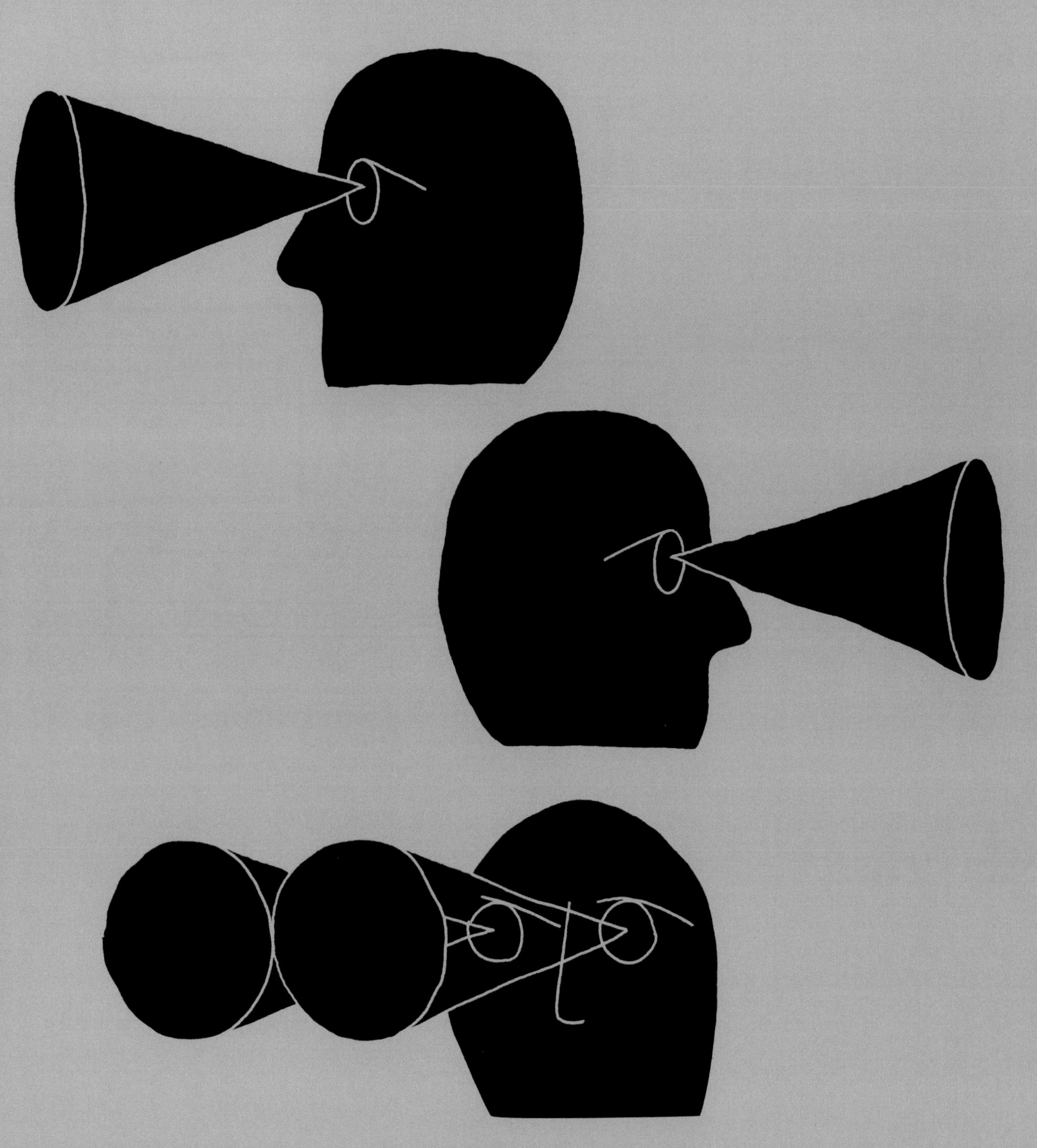

IN CONTEXT

APPROACH
Gestalt therapy

BEFORE
1920s Carl Jung says that people need to connect with their inner selves.

1943 Max Wertheimer explains the Gestalt idea of "productive thinking," which is distinctive for using personal insight.

1950 In *Neurosis and Human Growth,* Karen Horney identifies the need to reject the "shoulds" imposed by others.

AFTER
1961 Carl Rogers says that it is the client, not the therapist, who knows what form and direction therapy should take.

1973 American self-help author Richard Bandler, one of the founders of Neurolinguistic Programming (NLP), uses many of the Gestalt therapy techniques in his new therapy.

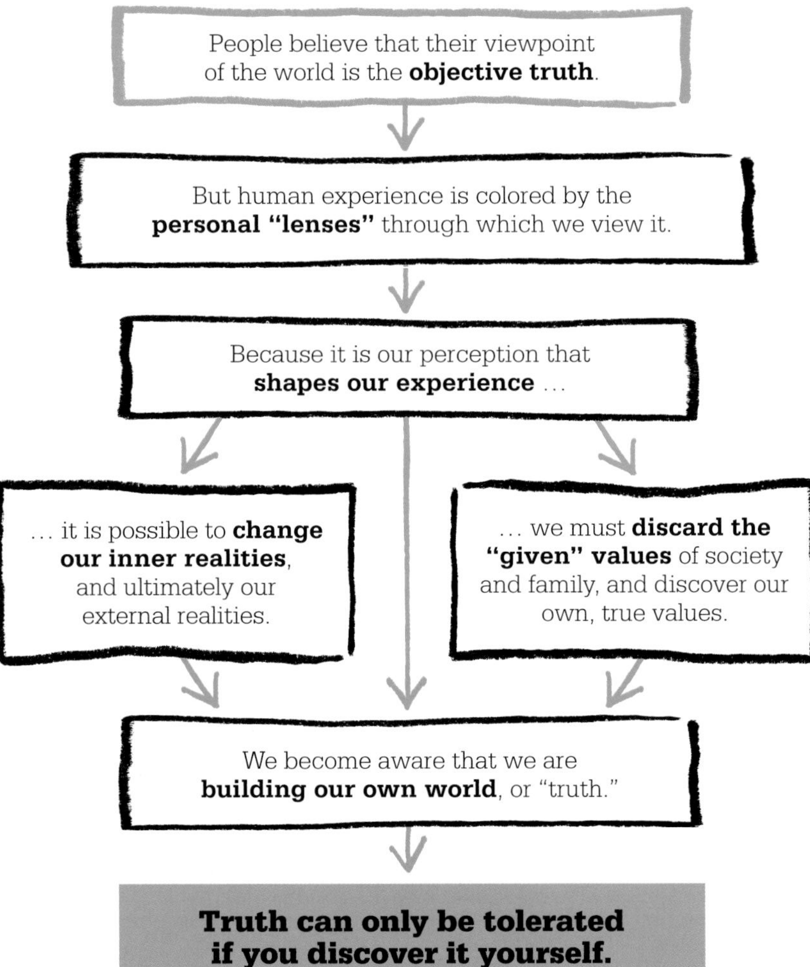

People believe that their viewpoint of the world is the objective truth.
But human experience is colored by the personal "lenses" through which we view it.
Because it is our perception that shapes our experience …
… it is possible to change our inner realities, and ultimately our external realities.
… we must discard the "given" values of society and family, and discover our own, true values.
We become aware that we are building our own world, or "truth."
Truth can only be tolerated if you discover it yourself.

In the 18th century, the German philosopher Immanuel Kant revolutionized our thinking about the world by pointing out that we can never really know what is "out there" beyond ourselves, because our knowledge is limited to the constraints of our minds and senses. We don't know how things are "in themselves," but only as we experience them. This view forms the basis of Gestalt therapy, which says that it is vitally important to remember that the complexity of the human experience—with its tragedies and traumas, inspirations and passions, and its nearly infinite range of possibilities—is coded by the individual "lenses" through which we view it. We do not automatically absorb all the sounds, feelings, and pictures of the world; we scan and select just a few.

Fritz Perls, one of the founders of Gestalt therapy, pointed out that this means our personal sense of reality is created through our perception; through the ways in which we view our experiences, not the events themselves. However, it is easy to forget this, or even fail to recognize it. He says we tend to mistake our viewpoint of the world for the absolute, objective truth, rather than acknowledging the role of perception and its influence in creating our perspective, together with all the ideas, actions, and beliefs that stem from it. For Perls, the only truth one can ever have is one's own personal truth.

Accepting responsibility

Perls developed his theories in the 1940s, when the dominant psychoanalytical view was that the human mind could be reduced to a series of biological drives seeking fulfillment. This approach was far too rigid, structured, simplified, and generalized for Perls; it did not

See also: Søren Kierkegaard 26–27 ▪ Carl Jung 102–107 ▪ Karen Horney 110 ▪ Erich Fromm 124–129 ▪ Carl Rogers 130–137 ▪ Abraham Maslow 138–139 ▪ Roger Shepard 192 ▪ Jon Kabat-Zinn 210 ▪ Max Wertheimer 341

allow for individual experience, which Perls held paramount. Nor did its analysts enable their patients to recognize and take responsibility for the creation of their experience. The psychoanalytical model operates on the understanding that patients are at the mercy of their unconscious conflicts until an analyst enters to save them from their unconscious drives. Perls, on the other hand, feels it is essential for people to understand the power of their own roles in creation. He wants to make us aware that we can change our realities, and in fact are responsible for doing so. No one else can do it for us. Once we realize that perception is the backbone of reality, each of us is forced to take responsibility for the life we create and the way we choose to view the world.

The Gestalt prayer was written by Fritz Perls to encapsulate Gestalt therapy. It emphasizes the importance of living according to our own needs, and not seeking fulfillment through others.

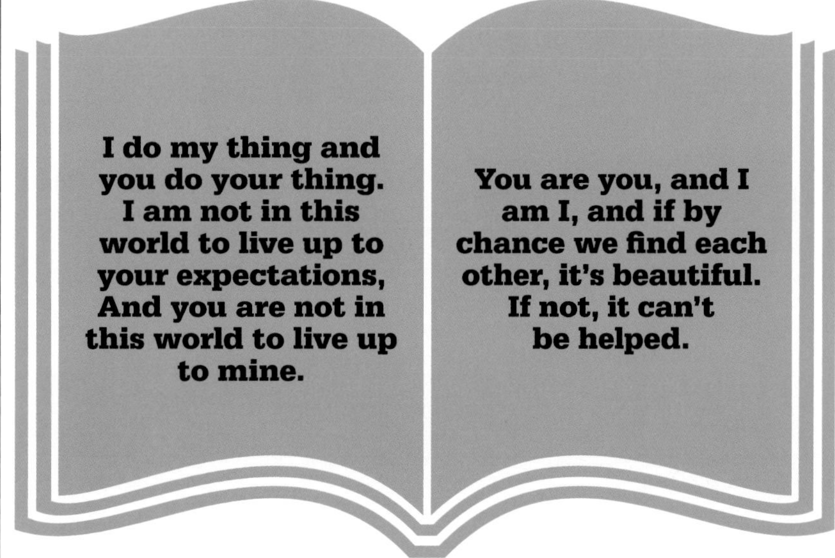

I do my thing and you do your thing. I am not in this world to live up to your expectations, And you are not in this world to live up to mine.
You are you, and I am I, and if by chance we find each other, it's beautiful. If not, it can't be helped.

Acknowledging power

Gestalt theory uses the tenets of individual experience, perception, and responsibility—both for one's thoughts and feelings—to encourage personal growth by establishing a sense of internal control. Perls insists that we can learn to control our inner experience, regardless of our external environment. Once we understand that our perception shapes our experience, we can see how the roles we play and the actions we take are tools, which we can then use consciously for changing reality. Control of our own inner psychic environment gives us power through two layers of choice: in how to interpret the environment, and how to react to it. The adage, "no one can make you angry other than yourself," perfectly exemplifies this philosophy, and its truth can be seen played out in the different ways that people react to traffic jams, bad news, or personal criticism, for example.

Learning is the discovery that something is possible.
Fritz Perls

In Gestalt therapy, individuals are forced to take direct responsibility for how they act and react, regardless of what may seem to be happening. Perls refers to this ability to maintain emotional stability regardless of the environment as "homeostasis," using a biological term normally used to describe the maintenance of a stable physical environment within the body. It implies a fine balancing of many systems, and this is how Gestalt therapy views the mind. It looks for ways of balancing the mind through the many thoughts, feelings, and perceptions that make up the whole human experience. It views a person holistically and places the focus firmly on the whole, not the parts.

Perls saw his task as helping his patients to cultivate an awareness of the power of their perceptions, and how they shape reality (or what we describe as "reality"). In this way, his patientsbecame able to take control of shaping their interior landscape. In taking »

Like Buddhism, Gestalt therapy encourages the development of mindful awareness and the acceptance of change as inevitable. Perls called change "the study of creative adjustments."

responsibility for their perceived sense of reality, they could create the reality they wanted.

Perls helped his patients achieve this through teaching them the integral processes of Gestalt therapy. The first and most important process is learning to cultivate awareness and to focus that awareness on the feelings of the present moment. This allows individuals to directly experience their feelings and perceived reality in the present moment. This ability to "be here now" is critical to the Gestalt process; it is an acute emotional awareness, and one that forms the foundation for understanding how each of us creates and reacts to our own environment. It also offers a pathway for learning how to change the ways we experience ourselves and our environment.

As a tool for personal growth, the ability to get in touch with authentic feelings—true thoughts and emotions—is more important to Perls than the psychological explanations or analytic feedback of other forms of therapy. The "why" behind behavior holds little significance for Perls; what is important is the "how" and "what." This devaluing of the need to find out "why" and the shift of responsibility for meaning from analyst to patient brought with it a profound change in the therapist–patient hierarchy. Where previous approaches in therapy generally involved a therapist manipulating the patient toward the therapeutic goal, the Gestalt approach is characterized by a warm, empathic relationship between therapist and patient, who work together as partners toward the goal. The therapist is dynamic but does not lead the patient; the Gestalt approach of Perls would later form the basis of Carl Rogers' humanistic, person-centered approach.

A denial of fate

Another component in the Gestalt method involves the use of language. One critical tool patients are given for increasing self-awareness is the instruction to notice and change the use of the word "I" within speech. Perls says that to take responsibility for our reality, we must recognize how we use language to give the illusion that we have no control when this is not the case. By simply rephrasing "I can't do that" to "I won't do that," it becomes clear that I am making a choice. This also helps to establish ownership of feeling; emotions arise in and belong to me; I cannot blame someone or something else for my feelings.

Other examples of language change include replacing the word "should" with "want," changing, for example, "I should leave now" to "I want to leave now." This also acts to reveal the element of choice. As

Fritz Perls

Frederick "Fritz" Salomon Perls was born in Berlin at the end of the 19th century. He studied medicine, and after a short time in the German army during World War I, graduated as a doctor. He then trained as a psychiatrist, and after marrying the psychologist Laura Posner in 1930, emigrated to South Africa, where he and Laura set up a psychoanalytic institute. Becoming disenchanted with the overintellectualism of the psychoanalytic approach, they moved to New York City in the late 1940s and became immersed in a thriving culture of progressive thought. In the late 1960s, they separated, and Perls moved to California, where he continued to change the landscape of psychotherapy. He left the US to start a therapy center in Canada in 1969, but died one year later of heart failure while conducting a workshop.

Key works

1946 *Ego Hunger and Aggression*
1969 *Gestalt Therapy Verbatim*
1973 *The Gestalt Approach and Eye Witness to Therapy*

Lose your mind and come to your senses.
Fritz Perls

Perls' Gestalt ideas of finding oneself jibed with events such as the Burning Man festival, but he warned against the "peddlers of instant joy" and the "so-called easy road of sensory liberation."

we learn to take responsibility for our experience, Perls says, we develop authentic selves that are free from society's influence. We also experience self-empowerment as we realize that we are not at the mercy of things that "just happen." Feelings of victimization dissolve once we understand that what we accept for ourselves in our lives—what we selectively perceive and experience—is a choice; we are not powerless.

If you need encouragement, praise, pats on the back from everybody, then you make everybody your judge.
Fritz Perls

With this personal responsibility comes the obligation to refuse to experience events, relationships, or circumstances that we know to be wrong for our authentic selves. Gestalt theory also asks us to look closely at what we choose to accept among our society's norms. We may have acted under the assumption of their truth for so long that we automatically accept them. Perls says we need instead to adopt beliefs that best inspire and develop our authentic self. The ability to write our own personal rules, determine our own opinions, philosophies, desires, and interests is of the essence. As we increase our awareness of self-accountability, self-reliance, and self-insight, we understand that we are building our own world, or truth. The lives we are living become easier to bear, because "truth can be tolerated only if you discover it yourself."

The possibility of intimacy

Gestalt therapy's emphasis on "being in the present" and finding one's own path and one's own ideas fitted perfectly within the 1960s counter-culture revolution of the Western world. But this focus on individualism was seen by some psychologists and analysts as a weakness within the therapy, especially by those who view human beings as, above all, social beings. They claim that a life lived along Gestalt principles would exclude the possibility of intimacy with another, and that it focuses too much on the individual at the expense of the community. In response, supporters of Gestalt therapy have claimed that without the development of an authentic self, it would not be possible to develop an authentic relationship with another.

In 1964, Perls became a regular lecturer at the Esalen Institute in California, becoming a lasting influence on this renowned center for spiritual and psychological development. After an explosion of popularity in the 1970s, Gestalt therapy fell out of favor, but its tenets were accepted into the roots of other forms of therapy. Gestalt is today recognized as one of many "standard" approaches to therapy. ■

IT IS NOTORIOUSLY INADEQUATE TO TAKE AN ADOPTED CHILD INTO ONE'S HOME AND LOVE HIM

DONALD WINNICOTT (1896–1971)

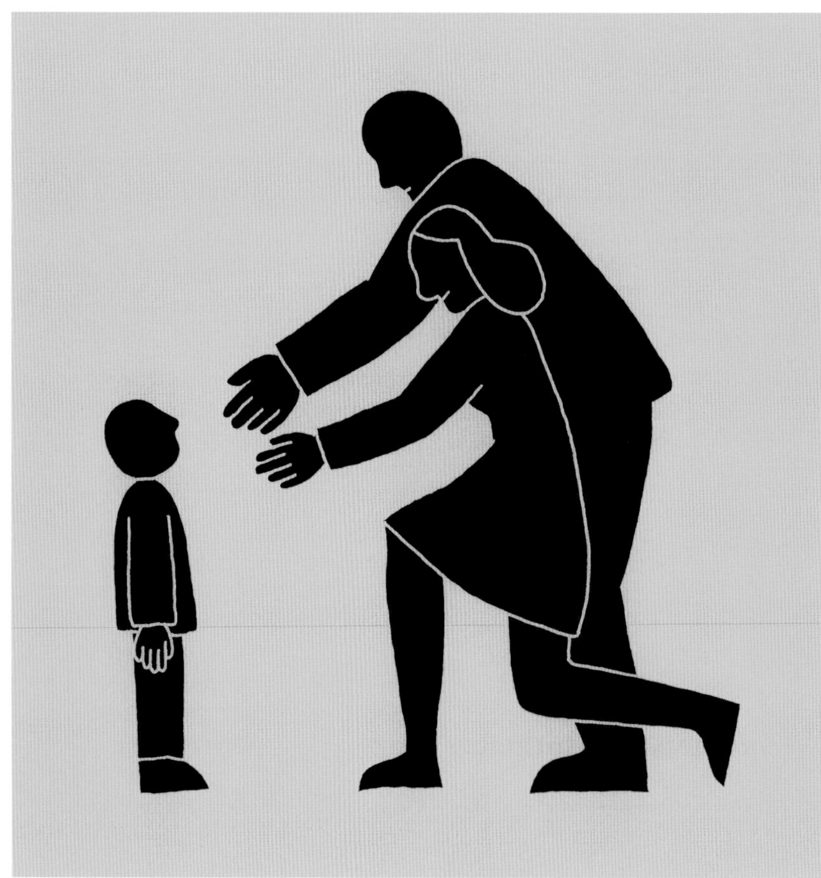

IN CONTEXT

APPROACH
Psychoanalysis

BEFORE
1900s Sigmund Freud suggests that neurotic conflicts (and the superego) arise in the Oedipal period—between ages three and six.

1930s Melanie Klein claims that a primitive form of the superego develops during the first year of life, and that love and hate are inherently linked.

AFTER
1947 Psychologist and play therapist Virginia Axline develops her eight principles of play therapy, which include: "Accept the child as she or he is."

1979 Swiss psychoanalyst Alice Miller says in *The Drama of the Gifted Child* that we are encouraged to "develop the art of not experiencing feelings."

Many people believe that if a child has suffered an upbringing that was lacking in love and support, they will be able to settle and flourish with a new family that provides what is needed. However, while stability and acceptance help to give a foundation in which a child can grow and find a healthy state of being, these qualities make up only one part of what is required.

As the first pediatrician in England to train as a psychoanalyst, Donald Winnicott had a unique insight into the mother-infant relationship and the developmental process of children. He was strongly influenced by Sigmund

See also: Sigmund Freud 92–99 ▪ Melanie Klein 108–109 ▪ Virginia Satir 146–147 ▪ John Bowlby 282–285

Children originally from neglectful or abusive homes are **afraid that they will not be loved** by their adoptive family …

… so in defense, they **act out in hatred**, even when placed with good parents.

This naturally evokes feelings of **hatred in the parents**.

If parents **acknowledge their hatred** and tolerate these feelings …

… the adopted child **knows that they are loved** and lovable even when child and adult are both experiencing hatred.

The child will be able to form strong attachments.

Freud but also by the writings of Melanie Klein, particularly regarding the unconscious feelings of the mother or carer for the infant. Winnicott began his career by working with children displaced by World War II and he examined the difficulties faced by children who are trying to adapt to a new home.

As Winnicott notes in his paper, *Hate in the Countertransference*: "It is notoriously inadequate to take an adopted child into one's home and love him." In fact, the parents must be able to take the adopted child into their home and be able to tolerate hating them. Winnicott states that a child can believe they are loved only after being hated; he stresses that the role that "tolerance of hate" plays in healing cannot be underestimated.

Winnicott explains that when a child has been deprived of proper parental nurturing, and is then granted a chance of this in a healthy family environment, such as with an adoptive or foster family, the child begins to develop unconscious hope. But fear is associated with this hope. When a child has been so devastatingly disappointed in the past, with even basic emotional or physical needs unsatisfied, defenses arise. These are unconscious forces that protect the child against the hope that »

Donald Winnicott

The English pediatrician and psychoanalyst Donald Woods Winnicott was the youngest child and only son born to a prominent, prosperous family living in Plymouth, England. His father, Sir John Frederick Winnicott, was an encouraging influence, although his mother suffered from depression. Winnicott first trained as a physician and pediatrician, completing psychoanalytic training later, in the 1930s.

Winnicott married twice, meeting his second wife Clare Britton, a psychiatric social worker, while working with disturbed children who had been evacuated during World War II. He continued to work as a pediatrician for more than 40 years and this gave his ideas a unique perspective. He twice served as president of the British Psychoanalytical Society, and sought to widen public knowledge through his many lectures and broadcasts.

Key works

1947 *Hate in the Countertransference*
1951 *Transitional Objects and Transitional Phenomena*
1960 *The Theory of the Parent–Infant Relationship*

It seems that an adopted child can believe in being loved only after reaching being hated.
Donald Winnicott

may lead to disappointment. The defenses, maintains Winnicott, explain the presence of hatred. The child will "act out" in an outburst of anger against the new parental figure, expressing hatred and, in turn, invoking hatred from the carer. He termed the behavior an "antisocial tendency."

According to Winnicott, for a child who has suffered, the need to hate and be hated is deeper even than the need for rebellion, and the importance of the carer tolerating the hate is an essential factor in the healing of the child. Winnicott says that the child must be allowed to express the hatred, and the parent must be able to tolerate both the child's and their own hatred as well.

The idea may be shocking, and people may struggle with the notion that they feel hatred rising within them. They may feel guilty, because the child has been through such difficulties already. Yet the child is actively behaving hatefully toward the parent, projecting past experiences of being neglected and ignored onto present-day reality.

The child of a broken home or without parents, Winnicott says, "spends his time unconsciously looking for his parents" and so feelings from past relationships are displaced onto another adult. The child has internalized the hate, and sees it even when it is no longer present. In their new situation, the child needs to see what happens when hatred is in the air. Winnicott explains: "What happens is that after a while a child so adopted gains hope, and then he starts to test out the environment he has found, and to seek proof of his guardian's ability to hate objectively."

There are many ways for a child to express hatred and prove that they are indeed not worthy of being loved. This worthlessness is the message that was imparted by earlier, negative parental experiences. From the child's point of view, they are attempting to protect themselves from the risk of ever having to feel love or to be loved because of the potential disappointment that accompanies that state of being.

Dealing with the hatred

The emotions that the child's hatred invokes in the parents, as well as in the child's teachers and other authority figures, are very real. Winnicott believes that it is essential that adults acknowledge these feelings, rather than deny them, which might seem easier. They also need to understand that the child's hatred is not personal; the child is expressing anxiety about their previous unhappy situation with the person who is now on hand.

What the authority figure does with their own hatred, of course, is of critical importance. The child's belief that they are "bad" and unworthy of being loved must not be reinforced by the response from the adult; the adult must simply tolerate the feelings of hatred and realize that these feelings are part of the relationship. This is the only way the child will feel secure and be able to form an attachment.

No matter how loving a new environment may be, it does not erase the past for the child; there will still be residual feelings as a result of their past experience. Winnicott sees no short cuts to a

The "antisocial tendency" in children is a way they express anxieties about their world, testing out their caregivers who must continue to provide a supportive and caring home.

Despite feeling the unconscious and natural negative feelings provoked by the child, a parent must provide an environment that "holds" the child, making them feel secure.

resolution. The child is expecting that the adult's feelings of hatred will lead to rejection, because that is what has happened before; when the hatred does not lead to rejection and is tolerated instead, it can begin to dissipate.

Healthy hatred

Even in psychologically healthy families with children who have not been displaced, Winnicott believes unconscious hatred is a natural, essential part of the parenting experience and speaks of "hating appropriately." Melanie Klein had suggested that a baby feels hatred for its mother, but Winnicott proposes that this is preceded by the mother hating the baby—and that even before this, there is an extraordinary primitive or "ruthless" love. The baby's existence places huge demands on the mother psychologically and physically and these evoke feelings of hatred in the mother. Winnicott's list of 18 reasons why the mother hates the baby include: that the pregnancy and birth have endangered her life; that the baby is an interference with her private life; that the baby hurts her when nursing, even biting her; and that the baby "treats her as scum, an unpaid servant, a slave." Despite all of this, she also loves this baby, "excretions and all," says Winnicott, with a hugely powerful, primitive love, and has to learn how to tolerate hating her baby without in any way acting on it. If she cannot hate appropriately, he claims, she turns the feelings of hatred toward herself, in a way that is masochistic and unhealthy.

Therapeutic relationship

Winnicott also used the relationship between the parent and child as an analogy for the therapeutic relationship between therapist and client. The feelings that arise in a therapist during analysis are part of a phenomenon known as "countertransference." Feelings that are aroused in the client during therapy—usually feelings about parents or siblings—are transferred onto the therapist. In his paper, Winnicott described how as part of the analysis, the therapist feels hate toward the client, though this hate was generated by the patient as a necessary part of testing that the therapist can bear it. The patient needs to know that the therapist is strong and reliable enough to withstand this onslaught.

Sentimentality in a mother is no good at all from the infant's point of view.
Donald Winnicott

A realistic approach

While some of Winnicott's ideas may appear shocking, he believes we should be realistic about bringing up children, avoiding sentimentality in favor of honesty. This enables us as children, and later as adults, to acknowledge and deal with natural, unavoidable negative feelings. Winnicott is a realist and pragmatist; he refuses to believe in the mythical idea of "the perfect family" or in a world where a few kind words wipe away all of the horrors that may have preceded it. He prefers to see the real environment and mental states of our experience, and asks us to do likewise, with courageous honesty. His ideas did not fit neatly into one school of thought, though they were hugely influential, and continue to impact on social work, education, developmental psychology, and psychoanalysis around the world. ■

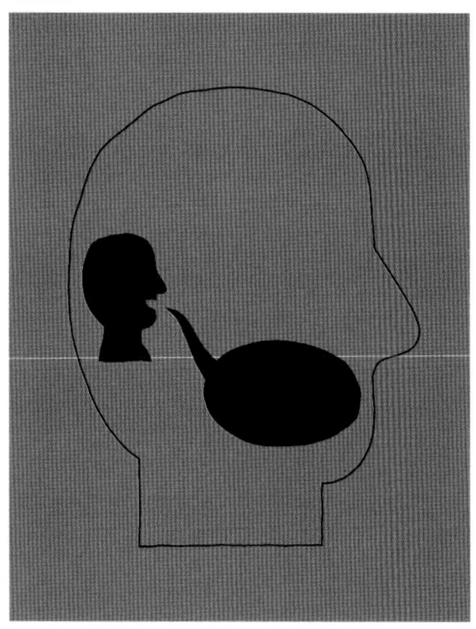

THE UNCONSCIOUS IS THE DISCOURSE OF THE OTHER

JACQUES LACAN (1901–1981)

IN CONTEXT

APPROACH
Psychoanalysis

BEFORE
1807 German philosopher Georg Hegel states that consciousness of self depends on the presence of the Other.

1818 German philosopher Arthur Schopenhauer claims that there can be no object without a subject to observe it, and that perception of the object is limited by personal vision and experience.

1890 William James in *The Principles of Psychology* distinguishes between the self as the knower, or "I," and the self as the known, or "me."

AFTER
1943 French philosopher Jean-Paul Sartre states that our perception of the world around us, or the Other, alters when another person appears; we absorb their concept of the Other into our own.

The Other is everything that lies beyond the boundaries of ourselves.

↓

We **define and redefine ourselves** through the existence of the Other.

↓

We understand the world through the **language** (discourse) of the Other.

↓

We also use that language for our innermost **thoughts**.

↓

The unconscious is the discourse of the Other.

Psychoanalysts explain the unconscious as the place where all the memories that we wish to push aside are stored, and cannot be retrieved consciously. The unconscious sometimes speaks to the conscious self in limited ways: Carl Jung believed that the unconscious presents itself to the waking self through dreams, symbols, and in the language of archetypes, while Freud saw it as expressing itself through motivational behavior and accidental "slips of the tongue." The one thing that the various psychoanalytical schools do agree on is that the unconscious holds a bigger picture than that retained by the conscious self. For French psychiatrist Jacques Lacan, however, the language of the unconscious is not that of the self, but of the "Other."

A sense of self

We easily take for granted the notion of the self—that each of us exists as a separate, individual being, who views the world through our own eyes, is familiar with the boundaries that separate us from others and from the world around us, and assumes a separateness

See also: William James 38–45 ▪ Sigmund Freud 92–99 ▪ Carl Jung 102–107 ▪ Donald Hebb 163

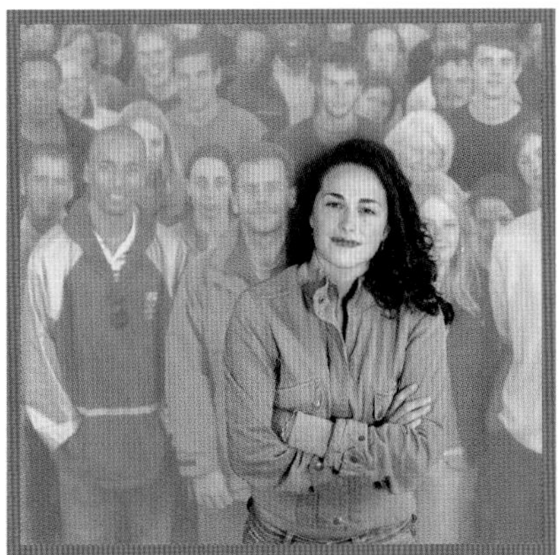

Our sense of self is shaped by our awareness of the "Other," or the world outside ourselves. However, Lacan stated, it is the language of the Other that forms our deepest thoughts.

in thinking and in the way we interact with our environment. But what if there was nothing out there that we could recognize as being separate from ourselves? We would then be unable to conceptualize our sense of self, because there would be no delineated being to think about. The only way we have of determining that as individuals we are distinct from the world all around us is our ability to recognize the separateness of ourselves from our environment, or from the Other, which allows us to become the subject "I." Lacan therefore concluded that each of us is a "self" only because we have a concept of the Other.

For Lacan, the Other is the absolute otherness that lies beyond the self; it is the environment into which we are born and which we have to "translate" or make sense of in order to survive and thrive. Infants must learn to assemble sensations into concepts and categories in order to function in the world, and they do this through gradually acquiring an awareness and understanding of a series of signifiers—signs or codes. But these signifiers can only come to us from the external world that lies beyond the self, therefore they must have been formed from the language—or what Lacan prefers to call the "discourse"—of the Other.

The I is always in the field of the Other.
Jacques Lacan

We are only able to think or to express our ideas and emotions through language, and the only language we have, according to Lacan, is that of the Other. The sensations and images that translate into the thoughts of our unconscious must therefore be constructed from this language of the Other, or, as Lacan stated, "the unconscious is the discourse of the Other." This idea has had a wide influence on the practice of psychoanalysis, leading to a more objective and open interpretation of the unconscious. ■

Jacques Lacan

Jacques Marie Émile Lacan was born in Paris, where he was educated at the Collège Stanislas. He went on to study medicine, specializing in psychiatry. Lacan remained in occupied Paris during World War II, working at the Val-de-Grâce military hospital.

After the war, psychoanalysis became the key tool in Lacan's work. However, he was expelled by the International Psychoanalytical Association in 1953, after an argument over his "deviant" use of shorter length therapy sessions. Lacan then set up La Société Française de Psychanalytique.

Lacan's writings extend into philosophy, art, literature, and linguistics, and he gave weekly seminars that were attended by eminent thinkers such as Roland Barthes and Claude Lévi-Strauss. A keen Freudian, Lacan formed the École Freudienne de Paris in 1963, and the École de la Cause Freudienne in 1981.

Key works

1966 *Écrits*
1968 *The Language of the Self*
1954–1980 *The Seminars* (27 volumes)

MAN'S MAIN TASK IS TO GIVE BIRTH TO HIMSELF

ERICH FROMM (1900–1980)

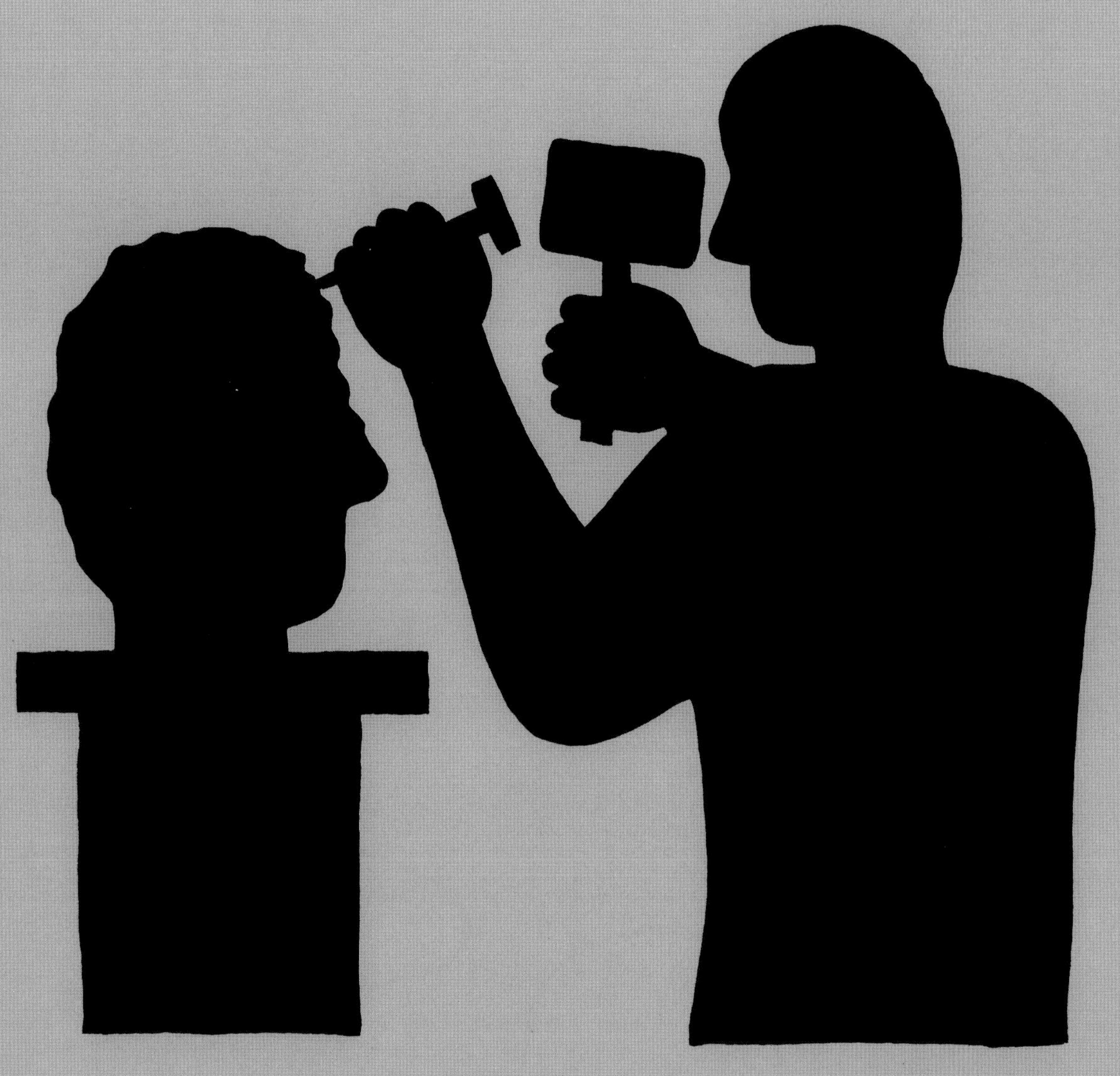

IN CONTEXT

APPROACH
Humanistic psychoanalysis

BEFORE
1258–1261 The Sufi mystic Rumi says that the longing of the human soul comes from separation from its source.

1950s Rollo May says that the "true religion" consists of facing life's challenges with purpose and meaning, through accepting responsibility and making choices.

AFTER
1950 Karen Horney says that the neurotic self is split between an idealized and a real self.

1960s Abraham Maslow defines creativity and thinking of others as characteristics of self-actualized people.

1970s Fritz Perls says that we must find ourselves in order to achieve self-actualization.

The ability to find meaning in our lives is the defining characteristic of humankind. According to the German-American psychoanalyst Erich Fromm, it also determines whether we follow a path of joy and fulfilment or tread a road of dissatisfaction and strife. Fromm believed that although life is inherently painful, we can make it bearable by giving it meaning, through pursuing and constructing an authentic self. The ultimate aim of a human life is to develop what Fromm described as "the most precious quality man is endowed with—the love of life."

Life is inherently fraught with emotional frustration, according to Fromm, because humans live in a state of struggle. We are constantly trying to balance our individual nature—our existence as a separate being—with our need for connection. There is a part of our inherent self that only knows how to exist in a united state with others; it lives at one with nature and at one with other people. Yet we see ourselves as separated from nature and isolated from one another. Worse still, we have the unique capacity to ponder the fact of this separation and think about our isolation. Humans, gifted with reason, are life being aware of itself.

Fromm suggests that our separation from nature originated with the growth of intellect, which has made us aware of our separateness. It is our ability to reason and relate that lets us transcend nature. It provides the capabilities for productive living and affords us intellectual superiority, but it also makes us realize that we exist alone in this world. Reason makes us aware of our own mortality and the mortality of our

It seems that nothing is more difficult for the average man to bear than the feeling of not being identified with a larger group.
Erich Fromm

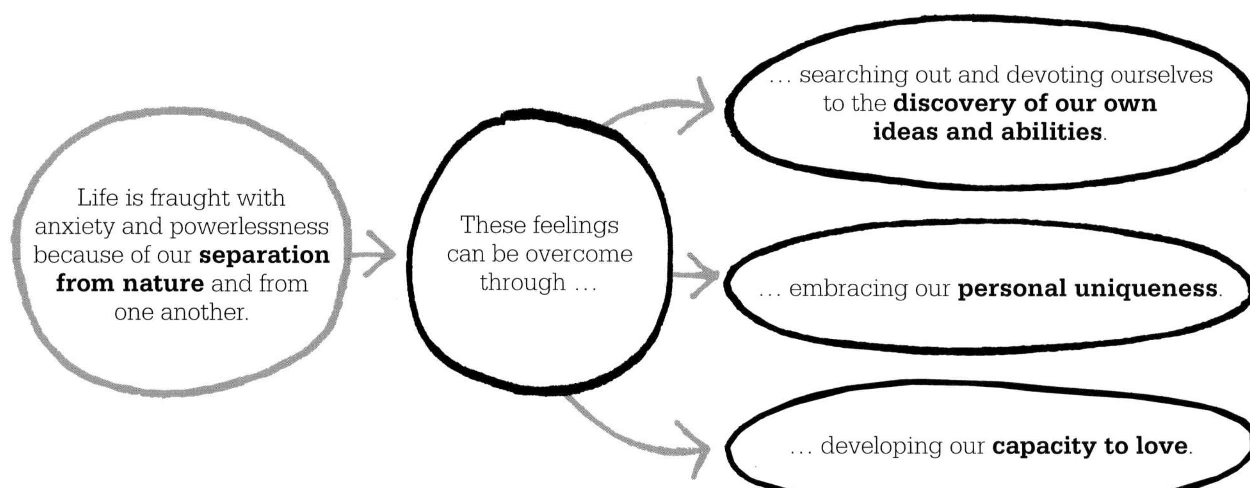

Life is fraught with anxiety and powerlessness because of our **separation from nature** and from one another.
These feelings can be overcome through …
… searching out and devoting ourselves to the **discovery of our own ideas and abilities**.
… embracing our **personal uniqueness**.
… developing our **capacity to love**.

See also: Alfred Adler 100–101 ▪ Karen Horney 110 ▪ Fritz Perls 112–117 ▪ Carl Rogers 130–137 ▪ Abraham Maslow 138–139 ▪ Rollo May 141

The creativity of artists encourages them to interpret the world around them in new ways. The world's most highly acclaimed artists have always essentially been nonconformist.

loved ones. This understanding creates a chronic source of tension and an unbearable loneliness that we are always seeking to overcome; man's inherent state of being is one of anxiety and hopelessness. But there is hope, Fromm insists, because we can overcome our sense of isolation and alienation through finding our purpose.

However, as we strive to become free, unique individuals, we still feel the need for unity with others; in trying to balance these needs, we may seek out the comfort of conforming to a group or an authority. Fromm argues that this a misguided approach, and that it is imperative to discover one's own independent sense of self and one's own personal views and value systems rather than adhering to conventional or authoritarian norms. If we try to hand responsibility for our choices to other people or institutions, we become alienated from ourselves, when the very purpose of our lives is to define ourselves through embracing our personal uniqueness, discovering our own ideas and abilities, and embracing that which differentiates each of us from other people. Humankind's main task is to give birth to themselves. In doing so, they free themselves from confusion, loneliness, and apathy.

Creativity and love

Paradoxically, Fromm believes that the only way we can find the sense of wholeness we seek is through the discovery of our individuality. We can achieve this by following our own ideas and passions, and through creative purpose, because "creativity requires the courage to let go of certainties."

One of the critical ways in which we deliver ourselves from isolation is through our capacity to love. Fromm's concept of love is vastly different from popular understandings of the word. To Fromm, love is not an emotion, nor is it dependent on finding an object to love. It is an interpersonal creative capacity that one must actively develop as part of one's personality. He says "it is an attitude, an ordination of character which determines the relatedness of the person to the whole world."

In terms of personal love for another, Fromm says that the main tenets are responsibility, respect, care, and knowledge—an objective knowledge of what other people truly want and need. Love is only possible through respecting the separateness and uniqueness of ourselves and of another; this is, paradoxically, how we develop the ability to create connectedness. Love demands a great amount of respect for the other person as an individual, and it is based on autonomy, not a blending of personalities. In our overwhelming desire to connect and unify, our relationships often result in an unloving imbalance. We think we are loving, but in reality we may be seeking another form of conformity. We say "I love you" when really we mean "I see me in you," "I will become you," or "I will possess you." In loving, we try to lose our uniqueness or steal it from the other person. Our yearning to exist "as one" makes us want to see ourselves reflected in other people, which in turn leads us to artificially impose our own traits onto someone else. »

The Four Nonproductive Personality Types

Receptive types have no choice but to accept their roles, and never fight for change or betterment.

Exploitative types are aggressive and self-centered, and typically engage in acts of coercion and plagiarism.

Hoarding types fight to retain what they have, and are always seeking to acquire more.

Marketing types "sell" everything, especially their own image.

The only way to love, says Fromm, is to love freely, granting the other person their full individuality; to respect the other person's differing opinions, preferences, and belief systems. Love is not found by fitting one person into another's mold, and it is not a question of finding the perfect "match." It is, he says, "union with somebody, or something, outside oneself, under the condition of retaining the separateness and integrity of one's own self."

Many people spend vast amounts of time and money attempting to cultivate the self that they feel is most worthy of acceptance, and most likely to result in being loved or desired. This is futile, because only a person who has a strong sense of self, and can stand firmly within their own understanding of the world, is able to give freely to others and love in an authentic way. Those who tend to orient themselves toward receiving love instead of being loving will fail; they will also seek to establish a receiving relationship in other ways, always wanting to be given things—material or immaterial—rather than to give. These people believe the source of all good things lies outside themselves, and they constantly feel the need to acquire, though this brings no relief.

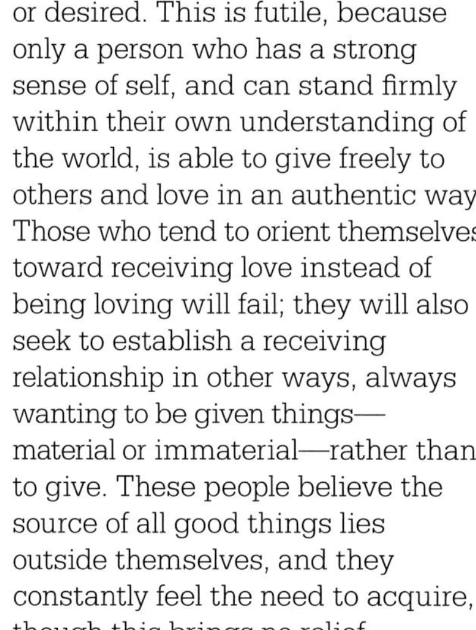

'Know thyself' is one of the fundamental commands that aim at human strength and happiness.
Erich Fromm

Personality types

Fromm identified several personality types that he called "nonproductive," because they enable people to avoid assuming true responsibility for their actions and prevent productive, personal growth. Each of the four main nonproductive types—receptive, exploitative, hoarding, and marketing—have both positive and negative sides. A fifth type, necrophilous, is unremittingly negative, and a sixth type—the productive personality—is Fromm's ideal. In reality, our personalities are generally drawn from a mix of the four main types.

A person with a "receptive" orientation is said to live passively in the status quo, accepting the lot handed to them. These people follow rather than lead; they have things done to them. In extremes, this is the stance of the victim, but on the positive side, it is rich in devotion and acceptance. Fromm compares this type to the peasants and migrant workers of history.

The "exploitative" orientation thrives on taking from others; exploitative people take what they need instead of earning or creating. However, they show extreme self-confidence and strong initiative. This type is typified by historical aristocracies who took power and wealth from indigenous populations to line their own pockets.

"Hoarders" are always seeking friends in high places and rank even loved ones in terms of their value, seeing them as something owned. Power-hungry and ungenerous, at best they are pragmatic and economical. Historically, these are the middle classes, or bourgeoisie, that rise in great numbers during economic depressions.

The last of the main types is the "marketing" orientation. These people are obsessed with image and with how to successfully advertise and sell themselves. Every choice is evaluated in terms of reflected status, from the clothes, cars, and vacations they buy to marriage into the "right" family. At worst, they are opportunistic, tactless, and shallow; at best, they are highly motivated, purposeful, and energetic. This type is most representative of modern society, in its ever-growing acquisitiveness and self-consciousness.

The most negative personality type—necrophilous—seeks only to destroy. Deeply afraid of the disorderly and uncontrollable nature of life, necrophilous types love to talk about sickness and death, and are obsessed with the need to impose "law and order." They prefer mechanical objects to other people. In moderation, these people are pessimistic nay-sayers whose glasses are perpetually half empty, never half full.

Life has an inner dynamism of its own; it tends to grow, to be expressed, to be lived.
Erich Fromm

Fromm's last personality type, the productive orientation, genuinely seeks and finds a legitimate solution to life through flexibility, learning, and sociability. Aiming to "become one" with the world and so escape the loneliness of separation, productive people respond to the world with rationality and an open mind, willing to change their beliefs in the light of new evidence. A productive person can truly love another for who they are, not as a trophy or safeguard against the world. Fromm calls this brave person "the man without a mask."

Fromm's work has a unique perspective, drawing on psychology, sociology, and political thinking, especially the writings of Karl Marx. His writing, aimed at a mainstream audience, influenced the general public more than academia—mainly because of his insistence on the freedom of ideas. He is nonetheless recognized as a leading contributor to humanistic psychology. ■

Hitler's fascination with death and destruction marks him out as an example of Fromm's necrophilous personality type, which is obsessed with control and the imposition of order.

Erich Fromm

Erich Fromm was the only child of his orthodox Jewish parents, and grew up in Frankfurt am Main, Germany. A thoughtful young man, he was initially influenced by his Talmudic studies, but later turned toward Karl Marx and socialist theory, together with Freud's psychoanalysis. Driven by the need to understand the hostility he witnessed during World War I, he studied jurisprudence, then sociology (to PhD level), before training in psychoanalysis. After the Nazis took power in Germany in 1933, Fromm moved to Switzerland and then New York, where he established a psychoanalytic practice and taught at Columbia University.

Fromm married three times and had a well-documented affair with Karen Horney during the 1930s. In 1951, he left the US to teach in Mexico, returning 11 years later to become professor of psychiatry at New York University. He died in Switzerland at the age of 79.

Key works

1941 *The Fear of Freedom*
1947 *Man for Himself*
1956 *The Art of Loving*

THE GOOD LIFE IS A PROCESS NOT A STATE OF BEING

CARL ROGERS (1902–1987)

IN CONTEXT

APPROACH
Person-centered therapy

BEFORE
1920s Austrian psychoanalyst Otto Rank proposes that separation from outdated thoughts, emotions, and behaviors is essential for psychological growth and development.

1950s Abraham Maslow says that people must not be viewed as a collection of symptoms but first and foremost as people.

AFTER
1960s Fritz Perls popularizes the concept of externalizing other people's expectations to find one's truest self.

2004 American humanistic psychologist Clark Moustakas explores the uniquely human components of life: hope, love, self, creativity, individuality, and becoming.

During the 19th and into the early 20th century, much of the approach to psychological treatment was based on the idea that mental illness was a fixed pathological malady that needed to be cured. Popular psychoanalytic theory, for example, defined people struggling with their mental health as "neurotic." Mental illness was seen in a negative light and most psychological practices and theories of the time offered strict definitions with structured explanations of the underlying causes of the mental illness, and fixed methods to cure it.

American psychologist Carl Rogers took a much more esoteric route to mental health, and in so doing expanded the approach of psychotherapy forever. He felt that the philosophies of the time were too structured and rigid to account for something as dynamic as the human experience, and that humanity is much too diverse to be fitted into delineated categories.

Achieving mental health

Rogers takes the view that it is absurd to view mental well-being as a specific fixed state; good mental health is not something that is suddenly achieved at the end of a series of steps. Nor is it attained because an individual's previously neurotic state of tension has been reduced by the satisfaction of biological drives and impulses, as the psychoanalysts insisted. Neither is it cultivated by following a specific program designed to develop and preserve a state of inner impermeable homeostasis, or balance, reducing the effect of the world's external chaos on the self, as the behaviorists recommended.

Rogers does not believe that anyone exists in a defective state that needs to be fixed in order to provide them with a better state, preferring to view human experience, and our minds and environment, as alive and growing. He talks about the "ongoing process of organismic experience"—seeing life as instantaneous and ongoing; life exists in the experience of every moment.

For Rogers, a healthy self-concept is not a fixed identity but a fluid and changing entity, open to possibilities. Rogers embraces an authentic, unprescribed, free-flowing definition

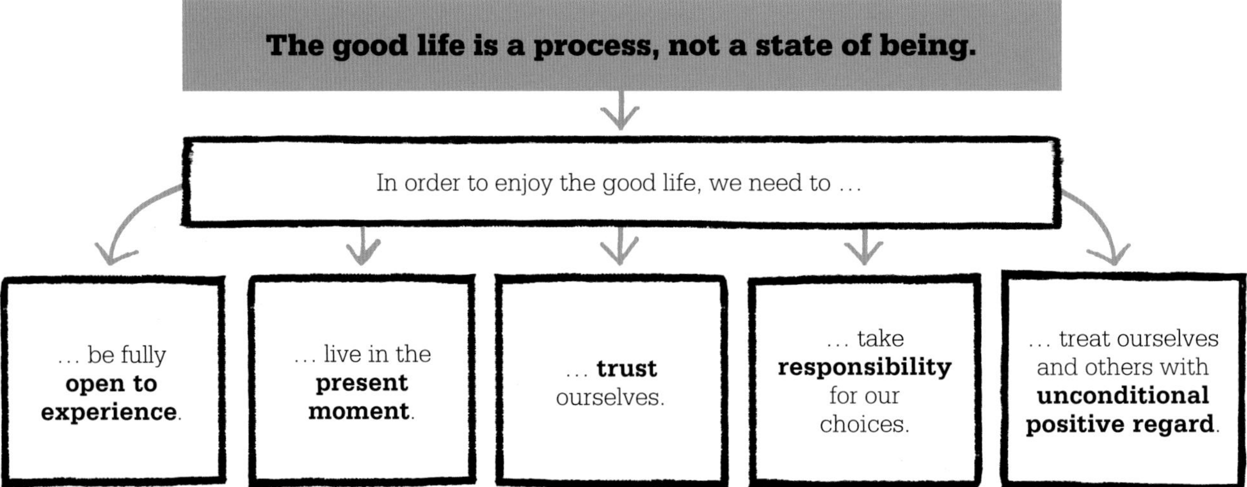

The good life is a process, not a state of being.
In order to enjoy the good life, we need to …
… be fully open to experience.
… live in the present moment.
… trust ourselves.
… take responsibility for our choices.
… treat ourselves and others with unconditional positive regard.

See also: Fritz Perls 112–117 ▪ Erich Fromm 124–129 ▪ Abraham Maslow 138–139 ▪ Rollo May 141 ▪ Dorothy Rowe 154 ▪ Martin Seligman 200–201

Unlike a maze with only one route across, Rogers asserts that life is full of possibilities and offers multiple routes—but individuals are often unable or unwilling to see them. To experience "the good life" we need to stay flexible and open to what life brings, by experiencing it fully moment by moment.

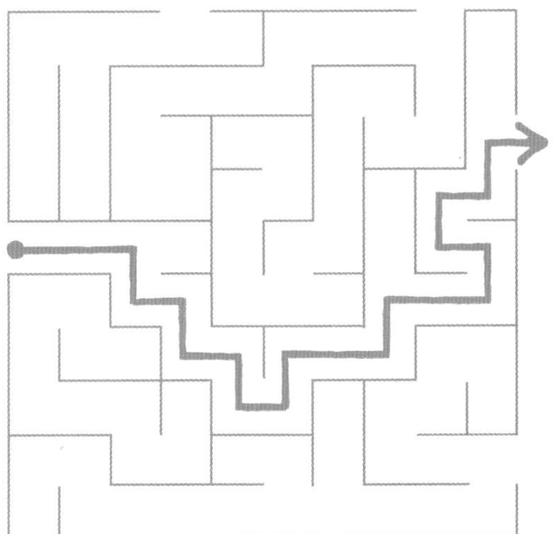

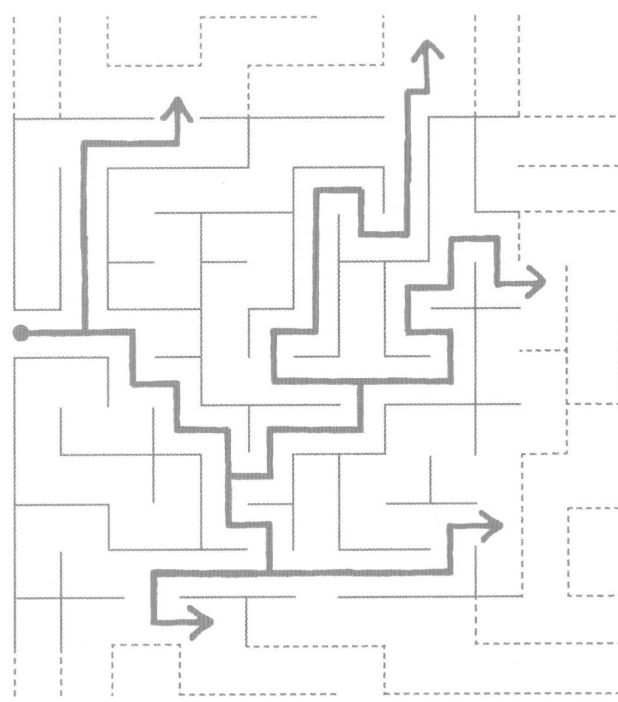

of healthy human experience, with limitless possibilities. Humans are not traveling a road where the destination is to become "adjusted" or "actualized," as fellow humanistic psychologist Abraham Maslow had suggested. Indeed, the purpose of existence is not about reaching any kind of destination, Rogers claims, because existence is less a journey toward an endpoint and more an ongoing process of growth and discovery that does not stop until we die.

Living "the good life"

Rogers uses the phrase living "the good life," to refer to the range of characteristics, attitudes, and behaviors displayed by people who have embraced the foundations of his approach—people who are "fully in the stream of life." One essential ingredient is the ability to stay wholly present in the moment. Since self and personality emerge out of experience, it is of the utmost importance to stay fully open to the possibilities offered by each moment, and to let experience shape the self. The individual lives in an environment of constant change, yet frequently and all too easily, people deny this fluidity and instead create constructs of how they think things should be. They then try to mold themselves and their idea of reality to fit the constructs they have made. This way of being is the very opposite of the fluid, flowing, and changing organization of self that Rogers believes the nature of our existence requires.

Our preconceptions about how the world is, or should be, and our own role within it, define the limits of our world and reduce our ability to stay present and open to experience. In living the good life and remaining open to experience, Rogers believes we adopt a way of being that prevents us from feeling trapped and stuck. The aim, as Rogers sees it, is for experience to be the starting »

What I will be in the next moment, and what I will do, grows out of the moment, and cannot be predicted.
Carl Rogers

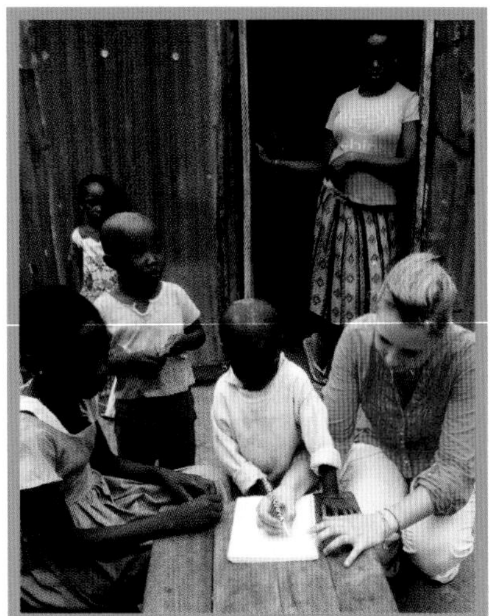

Spending time working in another country can be a rewarding way to open up to new experiences, challenge fixed ideas about the world, and find out more about ourselves.

point for the construction of our personalities, rather than trying to fit our experiences into a preconceived notion of our sense of self. If we hold on to our ideas of how things should be, rather than accepting how they really are, we are likely to perceive our needs as "incongruent" or mismatched to what is available.

When the world does not "do what we want," and we feel unable to change our ideas, conflict arises in the form of defensiveness. Rogers explains defensiveness as the tendency to unconsciously apply strategies to prevent a troubling stimulus from entering consciousness. We either deny (block out) or distort (reinterpret) what is really happening, essentially refusing to accept reality in order to stick with our preconceived ideas. In so doing, we deny ourselves the full range of potential reactions, feelings, and ideas, and we dismiss a wide range of options as wrong or inappropriate. The defensive feelings and thoughts that rise up in us when reality conflicts with our preconceptions create a limited, artificial interpretation of experience. In order to really participate in what Rogers calls the "ongoing process of organismic experience," we need to be fully open to new experience, and be completely without defensiveness.

A full range of emotions

By tuning in to our full range of emotions, Rogers argues, we allow ourselves a deeper, richer experience in every part of our lives. We may think we can selectively block emotion, and dampen down disturbing or uncomfortable feelings, but when we repress some of our emotions, we inevitably turn down the volume of all our emotions, denying ourselves access to the whole of our nature. If on the other hand, we allow ourselves to be more comfortable with our emotions, including those we have deemed to be negative, the flow of positive feelings emerges more strongly; it is as if by permitting ourselves to feel pain, we allow for a more intense experience of joy.

By always remaining open to everything that occurs, Rogers says that we allow our fullest abilities to function, and in turn

Self and personality emerge from experience, rather than experience being translated … to fit preconceived self-structure.
Carl Rogers

A fixed view of the world often leads to unhappiness; we can feel like "a square peg in a round hole," constantly frustrated that our life is not how we expected it to be. Rogers urges us to abandon our preconceived ideas and see the world as it really is.

we can get the greatest satisfaction from our experiences. We have not raised our defenses to shut off any part of the self, so we are able to experience everything fully. Once we escape from the rut of the preconceptions of the mind, we can allow ourselves to soar. Rather than organizing our experience to suit our idea of the world, we "discover structure *in* experience."

This openness is not for the faint-hearted, Rogers states; it requires a level of bravery on the part of the individual. We don't need to fear any type of feeling, he says—we need only to allow the full flow of cognition and experience. With true access to a fuller range of processing experience, each of us is more able to find the path that truly suits our authentic self—this is the fully functioning individual that Rogers urges us to become. We are always growing, and Rogers emphasizes that the direction in which people move—when there is freedom to move in any direction—is generally the direction they are best suited for, and that is best suited for them.

Unconditional acceptance

In contrast to the views of many of his predecessors in the field of psychotherapy, Rogers believed that people are, in their essence, healthy and good; and that mental and emotional well-being is the natural progression for human nature. These beliefs are the foundation of an approach that regards patients in an entirely positive light, one of absolute, unconditional acceptance. Rogers asked that his patients learn to do the same for themselves and for others. This perspective, grounded in compassion and the recognition of the potential of each and every individual, is famously termed "unconditional positive regard." Rogers believed that all people, not just his patients, needed to be able to view themselves in this way, as well as those around them and their environment.

Unconditional self-acceptance and unconditional acceptance of others are vital, and when these are lacking, people fail to remain open to experience. Rogers maintained that many of us have very strong, strident, specific conditions that must be met before we will grant approval or acceptance. We also base self-worth and regard for others on achievements or appearance, rather than accepting people as they are.

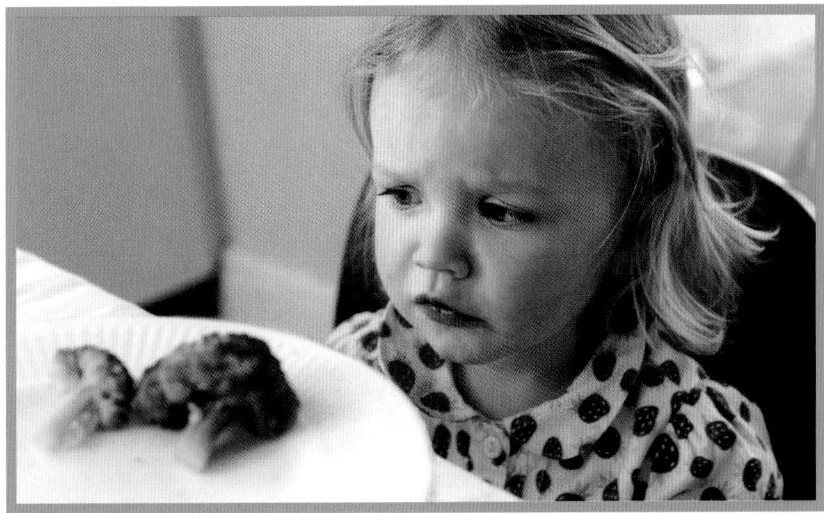

Love that is conditional on an action or situation—for example, on achieving A grades at school or eating the right foods—can leave children feeling unworthy and unaccepted.

No other person's ideas, and none of my own ideas, are as authoritative as my experience.
Carl Rogers

Parents may inadvertently teach children that they are worthy of affection only if certain requirements are met, offering them rewards and praise when they eat their vegetables or get an A grade in physics, but fail to love them openly just for themselves. Rogers calls these requirements "conditions of worth," believing that the tendency of humankind to demand that people and things match our arbitrary expectations does all of us a great disservice.

Achievements are to be respected, he says, but they are both separate and secondary to acceptance, which is a basic human need, and does not have to be "earned" through deeds or action. Rogers says that the value of an individual is inherently granted merely by the miracle of »

The subjective human being has an important value ... that no matter how he may be labeled and evaluated he is a human person first of all.
Carl Rogers

existence. Acceptance must never be thought of as conditional; unconditional positive regard is key to how we might all live "the good life."

As people become more accepting of themselves, they also become more patient with themselves. Acceptance alleviates the pressure to do, see, and acquire, which builds when we live with the mistaken idea that these activities define our worth. We can begin to realize that each of us is a continual work-in-progress; that we are in a process of change, as Rogers says in his seminal work, *On Becoming A Person*—we are all in a constant "state of becoming." The irony is that with greater self-acceptance, and with less unhealthy pressure and constant criticism, we can actually become much more productive.

Trusting oneself

To live "the good life," as Rogers sees it, is to learn to trust ourselves. As an individual moves toward openness, they find that they simultaneously make progress in their ability to trust themselves and their instincts and begin to rely more comfortably on their decision-making capabilities. With no need to repress any part of themselves, they have a greater ability to tune in to all the parts of themselves. This gives him access to a variety of perspectives and feelings, and in turn they are better able to evaluate choices that will truly realize their potential. They are able to see more clearly what direction their authentic self wishes to take, and can make choices that are truly in congruence with their needs. No longer at the mercy of what they think they should be doing, nor of what society or parents may have conditioned them to think they want, they can much more easily simply exist in the moment and be truly aware of what they actually want. And now they can trust themselves, not because they are infallible, but because they can be fully open to the consequences of each of their actions and correct them if they prove to be less than satisfying, Rogers explains.

In living "the good life" we also have a sense of owning our lives and taking responsibility for ourselves—this is another tenet of Rogers' philosophy and comes from an existential viewpoint. What we choose to think or do is down to us; there can be no residual resentments when we have truly identified for ourselves what we want and need, and taken the steps to create it. At the same time, there is greater accountability and an increased tendency to truly invest in our lives. It is not uncommon to hear about a doctor who hates medicine but practices because their parents said that being a doctor was the way to earn respect

Carl Rogers

Carl Rogers was born in Oak Park, Illinois, to a strictly Protestant family, and apparently had few friends outside the family before going to college. Initially, Rogers majored in agriculture, but after marrying his childhood sweetheart, Helen Elliott, in 1924, he enrolled at a theological seminary, before withdrawing to pursue a course in psychology. Rogers worked at the universities of Ohio, Chicago, and Wisconsin, developing his client-centered therapy based on humanistic psychology. He also spent time with the United Service Organizations (USO), offering therapy to returning army personnel during World War II. In 1964, he was awarded "Humanist of the Year" by the American Humanist Association, and devoted the last ten years of his life to working for world peace. He was nominated for a Nobel Peace Prize in 1987.

Key works

1942 *Counseling and Psychotherapy*
1951 *Client-centered Therapy*
1961 *On Becoming a Person*

Teaching a child to ride a bicycle requires encouragement and support, but ultimately the child must be brave and have self-belief. Rogers likened his person-centered therapy to this process.

and approval—both from them and from society. In direct contrast, the rates of students who drop out or fail university courses are strikingly low among those who have received little support but worked to pay for their own tuition.

The ways in which people can influence our desires and how we define ourselves can be intensely complex. Resentment can be buried deep within us when we act in accordance with someone else's wishes rather than our own. If our actions are free of external influences, we feel more authentic, more solidly in control of creating our own destiny, and more satisfied with the results.

Person-centered approach

Rogers' philosophy became the cornerstone of a new approach called humanistic psychology, which he founded in the 1950s with Abraham Maslow and Rollo May. It was based on a positive view of humanity as basically healthy and capable of growing and realizing its potential. This approach was in contrast to the other main psychological therapies of the time—psychoanalysis and behaviorism—both of which focus on the pathology of the individual and how to fix it.

Rogers initially called his approach "client-centered," and then changed it to "person-centered," and it has since been hugely influential in education, parenting, business, and other areas as well as in clinical work. In person-centered therapy, which Rogers described as "non-directive therapy," the therapist takes the role of a facilitator who helps the client find their own answers, based on the belief that the client knows themselves best. In person-centered therapy, the client identifies their problems and what direction the therapy should take. For example, the client may not wish to focus on their childhood but rather deal with issues they are facing at work, and the therapist may help them find what sort of role they would really like to take. Rogers describes the process as "supportive, not reconstructive;" the client must not come to rely on the therapist for support, but instead needs to learn how to become sufficiently self-aware and self-trusting to be independent and able to live "the good life."

Rogers' legacy

Rogers was one of the most influential psychotherapists of the 20th century, and his new client-centered, nondirective therapy marked a turning point in the development of psychotherapy. He was instrumental in the encounter-group philosophy of the 1960s, which encouraged open communication between individuals. He was responsible for the spread of professional counseling into areas such as education and social work, and was a pioneer in attempting to resolve international conflict through more effective communication. ■

The process of the good life … means launching oneself fully into the stream of life.
Carl Rogers

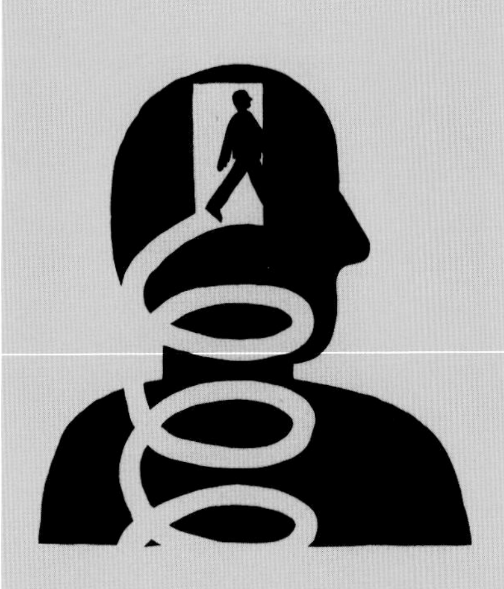

WHAT A MAN CAN BE, HE MUST BE

ABRAHAM MASLOW (1908–1970)

IN CONTEXT

APPROACH
Humanistic psychology

BEFORE
1920s Alfred Adler claims there is only one motivating force behind all our behavior and experience: the striving for perfection.

1935 Henry Murray develops the Thematic Apperception Test, which measures personality and motivation.

AFTER
1950s Kurt Goldstein defines self-actualization as the tendency to actualize, as much as possible, the organism's individual capacities, and proclaims that the drive to self-actualize is the only drive that determines the life of an individual.

1974 Fritz Perls says that every living thing "has only one inborn goal—to actualize itself as it is."

Throughout recorded history, questions have been posed about why we are here, and what the purpose is of our lives. Underlying these questions is a need to identify what will make us truly satisfied, and a confusion about how to find it. Psychoanalysts would claim that the fulfillment of innate biological drives leads toward satisfaction, and behaviorists would describe the importance of meeting physiological needs with food, sleep, and sex, but the new wave of psychotherapeutic thought in the early to mid-20th century believed that the path to inner fulfillment was much more complex.

One of the main proponents of this new approach to the problem was Abraham Maslow, a psychotherapist who is considered one of the founders of the humanist movement in psychology. He examined human experience by looking at the things that are most important to us: love, hope, faith, spirituality, individuality, and existence. One of the most crucial aspects of his theories was that in order to reach the most highly developed state of consciousness and realize the greatest potential, individuals must discover their true purpose in life and pursue it. Maslow refers to this ultimate state of being as self-actualization.

Toward self-actualization

Maslow created a highly structured plan to explain the path of human motivation, defining the steps that humans need to follow as they move toward self-actualization. His famous Hierarchy of Needs, which is often drawn as a pyramid, positions the most basic needs at the base and each of the other essential requirements for a fulfilled life in groups on top.

Maslow's hierarchy is split into two distinct sections: at the beginning are the four stages that make up the "deficiency needs" and all of these must be met before a person is able to reach for greater intellectual satisfaction through the "growth needs." The deficiency needs are simple and basic; they include physiological necessities (such as food, water, and sleep), the need for safety (to be safe and out of danger), love and belongingness needs (our need to be close to and accepted by others), and self-esteem requirements (our need to achieve in our lives and be recognized).

See also: Alfred Adler 100–101 ▪ Erich Fromm 124–129 ▪ Carl Rogers 130–137 ▪ Rollo May 141 ▪ Martin Seligman 200–201

The Hierarchy of Needs

Maslow's hierarchy of needs lists the qualities he observed in successful individuals who aimed high but kept their feet on the ground.

Self-transcendence
Helping others, connecting with something outside ourselves

Self-actualization
Fulfilling personal potential

Aesthetic
Order, beauty, symmetry

Cognitive
Knowing, understanding

Growth needs

Self-esteem
Achievement, recognition, respect, competence

Love and Belongingness
Acceptance, friendship, intimacy, relationships

Safety
Security, stability, health, shelter, money, employment

Physiological
Air, food, drink, sleep, warmth, exercise

Deficiency needs

At the higher level, the growth needs are cognitive (a need to know and understand), aesthetic (a desire for order and beauty), and lastly, two requirements that define the purpose of life, and lead to intense spiritual and psychological fulfillment: self-actualization and self-transcendence. Self-actualization is the desire for self-fulfillment, and self-transcendence is the need to move beyond the self, and connect to something higher than ourselves—such as God—or to help others realize their potential.

Maslow also proposes that each one of us has an individual purpose to which we are uniquely suited, and part of the path to fulfillment is to identify and pursue that purpose. If someone is not doing what they are best suited to do in life, it will not matter if all their other needs are fulfilled, he or she will be perpetually restless and unsatisfied. Each of us must discover our potential and seek out experiences that will allow us to fulfill it—"What a man can be, he must be," proclaims Maslow. ▪

Abraham Maslow

Abraham Maslow was born the eldest of seven children in Brooklyn, New York. His parents were Jewish immigrants who had left Russia for the US to escape the tumultuous political situation there. They had high expectations of Maslow and forced him to study law—a parental dominance that continued until 1928, when Maslow decided to take control of his life and pursue psychology instead. In the same year, he disobeyed his parents by marrying his cousin, Bertha Goodman, with whom he had two children.

Maslow moved to the University of Wisconsin and worked under Harry Harlow, the behavioral psychologist famous for his work with primates. Later, at Columbia University, Maslow found a mentor in psychoanalyst and former colleague of Freud's, Alfred Adler.

Key works

1943 *A Theory of Human Motivation*
1954 *Motivation and Personality*
1962 *Toward a Psychology of Being*

SUFFERING CEASES TO BE SUFFERING AT THE MOMENT IT FINDS A MEANING

VIKTOR FRANKL (1905–1997)

IN CONTEXT

APPROACH
Logotherapy

BEFORE
600–500 BCE In India, Gautama Buddha teaches that suffering is caused by desire, and can be alleviated by releasing desire.

458 BCE Ancient Greek dramatist Aeschylus explores the idea that "wisdom comes alone through suffering."

AFTER
1950s French existentialist philosophers, such as Jean-Paul Sartre, say our lives do not have a God-given purpose; we must find it for ourselves.

2003 Martin Seligman says a "full life" encompasses pleasure, engagement (flow), and meaning.

2007 US psychologist Dan Gilbert explains that people are unhappy because of the way they think about happiness.

Viennese psychiatrist Viktor Frankl had already begun to specialize in suicide prevention and the treatment of depression when, in 1942, he and his wife, brother, and parents were taken to a concentration camp. He spent three years there and endured many horrors and losses before emerging as the only survivor of the group. In his book *Man's Search for Meaning* (1946), written after these experiences, Frankl explains that humans have two psychological strengths that allow us to bear painful and possibly devastating situations and to move forward; these are the capacity for decision, and freedom of attitude. Frankl stresses that we are not at the mercy of our environment or events, because we dictate how we allow them to shape us. Even suffering can be seen differently, depending on our interpretation of events.

A man who has nothing else in this world may still know bliss.
Viktor Frankl

Frankl cites the case of one of his patients who suffered because he missed his dead wife. Frankl asked how it would have been if the patient had died first, and he replied that his wife would have found it very difficult. Frankl pointed out that the patient has spared her this grief, but must now suffer the grief himself. In giving meaning to the suffering it becomes endurable; "suffering ceases to be suffering at the moment it finds a meaning."

Meaning is something we "discover rather than invent," according to Frankl, and we must find it for ourselves. We find it through living, and specifically through love, creating things, and the way we choose to see things. ■

See also: Rollo May 141 ▪ Boris Cyrulnik 152–153 ▪ Martin Seligman 200–201

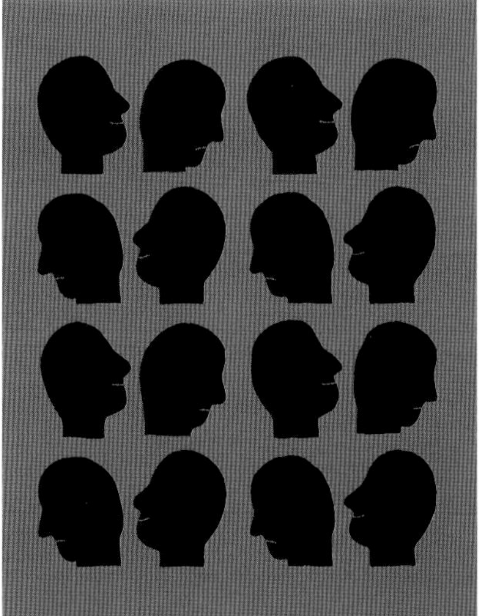

ONE DOES NOT BECOME FULLY HUMAN PAINLESSLY

ROLLO MAY (1909–1994)

IN CONTEXT

APPROACH
Existential psychotherapy

BEFORE
1841 Søren Kierkegaard claims that people misinterpret Christian ideology and misuse science to falsely defend against the anxiety inherent in existence.

1942 Swiss physician Ludwig Binswanger combines existential philosophy with psychotherapy in his *Basic Forms and the Realization of Human "Being-in-the-World."*

1942 Carl Rogers, a pioneer of humanistic psychology, publishes *Counseling and Psychotherapy.*

AFTER
1980 Irvin Yalom discusses in *Existential Psychotherapy* the four ultimate concerns of life: death, freedom, existential isolation, and meaninglessness.

In the mid-19th century, philosophers such as Martin Heidegger, Frederick Nietzsche, and Søren Kierkegaard challenged social dogma and demanded that people expand their ways of thinking to incorporate a fuller understanding of human experience, in a movement now known as existentialism. The notions of free will, personal responsibility, and how we interpret our experience were all of interest to the existentialists, who wanted to ask what it means, fundamentally, for a human to exist.

Psychologist Rollo May's *The Meaning of Anxiety* (1950) brought this human-centered philosophical approach into psychology for the first time, and May is often referred to as the father of existential psychology.

An existential approach

May viewed life as a spectrum of human experience, including suffering as a normal part of life, not as a sign of pathology. It is self-evident that as human beings, we tend to seek experiences that allow us to be comfortable. We enjoy our familiar environments, and favor experiences that keep the mental and physical senses in a state of balance and ease. This tendency, however, leads us to judge and label experiences as "good" or "bad," depending only on the levels of pleasure or discomfort they may bring. May says that in doing so, we do ourselves a disservice, since we are fighting against processes that lead to immense growth and development if we can accept them as a natural part of life.

May proposes an approach to life that echoes Buddhist thought, where we accept all forms of experience equally, rather than shunning or denying those we judge to be uncomfortable or unpleasant. We also need to accept our "negative" feelings, rather than avoid or repress them. Suffering and sadness are not pathological issues to be "fixed," he says; they are natural and essential parts of living a human life, and are also important because they lead to psychological growth. ■

See also: Søren Kierkegaard 26–27 ▪ Alfred Adler 100–101 ▪ Carl Rogers 130–137 ▪ Abraham Maslow 138–139 ▪ Viktor Frankl 140 ▪ Boris Cyrulnik 152–153

RATIONAL BELIEFS CREATE HEALTHY EMOTIONAL CONSEQUENCES

ALBERT ELLIS (1913–2007)

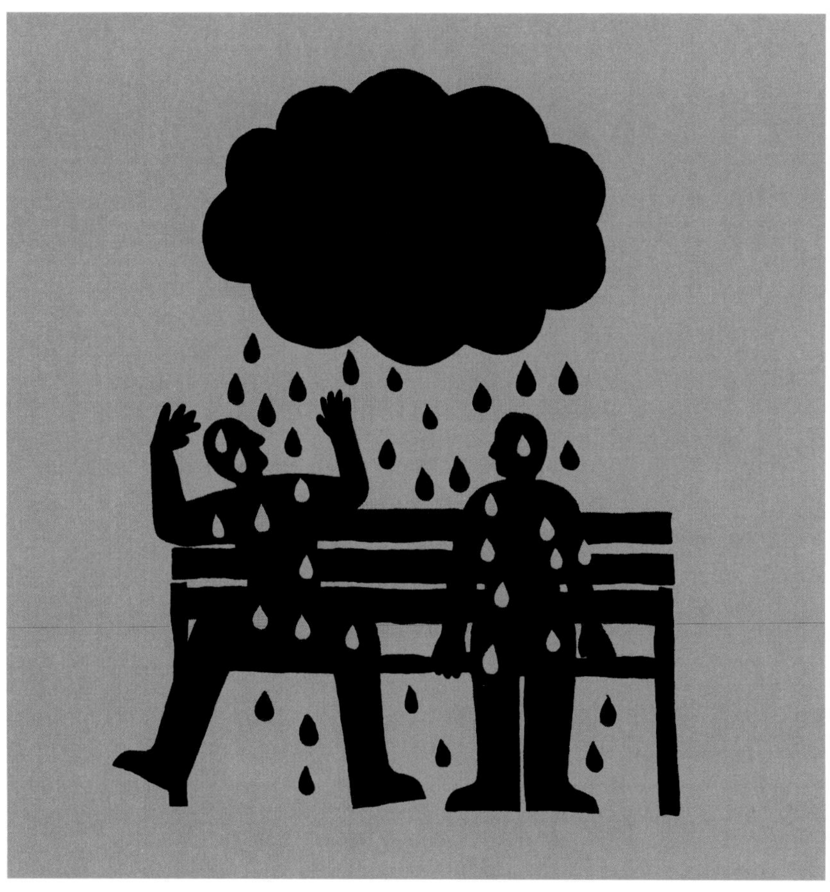

IN CONTEXT

APPROACH
Rational Emotive Behavior Therapy

BEFORE
1927 Alfred Adler says that a person's behavior springs from their ideas.

1940s The role of perception in creating reality is popularized by the Gestalt Therapy movement.

1950 Karen Horney suggests we escape from the "tyranny of the shoulds."

AFTER
1960s Aaron Beck says that depression is a result of unrealistic negative views about the world.

1980 American psychiatrist David Burns gives labels to cognitive distortions such as: Jumping to Conclusions, All or Nothing Thinking, Always Being Right, Over Generalizing, and Catastrophizing.

Epictetus, an ancient Greek philosopher, proclaimed in 80 CE, that "men are disturbed not by events, but by the views which they take of them." This principle is the foundation of Rational Emotive Behavior Therapy (REBT), devised by Dr. Albert Ellis in 1955, which asserts that experiences do not cause any specific emotional reaction; instead it is the individual's belief system that produces the reaction.

Practicing as a psychoanalyst in the 1940s and '50s, Ellis began to realize that while many of his patients gained an insight into

See also: Alfred Adler 100–101 ▪ Karen Horney 110 ▪ Erich Fromm 124–129 ▪ Carl Rogers 130–137 ▪ Aaron Beck 174–177 ▪ Martin Seligman 200–201

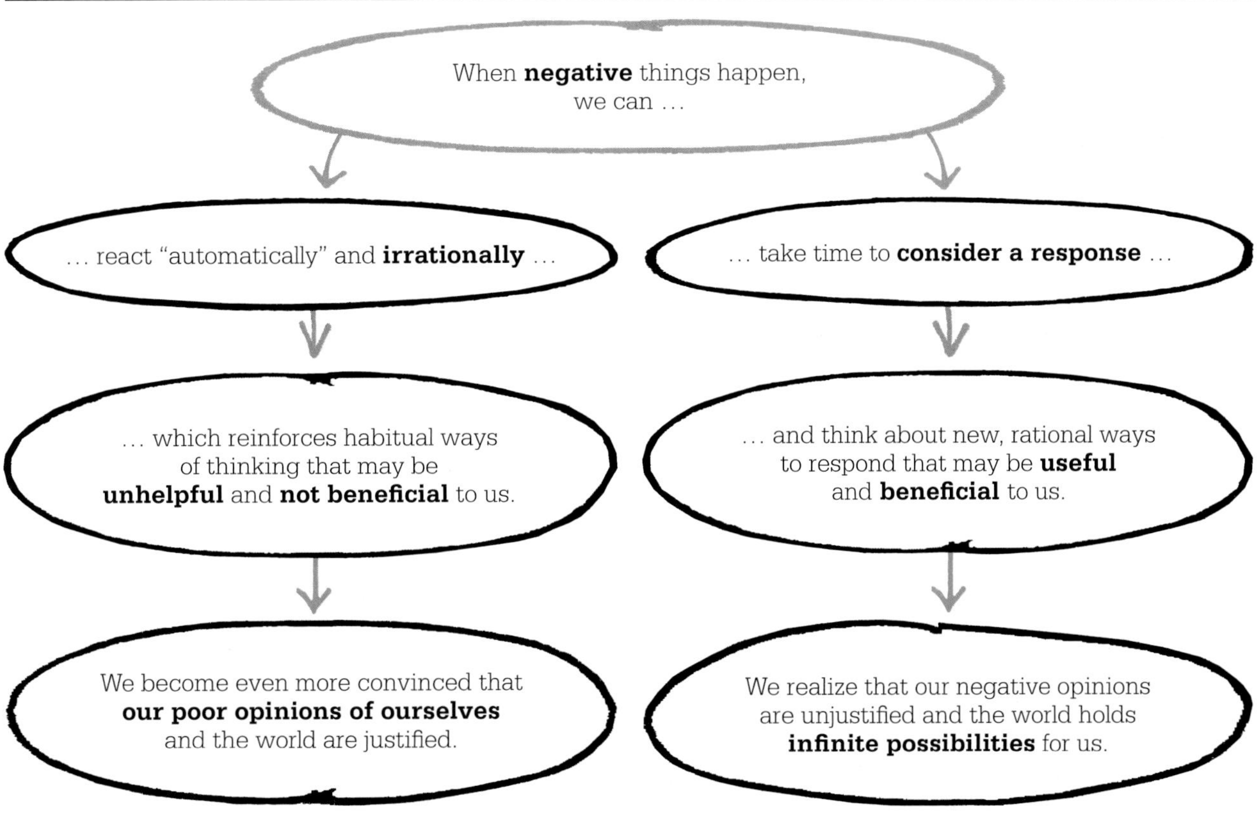

When **negative** things happen, we can …
… react "automatically" and **irrationally** …
… take time to **consider a response** …
… which reinforces habitual ways of thinking that may be **unhelpful** and **not beneficial** to us.
… and think about new, rational ways to respond that may be **useful** and **beneficial** to us.
We become even more convinced that **our poor opinions of ourselves** and the world are justified.
We realize that our negative opinions are unjustified and the world holds **infinite possibilities** for us.

themselves and their childhood, their symptoms unfortunately remained. It seemed that when one problem was resolved, the patient would put another in its place. The issue, Ellis decided, lay in the way the person was thinking (their cognition), and it required more than insight to change it.

Irrational thinking

Ellis began to describe his way of working as Rational Therapy because he believed that the majority of long-standing emotional problems are almost always due to irrational thinking. One of the most common ways in which irrationality occurs, he says, is the tendency to draw extreme conclusions, especially negative ones, about events. For example, if a man who is an irrational thinker loses his job, to him it is not merely unfortunate, but *awful*. He believes that he is worthless because he was fired, and that he will never find another job. Ellis describes irrational beliefs as illogical, extreme, damaging, and self-sabotaging because they cause unhealthy emotional consequences.

Rational thinking creates the opposite effect. Ellis defines rational thinking as helpful to the self. It is based on tolerance and the ability to bear distress without assuming catastrophic negative conclusions, and is rooted in a belief in positive human potential. This is not to say one turns a blind eye to negative factors in favor of naïve, positive beliefs—rational thinking does acknowledge reasonable feelings of sorrow, guilt, and frustration. The rational thinker may lose their job; it may have even been their fault that they lost their job. But they know they are not worthless. They may be upset with themselves, but they know that rationally there is the possibility of another job. Rational thinking is balanced and always allows room for optimism and possibilities; it creates healthy emotional consequences.

Ellis's notion of irrational thinking is influenced by Karen Horney's idea of the "tyranny of the shoulds"—a preoccupation »

People and things do not upset us. Rather, we upset ourselves by believing that they can upset us.
Albert Ellis

with the idea that something should (magically) be different from how it is. The struggle to reconcile these thoughts with reality is a painful and unending one. Rational thinking, on the other hand, focuses on acceptance; it maintains the balanced sense that sometimes things happen that we would prefer not to, but they are a part of life.

Conditioned response

We become so used to our responses to people and events that they appear to be almost automatic; our reaction becomes inextricably linked to the event itself. However, Ellis aimed to teach people to recognize how an event may contribute to a feeling, but it does not directly cause that feeling. Our emotional response depends on the meaning we put on what took place, which in turn is governed by rational or irrational thinking.

As the name implies, Rational Emotive Behavior Therapy examines both the emotional response (a cognitive process) and the behavior. The links between these two flow in both directions: it is possible to change your thinking through changing your behavior, and to change your behavior through changing your thinking. Ellis suggests that the way to change one's thinking involves being able to recognize and then dispute irrational beliefs, challenging them with rational thoughts.

Challenging beliefs

During REBT, an individual is asked to consider whether they have several overriding beliefs about themselves and their position in life as these contribute

If someone has been unlucky in love they may feel sad and rejected. However, there is a difference between feeling these emotions and allowing them to become a belief system.

to irrational responses. This process is known as "disputing." For instance, some people hold the belief that "I am the only really dependable person I know" or "I am destined to be always alone in this world." In therapy, the individual is encouraged to search their personal history to find rationalizations for these belief systems. Someone who has been through the break-up of several relationships may have the delusion that it is their "destiny to be alone" or that they are somehow "unlovable." REBT encourages

Albert Ellis

Albert Ellis was born in Pittsburgh, Pennsylvania. His father was often away on business and his mother suffered from bipolar disease; Ellis frequently took care of his two younger siblings. Ellis began a career in business and then became an author, before his writing on sexuality led him to start studying clinical psychology at Columbia University in 1942. Initially, Ellis practiced psychoanalysis and was influenced by Sigmund Freud, Albert Adler, and Erich Fromm. However, his Rational Therapy broke away from psychoanalytic theory and is considered to have led the shift toward cognitive behavioral therapy. He is recognized as one of the most influential psychologists in the US. He wrote more than 70 books, continuing to write and teach until his death at the age of 93.

Key works

1957 *How to Live with a Neurotic*
1961 *A Guide to Rational Living*
1962 *Reason and Emotion in Psychotherapy*
1998 *Optimal Aging*

people to allow for the pain of loss or loneliness, and to logically evaluate factors that led to the loss; but discourages the practice of believing that one or two instances mean that something will always happen, and therefore being happy is impossible.

One of the difficulties inherent in irrational thinking is that it tends to perpetuate itself, because in thinking, for instance, "nothing good ever happens to me," there is little or no motivation to seek opportunities where good things might happen. The irrational thinker sees the possibilities of having a good experience as so unlikely that they give up searching for them. It also makes them blind to the good things that do happen. Many people express the self-perpetuating belief: "Yes, I have tried, and *I know* that good things never happen," which rationalizes and reinforces their belief system.

Irrational thinking is "black and white;" it stops an individual from recognizing the full spectrum of possible experiences. If a faulty belief system leads us to always interpret situations negatively, then it prevents the possibility of alternate positive experiences. Though it often appears that "seeing is believing," the reality is that what we believe is what we see.

Constructivist theory

REBT is a constructivist theory, suggesting that although our preferences are influenced by our upbringing and culture, we construct our own beliefs and reality. As a therapy, it attempts to reveal people's inflexible and absolutist thoughts, feelings, and actions; and helps them see how they are choosing to "disturb themselves," as Ellis puts it. It suggests how to think of and choose healthier pathways; and how to internalize and habituate new, more beneficial beliefs. In so doing, the therapist becomes obsolete—once the client grasps the idea of becoming self-aware in decision-making, and choosing deliberately (and often differently), the therapist is no longer needed.

An active therapy

Albert Ellis's theories challenged the slow-moving methodology of psychoanalysis and created the first form of cognitive behavioral therapy, an approach that is popular today. He was an active and directive therapist and in place of long-term, passive psychoanalysis, he put the work and power squarely in the hands of the client—an approach that prefigured Carl Rogers. He also emphasized that theorizing was not enough—"you have to back it up with action, action, action," he said. REBT became one of the most popular therapies of the 1970s and '80s, and was highly influential on the work of Aaron Beck, who described Ellis as an "explorer, revolutionary, therapist, theorist, and teacher." ■

The best years of your life are the ones in which you decide your problems are your own … You realize that you control your own destiny.
Albert Ellis

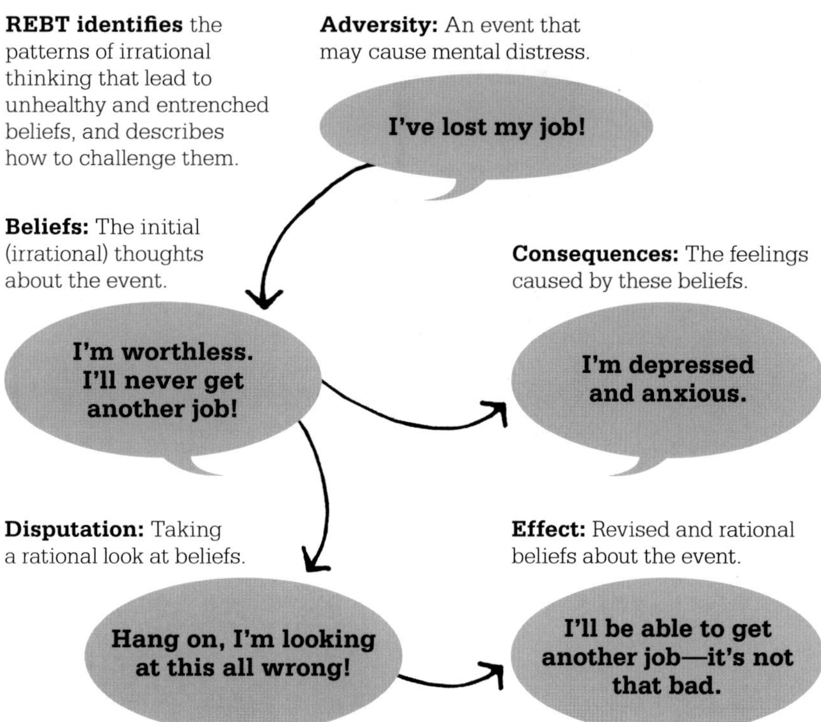

REBT identifies the patterns of irrational thinking that lead to unhealthy and entrenched beliefs, and describes how to challenge them.
Adversity: An event that may cause mental distress.
I've lost my job!
Beliefs: The initial (irrational) thoughts about the event.
I'm worthless. I'll never get another job!
Consequences: The feelings caused by these beliefs.
I'm depressed and anxious.
Disputation: Taking a rational look at beliefs.
Hang on, I'm looking at this all wrong!
Effect: Revised and rational beliefs about the event.
I'll be able to get another job—it's not that bad.

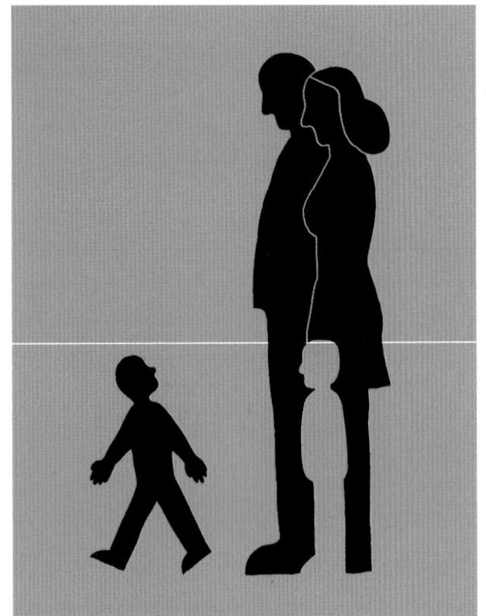

THE FAMILY IS THE "FACTORY" WHERE PEOPLE ARE MADE

VIRGINIA SATIR (1916–1988)

IN CONTEXT

APPROACH
Family therapy

BEFORE
1942 Carl Rogers publishes *Counseling and Psychotherapy*, emphasizing the role of respect and a nonjudgmental approach in mental health treatment.

AFTER
1953 US psychiatrist Harry Stack Sullivan publishes *The Interpersonal Theory of Psychiatry*, which states that people are products of their environment.

1965 Argentinian-born psychiatrist Salvador Minuchin brings family therapy to prominence at the Philadelphia Child Guidance Clinic.

1980 Italian psychiatrist Mara Selvini Palazzoli and her colleagues publish articles about their "Milan systems" approach to family therapy.

We **learn to react** in certain ways to the members of our family.

↓

These reactions **shape a role** that we adopt, especially when under stress.

↓

This role may **overwhelm our authentic self** and be taken with us into adulthood.

↓

The family is the "factory" where people are made.

The role that a person assumes in their "family of origin" (the family they grew up in) tends to be the seed from which the adult will grow. American psychologist Virginia Satir recognized the importance that the original family plays in shaping personality, and looked at differences between a healthy, functioning family and one that was dysfunctional. She was especially interested in the roles that people tend to adopt in order to compensate when healthy dynamics are lacking between family members.

A healthy family life involves open and reciprocated displays of affection, and expressions of positive regard and love for one another. More than any previous therapist, Satir emphasized the power that compassionate, nurturing relationships have in developing well-adjusted psyches.

Role playing

When family members lack the ability to openly express emotion and affection, Satir suggested that personality "roles" tend to emerge in place of authentic identities. She noted five commonly played roles

See also: Carl Rogers 130–137 ▪ Lev Vygotsky 278 ▪ Bruno Bettelheim 279

The Five Family Roles

Distractor

Computer

Leveler

Blamer

Placator

Five distinct personality roles, according to Satir, are commonly played out by individual family members in order to cover up difficult emotional issues.

that individual family members are likely to adopt, especially in times of stress. These are: the family member who constantly finds fault and criticizes ("the blamer"); the nonaffectionate intellectual ("the computer"); the person who stirs things up in order to shift the focus away from emotional issues ("the distractor"); the apologetic people-pleaser ("the placator"); and the open, honest, and direct communicator ("the leveler").

Only levelers maintain a healthy, congruent position, with their inner feelings matching their communications with the rest of the family. Others adopt their various roles because low self-esteem makes them afraid to show or share their true feelings. Placators are afraid of disapproval; blamers attack others to hide feelings of unworthiness; computers rely on their intellect to stop them acknowledging their feelings; and distracters—often the youngest in the family—believe they will only be loved if they are seen as cute and harmless.

These adopted roles may allow the family to function, but they can overwhelm each individual's ability to be their authentic self. Satir believed that in order to cast aside these false identities, whether as children or as adults, we must accept self-worth as a birthright. Only then will it be possible to start moving toward a truly fulfilling existence. This begins with a commitment to straightforward, open, and honest communication.

The need for basic, positive, emotional connections lies at the root of Satir's pioneering work. She believed that love and acceptance are the most potent healing forces for any dysfunctional family. By fostering close, compassionate relationships with her patients, she mimicked the dynamic she was encouraging them to adopt. ■

By knowing how to heal the family, I know how to heal the world.
Virginia Satir

Virginia Satir

Virginia Satir was born on a farm in Wisconsin and is said to have decided she wanted to be a "detective of people's parents" at the age of six. Losing her hearing for two years due to an illness helped to make her acutely observant of nonverbal communication, and gave her a sensitive insight into human behavior. Her father was an alcoholic, and she was well aware of the dynamics of caretaking, blaming, and pleasing that went on around her during her own childhood.

Satir trained as a teacher, but her interest in problems of self-esteem in children led her to take a master's degree in social work. She set up the first formal family therapy training programme in the US and the "Satir Model" is still hugely influential in personal and organizational psychology.

Key works

1964 *Conjoint Family Therapy*
1972 *Peoplemaking*

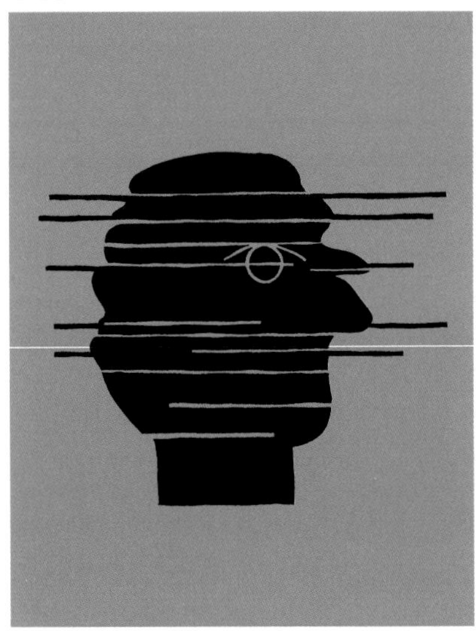

TURN ON, TUNE IN, DROP OUT

TIMOTHY LEARY (1920–1996)

IN CONTEXT

APPROACH
Experimental psychology

BEFORE
1890s William James says that the self has four layers: the material, the social, the spiritual, and the pure ego.

1956 Abraham Maslow stresses the importance of "peak experiences" in the route to self-actualization.

AFTER
1960s British psychiatrist Humphry Osmond coins the term "psychedelic" to describe the emotional effects of the drugs LSD and mescaline.

1962 In his "Good Friday Experiment," US psychiatrist and theologian Walter Pahnke tests if psychedelic drugs can deepen religious experience.

1972 US psychologist Robert E. Ornstein argues in *The Psychology of Consciousness* that only personal experience can unlock the unconscious.

Timothy Leary was an American psychologist who became an iconic figure of the 1960s counterculture, coining possibly the most widely used catchphrase linked with that era: "Turn On, Tune In, Drop Out."

However, the order in which Leary wished us to do these three things is slightly different. He felt that society was polluted by politics, and made up of sterile, generic communities that do not allow the depth of meaning needed by true individuals. The first thing he thought we should do is "Drop Out," by which he meant that we should detach ourselves from artificial attachments and become self-reliant in thought and deed. Unfortunately, "Drop Out" has been misinterpreted as urging people to halt productivity, which was never his intention.

Next, Leary tells us to "Turn On," or delve into our unconscious, and "find a sacrament which returns you to the temple of God, your own body." This is a command to explore deeper layers of reality, as well as the many levels of experience and consciousness. Drugs were one way to do this, and Leary, a Harvard professor, began experimenting with the hallucinogenic drug LSD.

To "Tune In," Leary asks us to return to society with a new vision, seeking fresh patterns of behavior that reflect our transformation, and to teach others our newfound ways. ■

The psychedelic movement of the 1960s was heavily influenced by Leary's call to create a better, more satisfying society by exploring the unconscious to uncover our true emotions and needs.

See also: William James 38–45 ▪ Abraham Maslow 138–139

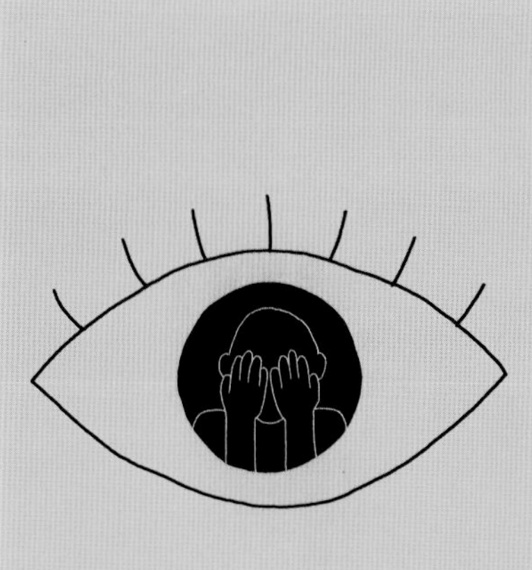

INSIGHT MAY CAUSE BLINDNESS

PAUL WATZLAWICK (1921–2007)

IN CONTEXT

APPROACH
Brief therapy

BEFORE
1880s Psychodynamic therapy, also known as insight-oriented therapy, emerges. It focuses on unconscious processes as manifested in a person's present behavior.

1938 B. F. Skinner introduces "radical" behaviorism, which does not accept that thinking, perception, or any other kind of unobservable emotional activity can trigger a particular pattern of behavior.

AFTER
1958 American psychiatrist Leopold Bellak sets up a brief therapy clinic, where therapy is limited to a maximum of five sessions.

1974 US psychotherapist Jay Haley publishes *Uncommon Therapy*, describing Milton Erickson's brief therapy techniques.

Psychotherapy often relies heavily on patients gaining an understanding of themselves, their history, and their behavior. This is based on the belief that to counter emotional pain and change behavior, we need to understand where our emotional patterns are rooted. Austrian-American psychologist Paul Watzlawick described this process as "insight." For example, a man who grieves for an abnormally long time after his partner leaves him might come to realize that he has deep issues with abandonment, because his mother left him when he was a child. But a number of therapists have concluded that insight may be unnecessary to counter emotional pain, and some, including Watzlawick, have claimed that it can make a patient worse.

Watzlawick famously stated he could not think of a single case in which someone changed as a result of a deepening understanding of self. The belief that understanding past events helps to shed light on present problems is based on a "linear" view of cause and effect. Watzlawick was drawn to the idea of circular causality of human behavior, which shows people tend to return to the same actions again and again.

Insight, Watzlawick suggested, may even cause blindness, both to the real problem and its potential solution. He supported the brief therapy approach, which targets and tackles specific problems more directly in order to achieve quicker results. But he also felt that for any therapy to succeed, it must offer the patient a supportive relationship. ■

Anybody can *be* happy, but to *make* oneself unhappy needs to be learned.
Paul Watzlawick

See also: B. F. Skinner 78–85 ▪ Elizabeth Loftus 202–207 ▪ Milton Erickson 343

MADNESS NEED NOT BE ALL BREAKDOWN IT MAY ALSO BE BREAK-THROUGH

R. D. LAING (1927–1989)

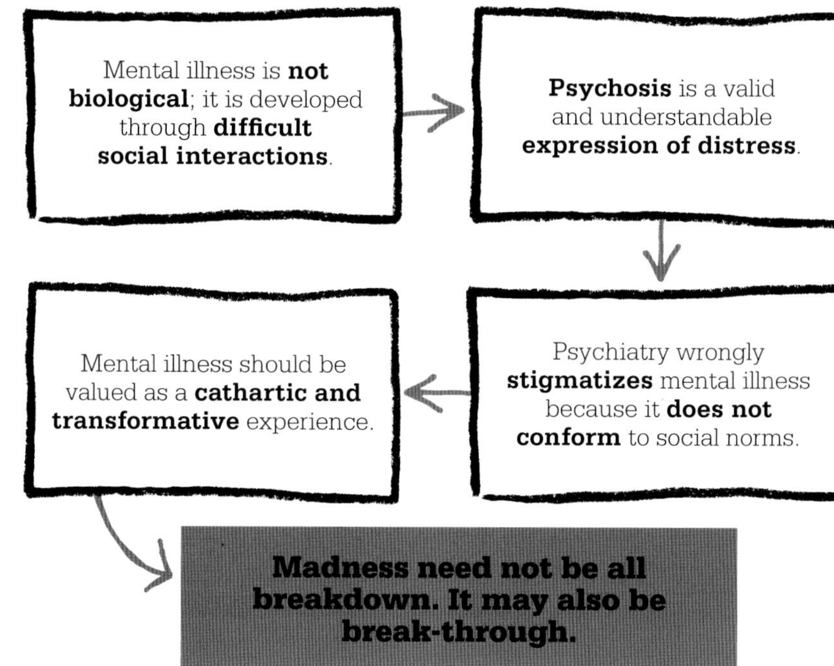

Mental illness is **not biological**; it is developed through **difficult social interactions**.
Psychosis is a valid and understandable **expression of distress**.
Psychiatry wrongly **stigmatizes** mental illness because it **does not conform** to social norms.
Mental illness should be valued as a **cathartic and transformative** experience.
Madness need not be all breakdown. It may also be break-through.

IN CONTEXT

APPROACH
Anti-psychiatry

BEFORE
1908 Swiss psychiatrist Eugen Bleuler coins the term "schizophrenia" to refer to the splitting of mental functions.

1911 Sigmund Freud proposes that schizophrenia is purely psychological, though it cannot be treated with psychoanalysis.

1943 French philosopher Jean-Paul Sartre introduces the distinction between the true self and the false self.

1956 Gregory Bateson, British social scientist, defines a "double bind" as an emotionally distressing dilemma in which all the potential resolutions lead to negative consequences.

AFTER
1978 CT brain scans reveal physical differences between chronic schizophrenics and nonschizophrenics.

At the end of the 19th century, the notion that mental illness was different in degree—rather than in kind—from the psychological suffering of normal people began to gain acceptance. Sigmund Freud suggested that neurosis and normality are part of the same scale, and that anyone is capable of experiencing mental disturbance in dire circumstances. It was from this context that R. D. Laing emerged as the preeminent icon of a new cultural trend.

Biology and behavior

Like Freud, Laing challenged the fundamental values of psychiatry, rejecting its focus on mental illness as a biological phenomenon and highlighting the significance of the

See also: Emil Kraepelin 31 ■ Sigmund Freud 92–99 ■ David Rosenhan 334–335

social, cultural, and familial influences that shape personal experience. Although he never denied the grim reality of mental illness, his views were in stark contrast to the accepted medical basis and practice of psychiatry.

Laing's work calls into question the validity of psychiatric diagnosis on the grounds that the accepted process of diagnosing mental disorders does not follow the traditional medical model. Doctors perform examinations and tests to diagnose physical illness, whereas psychiatric diagnosis is based on behavior. According to Laing, there is also an inherent problem in diagnosing mental illness based on conduct, but treating it biologically with drugs. If a diagnosis is based on behavior, then so too should be the treatment. He argues that drugs also hinder the ability to think, and as a result interfere with the natural process of true recovery.

Shakespeare's King Lear is an iconic example of a man driven mad by difficult circumstances. In Laing's view, Lear's madness is an attempt to return to his natural, healthy, state.

Approach to schizophrenia

Laing's main work centers on the understanding and treatment of schizophrenia—a serious mental disorder characterized by severe disruptions in psychological functioning—and on explaining it to ordinary people. Schizophrenia, he says, is not inherited, but is an understandable reaction to unlivable situations. He applies social scientist Gregory Bateson's theory of the "double bind," in which people are put into situations where they face conflicting expectations, and every action leads to negative consequences, resulting in extreme mental distress.

Illness as breakthrough

Laing was revolutionary in viewing the abnormal behavior and confused speech of schizophrenics as valid expressions of distress. For him, psychotic episodes represent attempts to communicate concerns, and should be seen as cathartic and transformative experiences that could lead to important personal insights. Laing accepts that these expressions are difficult to comprehend, but he explains that this is merely because they are wrapped in the language of personal symbolism, which is only meaningful from within. Laing's drug-free psychotherapy tries to make sense of a patient's symbolism by listening in an attentive and empathetic spirit. This is based on the belief that people are healthy in their natural state, and that so-called mental illness is an attempt to return to it. ■

R. D. Laing

Ronald David Laing was born in Glasgow, Scotland. After studying medicine at Glasgow University, he became a psychiatrist in the British Army, developing an interest in working with the mentally distressed. He later trained at the Tavistock Clinic, London, England. In 1965, Laing and a group of colleagues created the Philadelphia Association and started a radical psychiatric project at Kingsley Hall, London, where patients and therapists lived together.

Laing's erratic behavior and spiritual preoccupations in later life led to a decline in his reputation. As he was unable to develop a workable alternative to conventional medical treatment, his ideas are not generally accepted by the psychiatric establishment. Yet his contributions to the anti-psychiatry movement, particularly in family therapy, have had a lasting impact. He died of a heart attack in 1989.

Key works

1960 *The Divided Self*
1961 *The Self and Others*
1964 *Sanity, Madness and the Family*
1967 *The Politics of Experience*

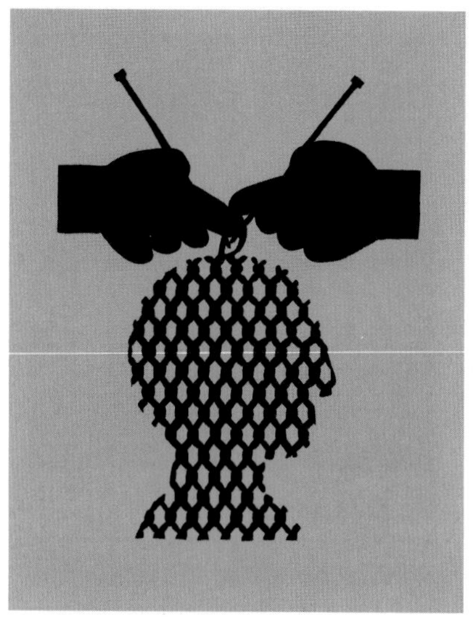

OUR HISTORY DOES NOT DETERMINE OUR DESTINY

BORIS CYRULNIK (1937–)

IN CONTEXT

APPROACH
Positive psychology

BEFORE
1920s Freud says that early trauma negatively impacts an infant's brain and can override any genetic, social, or psychological resilience factor.

1955–1995 A longitudinal study by psychologist Emmy Werner following traumatized children into adulthood suggests that one-third of the population tends toward resilience.

1988 John Bowlby asks for a study of resilience.

AFTER
2007 The UK government starts the UK Resilience Programme in schools.

2012 The American Psychological Association forms a task force on psychological resilience.

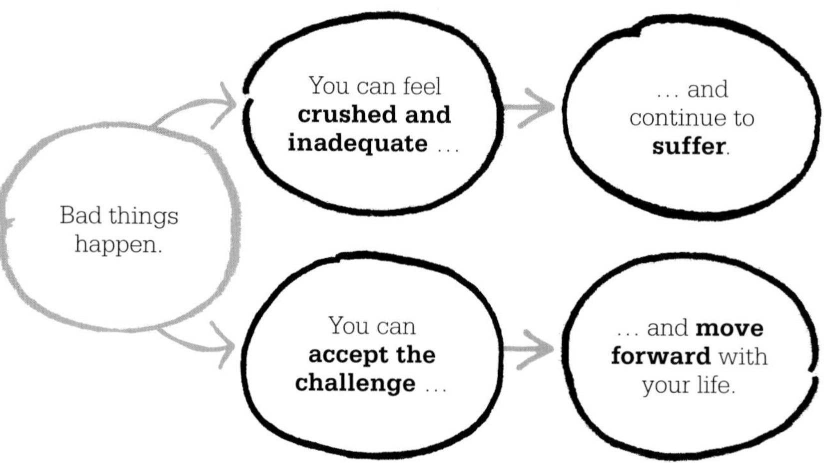

Bad things happen.
You can feel **crushed and inadequate** ...
... and continue to **suffer**.
You can **accept the challenge** ...
... and **move forward** with your life.

When tragedy strikes, some people are devastated. Unable to summon their coping mechanisms, they fall into deep depression or despondency, sometimes losing hope and even the will to carry on. They may become entirely preoccupied with the disaster and suffer nightmares, flashbacks, and anxiety attacks. Other people, however, react differently. They seem to manage not only the normal ups and downs of their lives, but also potentially overwhelming losses and traumas. Instead of becoming depressed and unable to cope, somehow they are able to deal with painful circumstances and move on.

Boris Cyrulnik is interested in this difference of reaction. To find out why some people are so deeply affected, while others are seemingly able to "bounce back," he has devoted his career to the study of psychological resilience.

Resilience is not a quality inherent within a person, Cyrulnik found, but one that builds through a natural process. He says that "alone, a child has no resilience ... it is an interaction, a relationship." We build resilience from developing

See also: Sigmund Freud 92–99 ▪ John Bowlby 282–285 ▪ Charlotte Bühler 342 ▪ George Kelly 343 ▪ Jerome Kagan 345–346

After disasters such as tsunamis psychologists have witnessed the formation of resilient communities, characterized by the residents' determination to overcome adversity.

relationships. We are constantly "knitting" ourselves from people and situations that we encounter, through the words we exchange and the feelings that arise. We might feel that if one "stitch" is dropped, our lives will unravel. In fact, "if just one stitch holds, we can start all over again."

Positive emotions and humor are key factors in resilience. Cyrulnik's research has shown that people who are better able to cope with life's difficulties or traumas are able to find meaning in hardship, seeing it as a useful and enlightening experience, and even to find ways to laugh. Resilient people always remain able to see how things may turn out for the better in future, even if the present is painful.

Meeting the challenge

It had previously been thought that people who show more resilience are less emotional in general, but Cyrulnik believed that the pain is no less for resilient people than it is for others; it is a matter of how they choose to use it. The pain may continue, even over a whole lifetime, but for these people it raises a challenge that they decide to meet. The challenge is to overcome what has happened, to find strength in the experience instead of letting it defeat them, and to use the strength to move defiantly forward. Given the right support, children are especially capable of complete recovery from trauma. Cyrulnik has shown that the human brain is malleable and will recover if allowed. The brain of a traumatized child shows shrinkage of the ventricles and cortex, but where the child is well supported and loved after the trauma, brain scans have shown the brain to be capable of returning to normal within a year.

Cyrulnik stresses the importance of not labeling children who have suffered a trauma, thereby sidelining them to a seemingly hopeless future. Trauma consists of the injury and the representation of that injury. Enduring humiliating adult interpretations of events can be the most traumatic experience. Labels, he says, can be more damaging and damning than the experience. ■

Resilience is a person's ability to grow in the face of terrible problems.
Boris Cyrulnik

Boris Cyrulnik

Boris Cyrulnik was born to Jewish parents in Bordeaux, France, shortly before the outbreak of World War II. In 1944, when the Vichy regime controlled unoccupied southern France by arrangement with Germany, his home was raided and his parents were taken to Auschwitz concentration camp. His parents had placed him with a foster family for safety, but within days they turned him over to the authorities for a small reward. He escaped while awaiting transfer to a concentration camp and worked on farms until the age of ten, when he was taken into care. He grew up in France, without any relatives. Largely self-taught, Cyrulnik eventually studied medicine at the University of Paris. Realizing he wanted to reevaluate his own life, he began to study psychoanalysis and later neuropsychiatry. He has devoted his career to working with traumatized children.

Key works

1992 *The Dawn of Meaning*
2004 *The Whispering of Ghosts*
2009 *Resilience*

ONLY GOOD PEOPLE GET DEPRESSED

DOROTHY ROWE (1930–2019)

IN CONTEXT

APPROACH
Personal construct theory

BEFORE
1940s Gestalt therapy is founded, introducing the notion that perception influences meaning.

1955 George Kelly publishes *The Psychology of Personal Constructs*, outlining the theory that everyone has a set of constructs (beliefs) about the world and the people in it.

1960 Psychologist and statistician Max Hamilton constructs the Hamilton Depression Rating Scale (HAM-D), a tool used to measure clinical depression.

AFTER
1980 Psychologist Melvin Lerner publishes *The Belief in a Just World: A Fundamental Delusion,* explaining how we wrongly believe that people get what they deserve.

If people could stop blaming themselves for things that have happened in their lives, the rate of depression would decrease dramatically. This premise is the foundation of Dorothy Rowe's success in treating the problem.

We are generally brought up to believe that the world is a fair and rational place; that if we are good, good things will happen to us. But if things go well when we are good, what does that say about us when things go wrong? Our belief in a "Just World"—where the good are rewarded and the bad punished—makes us blame ourselves for the bad things that happen to us.

When we are wronged or hurt in some way, there is a tendency to ask, "Why did this happen to me?" People look back to see what they did to cause the situation, even in the case of a natural disaster. Self-blame, guilt, helplessness, and shame irrationally arise when bad things happen, and these can lead to depression.

Rowe explained that we create and choose our beliefs. Once we understand this, we can let go of the idea of a Just World and think more rationally about negative experiences. We might suffer from bad parenting, job loss, or even a devastating tornado, but these things did not happen because we are doomed to misfortune, nor do we deserve to be treated badly. To recover from these setbacks, we need to stop personalizing events, start externalizing them, and realize that sometimes bad things just happen. ■

To turn natural sadness into depression, all you have to do is blame yourself for the disaster that has befallen you.
Dorothy Rowe

See also: Fritz Perls 112–117 ▪ Carl Rogers 130–137 ▪ Albert Ellis 142–145 ▪ Melvin Lerner 248–249 ▪ George Kelly 343

FATHERS ARE SUBJECT TO A RULE OF SILENCE

GUY CORNEAU (1951–2017)

IN CONTEXT

APPROACH
Masculine psychology

BEFORE
1900s Freudian analysts describe the Oedipus complex, which states that sons feel naturally competitive with their father.

1950s French psychoanalyst Jacques Lacan argues that the son sees the father as embodying the law.

AFTER
1991 In *Iron John: A Book About Men*, American author Robert Bly says that fathers fail to give their sons what they need to become men, and suggests that they need to reawaken the "Wild Man" within.

1990s American writers Douglas Gillette and Robert L. Moore publish five books exploring Jungian archetypes and the male psyche.

Before French-Canadian analyst Guy Corneau published *Absent Fathers, Lost Sons* in 1991, psychology had given little attention to emotional communication between men. Corneau's book examined the difficulties of intimate conversations between the male generations. He recounts his attempts to make an emotional connection with his own father: reaching out, seeking approval, but receiving only silence.

Communication between fathers and sons is often characterized by silences. While sons long for recognition and approval from their fathers, fathers are reluctant to give this approval freely.

Withholding approval

Corneau recognizes that this sequence of events is a familiar pattern in men, who are often unable to shower their sons with the praise, affection, or recognition craved by their offspring. When the son experiences this silence, he may try harder to impress, or he might withdraw, but the silence remains irrevocably imprinted in his mind, according to Corneau. The phenomenon may stem from a competitive interplay of male egos; a man who showers his son with praise would somehow be compromising his own power, making it less valuable. From the son's point of view, if approval is given too easily, without some degree of withholding, the father is then no longer worthy of impressing. It appears that in most forms of society there is a belief that men cannot be both strong and open.

Corneau says that this behavior does a disservice to men. They are denied the opportunity to express affection toward their sons—and the sons are forced to go without that affection. ■

See also: Sigmund Freud 92–99 ▪ Carl Jung 102–107 ▪ Jacques Lacan 122–123

COGNITIV PSYCHOL

THE CALCULATING BRAIN

E

OGY

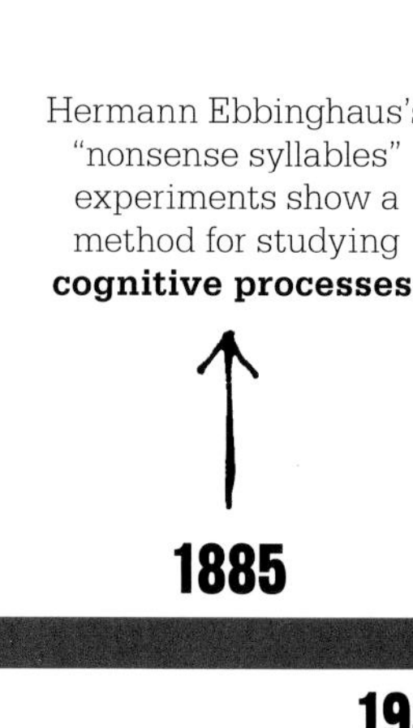

1885

Hermann Ebbinghaus's "nonsense syllables" experiments show a method for studying **cognitive processes**.

1932

Frederic Bartlett studies **reconstructive memory** in *The War of the Ghosts*.

1947

Jerome Bruner and Cecile Goodman publish *Value and Need as Organizing Factors in Perception,* arguing that **motivated reasoning affects perception**.

1949

Donald Hebb explains learning in terms of connections between **stimuli and neurons**.

1950

Alan Turing publishes *Computing Machinery and Intelligence*, in which he describes the human brain as an **"organized machine"** that learns through experience.

1956

George Armitage Miller argues that the human brain can only hold **seven chunks of information** at once.

1957

Leon Festinger's *A Theory of Cognitive Dissonance* suggests there is a human drive for **consistency of beliefs**.

1958

Donald Broadbent publishes *Perception and Communication*, introducing the **information-processing model** of cognition.

The first half of the 20th century was dominated by two strands of thinking in psychology: behaviorism (which concentrated on learning theory) and psychoanalysis (which focused on the unconscious and development in early childhood). The mental processes that had preoccupied psychologists in the previous century, such as perception, consciousness, and memory, were largely neglected.

There were inevitably some exceptions. Psychologists Frederic Bartlett of the UK and Bluma Zeigarnik of Russia were both studying the process of memory in the 1920s and '30s, anticipating the work of later cognitive psychologists. In Germany, Wolfgang Köhler's work on problem-solving and decision-making drew on Gestalt psychology—a German school of thought that concentrated on perception and perceptual organization—and was also a precursor of cognitive psychology.

The cognitive revolution

What eventually swung the balance from interest in behavior to the study of mental processes came from outside psychology. Improvements in communications and computer technology, and possibilities opened up by artificial intelligence—then a growing field thanks to advances made during World War II—led to a new way of thinking about the brain: as an information processor. The mental processes, referred to as "cognitive processes" or "cognition," which behaviorism would not or could not examine, now had a model for psychologists to work from. At the same time, advances in neuroscience led to a greater understanding of the functions of the brain and nervous system. This allowed psychologists, notably Donald Hebb, to examine mental processes directly, rather than merely inferring them from observations of behavior.

One of the first to apply the information-processing analogy to psychology was a student of Frederic Bartlett's at Cambridge, Donald Broadbent, who had been inspired by the work of computer scientist Alan Turing and communications expert Colin Cherry in the 1940s and '50s. But the turning point came in the US, where behaviorism began to be criticized for its limitations, leading to a so-called "cognitive revolution" in the late 1950s. In the vanguard of this

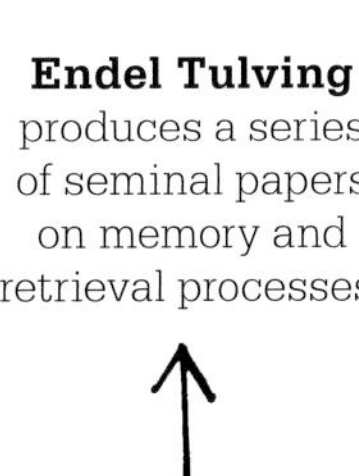

1960s

Endel Tulving produces a series of seminal papers on memory and retrieval processes.

1967

Aaron Beck outlines **cognitive behavior therapy** (CBT) in *Depression: Causes and Treatment.*

1967

Ulric Neisser coins the term **"cognitive psychology"** in his book of the same title.

1971

Roger Shepard and Jacqueline Metzler publish research showing that people are able to mentally rotate a 3D object.

1978

In *Mood and Memory*, Gordon H. Bower reports experiments that suggest **memory retrieval** is mood-dependent.

1979

Elizabeth Loftus's book *Eyewitness Testimony* exposes the **fallibility of eyewitness memory** as evidence.

1992

In *Facial Expressions of Emotion*, Paul Ekman suggests that certain **facial expressions are universal** and therefore biological.

2001

In *The Seven Sins of Memory,* Daniel Schacter details ways our **memories can be erroneous**.

dramatic shift of approach were the Americans George Armitage Miller and Jerome Bruner, who in 1960 co-founded the Center for Cognitive Studies at Harvard University.

A new direction

Miller and Bruner's ground-breaking work led to a fundamental change of direction in psychology. Areas that had been neglected by behaviorists, such as memory, perception, and emotions, became the central focus. While Bruner incorporated the concepts of cognition into existing theories of learning and developmental psychology, Miller's application of the information-processing model to memory opened up the field, making memory an important area of study for cognitive psychologists, including Endel Tulving, Elizabeth Loftus, Daniel Schacter, and Gordon H. Bower. There was also a reappraisal of Gestalt psychology: Roger Shepard reexamined ideas of perception, and Wolfgang Köhler's work on problem-solving and decision-making resurfaced in the theories of Daniel Kahneman and Amos Tversky. And, perhaps for the first time, cognitive psychologists, including Bower and Paul Ekman, made a scientific study of emotion.

But it wasn't only the theories of behaviorists that were overturned; Freud's psychoanalytic theory and its followers were also criticized for being unscientific. Aaron Beck found that cognitive psychology could provide a more effective therapy—and that it was more amenable to objective scrutiny. The cognitive therapy he advocated, later incorporating elements of behavioral therapy and meditation techniques, soon became standard treatment for disorders such as depression and anxiety, and led to a movement of positive psychology advocating mental well-being rather than just treating mental illness.

At the beginning of the 21st century, cognitive psychology is still the dominant approach to the subject, and has had an effect on neuroscience, education, and economics. It has even influenced the nature–nurture debate; in the light of recent discoveries in genetics and neuroscience, evolutionary psychologists such as Steven Pinker have argued that our thoughts and actions are determined by the make-up of our brains, and that they are like other inherited characteristics: subject to the laws of natural selection. ■

INSTINCT IS A DYNAMIC PATTERN

WOLFGANG KÖHLER (1887–1967)

IN CONTEXT

APPROACH
Gestalt psychology

BEFORE
1890 Austrian philosopher Christian von Ehrenfels introduces the concept of Gestalt in his book, *On the Qualities of Form*.

1912 Max Wertheimer publishes *Experimental Studies of the Perception of Movement*, a landmark in Gestalt psychology.

AFTER
1920s Edward Tolman brings together ideas from Gestalt and behaviorist psychology in his purposive behaviorism (now cognitive behaviorism).

1935 *Psychology of Productive Thinking* by Karl Duncker—a German Gestalt psychologist—describes experiments in problem-solving and mental restructuring.

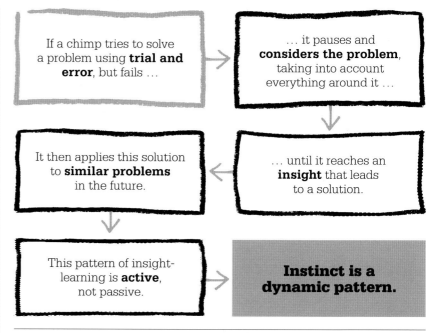

If a chimp tries to solve a problem using **trial and error**, but fails …

… it pauses and **considers the problem**, taking into account everything around it …

… until it reaches an **insight** that leads to a solution.

It then applies this solution to **similar problems** in the future.

This pattern of insight-learning is **active**, not passive.

Instinct is a dynamic pattern.

In the late 19th century, a group of German psychologists who disagreed with the prevailing schools of thought developed a new, scientific, and distinctly holistic approach, which they called Gestalt. Wolfgang Köhler, who founded the new movement along with Max Wertheimer and Kurt Koffka, explained that the word means both "pattern" and, when applied to their theory, "organized whole." Gestalt psychology (not to be confused with Gestalt therapy, a much later development) took as its starting point the idea that concepts such as perception, learning, and cognition should be considered as wholes, not studied by investigating their various parts.

Köhler thought the dominant branch of psychology, behaviorism, was too simplistic and overlooked the dynamic nature of perception.

See also: Ivan Pavlov 60–61 ▪ Edward Thorndike 62–65 ▪ Edward Tolman 72–73 ▪ Max Wertheimer 341

Köhler studied chimpanzees solving task-related problems. He realized they could actively perceive several possible solutions before finding the answer through a moment of insight.

Pavlov and Thorndike claimed that animals learn by trial and error through simple stimulus–response conditioning, but Köhler believed they were capable of insight and intelligence. He was able to put this to the test when he became director of an anthropoid research center on Tenerife from 1913–1920, where he studied chimpanzees tackling a number of problem-solving tasks.

Insightful learning

What Köhler observed confirmed his belief, and also demonstrated that problem-solving and learning could be explained in terms of Gestalt. When faced with a problem, such as how to reach food in an inaccessible place, the chimpanzees were frustrated in their initial attempts, but would then pause and apparently take stock of the situation before attempting some kind of solution. This often involved using tools—such as sticks or crates that were lying around in their play area—to reach the food. When subsequently faced with the same problem, they instantly applied the same solution. Köhler concluded that the chimps' behavior showed a cognitive trial-and-error process rather than an actual one; they were solving the problem in their minds first, and only after an insight (the "aha" moment) tried out their solution. This is contrary to the behaviorist view that learning is conditioned by response to a stimulus, and reinforced by reward. The chimps learned by perceiving the problem, not by receiving rewards.

This was a demonstration of Köhler's dynamic model of behavior, involving organization within perception, rather than passive learning through response to rewards. The pattern (Gestalt) of learning by insight—failure, pause, perception, insight, and attempt—is an active one; but this is not necessarily apparent to someone watching the chimps' separate attempts to solve the problem, mainly because it is not possible to see the organization of perception in the chimp's mind. What we call instinct, the apparently automatic response to solving a problem, is affected by this process of insight learning, and is itself an active, dynamic pattern. ■

Insight has the appearance of a complete solution with reference to the whole layout of the field.
Wolfgang Köhler

Wolfgang Köhler

Wolfgang Köhler was born in Estonia, but his family returned to their native Germany soon after his birth. He studied at various colleges before completing a PhD in Berlin. In 1909, he and Kurt Koffka worked with Max Wertheimer at the Frankfurt Academy on his perception experiments; these formed the basis of Gestalt psychology.

In 1913, Köhler became director of the Prussian Academy of Sciences research station in Tenerife, where he became stranded at the start of World War I, remaining there until 1920. On his return to Berlin, he served as director of the Psychological Institute until 1935, when he emigrated to the US to escape the Nazi regime. He taught at several US colleges, and was elected president of the American Psychological Association for 1959. Ulric Neisser described him as "a genuinely creative thinker as well as a person of great dignity and honor."

Key works

1917 *The Mentality of Apes*
1929 *Gestalt Psychology*
1938 *The Place of Values in a World of Facts*

INTERRUPTION OF A TASK GREATLY IMPROVES ITS CHANCES OF BEING REMEMBERED

BLUMA ZEIGARNIK (1901–1988)

IN CONTEXT

APPROACH
Memory studies

BEFORE
1885 Hermann Ebbinghaus publishes his pioneering book, *Memory: A Contribution to Experimental Psychology.*

1890 William James in *The Principles of Psychology* makes the distinction between primary (short-term) and secondary (long-term) memory.

AFTER
1956 George Armitage Miller's *The Magical Number Seven, Plus or Minus Two* revives interest in the study of memory.

1966 Jerome Bruner stresses the importance of organization and categorization in the learning process.

1972 Endel Tulving distinguishes between episodic memory (of specific events) and semantic memory (of factual information unrelated to an event or situation).

While researching for her doctorate in Berlin, Russian psychologist Bluma Zeigarnik was told by her professor, Kurt Lewin, that he had noticed waiters could recall details of orders that were still not paid for better than details of orders they had completed. This led Zeigarnik to wonder whether unfinished tasks have a different status in memory, and are remembered better, than finished ones. She devised an experiment in which participants were given simple puzzles or tasks to do. They were interrupted during about half these tasks. Later, when asked how well they could remember the activities, it became clear that they were twice as likely to recall details of the interrupted tasks, whether these were ultimately completed or not. Zeigarnik reasoned that this could be due to the task lacking closure, leading to the memory being stored differently, and more effectively.

The "Zeigarnik effect" can be demonstrated by the fact that a waiter is more likely to remember details of an order that has not yet been paid for, than one that has been completed.

This phenomenon, which became known as the "Zeigarnik effect," had important implications. Zeigarnik proposed that students, especially children, retained more if they had frequent breaks while studying. But little notice was taken of her ideas until memory once again became a key subject for research in the 1950s. Since then, Zeigarnik's theory has been accepted as a major step in the understanding of memory, and has found practical application not only in education but also in advertising and the media. ■

See also: Hermann Ebbinghaus 48–49 ▪ Jerome Bruner 164–165 ▪ George Armitage Miller 170–173 ▪ Endel Tulving 186–191 ▪ Daniel Schacter 208–209

WHEN A BABY HEARS FOOTSTEPS, AN ASSEMBLY IS EXCITED

DONALD HEBB (1904–1985)

IN CONTEXT

APPROACH
Neuropsychology

BEFORE
1890 William James puts forward a theory about neural networks in the brain.

1911 Edward Thorndike's Law of Effect proposes that connections between stimulus and response are "stamped in," creating a neural link, or association.

1917 Wolfgang Köhler's study of chimps shows that learning by insight is longer-lasting than learning by trial and error.

1929 Karl Lashley publishes *Brain Mechanisms and Intelligence.*

AFTER
1970s George Armitage Miller coins the term "cognitive neuroscience."

1980s Neuroscientists devise imaging techniques, allowing them to map brain functions.

In the 1920s, a number of psychologists turned to neuroscience for answers to questions about learning and memory. Prominent among these was Karl Lashley, who led the way in examining the role played by neural connections, but it was his student, the Canadian psychologist Donald Hebb, who formulated a theory to explain what actually happens during the process of associative learning.

Hebb argued that nerve cells become associated when they are simultaneously and repeatedly active; the synapses, or links, that connect them become stronger. Repeated experiences lead to the formation of "cell assemblies," or groups of connected neurons, in the brain—a theory often summed up as "cells that fire together, wire together." Similarly, separate cell assemblies can also become linked, forming a "phase sequence," which we recognize as a thought process.

This associative process, Hebb found, is especially noticeable in childhood learning, when new cell assemblies and phase sequences are being formed. In his book, *The Organization of Behavior* (1949), he gave the example of a baby hearing footsteps, which stimulates a number of neurons in its brain; if the experience is repeated, a cell assembly forms. Subsequently, "when the baby hears footsteps ... an assembly is excited; while this is still active he sees a face and feels hands picking him up, which excites other assemblies—so the 'footsteps assembly' becomes connected with the 'face assembly' and with the 'being-picked-up assembly.' After this has happened, when the baby hears footsteps only, all three assemblies are excited." In adults, however, learning tends to involve the rearrangement of existing cell assemblies and phase sequences, rather than the formation of new ones.

Hebb's theory of cell assembly was a cornerstone of modern neuroscience, and his explanation of neural learning, which became known as Hebbian learning, remains the accepted model. ■

See also: Edward Thorndike 62–65 ▪ Karl Lashley 76 ▪ Wolfgang Köhler 160–161 ▪ George Armitage Miller 170–173 ▪ Daniel Schacter 208–209

KNOWING IS A PROCESS NOT A PRODUCT

JEROME BRUNER (1915–2016)

IN CONTEXT

APPROACH
Cognitive development

BEFORE
1920s Lev Vygotsky develops his theory that cognitive development is both a social and a cultural process.

1952 Jean Piaget publishes his developmental theories in his book, *The Origins of Intelligence in Children*.

AFTER
1960s The teaching program "Man: A Course of Study (MACOS)," based on Bruner's theories, is adopted in schools in the US, the UK, and Australia.

1977 Albert Bandura publishes *Social Learning Theory*, which looks at development through a mixture of behavioral and cognitive aspects.

We learn things by **active experience**.

Instructing someone is not just telling them something but **encouraging them to participate**.

We acquire knowledge through the use of reasoning, by **constructing meaning** from the information.

This is a form of **information processing**.

Knowing is a process, not a product.

The field of developmental psychology was dominated throughout much of the 20th century by Jean Piaget, who explained how a child's thinking develops and matures in stages, as a result of a natural curiosity to explore the environment. Lev Vygotsky's theory, which appeared in English shortly after Piaget's, also claimed that a child finds meaning through experience, but widened the meaning of the word "experience" to encompass cultural and social experience. Children, he said, learn mainly through interaction with other people.

At this point in the 1960s, the "cognitive revolution" was gaining momentum; mental processes were increasingly being explained by the analogy of the brain as an "information processor." Jerome Bruner was a key figure in this new

See also: Jean Piaget 270–277 ▪ Lev Vygotsky 278 ▪ Albert Bandura 294–299

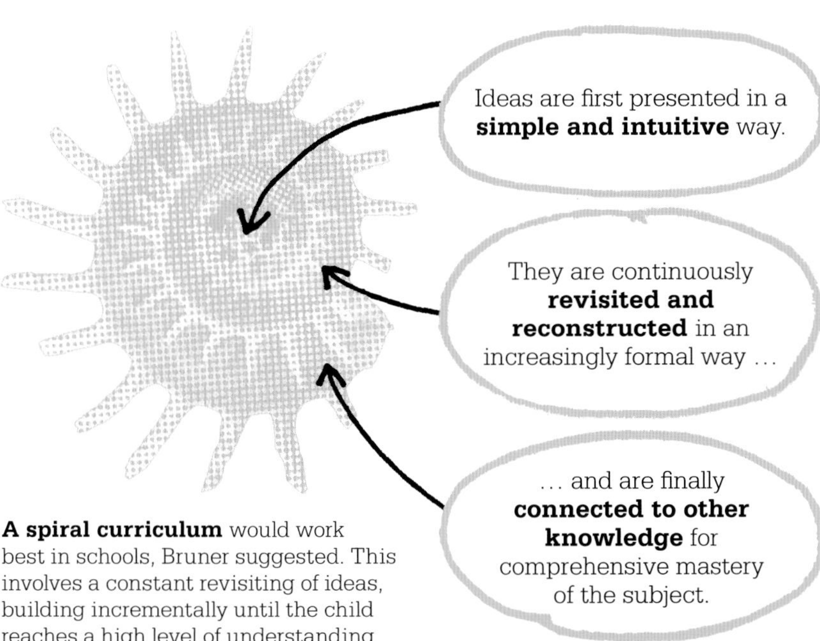

Ideas are first presented in a **simple and intuitive** way.
They are continuously **revisited and reconstructed** in an increasingly formal way …
… and are finally **connected to other knowledge** for comprehensive mastery of the subject.

A spiral curriculum would work best in schools, Bruner suggested. This involves a constant revisiting of ideas, building incrementally until the child reaches a high level of understanding.

approach, having previously studied the ways that our needs and motivations influence perception—and concluding that we see what we need to see. He became interested in how cognition develops, and so began to study cognitive processes in children.

The mind as processor

Bruner began his investigations by applying cognitive models to Piaget and Vygotsky's ideas, shifting the emphasis in the study of cognitive development from the construction of meaning to the processing of information: the means by which we acquire and store knowledge. Like Piaget, he believes that acquiring knowledge is an experiential process; but like Vygotsky, sees this as a social occupation, not a solitary one. He maintains that learning cannot be conducted unassisted: some form of instruction is essential to a child's development, but "to instruct someone … is not a matter of getting him to commit results to mind. Rather, it is to teach him to participate in the process." When we acquire knowledge, we need to actively participate and reason, rather than passively absorb information, because this is what gives knowledge meaning. In terms of cognitive psychology, reasoning is seen as "processing information," so the acquisition of knowledge should be seen as a process, not a product or end result. We need encouragement and guidance in that process, and for Bruner, that is the role of a teacher.

In *The Process of Education* (1960), Bruner presented the idea that children should be active participants in the process of education. The book became a landmark text, altering educational policy in the US at governmental and schoolteacher level. ■

Jerome Bruner

The son of Polish immigrants in New York City, Jerome Seymour Bruner was born blind, but regained his sight after cataract operations at the age of two. His father died when Bruner was 12, and his grief stricken mother moved the family frequently during his subsequent school years. He studied psychology at Duke University, then at Harvard, where he attained a PhD in 1941 alongside Gordon Allport and Karl Lashley.

Bruner served in the US army's Office for Strategic Studies (an intelligence unit) during World War II, then returned to Harvard, where he collaborated with Leo Postman and George Armitage Miller. In 1960, he cofounded the Center for Cognitive Studies with Miller at Harvard, staying until it closed in 1972. Bruner taught at Oxford University in England for ten years, before returning to the US. He continued to teach into his nineties, and died at the age of 100.

Key works

1960 *The Process of Education*
1966 *Studies in Cognitive Growth*
1990 *Acts of Meaning*

A MAN WITH A CONVICTION IS A HARD MAN TO CHANGE

LEON FESTINGER (1919–1989)

IN CONTEXT

APPROACH
Learning theory

BEFORE
1933 Gestalt psychologist Kurt Lewin leaves the Berlin School of Experimental Psychology and emigrates to the US.

AFTER
1963 Stanley Milgram publishes his experiments on willingness to obey authority figures, even when orders conflict with one's conscience.

1971 Philip Zimbardo's Stanford prison study shows how people adapt to the roles they are assigned.

1972 US social psychologist Daryl Bem proposes the alternative self-perception theory of attitude change.

1980s Elliot Aronson defends Festinger's theory, conducting experiments into initiation rites.

Alongside the two main movements in psychology that emerged in the early 20th century—behaviorism and psychoanalysis—there was also a slowly growing interest in the way in which human thought and behavior are influenced by social factors. By the end of World War II, this had become an important field of research, spearheaded in the US by Kurt Lewin, the founder of the Research Center for Group Dynamics at the Massachusetts Institute of Technology in 1945.

On the staff at the center was one of Lewin's former students, Leon Festinger. Originally attracted by Lewin's work exploring Gestalt

See also: Kurt Lewin 222–227 ▪ Solomon Asch 228–231 ▪ Elliot Aronson 250–251 ▪ Stanley Milgram 252–259 ▪ Philip Zimbardo 260–261 ▪ Stanley Schachter 345

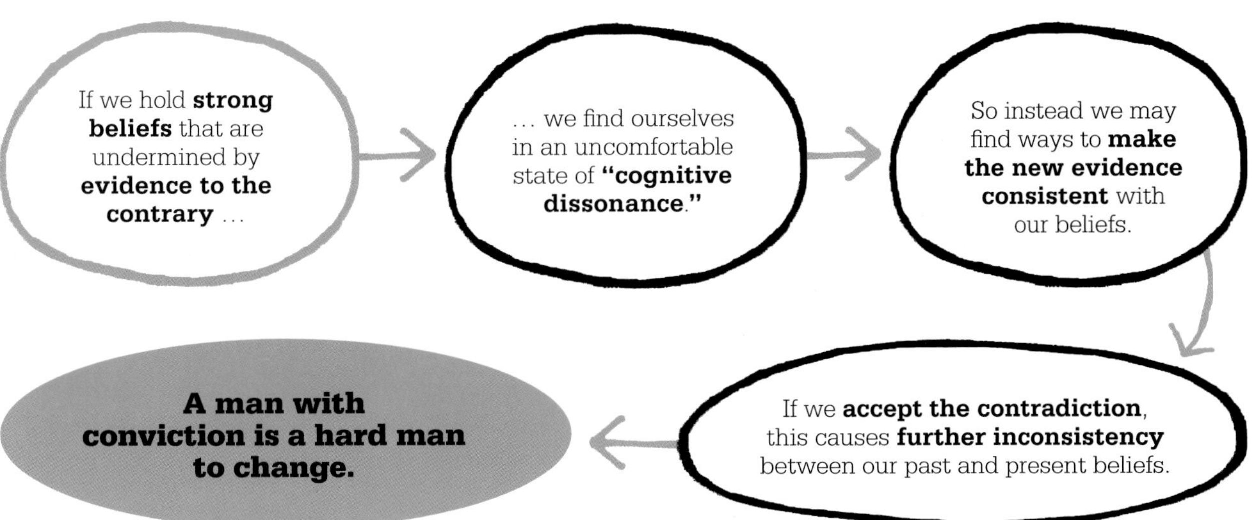

psychology, he later also took an interest in social psychology. In the course of his research, Festinger observed that people continually seek to bring order to their world, and a key part of that order is consistency. To achieve this, they develop routines and habits, such as establishing regular mealtimes and choosing favorite seats on their daily commute to work. When these routines are disrupted, people feel very uneasy. The same is true, he found, of habitual thought patterns or beliefs. If a very strong opinion is met with contradictory evidence, it creates an uncomfortable internal inconsistency; Festinger called this "cognitive dissonance." He reasoned that the only way to overcome this discomfort is to somehow make the belief and the evidence consistent.

If we hold strong beliefs that are undermined by evidence to the contrary …
… we find ourselves in an uncomfortable state of "cognitive dissonance."
So instead we may find ways to make the new evidence consistent with our beliefs.
If we accept the contradiction, this causes further inconsistency between our past and present beliefs.
A man with conviction is a hard man to change.

Unshakable conviction

After reading a report in a local newspaper in 1954, Festinger saw an opportunity to study the reaction to just such a cognitive dissonance. A cult claimed to have received messages from aliens warning of a flood that would end the world on December 21; only true believers would be rescued by flying saucers. Festinger and some of his colleagues at the University of Minnesota gained access to the group, interviewing them before the designated apocalyptic date and again afterward, when the events had failed to transpire. The study of this group, known as the Oak Park study, was written up by Festinger, Henry Riecken, and Stanley Schachter in *When Prophecy Fails* and describes the reaction of the cult members. Where common sense might lead us to expect that the failure of their prediction and consequent cognitive dissonance would cause cult members to abandon their beliefs, the opposite occurred. As the time neared, another "message" came through, declaring that, due to the group's dedication, the world was to be spared. Cult members became even more fervent believers. Festinger had anticipated this because, he argued, to accept the contradictory evidence would set up an even greater dissonance between past belief and present denial—especially if a great deal (reputation, jobs, and money) had been invested in the original belief.

When dissonance is present, in addition to trying to reduce it, the person will actively avoid situations and information which would likely increase the dissonance.
Leon Festinger

Drawing on the Oak Park study, Festinger hypothesized that this cognitive dissonance presented »

itself in two ways. First, the dissonance between a belief or conviction and any contradictory evidence will cause psychological discomfort, and to overcome this, the person experiencing it will try to reduce the inconsistency. Second, as well as trying to minimize the inconsistency, that person will deliberately ignore information and avoid situations that reinforce or increase the contradictions. For example, a smoker might decide to give up smoking in order to avoid the dissonance between their habit and the evidence of harm to their health; alternatively, they could simply ignore the warnings or even choose to convince themselves of the lie that tobacco has some health benefits.

Incontrovertible evidence wasn't enough to persuade some people, fueled by online misinformation, that the moon landings weren't lies propagated by the US government.

Controlled dissonance

After transferring to Stanford University, Festinger wanted to take the hypothesis he had gleaned from the Oak Park study and test it in controlled conditions. He collaborated with a colleague, James M. Carlsmith, to devise an experiment using volunteer subjects. The participants were asked to do a series of mindless and repetitive manual tasks under observation for one hour, then rate the enjoyability of the task. Unbeknownst to them, however, this was not actually the point of the experiment. At the end of the allotted time, some of the participants were taken aside and were asked by the control team to do a small favor: Would they please tell the next participant (who was in fact one of the control team) that the task was really satisfying and enjoyable—thus creating a dissonance between their professed enthusiasm for the task and the reality of their experience?

In return for the favor, these participants were offered payment: half of them were given $1, and the other half $20. When asked to rate the task, those participants who had been paid $1 claimed to have found the experience more enjoyable than those who had been paid $20. This confirmed Festinger's hypotheses; those paid only $1 experienced greater dissonance than those paid $20, so to reduce the inconsistency, they exaggerated their enjoyment

People come to love things for which they have suffered.
Leon Festinger

of the task. The payment of $20, on the other hand, lessened the dissonance felt, so the higher-paid participants gave a more realistic assessment of the task, and their ratings were similar to those given by participants who had not been asked to do the favor.

Fact vs. fantasy

Festinger's idea of minimizing and avoiding cognitive dissonance provided an explanation for the apparently irrational behavior seen in the Oak Park study and moreover demonstrated that incontrovertible evidence and reasoned argument to the contrary can actually cause strongly held beliefs to become even more entrenched. Logic and evidence are unlikely to change the opinions of people with strong convictions, as this would cause yet more inconsistency; it is in fact more likely that the conviction will become stronger. Cognitive dissonance, or at least the avoidance of it, makes them immune to evidence and rational argument, as Festinger explains: "Tell him you disagree and he turns away. Show him facts or figures and he questions your sources. Appeal to logic and he fails to see your point."

A case in point is that of the so-called "young Earth creationists," who believe that the Earth was created in its present form about 6,000 years ago and who deny the validity of the theory of evolution. When faced with fossil evidence challenging their view, the response has been increasingly complex pseudoscience rather than any acceptance that their original belief might have been mistaken.

Similarly, especially with the widespread misinformation and disinformation made possible by the internet, implausible conspiracy theories have thrived online, fueled rather than quashed by contradiction, and increasingly populist opinions—based on unshakable conviction rather than rational argument—have become a feature of modern politics. ■

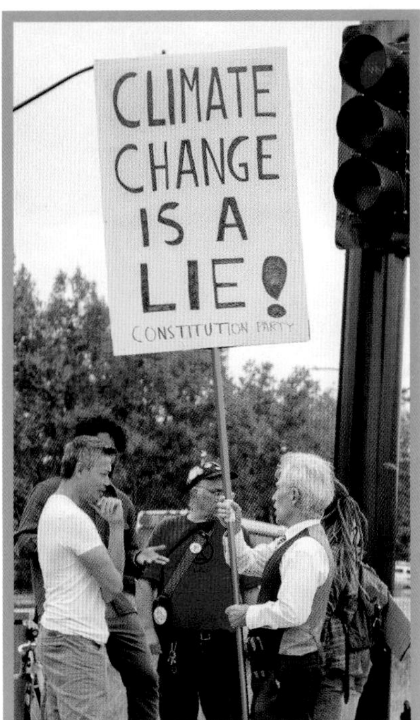

Despite overwhelming scientific evidence of climate change, cognitive dissonance causes some people to deny it as a hoax, convinced they know more than the expert scientists.

Leon Festinger

Leon Festinger was born in Brooklyn, New York, to a Russian immigrant family. He graduated from City College of New York in 1939, then studied at the University of Iowa under Kurt Lewin, finishing his PhD in Child Psychology in 1942. After spending the later years of World War II in military training, he rejoined Lewin in 1945 at the Research Center for Group Dynamics at the Massachusetts Institute of Technology (MIT).

It was during his tenure as professor at the University of Minnesota that Festinger made his famous Oak Park study of a cult predicting the end of the world. He moved to Stanford University in 1955, continuing his work in social psychology, but in the 1960s, he turned to research into perception. He later focused on history and archaeology at the New School for Social Research in New York. He died of liver cancer, aged 69.

Key works

1956 *When Prophecy Fails*
1957 *A Theory of Cognitive Dissonance*
1983 *The Human Legacy*

THE MAGICAL NUMBER 7 PLUS OR MINUS 2

GEORGE ARMITAGE MILLER (1920–2012)

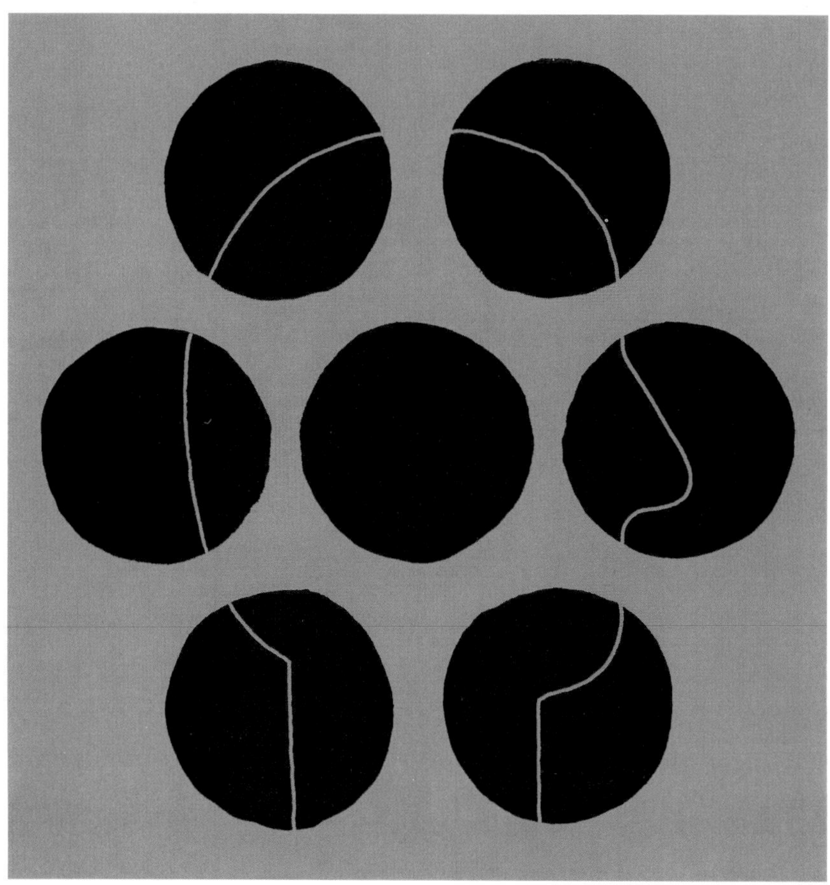

IN CONTEXT

APPROACH
Memory studies

BEFORE
1885 Hermann Ebbinghaus publishes his pioneering book *Memory: A Contribution to Experimental Psychology.*

1890 William James makes the distinction between primary (short-term) and secondary (long-term) memory in *The Principles of Psychology.*

1950 Mathematician Alan Turing's test suggests that a computer can be considered a thinking machine.

AFTER
1972 Endel Tulving makes the distinction between semantic and episodic memory.

2001 Daniel Schacter proposes a list of the different ways we misremember in *The Seven Sins of Memory.*

George Armitage Miller once famously complained: "My problem is that I have been persecuted by an integer. For seven years, this number has followed me around." So begins his now-famous article *The Magical Number Seven, Plus or Minus Two: Some Limits on our Capacity for Processing Information*. He goes on: "There is … some pattern governing its appearances. Either there really is something unusual about the number or I am suffering from delusions of persecution." Despite the whimsical nature of his title and introduction, Miller had a serious intent, and the article was

See also: Hermann Ebbinghaus 48–49 ▪ Bluma Zeigarnik 162 ▪ Donald Broadbent 178–185 ▪ Endel Tulving 186–191 ▪ Gordon H. Bower 194–195 ▪ Daniel Schacter 208–209 ▪ Noam Chomsky 302–305 ▪ Frederic Bartlett 342

The persistence with which this number plagues me is far more than a random accident.
George Armitage Miller

to become a landmark of cognitive psychology and the study of working memory (the ability to remember and use pieces of information for a limited amount of time).

Miller's paper was published in *The Psychological Review* in 1956, when behaviorism was being superseded by the new cognitive psychology—which Miller fully embraced. Its focus on the study of mental processes, such as memory and attention. Also, advances in computer science had brought the idea of artificial intelligence closer to reality, and while mathematicians such as Alan Turing were comparing computer processing with the human brain, cognitive psychologists were engaged in the reverse: the computer as a possible model for explaining the workings of the human brain. Mental processes were being described in terms of information processing.

His doctoral thesis study during World War II on speech perception fueled Miller's interest in the field of psycholinguistics. Exploring the growing field of communications ultimately introduced him to information theory, particularly the work of Claude Shannon, a leading figure in communications, who was investigating effective ways of turning messages into electronic signals. Shannon's communication model, which involved translating ideas into codes made up of "bits," underpins all digital communication. Miller was inspired to look at mental processes in a similar way and to establish the ground rules for the modern field of psycholinguistics in his 1951 book, *Language and Communication*.

Seven categories

Miller took Shannon's method of measuring information and his idea of "channel capacity" (the amount of information that can be processed by a system) and applied it to the model of short-term memory as an information processor. This was when he began to be "persecuted" by the recurrence and possible significance of the number seven—"sometimes a little larger and sometimes a little smaller than usual, but never changing so much as to be unrecognizable."

The first instance of the "magical" number came from experiments to determine the span of absolute judgment—how accurately we can distinguish a number of different stimuli. In one experiment cited in Miller's paper, the physicist and acoustic specialist Irwin Pollack played a variety of musical tones to participants who were then asked to assign a number to each tone. When up to around seven different tones were »

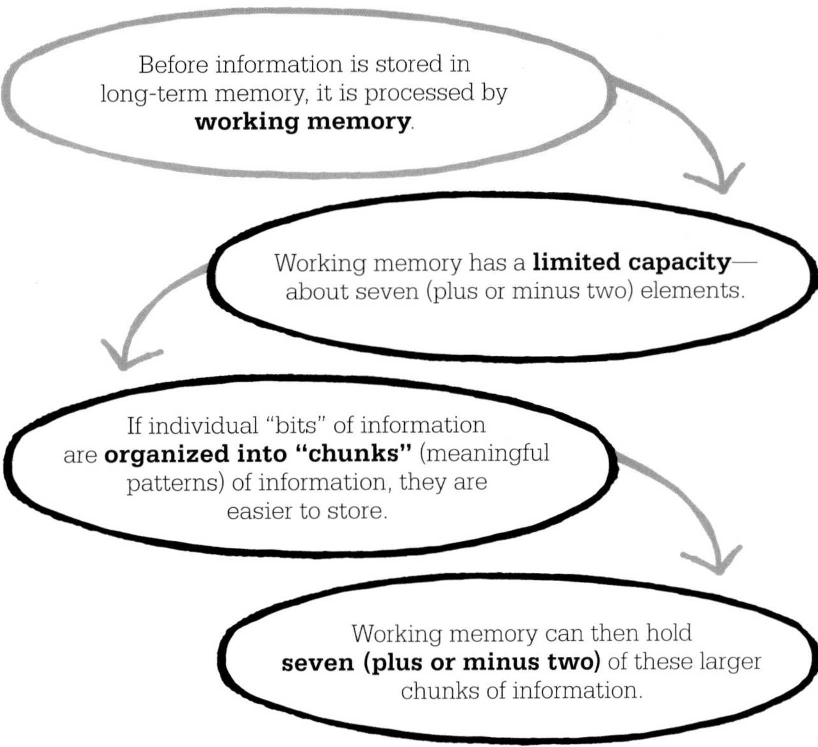
Before information is stored in long-term memory, it is processed by **working memory**.
Working memory has a **limited capacity**—about seven (plus or minus two) elements.
If individual "bits" of information are **organized into "chunks"** (meaningful patterns) of information, they are easier to store.
Working memory can then hold **seven (plus or minus two)** of these larger chunks of information.

played, the subjects had no difficulty in accurately assigning numbers to each of them, but above seven (give or take one or two), the results deteriorated dramatically.

In another experiment, by Kaufman, Lord, *et al* in 1949, researchers flashed varying numbers of colored dots onto a screen in front of participants. When there were fewer than seven dots, participants could accurately number them; when there were more than seven, participants were only able to estimate the number of dots. This suggests that the span of attention is limited to around six, and it caused Miller to wonder whether the same basic process might be involved in both the span of absolute judgment and the span of attention. The tones and dots in these experiments are what Miller calls "unidimensional stimuli" (objects that differ from one another in only one respect). What interested Miller is the amount of information in speech and language we can effectively process, and items such as words are "multidimensional stimuli." He looks to later studies by Pollack in which the simple tones were replaced by tones that varied in six ways (such as pitch, duration, volume, and location). Surprisingly, despite the apparently larger amount of information, the results still pointed to a differential limit of seven, plus or minus two. The difference is that, as more variables are added, accuracy slightly decreases. Miller claims this lets us make "relatively crude judgments of several things simultaneously," so we recognize and distinguish such complex things as spoken words and people's faces without having to process the individual sounds or features.

The process of memorizing may be simply the formation of chunks … until there are few enough chunks so that we can recall all the items.
George Armitage Miller

For Miller, the human mind is a communication system: as input information increases, so the amount transmitted to the brain increases initially before leveling off at a person's "channel capacity." He then applied this idea of channel capacity to the model of short-term memory. This notion, first proposed by William James, had long been an accepted part of the model of the brain as an information processor, coming between the sensory input of information and long-term memory. Hermann Ebbinghaus and Wilhelm Wundt had even suggested that short-term memory had a capacity limited to around seven items (seven, again). Miller believed that what he called working memory had a capacity that corresponded to the limits of absolute judgment and span of attention.

Bits and chunks

In terms of our ability to process information, if working memory is limited to about seven elements, there is a potential bottleneck restricting how much can be put into long-term memory. But Miller suggested that there was more to the correspondence than just the number seven, no matter how magical it seemed. Multidimensional stimuli could be seen as several "bits" of related information but treated as a single item. Miller believed that by the same principle, working memory organizes "bits" of information into "chunks" to overcome the bottleneck

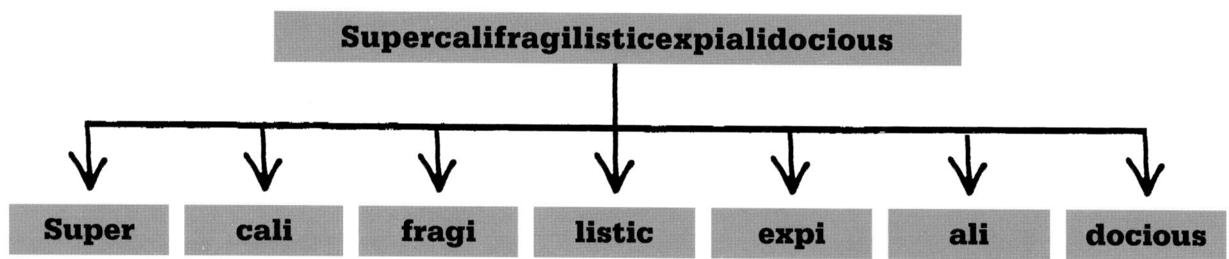

Miller's theory of chunking says that by building up or breaking down long streams of numbers or letters into memorable chunks, we increase the amount of information we can hold in working memory.

Binary code is a way of recoding information into increasingly tightly packed parcels (through multibase arithmetic). Miller claims our chunking process operates in a similar way.

of our limited spans of judgment and short-term memory. A chunk is not, however, just an arbitrary grouping, but an encoding of bits into a meaningful unit; for example, a string of 21 letters represents 21 bits of information, but if broken down into a sequence of three-letter words, it becomes seven chunks. Chunking is dependent on our ability to find patterns and relationships in the bits of information. To someone who does not speak the same language, the seven words might be meaningless and would not constitute seven chunks, but 21 bits.

Miller's theory was backed up by the earlier work of psychologists such as Sidney Smith. In 1954, Smith's experiments in memorizing a sequence of binary digits (a string of ones and zeroes) broke the series down into chunks—at first into pairs of digits, then into groups of three, four, and five—and then "recoded" them by translating the binary chunks into decimal numbers: 01 became 1, 10 became 2, and so on. He found that, using this system, it was possible to memorize and accurately reproduce a string of 40 digits or more, as long as the number of chunks was limited to the span of working memory.

As an aid to memorizing large amounts of information, chunking and recoding is an obvious boon, but it is not just a mnemonic trick—it is an "extremely powerful weapon for increasing the amount of information we can deal with."

The study of memory

Miller himself moved away from the subject of memory in his later research, but his theory prompted others to examine it in more detail. Donald Broadbent argued that the real figure for working memory is probably less than seven, and this was later confirmed in experiments by Nelson Cowan, who found it to be around four chunks, depending on the length and complexity of the chunks and the age of the subject.

In the conclusion to his paper, Miller is dismissive of the significance of the number that originally prompted it. He concludes by saying: "Perhaps there is something deep and profound behind all these sevens … but I suspect that it is only a pernicious, Pythagorean coincidence." ■

The kind of linguistic recoding that people do seems to me to be the very lifeblood of the thought processes.
George Armitage Miller

George Armitage Miller

George Armitage Miller, born in West Virginia, graduated from the University of Alabama in 1941 with an MA in speech pathology and went to Harvard to study for a PhD in psychology in Stanley Smith Stevens' Psychoacoustic Laboratory, with Jerome Bruner and Gordon Allport. World War II was then at its height, and the laboratory was called upon to help with military tasks, such as radio jamming.

In 1951, Miller left Harvard for the Massachusetts Institute of Technology (MIT), then returned to Harvard in 1955, where he worked closely with Noam Chomsky. In 1960, he co-founded the Harvard Center for Cognitive Studies. He later worked as a professor of psychology at Rockefeller University, New York, and Princeton University. In 1991, he was awarded the National Medal of Science.

Key works

1951 *Language and Communication*
1956 *The Magical Number Seven, Plus or Minus Two*
1960 *Plans and the Structure of Behavior* (with Eugene Galanter and Karl Pribram)

THERE'S MORE TO THE SURFACE THAN MEETS THE EYE

AARON BECK (1921–2021)

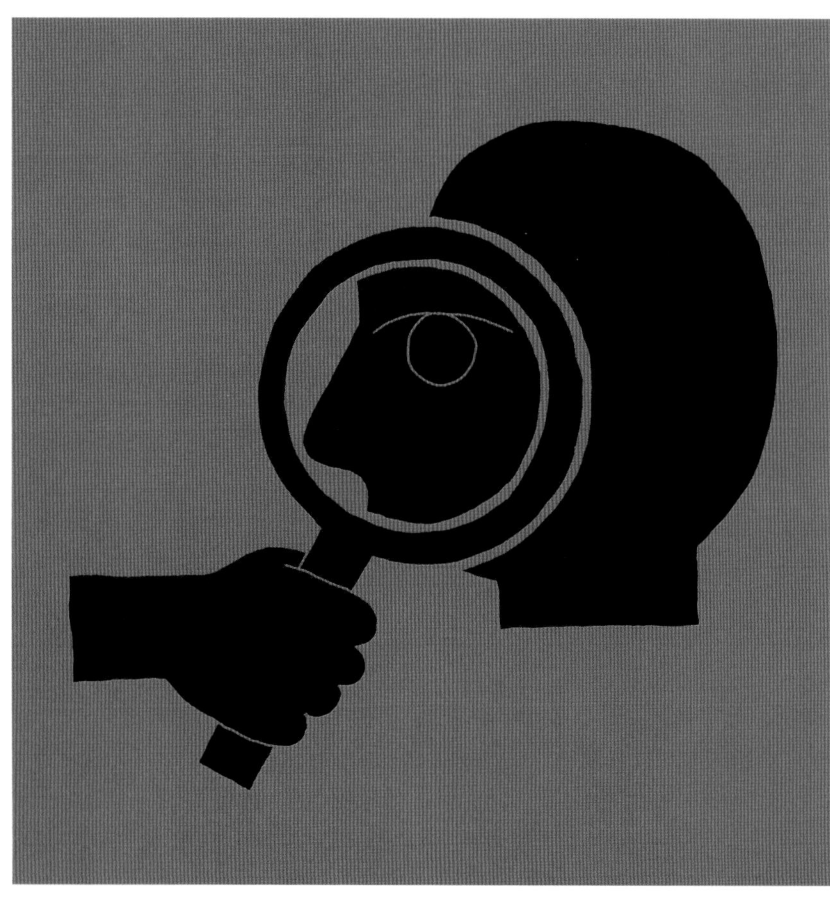

IN CONTEXT

APPROACH
Cognitive therapy

BEFORE
1890s Sigmund Freud proposes an analytic approach to psychotherapy.

1940s and 1950s Fritz Perls, with Laura Perls and Paul Goodman, develops Gestalt therapy—a cognitive approach to psychotherapy.

1955 Albert Ellis introduces Rational Emotive Behavior Therapy (REBT), breaking with the tradition of analysis.

AFTER
1975 Martin Seligman defines "learned helplessness" in *Helplessness: On Depression, Development, and Death*.

1980s A blend of Beck's ideas and the behavior therapies of Joseph Wolpe give rise to new cognitive behavioral therapies.

After psychology had become established as a distinct field of study, around the turn of the 20th century, two main schools, or approaches, emerged. These were experimental psychology, which was dominated by the behaviorism originating from Ivan Pavlov's experiments, and which was enthusiastically championed in the US; and clinical psychology, which was largely based on the psychoanalytical approach of Sigmund Freud and his followers. The two had little in common. Behaviorists rejected the introspective, philosophical approach of earlier psychologists, and strove to put the subject on a

See also: Joseph Wolpe 86–87 ▪ Sigmund Freud 92–99 ▪ Fritz Perls 112–117 ▪ Albert Ellis 142–145 ▪ Martin Seligman 200–201 ▪ Paul Salkovskis 214–215

Psychoanalytic therapy places an emphasis on delving into the patient's **unconscious** to solve current disorders.

Cognitive therapy places an emphasis on examining people's **perceptions** of their experiences.

The evidence for the success of psychoanalytic therapy is based on **personal accounts** rather than facts or research.

There is **strong empirical evidence** for the success of cognitive therapy.

The key to **effective treatment** lies not in the unconscious, but in the examination of **how a disorder manifests itself** in a patient's perceptions.

There's more to the surface than meets the eye.

more scientific, evidence-based footing. The psychoanalysts explored those very introspections, with theories, rather than proof, to support their case.

Cognitive revolution

By the mid-20th century, both approaches to psychology were being critically examined. But although behaviorism was being overtaken by cognitive psychology in experimental work, the clinical sphere was offering no alternative to the psychoanalytical model. Psychotherapy had evolved into many forms, but the basic idea of psychoanalysis and exploration of the unconscious was common to all of them. Some psychologists were beginning to question the validity of this kind of therapy, and Aaron Beck was among them.

When Beck qualified as a psychiatrist in 1953, experimental psychology was focused on the study of mental processes—it was the dawn of the "cognitive revolution." However, the practical approach of cognitive psychologists remained much the same as that of the behaviorists. If anything, they were frequently even more rigorous in establishing evidence for their theories. Beck was no exception to this. He had trained in and practiced psychoanalysis, but grew skeptical of its effectiveness as a »

Aaron Beck

Born in Providence, Rhode Island, Aaron Temkin Beck was the son of Russian Jewish immigrants. Athletic and outgoing as a young child, he became introspective and studious after a serious illness at the age of eight. He also acquired a fear of all things medical and, to overcome this, decided to train as a doctor, graduating from Yale in 1946. Beck then worked at Rhode Island Hospital, before qualifying as a psychiatrist in 1953. Disillusioned with the psychoanalytical approach to clinical psychology, he instigated cognitive therapy and later established the Beck Institute for Cognitive Therapy and Research in Philadelphia, now run by his daughter, Dr. Judith Beck. At the age of 100, he passed away at his home in Pennsylvania.

Key works

1972 *Depression: Causes and Treatment*
1975 *Cognitive Therapy and the Emotional Disorders*
1980 *Depression: Clinical, Experimental, and Theoretical*
1999 *Prisoners of Hate: The Cognitive Basis of Anger, Hostility, and Violence*

I concluded that psychoanalysis was a faith-based therapy.
Aaron Beck

therapy. He could find no reliable studies of the success rates of psychoanalysis—only anecdotal evidence of case reports. In his experience, only a minority of patients showed improvement under analysis, and the general consensus among therapists was that some got better, some got worse, and some stayed about the same, in almost equal numbers.

Of particular concern was the resistance of many psychoanalysts to objective scientific examination. Compared with experimental psychology, or with medicine, psychoanalysis seemed largely faith-based, with widely different results between individual practitioners. Reputation was frequently based solely on the charisma of a particular analyst. Beck concluded that "the psychoanalytic mystique was overwhelming ... It was a little bit like the evangelical movement." Many psychoanalysts regarded criticism of their theories as a personal attack, and Beck soon discovered that any questioning of the validity of psychoanalysis was likely to be countered with universal denouncement. At one time, he was turned down for membership of the American Psychoanalytic Institute on the grounds that his "desire to conduct scientific studies signaled that he'd been improperly analyzed." Those who found fault with the idea of analysis did so, some analysts argued, because of insufficient analysis of themselves.

Beck was suspicious of both the circularity of these arguments, and the link with the therapist's own personality. Coupled with his personal experience as a practicing psychoanalyst, this led him to examine thoroughly every aspect of therapy, looking for ways in which it could be improved. He carried out a series of experiments designed to evaluate the basis and treatment of depression, one of the most common reasons for seeking psychotherapy, and found that far from confirming the idea that this condition could be treated by examination of unconscious emotions and drives, his results pointed to a very different interpretation.

Changing perceptions

In describing their depression, Beck's patients often expressed negative ideas about themselves, their future, and society in general, which came to them involuntarily. These "automatic thoughts," as Beck called them, led him to conclude that the way the patients perceived their experiences—their cognition of them—was not just a symptom of their depression, but also the key to finding an effective therapy. This idea, which came to him in the 1960s, chimed with concurrent developments in experimental psychology, which had established the dominance of cognitive psychology by studying mental processes such as perception.

When Beck applied a cognitive model to treatment, he found that helping his patients to recognize and evaluate how realistic or distorted their perceptions were was the first step in overcoming depression. This flew in the face of conventional psychoanalysis, which sought and examined underlying drives, emotions, and repressions. Beck's "cognitive therapy" saw this as unnecessary or even counterproductive. The patient's perception could be taken at face value because, as he was fond of putting it, "there's more to the surface than meets the eye."

What Beck meant by this was that the immediate manifestations of depression—the negative "automatic thoughts"—provide all the information needed for therapy. If these thoughts are examined and compared with an objective, rational view of the same situation, the patient can recognize how his perception is distorted. For example, a patient who has been offered a promotion at work might express negative thoughts such as "I'll find the new job too difficult, and fail," a perception of the

A distorting mirror creates a view of the world that can seem terrifying and ugly. Similarly, depression tends to cast a negative perspective on life, making sufferers feel more hopeless.

By correcting erroneous beliefs, we can lower excessive reactions.
Aaron Beck

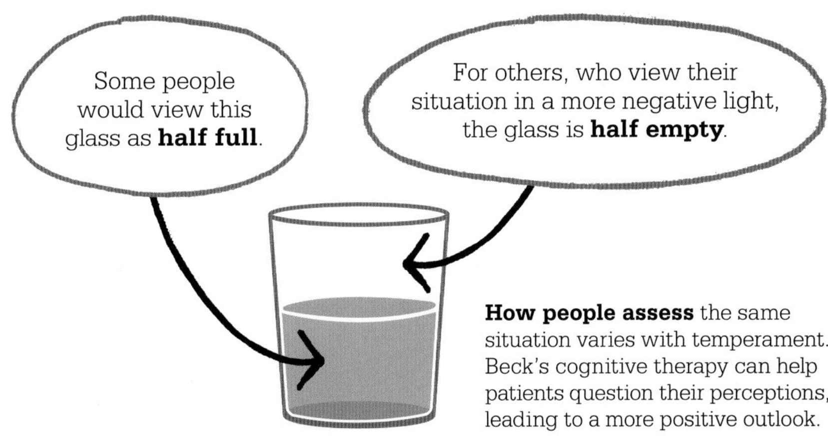
Some people would view this glass as **half full**.
For others, who view their situation in a more negative light, the glass is **half empty**.

How people assess the same situation varies with temperament. Beck's cognitive therapy can help patients question their perceptions, leading to a more positive outlook.

situation that leads to anxiety and unhappiness. A more rational way of looking at the promotion would be to see it as a reward, or even a challenge. It is not the situation that is causing the depression, but the patient's perception of it. Cognitive therapy could help him to recognize how distorted it is, and find a more realistic and positive way of thinking about the situation.

Empirical evidence

Beck's cognitive therapy worked for a large number of his patients. What is more, he was able to demonstrate that it worked, as he applied scientific methods to ensure that he had empirical evidence for his findings. He designed special assessments for his patients, so that he could monitor their progress closely. The results showed that cognitive therapy was making his patients feel better, and feel better more quickly, than was the case under traditional psychoanalysis. Beck's insistence on providing evidence for any claims he made for his therapy opened it up to objective scrutiny. Above all, he was most anxious to avoid acquiring the gurulike status of many successful psychoanalysts, and was at great pains to demonstrate that it was the therapy that was successful, and not the therapist.

Beck was not the only, or even the first, psychologist to find traditional psychoanalysis unsatisfactory, but his use of a cognitive model was innovatory. He had been influenced in his reaction against psychoanalysis by the work of Albert Ellis, who had developed Rational Emotive Behavior Therapy (REBT) in the mid-1950s, and he was no doubt aware of the work of behaviorists elsewhere in the world, including the South Africans Joseph Wolpe and Arnold A. Lazarus. Although different in approach, their therapies shared with Beck's a thoroughly scientific methodology and a rejection of the importance of unconscious causes of mental and emotional disorders.

Once the success of cognitive therapy had been established, it was used increasingly for treating depression, and later Beck found that it could also be helpful for other conditions, such as personality disorders and even schizophrenia. Always open to new ideas—as long as it could be shown that they were effective—Beck also incorporated elements of behavior therapy into his treatments, as did many other psychotherapists in the 1980s. This has resulted in the varied forms of cognitive behavioral therapy that are used by psychologists today.

Beck's pioneering work marked a turning point for psychotherapy, and his influence is considerable. As well as bringing a cognitive approach into clinical psychology, Beck subjected it to scientific scrutiny, exposing the weaknesses of psychoanalysis. In the process, he introduced several methods for assessing the nature and severity of depression that are still used: the Beck Depression Inventory (BDI), the Beck Hopelessness Scale, the Beck Scale for Suicidal Ideation (BSS), and the Beck Anxiety Inventory (BAI). ■

Don't trust me, test me.
Aaron Beck

WE CAN LISTEN TO ONLY ONE VOICE AT ONCE

DONALD BROADBENT (1926–1993)

IN CONTEXT

APPROACH
Attention theory

BEFORE
1640s René Descartes says the human body is a kind of machine with a mind, or soul.

1940s British psychologist and APU director Kenneth Craik prepares flow diagrams comparing human and artificial information processing.

AFTER
1959 George Armitage Miller's studies suggest that short-term memory can hold a maximum of seven pieces of information.

1964 Anne Treisman suggests that less important information is not eliminated at the filter stage, but attenuated and still "shadowed" by the mind.

1975 Ulric Neisser and Robert Becklen devise experiments to examine "selective looking," now known as inattentional blindness.

In Britain prior to World War II, psychology as an academic discipline lagged behind Europe and the US. Britain's psychologists had tended to follow in the footsteps of the behaviorist and psychotherapeutic schools of thought that had evolved elsewhere. In the few university psychology departments that existed, the approach followed that of the natural sciences: the emphasis was on practical applications rather than theoretical speculations.

It was in this unpromising academic environment that Donald Broadbent, who went on to become one of the most influential of the early cognitive psychologists, found himself when he left the Royal Air Force after the war and decided to study psychology. However, the practical approach proved ideal for Broadbent, who was able to make perfect use of his wartime experience as an aeronautical engineer and pilot.

Practical psychology

Broadbent had enlisted in the RAF when he was 17, and he was sent to the US as part of his training. Here he first became aware of psychology and the kind of problems it addresses, which led him to look at some of the problems encountered by pilots in a different way. He thought these problems might have psychological causes and answers, rather than simply mechanical ones, so after leaving the RAF, he went to Cambridge University to study psychology.

Broadbent's mentor at Cambridge, Frederic Bartlett, was a kindred spirit: a thoroughgoing scientist, and England's first professor of experimental psychology. Bartlett believed that the most important theoretical discoveries are often made while attempting to find solutions to practical problems. This idea appealed to Broadbent, and prompted him to continue working under Bartlett at the new Applied Psychology Unit (APU) after it opened in 1944. It was during his time there that Broadbent was to do his most groundbreaking work. He chose to ignore the then-dominant behaviorist approach to psychology and to concentrate on the practical problems he had come across in his time in the RAF. For example, pilots sometimes confused similar-looking controls; in some

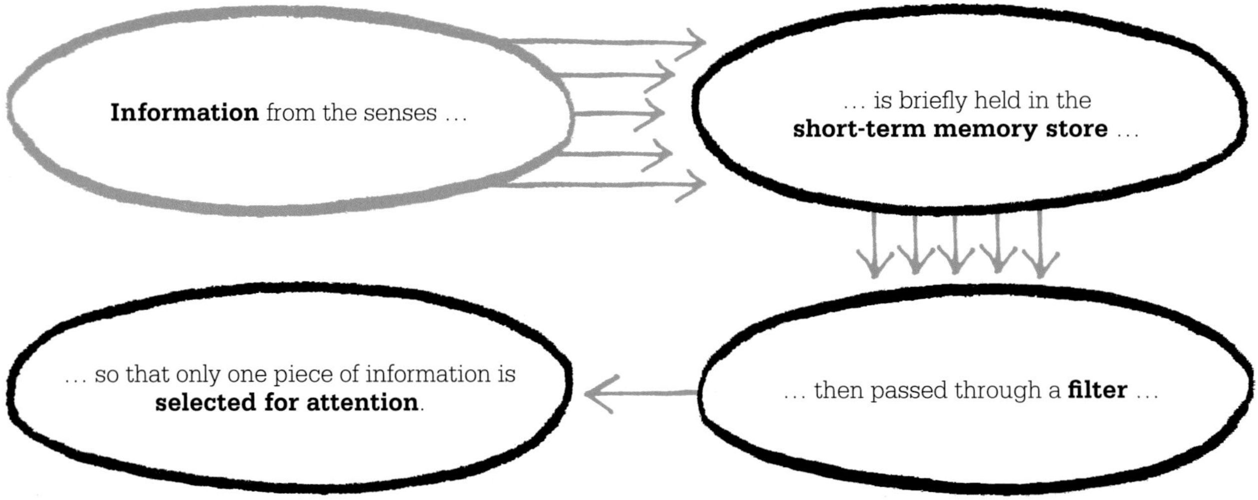

Information from the senses …

… is briefly held in the **short-term memory store** …

… then passed through a **filter** …

… so that only one piece of information is **selected for attention**.

See also: René Descartes 20–21 ▪ George Armitage Miller 170–173 ▪ Daniel Schacter 208–209 ▪ Christopher Chabris & Daniel Simons 216–217 ▪ Frederic Bartlett 342

A World War II plane incorporates a dazzling display of informational data; Broadbent was interested in discovering how pilots prioritized information and what design changes would aid this.

planes, the lever for pulling up the wheels was identical to the one for pulling up the flaps, and the two were situated together under the seat; this led to frequent accidents. Broadbent thought these incidents could be avoided if the capacities and limitations of the pilots were taken into consideration during the design process, rather than surfacing at the point of use.

Broadbent was interested in using psychology not only to design better equipment, but also to reach a better understanding of what affected the pilots' capabilities. They clearly had to cope with large amounts of incoming information, and then had to select the relevant data they needed to make good decisions. It seemed to him that mistakes were often made when there were too many sources of incoming information.

Broadbent was influenced in his thinking about how we process information by another product of wartime research: the development of computers and the idea of "artificial intelligence." The first director of the APU, Kenneth Craik, had left the unit important manuscripts and flow diagrams comparing human and artificial information processing, which Broadbent clearly studied.

At the same time, code breakers such as the mathematician Alan Turing had been tackling the notion of information processing, and in the postwar period he applied this to the idea of a "thinking machine." The comparison of a machine to the workings of the brain was a powerful analogy, but it was Broadbent who turned the idea around, considering the human brain as a kind of information-processing machine. This, in essence, is what distinguishes cognitive psychology from behaviorism: it is the study of mental processes, rather than their manifestation in behavior. »

Donald Broadbent

Born in Birmingham, England, Donald Broadbent considered himself to be Welsh, since he spent his teenage years in Wales after his parents' divorce. He won a scholarship to the prestigious Winchester College, then joined the Royal Air Force aged 17, where he trained as a pilot and studied aeronautical engineering.

After leaving the RAF in 1947, he studied psychology under Frederic Bartlett at Cambridge, then joined the newly founded Applied Psychology Unit (APU), becoming its director in 1958. Married twice, he was a shy, famously generous man whose "puritanical streak" led him to believe that his work was a privilege and should always be of real use. In 1974, he was awarded the CBE and appointed a fellow of Wolfson College, Oxford, where he remained until his retirement in 1991. He died two years later of a heart attack, aged 66.

Key works

1958 *Perception and Communication*
1971 *Decision and Stress*
1993 *The Simulation of Human Intelligence*

To study how our attention works, Broadbent needed to design experiments that would back up his hunches. His background in engineering meant that he would not be satisfied until he had evidence on which to base a theory, and he also wanted that research to have a practical application. The APU was dedicated to applied psychology, which for Broadbent referred not only to therapeutic applications, but also to applications that benefited society as a whole; he was always very conscious that his research was publicly funded.

Our mind can be conceived as a radio receiving many channels at once.
Donald Broadbent

One voice at a time

One of Broadbent's most important experiments was suggested by his experience with air traffic control. Ground crew often had to deal with several streams of incoming information simultaneously, sent from planes arriving and departing, which was relayed to the operators by radio and received through headphones. The air traffic controllers then had to make quick decisions based on that information, and Broadbent had noticed that they could only effectively deal with one message at a time. What interested him was the mental process that must take place in order for them to select the most important message from the various sources of incoming information. He felt that there must be some kind of mechanism in the brain that processes the information and makes that selection.

The experiment that Broadbent devised, now known as the dichotic listening experiment, was one of the first in the field of selective attention—the process our brains use to "filter out" the irrelevant information from the masses of data we receive through our senses all the time. Following the air traffic control model, he chose to present aural (sound-based) information through headphones to the subjects of his experiment. The system was set up so that he could relay two different streams of information at the same time—one to the left ear and one to the right—and then test the subjects on their retention of that information.

As Broadbent had suspected, the subjects were unable to reproduce all the information from both channels of input. His feeling that we can only listen to one voice at once had been confirmed, but still the question remained as to exactly how the subject had chosen to retain some of the incoming information and effectively disregard the rest.

Thinking back to his initial training as an engineer, Broadbent suggested a mechanical model to explain what he felt was happening in the brain. He believed that when there are multiple sources of input, they may reach a "bottleneck" if the brain is unable to continue to process all the incoming information; at this point, there must be some kind of "filter" that lets through only one channel of input. The analogy he uses to explain this is typically practical: he describes a Y-shaped tube, into which two flows of ping-pong balls are channeled. At the junction of the two branches of the tube, there is a flap that acts to block one flow of balls or the other; this allows balls from the unblocked channel into the stem of the tube.

Air traffic controllers have to deal with a multitude of simultaneous signals. By recreating this problem in listening experiments, Broadbent was able to identify attention processes.

A question still remained, however: at what stage does this filter come into operation? In a series of experiments that were variations on his original dichotic listening tasks, Broadbent established that information is received by the senses and then passed on in its entirety to some kind of store, which he called the short-term memory store. It is at this stage, he believes, that the filtering occurs. His description of how and when information is selected for attention is known as the "Broadbent Filter Model," and it demonstrated a completely new approach to experimental psychology, not only in combining the theoretical with the practical, but also in considering the workings of the brain as a form of information processing.

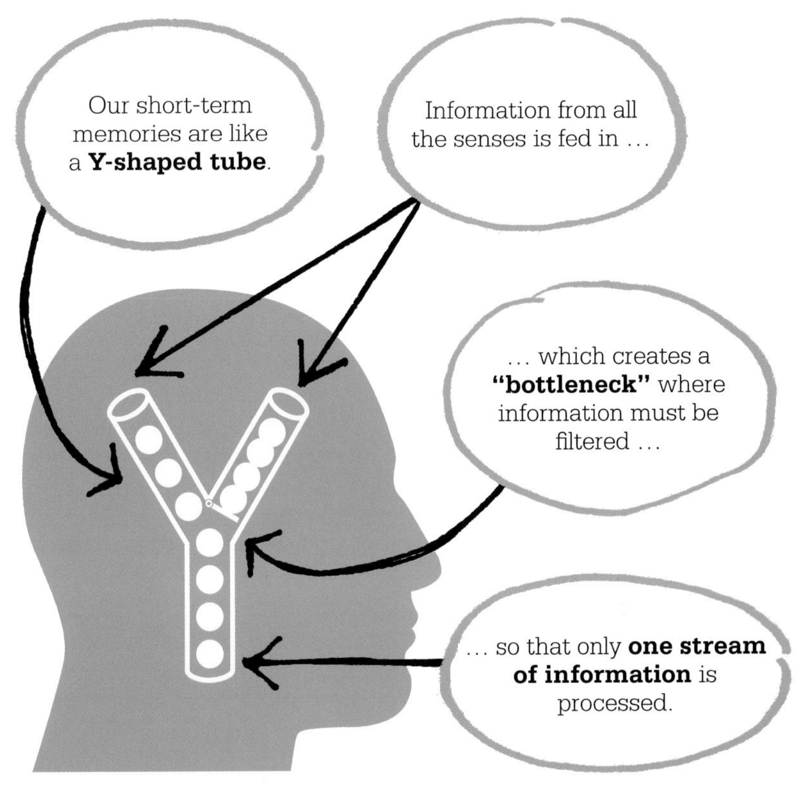

Our short-term memories are like a **Y-shaped tube**.
Information from all the senses is fed in …
… which creates a **"bottleneck"** where information must be filtered …
… so that only **one stream of information** is processed.

The cocktail party problem

Broadbent was not the only person to address the problem of selective attention. Another British scientist, Colin Cherry, also investigated the subject during the 1950s. Working in communication rather than psychology, Cherry posed what he called the "cocktail party problem:" how, at a party where lots of people are talking, do we select which of many conversations to give our attention to, and which to ignore? And how is it possible to be distracted from our focused attention on conversation "A" by conversations "B" or "C"?

> One of the two voices is selected for response without reference to its correctness, and the other is ignored.
> **Donald Broadbent**

To help answer these questions, Broadbent turned his attention to the nature of the filter in his model. Precisely what information does it filter out, and what does it allow through? Following another process of rigorous experimenting, he found that the selection is made not on the content of the information (what is being said), but on the physical characteristics of any message, such as clarity or tone of voice. This suggests that even though information is stored, albeit very briefly, in short-term memory, it is only after filtering that it is processed for meaning and actually understood. This finding had important implications when applied to air traffic control, for example, where decisions could be made on possibly irrelevant or inaccurate information, rather than being prioritized according to meaning and importance.

Broadbent and Cherry worked together on many dichotic listening experiments to test the filtering process. They realized that filtering is also affected by expectation. In one experiment, participants were asked to listen to different sets of numbers presented simultaneously to each ear. In some cases, they were instructed which ear (the information channel) they would be asked about first; in others, no instructions were given. The results showed that when people know which ear is receiving the stream of information they will be asked for first, they switch » attention to that ear, and the information that enters the other ear is not always accurately retrieved from memory. In all cases the information that people chose or were asked to remember first seemed to be processed more accurately than the later material; it was thought this might be due to parts of the information being lost from the short-term memory store before the participant tried to retrieve it. In 1957, Broadbent wrote: "We can listen to only one voice at once, and the first words we hear are the best recalled."

Modifying the model

In 1958, Broadbent published the results of his research in a book, *Perception and Communication*, which effectively outlined a framework for studying attention, comprehension, and memory. The timing was significant, as it coincided with a divergence of opinion about the importance of behaviorism in the US, and the book slowly became known as one of the landmarks in the development of the new cognitive psychology. As a result, Broadbent was recognized, by his peers if not the public, as the first major psychologist Britain had produced, and was rewarded the same year by being appointed director of the APU to succeed Bartlett.

Not one to rest on his laurels, however, Broadbent saw his new appointment as an opportunity to continue his work on attention, widening the scope of his research and refining the theory. From the starting point of his filter model, he returned to the cocktail party problem, and in particular one phenomenon Cherry had identified concerning the nature of information that is selected for attention. When an overheard conversation includes information that has some kind of special significance for a person—such as a personal name—the attention is switched toward that conversation, and away from the one previously attended to.

Further dichotic listening experiments at the APU bore out Cherry's findings: attention is filtered by physical characteristics but also by meaning, using feedback from memory stores, prior experience, and expectations. The sound of a siren, for instance, would divert attention on to that stream of sound. This suggests that information is in some way understood before being selected for attention.

People at a party may be listening to one conversation but then become aware of (and switch attention to) another if it includes personally significant information.

The test of a psychological theory, as well as its moral justification, lies in its application to concrete practical considerations.
Donald Broadbent

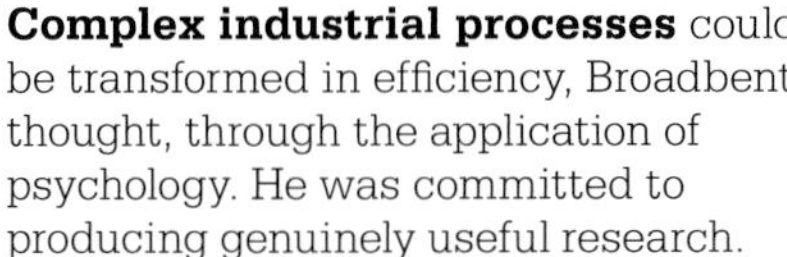

Complex industrial processes could be transformed in efficiency, Broadbent thought, through the application of psychology. He was committed to producing genuinely useful research.

Broadbent realized that his filter model needed modification, but was pleased rather than dismayed to have to make the changes. As a scientist, he felt that all scientific theories are temporary, derived from the evidence available at the time, and so susceptible to change in the light of new evidence; this is how science progresses.

The work of the APU centered around Broadbent's research into attention, but this allowed for a constantly widening range of applications. Broadbent worked tirelessly to ensure that his work was practically useful, examining the effects of noise, heat, and stress on attention in work environments, and he constantly reviewed his ideas as he worked. In the process, he gained government support for his ideas, and the respect of many industries whose practices were improved by his work. This led to yet more research into areas such as differences of attention between individuals, and lapses of attention and their causes. In each case the results of his experiments led to refinements of his theories. In 1971, he published a second book, *Decision and Stress*, which detailed an extended version of his filter theory. Like its predecessor, this book became a classic textbook of cognitive psychology.

The cognitive approach

Broadbent's books did not reach the general public, but were widely read by scientists from other disciplines. His comparison of the workings of the human brain with electronic machines became more and more relevant as interest in computing increased. His model of the various stages of human information processing—acquisition, storage, retrieval, and use—echoed the work on artificial intelligence at that time.

Broadbent was instrumental in setting up a Joint Council Initiative on Cognitive Science and Human-Computer Interaction, which helped shape the development of cognitive science. His work also established applied psychology as an important approach for problem-solving, increasing its impact well beyond the confines of the laboratory. A key figure in the founding of cognitive psychology, his research into attention laid the groundwork for a new field of enquiry that continues to yield rich results today. ■

His psychology was intended for society and its problems, not merely for the dwellers in ivory towers.
Fergus Craik & Alan Baddely

TIME'S ARROW IS BENT INTO A LOOP

ENDEL TULVING (1927–2023)

IN CONTEXT

APPROACH
Memory studies

BEFORE
1878 Hermann Ebbinghaus conducts the first scientific study of human memory.

1927 Bluma Zeigarnik describes how interrupted tasks are better remembered than uninterrupted ones.

1960s Jerome Bruner stresses the importance of organization and categorization in the learning process.

AFTER
1979 Elizabeth Loftus looks at distortions of memory in her book *Eyewitness Testimony.*

1981 Gordon H. Bower makes the link between events and emotions in memory.

2001 Daniel Schacter publishes *The Seven Sins of Memory: How the Mind Forgets and Remembers.*

Episodic memory is made up of events and experiences that are stored in long-term memory.

It is distinct from **semantic memory**, which is our long-term memory store for facts and knowledge.

Memories of our experiences are **associated with particular times and places** and can be triggered by these cues.

Associated **sensory cues** such as a particular song or scent can also help us recall seemingly complete memories of past events.

Only humans can **"travel back in time"** to reflect on their experiences in this way …

… as if time's arrow is bent into a loop.

Memory was one of the first fields of study for psychologists in the 19th century, as it was closely connected with the concept of consciousness, which had formed the bridge between philosophy and psychology. Hermann Ebbinghaus in particular devoted much of his research to the scientific study of memory and learning, but the next generation of psychologists turned their attention to a behaviorist study of learning, and "conditioning" replaced memory as the focus of research. Apart from a few isolated studies, notably by Bluma Zeigarnik and Frederic Bartlett in the 1920s and '30s, memory was largely ignored as a topic until the "cognitive revolution" took place following World War II. Cognitive psychologists began to explore the idea of the brain as an information processor, and this provided a model for the storage of memory: it was seen as a process, whereby some items passed from short-term or working memory into long-term memory.

By the time Endel Tulving finished his doctorate in 1957, memory was once more a central area of study. Forced to abandon the study of visual perception due to a lack of facilities, Tulving turned his attention to memory. The funding deficit also shaped his approach to the subject, designing experiments that used no more than a pen, some paper, and a supply of index cards.

The free-recall method

Learning about the subject as he went along, Tulving worked in a rather unorthodox way, which occasionally earned him criticism from his peers, and was to make

See also: Hermann Ebbinghaus 48–49 ▪ Bluma Zeigarnik 162 ▪ George Armitage Miller 170–173 ▪ Gordon H. Bower 194–195 ▪ Elizabeth Loftus 202–207 ▪ Daniel Schacter 208–209 ▪ Roger Brown 243 ▪ Frederic Bartlett 342

publishing his results difficult. His maverick instincts did, however, lead to some truly innovative research. One hurriedly designed, *ad hoc* demonstration to a class of students in the early 1960s was to provide him with the model for many later experiments. He read out a random list of 20 everyday words to the students, and then asked them to write down as many as they could recall, in any order. As he expected, most of them managed to remember around half of the list. He then asked them about the words that they had not remembered, giving hints such as "Wasn't there a color on the list?," after which the student could often provide the correct answer.

Tulving developed a series of experiments on this "free recall" method, during which he noticed that people tend to group words together into meaningful categories; the better they organize the information, the better they are able to remember it. His subjects were also able to recall a word when given a cue in the form of the category (such as "animals") in which they had mentally filed that word. Tulving concluded that although all the words memorized from the list were actually available for remembering, the ones that were organized by subject were more readily accessible to memory, especially when the appropriate cue was given.

Memory types

Where previous psychologists had concentrated on the process of storing information, and the failings of that process, Tulving made a distinction between two different processes—storage and retrieval of information—and showed how the two were linked.

In the course of his research, Tulving was struck by the fact that there seemed to be different kinds of memory. The distinction between long-term memory and short-term memory had already been established, but Tulving felt there was more than one kind of long-term memory. He saw a difference between memories that are knowledge-based (facts and data) and those that are experience-based (events and conversations). He proposed a division of long-term memory into two distinct types: semantic memory, the store of facts; and episodic memory, the repository of our personal history and events.

Tulving's experiments had demonstrated that organization of semantic information, such as lists of words, helps efficient recollection, and the same appeared to be true of episodic memory. But where »

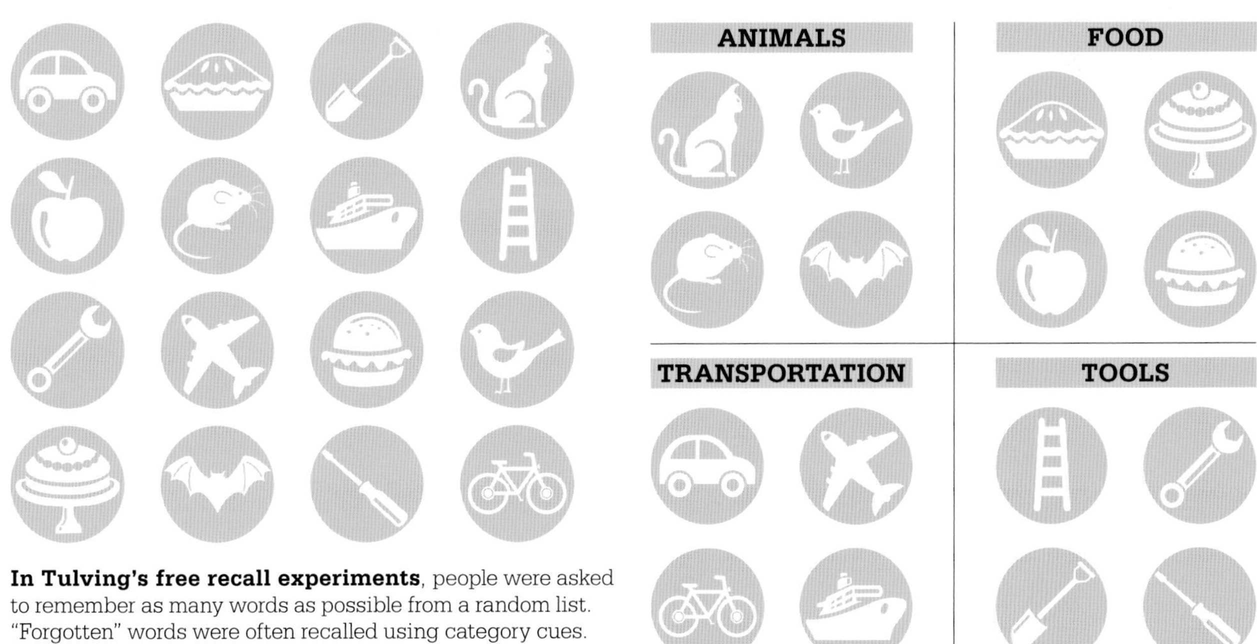

In Tulving's free recall experiments, people were asked to remember as many words as possible from a random list. "Forgotten" words were often recalled using category cues. They were stored in memory but temporarily inaccessible.

Emotional events such as weddings give rise to episodic memories. These are stored in such a way that the person remembering relives the event, in a form of "time travel."

Remembering is mental time travel.
Endel Tulving

semantic memories are organized into meaningful categories of subject matter, episodic memories are organized by relation to the specific time or circumstances in which they were originally stored. For example, a particular conversation may have taken place during a birthday dinner, and the memory of what was said would be stored in association with that occasion. Just as the category of "city" might provide a retrieval cue for the semantic memory "Beijing," the mention of "40th birthday" might act as a cue for the retrieval of what had been said over that dinner. The more strongly these autobiographical memories are associated with the time and circumstances of their occurrence, the greater their accessibility is likely to be. "Flashbulb memories," which are stored when a highly memorable event—such as the 9/11 terrorist attacks—occurs, are an extreme example of this.

Tulving described recollection from episodic memory as "mental time travel," involving us in a revisiting of the past to access the memory. In his later work he pointed out that episodic memory is unique in featuring a subjective sense of time. Specific to humans, it involves not merely awareness of what has been, but also of what may come about. This unique ability allows us to reflect on our lives, worry about future events, and make plans. It is what enables humankind to "take full advantage of its awareness of its continued existence in time" and has allowed us to transform the natural world into one of numerous civilizations and cultures. Through this facility, "time's arrow is bent into a loop."

Encoding information

Tulving realized that organization is the key to efficient recall for both semantic and episodic memory, and that the brain somehow organizes information so that specific facts and events are "pigeonholed" with related items. Recalling that specific

Endel Tulving

Born in Tartu, Estonia, as a boy, Endel Tulving was more interested in sports than academic subjects. When Russia invaded in 1944, he and his brother fled to Germany to finish their studies and did not see their parents again until after the death of Stalin nine years later. After World War II, Tulving was a translator for the US Army and briefly attended medical school before emigrating to Canada in 1949. Studying at the University of Toronto, in 1953, he graduated in psychology and took his MA in 1954. He then moved to Harvard, gaining a PhD for his thesis on visual perception. He returned to the University of Toronto in 1957 and taught there until 1992, when he moved to the Rotman Research Institute, although he remained Professor Emeritus at the university until 2019. In 2023, Tulving died from complications of a stroke at his nursing home.

Key works

1972 *Organization of Memory*
1983 *Elements of Episodic Memory*
1999 *Memory, Consciousness, and the Brain*

information is then made easier by direction to the appropriate pigeonhole—the brain "knows where to look" for the memory it wants and can narrow down the search. The implication, he believed, is that the brain encodes each memory for storage in long-term memory, so that specific memories can be located for recollection by a more general retrieval cue. The cues that prompt episodic memory are usually sensory. A specific sound, such as a piece of music, or a scent can trigger a complete memory.

Tulving's theory of the "encoding specificity principle" was especially applicable to episodic memory. Memories of specific past events are encoded according to the time of their occurrence, along with other memories of the same time. He found that the most effective cue for retrieving any specific episodic memory is the one which overlaps with it most, since this is stored together with the memory to be retrieved. Retrieval cues are necessary to access episodic memory, but not always sufficient, because sometimes the relationship is not close enough to allow recollection, even though the information is stored and available in long-term memory.

Unlike previous theories of memory, Tulving's encoding principle made a distinction between memory that is available and that which is accessible. When someone is unable to recall a piece of information, it does not mean that it is "forgotten" in the sense that it has faded or simply disappeared from long-term memory; it may still be stored, and therefore be available—the problem is one of retrieval.

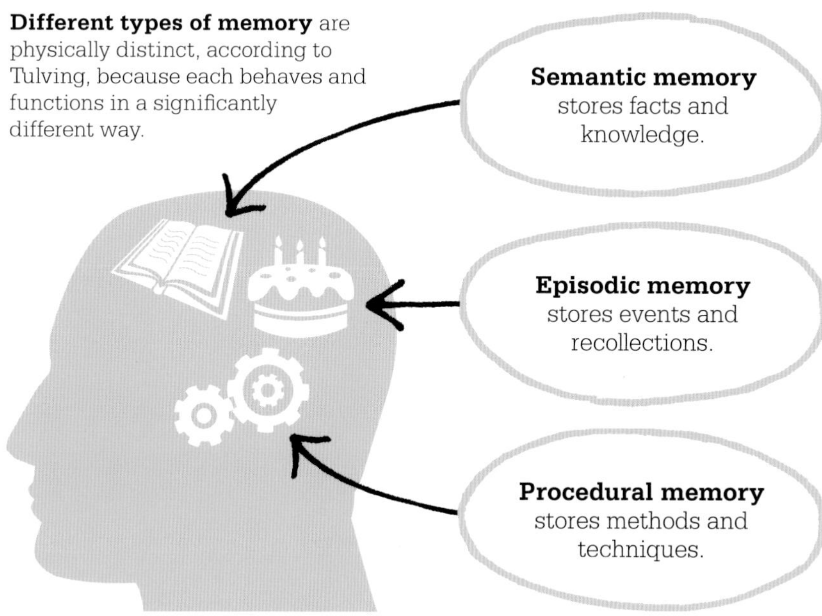

Semantic memory stores facts and knowledge.
Episodic memory stores events and recollections.
Procedural memory stores methods and techniques.

Different types of memory are physically distinct, according to Tulving, because each behaves and functions in a significantly different way.

Relating what we know about the behavior of memory to the underlying neural structures is not at all obvious. That's real science.
Endel Tulving

Scanning for memory

Tulving's research into the storage and retrieval of memory opened up a whole new area for psychological study. The publication of his findings in the 1970s coincided with a new determination by many cognitive psychologists to find confirmation of their theories in neuroscience, using brain-imaging techniques that had just become available. In conjunction with neuroscientists, Tulving was able to map the areas of the brain that are active during encoding and retrieval of memory, and establish that episodic memory is associated with the medial temporal lobe and, specifically, the hippocampus.

Partly due to his unorthodox and untutored approach, Tulving made innovative insights that proved inspirational to other psychologists, including some of his former students such as Daniel Schacter. Tulving's focus on storage and retrieval provided a new way of thinking about memory, but it was perhaps his distinction between semantic and episodic memory that was his breakthrough contribution. It allowed subsequent psychologists to increase the complexity of the model to include such concepts as procedural memory (remembering how to do something) and the difference between explicit memory (of which we are consciously aware) and implicit memory (of which we have no conscious awareness, but which nonetheless continues to affect us). These topics remain of great interest to cognitive psychologists today. ■

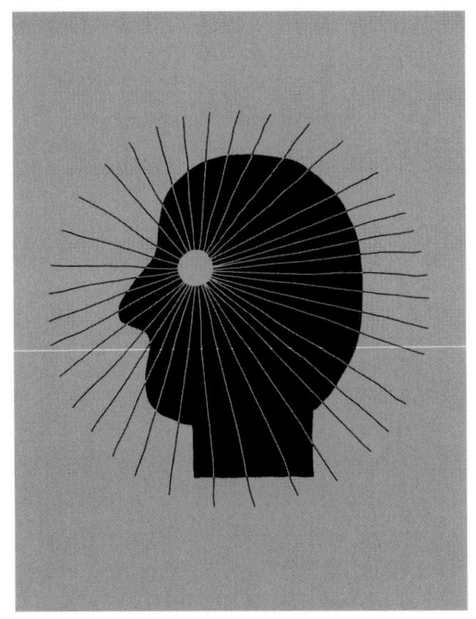

PERCEPTION IS EXTERNALLY GUIDED HALLUCINATION

ROGER N. SHEPARD (1929–2022)

IN CONTEXT

APPROACH
Perception

BEFORE
1637 René Descartes in his treatise *Discourse on the Method* suggests that though our senses can be deceived, we are thinking beings with innate knowledge.

1920s Gestalt theorists study visual perception, finding that people tend to view objects comprising composite parts as a unified whole.

1958 Donald Broadbent's book *Perception and Communication* introduces a truly cognitive approach to the psychology of perception.

AFTER
1986 American experimental psychologist Michael Kubovy publishes *The Psychology of Perspective and Renaissance Art.*

How the mind makes use of information gathered from the external world has been a major concern for philosophers and psychologists throughout history. Exactly how do we use the information gained through our senses? In the early 1970s, cognitive and mathematical psychologist Roger Shepard proposed new theories of how the brain processes "sense data."

Shepard argued that our brains not only process sense data, but also make inferences from it, based on an internal model of the physical world where we can visualize objects in three dimensions. The experiment he used to prove this, in which subjects tried to ascertain whether two tables—each drawn from a different angle—were the same, showed that we are able to perform what Shepard called "mental rotation:" turning one of the tables in our mind's eye for comparison.

Shepard used a series of optical (and aural) illusions to demonstrate that our brains interpret sense data using both knowledge of the external world and mental visualization. Perception, Shepard said, is "externally guided hallucination," and he described the processes of dreaming and hallucination as "internally simulated perception."

An optical illusion creates confusion in the viewer, demonstrating that we are not just perceiving, but also attempting to fit the sensory data to what we already understand in the mind's eye.

Shepard's research introduced revolutionary techniques for identifying the hidden structure of mental representations and processes. His work in visual and auditory perception, mental imagery, and representation has influenced generations of psychologists. ■

See also: René Descartes 20–21 ▪ Wolfgang Köhler 160–161 ▪ Jerome Bruner 164–165 ▪ Donald Broadbent 178–185 ▪ Max Wertheimer 341

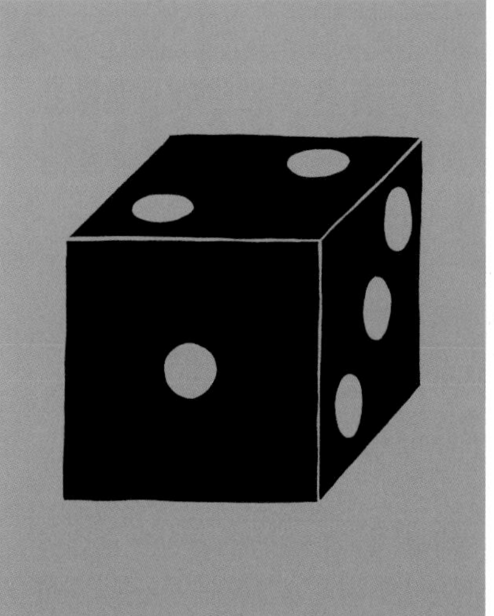

WE ARE CONSTANTLY ON THE LOOKOUT FOR CAUSAL CONNECTIONS

DANIEL KAHNEMAN (1934–)

IN CONTEXT

APPROACH
Prospect theory

BEFORE
1738 The Dutch-Swiss mathematician Daniel Bernoulli proposes the expected utility hypothesis to explain decision-making preferences in situations involving risk.

1917 Wolfgang Köhler publishes *The Mentality of Apes*—his study of problem-solving in chimpanzees.

1940s Edward Tolman's studies on animal behavior open up a new area of research into motivation and decision-making.

AFTER
1980 US economist Richard Thaler publishes the first paper on the subject of behavioral economics: *Toward a Positive Theory of Consumer Choice*.

Until very recently, our perception of risk and the way that we make our decisions was considered to be more a matter of probability and statistics than psychology. However, cognitive psychology, with its emphasis on mental processes, brought the concepts of perception and judgment to the field of problem-solving, with some surprising results.

After observing a long run of red on the roulette wheel, most people erroneously believe that black is now due.
Daniel Kahneman & Amos Tversky

Israeli-American Daniel Kahneman, with Amos Tversky, reexamined theories of how we make decisions when faced with uncertainty, in *Judgment under Uncertainty: Heuristics and Biases* (1974). They found the general belief that people made decisions based on statistics and probability was not true in practice. Instead, people base their decisions on "rule of thumb"—on specific examples or small samples. Consequently, judgments can frequently be wrong, because they are based on information that comes easily to mind, rather than that has actual probability.

Kahneman and Tversky noticed this experience-based method of problem-solving has a pattern: we tend to overestimate the likelihood of things with low probability (such as a plane crash), and underestimate those with a higher probability (such as crashing while driving drunk).

These findings formed the basis of Kahneman and Tversky's prospect theory, proposed in 1979, and led to the collaborative field of psychology known as behavioral economics. ■

See also: Edward Tolman 72–73 ▪ Wolfgang Köhler 160–161

EVENTS AND EMOTION ARE STORED IN MEMORY TOGETHER

GORDON H. BOWER (1932–2020)

IN CONTEXT

APPROACH
Memory studies

BEFORE

1927 Bluma Zeigarnik describes the "Zeigarnik effect" of interrupted tasks being better remembered than uninterrupted ones.

1956 George Armitage Miller's *The Magical Number 7, Plus or Minus 2* provides a cognitive model for storage in short-term memory.

1972 Endel Tulving makes a distinction between semantic and episodic memory.

AFTER

1977 Roger Brown coins the term "flashbulb memory" for autobiographical memory connected with highly emotional events.

2001 Daniel Schacter publishes *The Seven Sins of Memory*, which categorizes the ways that memory can fail.

When we are in a **happy mood**, we tend to store in memory the **positive things** that happen …

When we are in an **unhappy mood**, we tend to store in memory the **negative things** that happen …

… because we **pay more attention** to the information that **agrees with our mood**.

Events and emotion are stored in memory together.

When we are **happy**, we find it easier to recall memories from a **happy time**.

When we are **unhappy**, we find it easier to recall memories from an **unhappy time**.

See also: Bluma Zeigarnik 162 ▪ George Armitage Miller 170–173 ▪ Endel Tulving 186–191 ▪ Paul Ekman 196–197 ▪ Daniel Schacter 208–209 ▪ Roger Brown 243

The 1950s saw a revival of interest in the study of memory. Increasingly sophisticated models of short- and long-term memory were developed, in order to explain how information is selected, organized, stored, and retrieved. The ways in which memories could be forgotten or distorted were also identified.

Memory and mood

By the 1970s, the focus in learning theory and memory had moved to investigating why some memories are better stored or more easily retrieved than others. One of the foremost psychologists in the field, Gordon H. Bower, had noticed that emotion appeared to impact on memory. Bower carried out studies in which people learned lists of words while in different moods and later had to recall them again when in varying emotional states. He uncovered what he called "mood-dependent retrieval": whatever a person has learned when unhappy is easier to recall when they are again unhappy. Bower concluded that we form an association between our emotional state and what is going on around us, and the emotion and the information are stored in memory together. It is then easier to recall facts that we learned when we were in the same mood as we are when recollecting them.

Bower also discovered that emotion plays a part in the type of information that the brain stores. When we are happy, he observed that we tend to notice—and therefore remember—positive things; when we are sad, negative things attract our attention and are committed to memory more easily. For example, Bower found that unhappy people recalled details of a sad story better than those who were happy when they read it. He called this "mood-congruent processing" and concluded that episodic memory—of events, not just words or facts—is especially linked to emotions. The events and emotions are stored together, and we remember best the events that match our mood both when they occurred and when recalling them.

An idyllic vacation, according to Bower, is more easily recalled when we are in a happy mood. Bad memories of the trip are likely to be forgotten or only remembered when we are unhappy.

Bower's findings led him to study people in various emotional states, retrospectively observing their videotaped interactions with others. Memory and judgment of past behavior varied with current mood. This research helped Bower refine his ideas about emotion and memory and inspired further psychological examination of the role emotions play in our lives. ■

Gordon H. Bower

Gordon H. Bower was brought up in Scio, Ohio. In high school, he was more interested in baseball and playing jazz than studying until a teacher introduced him to the works of Sigmund Freud. He went on to graduate in psychology at Case Western Reserve University, Cleveland, switching to Yale for his PhD in learning theory, which he completed in 1959.

From Yale, Bower moved to Stanford University, California, where he taught until his retirement in 2005. His research there helped develop the field of cognitive science, and in 2005, Bower was awarded the US National Medal of Science for his contributions to cognitive and mathematical psychology. He lived in Stanford until his death in 2020.

Key works

1966, 1975 *Theories of Learning* (with Ernest Hilgard)
1981 *Mood and Memory*
1991 *Psychology of Learning and Motivation* (Volume 27)

People who are happy during the initial experience learn the happy events better; angry people learn anger-provoking events better.
Gordon H. Bower

EMOTIONS ARE A RUNAWAY TRAIN

PAUL EKMAN (1934–)

IN CONTEXT

APPROACH
Psychology of emotions

BEFORE
1960s The study of isolated Samoan communities by American anthropologist Margaret Mead suggests that facial expressions are culture-specific.

1960s American psychologist Silvan Tomkins (Ekman's mentor) proposes his Affect Theory of Emotions, distinct from the basic Freudian drives of sex, fear, and the will to live.

1970s Gordon H. Bower uncovers and defines the links between emotional states and memory.

AFTER
2000s The findings of Ekman's work on facial expressions and deception are incorporated into security procedures used by public transport systems.

Emotions, and more especially emotional disorders, played a large part in psychotherapy from its beginnings, but they were seen more as symptoms to be treated than as something to be examined in their own right. One of the first to realize that emotions deserved as much attention as thought processes, drives, and behavior was Paul Ekman, who came to the subject through his research into nonverbal behavior and facial expressions.

When Ekman began his research in the 1970s, it was assumed that we learn to physically express emotions according to a set of social conventions, which differ from culture to culture. Ekman traveled widely to all corners of the world, first photographing people in the "developed countries," such as Japan and Brazil, and then people in places without access to radio or television, such as the jungles of Papua New Guinea. He found tribespeople could interpret facial expressions as well as anyone in

Emotions can and often do **start before our conscious mind is aware** of them.

Emotions can **override** some of our most **fundamental drives** (disgust can override hunger).

It is therefore **difficult to control** what we become emotional about.

Emotions are powerful and difficult to hold back, like a runaway train.

See also: William James 38–45 ▪ Sigmund Freud 92–99 ▪ Gordon H. Bower 194–195 ▪ Nico Frijda 330–331 ▪ Charlotte Bühler 342 ▪ René Diatkine 344–345 ▪ Stanley Schachter 345

The Six Basic Emotions

Anger

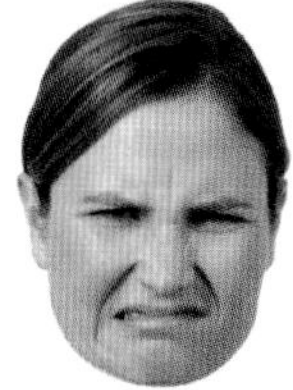

Disgust

Fear

Happiness

Sadness

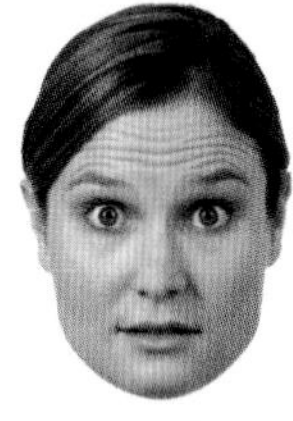

Surprise

more globally aware countries, which suggests that facial expressions are universal products of human evolution.

Basic emotions

Ekman came up with six basic emotions—anger, disgust, fear, happiness, sadness, and surprise—and because of their ubiquity, concluded they must be important to psychological make-up. He noted that facial expressions linked to these emotions are involuntary—we react automatically to things that trigger these emotional responses—and that this reaction often happens before our conscious mind has time to register the causes of that emotion. Ekman inferred not only that our faces can reveal our inner emotional state, but that the emotions responsible for these involuntary expressions are more powerful than psychologists had previously thought.

In *Emotions Revealed*, Ekman states that emotions can be more powerful than the Freudian drives of sex, hunger, and even the will to live. For example, embarrassment or fear can override libido, preventing a satisfactory sex life. Extreme unhappiness can override the will to live. The power of the "runaway train" of emotions convinced Ekman that a better understanding of emotions would help overcome some mental disorders. We may be unable to control our emotions, but we may be able to make changes to the things that trigger them and the behavior they lead to.

Running parallel to his work on emotions, Ekman pioneered research into deception and the ways we try to hide our feelings. He identified small tell-tale signs, which he called "microexpressions," detectable when someone is either consciously or unconsciously concealing something. This has proved useful in devising security measures to counter terrorism. ■

Paul Ekman

Paul Ekman was born and spent his early childhood in Newark, New Jersey. At the outbreak of World War II, his family moved west to Washington, then Oregon, and eventually southern California. Aged just 15, Ekman took up a place at the University of Chicago, where he became interested in Freud and psychotherapy, and went on to study for his doctorate in clinical psychology at Adelphi University, New York. After a brief spell working for the US Army, he moved to the University of California, San Francisco (UCSF), where he began his research into nonverbal behavior and facial expressions. This work led to his studies of the concealment of emotions in facial expressions, which in turn took Ekman deep into the then-unexplored field of the psychology of emotions. He was appointed Professor of Psychology at UCSF in 1972, and remained there until his retirement in 2004.

Key works

1985 *Telling Lies*
2003 *Emotions Revealed*
2008 *Emotional Awareness*

ECSTASY IS A STEP INTO AN ALTERNATIVE REALITY

MIHÁLY CSÍKSZENTMIHÁLYI (1934–2021)

IN CONTEXT

APPROACH
Positive psychology

BEFORE
1943 Abraham Maslow's *A Theory of Human Motivation* lays the foundations for a humanistic psychology.

1951 Carl Rogers publishes *Client-Centered Therapy*, a humanistic approach to psychotherapy.

1960s Aaron Beck introduces cognitive therapy as an alternative to psychoanalysis.

1990s Martin Seligman switches from "learned helplessness" and depression to "positive psychology."

AFTER
1997 Csíkszentmihályi works on The GoodWork Project with William Damon and Howard Gardner, publishing *Good Work: When Excellence and Ethics Meet* and *Good Business: Leadership, Flow, and the Making of Meaning* in 2002.

During the "cognitive revolution," there was a growing movement in clinical psychology away from seeing patients solely in terms of their disorders, toward a more holistic, humanistic approach. Psychologists such as Erich Fromm, Abraham Maslow, and Carl Rogers were beginning to think about what constituted a good and happy life, rather than merely alleviating the misery of depression and anxiety. From this grew a movement of "positive psychology," which concentrated on finding ways to achieve this good and happy life.

When we engage in an **activity that we enjoy** and that gives enough challenge to our skills …

… we become absorbed in that activity and reach **a state of "flow"** in which …

… we are totally **focused**.

… we feel a sense of **serenity**.

… we feel a sense of **timelessness**.

… we have a feeling of inner **clarity**.

Above all, we are **not conscious of ourselves** or the world around us.

Flow is similar to a **state of ecstasy**.

See also: Erich Fromm 124–129 ▪ Carl Rogers 130–137 ▪ Abraham Maslow 138–139 ▪ Aaron Beck 174–177 ▪ Martin Seligman 200–201 ▪ Jon Kabat-Zinn 210

A good jazz musician will pass into an almost trancelike state while playing. Engulfed by the ecstatic feeling of "flow," musicians become absorbed in their music and performance.

Central to the new psychology was the concept of "flow," devised by Mihály Csíkszentmihályi in the 1970s, and fully explained in his book *Flow: The Psychology of Optimal Experience* in 1990. The idea came to him from interviewing people who appeared to get a lot out of life, either in their work or their leisure activities—not only creative professionals such as artists and musicians, but people from all walks of life, including surgeons and business leaders, and those who found satisfaction in pursuits such as sports and games. Csíkszentmihályi found that all these people described a similar sensation when they were totally engaged in an activity they enjoyed and could do well. They all reported achieving a state of mind with no sense of self, in which things came to them automatically—a feeling of "flow." It starts, he said, with "a narrowing of attention on a clearly defined goal. We feel involved, concentrated, absorbed. We know what must be done, and we get immediate feedback as to how well we are doing." Musicians know instantly if the notes they play sound as they should; tennis players know whether the ball they hit will reach its destination.

State of ecstasy

People experiencing flow also describe feelings of timelessness, clarity, and serenity, which led Csíkszentmihályi to liken it to a state of ecstasy (in its truest sense, from the Greek *ekstasis*, meaning "being outside oneself"). A major part of the enjoyment of flow is the sense of being outside everyday reality, totally separated from the cares and worries of ordinary life. Flow, Csíkszentmihályi felt, is key to optimal enjoyment of any activity, and consequently to a fulfilling life.

But how can flow be achieved? Csíkszentmihályi studied cases of people who regularly reached this "ecstatic" state, and realized that it always occurred when the challenge of an activity matched a person's skills; the task was doable, but also extended their capabilities and demanded total concentration. Only a reasonable balance of ability and difficulty could lead to flow. If someone's skills were not up to the task, this led to anxiety, and if the task was too easily done, it led to boredom or apathy.

Csíkszentmihályi's concept of flow was eagerly picked up by other advocates of positive psychology, and became an integral part of this new, optimistic approach. Csíkszentmihályi himself saw flow as a vital element in activity of all kinds, and thought it especially important in making work more rewarding and meaningful. ■

Mihály Csíkszentmihályi

Mihály Csíkszentmihályi was born in Fiume, Italy (now Rijeka, Croatia), where his father was posted as a Hungarian diplomat. The family became exiles in Rome when Hungary was taken over by the Communists in 1948.

As a teenager, Csíkszentmihályi attended a talk given by Carl Jung in Switzerland, which inspired him to study psychology. A scholarship brought him to the University of Chicago; he graduated in 1959, and received his PhD in 1965. While a student, he married the writer Isabella Selenga, and in 1968 became a US citizen. From 1969, Csíkszentmihályi taught at the University of Chicago, and developed his ideas on "flow." In 2000, he was made Distinguished Professor of Psychology and Management at Claremont Graduate University, California. He died in Claremont in 2021.

Key works

1975 *Beyond Boredom and Anxiety*
1990 *Flow: The Psychology of Optimal Experience*
1994 *The Evolving Self*
1996 *Creativity*

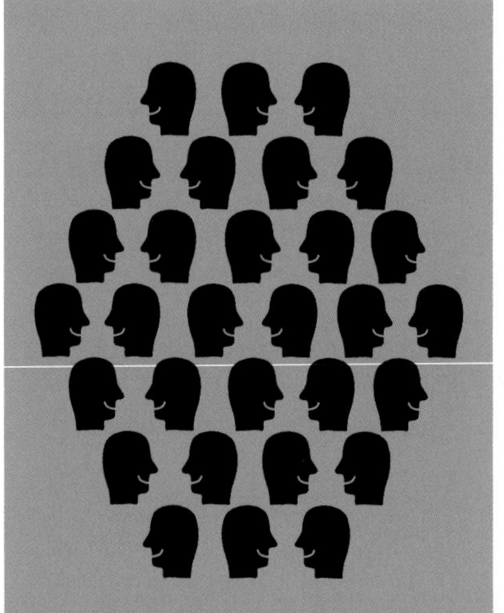

HAPPY PEOPLE ARE EXTREMELY SOCIAL

MARTIN SELIGMAN (1942–)

IN CONTEXT

APPROACH
Positive psychology

BEFORE
1950s Carl Rogers develops the concept and practice of "client-centered" therapy.

1954 Abraham Maslow uses the term "positive psychology" for the first time, in his book *Motivation and Personality.*

1960s Aaron Beck exposes the weaknesses of traditional psychoanalytical therapy, and proposes cognitive therapy.

AFTER
1990 Mihály Csíkszentmihályi publishes *Flow: The Psychology of Optimal Experience*, based on his research into the links between meaningful, engaging activity and happiness.

1994 Jon Kabat-Zinn's *Wherever You Go, There You Are* introduces the idea of "mindfulness meditation" to cope with stress, anxiety, pain, and illness.

There are three kinds of happy life.

The Good Life—pursuing personal growth and achieving "flow."

The Meaningful Life—acting in the service of something greater than yourself.

The Pleasant Life—socializing and seeking pleasure.

These **bring lasting happiness**, but this happiness cannot be achieved without social relationships.

Social relationships do not guarantee high happiness, but it does not appear to occur without them.

While experimental psychology after World War II became deeply concerned with the cognitive processes of the brain, clinical psychology continued to examine ways to treat disorders such as depression and anxiety. The new cognitive therapies still focused largely on alleviating unhappy conditions rather than on creating and promoting happier ones. Martin Seligman, whose theory of "learned helplessness" (the spiral of acquiring pessimistic attitudes in illnesses such as depression) had

See also: Erich Fromm 124–129 ▪ Carl Rogers 130–137 ▪ Abraham Maslow 138–139 ▪ Aaron Beck 174–177 ▪ Mihály Csíkszentmihályi 198–199 ▪ Jon Kabat-Zinn 210

Good social relationships are, like food and thermoregulation, universally important to human mood.
Martin Seligman

led to more successful treatments in the 1980s, believed that what psychology offered was good, but it could offer more. He felt that therapy should be "as concerned with strength as with weakness; as interested in building the best things in life as repairing the worst." Having studied philosophy, he likened the task of his "positive psychology" to that of Aristotle seeking *eudaemonia*—"the happy life." Like his philosophical forebears, Seligman found this was not a matter of relieving or removing things that make us unhappy, but of encouraging those things that might make us happy—and first he had to discover what they were.

"Happy" lives

Seligman noticed that extremely happy, fulfilled people tend to get on with others, and enjoy company. They seemed to lead what he called "the pleasant life," one of the three distinct types of "happy" life that he identified, the others being "the good life" and "the meaningful life." The pleasant life, or seeking as much pleasure as possible, appeared to bring happiness, though Seligman found this was often short-lived. Less obviously, the good life, or being successfully engaged in relationships, work, and play, gave a deeper, more lasting happiness. Similarly, the meaningful life, or acting in the service of others or something bigger than oneself, led to great satisfaction and fulfilment.

Seligman also observed that good and meaningful lifestyles both involve activities that his colleague Mihály Csíkszentmihályi had described as generating "flow," or deep mental engagement. The pleasant life clearly does not involve "flow," but Seligman did find that all the "extremely happy people" he studied were also very sociable, and in a relationship. He concluded that "social relationships do not guarantee high happiness, but it does not appear to occur without them." A good and meaningful life may bring *eudaemonia,* but having a pleasant life as well will intensify whatever happiness you achieve. ■

Enjoying social events and the company of others may not offer deep intellectual or emotional satisfaction, but Seligman observed that it was an essential part of being truly happy.

Martin Seligman

Born in Albany, New York, Martin Seligman took his first degree in philosophy at Princeton University in 1964. He then turned his attention to psychology, gaining a doctorate from the University of Pennsylvania in 1967. He taught at Cornell University, New York, for three years, before returning in 1970 to Pennsylvania, where he has been Professor of Psychology since 1976.

Seligman's research into depression during the 1970s led to a theory of "learned helplessness," and a method of countering the pervasive pessimism associated with it. But after an incident with his daughter that highlighted his own innate negativity, he was persuaded that focusing on positive strengths, rather than negative weaknesses, was key to happiness. Regarded as one of the founding fathers of modern positive psychology, Seligman instigated the Positive Psychology Center at the University of Pennsylvania.

Key works

1975 *Helplessness*
1991 *Learned Optimism*
2002 *Authentic Happiness*

WHAT WE BELIEVE WITH ALL OUR HEARTS IS NOT NECESSARILY THE TRUTH

ELIZABETH LOFTUS (1944–)

IN CONTEXT

APPROACH
Memory

BEFORE
1896 Sigmund Freud proposes the notion of repressed memory.

1932 Frederic Bartlett claims that memory is subject to elaboration, omission, and distortion in *Remembering*.

1947 Gordon Allport and Leo Postman conduct experiments that demonstrate various types of nondeliberate misreporting.

AFTER
1988 The self-help book for sexual abuse survivors, *The Courage to Heal*, by Ellen Bass and Laura Davis, is influential in popularizing recovered memory therapy in the 1990s.

2001 In *The Seven Sins of Memory*, Daniel Schacter describes the seven different ways in which our memories can malfunction.

Toward the end of the 19th century, Sigmund Freud claimed that the mind has a way of defending itself against unacceptable or painful thoughts and impulses by using an unconscious mechanism that he called "repression" to keep them hidden from awareness. Freud later modified his thinking to a more general theory of repressed desires and emotions. However, the idea that the memory of a traumatic event could be repressed and stored beyond conscious recall became accepted by many psychologists.

The rise of various forms of psychotherapy in the 20th century focused attention on repression, and the possibility of retrieving repressed memories became associated with psychoanalysis so strongly that even Hollywood dramas began to explore the link. Memory in general was a popular subject among experimental psychologists, too, particularly as behaviorism began to wane after World War II, and the "cognitive revolution" was suggesting new models for how the brain processed information into memory. By the time Elizabeth Loftus began her studies, long-term memory in particular was an attractive area for research, and repressed and recovered memory was about to become a hot topic, as a number of high-profile child abuse cases reached the courts in the 1980s.

Human remembering does not work like a videotape recorder or a movie camera.
Elizabeth Loftus

Suggestible memory

During the course of her research, Loftus grew skeptical about the idea of recovering repressed memories. Previous research by Frederic Bartlett, Gordon Allport, and Leo Postman had already shown that even in the normal working of the human brain, our ability to retrieve

Elizabeth Loftus

Born Elizabeth Fishman in Los Angeles in 1944, Loftus received her first degree at the University of California, intending to become a high school math teacher. While at UCLA, however, she started classes in psychology, and in 1970 received a PhD in psychology at Stanford University. Here, she first became interested in the subject of long-term memory, and met and married fellow psychology student Geoffrey Loftus, whom she later divorced. For 29 years, she taught at the University of Washington, Seattle, becoming professor of psychology and adjunct professor of law. In 2002, she moved to the University of California, appointed distinguished professor. Awarded numerous honors, Loftus was the highest-ranked woman in a scientifically quantified ranking of the 20th century's most important psychologists.

Key works

1979 *Eyewitness Testimony*
1991 *Witness for the Defense* (with Katherine Ketcham)
1994 *The Myth of Repressed Memory* (with Katherine Ketcham)

See also: Sigmund Freud 92–99 ▪ Bluma Zeigarnik 162 ▪ George Armitage Miller 170–173 ▪ Endel Tulving 186–191 ▪ Gordon H. Bower 194–195 ▪ Daniel Schacter 208–209 ▪ Roger Brown 243 ▪ Frederic Bartlett 342

information from memory can be unreliable; Loftus believed that this must also be true of the recollection of events that are so traumatic that they are repressed—perhaps even more so, given the emotive nature of the events.

Loftus began her research into the fallibility of recollection in the early 1970s, with a series of simple experiments designed to test the veracity of eyewitness testimony. Participants were shown film clips of traffic accidents and then asked questions about what they had seen. Loftus found that the phrasing of questions had a significant influence on how people reported events. For example, when asked to estimate the speed of the cars involved, the answers varied widely, depending on whether the questioner had used the words "bumped," "collided," or "smashed" to describe the collision. They were also asked if there was any broken glass after the accident, and the answers again correlated to the wording of the question of speed. In later versions of the experiment, participants were verbally given false information about some details of the accident (such as road signs around the scene), and these appeared as recollections in many of the participants' reports.

Legal implications

It became clear to Loftus that recollection can be distorted by suggestions and leading questions, made after the event in question. Misinformation can be "planted" into the recollection of an observer. »

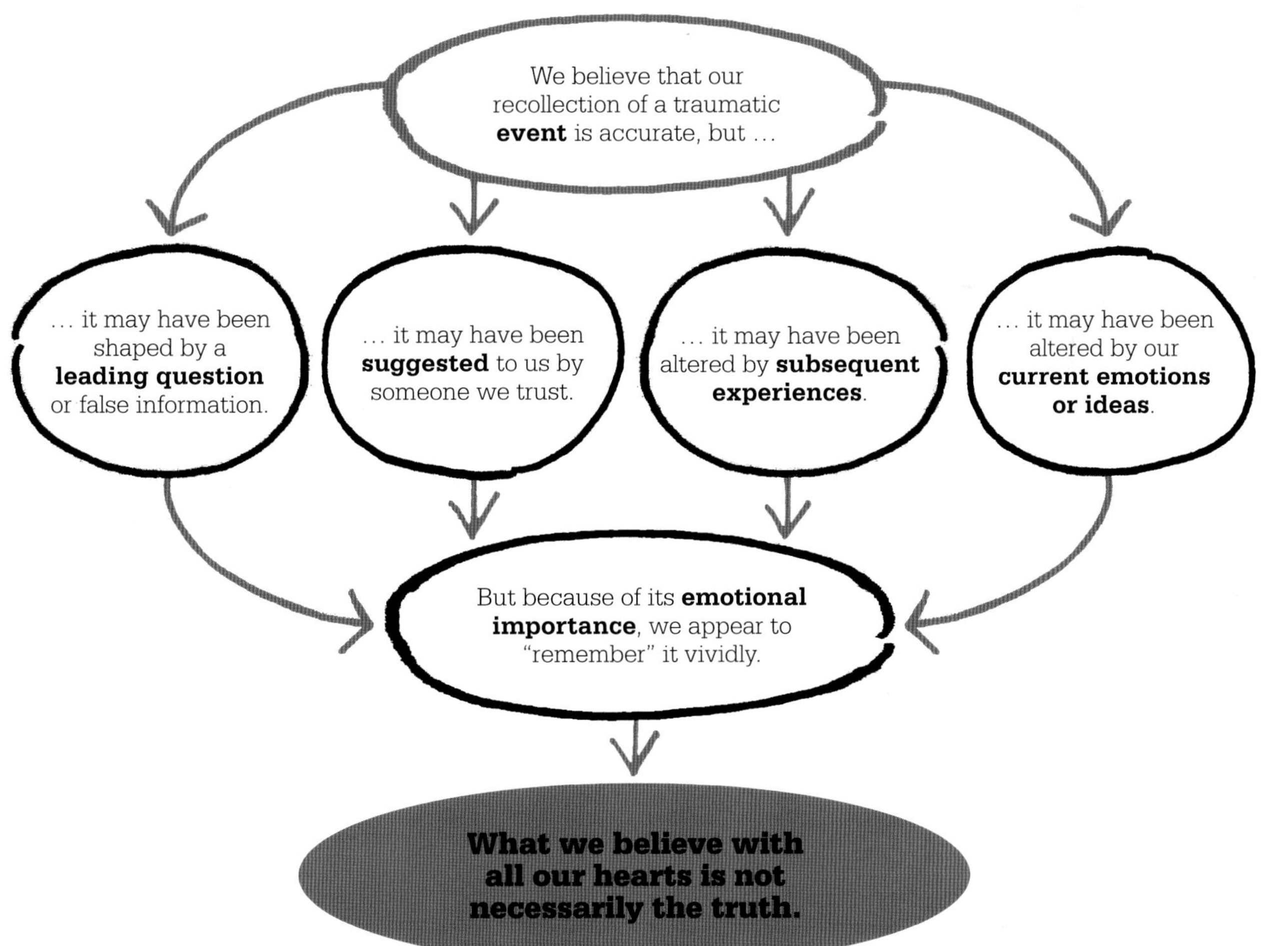

We believe that our recollection of a traumatic **event** is accurate, but …
… it may have been shaped by a **leading question** or false information.
… it may have been **suggested** to us by someone we trust.
… it may have been altered by **subsequent experiences**.
… it may have been altered by our **current emotions or ideas**.
But because of its **emotional importance**, we appear to "remember" it vividly.
What we believe with all our hearts is not necessarily the truth.

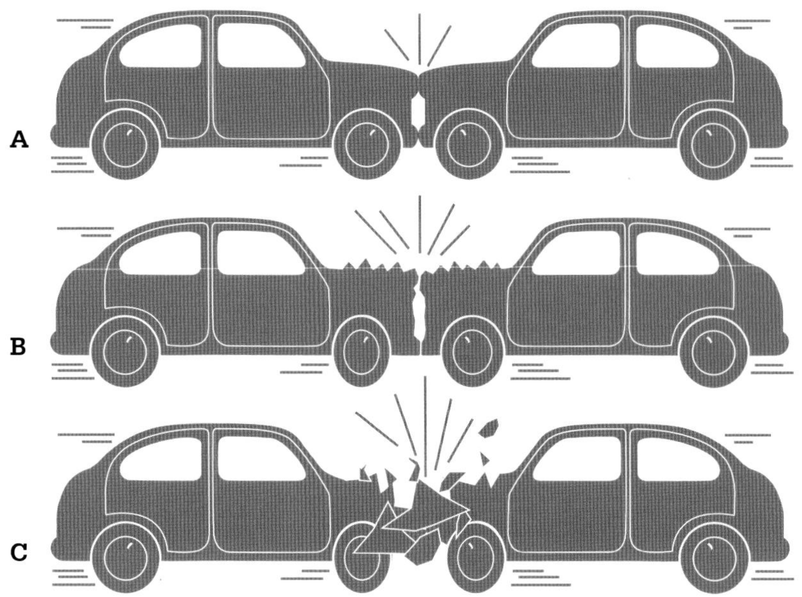

In a 1974 experiment, Loftus showed a group of people a film of cars colliding, then asked them how fast the cars "bumped," "collided," or "smashed" into each other. Her choice of verb determined their estimate of car speeds.

The title of her 1979 book describing her experiments, *Eyewitness Testimony*, shows that Loftus was well aware of the implications of this "misinformation effect," not only for the psychological theory of memory, but also for the legal process. Anticipating the controversy that was to follow, she wrote that "the unreliability of eyewitness identification evidence poses one of the most serious problems in the administration of criminal justice and civil litigation."

False memory syndrome

Loftus was soon to be increasingly involved in forensic psychology as an expert witness in the spate of child abuse cases of the 1980s. What she realized then was that memories could not only be distorted by subsequent suggestion and incorrect details introduced by misinformation, but may even be totally false. Among the many cases in which she was involved, that of George Franklin perfectly illustrates the different aspects of what came to be known as "false memory syndrome." Franklin was convicted in 1990 for the murder of a child who was best friends with his daughter, Eileen. Her eyewitness testimony, 20 years after the murder, was crucial to the conviction. Loftus found numerous discrepancies in Eileen's evidence and proved her memories to be incorrect and unreliable in several respects, but the jury nonetheless found Franklin guilty.

In 1995, the conviction was overturned because the court had been deprived of "crucial evidence": the fact that Eileen had "recovered" the memory during hypnotherapy. Loftus believed that Eileen's memory of seeing her father commit the murder was sincerely believed, but false, and had evolved because Eileen had witnessed her father commit other cruel actions, and "one brutal image overlapped another." Loftus successfully argued in court that a combination of suggestion during hypnosis, existing frightening memories, and Eileen's rage and grief had created a completely false "repressed memory."

The case of Paul Ingram (which Loftus was not involved in) also pointed toward the possibility of implanting false memories. Arrested in 1988 for sexually abusing his daughters, Ingram initially denied the charges, but after several months of questioning confessed to them along with a number of other cases of rape and even murder. A psychologist involved in the case, Richard Ofshe, grew suspicious and suggested to Ingram he was guilty of another sexual offense—but this time, one that was provably fabricated. Ingram again initially denied the allegation, but later made a detailed confession.

Lost in the mall

The evidence for the implantation of false memories was still anecdotal, however, and far from conclusive; Loftus suffered harsh criticism for what were then considered to be controversial opinions. So she decided to collect irrefutable evidence through an experiment that aimed to deliberately implant false memories. This was her 1995 "Lost in the Mall" experiment.

Loftus presented each of the participants with four stories from their own childhood that had apparently been remembered and supplied by members of the participant's family. In fact, only three of the four stories were true; the fourth, about getting lost in a shopping mall, was concocted for the experiment. Plausible details, such as a description of the mall, were worked out in collaboration with the relatives. Interviewed about these stories one week later and then again two weeks later, the participants were asked to rate how well they remembered the events in the four stories. At both interviews, 25 percent of the participants claimed to have some memory of the mall incident. After the experiment, participants were debriefed and told that one of the stories was false—did they know which it was? Of the 24 participants, 19 correctly chose the mall as the false memory, but five participants had grown to sincerely believe in a false memory of a mildly traumatic event.

Loftus had provided an insight into how false memories might form in real, everyday settings. For ethical reasons, Loftus could not devise an experiment to test whether a truly traumatic false memory (such as child abuse) would be even more vividly recalled and sincerely believed, but she suggested that it would, in the same way that a more disturbing dream is more vividly recalled and even mistaken for reality. It was this idea that prompted her to say, "What we believe with all our hearts is not necessarily the truth."

However, in 1986, psychologists John Yuille and Judith Cutshall did manage to conduct a study of memory following a traumatic situation. They found that witnesses to an actual incident of gun shooting had remarkably accurate memories, even six months after the event, and resisted attempts by the researchers to distort their memories through misleading questions.

Questionable therapy

Loftus points out that her findings do not deny that crimes such as abuse may have taken place, nor can she prove that repressed memories do not exist; she merely stresses the unreliability of recovered memory and insists that courts must seek evidence beyond this. Her work has also called into question the validity of the various methods used to recover memory, including psychotherapeutic techniques such as regression, dream work, and hypnosis. Consequently, it raised the possibility that false memories can be implanted during the therapeutic process by suggestion, and in the 1990s, several US patients who claimed they were victims of "false memory syndrome" successfully sued their therapists. Unsurprisingly, this apparent attack on the very idea of repressed memory earned an adverse reaction from some psychotherapists and split opinion among psychologists working in the field of memory. Reaction from the legal world was also divided, but after the hysteria surrounding a series of child abuse scandals in the 1990s had died down, guidelines incorporating Loftus's theories on the reliability of eyewitness testimony were adopted by many legal systems.

Today, Loftus is acknowledged as an authority on the subject of false memory. Her theories have become accepted by mainstream psychology and have inspired further research into the fallibility of memory in general, notably by Daniel Schacter in his book, *The Seven Sins of Memory.* ■

Despite the unreliability of eyewitness testimony, Loftus found that jurors tend to give more weight to it than any other form of evidence when reaching a verdict.

Do you swear to tell the truth, the whole truth, or whatever it is you think you remember?
Elizabeth Loftus

In real life, as well as in experiments, people can come to believe things that never really happened.
Elizabeth Loftus

THE SEVEN SINS OF MEMORY

DANIEL SCHACTER (1952–)

IN CONTEXT

APPROACH
Memory studies

BEFORE
1885 Hermann Ebbinghaus describes the "forgetting curve" in *Memory.*

1932 Frederic Bartlett lists seven ways in which a story may be misremembered in his book *Remembering.*

1956 George Armitage Miller publishes his paper *The Magical Number Seven, Plus or Minus Two.*

1972 Endel Tulving makes the distinction between semantic and episodic memory.

AFTER
1995 Elizabeth Loftus studies retroactive memory in *The Formation of False Memories.*

2005 US psychologist Susan Clancy studies apparent memories of alien abduction.

Forgetting, Daniel Schacter believes, is an essential function of human memory, allowing it to work efficiently. Some of the experiences we go through and the information we learn may need to be remembered, but much is irrelevant and would take up valuable "storage space" in our memory, so is "deleted," to use an analogy with computers that is often made in cognitive psychology.

Sometimes, however, the process of selection fails. What should have been tagged as useful information and stored for future use is removed from memory and therefore forgotten; or—conversely—trivial or unwanted information that should have been removed is kept in our memory.

Storage is not the only area of memory functioning with potential problems. The process of retrieval can cause confusion of information, giving us distorted recollections. Schacter lists seven ways in which memory can let us down: transience, absent-mindedness, blocking, misattribution, suggestibility, bias, and persistence. In a reference to the Seven Deadly Sins, and with a nod to George Armitage Miller's "magical number seven," he calls these the "seven sins of memory." The first three Schacter calls "sins of omission," or forgetting, and the last four are "sins of commission," or remembering. Each sin can lead to a particular type of error in recollecting information.

The first of the sins, transience, involves the deterioration of memory, especially of episodic memory (the memory of events), over time. This is due to two factors: we can recall more of a recent event than one in the distant past; and each time we remember the event (retrieve the memory), it is reprocessed in the brain, altering it slightly.

We don't want a memory that is going to store every bit of every experience. We would be overwhelmed with clutter of useless trivia.
Daniel Schacter

See also: Hermann Ebbinghaus 48–49 ▪ Bluma Zeigarnik 162 ▪ George Armitage Miller 170–173 ▪ Endel Tulving 186–191 ▪ Gordon H. Bower 194–195 ▪ Elizabeth Loftus 202–207 ▪ Frederic Bartlett 342

Absent-mindedness, the sin that manifests itself in mislaid keys and missed appointments, is not so much an error of recollection but of selection for storage. Sometimes we do not pay enough attention at the time we do things (such as when we put down keys), so the information is treated by the brain as trivial and not stored for later use. In contrast to this is the sin of blocking, where a stored memory cannot be retrieved, often because another memory is getting in its way. An example of this is the "tip-of-the-tongue" syndrome, where we can nearly—but not quite—grasp a word from memory that we know very well.

Sins of commission

The "sins of commission" are slightly more complex, but no less common. In misattribution, the information is recalled correctly, but the source of that information is wrongly recalled. It is similar in its effect to suggestibility, where recollections are influenced by the way in which they are recalled, for example, in response to a leading question. The sin of bias also involves the distortion of recollection: this is when a person's opinions and feelings at the time of recalling an event color its remembrance.

Finally, the sin of persistence is an example of the memory working too well. This is when disturbing or upsetting information that has been stored in memory becomes intrusively and persistently recalled, from minor embarrassments to extremely distressing memories.

However, the sins aren't flaws, Schacter insists, but the costs we pay for a complex system that works exceptionally well most of the time. ■

The Seven Sins of Memory

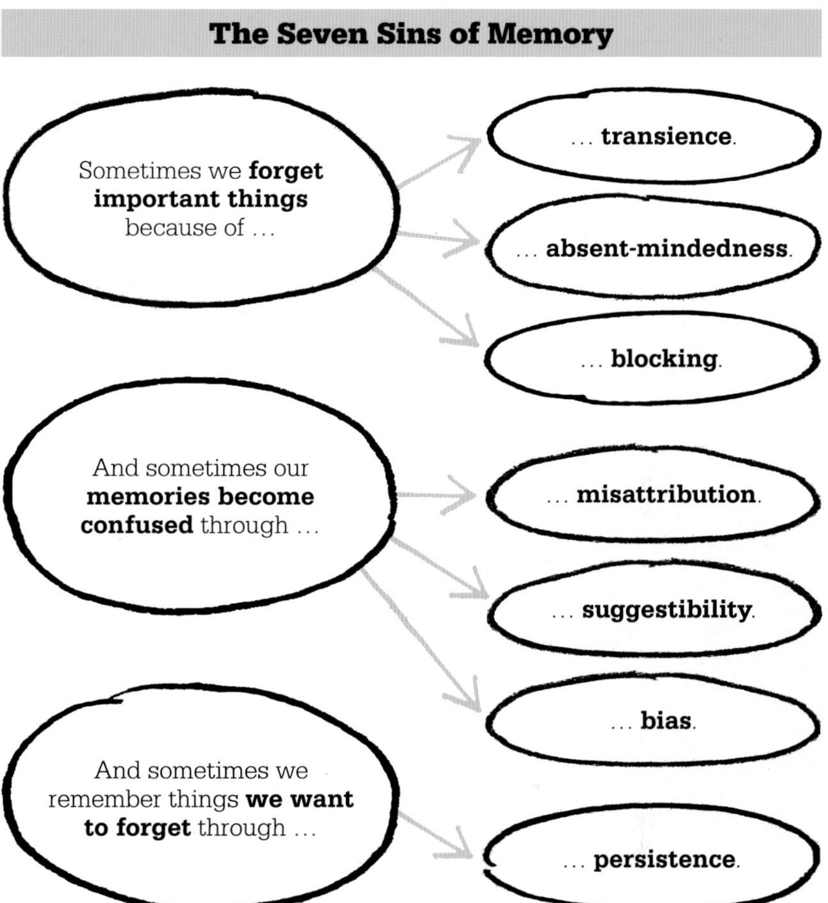
Sometimes we forget important things because of …
… transience.
… absent-mindedness.
… blocking.
And sometimes our memories become confused through …
… misattribution.
… suggestibility.
… bias.
And sometimes we remember things we want to forget through …
… persistence.

Daniel Schacter

Daniel Schacter was born in New York in 1952. A high-school course sparked his interest in psychology, which he went on to study at the University of North Carolina. After graduation, he worked for two years in the perception and memory laboratory of Durham Veterans Hospital, observing and testing patients with organic memory disorders. He then began postgraduate studies at Toronto University, Canada, under the supervision of Endel Tulving, whose work on episodic versus semantic memory was causing lively debate at the time. In 1981, he established a unit for memory disorders at Toronto, with Tulving and Morris Moscovitch. Ten years later, he became Professor of Psychology at Harvard, where he set up the Schacter Memory Laboratory.

Key works

1982 *Stranger Behind the Engram*
1996 *Searching for Memory*
2001 *The Seven Sins of Memory*

ONE IS NOT ONE'S THOUGHTS

JON KABAT-ZINN (1944–)

IN CONTEXT

APPROACH
Mindfulness meditation

BEFORE
c.500 BCE Siddhartha Gautama (the Buddha) includes right mindfulness as the seventh step of the Eightfold Path to end suffering.

1960s Vietnamese Buddhist monk Thich Nhat Hanh popularizes mindful meditation in the US.

AFTER
1990s Mindfulness-Based Cognitive Therapy (MBCT) is developed by Zindel Segal, Mark Williams, and John D. Teasdale for the treatment of depression and is based on Kabat-Zinn's MBSR.

1993 Dialectical Behavior Therapy uses mindfulness without meditation for people too disturbed to achieve the necessary state of mind.

Following World War II, there was an increased interest in Eastern philosophies throughout Europe and America, bringing ideas such as meditation into mainstream culture. The medical benefits of meditation attracted the interest of American biologist and psychologist Jon Kabat-Zinn, who went on to pioneer an approach known as Mindfulness-Based Stress Reduction (MBSR), which integrates meditation into the framework of cognitive therapy.

Buddhist meditation has encouraged the practice of mindfulness for more than 2,000 years, but its mental and physical health benefits were not clinically tested and proven until the early 1990s.

Practicing mindfulness

Central to Kabat-Zinn's approach is "mindfulness." In this form of meditation, the object is to observe thoughts and mental processes (as well as body or physical processes) in a detached, decentered, and nonjudgmental way—"to stay in the body and to watch what's going on in the mind, learning neither to reject things nor to pursue things, but just to let them be and let them go."

In mindfulness meditation, we learn to observe thought processes calmly without identifying with them and realize that our minds have a life of their own. A thought of failure, for instance, is seen as simply an event in the mind, not as a springboard to the conclusion "I am a failure." With practice, we can learn to see mind and body as one thing: a "wholeness." Each of us is more than just a body, says Kabat-Zinn, and more than the thoughts that go through our minds. ■

See also: Joseph Wolpe 86–87 ▪ Fritz Perls 112–117 ▪ Erich Fromm 124–129 ▪ Aaron Beck 174–177 ▪ Neal Miller 344 ▪ John D. Teasdale 346

WITHOUT THE BIOLOGICAL CLOCKS IN OUR BRAINS, OUR LIVES WOULD BE CHAOTIC

COLIN BLAKEMORE (1944–2022)

IN CONTEXT

APPROACH
Neurological science

BEFORE
1900 In *The Interpretation of Dreams*, Sigmund Freud suggests that the unconscious makes itself known in sleep through our dreams.

1935 A team led by Alfred Lee Loomis describes the stages of sleep for the first time.

AFTER
2009 Psychiatrist John Allan Hobson develops the theory that different aspects of the conscious mind interact during dreaming.

2017 The Nobel Prize in Physiology or Medicine is awarded to Jeffrey C. Hall, Michael Rosbash, and Michael W. Young "for their discoveries of molecular mechanisms controlling the circadian rhythm" in fruit flies.

Humans spend about one third of their time asleep, defenseless and vulnerable. Why, neurobiologist Colin Blakemore asked, did we not evolve to be awake longer, unless sleep has a vital purpose? An indicator of its necessity, he argues, is the regularity of our pattern of sleeping. Although it follows a roughly 24-hour cycle, known as the circadian rhythm, this pattern is not dependent on the change of light from day to night; instead, it is our body's internal "biological clock" that determines when and how long we sleep.

Patterns of brain activity

Within our sleep, there is also an internal pattern. While our bodies are largely inactive, our brains continue to function, rotating through a cycle of stages, each of about 90 minutes, with three or four cycles in a typical night's sleep. A period of deep sleep, characterized by a slowing of brain activity, is followed by a period of brain activity similar to the waking state, characterized by rapid eye movements (REM). During this stage, the brain is at its most active (it is the phase in which we dream), but the body is paralyzed.

Blakemore argues that disrupting our sleep patterns, which are governed by our internal biological clock, has a detrimental effect on our well-being.

Sleep studies have confirmed Blakemore's theory that disrupting our biological clock impairs both physical health and cognitive function. It causes mental distress, and interruption of sleep—especially REM sleep—is similarly unsettling. While Blakemore highlights the importance of sleep and the vital role of our biological clock, research is still ongoing as to the precise purpose of our sleeping and dreaming beyond simple physical rest. ■

See also: William James 38–45 ▪ Sigmund Freud 92–99 ▪ Carl Jung 102–107

A NUDGE IS SOME SMALL FEATURE OF THE ENVIRONMENT THAT ATTRACTS OUR ATTENTION AND ALTERS OUR BEHAVIOR

RICHARD THALER (1945–)

IN CONTEXT

APPROACH
Nudge theory

BEFORE
1920s After leaving his academic post in disgrace, behaviorist John B. Watson turns to a career in advertising.

1968 Robert Zajonc explains how mere exposure to a stimulus brings about a change in attitude.

2000 Daniel Kahneman and Amos Tversky argue that our decision-making is based largely on "rules of thumb" rather than consideration of statistics and probability.

AFTER
2010 The British government establishes a "nudge unit." In the US, President Obama follows suit, as do many other countries.

2021 Thaler and Sunstein's bestselling *Nudge: Improving Decisions about Health, Wealth, and Happiness* is updated, with a subtitle, "The Final Edition."

During the 20th century, the theories of behaviorist and social psychologists began to provide useful techniques of persuasion for advertisers and governments trying to influence public behavior—for example, during World War II—to encourage particular behaviors and warn against others. By the 21st century, however, with a more sophisticated public possibly inured to such explicit persuasion, new techniques were needed.

Subtle persuasion

While not psychologists, Americans Richard Thaler (a behavioral economist) and Cass Sunstein (a legal scholar) built on psychological studies of persuasion to develop their "nudge" theory: the idea that small changes to the environment can catch people's attention to provide a "nudge" that makes the desired behavior more likely. As Daniel Kahneman had explained, we tend not to weigh up all the options rationally when making decisions, but instead use rules of thumb—a technique widely adopted by supermarkets that position candy, for example, by checkouts to tempt customers to buy such nonessentials.

Since the publication of Thaler and Sunstein's *Nudge: Improving Decisions about Health, Wealth, and Happiness* in 2008, nudge theory has been widely adopted in various fields to encourage positive change in behavior—for example, by printing health warnings on the packaging of tobacco products or by making organ donation after death the default option rather than something people have to opt into. ■

Signposts such as "School ahead" influence drivers to drive slowly, even if the road is empty, and to sound their horn less, even in heavy traffic.

See also: Jerome Bruner 164–165 ▪ Daniel Kahneman 193 ▪ Robert Zajonc 236–241

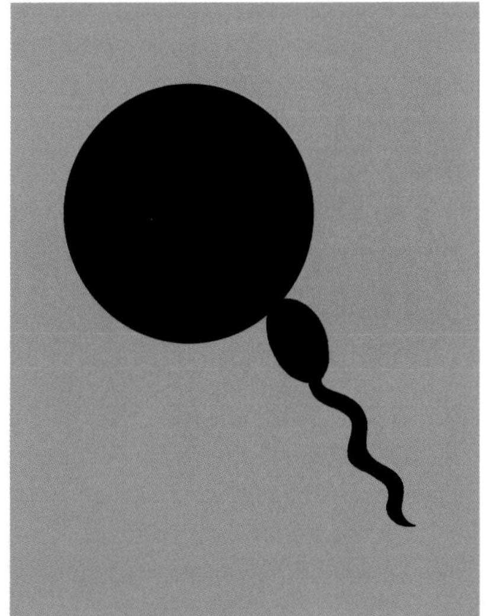

THE FEAR IS THAT BIOLOGY WILL DEBUNK ALL THAT WE HOLD SACRED

STEVEN PINKER (1954–)

IN CONTEXT

APPROACH
Evolutionary psychology

BEFORE
1859 Biologist Charles Darwin says that emotion, perception, and cognition are evolutionary adaptations.

1960s Noam Chomsky claims that the capacity for language is an innate ability.

1969 John Bowlby argues that the attachment of newborn babies to their mothers is genetically programmed.

1976 In *The Selfish Gene*, British biologist Richard Dawkins states that behavioral tendencies evolve through interaction with others over a long period of time.

AFTER
2000 In *The Mating Mind*, American evolutionary psychologist Geoffrey Miller says that human intelligence is shaped by sexual selection.

The debate over how much of our behavior is innate (inborn) and how much can be attributed to our environment dates back thousands of years. Some cognitive psychologists have claimed that not only do we inherit certain psychological characteristics, they are also subject to the same sort of natural selection as our physical characteristics. They point out that the mind is a product of the brain, and the brain is shaped by genetics.

This new field of evolutionary psychology has met with strong opposition, but one of its champions is the Canadian psychologist Steven Pinker, who has identified four fears that lie behind our reluctance to accept evolutionary psychology despite the empirical evidence. The first fear is one of inequality: if the mind is a "blank slate" when we are born, we are all born equal. But if we inherit mental traits, some people have a natural advantage. The second fear is that if certain imperfections are innate, they are not susceptible to change, so social reform to help the disadvantaged is futile. The third fear is that if our behavior is determined by genes, we can abdicate responsibility for our misdemeanors and blame them on our genetic make-up. The final fear, Pinker says, is the most fundamental. This is the fear that if we accept that we are shaped by evolutionary psychology, our "finer feelings"—our perceptions, motives, and emotions—will be reduced to mere processes of our genetic evolution, so biology will "debunk all that we hold sacred." ■

The Blank Slate … promised to make racism, sexism, and class prejudice factually untenable.
Steven Pinker

See also: Francis Galton 28–29 ▪ Konrad Lorenz 77 ▪ John Bowlby 282–285 ▪ Noam Chomsky 302–305

COMPULSIVE BEHAVIOR RITUALS ARE ATTEMPTS TO CONTROL INTRUSIVE THOUGHTS

PAUL SALKOVSKIS (1950s–)

IN CONTEXT

APPROACH
Cognitive behavioral therapy

BEFORE

1950s Joseph Wolpe applies behaviorist ideas to clinical psychology in techniques such as systematic desensitization.

1952 Behavior and personality theorist Hans J. Eysenck causes controversy with claims that psychotherapy has no beneficial effect.

1955 Albert Ellis offers an alternative to traditional psychotherapy with his Rational Emotive Behavior Therapy (REBT).

1960s Aaron Beck questions whether psychoanalytical therapy is effective; he goes on to develop cognitive therapy.

AFTER

2000s Cognitive behavioral therapy becomes a standard treatment for anxiety, panic attacks, and other disorders.

The second half of the 20th century saw a profound change in clinical psychology. Psychoanalysis was seen by many psychologists as less than scientific, and by the 1960s, it was replaced as the treatment for some disorders by behaviorist therapies, or the newer cognitive therapy developed by Aaron Beck. Combinations of these approaches, under the umbrella term cognitive behavioral therapy (CBT), evolved in the 1980s, pioneered in Britain by Paul Salkovskis. CBT, he found, was especially successful in treating obsessive-compulsive disorder (OCD); where psychoanalysis had failed to find a root cause for the disorder in repression or past trauma, Salkovskis explained the problem in terms of cognitive psychology, and offered a cognitive and behavioral treatment.

In the film *As Good As It Gets*, Jack Nicholson's character Melvin exhibits compulsive activities such as wearing gloves to avoid potential "contamination" by the outside world.

Obsessive thoughts

Salkovskis suggests that obsessive-compulsive disorder has its basis in the sort of unwelcome and intrusive thoughts that we all have from time to time—the idea that something terrible is about to happen, or that we will suffer or cause some awful misfortune. Most of the time, we can put these thoughts out of our minds and carry on with life, but sometimes they are more difficult to shake off. At the extreme end of the scale, the thoughts become obsessive and bring with them a feeling of dread and responsibility. People predisposed to these kinds of obsessive thoughts find it difficult to make a rational appraisal of their importance, and overestimate not only any risk of harm, but also the amount of control they have to prevent it. Obsessive thoughts

See also: Joseph Wolpe 86–87 ▪ Fritz Perls 112–117 ▪ Albert Ellis 142–145 ▪ Aaron Beck 174–177

We all have unwelcome **intrusive thoughts**.

↓

But some people have trouble shaking them off, and the thoughts become **overimportant and obsessional**.

↓

They overestimate the **threat** posed by these thoughts.

They feel **responsible** for any harm implied by these intrusive thoughts.

↓

They therefore feel compelled to take action to counter the threats and control the thoughts.

↓

Compulsive behavior rituals are attempts to control intrusive thoughts.

and ritualized behavior patterns can dominate, such as locking and relocking doors or switching lights on and off. There is also a feeling of a responsibility to act, even if the action is out of proportion to the risk. The resulting compulsive actions can become ritual behavior patterns, carried out repeatedly in an attempt to gain control over a perceived threat.

Cognitive behavioral therapy combines cognitive and behavioral techniques to address both the cause and the symptoms of OCD to great effect. First, patients are helped through cognitive therapy to recognize the obsessional thoughts for what they are, making a more rational appraisal of the risk and, crucially, of how much responsibility they themselves have for taking preventative action. This cognitive approach helps reduce the distress. Alongside this, behavioral therapy techniques, such as desensitization (gradual exposure to the perceived threat), help patients control their compulsive behavior. Salkovskis successfully uses CBT techniques to treat anxiety, panic attacks, and phobias. ■

Paul Salkovskis

A graduate of the Institute of Psychiatry, London in 1979, Paul Salkovskis took up a post at the University of Oxford in 1985 to research panic disorders. His interest in using cognitive theory on anxiety disorders led ultimately to his appointment as Professor of Cognitive Psychology.

While at Oxford, his work refocused on the treatment of obsessive-compulsive disorder using cognitive behavioral therapy. In 2000, he became Professor of Clinical Psychology and Applied Science at the Institute of Psychiatry, and Clinical Director in the Centre for Anxiety Disorders and Trauma. Salkovskis moved to the University of Bath in 2010 to establish a specialist CBT center. He returned to Oxford in 2018 to become Director of the Oxford Institute of Clinical Psychology, and has led CBT skills training both nationally and throughout the world.

Key works

1998 *Panic Disorder*
1999 *Understanding and Treating Obsessive-Compulsive Disorder*
2000 *Causing Harm and Allowing Harm* (with A. Wroe)

WE PAY ATTENTION TO WHAT WE'RE LOOKING FOR … WHAT WE SEE IS AMAZINGLY LIMITED

CHRISTOPHER CHABRIS (1966–) & DANIEL SIMONS (1969–)

IN CONTEXT

APPROACH
Inattentional blindness

BEFORE
1890 In *The Principles of Psychology*, William James describes selective attention, remarking that "without selective interest, experience is utter chaos."

1950s Donald Broadbent's dichotic listening experiments (simultaneously stimulating each ear with different sounds) confirm that we can only listen to one voice at a time.

1992 Arien Mack and Irvin Rock coin the term "inattentional blindness," which is also the title of their 1998 book on the subject.

AFTER
2011 A repeat of the invisible gorilla experiment by Elizabeth Graham and Deborah Burke shows that age is a factor in the extent of inattentional blindness.

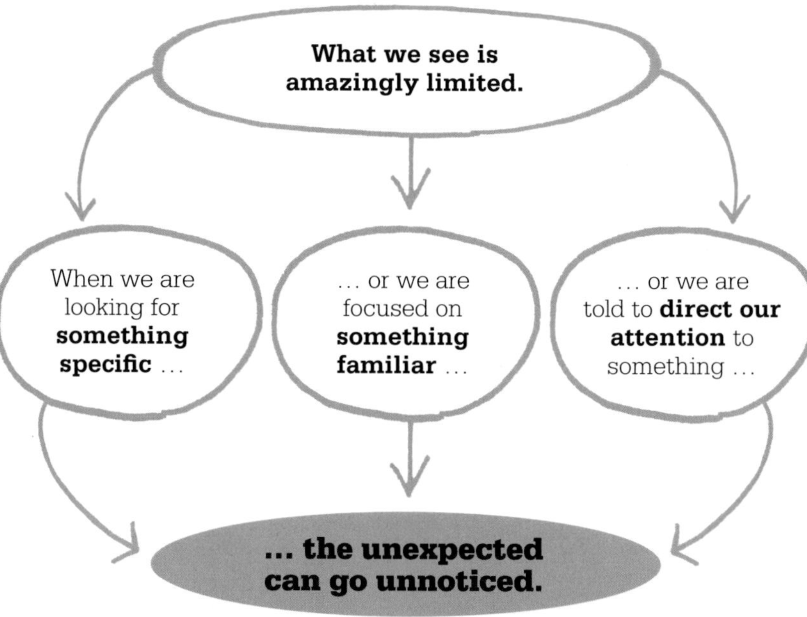

What we see is amazingly limited.
When we are looking for something specific …
… or we are focused on something familiar …
… or we are told to direct our attention to something …
… the unexpected can go unnoticed.

In an experiment that gained international attention when it was later used in a television advertisement, Christopher Chabris and Daniel Simons demonstrated strikingly just how easily we can fail to see what is happening right in front of us. Participants were asked to watch a video of basketball players passing a ball to one another and to count the number of passes the players in white shirts made. After viewing the video, they were then asked if they had noticed the gorilla, and a surprising majority admitted they had failed to notice a person in a gorilla suit walking through the group of basketball players and even waving to the camera.

Their experiment was developed from a similar scenario devised in 1975 by Ulric Neisser and Robert Becklen, who were researching what they called "selective looking." They

See also: George Armitage Miller 170–173 ▪ Donald Broadbent 178–185 ▪ Roger N. Shepard 192

were trying to create a visual equivalent of the dichotic listening studies created by Donald Broadbent. To achieve this, they superimposed videos of different events on a single screen. What they discovered was that when viewers actively followed one event, they would often miss unexpected and conspicuous additions, such as a woman with an umbrella or a gorilla-suited man walking through a basketball game.

Interest in this "selective looking," or "inattentional blindness" as it became known, was renewed when a group of psychologists including Chabris and Simons explored the case of a police officer, Kenny Conley. He'd been convicted in 1995 for failing to come to the aid of a fellow police officer involved in a fight. Conley maintained he had not seen the incident, even though he had passed nearby, as he was focused on chasing a suspect; nevertheless, he was found guilty. The psychologists devised a series of experiments, with participants chasing an experimenter and counting the number of times he touched his head. They were then asked if they had noticed the fight that they had run past. The results confirmed that Conley had probably been telling the truth and had not noticed his colleague's predicament.

Inattentional blindness calls into question the notion of people's ability to "multitask," especially in situations such as using a mobile device while driving a car.

Paying attention is not just analyzing carefully; rather, it is a constructive act ... What we build has only the dimensions we have given it.
Ulric Neisser

Taking it further

Chabris and Simons researched further into inattentional blindness, reviving and popularizing Neisser's "invisible gorilla" experiment, but also developing new experiments using randomly moving objects on a computer screen: when asked to concentrate on either the black or the white objects, participants missed the prominent red cross moving across the screen.

Their work found that inattentional blindness is the result of a lack of attention rather than poor cognitive processing. Unexpected things go unnoticed because our visual attention is fully engaged elsewhere. It raises practical questions about how we process visual information, about the potential unreliability of eyewitness testimony, and about the ability of people to "multitask." ■

Christopher Chabris & Daniel Simons

Christopher Chabris was born in New York City in 1966 and has spent most of his career at Harvard University, from which he graduated with a BA in computer science and where he gained his PhD cognitive neuroscience. Since then, he has held teaching and research posts in the Harvard Medical School and the university department of psychology. He has also been appointed to positions at the Institute for Advanced Study in Toulouse, France, and Union College in Schenectady, New York.

Daniel Simons (born 1969) studied psychology at Carleton College and Cornell University before beginning his teaching career as an experimental psychologist and cognitive scientist at Harvard University in 1997. After rising to the level of Associate Professor, he moved to the University of Illinois, where since 2002 he has been professor in charge of the Visual Cognition Laboratory, conducting research into perception, attention, and awareness.

Key works:

2010 *The Invisible Gorilla, and Other Ways Our Intuitions Deceive Us*
2023 *Nobody's Fool: Why We Get Taken In and What We Can Do About It*

SOCIAL PSYCHOL

BEING IN A WORLD OF OTHERS

OGY

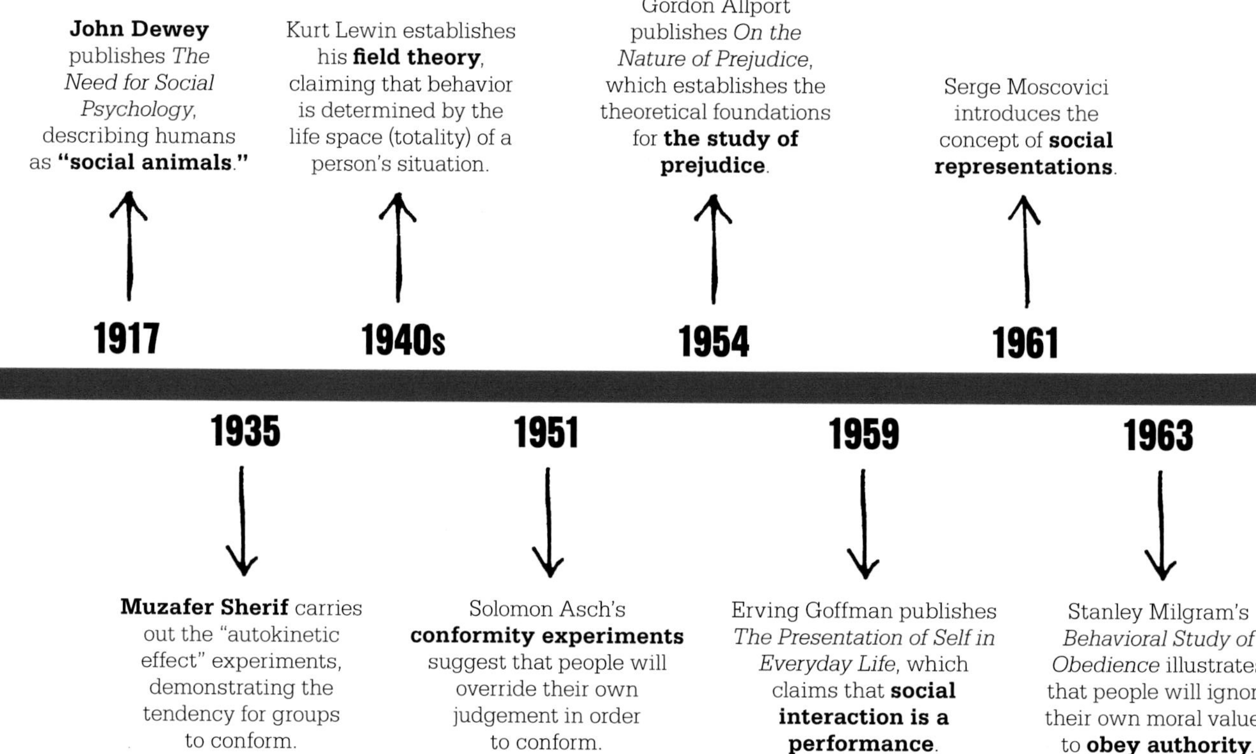

1917
John Dewey publishes *The Need for Social Psychology*, describing humans as **"social animals."**
1935
Muzafer Sherif carries out the "autokinetic effect" experiments, demonstrating the tendency for groups to conform.
1940s
Kurt Lewin establishes his **field theory**, claiming that behavior is determined by the life space (totality) of a person's situation.
1951
Solomon Asch's **conformity experiments** suggest that people will override their own judgement in order to conform.
1954
Gordon Allport publishes *On the Nature of Prejudice*, which establishes the theoretical foundations for **the study of prejudice**.
1959
Erving Goffman publishes *The Presentation of Self in Everyday Life*, which claims that **social interaction is a performance**.
1961
Serge Moscovici introduces the concept of **social representations**.
1963
Stanley Milgram's *Behavioral Study of Obedience* illustrates that people will ignore their own moral values to **obey authority**.

As psychology became established as a scientific discipline, its scope was at first limited to the examination of the mind and its workings, before broadening to include the study of behavior. For much of the first half of the 20th century, this meant the emphasis was very much on a study of the mind and behavior of individuals and their responses to their environment, though it became increasingly clear to some psychologists that "the environment" includes other people.

The field of social psychology emerged in the 1930s, when psychologists began to explore the interactions of individuals within groups and society as a whole. They examined the effect of social organizations on the individual, and the way that social structures are influenced by the psychology of their individual members. Social psychologists, as they were called, also studied the relationships between individuals within these groups and between different groups. This introduced a new set of topics to psychology, including group dynamics, attitudes, and prejudice, as well as social conflict, conformity, obedience, and social change.

Social environment

Among the first to make a systematic study of the psychology of social groups was German–American Kurt Lewin, considered the "father of social psychology." Lewin took a fresh look at the dominant behaviorist approach, examining how behavior results from the interaction between the individual and his environment, as well as the nature of that environment. In his studies of small groups, he laid the foundations for later examinations of group dynamics and how groups and their members bring about change.

Behaviorism fell out of favor after World War II, and Lewin's ideas about the effect of the social environment provided an alternative that was enthusiastically taken up by the next generation. The concept of "attribution"—the way we see and interpret the behavior of others—became an area of specific research, and from that came theories of conformity and cultural norms such as those of Solomon Asch. Erving Goffman's best-known theory—that we act out certain behaviors to suit the impression we want to give

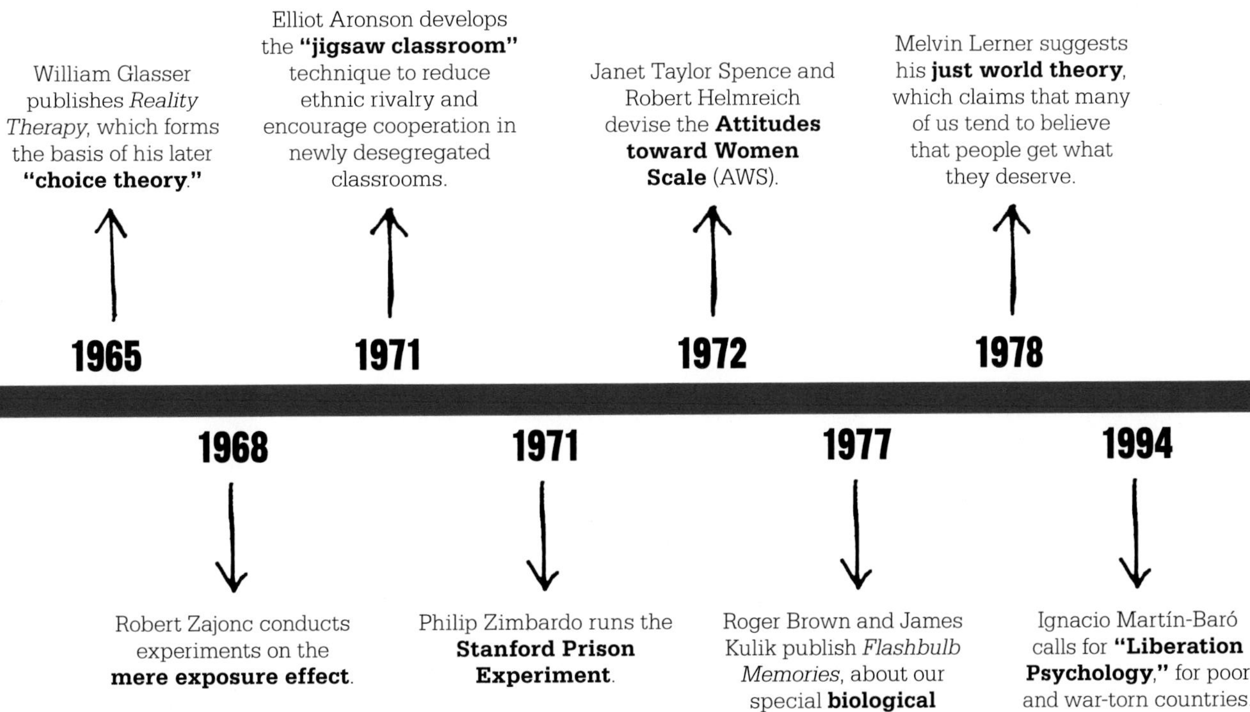

to others—also came out of this new emphasis on the importance of social interaction.

1965
William Glasser publishes *Reality Therapy*, which forms the basis of his later **"choice theory."**
1971
Elliot Aronson develops the **"jigsaw classroom"** technique to reduce ethnic rivalry and encourage cooperation in newly desegregated classrooms.
1972
Janet Taylor Spence and Robert Helmreich devise the **Attitudes toward Women Scale** (AWS).
1978
Melvin Lerner suggests his **just world theory**, which claims that many of us tend to believe that people get what they deserve.
1968
Robert Zajonc conducts experiments on the **mere exposure effect**.
1971
Philip Zimbardo runs the **Stanford Prison Experiment**.
1977
Roger Brown and James Kulik publish *Flashbulb Memories*, about our special **biological memory mechanism**.
1994
Ignacio Martín-Baró calls for **"Liberation Psychology,"** for poor and war-torn countries.

Research in the 1960s shed light on the darker aspects of behavior; Melvin Lerner showed how victims can be blamed for their misfortunes, and Elliot Aronson explained that aberrant behavior may be caused by circumstances, not insanity. And, while the atrocities of World War II were still fresh in people's minds, Stanley Milgram and Philip Zimbardo showed the need to conform and obey in controversial studies that prompted a thorough examination of experimental ethics.

Applying psychology

The advent of cognitive psychology brought a new influence on social psychology. The effects of cognitive processes such as memory and emotion were highlighted by Roger Brown and Robert Zajonc, and these findings were exploited widely by the mass media and advertising, which increasingly affected social structures, prompting theories of social constructivism by psychologists such as Serge Moscovici. These in turn became increasingly relevant as the impact of internet communication and social media became apparent in the first decades of the 21st century. As a result, social psychology has rapidly become more applicable to many different situations. It has influenced other areas of psychology—in particular psychotherapy—through William Glasser's "reality therapy." It has also impacted on other disciplines, including sociology, anthropology, and even politics and economics. The 1960s saw the rise of the civil rights movement and feminism, both of which challenged the status quo. Issues surrounding prejudice, cultural norms, and beliefs came to the fore, and the work of social psychologists such as Janet Taylor Spence did much to alter attitudes toward women, while others used Lewin's process of social transformation to bring about organizational changes. Business, industry, and social organizations now use models pioneered by social psychologists, such as the "nudge" theory, and they have been adopted as a means of achieving social and political reform in societies suffering from oppression, most notably in the "Liberation Psychology" espoused by Ignacio Martín-Baró. ■

YOU CANNOT UNDERSTAND A SYSTEM UNTIL YOU TRY TO CHANGE IT

KURT LEWIN (1890–1947)

IN CONTEXT

APPROACH
Field theory

BEFORE
Early 1900s Sigmund Freud and other psychotherapists argue that human behavior is a result of past experience.

1910s Wolfgang Köhler, among other Gestalt psychologists, argues that people must be understood holistically, according to all of their elements and their interactions with the surrounding environment.

AFTER
1958 In *The Dynamics of Planned Change*, Ronald Lippitt, Jeanne Watson, and Bruce Westley create a seven-step change theory that focuses on the role of the change agent rather than on the evolution of change itself.

The behaviorists believed that behavior is dictated by the environment alone, but in the 1920s Kurt Lewin made the claim that behavior is a result of both the individual and the environment. His revolutionary ideas developed and evolved into the study of group dynamics that is invaluable to organizations today.

In his investigation of human behavior, Lewin developed field theory, which explores the forces and factors that influence any given situation. Lewin's "field" refers to the psychological environment of the individual or the collective group at a particular point in time, and he identified two opposing forces present in any given field: helpful forces, which drive people toward achieving their goals, and hindering forces, which inhibit movement toward these goals.

Lewin's change model

Field theory provided the basis for Lewin's model of change, which offers an invaluable guide for successful transformation, both for individuals and organizations. The model shows that in order to carry out the process of change successfully, a person or organization leader must take into account the various influences at play both within the minds of individuals and within their environment.

In explaining his change model, Lewin emphasizes that the entire situation, including all the relevant personal and environmental details, must be taken into account, as focusing on isolated facts can lead to a skewed perception of the circumstances. Not only must you have a thorough and holistic

A person who has learned to see how much his own fate depends upon the fate of his entire group will be eager to take over a fair share of responsibility for its welfare.
Kurt Lewin

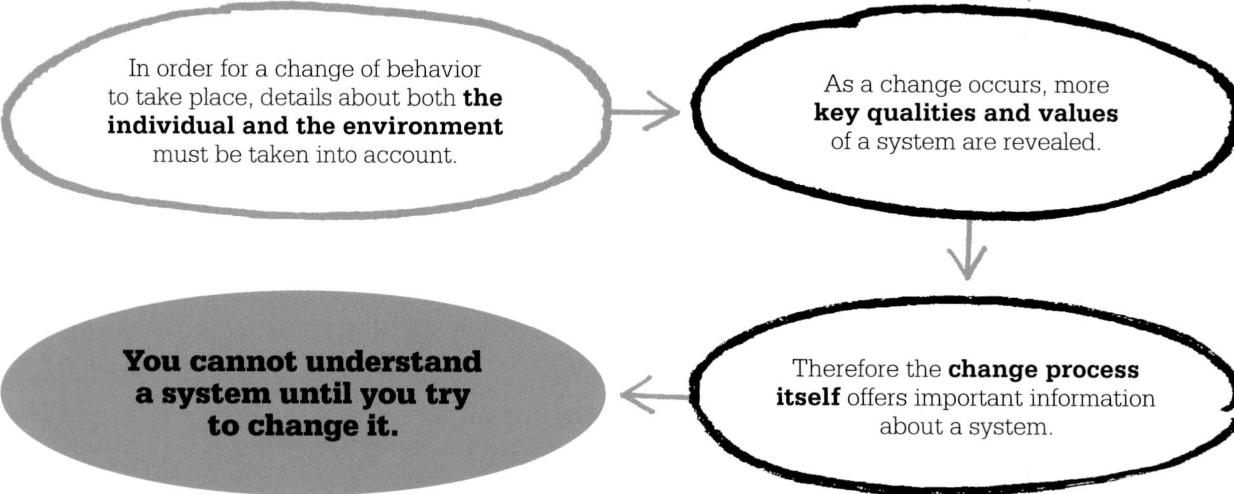

In order for a change of behavior to take place, details about both **the individual and the environment** must be taken into account.
As a change occurs, more **key qualities and values** of a system are revealed.
Therefore the **change process itself** offers important information about a system.
You cannot understand a system until you try to change it.

See also: Sigmund Freud 92–99 ▪ Wolfgang Köhler 160–161 ▪ Leon Festinger 166–169 ▪ Max Wertheimer 341 ▪ Elton Mayo 341

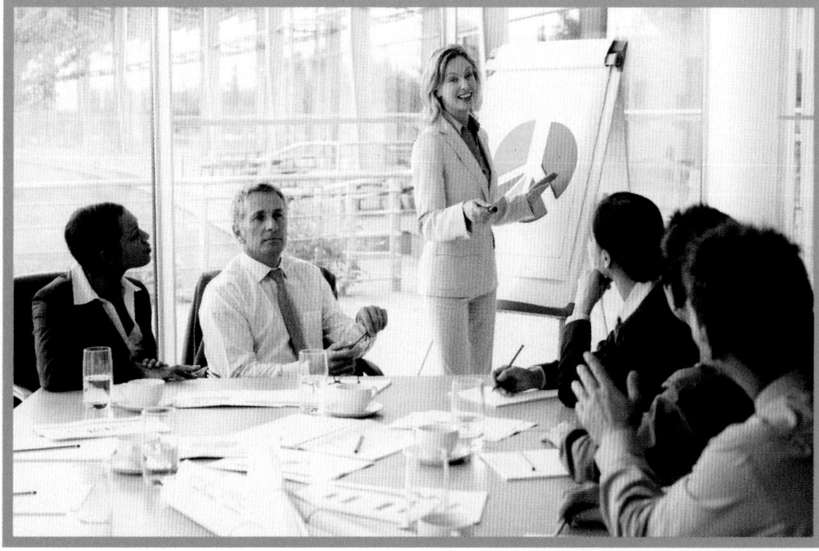

Successful organizational change is engendered by making a unique diagnosis of the people and situational forces involved, and understanding the interplay between them.

understanding of a situation in order to change it, but that understanding actually deepens throughout the change process, and therefore "you cannot understand a system until you try to change it."

Lewin's model describes a three-step process for achieving personal or organizational transformation. The first stage—which he called "unfreezing"—involves recognizing that change is necessary, and dismantling old beliefs and practices. Change occurs in the second stage, and is often accompanied by confusion and distress as the old mindset or system breaks down. The third and final stage, "freezing," occurs when a new mindset is crystallized and there is an accompanying sense of comfort and stability within the new framework. The process is difficult because it involves painful unlearning, difficult relearning, and the restructuring of thoughts, feelings, attitudes, and perceptions.

We all need each other. This type of interdependence is the greatest challenge to the maturity of individual and group functioning.
Kurt Lewin

Unfreezing beliefs

The unfreezing stage is perhaps the most complex stage of the process, as people are naturally inclined to resist changes to their established mindsets and routines. It requires careful preparation; many change efforts within organizations fail simply because employees are not adequately prepared, making them more resistant to change and less likely to function effectively under the new system. Preparation might include creating an exciting vision for change that employees can rally around, communicating it effectively, developing a sense of urgency and necessity for change, providing employees with support, and allowing them to participate actively in the process.

On an individual level, people may react to this stage defensively, not wanting to leave their comfort zone and undergo the challenge of learning new skills or accepting a new set of beliefs. This natural resistance can be overcome if the individual is helped to accept that the change is necessary, valid, and will lead to the best outcome, and if support is given to engender a feeling of psychological safety.

Lewin demonstrated the positive effect of creating an environment of psychological safety during the unfreezing stage (and of allowing active participation in the change process) in his efforts to convince American housewives to serve animal organs as food at home during World War II. Historically, offal had only been eaten by low-income families, but the American government wanted to ensure that nutritious food was not going to waste during a time of food shortages, especially as kidneys, livers, and hearts are all high-protein foods. The US Department of Agriculture called upon Lewin to help convince housewives to include these »

Learning is more effective when it is an active rather than a passive process.
Kurt Lewin

meats in their family meals. During interviews with housewives, Lewin realized that there were both helpful and hindering forces at play. The helpful forces, or incentives, toward changing the housewives' view of organ meat was its high nutritional value. The hindering forces, or barriers, to change centered around the women's view that the meat was inappropriate for them and their families, and to a lesser degree, that it would not taste good.

Lewin set up a study using two groups of housewives to explore the best ways of initiating change. The first group was told repeatedly that eating offal was beneficial for them, while the other group took part in a small group discussion focusing on how the food shortage problem could be eased if women like themselves could be convinced to take part in a program of using secondary cuts of meat such as livers, kidneys, and hearts. When around one-third of the women who had participated in the discussion group later served offal for dinner, Lewin concluded that increasing the level of people's involvement also increases the likelihood of changing their attitudes and behaviors. Lecturing to the first group had proved ineffective, but in the discussion group he had created an environment in which women felt psychologically safe enough to express their concerns and opinions. Through exploring their beliefs as well as the realities of the food shortages, he helped them change their opinions about which meats were edible and guided them toward a new belief: that offal is acceptable to buy and serve at home.

Making the change

During Lewin's second stage—the actual change process—people are confronted with the daunting and confusing task of implementing a new system. They must give up familiar routines and practices and master new skills (which itself can arouse feelings of uncertainty or a fear of failure). In an organization, the new system will be defined by the leadership, and often relates to technology, structure, procedures, or culture. It is important at this stage to provide sufficient support for employees and ensure the elimination of obstacles.

At the level of personal change, people cannot be given a new belief system, but must find and accept one for themselves. When an old belief has been proven wrong or ineffective, we are naturally inclined to replace the old value system with a new one, filling the uncomfortable void left by the unfreezing process. We do this in a combination of ways: relying on our instinctive feelings, studying role models, and looking more generally to the vast array of information available. We hope in this way to expose ourselves to a new piece of information that will solve the problem. Once this insight is achieved, we have accepted and established a new mindset.

In the case of the American housewives during World War II, Lewin provided the women with new information by educating them about the good taste and nutritional value of offal (thereby replacing their old belief that it was an inferior meat), and convincing them that given the reality of wartime food shortages, there was absolutely no shame in serving it to their families (thereby replacing their prewartime belief that they would be viewed as social inferiors for eating it).

The freezing stage

After change has been implemented within an organization, it must become part of the company's culture (or "frozen") in order for it to be successful in the long term. The new thought processes, practices, and behaviors adopted during the transition must become routine. Management can help to ensure changes become more firmly established by publicizing the ways in which change has benefited the company, and by nurturing positive

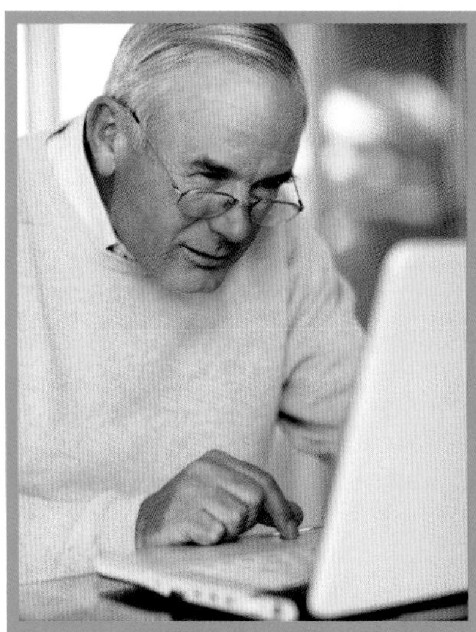

Learning to use new technologies in place of old ones is made easier by an increase in driving forces—such as the ability to contact friends and family worldwide, instantly and inexpensively.

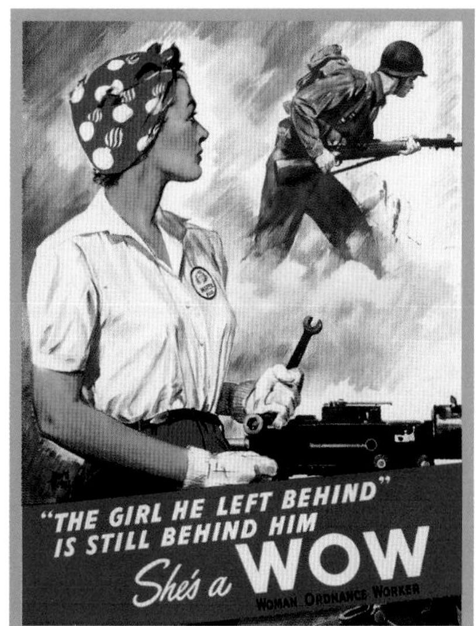

"THE GIRL HE LEFT BEHIND" IS STILL BEHIND HIM
She's a WOW
WOMAN ORDNANCE WORKER

During World War II, housewives were encouraged to change many of their beliefs, from the types of food and clothing that were acceptable to their capability to do "men's jobs."

feelings toward the change among employees, perhaps by delivering rewards for implementing the new skills or processes. For example, in the 1990s, Continental Airlines was forced to file for bankruptcy. In order to stay in business, the management implemented a major change: they shifted the company focus from saving costs to putting out a quality product that met high customer standards. They decided to reward employees for adopting the new policies and practices (to ensure compliance to the new priorities) by offering them a $65 bonus if the US Department of Transportation rated the company among the top five airlines. The use of Lewin's change model marked Continental's evolution from being the poorest-performing airline to being named Airline of the Year.

At the individual level, the freezing stage marks a time when new beliefs and practices are tested through trial and error; this either reinforces the changes or starts a new change cycle. For example, after a week of serving offal to her family, a wartime housewife might assess whether her family seems to enjoy the meat, whether they seem healthy, and whether other families seem to be judging her positively or negatively based on her meal choices. If the answers to these questions are positive, she will continue to serve offal at dinnertime. If, however, her children do not appear to be as healthy as they were when eating chicken or steak, or if other women are criticizing her choice of meat, she may decide to abandon offal and look for other ways to feed her family, starting the unfreezing and change processes all over again.

Lewin's pioneering experimental work into social systems has led him to be widely recognized as the founder of social psychology. He was the first psychologist to study "group dynamics" and organizational development in a methodical way. He applied rigorous social science to effect useful social transformation, and his work has been influential across the fields of experimental and social psychology. ■

There is nothing so practical as a good theory.
Kurt Lewin

Kurt Lewin

German-American psychologist Kurt Lewin was born in 1890 into a middle-class Jewish family in Mogilno, Poland (then Prussia). In 1905, his family moved to Berlin, where he studied medicine at the University of Freiburg before transferring to the University of Munich to study biology. During World War I, he served in the German army, but returned to Berlin to complete his PhD after being injured. He worked at the Psychological Institute, Berlin, from 1921 to 1933, when restrictions on the Jewish population compelled him to resign and seek refuge in the US. He began working at Cornell University, then moved to the University of Iowa where he became a professor. In 1944, he became director of the Center for Group Dynamics at the Massachusetts Institute of Technology, but died of a heart attack just three years later.

Key works

1935 *A Dynamic Theory of Personality*
1948 *Resolving Social Conflicts*
1951 *Field Theory in Social*

HOW STRONG IS THE URGE TOWARD SOCIAL CONFORMITY?

SOLOMON ASCH (1907–1996)

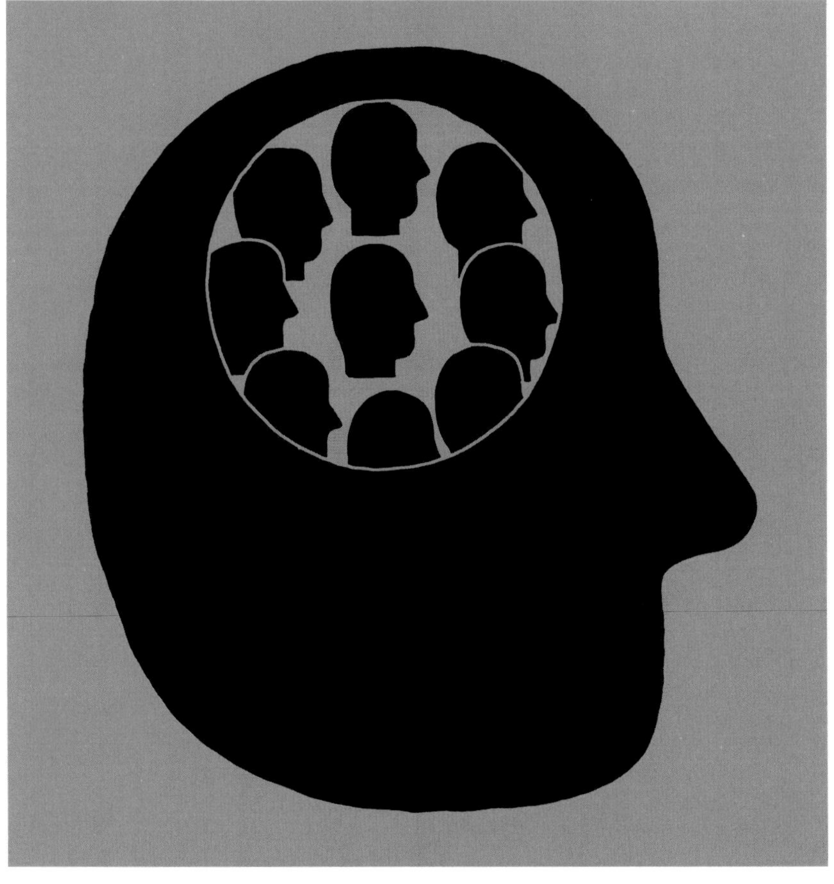

IN CONTEXT

APPROACH
Conformism

BEFORE
1880s Hippolyte Bernheim, a French physician, uses hypnosis to demonstrate the concept of "suggestibility."

1935 Muzafer Sherif's conformism experiment leads Asch to develop the Asch Paradigm.

AFTER
1963 Stanley Milgram's obedience experiments show that people conform for an authority figure despite experiencing a moral conflict.

1976 Serge Moscovici argues that a consistent minority can be influential.

1979 Knud S. Larsen, a Danish psychologist, shows that conformity may be tied to cultural climate.

Social psychologist Solomon Asch challenged our idea of ourselves as autonomous beings when he devised an experiment to demonstrate our urge to conform. His famous experiment showed that when people are confronted with a majority opinion, the tendency to conform may be stronger than their commitment to what they perceive to be true. He detailed his findings in his 1955 paper *Opinions and Social Pressure*, which also discusses the social influences that shape a person's beliefs, judgments, and practices. Asch wanted to investigate the effects of group pressure on individual decision-making, and

See also: Serge Moscovici 244–245 ▪ Stanley Milgram 252–259 ▪ Philip Zimbardo 260–261 ▪ Max Wertheimer 341 ▪ Muzafer Sherif 343–344

A group exerts **profound social effects** on its members.

A certain amount of **conformity** serves important social functions.

People feel **compelled** to conform in order to **fit in**.

They will pretend or even convince themselves that they **agree with the majority**.

Their tendency to conform can be **stronger** than their **values or basic perceptions**.

how and to what extent people's attitudes were influenced by social forces around them.

Turkish psychologist Muzafer Sherif set out to answer similar questions in 1935, using a visual illusion called the autokinetic effect, whereby a stationary spot of light seen in a dark room appears to move. He told the subjects of his study that he was going to move the light and asked them how far they thought it had shifted. Tested in groups, the participants' estimates converged into a group norm, revealing that they used others' estimates as a frame of reference in an ambiguous situation. Although Sherif believed that he had demonstrated the principles of conformity, Asch contended that—because there was no right or wrong answer to the task—no definitive conclusions could be drawn. Conformity, he believed, could only be measured in terms of an individual's tendency to agree with group members who unanimously give the wrong answer on a task that has an unambiguous solution. The simple perceptual task that became known as the Asch Paradigm was designed to offer this.

The Asch Paradigm

The experiment was conducted with 123 male subjects, each of whom was put individually into a »

Solomon Asch

Solomon Elliott Asch was a pioneer in the field of social psychology. He was born into a Jewish family in Warsaw (then part of the Russian Empire) in 1907. At the age of 13 he emigrated to the US and studied psychology. He received a PhD in 1932 from Columbia University, where he was influenced by Max Wertheimer.

Asch became a professor at Swarthmore College in 1947, and worked closely with Wolfgang Köhler. He held visiting posts at Massachusetts Institute of Technology (MIT) and Harvard, where he supervised Stanley Milgram's PhD, before moving to the University of Pennsylvania. His many awards include the Distinguished Scientific Contribution Award from the American Psychological Association. He died aged 88.

Key works

1951 *Effects of Group Pressure Upon the Modification and Distortion of Judgment*
1952 *Social Psychology*
1955 *Opinions and Social Pressure*
1956 *Studies of Independence and Conformity*

group of five to seven "confederates" (people who were aware of the real aims of the experiment but were introduced as fellow participants). The group was shown one card with a line on it, followed by another card with three lines labeled A, B, and C, and asked which one of those three lines was the same length as the line on the first card.

The room was always organized so that the subject would give either the last or the penultimate answer. Over the course of 18 trials, confederates were instructed to provide the correct answers for the first six, but then to give identical but incorrect answers for another 12. This was to test whether or not the subject would answer correctly or whether he would match his response to that of the confederates when all gave the same—incorrect—answer. Initially, Asch thought that only a few of the subjects would comply with the confederates' answers. After all, the task was simple and the answers obvious; during the pilot study in which there was no pressure to yield to an erroneous group, only three errors were made out of 720 total trials. The results of the actual study were surprising. When surrounded by a group of people all giving the same incorrect answer, subjects gave incorrect answers on almost a third (32 percent) of the questions; 75 percent of them provided an incorrect response for at least one question. One person complied with the group giving a wrong answer on 11 out of 12 trials. Because the task was both simple and unambiguous, these figures indicate a high degree of conformity by the subjects. However, not a single participant conformed on all critical trials, and 13 of the 50 participants (26 percent) never conformed.

The results proved that the subjects themselves were highly consistent. Those who broke away from the group opinion and provided an independent answer did not succumb to the majority even over many trials, while those who chose to comply with the majority seemed unable to break this pattern.

Explanations

To get a deeper understanding of his results, Asch interviewed his subjects to find out why they offered incorrect answers. Some said they wanted to go along with what they believed to be the experimenter's wishes and avoid upsetting the overall experiment. A few actually wondered if they were perhaps suffering from eye strain or were seated at a misleading angle. Some denied that they were aware of having given incorrect answers. Eventually, some admitted to knowing their answers were incorrect, adding that they did not want to stand out or appear different and foolish: they wanted to fit in.

"All the yielding subjects underestimated the frequency with which they conformed."
Solomon Asch

In the Asch Paradigm experiment, participants were given a visual test. They had to decide which of the three lines on the second card was the same length as the one on the first card. Each question was called a "trial" and there were 18 trials in all.

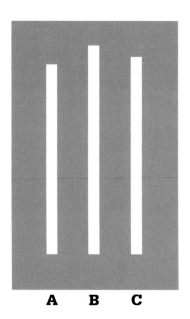

Asch also spoke to the subjects who had maintained correct and independent responses, and found that they had not been unresponsive to the majority, but had been able to recover from the doubt that they felt in order to give an honest account of what they saw.

Asch performed variations on the experiment to test what difference the size of the majority group made to levels of conformity. He found that just one confederate had virtually no influence on the subject's conformity, two had only a small influence, but three or more encouraged a relatively stable tendency to conform. Unanimity in the confederates' responses was a more powerful factor; but even if only one confederate offered an alternative answer, the subjects were much more likely to provide an independent (and correct) response. This finding highlights the power of even a very small dissenting minority. Furthermore, Asch discovered that if he allowed the participants to give their answers privately, by writing them down on a piece of paper, conformity noticeably decreased, and this held true even if the confederates were still giving their answers aloud.

US Senator Joseph McCarthy launched a Communist witch hunt during the 1950s, generating an environment of fear and high levels of political and social conformity.

Cultural norms

Some psychologists hypothesized that Asch's findings reflected the cultural climate of 1950s America during McCarthyism, when dissent was seen as anti-American and people were imprisoned for their opinions. Later studies found variations in levels of conformity. For instance, a study conducted in the early 1970s (a time of liberal, progressive thinking in the US) found far lower rates of conformity. However, a study in the late 1970s showed a return to higher rates.

Conformity rates for cultures worldwide also differ. Researchers found that individualist cultures such as the US, the UK, and other Western European countries, where personal choice and individual achievements are valued highly, show lower levels of conformity than collectivist cultures such as Japan, Fiji, and African countries, where group belonging is valued highly.

Psychologists have criticized Asch's methods on the grounds that he focused on a stripped-down version of group behavior that does not feature much interaction between participants, or that he was more focused on the individuals within a group than on the group dynamic. Others wonder if he overstated the power of the majority to influence the minority. Serge Moscovici, in particular, disagreed with Asch's analysis and argued that an active minority could influence the majority and bring about change. Moscovici was inspired to develop his own studies to demonstrate how a consistent minority can affect the thinking of the majority.

A member of a tribe of cannibals accepts cannibalism as altogether fitting and proper.
Solomon Asch

Although Asch acknowledges that social life requires some consensus, he also emphasizes that this is most productive when each individual contributes his independent insight and experience. Consensus should not come out of fear or conformity; the fact that he found the tendency to conform was strong even among intelligent people raised questions about societal values and the quality of education.

Asch's conclusions note the power (and danger) of social influence to shape a person's beliefs and behavior. If something becomes normal for a group, social pressure will ensure conformity. Inspired by Asch's theory, Stanley Milgram's experiment on obedience showed that ordinary people are capable of cruelty when under pressure to conform.

However, the majority of participants in Asch's study, even those who had conformed, stated that they valued independence of mind, leaving him optimistic about humanity. ■

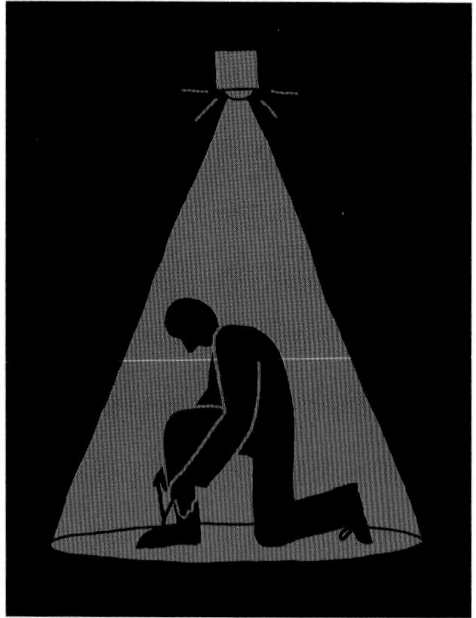

LIFE IS A DRAMATICALLY ENACTED THING

ERVING GOFFMAN (1922–1982)

IN CONTEXT

APPROACH
Impression management

BEFORE
1890 William James first makes the distinction between the private self-as-subject ("I") and the public self-as-object ("me").

1902 American sociologist Charles Cooley posits the looking-glass self theory, which states that the self is reflected in the reactions of other people.

AFTER
1990 US psychologists Mark Leary and Robin Kowalski define three ways in which impression management can increase well-being: belonging, self-enhancement, and self-understanding.

1995 Psychologist Sarah Hampson argues that our behavior changes according to who we are with, and different people bring out various aspects of our personality.

Social interaction is comparable to a theatrical play.

People, like actors, try to create a **favorable impression** of themselves through their choice of script, setting, wardrobe, skills, and props.

There are **"front stage"** areas for our public personas, and **"backstage"** areas for our private lives.

There is an **audience** for the performance.

Life is a dramatically enacted thing.

Devised by Erving Goffman, impression management is a theory that relates to how we create, maintain, and enhance our social identities. A fundamental aspect of social interaction, Goffman says, is that we try—either consciously or subconsciously—to manipulate and control the way that others perceive us. Whenever we interact with other people, we present a public image of ourselves. In some instances, we may be trying to influence a particular person (such as a job interviewer); in other situations, we may simply be trying to maintain a favorable image of ourselves. In his 1959 book, *The Presentation of Self in Everyday Life*, Goffman draws a parallel between impression management

See also: William James 38–45 ▪ William Glasser 246–247 ▪ Stanley Milgram 252–259 ▪ David D. McClelland 328–329 ▪ Walter Mischel 332–333

and theater, showing how the ways we present ourselves in the real world are similar to the performances of dramatic actors on stage. Each social interaction is driven as much toward having a particular effect on the audience as it is toward honest self-expression.

In fact, according to Goffman's theory, personality is the sum of the various roles that individuals play in their lives. This implies that the true self is not a private or internal phenomenon, but rather the dramatic effect of the ways in which people present themselves publicly. "Life is a dramatically enacted thing," Goffman says: creating a successful impression requires the right setting, props, wardrobe, skills, and a shared understanding of what constitutes being on stage (in the public sphere) versus backstage (in the personal, private sphere).

Performance skills

Goffman believes that in real life, everyone has the ability to choose their own stage, props, and costumes to display to the audience. The main goal of both the social actor and the onstage actor is to maintain a sense of coherence through interactions with other actors. This can only be achieved when everyone agrees upon the "definition of the situation," and on the characteristics, expectations, and limitations of a particular performance or interaction, signaling to each other the appropriate ways of reacting and fitting into the social setting.

To be in proper accord, people must agree on their personal identities, the social context, and the collective expectations of behavior within that context. For example, celebrities attending an elite party have all implicitly agreed to understand that they are "celebrities at an elite party"; each will accept their defined role in that situation and encourage other actors and observers (or audience members) alike to accept this definition. However, if the particular definition of the situation becomes discredited—for instance, if the food at the party turns out to be nothing more special than pizza, or there are noncelebrities also in attendance—there is a tendency for people to pretend that nothing has changed, thereby encouraging an artificial sense of believability in order to keep the peace or to avoid embarrassment.

Goffman himself was said to enjoy testing the limits of the rules that shaped encounters in restaurants, lecture theaters, and movie theater lines. ■

Hotel staff are "front stage" when they are interacting with the public. Their behavior may change, becoming less formal, when they are not on duty "backstage."

Erving Goffman

Erving Goffman, a Canadian sociologist and writer, was born in Mannville, Alberta. His ancestors were Ukrainian Jews who had emigrated to Canada. Goffman gained a bachelor's degree in sociology and anthropology at the University of Toronto, then obtained a master's and PhD in sociology at the University of Chicago. In 1962, he was made a full professor at the University of California, and by 1969 had published seven significant books. Tragedy struck in 1964 when his first wife died by suicide; Goffman wrote about this experience in his 1969 paper, *The Insanity of Place*. In 1981, he married again, and in 1982—despite being seen as something of a maverick—became president of the American Sociological Association. He died of stomach cancer just a few months later.

Key works

1959 *The Presentation of Self in Everyday Life*
1961 *Asylums*
1971 *Relations in Public*
1974 *Frame Analysis*

THE MORE ESPRIT DE CORPS THERE IS … THE GREATER THE DANGER OF GROUPTHINK

IRVING JANIS (1918–1990)

IN CONTEXT

APPROACH
Conformity

BEFORE
1952 Sociologist and journalist William H. Whyte Jr. coins the term "groupthink" to describe "a rationalized conformity … which holds that group values are not only expedient but right and good as well."

1955 Solomon Asch examines how far the desire to conform affects decision-making.

1961 Muzafer Sherif's study of boys at a summer camp shows the formation of "ingroups" and "outgroups."

AFTER
1963 Stanley Milgram's controversial experiments test the limits of subjects' obedience to authority.

1981 Bibb Latané develops his social impact theory describing how individuals can be sources or targets of social influence.

Coined in 1952 by William H. Whyte Jr., "groupthink" is a term to describe the way that, in decision-making, groups tend to place a higher value on conformity than on reaching the right conclusions. Although it was a widely accepted phenomenon, only later did psychologists begin to study groupthink. Conscious of its Orwellian connotations (George Orwell had used similar language in his dystopian novel, *1984*), Irving Janis adopted the term and pioneered research into it, analyzing its causes and symptoms.

Taking as examples US foreign-policy decisions such as the failed invasion of Cuba in 1961, he showed how, in order to minimize conflict, groups tended to strive for consensus without adequately examining the options. This urge for conformity, he argued, prevented independent thinking and critical analysis and led sometimes to disastrously simplistic decisions.

While acknowledging the benefits of group decision-making, such as discussion and debate, Janis saw that social influences within the group could put these at risk. He identified several features that could lead to groupthink and stifle creative thought and debate, not least of which was the severity and urgency of the situation being considered: in a crisis, consensus is often paramount. But equally important as sources of groupthink are the relationships within the group, the nature of its leadership, and whether the group members form a cohesive social unit, with individuals feeling that they are equal partners. In addition to these causes of groupthink, Janis listed the typical features of groups liable to fall into this trap, such as a large element of self-delusion—especially

Janis warned that the greater the social cohesion and camaraderie within a group, the greater the danger of groupthink.

See also: Kurt Lewin 222–227 ▪ Solomon Asch 228–231 ▪ Stanley Milgram 252–259 ▪ Philip Zimbardo 260–261 ▪ Muzafer Sherif 343–344

The advantages of having decisions made by groups are often lost … when the members … face a crisis situation.
Irving Janis

the illusion that the group's view is unanimous—and the belief that this unanimous view is undoubtedly right and good. Having claimed the moral high ground, the group not only considers itself justified in its decisions, but also acquires a degree of invulnerability and will collectively rationalize its position in the face of any warnings. To maintain this unanimity, however, pressure is brought to bear on any dissent from the consensus, and individual members feel the need to self-censor rather than voice their disagreement. Thus is an "ingroup" free of dissent created. To protect itself from criticism or information that might upset its consensus, the ingroup will characterize any group with conflicting opinions as rivals or enemies—reinforcing the ingroup's esprit de corps.

Wider applications

Janis's work on groupthink was based on decision-making by government departments but is equally applicable to many other groups, such as corporate boards and teams in competitive sports. With the vastly increased influence of the internet and especially social media, however, the scope of groups has broadened. Groups on platforms such as Facebook, Instagram, and TikTok can instill a false sense of camaraderie that allows elements of groupthink to thrive among large numbers of people, stifling critical thinking and influencing their opinions and attitudes. ▪

We are often **reluctant to disagree** with our friends.

→ We are also often eager to be **seen as team players**.

→ The urge to **"go with the flow"** can override our true opinions and feelings.

→ The more **amiability** and **esprit de corps** there is, the greater the danger that **independent critical thinking** will be **replaced by groupthink**.

Irving Janis

Born in Buffalo, New York, in 1918, Irving Janis graduated from the University of Chicago in 1939 and went on to gain a PhD from Columbia University in New York. When the US entered World War II, he was drafted into the army, applying his knowledge of psychology in studies of morale among the troops. After the war, he pursued an academic career, becoming a teacher at Yale University in 1947, where he remained until his retirement. While at Yale, he worked primarily in the field of social psychology, earning several prestigious awards for his contributions to the study of decision-making and group dynamics. He is best known for his work, beginning in the 1960s, on the phenomenon of "groupthink." He retired from Yale in 1985 and moved to California, where he was appointed Adjunct Professor of Psychology Emeritus at the University of California, Berkeley. He died, aged 72, of lung cancer in Santa Rosa, California, in 1990.

Key works

1969 *Personality: Dynamics, Development, and Assessment*
1972 *Victims of Groupthink: A Psychological Study of Foreign-Policy Decisions and Fiascoes*
1989 *Crucial Decisions: Leadership in Policymaking and Crisis Management*

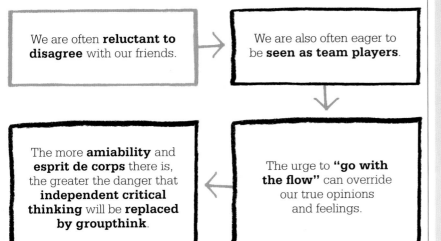

THE MORE YOU SEE IT THE MORE YOU LIKE IT

ROBERT ZAJONC (1923–2008)

IN CONTEXT

APPROACH
Familiarity

BEFORE
1876 German experimental psychologist Gustav Fechner suggests familiarity increases positive feeling toward art objects, but "supersaturation" leads to aversion.

1910 Edward B. Titchener documents the mere exposure effect, describing it as a "glow of warmth" that people experience in the presence of familiar things.

AFTER
1971 Psychologists T. T. Faw and D. Pien find that adults and children prefer unfamiliar line drawings and patterns to familiar ones.

1989 Robert Bornstein finds that the mere exposure effect is strongest when unfamiliar stimuli are presented briefly.

Repeated exposure to a stimulus breeds **familiarity** with it.

Familiarity brings about an **attitude change** toward the stimulus …

… taking the form of **preference**, **or affection**.

This preference is emotional and forms on a **subconscious level** before a person is even aware of it.

The more you see it, the more you like it.

Until the middle of the 20th century, social scientists tended to base their explanations of human behavior on environmental factors. However, the Polish-born psychologist Robert Zajonc believed that to develop a more complete understanding, it is necessary to take into account the functions of the mind as well. Zajonc's main interest was in the relationship between feeling and thought—the intersection of emotion and cognition—and he devoted much of his career toward exploring which of these factors has a stronger influence on behavior. To this end, he performed a seminal experiment in 1968 that led to his discovery of the "mere exposure effect," which is arguably his best-known contribution to the field of social psychology.

Familiarity experiments

Mere exposure, Zajonc explained, simply refers to a condition in which the given stimulus is accessible to the subject's perception, either consciously or subconsciously. The effects of mere exposure had been documented previously by the psychologist Edward B. Titchener who, in 1910, described the "glow of warmth" and feeling of intimacy that a person experiences in the presence of something familiar. However, Titchener's hypothesis was rejected at the time, and the idea faded into relative obscurity.

Zajonc's interest in the effect was aroused by a newspaper article that described a curious experiment that took place at Oregon State University in 1967. The article stated that a "mysterious student" had been attending class for two months, enveloped in a black bag. The professor, Charles Goetzinger, knew the identity of the person

See also: Leon Festinger 166–169 ▪ Edward B. Titchener 340 ▪ Stanley Schachter 345

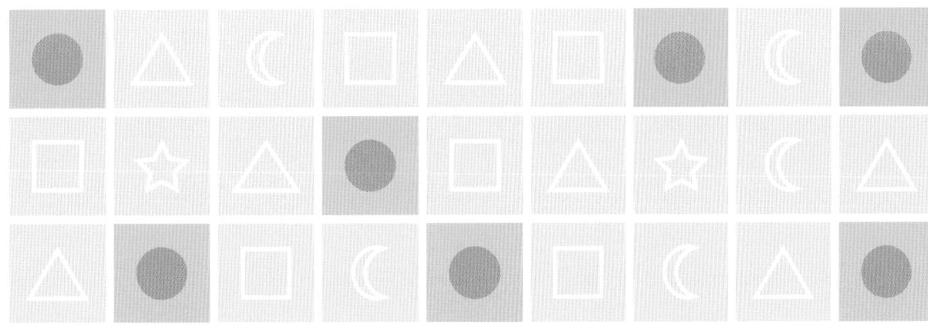

Zajonc's 1968 experiment tested the mere exposure effect by showing people slides of symbols with uneven rates of repetition; the more frequently someone saw a symbol, the more they claimed to like it.

inside, but none of the class had any idea who it might be. Goetzinger then observed the class to gauge their reactions over time. Initially, the students treated the black bag with hostility, but this softened in time and they were eventually friendly and even protective toward the person in the bag. Goetzinger noted that the students' attitude gradually "changed from hostility toward the black bag to curiosity and finally to friendship."

Zajonc's groundbreaking paper, *Attitudinal Effects of Mere Exposure*, was published in *The Journal of Personality and Social Psychology* in 1968. Zajonc's paper describes a series of experiments in which he showed participants a sequence of random images—geometric shapes, Chinese symbols, paintings, and pictures of faces—that were flashed in front of them so rapidly that they were unable to discern which were shown repeatedly. When subjects were later asked which images they preferred, they consistently chose the ones to which they had been most frequently exposed, although they were not consciously aware of this fact. What Zajonc seemed to have discovered was that familiarity brings about an attitude change, breeding affection or some form of preference for the familiar stimulus. This increases with exposure: the greater your number of exposures to something, the more affection you will feel toward it. To put it simply, "the more you see it, the more you like it."

Researchers into the mere exposure phenomenon since Zajonc's experiment have found that it is even possible to recreate this effect using sound rather than images. In 1974, the social psychologist D. W. Rajecki used fertile chicken eggs as test subjects, playing tones of different frequencies to different groups of eggs before they hatched, and then playing these tones to both groups of chicks again after hatching. Without exception, the chicks preferred the tones that had been played to them prenatally.

Preferences are not rational

Zajonc's findings indicate that this preference for familiar things is based purely on the history of exposure to it, and is not affected by a person's expressed personal beliefs or attitudes. This holds true even when exposures take place only on the subliminal level, when subjects are completely unaware that they are being presented with a stimulus. This discovery led to Zajonc's claim that "preferences need no inferences," meaning that affectionate feeling is not based on reasoned judgement. This is contrary to what most of us might imagine to be the case.

In a paper called *Feeling and Thinking*, written in 1980, Zajonc argued that feelings and thoughts are actually very independent of one another. Feelings not only precede thoughts during a person's complex response to a stimulus, but are actually the most powerful determinants of a person's attitudes and decisions. This paper was widely debated, and it helped to bring the study of emotion back to the forefront of Western psychology, in part because the theory bears »

Novelty is commonly associated with uncertainty and conflict—states that are more likely to produce negative than positive affect.
Robert Zajonc

The advertising industry has always attributed to exposure formidable advertising potential.
Robert Zajonc

Repeated exposure to a brand can create a liking for it, even when it is presented without any factual information and requires no decision-making from the person viewing it.

important implications for the study of decision-making processes. It suggests that, contrary to what we may believe, it is not reason and logic that guide our decisions; in fact, we make fast, instinctive, emotion-based decisions before we have even had a chance to consider the choice cognitively—we make judgments without information. If this is true, it follows that our logical reasoning merely justifies and rationalizes the decisions we have already made, rather than actually serving to inform the choice in the first place.

The form of experience that we came to call "feeling" accompanies all cognitions.
Robert Zajonc

Zajonc concludes that "affect is always present as a companion to thought, whereas the converse is not true for cognition." We can never think about something without a feeling attached; as Zajonc says, we do not just see "a house," we see "a handsome house" or "a pretentious house." Every perception we have contains some affect, or feeling. The primacy of affect over cognition is also apparent in memory, he says, as Frederick Bartlett noted in his book, *Remembering*: "When a subject is being asked to remember, very often the first thing that emerges is something of the nature of attitude."

Interpersonal attraction

The impact of the mere exposure effect extends beyond the confines of the laboratory, and out into the area of interpersonal attraction. In this context, the phenomenon is referred to as the "propinquity effect," the way we tend to form friendships or romantic relationships with people we see regularly. One explanation for this focuses on evolution: when animals are exposed to something for the first time, they often respond with fear and aggression, but repeated exposures—during which the animal realizes the perceived threat does not materialize—lead to a reduction in negative responses. Zajonc explored this notion further with human subjects, discovering that people form very negative attitudes toward an imaginary group of unfamiliar people, attributing unpleasant qualities to them for no apparent reason other than the fact that they are complete strangers. However, as with shapes and symbols, repeated exposure is shown to increase trust and affection.

Another explanation for the propinquity effect focuses on the many factors involved in interpersonal attraction, which include familiarity, similarity of attitudes, physical attraction, and reciprocal affection. Frequent interactions between people may not only increase the level of familiarity, but also provide an increasing impression of similarity, thereby breeding positive feelings and ultimately attraction.

Exposure and advertising

Advertising is another arena in which the mere exposure effect plays a crucial role, although the picture here is less clear. Research seems to suggest that repeated exposure to a brand or corporate name would boost sales, but this assumption is evidently overly simplistic, as it doesn't take into account other possible effects of frequent exposure.

One study used banner ads to test the mere exposure effect on college-aged students. Subjects were presented with an article to read on a computer screen while banner ads flashed along the top of the screen. The results indicated that those who had been exposed more frequently to the banner ads did indeed rate the ads more favorably than those who had seen it less frequently or not at all. However, another study found that familiarity with a brand name can create an ambivalent attitude. This may be because people have both good and bad associations with familiar companies, and all of these associations are brought to mind with frequent exposure, leading to greater ambivalence. As a result, it is unclear whether mere familiarity, created through repeated advertising, is good for sales.

Familiar faces

Zajonc found that not only does exposure influence how a person feels about someone, but it can even change the way a person looks over time. With a group of colleagues, he conducted a study to find out whether the faces of spouses appear more similar after 25 years together. They compared photographs of couples taken during their first year of marriage with those taken 25 years later, and found that couples looked more alike after many years of being together. After ruling out several other potential explanations, the researchers decided that empathy was the most likely cause. Time had increased the couple's empathy for each other, and since human emotion is communicated through facial expressions, they may have begun to mimic each others' expressions in the process of empathizing, resulting in similar wrinkle patterns over time.

Known for the breadth of his work on the basic processes of social behavior, Zajonc helped to create the modern field of social psychology. He used his work on thought and feeling to explore issues such as racism, genocide, and terrorism, hoping that research could ultimately help to prevent war and human suffering. ■

Couples grow to resemble each other over time because they express empathy through reflecting each other's facial expressions; this leads to the formation of similar facial lines.

Robert Zajonc

Robert Zajonc was born in Lodz, Poland. When he was 16 his family fled to Warsaw during the Nazi invasion of Poland. Two weeks later, their building was bombed and both of his parents were killed. He spent six months recuperating in a hospital, after which he was arrested by Nazi soldiers and sent to a German labor camp. He escaped with two other prisoners and walked 200 miles (320km) to France only to be recaptured and imprisoned again. He broke out for a final time and made his way to the UK.

After World War II, Zajonc moved to the US, where he established himself as an eminent psychologist, gaining psychology degrees to PhD level at the University of Michigan. He worked there until his retirement in 1994, when he became an emeritus professor at Stanford University. Zajonc died of pancreatic cancer at the age of 85.

Key works

1968 *Attitudinal Effects of Mere Exposure*
1975 *Birth Order and Intellectual Development*
1980 *Feeling and Thinking*

WHO LIKES COMPETENT WOMEN?

JANET TAYLOR SPENCE (1923–2015)

IN CONTEXT

APPROACH
Gender studies

BEFORE
1961 Albert Bandura develops social learning theory, which suggests that boys and girls behave differently because they are treated differently.

1970 Robert Helmreich and Elliot Aronson publish a study showing that men find competent men more likeable than incompetent ones.

AFTER
1992 US psychologist Alice Eagly finds that women are evaluated more negatively when they display leadership in a traditionally masculine way.

2003 Simon Baron-Cohen suggests the female brain is predominantly hardwired for empathy, whereas the male brain is hardwired for understanding systems.

Until the women's liberation movement took hold in the 1970s, Janet Taylor Spence's research had focused primarily on anxiety. However, after reading a study conducted by two of her colleagues about how competence in men correlated with likability, the American psychologist turned to issues relating to gender. Noticing that the study did not consider women, she decided to conduct a similar study that focused entirely on women. The resulting paper—*Who likes competent women?*—was published in 1972.

Working with Robert Helmreich, Taylor Spence set out to test whether men and women preferred competent women to incompetent ones. The two psychologists suspected that only people who believed in sexual equality would prefer competence. To test their hypothesis, they designed the Attitudes Toward Women Scale, which assesses attitudes toward the roles and rights of women by asking questions about education, marriage, professional life, habits, intellectual leadership, and social and economic freedom. The results were surprising. Contrary to the researchers' expectations, subjects not only preferred more competent to less competent women, but even awarded the highest ratings to the women who were competent in stereotypically masculine ways.

This landmark study was seminal in launching gender research as a subcategory within the field of social psychology. ■

Even our conservative subjects … rated highest the woman who was competent in stereotypically masculine areas.
Janet Taylor Spence

See also: Sigmund Freud 92–99 ▪ Guy Corneau 155 ▪ Eleanor E. Maccoby 292–293 ▪ Albert Bandura 294–299

FLASHBULB MEMORIES ARE FIRED BY EVENTS OF HIGH EMOTIONALITY

ROGER BROWN (1925–1997)

IN CONTEXT

APPROACH
Memory studies

BEFORE
1890 William James makes a distinction between short-term (primary) memory and long-term (secondary) memory.

1932 Frederic Bartlett's studies show that recollective memory is not simply a matter of retrieval; it is an active reconstruction of past events.

AFTER
1982 US psychologist Ulric Neisser argues that flashbulb memories do not use a special mechanism and can be inaccurate due to multiple "rehearsals" after the event.

1987 In *Autobiographical Memory,* American psychologist David Rubin suggests that we remember landmark events that define us as people.

In the late 1970s, Harvard University professor Roger Brown co-wrote a paper called *Flashbulb Memories* that became the classic study on a memory phenomenon. Brown and his colleague, James Kulik, coined this term to refer to a special kind of autobiographical memory in which people give a highly detailed, vivid account of the exact moment that they learned about an event with a high shock value.

The paper argues that culturally and personally significant events, such as the shooting of John F. Kennedy or Martin Luther King, trigger the operation of a special biological memory mechanism ("now print") that creates a permanent record of the event and the circumstances in which we first become aware of it. Almost like a flash photograph, we can picture where we were, who we were with, and what we were doing when we heard the shocking news—such as the destruction of the twin towers on 9/11. Brown and Kulik claim these memories are vivid, accurate, and enduring. However, researchers such as Ulric Neisser have contested the special mechanism theory, proposing that the memories' durability stems from the fact that they are thought about (or rehearsed) repeatedly after the event, by the individual and the wider world, and so are continually reinforced within memory. ■

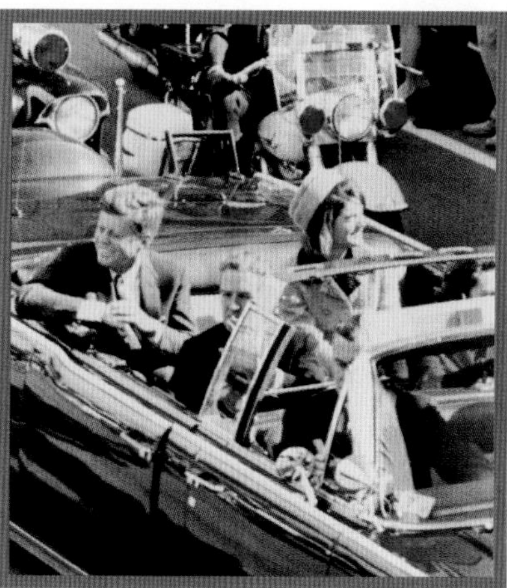

The assassination of President John F. Kennedy in 1963 was shocking and culturally significant. Brown claims these kinds of events cause the formation of "flashbulb" memories.

See also: William James 38–45 ▪ Jerome Bruner 164–165 ▪ Endel Tulving 186–191 ▪ Frederic Bartlett 342 ▪ Ulric Neisser 345

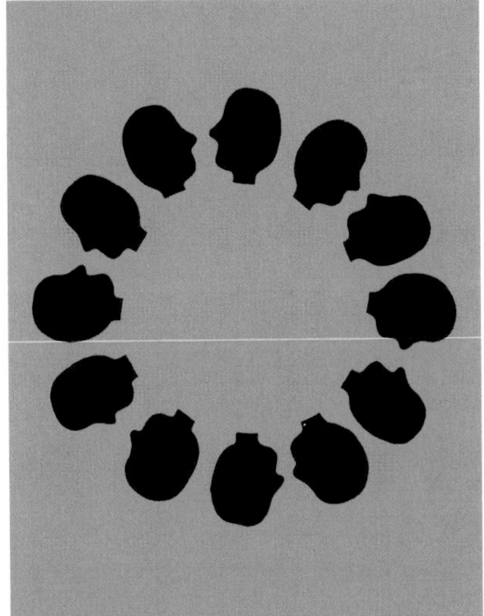

THE GOAL IS NOT TO ADVANCE KNOWLEDGE, BUT TO BE IN THE KNOW

SERGE MOSCOVICI (1925–2014)

IN CONTEXT

APPROACH
Social constructivism

BEFORE
1807 German philosopher Georg Hegel says that our ideas and values are fashioned by the *zeitgeist*, or spirit of the age, which constantly changes through the reconciliation of opposing views.

1927 German physicist Werner Heisenberg's "Uncertainty Principle" reveals that the observer affects the observed.

1973 American psychologist Kenneth Gergen writes *Social Psychology as History*, which marks the emergence of social constructivism.

AFTER
1978 In his zone of proximal development theory, Lev Vygotsky puts forward the idea that learning is fundamentally a socially mediated activity.

We overhear something that **arouses our curiosity**.

This **merges** with other things we know or have experienced.

We chatter about this with other people and **share our thoughts**.

Everyone is eager to transmit knowledge and **keep a place in the circle of conversation**.

The **collective conversations** continue, allowing everyone to know more.

Attitudes become organized and **values become established**.

Society begins to use new phrases and visions to describe a **collective common sense**.

The goal is not to advance knowledge, but to be "in the know."

See also: Friedrich Herbart 24–25 ▪ Kurt Lewin 222–227 ▪ Solomon Asch 228–231 ▪ Lev Vygotsky 278

In the late 1960s, some social psychologists, known as the social constructivists, argued that the voice of ordinary people was being lost from psychological research. The concern was that individuals were wrongly being portrayed as merely perceiving their social worlds rather than actually constructing them. In order to counteract these worrying trends, social psychologist Serge Moscovici conducted a piece of research that became a classic study of the way people absorb ideas and understand their world.

In his study, *Psychoanalysis: its image and its public*, published in France in 1961, Moscovici explored the belief that all thought and understanding is based on the workings of "social representations." These are the many concepts, statements, and explanations that are created in the course of everyday interactions and communications between people. They allow us to orientate ourselves in our social and material worlds and provide us with the means to communicate within a community. They are, in effect, a collective "common sense"—a shared version of reality—that is built through the mass media, science, religion, and interaction between social groups.

To test his theory, Moscovici looked at how the concepts of psychoanalytic theory had been absorbed within France since World War II. He studied mass-market publications and conducted interviews, searching for evidence of the type of information that had been floating around the collective consciousness. He discovered that psychoanalytic theory had trickled down both in the form of "high culture" and as popular common sense: people thought about and discussed complex psychoanalytic concepts in a way that seemed quite normal, but on the whole they were using simplified versions.

Molding common sense

The translation of difficult concepts into accessible and more easily transmissible language is not problematic, Moscovici contends, because "the goal is not to advance knowledge, but to be in the know"; to be an active participant in the collective circuit. The process allows the unfamiliar to become familiar and paves the way for science to become common sense. In this way, social representations provide a framework for groups of people to make sense of the world. They also affect how people treat each other within societies. For example, when debate arises over a potentially "controversial" social issue—such as the integration of immigrant people into a community—the impact and importance of social representations becomes apparent.

Moscovici insists that social representations are genuine forms of knowledge in their own right, not diluted versions of higher-level information. In fact, he makes it clear that these everyday thoughts (rather than the more abstract, scientific versions) are significant, because "shared representations are there to set up and build a common 'reality,' a common sense which becomes 'normal.'" ▪

Serge Moscovici

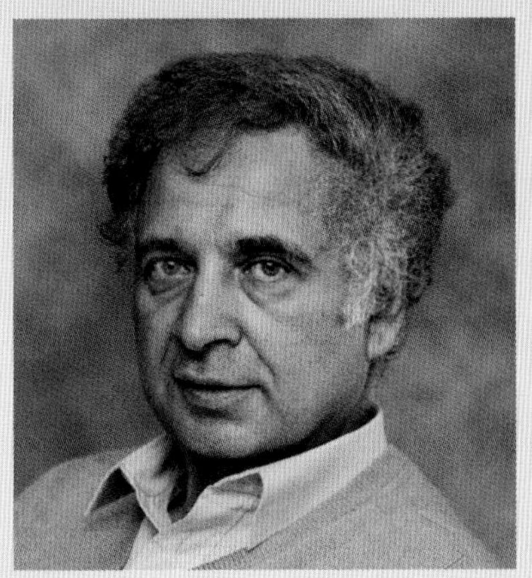

Born Srul Hersh Moskovitch to a Jewish family in Braila, Romania, Serge Moscovici attended school in Bucharest but was expelled due to antisemitic laws. After surviving the violent pogrom of 1941, in which hundreds of Jewish people were tortured and murdered, he and his father moved constantly around the country. He learned French during World War II, and co-founded an art journal, *Da*, which was banned due to censorship laws. In 1947, he left Romania and traveled via "displaced persons" camps until he reached France a year later.

In 1949, he gained a degree in psychology, then a PhD under the supervision of Daniel Lagache, with the support of a refugee grant. He co-founded the European Laboratory of Social Psychology in 1965, and as a professor of psychology he taught in prestigious universities across the US and Europe.

Key works

1961 *Psychoanalysis*
1976 *Social Influence and Social Change*
1981 *The Age of the Crowd*

WE ARE BY NATURE SOCIAL BEINGS

WILLIAM GLASSER (1925–2013)

CONTEXT

APPROACH
Choice theory

BEFORE
c.350 BCE Greek philosopher Aristotle says we are driven by three things: sensual appetite, anger, and *boulesis*, the rational desire for what is beneficial.

1943 Clark L. Hull says that all human behavior comes from four primary drives: hunger, thirst, sex, and the avoidance of pain.

1973 US scientist William T. Powers develops perceptual control theory (PCT), which suggests that our behavior is how we control our perceptions in order to keep them close to internally fixed reference levels.

AFTER
2000 US psychiatrist Peter Breggin publishes *Reclaiming Our Children*, criticizing the use of psychiatric drugs as "cures" for troubled children.

William Glasser openly rejected conventional psychiatry and the use of medication, claiming that most of the mental and psychological problems that people experience are actually on a spectrum of healthy human experience, and can be improved through changes in behavior. His ideas focus on achieving greater happiness and fulfilment through personal choice, responsibility, and transformation.

In 1965, he developed "reality therapy," a cognitive-behavioral, problem-solving approach to treatment that encourages clients to seek what they really want in the present moment, and to assess whether or not the behaviors

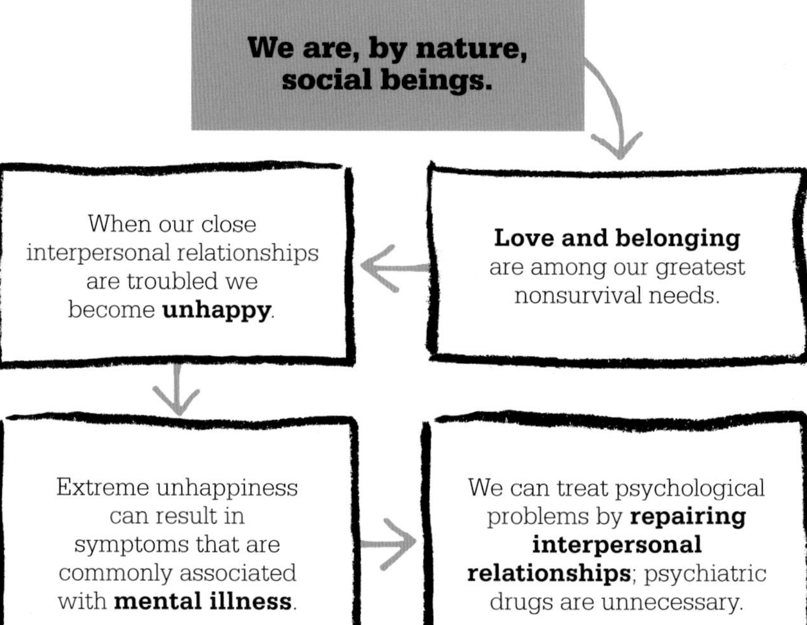
We are, by nature, social beings.
Love and belonging are among our greatest nonsurvival needs.
When our close interpersonal relationships are troubled we become unhappy.
Extreme unhappiness can result in symptoms that are commonly associated with mental illness.
We can treat psychological problems by repairing interpersonal relationships; psychiatric drugs are unnecessary.

See also: Emil Kraepelin 31 ▪ Sigmund Freud 92–99 ▪ David Rosenhan 334–335 ▪ Clark L. Hull 341

that they have chosen are bringing them closer to or further away from achieving their goals.

Choice theory

Over decades of practicing reality therapy, Glasser realized that his entire approach was based on the idea of people actively identifying what they want to do in order to be fulfilled, and this led him to develop "choice theory." This theory holds that we are all motivated to act in ways that increase pleasure and decrease pain—we want to think and behave in ways that will make us feel better. All pleasure and pain, he says, derives from our efforts to satisfy five genetically encoded needs: survival, love and belonging, power, freedom, and fun. Any behavior that satisfies one of these is pleasurable, and any that fails to do so is a source of pain, and ultimately, he explains, it is only through human relationships that we can satisfy these needs. When we are struggling to survive, the help of another makes us feel good; in order to feel love and belonging, we need at least one good relationship; to sense even the least of our power, we need someone to listen to what we say; to feel free, we must feel free from the control of others; and while it is possible to have fun on our own, it is much easier with other people. For these reasons, he argues, "we are, by nature, social beings."

Improving our relationships is improving our mental health.
William Glasser

Interpersonal strife with those close to us leads to rifts and resentments that produce symptoms of mental illness; these problems are, in fact, the logical consequences of troubled relationships.

Glasser emphasizes that lasting psychological problems are usually caused by problems in our personal relationships (rather than signifying a biochemical abnormality in the brain), and distress can be remedied through repairing these relationships without recourse to psychiatric drugs. He points toward the basic human need for power, which we try to satisfy by attempting to control other people. In fact, the only thing that we can control is the way we behave and think; we cannot control others. Trying to, he says, shows a lack of respect for others and is the cause of unhappiness. Choice theory is a self-control psychology designed to counteract this tendency and to help us find happiness within our relationships. ■

William Glasser

William Glasser was born in Cleveland, Ohio, in 1925. Originally trained as a chemical engineer, he attended medical school in Cleveland and trained in psychiatry in Los Angeles. He began practicing in 1957. Through the writings on perceptual control theory (PCT) by William T. Powers, Glasser was introduced to control theory systems. In 1967, Glasser founded the Institute for Reality Therapy in California (later renamed the William Glasser Institute), which trains students in choice theory. His approach is taught in more than 28 countries, and he has written on mental illness, counseling, and how to improve schools. He was the recipient of many awards, including the "A Legend in Counseling Award" and the Master Therapist designation by the American Psychiatric Association.

Key works

1965 *Reality Therapy*
1969 *Schools Without Failure*
1998 *Choice Theory*
2003 *Warning: Psychiatry Can Be Hazardous to Your Mental Health*

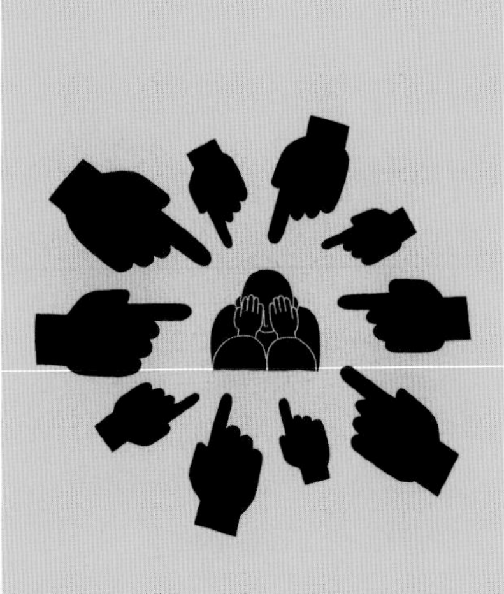

WE BELIEVE PEOPLE GET WHAT THEY DESERVE

MELVIN LERNER (1929–)

IN CONTEXT

APPROACH
Attribution theory

BEFORE
1958 Austrian psychologist Fritz Heider investigates the attribution process, or how people judge the factors that influence a situation.

1965 American psychologists Edward E. Jones and Keith Davis argue that the goal of attribution is to discover how behavior and intention reveal a person's basic nature.

AFTER
1971 US sociologist William J. Ryan coins the phrase "victim blaming," exposing how it is used to justify racism and social injustice.

1975 American psychologists Zick Rubin and Letitia Peplau find that firm believers in a "Just World" tend to be more authoritarian, more religious, and more admiring of existing social and political institutions.

People want to believe that they live in a safe, stable, and **orderly world** …

… where "bad" things only happen to "bad" people, and only "good" things happen to "good" people.

People blame the **victims of misfortune** in order to protect themselves from feeling **vulnerable**.

People operate under the assumption that "people get what they deserve" and deserve what they get.

People are most comfortable when they have a sense of control over their lives. We need to believe that we live in a world where the good are rewarded and the bad are punished, and this contributes significantly to our sense that it is possible to predict, guide, and ultimately control events. This "Just-World hypothesis" is a tendency to believe that "people get what they deserve." But, according to Melvin Lerner, this is a dangerous misconception that places undue importance on the supposed character traits of the people involved rather than on the actual facts of a situation. If someone is suffering or being punished, we find it easier to believe that that person must have done something to deserve such treatment. The Just-World theory becomes a comforting rationalization of seemingly inexplicable events and stops the world from appearing chaotic or random. It also allows people to believe that as long as

See also: Dorothy Rowe 154 ▪ Elizabeth Loftus 202–207

Homelessness, like many other social problems, is much easier to tolerate or be indifferent to if you believe that people are ultimately responsible for their own misfortunes.

they are "good," only "good" things will happen to them, generating a false sense of safety and control.

In his book, *The Belief in a Just World*, Lerner argued that we ask children to "be good" and promise them that in return for effectively putting their natural impulses and desires to one side, they will be rewarded in the future. For this contract to be fulfilled, we must live in a just world, so children grow into adults with this belief firmly in place.

Victim-blaming

In a 1965 study, Lerner found that students who were told that a fellow student had won the lottery rationalized this event by believing that the winner must have worked harder than his peers. It seems that belief in a Just World allows people to adjust the facts of a situation. This can be especially damaging when applied to the way we might view victims of crime or abuse. In rape cases, for example, it is often suggested that the female victim was "asking for it" because she wore a short skirt or was flirtatious, effectively absolving the perpetrator of responsibility and placing it in the hands of the victim. By blaming the victim, outsiders also protect their own sense of safety.

Lerner did emphasize, however, that belief in a Just World does not always lead to victim-blaming. The seeming innocence, attractiveness, status, and degree of similarity of the victim to those assessing them can affect whether or not people are held responsible for their misfortune.

Lerner's hypothesis became the foundation of important research into social justice. It also sparked debate over the effects of a Just-World approach to life. Does it help people stand up to difficulties? It may instead stimulate the feeling that any wrongdoing, however minor or unintentional, leads to disaster—a belief that Australian psychologist Dorothy Rowe has suggested can lead to an increased susceptibility to depression. ■

People need to believe they live in a Just World.
Melvin Lerner

Melvin Lerner

A pioneer of the psychological study of justice, Melvin Lerner studied social psychology at New York University, receiving his doctorate in 1957. He then moved to Stanford University, California, where he studied for his post-doctorate in clinical psychology.

From 1970 to 1994, Lerner taught social psychology at the University of Waterloo in Canada. He has also lectured at a number of universities in the US and Europe, including the University of California, Washington University, and the universities of Utrecht and Leiden in the Netherlands.

Lerner was editor of the journal *Social Justice Research*, and in 2008 was given a Lifetime Achievement Award by the International Society for Justice Research. He is a visiting scholar at Florida Atlantic University.

Key works

1980 *The Belief in a Just World: A Fundamental Delusion*
1981 *The Justice Motive in Social Behavior: Adapting to Times of Scarcity and Change*
1996 *Current Concerns about Social Justice*

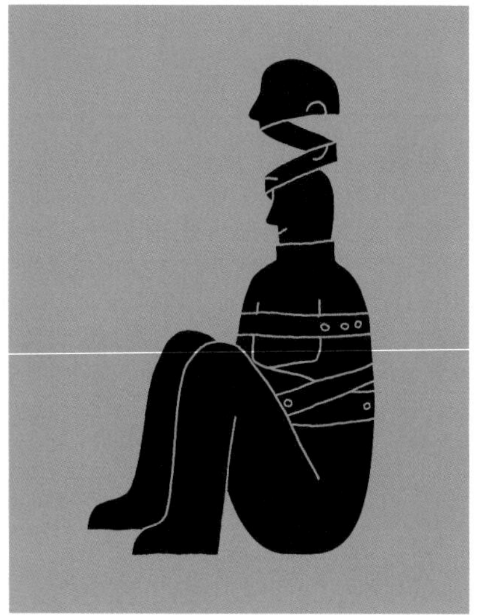

PEOPLE WHO DO CRAZY THINGS ARE NOT NECESSARILY CRAZY

ELLIOT ARONSON (1932–)

IN CONTEXT

APPROACH
Attitude change

BEFORE
1956 Social psychologist Leon Festinger states his theory of cognitive dissonance, which posits that having inconsistent beliefs causes uncomfortable psychological tension.

1968 The My Lai Massacre of civilians in Vietnam takes place, possibly because US soldiers dehumanized victims to reduce cognitive dissonance.

AFTER
1978 Elliot Aronson devises the jigsaw method of learning, involving highly interdependent small-group learning, to reduce prejudice and violence at school.

1980s Psychologists argue that dissonance experiments may not reflect real attitude changes, but a desire to seem consistent and hence socially acceptable.

In his 1972 book, *The Social Animal*, Elliot Aronson puts forward "Aronson's First Law:" people who do crazy things are not necessarily crazy. The "crazy things" he refers to include acts of violence, cruelty, or deep prejudice—acts so extreme that they seem to reflect a psychological imbalance on the part of the perpetrator. Aronson, however, argues that although psychotic people certainly exist, even people who are generally psychologically healthy can be driven to such extremes of human behavior that they appear insane. It

In some situations, sane people do crazy things.

If we are unaware of the **social circumstances** that prompted their actions …

… we are tempted to conclude that they are caused by a **deficiency in character** or **insanity**.

We must remember that people who do crazy things are not necessarily crazy.

See also: Leon Festinger 166–169 ▪ Solomon Asch 228–231 ▪ Melvin Lerner 248–249 ▪ Stanley Milgram 252–259 ▪ Philip Zimbardo 260–261

is therefore important that, before diagnosing people as psychotic, social psychologists make every effort to understand the situations people have been facing and the pressures that were operating on them when the abnormal behavior took place.

Cognitive dissonance

To illustrate his point, Aronson cites an incident that took place at Kent State University, Ohio, in 1970 in which members of the Ohio National Guard shot and killed four unarmed students, wounding nine others. Some of these students had been protesting against the American invasion of Cambodia, but others were simply crossing the campus. The reason for the shootings remains ambiguous, but the fact that it was tragically unnecessary is clear. However, in the aftermath, one Ohio schoolteacher (as well as National Guard members) asserted that the students had deserved to die, and rumors spread quickly that the slain girls were either pregnant, had syphilis, or were filthy. Aronson argues that these rumors, though false, did not reflect the beliefs of psychotic minds, but rather the attempt of pressured and conflicted minds to find relief.

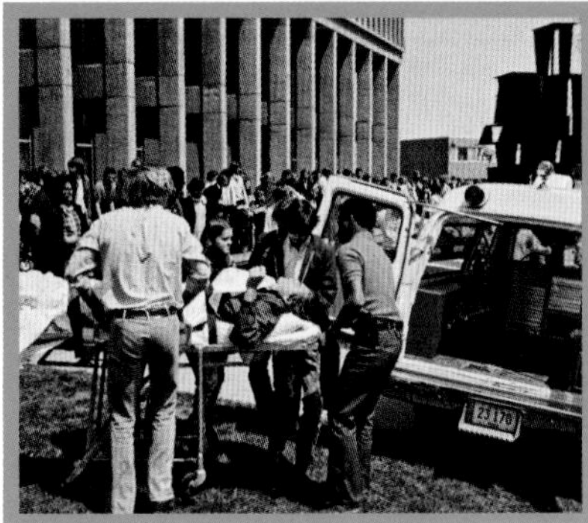

The Kent State University shootings, in which four students were shot dead by the National Guard, caused the emotionally conflicted townspeople to denigrate the victims.

Some situational variables can move a great proportion of us 'normal' adults to behave in very unappetizing ways.
Elliot Aronson

The conflict felt by these people is known as "cognitive dissonance," an unpleasant feeling experienced when two or more of one's beliefs are inconsistent. In order to reduce this dissonance, people change their attitudes, beliefs, and actions, even if this involves justifying or denying cruelty against others. This, Aronson claims, is what happened after the Kent massacre. The townspeople wanted to believe in their National Guards' goodness, and this meant believing their victims deserved to die. The idea that the slain had been "wanton" and "dirty" comforted the people, relieving the emotional conflict of believing that innocent students were needlessly killed.

Aronson claims that anyone could behave this way under similar circumstances. By understanding the reasons why people justify or deny the use of cruelty, we may be better placed to mediate or prevent it in wider social contexts, such as war or social prejudice. ▪

Elliot Aronson

Elliot Aronson grew up in Revere, Massachusetts, during the Great Depression. He won a scholarship to attend Brandeis University, where he initially majored in economics but soon switched to psychology after hearing a lecture by Abraham Maslow. He then earned a Master's degree at Wesleyan University, working with David McClelland, and a PhD at Stanford University under Leon Festinger. Aronson has since been a professor at several universities, including Harvard, the University of Texas, Stanford, and the University of California at Santa Cruz.

Throughout his career, Aronson has tried to use his research findings to improve the human condition and reduce prejudice. In recognition of his work, he was given the William James Award and the Gordon Allport Prize and was included in the list of the 100 most influential psychologists of the 20th century, published by the *Review of General Psychology*. He is the only person to have won all three awards offered by the American Psychological Association: for writing, teaching, and research.

Key works

1972 *The Social Animal* (12th edition, 2018)
1978 *The Jigsaw Classroom*
2007 *Mistakes Were Made (But Not By ME)* (3rd edition, 2020)

PEOPLE DO WHAT THEY ARE TOLD TO DO

STANLEY MILGRAM (1933–1984)

IN CONTEXT

APPROACH
Conformism

BEFORE
1939–1945 During World War II, approximately six million Jews are systematically killed on the orders of Nazi Germany.

1950 Solomon Asch demonstrates the power of social pressure to make people conform in his line-task experiments.

1961 Nazi war criminal Adolf Eichmann is tried, and claims he was just "following orders."

AFTER
1971 Philip Zimbardo conducts his prison experiment, which demonstrates that in certain situations, otherwise good people can perform evil deeds.

1989 American psychologists Herbert Kelman and V. L. Hamilton state that members of a group obey authority when they accept its legitimacy.

Social psychologist Stanley Milgram dramatically changed our understanding of human obedience when he published *Behavioral Study of Obedience* in 1963. This paper contained results of an experiment that seemed to suggest that the majority of people are capable of causing extreme harm to others when told to do so by a figure of authority. It also caused people to question the ethical limits of psychological experimentation.

Milgram became particularly interested in studying obedience during the trial of German Nazi war criminal Adolf Eichmann. The prevailing view was that there was something inherently different about the 20th-century Germans; in the 1950s, psychologists such as Theodor Adorno had suggested that the Germans had certain personality characteristics that made them specifically susceptible to committing the atrocities of the Holocaust. Eichmann, however, claimed he had just been "following orders," so Milgram set out to investigate if this could be true—would an ordinary person lay aside what he knew to be right or wrong merely because he was ordered to do so? His study went on to demonstrate important aspects of the relationship between authority and obedience, and it remains one of the most controversial experiments in the history of psychology.

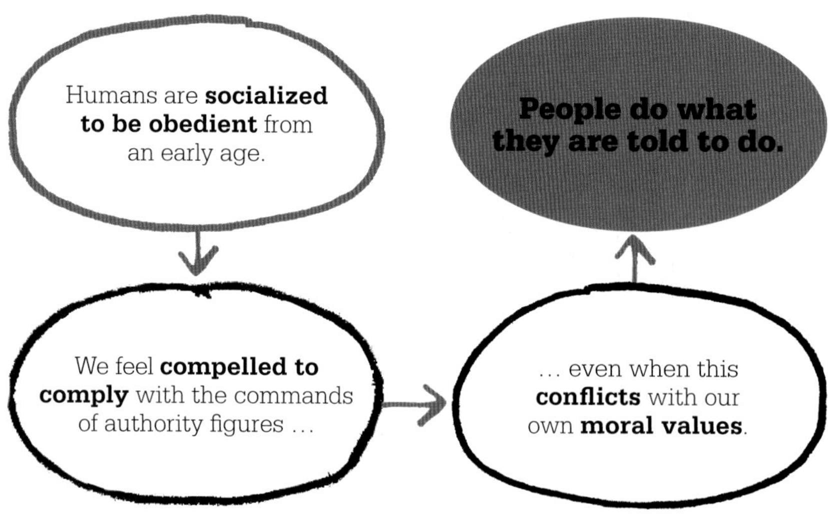

Humans are **socialized to be obedient** from an early age.
We feel **compelled to comply** with the commands of authority figures ...
... even when this **conflicts** with our own **moral values**.
People do what they are told to do.

The power of the group

Milgram believed that it was the situation of World War II and the compulsion to obey—rather than the dispositions of the Germans—that had enabled Nazi cruelty. He maintained that the behavior was a direct result of the situation, and any of us might have behaved identically in that very same context. In the late 1950s, Milgram had worked extensively with Solomon Asch on his conformity studies and had witnessed people agreeing with the decisions of a group, even when they knew these decisions to be wrong. The experiments showed that people are prepared to do or say things that conflict with their own sense of reality. Would they also allow their moral judgments to be affected by the authority of a group or even a single figure?

The Milgram experiment

Milgram set out to test whether normally kind, likeable people could be made to act against their own moral values in a setting where some kind of authority held sway. He devised an investigation of how obedient a selection of "ordinary" men would be when they were told by an authority figure to administer electric shocks to another person. The experiment took place in a laboratory at Yale University in 1961, where Milgram was a professor of psychology. The participants were recruited through a newspaper advertisement, and a total of 40 men were selected from a wide range of

See also: Solomon Asch 228–231 ▪ Serge Moscovici 244–245 ▪ Philip Zimbardo 260–261 ▪ Walter Mischel 332–333

The most famous and controversial of all obedience experiments.
Richard Gross

occupations, including teachers, postal workers, engineers, laborers, and salesmen. They were each paid $4.50 for their participation; the money was given to them as soon as they arrived at the laboratory, and they were told that the payment was theirs to keep regardless of what happened during the experiment.

In the laboratory, Milgram had created a phony (but very impressive and realistic-looking) electric shock generator. This had 30 switches marked in 15-volt increments with labels that indicated the intensity of different ranges of shock levels, from "slight shock" at one end, to "extreme intensity shock," "danger: severe shock," and finally, one marked simply "XXX," at the other.

The role of the experimenter or "scientist" was played by a biology teacher who introduced himself to the participants as Jack Williams. In order to give the impression of authority, he was dressed in a gray laboratory technician's coat and maintained a stern and emotionless demeanor throughout each of the experiments.

The participants were told that the study intended to investigate the effects of punishment on learning. They were told that of two volunteers, one would be the learner and the other the teacher. In fact, one of the two "volunteers" in each case was not a participant but a stooge: he was a likeable accountant called Mr. Wallace, who had been trained to play the role of the victim. When Mr. Wallace and the genuine participant drew paper from a hat to determine which role they would play, the draw was always rigged so that Mr. Wallace took on the role of "learner" in every instance. In full view of the participant, the "learner" (Mr. Wallace) was strapped into an "electric chair" with an electrode attached to his wrist; the participant was told that this electrode was attached to the shock generator »

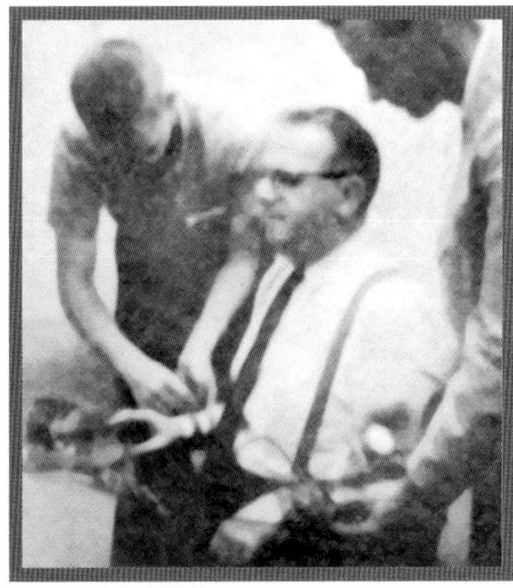

Convincingly wired up, Mr. Wallace pretended to be an innocent volunteer. His screams failed to prevent 65 percent of participants from administering the highest level of fake electric shock.

Stanley Milgram

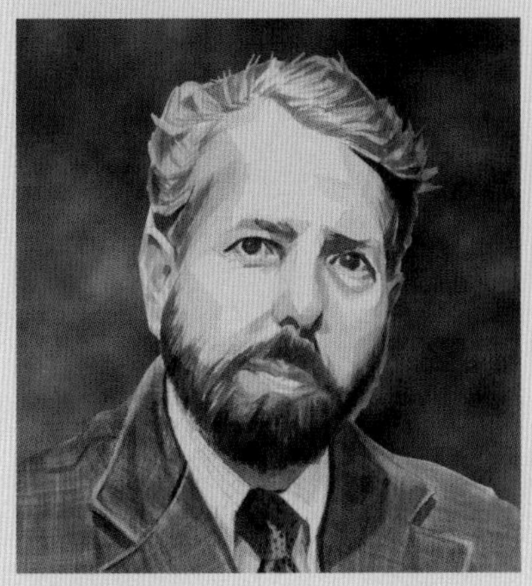

Stanley Milgram was born in 1933 to a Jewish family in New York City. His Hungarian parents ran a bakery in the Bronx, and he attended James Monroe High School with Philip Zimbardo.

A high academic achiever and a leader among his peers, Milgram initially studied political science, but went on to receive a PhD in psychology from Harvard in 1960 under Gordon Allport. After working with Solomon Asch on conformity studies at Harvard, he became assistant professor at Yale, where he carried out his obedience experiments. In 1961, he married Alexandra Menkin, with whom he had two children. In 1963, he returned to Harvard, but was denied tenure because of the controversy surrounding his experiment, so he moved to the City University of New York, where he taught until his death at the age of 51.

Key works

1963 *Behavioral Study of Obedience*
1967 *The Small World Problem*
1974 *Obedience to Authority: An Experimental View*

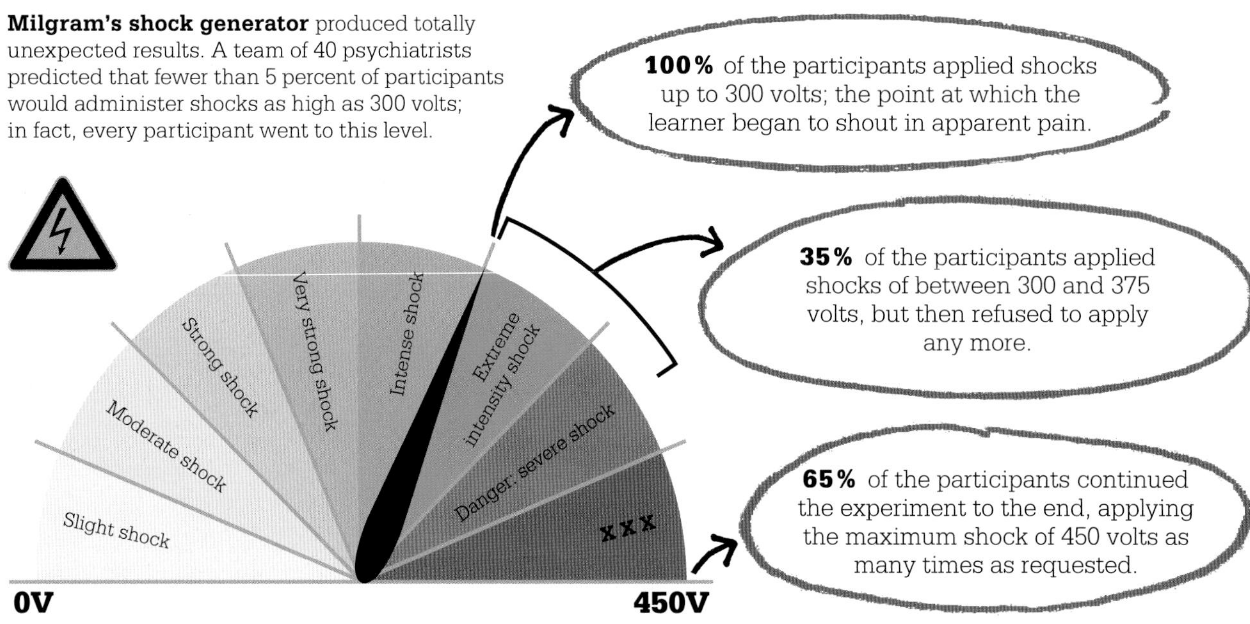

located in an adjacent room. The participant heard the "scientist" tell the "learner" (Mr. Wallace) that "although the shocks can be extremely painful, they cause no permanent damage." To make the situation appear more authentic, the scientist then wired up the participant and gave him a sample shock of 45 volts—which was in fact the only shock strength that the generator could produce.

Milgram's shock generator produced totally unexpected results. A team of 40 psychiatrists predicted that fewer than 5 percent of participants would administer shocks as high as 300 volts; in fact, every participant went to this level.
100% of the participants applied shocks up to 300 volts; the point at which the learner began to shout in apparent pain.
35% of the participants applied shocks of between 300 and 375 volts, but then refused to apply any more.
65% of the participants continued the experiment to the end, applying the maximum shock of 450 volts as many times as requested.
Slight shock
Moderate shock
Strong shock
Very strong shock
Intense shock
Extreme intensity shock
Danger: severe shock
XXX
0V
450V

At this point, the participant was moved to the room containing the shock generator and asked to assume the role of "teacher." He was asked to read a series of word pairs (such as "blue-girl," "nice-day") aloud for the learner to memorize. After this he was to read out a series of single words; the learner's task was to recall the pairing word in each case and to indicate his answer by pressing a switch that illuminated a light on the shock generator. If the learner's answer was correct, the questions continued; if the answer was incorrect, the participant was instructed to tell the learner the correct answer, announce the level of shock he was about to receive, and press a switch to administer the shock. Participants were instructed to increase the shock level by 15 volts (in other words, to keep moving up the shock scale on the machine) with every wrong answer.

Applying the shocks

As part of the experiment, the learner (Mr. Wallace) had been briefed to answer incorrectly to around one question in every four, to ensure that the participant would be required to start applying electric shocks. During the experiment, the learner would pound the wall once the voltage had reached 300, and shout: "I absolutely refuse to answer any more! Get me out of here! You can't hold me here! Get me out!" As the shock level increased, the learner would shout more frantically, and then eventually cease making any noise at all; questions would be met with nothing but an eerie silence. The participant was told to treat any unanswered question as an incorrectly answered question and apply the next level of shock voltage. If he expressed misgivings about continuing the experiment, he received a verbal prod from the "scientist" to encourage him, from a simple request to continue, to finally being told that he had no choice but to go on. If he refused to obey after the last prod, the experiment was terminated.

With numbing regularity, good people were seen to knuckle under the demands of authority and perform actions that were callous and severe.
Stanley Milgram

In advance of the experiment, Milgram had asked several different groups of people, including ordinary members of the public as well as psychologists and psychiatrists, how far they thought participants would go when asked to administer the electric shocks. Most people thought participants would stop at a level that caused pain, and the psychiatrists predicted that, at most, one in 1,000 would continue to the highest level of shock. Astonishingly, when the experiment took place, Milgram found that all 40 of the participants obeyed commands to administer shocks up to 300 volts. Only five people refused to continue at this point; 65 percent of the participants obeyed the instructions of the "scientist" right to the end, obeying commands to administer shocks to the top level of 450 volts.

Their discomfort at doing so was often evident: many showed signs of severe distress, tension, and nervousness over the course of the experiment. They stuttered, trembled, sweated, groaned, broke out into nervous laughing fits, and three people had full-blown seizures. In every instance of the experiment, the participant stopped and questioned it at some point; some even offered to refund the money they were paid at the beginning. Interviews after the experiments confirmed that, with only a few exceptions, participants had been completely convinced that the "learning experiment" was real.

All participants were fully debriefed so they understood what had actually taken place, and they were asked a series of questions to test that they were not emotionally harmed by the experience. The participants were also reunited with the "learner" (Mr. Wallace) so that they could see that no actual shocks had been administered.

Feeling obliged to obey

Milgram noted several features of the experiment that may have contributed to such high levels of obedience; for example, the fact that it took place at the prestigious Yale University gave it credibility. In addition, participants believed that the study was designed to advance knowledge, and they had been assured that the shocks were painful but not dangerous. Being paid may have increased their sense of obligation, as did the fact they had volunteered to take part. To test these explanations, Milgram ran many variations on the study, but changing the context had only minor effects on the results.

Milgram wanted to see if the inclination to obey authority figures can become the major factor in determining behavior, even in extreme circumstances. It is clear from the reactions and responses of the participants that obeying the "scientist" was violating their own sense of morality and negatively affecting them both physically and emotionally, but the pressure to comply was simply too powerful to defy in most cases.

> Ordinary people, simply doing their jobs, and without any particular hostility on their part, can become agents in a terrible destructive process.
> **Stanley Milgram**

This sense of obedience, Milgram felt, comes from the fact that people are socialized from a very young age (by parents and »

By the 1960s, Yale University was known to the general public as being highly prestigious; its authority may have seemed literally unquestionable to the participants of Milgram's study.

teachers) to be obedient and to follow orders—especially the rules set forth by authority figures. As Milgram says, "obedience is as basic an element in the structure of social life as one can point to … it serves numerous productive functions." But equally, the inhumane policies of the death camps in World War II "could only be carried out on a massive scale if a very large number of persons obeyed orders." His experiments clearly demonstrated that normally harmless people become capable of committing cruel acts when a situation pressures them to do so.

In describing his results, Milgram also turned to the theory of conformism, which states that when a person has neither the ability nor expertise to make a decision, he will look to the group to decide how to behave. Conformity can limit and distort an individual's response to a situation, and seems to result in a diffusion of responsibility—which Milgram felt was crucial to comprehending the atrocities carried out by the Nazis. However, the conflict between a person's conscience and external authority exerts a huge internal pressure, and Milgram felt that this accounted for the extreme distress experienced by the participants in his study.

Ethical concerns

There were many ethical concerns associated with Milgram's study. When it was first published, the ensuing controversy was so great that the American Psychological Association revoked his membership for a full year. However, it was eventually reinstated, and Milgram's 1974 book *Obedience to Authority* received the annual Social Psychology Award.

The major concern was that the participants in the experiment were explicitly deceived, both about the nature of the study and about the reality of the electric shocks. Milgram's defense was that he could not have obtained realistic results without employing deception, and all of the participants were debriefed after the experiment. Self-knowledge, he argued, is a valuable asset, despite the discomfort that the participants may have felt when forced to confront the fact that they behaved in a previously unthinkable way.

However, many psychologists remained uneasy, and the study was ultimately crucial in the development of ethical standards of psychological experimentation. It helped to define important principles such as the avoidance of intentional deceit of participants, and the need to protect experimental participants from emotional suffering.

Cross-cultural validity

Another criticism of Milgram's study was that he used an unrepresentative sample: American men do not necessarily reflect the general population. Even so, Milgram was able to conclude that obedience was not a particular feature found in the minds of 20th-century Germans, but something more universal. A number of cross-cultural replications

The behavior of Nazis during World War II had been attributed to a prevalence of the "authoritarian personality" in the population; this was questioned by Milgram's experiments.

Obedience to authority is not a feature of German culture, but a seemingly universal feature of human behavior.
Stanley Milgram

In wartime, a soldier does not ask whether it is good or bad to bomb a hamlet.
Stanley Milgram

Drone pilots ordered to bomb targets may become detached from the consequences of their actions due to the distance from the impact zone and any humans within it.

of the original experiment have demonstrated remarkably high consistency in results within societies, but slight differences between one country and another. For example, in most of Europe and North America, results are very similar to those found in Milgram's original experiment, with very high percentages of obedience. Asian studies, however, show even greater levels of obedience (in East Asian and Muslim countries in particular), while indigenous African and Latin American populations, as well as the Inuit peoples of Canada, show far less obedience.

Virtual torture

In 2006, the psychologist Mel Slater set out to see what the effect would be if participants were made explicitly aware that the situation was not real. His replication used a computer simulation of the learner and shock process, so participants administering the shocks were fully aware that the learner was computer-generated. The experiment was run twice: first with the virtual learner communicating only by text, and then with the computer-generated model visible on screen. Those with only text contact with the learner had little trouble administering the shocks; but when the virtual learner was visible, participants acted exactly as they had in Milgram's original experiment.

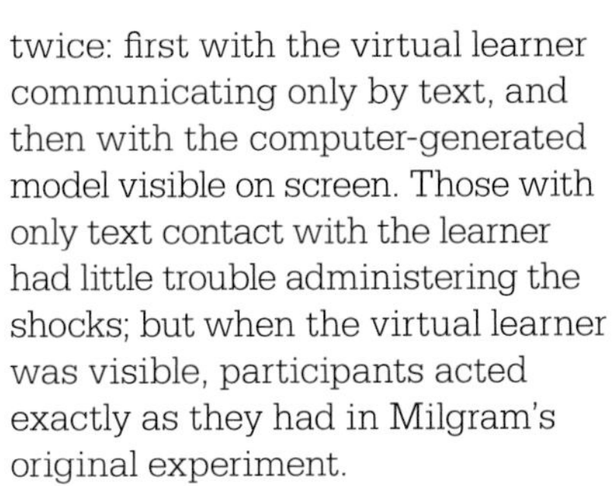

Society demands obedience

The notion of a society rests on an understanding that individuals are prepared to relinquish some personal autonomy and look to others of higher authority and social status to make decisions on a larger scale or from a higher, broader perspective. Even the most democratic of societies requires the rulings of a recognized, legitimate authority to take precedence over individual self-regulation, in pursuit of the greater collective good. In order for any society to function, its populace must agree to obey its rules. Legitimacy is, of course, the key, and there are countless historical examples of people using their authority to persuade others to commit crimes against humanity.

Equally importantly, Milgram showed that it is "not so much the kind of person a man is, as the kind of situation in which he finds himself that determines how he will act." Instead of examining personalities to explain crimes, he says, we should examine the context, or situation.

Milgram's seminal study was heavily criticized at the time, not least because it painted an unappealing and chilling portrait of human nature. It is easier to believe that there are fundamental differences between the Nazis and the rest of humanity than to accept that in certain situations, many of us are capable of committing extraordinary acts of violence. Milgram held up a light to the dark realities concerning power and the consequences of our tendency to obey authority figures, and in so doing, he simultaneously absolved and made villains of us all. ■

WHAT HAPPENS WHEN YOU PUT GOOD PEOPLE IN AN EVIL PLACE?

PHILIP ZIMBARDO (1933–)

IN CONTEXT

APPROACH
Conformity

BEFORE
1935 Muzafer Sherif demonstrates how groups quickly come to develop a "social norm" in his autokinetic effect experiments.

1940s Kurt Lewin shows how people's behavior changes as their situations are altered.

1963 Stanley Milgram conducts his obedience studies, which demonstrate that people will obey authority even if it means committing cruel acts.

AFTER
2002 British psychologists Stephen Reicher and Alex Haslam extend Zimbardo's study to explore positive rather than negative group behavior.

2004 Zimbardo defends a former Abu Ghraib prison guard in court, arguing that the circumstances caused the guard's cruel behavior.

Stanley Milgram's shocking obedience studies revealed that people will obey authority figures even if this entails acting against their own moral convictions. In the aftermath, Philip Zimbardo set out to discover how people would behave if they were put into a position of authority with unimpeded power. Would they willingly use (or abuse) the power granted to them? In 1971 he carried out the now-famous Stanford Prison experiment, using 24 middle-class American college students who had undergone tests to establish that they were mentally healthy.

On the flip of a coin the students were randomly assigned the role of either "guard" or "prisoner," and one

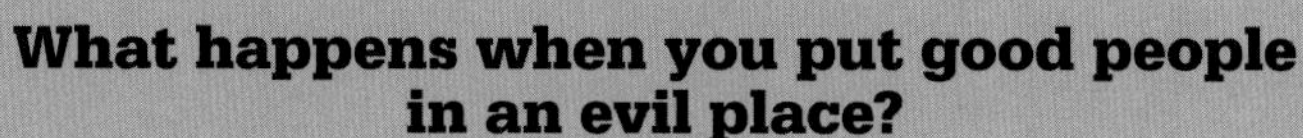
What happens when you put good people in an evil place?

Normal, healthy people start to behave according to the **social roles** assigned to them.

Those in the **position of power** will naturally use (and abuse) their authority.

Those in a **subordinate position** will submit to authority.

It is the **power of social situations**, rather than the dispositions of people, that leads to **evil behavior**.

See also: John B. Watson 66–71 ▪ Zing-Yang Kuo 75 ▪ Kurt Lewin 222–227 ▪ Elliot Aronson 250–251 ▪ Stanley Milgram 252–259 ▪ Muzafer Sherif 343–344

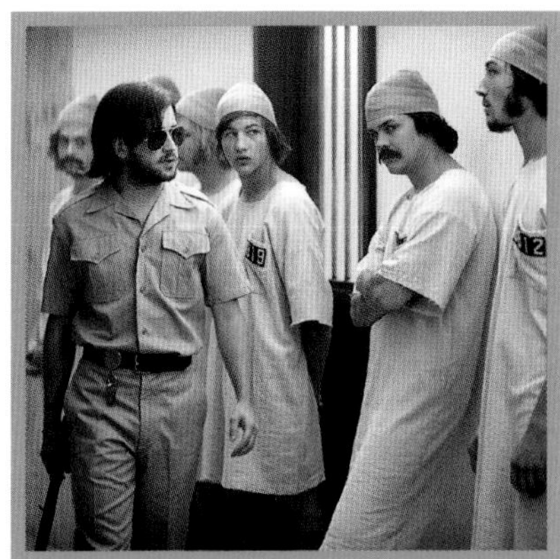

The "prisoners" rebelled against the "guards," but the guards' tactics became more aggressive. They began dividing the prisoners into groups, giving some rewards and others punishments.

Sunday morning soon afterward, the prisoners were arrested at their homes, booked at a real police station, then transferred to the basement of the Stanford University psychology department, which had been converted into a mock prison.

The prison environment

In order to make the experience as psychologically real as possible, prisoners were stripped, searched, deloused, and given uniforms and bedding upon their arrival. To heighten their sense of anonymity and dehumanization, they were addressed only by their given numbers, and each had a chain bolted around one ankle to serve as a reminder of their lack of freedom.

The guards wore military-style uniforms and sunglasses (to make eye contact impossible), and carried keys, whistles, handcuffs, and clubs. They were on duty 24 hours a day, and were given complete control over the prisoners, with permission to employ whatever tactics they saw fit in order to maintain order.

To the researchers' amazement, the environment quickly became so threatening to participants that the study had to be ended after only six days. Every guard became abusive and authoritarian; prisoners were denied food or bedding, hooded, chained, and made to clean toilet bowls with their hands. As the boredom increased, they used the prisoners as their playthings, making them take part in degrading games. After just 36 hours, one prisoner had to be released because of uncontrolled crying, fits of rage, and severe depression. When other prisoners showed symptoms of acute distress, Zimbardo realized the situation had become dangerous and ended the experiment.

Zimbardo's experiment showed that good people can be induced into behaving in evil ways by immersion in "total situations" that have an apparently legitimizing ideology and approved rules and roles. The implications are vast, as Zimbardo explains: "Any deed that any human being has ever done, however horrible, is possible for any of us to do—under the right or wrong situational pressures." ■

Our study … reveals the power of social, institutional forces to make good men engage in evil deeds.
Philip Zimbardo

Philip Zimbardo

Philip Zimbardo was born in New York City in 1933 to a Sicilian-American family, and was a classmate of Stanley Milgram at James Monroe High School in the Bronx. He went on to earn his BA degree from Brooklyn College, New York, and a PhD from Yale. He taught at several universities before moving to Stanford in 1968, where he is still a psychology professor.

In 2000, Zimbardo stated that he agreed with George Armitage Miller that it was time to "give psychology away to the public," and his career has reflected this idea. In the 1980s he presented a popular TV series on "discovering psychology." The American Psychological Foundation presented him with an award for Distinguished Lifetime Contributions to General Psychology in 2000, and two years later he was elected president of the American Psychological Association.

Key works

1972 *The Stanford Prison Experiment*
2007 *The Lucifer Effect*
2008 *The Time Paradox*
2010 *Psychology and Life*

THE EXPERIMENTER [MUST] BALANCE ... SCIENTIFIC INTERESTS AGAINST THE INTERESTS OF HIS PROSPECTIVE SUBJECTS

DIANA BAUMRIND (1927–2018)

IN CONTEXT

APPROACH
Experimental ethics

BEFORE

1920 A nine-month-old baby is the subject of John B. Watson's now-notorious "Little Albert" experiment.

1930 Edwin Tolman and other behaviorist psychologists use animals such as rats in their experiments.

1961 Subjects in Stanley Milgram's obedience experiments are told they are administering electric shocks to a volunteer.

AFTER

1971 Philip Zimbardo's Stanford Prison experiment is severely criticized as being dangerously unethical.

1978 "The Belmont Report: Ethical Principles and Guidelines for the Protection of Human Subjects of Research" is published.

Experiments have long been intrinsic to the scientific study of psychology, often involving animal or human subjects. After ethical concerns were raised by John B. Watson's controversial experiments on a human baby, however, such experiments were mostly carried out on animals.

More recently, the growth of the field of social psychology has led to scrutiny of the ethics of psychological experimentation, particularly the participation of human subjects. Stanley Milgram's study of obedience, and later Philip Zimbardo's famous Stanford Prison experiment, showed the dangers for human subjects in such experiments and prompted American clinical psychologist Diana Baumrind to spearhead an examination of their ethics.

Code of practice

Guidelines were appearing at this time, warning against causing "unnecessary suffering" to animals in research, but it was clear that more complex rules were needed for human subjects. Baumrind's study identified a number of issues, including those of consent, and more particularly informed consent, deception, protection of participants, debriefing, and confidentiality. Subsequently codified, these core principles have been adopted by professional associations of psychologists around the world, forming the basis for their codes of practice. Periodically, they are revised to reflect changes in social and political attitudes. ■

If there is a conflict of interest between the participants and the researcher, it is the interests of the subjects that should take priority
R. Rosenthal & R. L. Rosnow

See also: John B. Watson 66–71 ▪ B. F. Skinner 78–85 ▪ Stanley Milgram 252–259 ▪ Philip Zimbardo 260–261

THE UNRESPONSIVE BYSTANDER: WHY DOESN'T HE HELP?

BIBB LATANÉ (1937–) & JOHN M. DARLEY (1938–2018)

IN CONTEXT

APPROACH
Conformity

BEFORE
1935 Muzafer Sherif finds that people in a group feel the need to conform in order to fit in with the others.

1951 In the task known as the "Asch Paradigm," Solomon Asch shows that people's compulsion to conformity can override their perceptions and values.

AFTER
2019 A study by the Netherlands Institute for the Study of Crime and Law Enforcement finds that in analysis of 219 recorded street disputes, bystanders intervened in almost every case.

According to the *New York Times*, the rape and murder of Kitty Genovese in 1964 was witnessed by 38 people, yet none intervened. Although later shown to have wildly exaggerated the lack of response, the report prompted American social psychologists Bibb Latané and John M. Darley to study this "bystander effect." In a series of experiments, they put participants into staged emergency situations to see how quickly, if at all, they responded to various scenarios, such as smoke appearing in a room or a woman apparently being attacked. Some participants were the only witness to the incident, while others were with a friend or in a group of confederates of the experimenters.

Latané and Darley found that participants' responses depended on the nature and urgency of the incident and the action required, but was also affected by the presence of others. Lone participants were more likely to respond, and more quickly, than those in a group. They noted a high degree of social influence, with subjects checking the reactions of others before deciding to act themselves. As well as indicating a desire for conformity and group cohesion, participants experienced a diffusion of responsibility—a sense that someone else will intervene—when part of a group of witnesses.

The bystander effect suggested that a lone witness to an incident would be more inclined to help than a group.

Although these experiments demonstrated the "bystander apathy" apparently exhibited during the Genovese incident, Latané and Darley's findings have been challenged by real-life studies, which show a far greater tendency toward bystander intervention. ■

See also: Solomon Asch 228–231 ▪ Irving Janis 234–235 ▪ Stanley Milgram 252–259 ▪ Muzafer Sherif 343–344

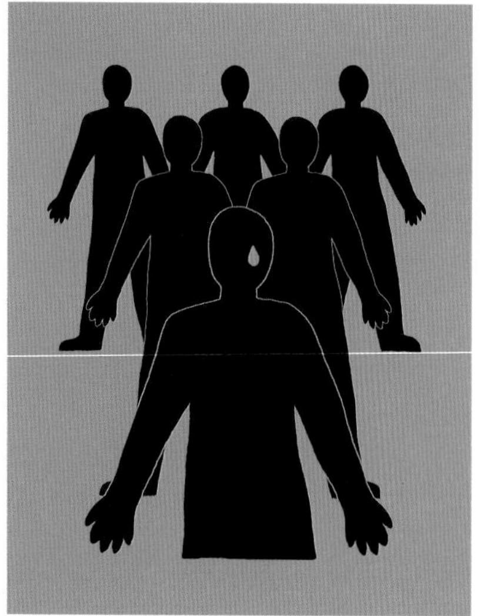

TRAUMA MUST BE UNDERSTOOD IN TERMS OF THE RELATIONSHIP BETWEEN THE INDIVIDUAL AND SOCIETY

IGNACIO MARTÍN-BARÓ (1942–1989)

IN CONTEXT

APPROACH
Liberation psychology

BEFORE
1965 Community psychology, a new discipline investigating the relationships between individuals and communities, arises from discussions at the Swampscott Conference, Massachusetts.

1970s A crisis over the relevance of social psychology, the study of links between social conditions, emotions, and behaviors, erupts in Britain, North America, and most acutely in Latin America.

AFTER
1988 The Latin American Institute of Mental Health and Human Rights is founded.

1997 US psychologists Isaac Prilleltensky and Dennis Fox publish *Critical Psychology*, highlighting how traditional psychology can help sustain injustice and social oppression.

Ignacio Martín-Baró made his claim that "trauma must be understood in terms of the relationship between the individual and society" after witnessing first-hand the social injustices and violence endemic to El Salvador in the 1980s. Rejecting the idea of an impartial, universal approach to psychology, he came to realize that psychologists must take into account the historical context and social conditions of the people they are studying. He believed that while some mental health problems reflect an abnormal reaction to

Because it aims to be **impartial and universal**, mainstream psychology does not address the way specific contexts and environments shape mental health.

But to understand and treat mental disorders, a psychologist should understand the **sociopolitical environment** of his subjects and patients.

Trauma must be understood in terms of the relationship between the individual and society.

See also: Lev Vygotsky 278 ▪ Jerome Kagan 345–346

reasonably normal circumstances, the problems specific to oppressed and exploited groups tend to reflect a perfectly understandable and normal reaction to abnormal circumstances. Martín-Baró decided that psychologists needed to be more aware of how living within a difficult context affects mental health, and that they should help the society being studied to transcend its history of oppression. In the mid-1980s, he launched the branch of liberation psychology, which is committed to improving the lives of all marginalized and oppressed people.

Liberation psychologists claim that traditional psychology has many inadequacies. It frequently fails to offer practical solutions to social problems; many of its principles are developed from artificial settings in wealthy countries, and so are unlikely to translate to different situations; it tends to ignore human moral qualities, such as hope, courage, and commitment; and its main goal seems to be to maximize pleasure, rather than considering how to awaken and drive the desire for justice or freedom.

Traumatized societies

His collection *Writings for a Liberation Psychology*, published posthumously in 1994, captures several decades of Martín-Baró's concerns. It addresses the use of psychology as an instrument of war and political manipulation, the role of religion in psychological warfare, and the impact of trauma and violence on mental health. Martín-Baró studied areas where dependent economies and severe inequalities had led to relentless poverty and social exclusion. He examined the psychological impact of civil war and oppression in El Salvador; the dictatorships in Argentina and Chile; and poverty in Puerto Rico, Venezuela, Brazil, and Costa Rica. Each involved a different set of circumstances, affecting the local population in unique ways. He concluded that the mental health issues that arise in one context will reflect the history of the place as well as its social and political environment, and that individuals must be treated with both these factors in mind.

The challenge is to construct a new person in a new society.
Ignacio Martín-Baró

Martín-Baró focused on Central America, but his ideas are relevant anywhere social and political turmoil disrupts daily life. His humane and impassioned perspective draws a crucial link between mental health and the struggle against injustice, and attempts to find fresh ways of addressing associated psychological issues more effectively. ■

Ignacio Martín-Baró

Ignacio Martín-Baró was born in Valladolid, Spain. In 1959, he joined the Jesuit order, and was sent to South America. There, he studied at the Catholic University in Quito, Ecuador, and at the Javeriana University in Bogotà, Colombia. In 1966, Martín-Baró, now a Jesuit priest, was sent to El Salvador. He continued his studies at the University of Central America in San Salvador, gaining a licentiate in psychology in 1975. He later earned a PhD in social psychology from the University of Chicago, before returning to the University of Central America and eventually becoming head of its psychology department. Martín-Baró was openly critical of El Salvador's rulers, and in 1986 set up the University Institute of Public Opinion. He and five others were murdered by an army death squad for their exposure of political corruption and injustice.

Key works

1983 *Action and Ideology*
1989 *System, Group and Power*
1994 *Writings for a Liberation Psychology*

DEVELOP
PSYCHOL
FROM INFANT TO ADULT

MENTAL

OGY

1915

In a new edition of *Three Essays on the Theory of Sexuality*, Freud adds a section outlining his theory of **psychosexual development**.

1920s

The psychoanalytic world is **divided on issues of child development** between Anna Freud's conservative approach and Melanie Klein's "revolutionary" one.

1930s

Lev Vygotsky's sociocultural theory of learning emphasizes the **importance of the community** in learning and development.

1936

Jean Piaget suggests that cognitive processes develop in **a series of well-defined stages** through childhood.

1946

Kenneth Clark and Mamie Phipps Clark found the Northside Center for Child Development in Harlem, New York, where they examine the formation of **racial bias**.

1950

Eric Erikson publishes *Childhood and Society*, which includes an exposition of the eight stages of **psychosocial development**.

1957

Noam Chomsky challenges traditional theories of **language learning** in *Syntactic Structures*.

1958-1960

John Bowlby publishes a series of articles rejecting psychoanalytic and behavioral theories of attachment.

In the early part of the 20th century, two main approaches in psychology examined the psychological development of humans from childhood to adulthood: the psychoanalytic theory of Freud gave an account of psychosexual development in children, and behaviorism explained the mechanics of the learning process. However, the study of development itself—the psychological, emotional, and perceptual changes that occur during a lifetime—did not evolve until the 1930s, when Jean Piaget overturned conventional thinking with the idea that a child is not just a "miniature adult" gaining knowledge as their body matures, but at the same time is also going through radical psychological changes. Piaget raised some fundamental questions: whether we acquire knowledge gradually or in distinct stages; whether certain abilities are innate or learned; and how the environment affects development. His cognitive development theory suggested that a child's growth into adulthood is divided into several developmental stages, and within each stage the child learns by doing rather than instruction. Piaget's ideas set the stage for the new field of developmental psychology and shaped the curricula of schools up to the present day.

Other developmental theories soon emerged. Although broadly agreeing with Piaget's findings, Lev Vygotsky argued that it was necessary for a child to have adult guidance at various stages in their learning, and also stressed the importance of a child's social and cultural environment. Erik Erikson also built on Piaget's ideas, identifying eight stages of psychosocial development, including the "identity crisis" of adolescence; while Lawrence Kohlberg came up with six stages of moral development in his studies.

With the "cognitive revolution" that followed World War II, psychologists such as Albert Bandura looked at the issue of development again, this time in the light of cognitive models of information processing. Bandura retained elements of both Piaget's stages of development and Vygotsky's social constructivism in his social learning theory. Cognitive psychology also brought new ideas about learning, especially the acquisition of

1959
Harry Harlow carries out experiments on monkeys proving that **contact comfort** is more important than the provision of food in forming attachments.

1961
Albert Bandura performs the **Bobo Doll experiments** into observational learning (modeling).

1970
Mary Ainsworth explores types of attachment in her **Strange Situation** studies.

1971
Lawrence Kohlberg identifies **six stages of moral growth** in *Stages of Moral Development*.

1973
A school opens in Neuville-du-Bosc, France, which follows the educational theories of **Françoise Dolto**.

1974
Eleanor E. Maccoby conducts a study into **gender differences** in *The Psychology of Sex Differences*.

1991
Jerome Bruner explores the way the developing mind structures its sense of reality in *The Narrative Construction of Reality*.

2010
In *Delusions of Gender*, **Cordelia Fine** challenges the scientific basis for assuming a difference between male and female minds.

language, and Noam Chomsky's suggestion that this is an innate capability once more opened the nature versus nurture debate.

Attachment theory

While much developmental psychology concerned itself with the process of learning, a growing area of interest arose from the research carried out by the British psychoanalyst and psychiatrist John Bowlby. His study of children who had been separated from their families during World War II led to the formulation of attachment theory, which deals with the way we build and maintain relationships with family and friends, placing a special importance on the attachments made by infants to the people who care for them; Bowlby saw this as a natural impulse for survival. In the US, the basic ideas of attachment theory were reinforced by psychologist Harry Harlow's experiments. He showed the effects of isolation and maternal separation on infants, and his experiments demonstrated that to build healthy cognitive and social development, infants needed companionship and care. Later research by Mary Ainsworth built on these findings, adding the concept of a "secure base" from which an infant can explore the world. Developing his own, more controversial, theories of childhood development from the basis of attachment theory, Bruno Bettelheim rejected the importance of the traditional family following his study of children brought up communally in kibbutzim. In the 1960s, social issues such as the civil rights movement and feminism were influencing thought in both social and developmental psychology. How our prejudices are acquired, and at what stage of development, became an area of interest for the Black Americans Kenneth Clark and Mamie Phipps Clark, who carried out studies of child development in Harlem, New York; while Eleanor Maccoby examined the differences in development between the genders—the first of many explorations in the new field of gender studies opening a debate that challenged the conventional assumption of different male and female minds. Current topics being explored in developmental psychology include the causes and treatment of learning difficulties, and with an increasingly aging population, the issues that confront us as we enter old age. ■

THE GOAL OF EDUCATION

IS TO CREATE MEN AND WOMEN WHO ARE CAPABLE OF DOING

NEW THINGS

JEAN PIAGET (1896–1980)

IN CONTEXT

APPROACH
Genetic epistemology

BEFORE
1693 English philosopher John Locke's *Some Thoughts Concerning Education* suggests a child's mind is a tabula rasa, or blank slate.

1780s German philosopher Immanuel Kant introduces the concept of the schema and suggests that morality develops independently of authority figures through interaction with peers.

AFTER
1907 Italian educator Dr. Maria Montessori opens the first Montessori school, which encourages independence and respect for natural developmental stages.

1970s–1980s Many Western education systems incorporate a more child-centered approach to learning.

Somewhere between his roots as a precocious young biologist and his later fascination with epistemology, Jean Piaget carved out his own niche in a discipline that he called genetic epistemology, the study of how intelligence changes as children grow. Piaget was not interested in comparing levels of intelligence between children of different ages (quantitative cognitive change); his interests lay in the natural development of mental skills over time (qualitative cognitive change). Quantitative studies make possible numerical comparisons, but Piaget wanted to explore differences in the types, experience, and qualities of children's learning, which required "qualitative" research. Breaking away from the prevalent behaviorist model, which had linked child development entirely with environmental factors, Piaget decided to explore the innate, or inborn, capacities that he believed guide children's progression through a series of age-defined developmental stages.

Piaget believed that children are active and autonomous learners, using their senses to interact with the world around them as they move through the developmental stages. He also believed that it is of primary importance to nurture and guide children on this journey, giving them the freedom to experiment and explore on their own, in a very individual, trial-and-error manner. The task of a good teacher is, therefore, simply to support children on their journey through these stages, constantly encouraging their creativity and imagination, because "the goal of education is to create men and women who are capable of doing new things."

Learning is active

One theme that pervades Piaget's theory of intellectual development is the concept of learning as an active personal process. From infancy through childhood, he says, learning arises from a child's natural desire to sense, explore, move, and then master. For this reason Piaget had many misgivings about the notion of standardized testing, in which children undergo preformatted tests that have "correct" answers to provide quantitative measures of intelligence. While working on

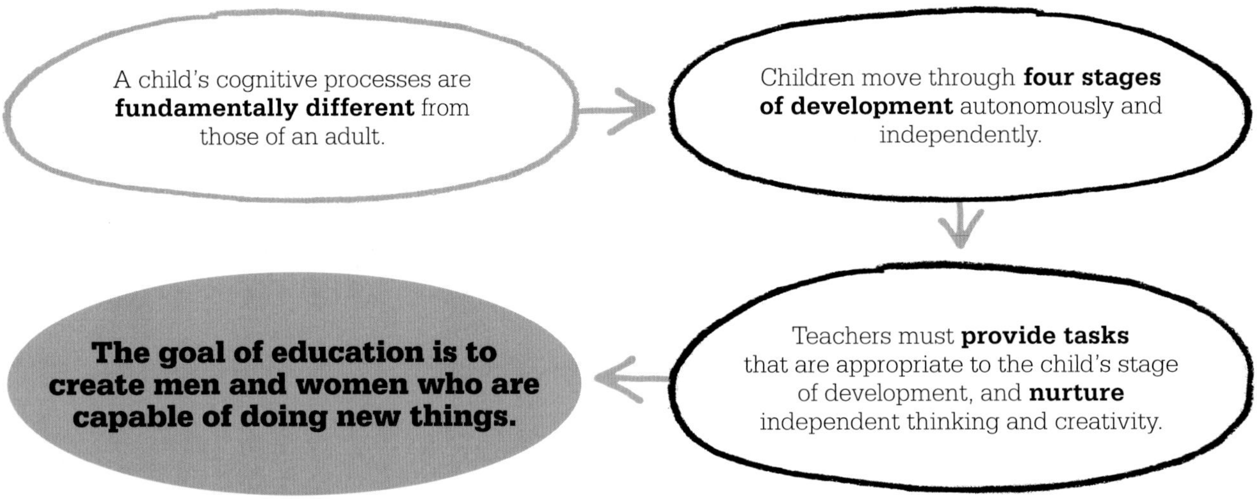

A child's cognitive processes are **fundamentally different** from those of an adult.

Children move through **four stages of development** autonomously and independently.

Teachers must **provide tasks** that are appropriate to the child's stage of development, and **nurture** independent thinking and creativity.

The goal of education is to create men and women who are capable of doing new things.

See also: Alfred Binet 50–53 ▪ Jerome Bruner 164–165 ▪ Lev Vygotsky 278 ▪ Erik Erikson 280–281 ▪ Françoise Dolto 287 ▪ Lawrence Kohlberg 300–301 ▪ Jerome Kagan 345–346

standardizing intelligence tests for Alfred Binet in the early 1920s, he became interested less in a child's ability to produce correct answers than in what those answers actually were. Their explanations revealed that children's assumptions about how the world works are very different to those of adults, leading Piaget to believe that children not only think differently to adults, but also that children of different ages have different methods of thinking.

The evolving mind

Since the 17th century, in Europe, the idea that a child is effectively a miniature adult had held sway. Empiricist philosophers of the time had suggested that a child's brain works exactly like an adult's, but has fewer associations. Another group of thinkers, the psychological nativists, claimed that certain concepts—such as the ideas of time, space, and number—are innate, or "hard-wired" into the brain, so babies are born with an ability to make use of them. Piaget's suggestion that children's mental processes—from infancy to adolescence—are fundamentally different to an adult's was a radical and controversial departure from this view.

Education, for most people, means trying to lead the child to resemble the typical adult of their society.
Jean Piaget

Children are not mini adults who simply do not yet know as much as adults; rather, they see the world differently and interact with it in a wholly distinct way.

Piaget himself claimed that it is vitally important to understand the formation and evolution of intelligence during childhood, because this is the only way we can reach a full understanding of human knowledge. His use of psychotherapeutic interviewing techniques to ask children to explain their answers was inspired, and it became an important tool in all his research. Rather than adhering to a predetermined and impersonal list of questions, this flexible method allowed the child's answers to determine the subsequent question. By following the child's line of thought, Piaget believed he could better understand the processes underlying it. His rejection of a notion of quantitative or measurable intelligence led to some groundbreaking theories of childhood cognitive development.

Developing the intellect

Piaget initially believed that social factors, such as language and contact with family members and peers, impacted most on children's intellectual development. However, while studying infants, he realized that for them language is less important and their own activity is paramount. In the first few days of life, babies have limited bodily movements—mainly crying and sucking—though they quickly begin to add new actions, such as reaching for a toy. So Piaget concluded that action, rather than social interaction, is the source of thought at this stage.

This discovery formed part of his theory that every child passes through various stages of cognitive development, and that these stages are different in quality and are hierarchical. A child only moves on to the next stage upon genuine completion of the current stage. In studies and observations, Piaget determined that all children pass through the stages in the same sequence, without skipping any or regressing to previous ones. This is not a process that can be rushed, and although children generally tend to go through the same stage at roughly the same age, each individual child has their own pace of development.

The four stages defined by Piaget represent levels in the development of intelligence »

The Four Stages of Development

1 At the **sensorimotor** stage, babies learn about the world through touch and their other senses.

2 Children begin to arrange objects logically during the **preoperational** stage.

3 During the **concrete operational** stage, children learn that quantities can take different forms.

4 Verbal reasoning and hypothetical thinking develop in the **formal operational** stage.

and, as such, they provide a list of the "schemas" that children make use of at that particular moment in their development. A schema is a representation in the mind of a set of ideas, perceptions, and actions that provide a mental structure to help us organize our past experiences, and prepare us for future experiences. During infancy and early childhood, a schema can be as simple as "things I can eat." However, as children grow, their schemas become more complex, offering an understanding of what constitutes "a kitchen," a "best friend," or "democratic government." Intelligent behavior, according to Piaget, is comprised of a growing collection of schemas.

Knowledge … is a system of transformations that become progressively adequate.
Jean Piaget

Four stages of development

Piaget's first stage is called the sensorimotor stage, and this spans the first two years of a child's life. During this period, infants learn about the world primarily through their senses (sensori-) and through physical action or movement (motor). Children at this stage are egocentric, able to see the world only from their own viewpoint. At the beginning of this stage, infants practice reflexes without understanding or intention; later they can extend and coordinate reflexes with objects. Then they begin to coordinate their senses in a way that anticipates events; for example, they can imagine objects that are not present and find hidden ones. They begin to experiment and set goals in their use of objects, and think about a problem before acting. These developments mark the completion of the first stage.

As the child moves toward the development of self-awareness, they now have the tools of representational thought and can begin to develop and use internal images, symbols, and language. This constitutes the second, or preoperational, stage when a child is primarily interested in how things look or appear. They will demonstrate skills such as arranging objects in a logical order (according to height, for example), or comparing two objects (such as blocks) through shared attributes, focusing on one perceptual quality (such as size or color) at a time. From years two to four, the child thinks in absolute terms (such as "big" or "biggest"); from four to seven, they begin to use relative terms (such as "bigger" or "heavier"). The ability to think logically is still limited and children remain egocentric, unable to see things from another's perspective.

The third stage is the concrete operational stage, and this is when a child becomes capable of performing logical operations, but only in the presence of actual (concrete) objects. The child now begins to grasp the concept of conservation, understanding that the quantity of an object remains the same despite physical changes in its arrangement. They realize that if you pour liquid from a short, wide glass into a tall, thin one, the amount of liquid remains the same despite the difference in height. Children can also understand that objects can be sorted according to many qualities simultaneously—a marble can be large, green, or clear. A little less egocentric now, children begin to incorporate more relativity into their viewpoints.

During the fourth stage—the formal operational stage—children begin to manipulate ideas (rather than simply objects) and are able to reason purely on the basis of verbal statements. They no longer need to refer to concrete objects, and can follow an argument. They start to think hypothetically, and this new capacity for imagination, and their ability to discuss abstract ideas, reveals that they have now become less egocentric.

Reaching equilibrium

In addition to defining the four stages, Piaget identified several fundamental facets of the developmental process that were 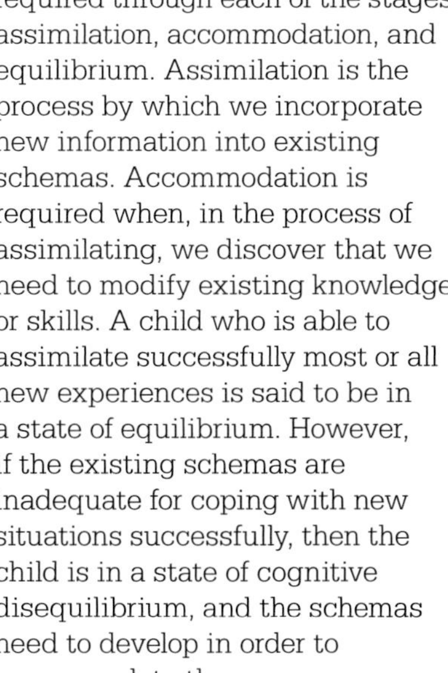required through each of the stages; assimilation, accommodation, and equilibrium. Assimilation is the process by which we incorporate new information into existing schemas. Accommodation is required when, in the process of assimilating, we discover that we need to modify existing knowledge or skills. A child who is able to assimilate successfully most or all new experiences is said to be in a state of equilibrium. However, if the existing schemas are inadequate for coping with new situations successfully, then the child is in a state of cognitive disequilibrium, and the schemas need to develop in order to accommodate the necessary information. Essentially, this is the process of adaptation, one of the most basic forms of learning.

Impact on education

Piaget's work inspired the transformation of the education systems of Europe and the US during the 1970s and '80s, bringing about a more child-centered

Intelligence is what you use when you don't know what to do.
Jean Piaget

approach to teaching, in theory and in practice. Rather than trying to teach a child to think and behave like an adult, educators were encouraged to view their work as an opportunity to engage children in novel and individual modes of thinking. Piaget believed that education should inspire people to create, invent, and innovate, and actively discourage them from conforming or following established guidelines at the expense of imagination. If the natural process of learning—from infancy onward—is individual, active, and exploratory, then so too should be a system of education that guides children's formal intellectual development.

Another vitally important aspect of a child-centered education is an awareness of the concept of "readiness," which involves setting limits on learning based on the child's stage of development. One of Piaget's most enduring contributions to the field of education, particularly with »

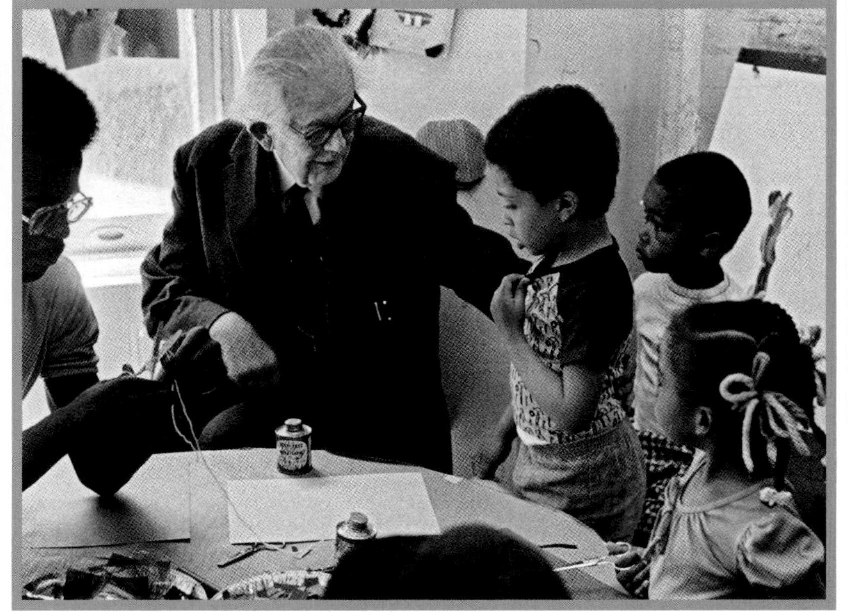

Educators should not insist on a particular way of doing or understanding something, Piaget (pictured left) asserted, but nurture children's natural learning processes.

Children at this Montessori school bring Piaget's ideas to life. They are encouraged to build their own learning with hands-on activities and plenty of discussion with their peers.

regards to mathematics and science, is the acknowledgement that teachers need to be aware of and honor an individual child's capacity to deal with a novel experience or to take on fresh information. The tasks that a teacher sets should reflect, and also be adapted as precisely as possible to, the individual student's cognitive level and capabilities.

Piaget believed that children learn from being active rather than from passive observation, and teachers must adapt to this. Interaction between students is of primary significance in the classroom, and having established that one of the best ways to secure knowledge is to teach it to somebody else, it follows that if children are allowed to discuss topics actively among themselves (rather than listening passively to lessons), they are more likely to deepen and consolidate their existing knowledge.

Moral education

As with intellectual development, Piaget believed that children also develop morally in stages and, for the most part, autonomously. Real moral growth is not the product of adult instruction, but is based on a child's own observations of the world. Piaget viewed peer interaction as absolutely crucial for the moral development of children. Peers, not parents or other authority figures, are seen as being vital to moral growth, providing a key source for understanding concepts such as reciprocity, equality, and justice. Consequently, Piaget

Children have real understanding only of that which they invent themselves.
Jean Piaget

eagerly promoted peer interaction within the classroom as an integral part of the learning experience.

The role of the teacher in Piaget's child-centered classroom is, therefore, almost one of a mentor and an enabler rather than that of a standard instructor. Teachers need to assess carefully each student's current level of cognitive development and then set tasks that are intrinsically motivating. Interestingly, teachers must also create cognitive disequilibrium in their students in order to help them advance to the next stage of

Jean Piaget

Born in Neuchâtel, Switzerland, Jean Piaget grew up with an insatiable interest in the natural world, and at the age of 11 he wrote his first scientific paper. He studied natural sciences and earned a PhD from the University of Neuchâtel at the age of 22. His interest moved to psychoanalysis and he developed his theories of genetic epistemology in France. In 1921, he became the director of the Jean-Jacques Rousseau Institute in Geneva. He married Valentine Châtenay and they had three children, who were the subjects of many of Piaget's observations about cognitive development. In 1955, he created the International Centre for Genetic Epistemology and was its director until his death in 1980. He was awarded prizes and honorary degrees worldwide.

Key works

1932 *The Moral Judgment of the Child*
1947 *The Psychology of Intelligence*
1952 *The Origins of Intelligence in Children*
1962 *The Psychology of the Child*

development, thereby providing genuine learning opportunities. They should focus on the process of learning, rather than on the achievement of end results, by encouraging their students to ask more questions, experiment, and explore, even if that means making some mistakes along the way. Above all, they must engender a collaborative space where students teach and learn from each other.

Criticisms of Piaget's work

Despite his popularity and the broad influence of his work in the fields of developmental psychology, education, morality, evolution, philosophy, and even artificial intelligence, Piaget's ideas were not accepted without scrutiny and criticism. As with all highly influential theories, years of exploration and research have brought to light its problems and weaknesses. Piaget's notion of egocentrism, for instance, has been called into question. Studies by the US psychologist Susan Gelman in 1979 demonstrated that four-year-olds were able to adjust their explanation of something in order to clarify it for a blindfolded person, and would use simpler forms of speech when talking to younger children, which is inconsistent with Piaget's description of an egocentric child who has no awareness of the needs of others.

Piaget's portrayal of children as primarily independent and autonomous in their construction of knowledge and their understanding of the physical world also met with some resistance, as it seemed to ignore the important contribution that other people make to a child's cognitive development. Pioneering psychologist Lev Vygotsky's work focused on proving that knowledge and thought are essentially social in nature, and disproving Piaget's assumption that a child was not really a part of the social whole. His theory suggests human development exists on three levels: the cultural and the interpersonal as well as the individual, and his main concern was with the first two levels. His "zone of proximal development" theory—which states that children require the help of adults or older children to complete some tasks—served as a response to Piaget.

Another area of exploration has been the assumed universality of the developmental stages identified by Piaget. Although he had no compelling evidence to support this assumption at the time, more recent cross-cultural investigations concerning the sensorimotor stage (including one study conducted by Pierre Dasen in 1994) indicated that the substages suggested by Piaget are indeed universal, though environmental and cultural factors seem to affect the rate at which these stages are reached, and how quickly they are then completed.

Piaget's work unquestionably paved the way for many new areas of enquiry into the nature of child development and human cognitive development. He created the context in which a vast body of research took shape in the 20th and 21st centuries, and fundamentally changed the nature of education in the Western world. ■

Indigenous Australian children aged between eight and 14 and living in remote parts of central Australia were found by Pierre Dasen to progress through the stages identified by Piaget.

> The deep structures, the basic cognitive processes, are indeed universal.
> **Pierre Dasen**

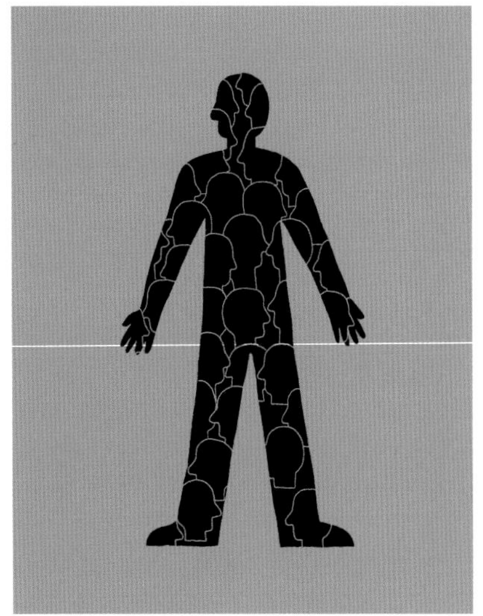

WE BECOME OURSELVES THROUGH OTHERS

LEV VYGOTSKY (1896–1934)

IN CONTEXT

APPROACH
Social constructivism

BEFORE
1860s Francis Galton sparks debate about whether nature (innate ability) or nurture (upbringing) has the most influence on personality.

AFTER
1952 Jean Piaget argues that the ability to absorb and process information develops through interaction between children's innate talents and their environment.

1966 Jerome Bruner suggests that any subject can be taught effectively to a child at any stage of development.

1990 American educational psychologist Robert Slavin designs his Student Teams Achievement Divisions (STAD) to promote more collaborative learning, and downgrade competitive, winner–loser approaches to education.

For Russian psychologist Lev Vygotsky, the skills needed to reason, understand, and remember all stem from a child's experiences with parents, teachers, and peers. Vygotsky saw human development as taking place on three levels—cultural, interpersonal, and individual. He focused on the cultural and interpersonal levels, believing that our most formative experiences are social; "we become ourselves through others."

All higher psychological functions are internalized relationships of the social kind.
Lev Vygotsky

Vygotsky believed that children absorb the accumulated wisdom, values, and technical knowledge of previous generations through interactions with their caregivers, and use these "tools" to learn how to conduct themselves effectively in the world. But it is only through social interaction that children can experience and internalize these cultural tools. Even our ability to think and reason on an individual level stems from social activities in the course of our development that foster our innate cognitive abilities.

Vygotsky's theories influenced approaches to both learning and teaching. He believed that teachers should play an instructive role, constantly guiding and nurturing their pupils in order to improve their attention span, concentration, and learning skills, and so build up their competence. This idea had a marked effect on education, particularly in the late 20th century, stimulating a shift from child-centered to curriculum-centered teaching, and to a greater use of collaborative learning. ■

See also: Francis Galton 28–29 ▪ Jerome Bruner 164–165 ▪ Jean Piaget 270–277

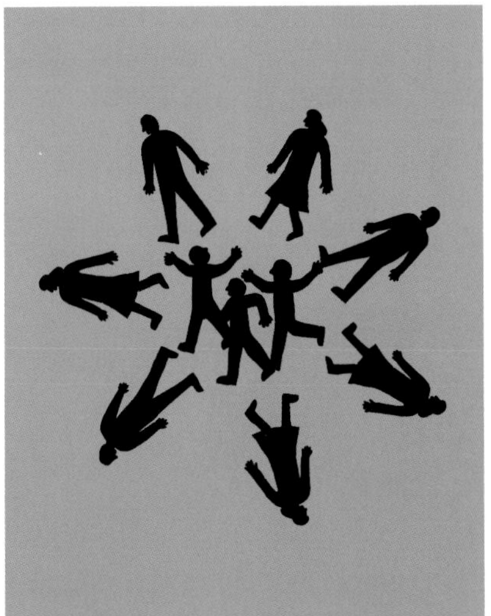

A CHILD IS NOT BEHOLDEN TO ANY PARTICULAR PARENT

BRUNO BETTELHEIM (1903–1990)

IN CONTEXT

APPROACH
Parenting systems

BEFORE
1945 American psychoanalyst René Spitz reports on the disastrous effects of bringing up children in institutions.

1951 John Bowlby concludes that an infant requires an intimate and continuous relationship with his mother.

1958 US anthropologist Melford Spiro writes *Children of the Kibbutz*, insinuating that Western child-rearing methods, with the focus on the mother as the main carer, work best in all cultures.

AFTER
1973 American psychiatrists Charles M. Johnston and Robert Deisher argue that communal child-rearing provides advantages that few nuclear families offer.

While running a center where disturbed children were raised successfully by professional carers, Bruno Bettelheim began to question the common assumption that the best upbringing involved a close mother–child relationship. He wondered if the Western world might have something to learn from communal child-rearing systems, such as the one used on an Israeli kibbutz.

In 1964, Bettelheim spent seven weeks on a kibbutz, where children were cared for in special houses, away from their family home. In his 1967 book *The Children of the Dream*, he stated that "a kibbutz child is not beholden to any particular parent," and although he observed that this led to fewer one-to-one relationships, it did encourage many less intimate friendships and an active social life.

Successful adults

Before his study, Bettelheim had predicted that a kibbutz might produce mediocre adults who had little cultural impact on society. Instead, he found that kibbutzniks often become accomplished adults. In fact, the children Bettelheim studied were tracked down in the 1990s by a journalist, who discovered that a high percentage were now successful professionals.

Bettelheim concluded that the kibbutz's communal approach was a huge success. By publishing his findings, he hoped to improve childcare systems in the US. ■

Kibbutz children, Bettelheim found, often develop closer bonds with each other than with adults. This ability to relate well to their peers may explain their professional success as adults.

See also: Virginia Satir 146–147 ▪ John Bowlby 282–285

ANYTHING THAT GROWS HAS A GROUND PLAN

ERIK ERIKSON (1902–1994)

IN CONTEXT

APPROACH
Psychosocial development

BEFORE
1905 Sigmund Freud develops his theory of psychosexual development, claiming there are five stages through which a child progresses toward sexual maturity.

1930s Jean Piaget proposes a stage-based theory of cognitive development.

AFTER
1980 Building on Erikson's work, American psychologist James Marcia explores identity formation in adolescence.

1996 In her bestselling book *New Passages*, American writer Gail Sheehy notes that adults are prolonging their adolescence into their thirties, pushing back all of Erikson's stages of adulthood by approximately 10 years.

Erik Erikson understood human development in terms of the epigenetic principle, which states that every organism is born with a certain purpose and its successful development results in the fulfillment of this purpose. In Erikson's own words, "anything that grows has a ground plan, and out of this the parts arise." He proposed that the human personality unfolds and evolves in eight predetermined stages. According to Erikson, this growth involves the constant interaction between heredity and environmental influences.

The eight stages

The first stage, which takes place during a baby's first year, is "trust versus mistrust." If the infant's needs are badly or inconsistently met, feelings of mistrust develop that can recur in later relationships. The second stage, "autonomy versus shame and doubt," takes place from 18 months to 2 years. This is when the child learns to explore, but also for the first time must deal with feelings of shame and doubt as a result of small failures or parental reprimands. Healthy willpower develops as a result of learning to negotiate both success and failure. Stage three, from three to six years, presents the crisis of "initiative versus guilt." This is when children learn to act creatively and playfully, but also with purpose. As they interact with others they discover that their actions can adversely affect someone else. Severe punishments at this stage can inflict paralyzing feelings of guilt.

From 6 to 12, children focus on education and learning social skills. This fourth stage is known as "industry versus inferiority," and it provides a feeling of competence, although an overemphasis on work can lead children mistakenly to equate self-worth with productivity.

Hope is both the earliest and the most indispensable virtue inherent in the state of being alive.
Erik Erikson

See also: G. Stanley Hall 46–47 ▪ Sigmund Freud 92–99 ▪ Kurt Lewin 222–227 ▪ Jean Piaget 270–277 ▪ Lawrence Kohlberg 300–301

Anything that grows has a ground plan, and out of this the parts arise.

The human personality develops through eight **distinct and predetermined stages** between birth and death.

By **negotiating each stage successfully**, we develop as mentally healthy individuals.

Failure at any stage results in a **mental deficiency** (such as lack of trust or an overwhelming sense of guilt) that stays with us throughout life.

From here we enter adolescence and the fifth stage of "ego-identity versus role confusion." This is when we develop a coherent sense of who we are, through consideration of our past, present, and future. When successfully negotiated, this stage ensures a unified sense of self, but problems here can lead to an "identity crisis"—a term coined by Erikson.

During the sixth stage of "intimacy versus isolation," between the ages of 18 and 30, we build close relationships and experience love. The penultimate stage, "generativity versus stagnation," from 35 to 60, sees us working on behalf of future generations, or contributing to society through cultural activities or social activism.

The final stage, "ego-integrity versus despair," starts at the age of around 60. It occurs when people reflect on their lives, becoming either satisfied and at peace with their old age, or despairing over physical disintegration and the reality of death. Successful negotiation of this stage results in the attainment of wisdom. ■

Erikson said that in our older years we achieve a sense of completeness and "personal wholeness" in direct proportion to the degree to which we successfully negotiated earlier stages.

Erik Erikson

Erik Erikson was born in Frankfurt, Germany, as the result of an extramarital affair. He was given the surname of his mother's husband (he never knew his biological father), and his mother married again when he was three years old. He was encouraged to study medicine, but rebelled and studied art, touring Italy in his youth as a "wandering artist." Having always struggled with identity issues, Erikson then suffered what he called an "aggravated identity crisis" and went to Vienna, where he taught art in a school run on psychoanalytic principles. Embracing these fully, he then trained as a psychoanalyst under Anna Freud. In 1933, he married Joan Serson and they emigrated to Boston, where he became the first child psychoanalyst in the city. He later taught at Harvard, Yale, and Berkeley. He changed his surname to the self-chosen "Erikson" when he became an American citizen in 1933.

Key works

1950 *Childhood and Society*
1964 *Insight and Responsibility*
1968 *Identity: Youth and Crisis*

EARLY EMOTIONAL BONDS ARE AN INTEGRAL PART OF HUMAN NATURE

JOHN BOWLBY (1907–1990)

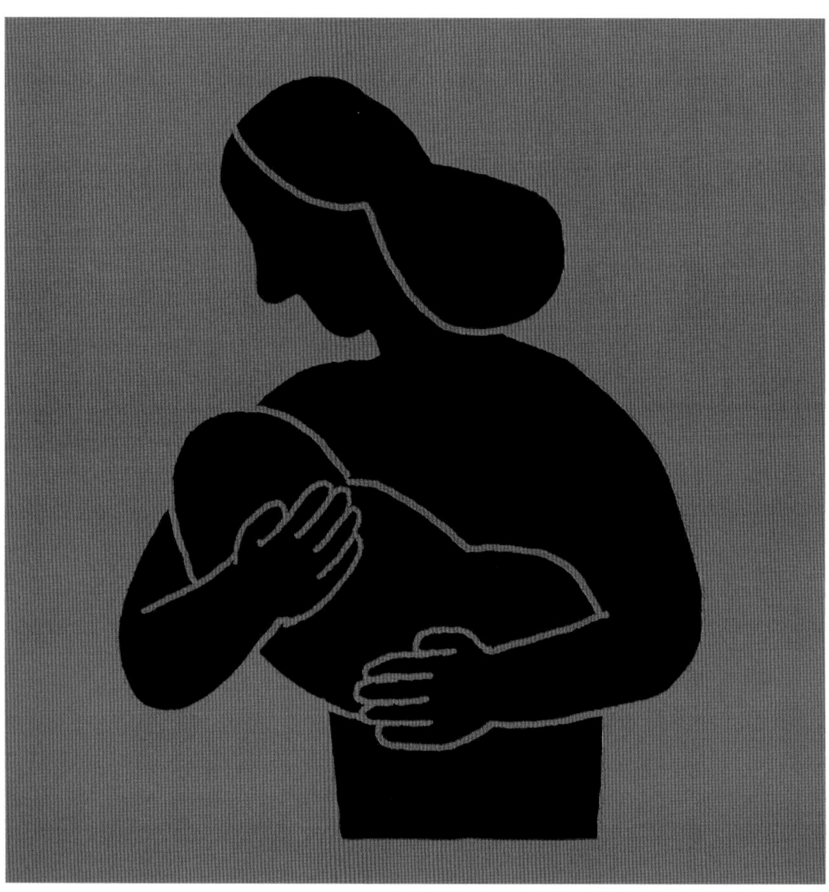

IN CONTEXT

APPROACH
Attachment theory

BEFORE
1926 Sigmund Freud presents the psychoanalytic theory of "cupboard love," suggesting that infants become attached to caregivers because they fulfil physiological needs.

1935 Konrad Lorenz's research shows that nonhumans form strong bonds with the first moving object they encounter.

AFTER
1959 Harry Harlow's work demonstrates that macaque monkeys separated from their mothers in infancy develop social and emotional problems.

1978 Michael Rutter shows that children can become strongly attached to a variety of attachment figures (such as fathers, siblings, peers, and inanimate objects).

In the 1950s, the prevailing theory on how infants form attachments was based on the psychoanalytical concept of "cupboard love." This suggested that babies form bonds with people who fulfil their physiological needs, such as feeding. At the same time, the animal studies of Konrad Lorenz suggested that animals simply bond with the first moving object they encounter, which is usually the mother.

It was against this background that John Bowlby took a distinctly evolutionary perspective on early attachment. He argued that because newborn infants are completely helpless, they are genetically

See also: Konrad Lorenz 77 ▪ Sigmund Freud 92–99 ▪ Melanie Klein 108–109 ▪ Anna Freud 111 ▪ Kurt Lewin 222–227 ▪ Lev Vygotsky 278 ▪ Bruno Bettelheim 279 ▪ Harry Harlow 286 ▪ Mary Ainsworth 288–289 ▪ Michael Rutter 346

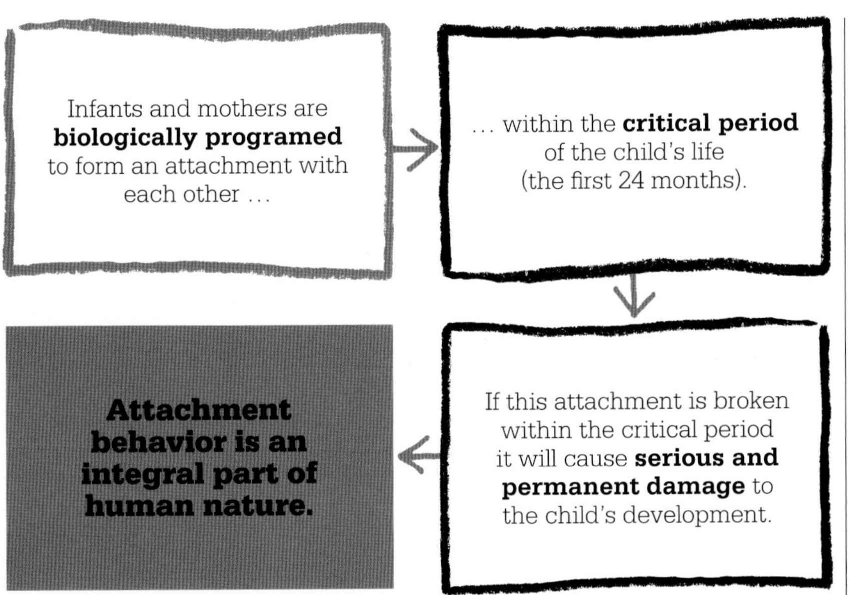

programed to form an attachment with their mothers in order to ensure their survival. Mothers, he believed, are also genetically programmed to bond with their babies, feeling the need to keep them in close proximity. Any conditions that threaten to separate mother and child activate instinctive attachment behaviors and feelings of insecurity and fear.

Infants and mothers are **biologically programed** to form an attachment with each other …
… within the **critical period** of the child's life (the first 24 months).
If this attachment is broken within the critical period it will cause **serious and permanent damage** to the child's development.
Attachment behavior is an integral part of human nature.

These ideas formed the basis of Bowlby's theory, which developed to explain the lifelong significance of the mother–infant bond as well as the psychological difficulties that children suffer if this bond is damaged or entirely broken.

Mothers only

One of the most controversial aspects of Bowlby's theory is that infants always attach to a woman, never a man. This female figure may not be the natural mother, but she certainly represents a mother-figure. The term he gave for this tendency to attach to a female is "monotropy," and he emphasized that, although an infant may have more than one attachment figure, their attachment to a mother-figure is simply different from and more significant than any other attachment they will form throughout their life. Both the infant and their mother behave in ways that secure this attachment. An infant, for instance, engages in sucking, cuddling, looking, smiling, and crying in order to shape and control their caregiver's behavior, and a caregiver would be both sensitive and responsive to the infant's needs. In this way, the two behavioral systems—attachment and caregiving—help shape one another and create a lifelong bond.

Bowlby believes that this bond is so deeply formative that if it fails to take place, or breaks down within the first few years of life, the child will go on to suffer serious negative consequences in later life. He also argues that there is a critical period during which a mother and infant should develop a secure attachment: it should take place during the first year, or at the very least before the child is two years old. Bowlby thought that any attempts at mothering beyond the age of three would be useless, and the child would be on course to suffer the effects of maternal deprivation.

Maternal deprivation

In 1950, Bowlby was commissioned by the World Health Organization to study children who had suffered maternal deprivation during World War II due to evacuation or being made homeless. He was also asked to investigate the effects of being raised in residential nurseries and other large institutions (such as orphanages). The result of this early work was Bowlby's 1951 report, *Maternal Care and Mental Health*, in which he observed that children deprived of maternal care for prolonged periods of time during early childhood suffered some degree of intellectual, social, or emotional retardation later in life.

Five years later, Bowlby began a second study, this time investigating children who had spent five months to two years in a tuberculosis »

Mother love in infancy is as important for mental health as are vitamins and proteins for physical health.
John Bowlby

Bowlby predicted that child evacuees would suffer long-term attachment problems as a result of enforced separation from their mothers; later studies found this to be the case.

sanatorium (which offered no substitute mothering) when they had been less than four years old. The children—aged seven to 13 by the time of the study—were rougher in play, showed less initiative and more overexcitement, and were less competitive than those with a more traditional upbringing.

In extreme cases, Bowlby found that maternal deprivation could even result in "affectionless psychopathy," a clinical condition in which people are unable to care deeply for others and so do not form meaningful interpersonal relationships. Those who suffer from it display a higher incidence of juvenile delinquency and antisocial behavior without any sign of remorse, since they are unable to experience feelings of guilt. In Bowlby's 1944 study of juvenile thieves, he found that many of the young criminals had been separated from their mothers for a period of more than six months before they were five years old, and of these, 14 had developed the condition of affectionless psychopathy.

Attachment behavior is held to characterize human beings from the cradle to the grave.
John Bowlby

The reason why this primary, secure attachment is so important, Bowlby says, is that it is essential for the development of an inner working model or framework that children use to understand themselves, others, and the world. This inner working model guides a person's thoughts, feelings, and expectations in all of their personal relationships, even into adulthood. Because the primary attachment serves as a prototype for all future relationships, the quality of the attachment will determine whether or not children grow to trust others, view themselves as valuable, and feel confident in society. These working models are resistant to change; once formed, they determine how people behave and the kind of bond they will form with their own children.

The father's role

Bowlby's attachment theory has been criticized for exaggerating the importance of the mother–child relationship and undervaluing the father's contribution. Bowlby sees the father as having no direct emotional significance for the infant, contributing only indirectly by supporting the mother financially and emotionally. The evolutionary basis of Bowlby's theory suggests that women are naturally inclined to be parents, with inborn maternal instincts that guide them through the process of child-rearing, whereas men are more naturally suited for being providers.

However, British psychologist Rudolph Schaffer—who worked under Bowlby at the Tavistock Clinic in London—found that there is considerable cultural variation in the extent to which fathers are involved in childcare. Increasing numbers of fathers are taking on the role of principal parent, which suggests that parenting roles are a consequence of social convention rather than biology.

Bowlby's view implies that men will inevitably be inferior parents, but research by Schaffer and the American psychologist Ross Parke suggests that men are equally capable of providing warmth and sensitivity to their infants. They also found that a child's developmental outcome is not determined by the parent's gender, but rather by the strength and

Direct observations of men in their fathering role has shown them to be as capable of as much warmth and sensitivity as women.
H. Rudolph Schaffer

quality of the bond that is forged. In a further study, Schaffer and psychologist Peggy Emerson found that infants and young children display a wide range of attachment behaviors toward many people besides their mothers, and that multiple attachments may actually be the rule rather than the exception.

These later findings were especially important for working women, because the implication of Bowlby's theories was that women should not work once they become mothers; they should stay with the child, fulfilling the role of essential primary caregiver. For decades after Bowlby's theory was posited, generations of working women were saddled with guilt, but many studies since then have questioned this aspect of Bowlby's theory. For instance, in the 1970s psychologists Thomas Weisner and Ronald Gallimore showed that mothers are the exclusive caregivers in only a very small percentage of human societies, and it is not uncommon for groups of people (including relatives and friends) to share responsibility for raising children. Schaffer also points to evidence suggesting that children of mothers who are happy in their work develop more successfully than children whose mothers are frustrated from staying at home.

Groundbreaking work

Despite the many criticisms and revisions that it has provoked, Bowlby's work remains the most comprehensive and influential account of human attachment to date, and led to the groundbreaking experiments of Harry Harlow and Mary Ainsworth. Psychologists have used Bowlby's basic premise to delve more deeply into childhood attachment patterns, and to develop theories of adult attachment by exploring how the bond between parent and child can influence the future bond between spouses and romantic partners. Bowlby's theories have also had many beneficial effects on various aspects of child-rearing, such as the improvement of institutional care and the growing preference for fostering as an alternative. ■

Bowlby claimed that day care centers are not suitable for the care of infants, as maternal deprivation leads to juvenile delinquency; this created a real dilemma for working mothers.

John Bowlby

John Bowlby was the fourth of six children born to a London-based, upper-middle-class family. He was raised primarily by nannies and sent to boarding school at the age of seven. These experiences made him particularly sympathetic to the attachment difficulties faced by young children. He studied psychology at Trinity College, Cambridge, then spent some time teaching delinquent children. He later earned a medical degree and qualified as a psychoanalyst.

During World War II, Bowlby served in the Royal Army Medical Corps and in 1938 married Ursula Longstaff, with whom he had four children. After the war he became director of the Tavistock Clinic, where he remained until retirement. In 1950, he carried out a major study for the World Health Organization. He died at his summer home on the Island of Skye in Scotland, aged 83.

Key works

1951 *Maternal Care and Mental Health (WHO Report)*
1959 *Separation Anxiety*
1969, 1973, 1980 *Attachment and Loss* (three volumes)

CONTACT COMFORT IS OVERWHELMINGLY IMPORTANT

HARRY HARLOW (1905–1981)

IN CONTEXT

APPROACH
Attachment theory

BEFORE
1926 Sigmund Freud's psychoanalytic theory of "cupboard love" suggests that an infant becomes attached to a caregiver because that person is a source of food.

1935 Konrad Lorenz states nonhumans form strong bonds with the first moving object they meet—often the mother.

1951 John Bowlby argues that human mothers and infants are genetically programmed to form a uniquely strong bond.

AFTER
1964 UK psychologists Rudolf Schaffer and Peggy Emerson show that infants are attached to people who do not perform feeding and caretaking duties.

1978 Michael Rutter shows that children bond with a variety of attachment figures, including inanimate objects.

Many psychologists have suggested that an infant becomes attached to its caregiver simply because that person fulfils its need for food. John Bowlby challenged this "cupboard love" idea theoretically, but Harry Harlow set out to prove it.

Harlow took infant macaque monkeys from their mothers, placing them in cages with surrogate "mothers"—one made of wire with a feeding bottle attached; the other made of soft, cuddly, terry cloth, but with no bottle. If the "cupboard love" theory was correct, the baby monkeys would remain with the mother that provided food. But in fact, they spent most of their time with the cloth mother, using her as a secure base, and clinging to her for safety when frightening objects were placed in the cage. Later tests, in which the cloth mother was also able to rock and provide food, showed this attachment was even stronger. Harlow, therefore, suggested that the main function of nursing might even be to ensure body contact with the mother.

Infant macaque monkeys in Harlow's experiment formed a strong attachment to their cuddly, cloth, surrogate "mother," despite her inability to provide any nourishment.

Harlow's work was enormously important, because contemporary advice from psychologists and doctors had warned parents against rocking or picking up a crying child. The results of his experiments were so conclusive that they changed the approach to parenting in the Western world. ■

See also: Konrad Lorenz 77 ▪ Sigmund Freud 92–99 ▪ Abraham Maslow 138–139 ▪ John Bowlby 282–285 ▪ Mary Ainsworth 288–289 ▪ Michael Rutter 346

WE PREPARE CHILDREN FOR A LIFE ABOUT WHOSE COURSE WE KNOW NOTHING

FRANÇOISE DOLTO (1908–1988)

IN CONTEXT

APPROACH
Psychoanalysis

BEFORE
1924 Sigmund Freud theorizes about the castration anxiety children face, which Dolto says is a factor in our unconscious image of our own bodies.

1969 Jacques Lacan investigates "otherness," which becomes central to Dolto's work focusing on the distinctiveness of individuals.

AFTER
1973 A school based on Dolto's theories opens in La Neuville-du-Bosc, France, emphasizing well-being and noncompulsory activities.

1978 La Maison Verte, a daycare center based on Dolto's ideas, opens in Paris, with the aim of helping parents and children to minimize the adverse effects of separation.

Following her own difficult childhood, French physician and psychoanalyst Françoise Dolto decided that her work should help children discover and release their desires, believing that this release would prevent neuroses. She felt that some of the illnesses commonly manifested by children were, in reality, reflections of a lack of connection between parents and their offspring. Adults, she observed, often seemed unable to understand children, in spite of once being children themselves.

Unique perspective

Dolto believed that every child possesses a unique perspective, which traditional education seeks to stifle. She condemned any system of morality or education that seeks to control children through obedience or imitation, and was dissatisfied with the techniques being used, both at school and at home, to anticipate a child's future when that future is fundamentally unknowable. Children, she stated, are different from the adults who teach them, simply because they must have had experiences that the older generation could never have had when they were that age.

For Dolto, the goal of education was to allow each child the freedom to explore his individual inclination. The adult, she believed, should serve as a role model, offering an example rather than attempting to impart a method. The educator's role, Dolto declared, was to teach children how to lead themselves. ■

It is too late to make a difference with adults; the work has to be done with children.
Françoise Dolto

See also: Sigmund Freud 92–99 ▪ Alfred Adler 100–101 ▪ Jacques Lacan 122–123 ▪ Daniel Lagache 343

A SENSITIVE MOTHER CREATES A SECURE ATTACHMENT

MARY AINSWORTH (1913–1999)

IN CONTEXT

APPROACH
Attachment theory

BEFORE
1950s John Bowlby emphasizes the significance of the mother-child bond.

1959 Harry Harlow's research with infant macaque monkeys demonstrates that they use an attachment figure as a secure base from which to explore their environment.

AFTER
1980 American psychologist Brian E. Vaughn shows that the attachment figure may change, according to variations in a family's circumstances.

1990 American psychologist Mary Main identifies a fourth attachment type in young children—"disorganized"—to describe an infant who is fearful of both the environment and the attachment figure.

In the early 1950s, Mary Ainsworth, working closely with attachment theorist John Bowlby, developed a particular interest in the relationship between mothers and infants. In 1969, she experimented with a procedure that became known as the "Strange Situation," which studied how babies balance their needs for attachment and exploration under varying levels of stress. In each experiment, Ainsworth placed a mother and her one-year-old baby in a room with toys for the baby to play with, and watched their

When **separated from its mother**, an infant displays one of three different kinds of attachment.

If the infant shows no signs of distress and can be comforted by a stranger, the attachment is **anxious-avoidant.**

If the infant shows intense signs of distress but resists contact with the mother on her return, the attachment is **anxious-resistant.**

If the infant is distressed, but upon the mother's return uses her as a secure base from which to explore, there is a secure attachment.

See also: Sigmund Freud 92–99 ▪ John Bowlby 282–285 ▪ Harry Harlow 286 ▪ Jerome Kagan 345–346 ▪ Michael Rutter 346

Attachment behavior is strongly activated under circumstances when the attachment figure is inaccessible.
Mary Ainsworth

interactions both before and after the introduction of a stranger to the room. The "situation" included periods when the mother left the baby alone with the stranger, then returned to the room.

Ainsworth found that the most important information about mother-child bonding was gleaned not from the baby's reaction to the mother leaving the room, but rather from the infant's reaction to her return. She suggested that a baby's reactions upon reunion with his mother indicate three distinct patterns, or types, of attachment.

Attachment types

Around 70 percent of the babies in Ainsworth's studies were "securely attached." These infants used their mothers "as a secure base from which to explore." They were distressed when she left the room, but played happily, even in the presence of a stranger, as long as the mother was on hand if needed.

The babies who appeared to be indifferent to their mothers, and were hardly affected when she left the room, Ainsworth classified as "anxious-avoidant." They were as easily comforted by the stranger as by the mother. About 15 percent of the infants fell into this group.

A further 15 percent, described as "anxious-resistant," were wary of the stranger, even with the mother present. They became intensely distressed when the mother left the room, but were also angry and resistant to contact on her return.

Mothers in non-Western cultures often keep their infants close to them at all times. Customs such as these can affect the incidence of different attachment types in a community.

Ainsworth claimed that a mother's sensitivity largely determines the type of attachment. A sensitive mother, she stated, understands her child's needs and responds appropriately to them, creating a secure attachment.

Criticism

Critics of Ainsworth's work have suggested that attachment types are not always permanent, and that babies do not fit neatly into a single type. Cultural differences have also been noted. A 1990 study in Japan uncovered an unusually high percentage of anxious-resistant infants, which may have been due to Japanese babies being less used to separation from their mothers than US infants. However, the Strange Situation is considered to be one of the most important studies in attachment research, and is still widely replicated today. ■

Mary Ainsworth

Mary Ainsworth was born in Glendale, Ohio, moving to Canada at the age of five. She gained her doctorate in psychology from the University of Toronto in 1939, and taught there briefly before joining the Canadian Women's Army Corps in 1942. After World War II, she returned to the University of Toronto, marrying graduate student Leonard Ainsworth in 1950 and moving to London, where Mary worked with John Bowlby at the Tavistock Clinic. In 1954, the couple moved to Uganda, where Leonard had accepted a post, and Mary took the opportunity to study mother-child bonding in tribal society. On returning to the US in 1956, she continued her academic career, eventually becoming a professor at the University of Virginia in 1975.

Key works

1967 *Infancy in Uganda*
1971 *Infant Obedience and Maternal Behavior*
1978 *Patterns of Attachment*

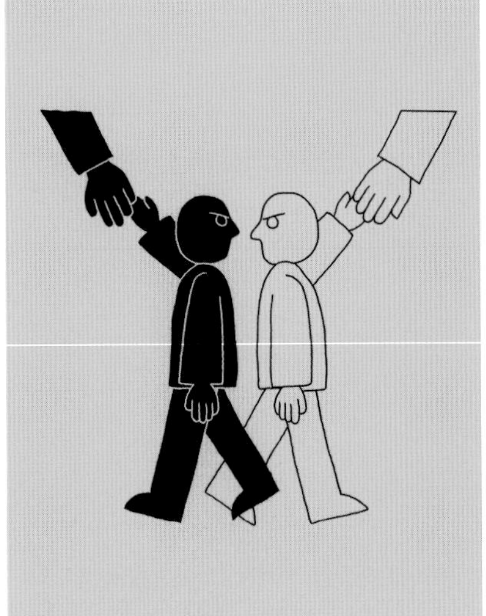

WHO TEACHES A CHILD TO HATE AND FEAR A MEMBER OF ANOTHER RACE?

KENNETH CLARK (1914–2005) & MAMIE PHIPPS CLARK (1917–1983)

IN CONTEXT

APPROACH
Race attitudes

BEFORE
1929 German-born writer and social worker Bruno Lasker publishes *Race Attitudes in Children*, setting up methods for the psychological study of children's views on race.

Early 1930s Canadian psychologist Otto Klineberg works with lawyers fighting for equal salaries for Black public-school teachers.

AFTER
1954 The US Supreme Court rules that racial segregation in schools is unconstitutional, in the *Brown v. Board of Education of Topeka* hearings.

1978 Elliot Aronson devises the "jigsaw method" of teaching—where mixed-race groups of students work interdependently—to help reduce racial prejudice in integrated classrooms.

During the late 1930s, Kenneth Clark and his wife, Mamie Phipps Clark, studied the psychological effects of segregation on Black American schoolchildren, particularly on their self-image. They designed a "doll test" that would indicate children's awareness of racial differences and their underlying attitudes about race. Working with children between the ages of three and seven, they used four dolls, each identical in appearance except for the color of their skin, which ranged from shades of white to dark brown. The children showed an undeniable awareness of race by correctly identifying the dolls on the basis of their skin color, as well as identifying themselves in racial terms by choosing the doll that looked most like them.

In order to explore the children's attitudes about race, the Clarks asked each of them to point out the doll they liked best or most wanted to play with; the doll that had a nice color; and the doll that looked bad. Distressingly, Black children showed a clear preference for the white dolls and a rejection of the Black dolls, which can be interpreted as indirect self-rejection. Convinced that this reflected the children's tendency to absorb racial prejudices that exist in society and then to turn this hatred inward, the Clarks asked a very important question: "Who teaches a child to hate and fear a member of another race?"

The Clarks' doll experiments showed that Black children in segregated schools often preferred white dolls, a sign that they had absorbed prevailing prejudices.

Passing on prejudice

The Clarks sought to understand the influences shaping prejudice in America, and decided that as children learn to evaluate racial differences, according to the standards of society, they are

See also: Elliot Aronson 250–251 ▪ Muzafer Sherif 343–344

By the age of three, children are **racially aware** and already forming **prejudices**.

In 1930s America, white and even black children showed a preference for whiteness and a **rejection of blackness**.

Who teaches a child to hate and fear a member of another race?

Segregation and social influences from parents, teachers, playmates, and the media lead to children internalizing racist attitudes.

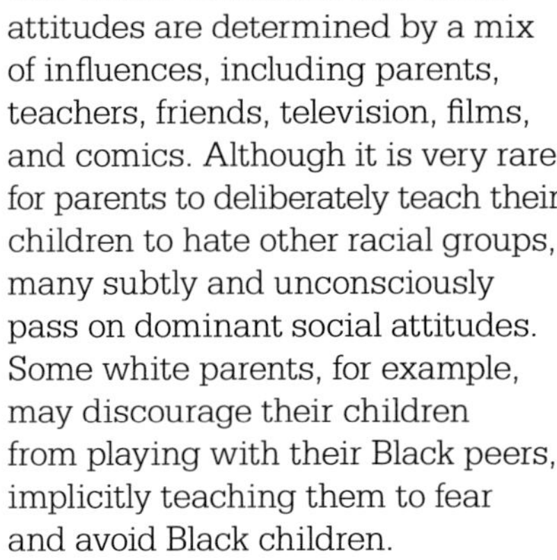

required to identify with a specific group, and each racial group has an implied status within a hierarchy. That young Black children preferred the white doll showed they were aware American society preferred white people and had internalized this. Children as young as three had expressed similar attitudes to those of adults in their community.

Segregation is a way in which society tells a group of human beings that they are inferior.
Kenneth Clark

The Clarks concluded that these attitudes are determined by a mix of influences, including parents, teachers, friends, television, films, and comics. Although it is very rare for parents to deliberately teach their children to hate other racial groups, many subtly and unconsciously pass on dominant social attitudes. Some white parents, for example, may discourage their children from playing with their Black peers, implicitly teaching them to fear and avoid Black children.

Clark's 1950 summary of his research insisted that segregation was damaging the personalities of white and Black children alike. His expert testimony in court cases tied into the 1954 *Brown v. Board of Education of Topeka* case, which determined that racial segregation was unconstitutional in public schools, contributed directly to desegregated schooling and to the Civil Rights Movement in America. ■

Kenneth Clark & Mamie Phipps Clark

Kenneth Clark grew up in Harlem, New York. Thanks to his mother's persistence, he attended high school, then earned a master's degree in psychology from Howard University, Washington DC. He married Mamie Phipps, who had grown up in Arkansas during racial segregation but had made it on a scholarship to Howard.

The pair carried out research together, becoming the first Black American man and woman to receive a PhD in psychology from Columbia University in New York City. They also founded child development and youth opportunity centers in Harlem.

Clark was also the first Black American to hold a permanent professorship at the City University of New York, and to serve as the president of the American Psychological Association.

Key works

1947 *Racial Identification and Preference in Negro Children*
1955 *Prejudice and Your Child*
1965 *Dark Ghetto*
1974 *Pathos of Power*

GIRLS GET BETTER GRADES THAN BOYS

ELEANOR E. MACCOBY (1917–2018)

IN CONTEXT

APPROACH
Feminist psychology

BEFORE
Early 20th century First research into sex differences by female psychologists.

1970s Studies of the genders tend to emphasize differences between men and women.

AFTER
1980s Studies suggest structural differences between the male and female brain.

1993 Anne Fausto-Sterling argues that a spectrum of sexes exists, with five gradations between "female" and "male."

2003 Simon Baron-Cohen claims the female brain is hard-wired for empathy, and the male brain for grasping systems.

2010 Cordelia Fine's book *Delusions of Gender* introduces "neurosexism": the assumption of differences between male and female minds.

There is no significant difference in the overall **intellectual aptitude** of boys and girls.

But because girls tend to put in a greater effort at school, and have greater interest and better work habits …

… girls get better grades than boys.

The emergence of feminist psychologists during the 1970s revived an interest in the study of sex differences, which had waned during the rise of behaviorism. Feminist concerns became increasingly important to US psychologist Eleanor Maccoby. Frustrated by the tendency of psychological literature to report on research findings that emphasized the differences between men and women rather than the similarities, Maccoby, with student Carol Jacklin, reviewed more than 1,600 studies of gender differences. They published their findings in *The Psychology of Sex Differences* (1974) with the aim of showing that what most consider essential differences between the genders are in fact myths, and that many gender stereotypes are untrue. Although some findings had shown boys to be more aggressive and more adept at mathematics and spatial reasoning than girls, and girls to have superior verbal abilities, subsequent studies revealed that these differences are either negligible or are more complex than they initially appear.

One difference that was consistent and undeniable was that "girls get better grades than boys" in school. Maccoby found this particularly interesting, especially considering that girls did not obtain higher aptitude test scores when all of the subject matter areas were reviewed.

See also: Janet Taylor Spence 242

Girls show greater responsiveness to teacher's expectations and are more willing to work, according to Maccoby's research, which makes them more likely to do better at school than boys.

Intellectual development in girls is fostered by their being assertive and active.
Eleanor E. Maccoby

Furthermore, previous research into achievement motivation seemed to suggest that boys should outperform their female peers. Boys were arguably more oriented toward achievement for its own sake than girls, showing greater task involvement and more exploratory behavior; girls were primarily interested in achievement relating to interpersonal relationships—exerting effort to please others and demonstrating low self-confidence with respect to many tasks.

Challenging stereotypes

Maccoby systemically argued against these assumptions, pointing to the fact that girls are higher academic achievers than boys, show greater interest in school-related skills from an early age, and are less likely to drop out before completing high school. Maccoby concluded that their better grades clearly reflect some combination of greater effort, greater interest, and better work habits than their male peers. Whatever discrepancy exists between boys and girls in terms of achievement motivation does not reflect school-related motivation. This motivation could prove significant throughout girls' lives, as performance at school is also relevant to job performance.

The ongoing debate over inherent sex differences is tied up with general political questions about how society should be organized, and the roles that men and women are "naturally" equipped to fill. By pointing out that psychological literature tends to publish results indicating sex differences, while ignoring those indicating equality, Maccoby has fought against the assignment of men and women to stereotypical professions. ■

Eleanor E. Maccoby

Born in Tacoma, Washington, Eleanor Maccoby (née Emmons) earned a bachelor's degree from the University of Washington and an MA and PhD in experimental psychology from the University of Michigan. In the 1940s, she worked at Harvard University, supervising research on child-rearing practices. Perceiving that gender bias was hindering her, Maccoby moved to Stanford University, where she was the first woman to serve as Chair of the Psychology Department. Considered one of the 100 most eminent psychologists of the 20th century, she received a Lifetime Achievement Award from the American Psychology Foundation, and The American Psychological Association created an award in her name. Maccoby's work to debunk stereotypes is viewed as key to understanding children's socialization and gender differences. She died aged 101.

Key works

1966 *The Development of Sex Differences*
1974 *The Psychology of Sex Differences*
1996 *Adolescents after Divorce*

MOST HUMAN BEHAVIOR IS LEARNED THROUGH MODELING

ALBERT BANDURA (1925–2021)

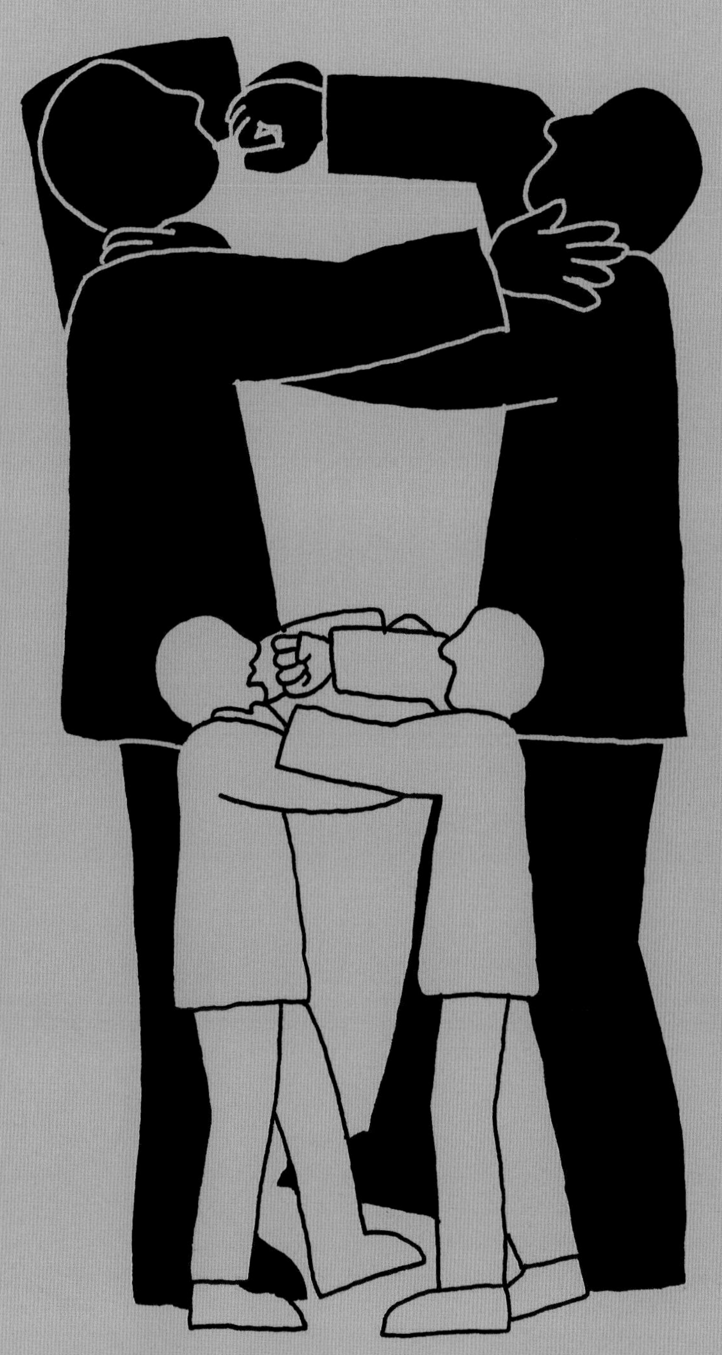

IN CONTEXT

APPROACH
Social learning theory

BEFORE
1938 B. F. Skinner proposes the behaviorist notion of operant conditioning, which explores positive and negative reinforcements in learning.

1939 US psychologist John Dollard argues that aggression is always a consequence of frustration, and that frustration always leads to aggression.

AFTER
1966 American psychologist Leonard Berkowitz claims environmental cues, such as those associated with aggressive behavior, must be present for aggression to follow anger.

1977 US psychologist Robert A. Baron suggests that Bandura's experiment implies that violence in the media contributes to violence in society.

In the 1940s and '50s, learning was understood primarily in behaviorist terms, with B. F. Skinner's theory of operant conditioning—in which learning is wholly determined by rewards and punishments—dominating the field. From this context emerged Albert Bandura's interest in studying childhood aggression—an area he felt was too complex to explain in terms of operant conditioning—as a learned behavior.

Bandura's hypothesis was that children learn aggression through observing and imitating the violent acts of adults—particularly family members. He believed that the key to the problem lies at the intersection of Skinner's operant conditioning and Freud's psychoanalytic theory of identification, which explores how people assimilate the characteristics of others into their own personalities. Bandura's work culminated in his famous Bobo doll experiment, and his hugely influential 1977 treatise *Social Learning Theory*.

Social learning theory

Bandura's belief that people learn not through reinforcement (rewards and punishments), but through observing others, is at the heart of social learning theory. This theory suggests that learning is achieved by mentally rehearsing and then imitating the observed actions of other people, who serve as models of appropriate or acceptable behavior. Bandura argued that "most human behavior is learned through modeling."

Bandura noted four conditions that are necessary for a person to successfully model the behavior of another: attention, retention, reproduction, and motivation. Learning requires that the learner is paying attention to the behavior in the first place, that they remember what they saw or heard, that they are actually able to physically reproduce the behavior, and that they have a good motive or reason to reproduce it, such as the expectation of reward.

Although the concept of reward is part of his social learning theory, Bandura's move away from behaviorism is evident in his radical, anti-behaviorist ideas about the relationship between a person's environment and their behavior. According to behaviorism, environmental circumstances

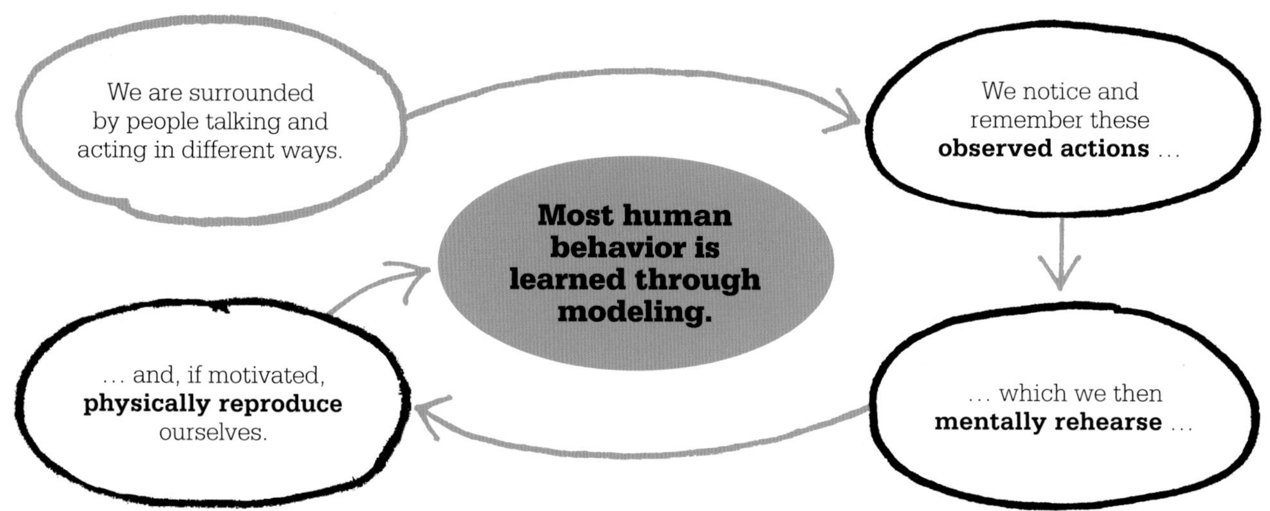

We are surrounded by people talking and acting in different ways.
We notice and remember these **observed actions** ...
... which we then **mentally rehearse** ...
... and, if motivated, **physically reproduce** ourselves.
Most human behavior is learned through modeling.

See also: Konrad Lorenz 77 ▪ B. F. Skinner 78–85 ▪ Sigmund Freud 92–99 ▪ Lev Vygotsky 278

entirely determine behavior, but Bandura believes in "reciprocal determinism"—the idea that a person influences the environment just as the environment influences them. He conceived of personality as an interaction between three different components: environment, behavior, and psychological processes (the ability to use language and entertain images in the mind). All of these components are relevant to the study of childhood aggression, which, Bandura argued, was learned by watching and modeling adults.

Bobo doll experiment

Bandura's social learning point of view was the basis for his 1961 Bobo doll experiment on childhood aggression, which sought to explain how aggressive behavior develops, what provokes people to aggressive acts, and what determines whether they continue to behave aggressively. By proving that a child will imitate the behavior of an adult role model, the experiment showed the power of examples of aggression in society.

Behavior partly created the environment, and the resultant environment, in turn, influenced the behavior.
Albert Bandura

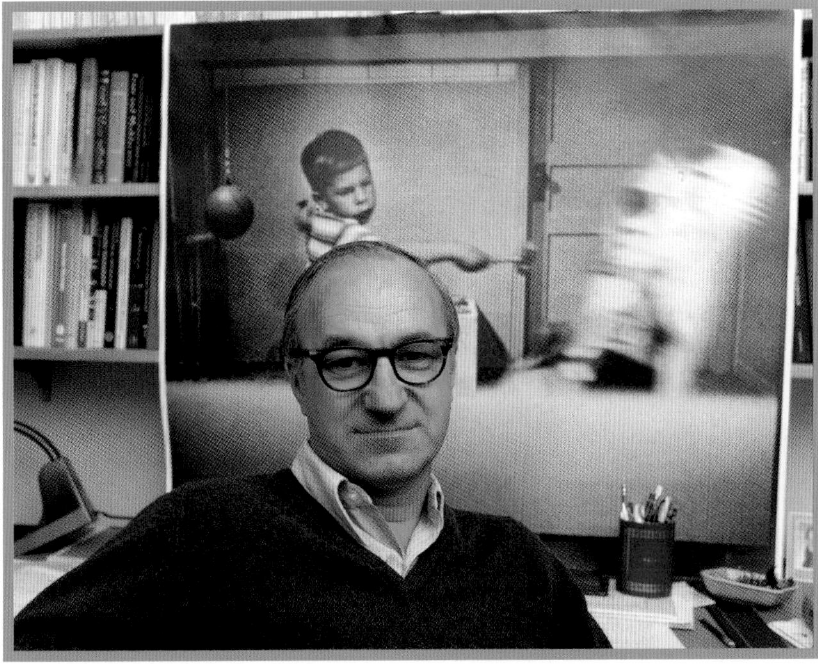

In Bandura's famous experiment on aggressive behavior (shown in the photograph on the wall behind him), children viciously attacked the Bobo doll.

For the experiment, 36 boys and 36 girls, all between the ages of three and six, were recruited from a local nursery school. They were divided up into three groups of 24, each comprising 12 boys and 12 girls. The first group was the control group (which did not see any adult role model); the second group was exposed to an adult modeling aggressive behavior toward an inflatable Bobo doll; the third group was exposed to a passive adult model. All of the children in the experiment were tested individually to ensure that they would not be influenced by their peers.

In the experiments on the second group, each child watched an adult performing physically and verbally aggressive acts toward the doll. The adult pummeled the large Bobo toy with a mallet, flung it in the air, kicked it, threw it down on the floor, and beat it. When each child was later left alone in a room of toys that included a Bobo doll, they imitated a good deal of the aggressive acts performed by the adult models, even creating novel acts of violence against the doll. Children in this group were also generally less inhibited than those in the other groups, showing an increased attraction to guns despite the fact that playing with guns was not modeled.

By contrast, children who were either in the control group or who were exposed to a passive adult model only rarely demonstrated any kind of physical or verbal aggression. Although Bandura did consider the possibility that observing aggressive acts merely »

Violence in computer games and the media has been cited as a potential source of behavior modeling, but psychologists are still debating this.

weakened any inhibitions that the children may have already had about behaving violently, the fact that they often imitated the exact behavior they had just seen suggests that observational learning was taking place.

Violence in the media

Bandura's research has raised many important questions surrounding the prevalence of violence in the media. If a stranger performing aggressive acts can be a model of aggression for children, you might argue that television programs could also be considered a source of behavior modeling. Modern films and television shows include graphic violence, which is often expressed as an acceptable (or at least expected) form of behavior, which children who are regularly exposed to the media may feel inclined to imitate. This idea has been hotly debated. Many studies indicate that violent films and television shows do not increase a child's tendencies toward violence. Some studies even indicate that exposure to violence can actually decrease the amount of aggression in children. This theory—known as the catharsis effect—suggests that an individual may be able to relate to a violent on-screen character and release negative feelings, thereby becoming less aggressive personally than prior to the viewing.

Exposure to aggressive modeling is hardly cathartic.
Albert Bandura

Other psychologists regard television as a form of education, and believe that, as characters often serve as role models for children, they should be positive models in order to help decrease the general level of violence prevalent in society.

Although Bandura himself does not believe in the catharsis effect of viewing aggressive behavior, he was careful to note that there was a distinction between learning and performance. Children, he thought, could certainly learn aggressive behavior from viewing it, but knowledge of violent acts would not necessarily result in committing these acts themselves. He warned against assuming a more direct and causal relationship between violence in the media and real-world aggression.

Social learning theorists accept that cognition has a part to play in modeling, and that cognitive factors mediate the process between viewing violence and actually imitating it. For instance, the perception and interpretation of TV violence, and how realistic the program is, are both important intervening variables. Bandura also considers that environmental experiences are another influence in the social learning of aggression in children. Unsurprisingly, people living in neighborhoods with high crime rates are more likely to commit acts of violence than those living in low-crime areas.

Gender development

The social learning theory underlying Bandura's research on childhood aggression has important implications for our understanding of the development of gender identity. According to the gender development theory, one reason why boys and girls tend to exhibit differences in their behavior is that they are treated differently by their parents (as well as other significant adults and peers). It has been shown that people unwittingly tailor their behavior toward children from birth to match their own gender-role expectations; this encourages children to behave according to what are considered gender norms.

According to Bandura's findings, children also learn how to behave through reinforcement and observation learning. By imitating the behavior of others, children are highly likely to receive positive reinforcement for the type of behavior that is considered most appropriate to their sex. They will also be either directly or subtly discouraged from behaving in ways that are not sex-appropriate.

Although there has been some criticism of Bandura's work (often centered on whether his idea is truly a theory of cognitive development), his findings and theories are still cited and debated half a century later, reflecting the breadth and scope of his influence. His groundbreaking contributions span many of the fields of psychology, including social cognitive theory, personality theory, and even therapeutic practices. His ideas also serve as a bridge between preceding behaviorist learning theories and subsequent cognitive learning theories.

Bandura's focus on processes such as attention, memory, and motivation marked a departure from studying only observable and measurable variables (the sole concern of behaviorists) and looked instead to the mental realm—the mind—for information about how people learn. For these reasons, Bandura is considered by many of his peers to be one of the most distinguished and influential psychologists of all time. ■

Behavior seen as sex-appropriate in children, such as independence (in boys) or empathy (in girls), is often positively reinforced by adults' expectations, as well as by children's imitation of adults and peers.

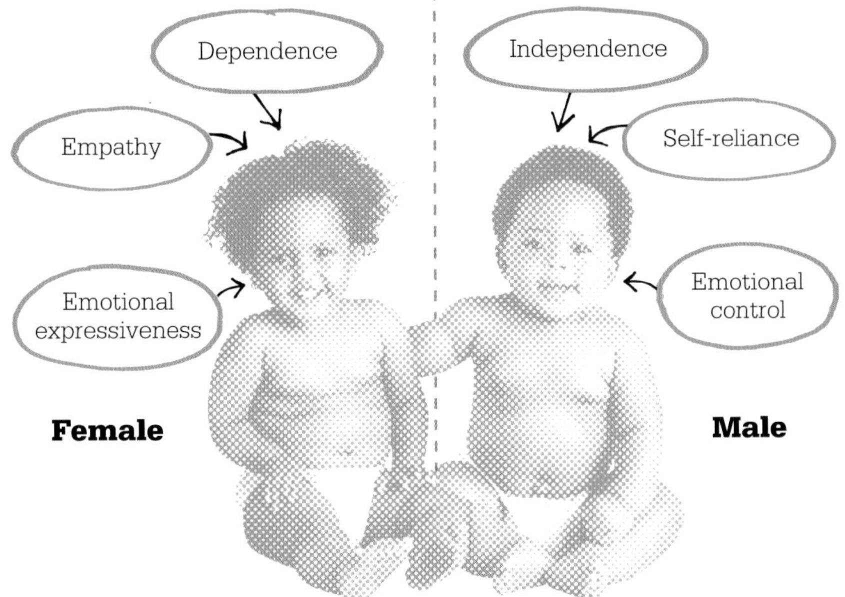

Albert Bandura

Born in Alberta, Canada, Albert Bandura graduated from the University of British Columbia, then earned a Master's degree and doctorate at the University of Iowa, where his interest in learning theory developed. In 1953, he took up a teaching post at Stanford University, California, and remained as professor emeritus. He also received 19 honorary degrees and was elected president of the American Psychological Association in 1974.

Considered one of the world's most eminent and influential psychologists, Bandura received many awards, including an Outstanding Lifetime Contribution to Psychology Award from the American Psychological Association (2004). He was made an Officer of the Order of Canada (2014), and in 2016 was awarded a US National Medal of Science by President Barack Obama.

Key works

1973 *Aggression: A Social Learning Analysis*
1977 *Social Learning Theory*
1986 *Social Foundations of Thought and Action: A Social Cognitive Theory*

MORALITY DEVELOPS IN SIX STAGES

LAWRENCE KOHLBERG (1927–1987)

IN CONTEXT

APPROACH
Moral development

BEFORE
1923 Sigmund Freud offers a psychoanalytic account of moral development.

1932 Jean Piaget argues that morality develops from two types of reasoning: one that is subject to the rules of others, and another that is subject only to a person's own rules.

AFTER
1977 American educational psychologist William Damon suggests that young children are able to take the needs of others into account, earlier than Kohlberg claims they are.

1982 American psychologist Nancy Eisenberg argues that in order to understand children's moral development, we must examine their reasoning when faced with conflict between their own needs and those of others.

Lawrence Kohlberg believed that morality develops gradually throughout childhood and adolescence. In 1956, he began a study involving 72 boys between the ages of 10 and 16. He presented the boys with moral dilemmas that required them to choose between two alternatives, neither of which could be considered completely acceptable, and noted their responses. One example was whether it was right or wrong for a man with no money to steal drugs that his sick wife desperately needed. Kohlberg followed up on 58 of the boys, testing them every three years over the course of 20 years, to

Morality develops in six stages throughout childhood, adolescence, and adulthood.

In the **two preconventional stages**, moral behavior is determined by the concepts of punishment, reward, and reciprocity.

In the **two conventional stages**, moral behavior is consistent with doing what others believe to be right, upholding laws, and maintaining social order.

In the **two postconventional stages**, individuals are the ultimate judge of moral behavior, based on their own conscience and universal moral principles rather than social norms.

See also: Sigmund Freud 92–99 ▪ Jean Piaget 270–277 ▪ Albert Bandura 294–299

Moral thought may be considered partially to generate its own data as it goes along.
Lawrence Kohlberg

observe how their moral inclinations changed with age. Based on the answers given by his subjects, Kohlberg identified six stages of moral development, which spanned three levels of moral reasoning: preconventional, conventional, and postconventional.

Building moral reasoning

The preconventional level of moral reasoning, which develops during our first nine years of life, considers rules as fixed and absolute. In the first of its two stages (the stage of obedience and punishment), we determine whether actions are right or wrong by whether or not they lead to a punishment. In the second stage (the stage of individualism and exchange), right and wrong are determined by what brings rewards. The desires and needs of others are important, but only in a reciprocal sense—"You scratch my back and I'll scratch yours." Morality at this level is governed by consequence.

The second level of moral reasoning starts in adolescence, and continues into early adulthood. It sees us starting to consider the intention behind behavior, rather than just the consequences. Its first stage, often called the "good boy–nice girl" stage, is when we begin classifying moral behavior as to whether it will help or please. Being seen as good becomes the goal. In the second stage (the law and order stage), we start to equate "being good" with respecting authority and obeying the law, believing that this protects and sustains society.

Mahatma Gandhi was among the few who reach the final stages of moral development described by Kohlberg. Throughout his adult life, he felt a duty to disregard unjust and oppressive laws.

The third level of moral development is when we move beyond simple conformity, but Kohlberg suggested that only around 10–15 percent of us ever reach this level. In its first stage (the social contract and individual rights stage), we still respect authority, but there is a growing recognition that individual rights can supersede laws that are destructive or restrictive. We come to realize that human life is more sacred than just following rules. The sixth and final stage (the stage of universal ethical principles) is when our own conscience becomes the ultimate judge, and we commit ourselves to equal rights and respect for all. We may even resort to civil disobedience in the name of universal principles, such as justice.

Kohlberg's six-stage theory was considered radical, because it stated that morality is not imposed on children (as psychoanalysts said), nor is it about avoiding bad feelings (as the behaviorists had thought). Kohlberg believed children developed a moral code and awareness of respect, empathy, and love through interaction with others. ■

Lawrence Kohlberg

The youngest of four children, Lawrence Kohlberg was born in Bronxville, New York. After completing high school at the end of World War II, he became a sailor, and helped smuggle Jewish refugees into Palestine.

In 1948, Kohlberg enrolled at the University of Chicago, where he completed his bachelor's degree in just one year, and went on to research and teach, gaining a doctorate in 1958. He also taught at Yale University, and finally Harvard.

While in Belize in 1971, Kohlberg contracted a parasitic infection that left him battling with persistent pain and depression. On January 19, 1987, after asking to leave a treatment session, he died by suicide, reportedly by walking into the icy waters of the Atlantic Ocean.

Key works

1969 *Stage and Sequence*
1976 *Moral Stages and Moralization*
1981 *The Philosophy of Moral Development*

THE LANGUAGE ORGAN GROWS LIKE ANY OTHER BODY ORGAN

NOAM CHOMSKY (1928–)

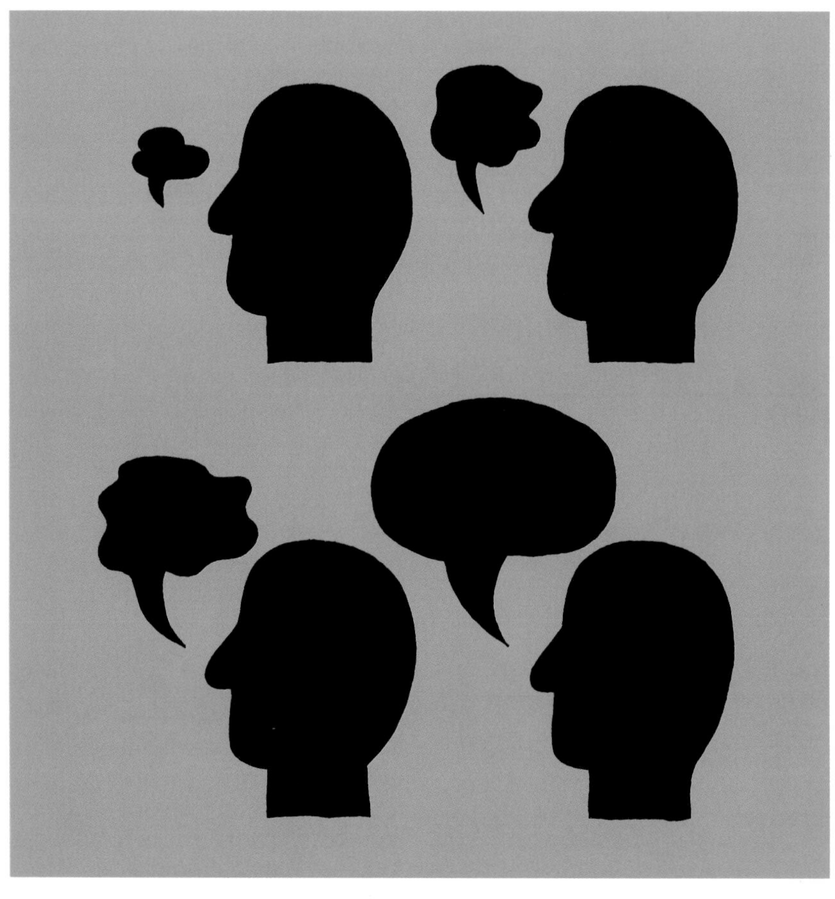

IN CONTEXT

APPROACH
Nativism

BEFORE
1958 B. F. Skinner uses operant conditioning to explain language development, arguing that children learn words and phrases through reinforcement.

1977 Albert Bandura argues that children may imitate the general form of sentences and fill in these with specific words.

AFTER
1994 Steven Pinker argues that language is an instinct from an innate program hard-wired in the brain, which arose because it was adaptive for human survival.

2003 Psychologists Stan Kuczaj and Heather Hill claim parents offer children better examples of grammatical sentences than Chomsky suggests.

In the middle of the 20th century, learning theory as explained by B. F. Skinner and Albert Bandura dominated psychologists' conception of language development. These behaviorists believed that language—like all other human faculties—was a direct result of environmental input and learning, developed through the reinforcement and reward techniques at the heart of operant conditioning. Skinner noted that when children imitate verbal sounds and form correct words, they receive immediate reinforcement and approval from their parents, which motivates

See also: B. F. Skinner 78–85 ▪ Jerome Bruner 164–165 ▪ Steven Pinker 213 ▪ Jean Piaget 270–277 ▪ Albert Bandura 294–299

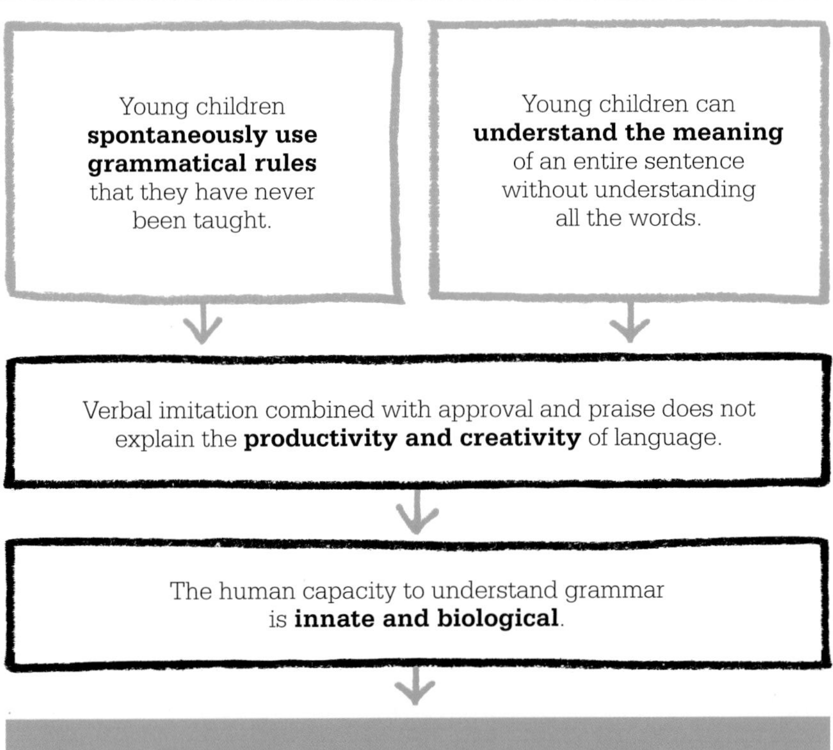

them to continue learning new words and phrases. Bandura broadened the concept of imitation, noting that children imitated not only specific words and sounds, but also the general form and structure of sentences, as though filling in templates with specific words.

Young children **spontaneously use grammatical rules** that they have never been taught.
Young children can **understand the meaning** of an entire sentence without understanding all the words.
Verbal imitation combined with approval and praise does not explain the **productivity and creativity** of language.
The human capacity to understand grammar is **innate and biological**.
The language organ grows like any other body organ.

Linguist Noam Chomsky, however, did not believe that operant conditioning adequately explained the productivity, creativity, and innovation of language. It also seemed insufficient to explain children's spontaneous use of grammatical rules that they have neither heard nor learned, as well as their ability to understand the meaning of an entire sentence without necessarily understanding the meaning of each word. For Chomsky, this ability is innate in humans—he claimed that "the language organ grows like any other body organ," likening it to other features acquired through heredity.

Nativism

Chomsky maintained that, although a child's environment supplies the content of language, grammar itself is a built-in and biologically determined human capacity. To illustrate his point, he refers to other aspects of human development that we accept as being an inevitable outcome of heredity. The onset of puberty, for instance, is an aspect of human growth that is like the "growth" of the language organ. We assume unquestioningly that it is a genetically determined milestone, and though the specific details of its onset depend on several variable environmental influences, the fundamental process is the same across the human species. We take for granted that this is a result of basic biological programming. Language growth, Chomsky emphasizes, is another genetically programmed inevitability of human development, on par with the processes that determine that we have arms instead of wings or that build the structure of our visual or circulatory systems.

The concept that language is a part of our growth process is important because it highlights Chomsky's belief that it is not a consequence of learning. He adopts a nativist perspective, focusing on the inherited contributions to behavior and minimizing the importance of environmental input. However, he believes that the environment plays a role in determining the specific direction of language »

Language is a process of free creation.
Noam Chomsky

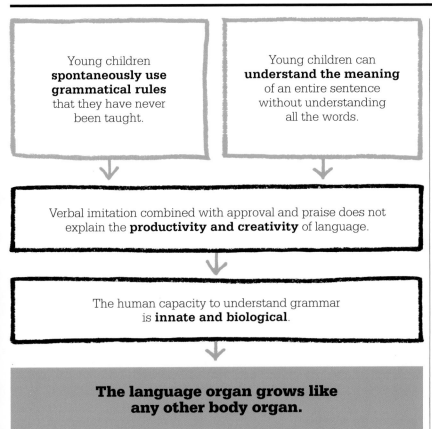

growth, insofar as an individual's language organ develops according to early experiences. For instance, because Chomsky grew up in Philadelphia, Pennsylvania, he absorbed knowledge of that particular English dialect and his language organ's structure was tailored accordingly. The same process occurs for everyone, whether they have grown up in Paris, Tokyo, or London.

Universal grammar

But where is the proof that language acquisition is inborn rather than learned? According to Chomsky, the most convincing evidence for this claim is that there are aspects of grammar that are so intuitive and self-evident that they need never be discussed or learned in order to be understood. (They are therefore part of our biological inheritance.) For instance, there are certain constructions in the English language that permit the dropping of pronouns, and others that do not. The difference between the two is subtle, yet even by the age of 6, native English-speaking children will use the constructions flawlessly. This implies that certain aspects of grammar are understood without requiring any instruction, and that the knowledge is therefore innate. This is the only way to explain how people have such a rich grammatical understanding and how children can use language so creatively by the age of 6.

Chomsky claims that "universal grammar" is found worldwide, with modifications according to people's native languages. It is a predefined mechanism that acts as the basis for the acquisition of any language. He argues that this is demonstrated by the way that all children are equally able to learn any language to which they are exposed. He says that a common set of linguistic features is built into the language organ through heredity, and it includes elements of grammar, meaning, and speech. It is what makes it possible for us to speak and learn human languages, and may make it impossible for us to learn any language that violates these principles.

We are designed to learn languages based upon a common set of principles, which we may call universal grammar.
Noam Chomsky

Language device

Chomsky proposes a name for our innate language organ: the Language Acquisition Device (LAD). He bases his claim for its existence on three things: the fact that children are born with the capacity to formulate and understand all kinds of sentences despite never having heard or learned them; that every human language appears to have certain universal elements; and that some grammatical principles are acquired by individuals regardless of their culture or intelligence. There is other supporting evidence as well, including the fact that the human vocal organs, breathing

Noam Chomsky

Linguist, philosopher, cognitive scientist, and social activist Noam Chomsky was born in Pennsylvania to Jewish parents. He studied philosophy and linguistics at the University of Pennsylvania, where he earned his bachelor's, master's, and doctoral degrees. Chomsky joined the Massachusetts Institute of Technology in 1955, becoming an Institute Professor in 1976.

Chomsky is widely known as one of the fathers of modern linguistics, but he is also a political dissident and anarchist. His criticisms of US foreign policy have made him a highly controversial figure. He has won several honorary degrees as well as being a recipient of the Distinguished Scientific Contribution Award, the Dorothy Eldridge Peacemaker Award, and the Orwell Award. He was married to linguist Carol Schatz for 59 years until her death in 2008.

Key works

1957 *Syntactic Structures*
1965 *Cartesian Linguistics*
1968 *Language and Mind*

Deaf children communicate using a "gestural language," which has the same characteristics as spoken language, suggesting that knowledge of grammar and syntax is innate.

apparatus, auditory system, and brain are all specialized for spoken communication. Chomsky argues that, in light of the frequency with which children are exposed to the ungrammatical and incomplete speech uttered by their parents and other adults, only some kind of LAD can explain the fact that children seem to possess knowledge of grammatical rules. Finally, studies of deaf children provide further evidence for an LAD, revealing the untutored emergence of a "gestural language" that shares the basic principles of spoken language.

Evaluation

Cognitive scientist Steven Pinker agrees that language is an instinct stemming from an innate program that is hard-wired in the human brain, but says that it arose through evolution and was therefore adaptive, helping our ancestors survive. Chomsky disagrees with Pinker about how language evolved, arguing that language represents a distinct mental module that is unique to human beings and completely independent of general cognitive ability.

Linguist Jean Aitchison is also in agreement with Chomsky's claim that children are hard-wired with knowledge of linguistic rules, but her view is that children have built-in problem-solving abilities that enable them to process linguistic data (and other forms of data). Chomsky maintains, however, that human beings' innate language ability exists independently of other abilities, and because the mind is constructed of mental organs similar to those of the body, language can easily be isolated from other mental faculties.

Criticism also comes from Robin Chapman, an expert in communicative disorders, who argues that the study of language development should also be understood within the context of children's social interactions. She notes that language structure is acquired piecemeal over several years, and that there are wide variations in how rapidly children acquire it, suggesting that social environment could also be a factor. There is also some degree of doubt surrounding Chomsky's assumption that language is unique to human beings. Data from studies with chimpanzees and gorillas has suggested that the difference between ape and human language is quantitative rather than qualitative, which raises questions about how species-specific language really is.

Chomsky's work has been highly influential across linguistics, psychology, philosophy, and even mathematics. Although the idea that children are predisposed to learn language is widely accepted, his claim that children have an innate knowledge of language that is not deeply influenced by their parents is highly controversial. He has been widely considered the most extreme nativist in the history of psychology, and although a biological source for language development is widely thought to be nearer to the truth than one involving operant conditioning, it is still unlikely to offer the complete picture. Chomsky's work has led to the emergence of more integrated views, which will no doubt lead to new research and understanding. ■

Studies of how chimpanzees communicate with each other shows that their language is complex, although it appears to have less content and variation than human language.

PSYCHOL
OF DIFFE
PERSONALITY AND INTELLIGENCE

OGY
RENCE

1871

In *The Descent of Man*, **Charles Darwin** argues that variations in intellectual abilities tend to be inherited.

1884

Francis Galton is the first to investigate **individual differences** scientifically, through large-scale questionnaires.

1904

Charles Spearman proposes that intelligent behavior is generated by a single, unitary quality within the brain, which he calls **"the general factor"** or "g."

1905

Alfred Binet and Theodore Simon develop the **first intelligence test**, which becomes known as the Binet-Simon scale.

1921

Floyd and Gordon Allport publish *Personality Traits: their Classification and Measurement.*

1937

Gordon Allport publishes his most significant work, *Personality: psychological interpretation.*

1941

Raymond Cattell suggests that intelligence is made up of two factors: **fluid and crystallized intelligence**.

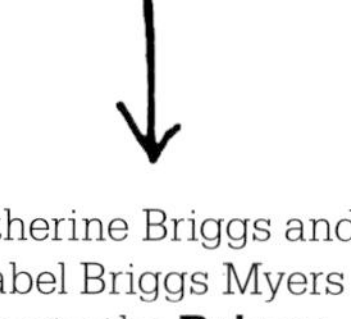

1942

Katherine Briggs and Isabel Briggs Myers create the **Briggs Myers Type Indicator**—a widely used psychometric test.

Theoretical psychology has largely been concerned with identifying and examining aspects of the mind and behavior that are common to us all, yet philosophers, and later scientists, have always recognized that there are differences in our psychological make-up that render us individuals. Some of the early philosophers explained differences in personality using the idea of the four humors or temperaments, but it was not until the 20th century that there was any truly scientific study of personality.

Behaviorists, as one would expect, saw personality as a product of conditioning, and psychoanalytical theory described personality as the effect of past experience on the unconscious—but these explanations resulted from research into more general theories rather than a study of personality itself. The first psychologist to systematically approach the subject was Gordon Allport, who felt that existing ideas of personality were inadequate. As one of the pioneers of what is now called "trait theory," he identified a number of different personality traits, which he suggested showed themselves in three different levels in a combination unique to each person. The idea of traits became central to personality psychology and, following Allport's work, it became a major new area of study.

Personality traits

New ways of analyzing traits, such as Raymond Cattell's factor analytical method, which identified 16 personality factors, led to refinement of Allport's theories: reducing the number of traits that combined to form an individual personality. The prominent traits of introversion and extraversion were common to most of these models, and the distinction between them was felt to be a major factor in determining personality. They were incorporated into Hans Eysenck's three-factor model, with its basic traits of extraversion–introversion, neuroticism, and psychoticism.

One assumption that was questioned was whether personality traits would result in consistent behavior. Research conducted by Walter Mischel showed that different situations produced different behavior, and suggested that personality traits should be considered in the context of an individual's perception of and

1947-1970s
Hans Eysenck develops an influential **three-factor model** of the theory of personality.

1950
J. P. Guilford suggests that the **Structure of Intellect** (SI) has three dimensions: content, products, and operations.

1954
Corbett H. Thigpen and Hervey M. Cleckley document a case of **multiple personality disorder** in *The Three Faces of Eve*.

1955
David Wechsler develops the **Wechsler Adult Intelligence Scale** (WAIS).

1968
Walter Mischel publishes *Personality and Assessment,* questioning the assumption that behavior is determined by personality traits **regardless of situation or context**.

1973
David Rosenhan questions the validity of psychiatric notions of normal or sane in his **pseudo-patient experiments**.

1986
Nico Frijda publishes *The Emotions*, describing them as changes in individuals that prepare them for action.

1990s
Researchers agree on the **"big five" personality traits**—openness, conscientiousness, extraversion, neuroticism, and agreeableness.

reaction to various circumstances. Not only was personality found to be less consistent than had been assumed, but in some cases there was the possibility of an individual having more than one distinct personality. In a case made famous by a book and film, *The Three Faces of Eve*, psychiatrists Corbett H. Thigpen and Hervey M. Cleckley described multiple personality disorder, now called dissociative identity disorder.

The intelligence factor

Another factor that distinguishes us as individuals is intelligence. This had been studied from the earliest days of psychology, but had proved difficult to define or measure. Studies are also frequently controversial; since the time of Darwin and Galton, intelligence was assumed to be an inherited characteristic (and carried with it connotations of racial stereotypes and eugenics) rather than one influenced by environment. The issue of nature versus nurture in determining intelligence became key, with psychologists including Raymond Cattell and Hans Eysenck defending a hereditary viewpoint, and others arguing that not only is intelligence affected by environment, but the way it is tested is culturally biased, giving distorted results.

In the early 20th century, British psychologist Charles Spearman had laid the foundations for a more objective, scientific study of intelligence by using statistical techniques to test and measure intelligence. He identified a single factor, the "g factor," that correlated to all the mental abilities that make up general intelligence. This notion of a single measure of intelligence was challenged by J. P. Guilford, who believed that intelligence consists of a number of different abilities, an idea that led to Raymond Cattell's theory of fluid and crystallized intelligence—two levels of reasoning and critical thinking.

Research into other areas of psychological difference has included emotions and facial expressions, pioneered by Paul Ekman and Nico Frijda, and psychological disorders, but David Rosenhan's experiment showed that it is not easy to distinguish the "normal" from the "abnormal." Individual differences appear to be points on a spectrum, rather than easily labeled divisions—highlighting the complexity and diversity of human psychology. ■

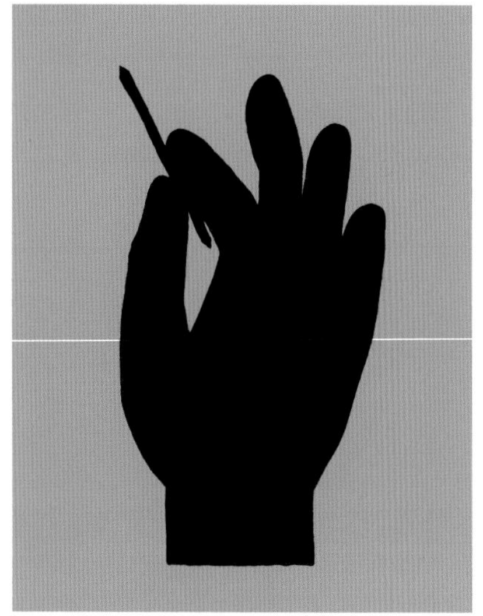

NAME AS MANY USES AS YOU CAN THINK OF FOR A TOOTHPICK

J. P. GUILFORD (1897–1987)

IN CONTEXT

APPROACH
Intelligence psychometrics

BEFORE
19th century Wilhelm Wundt, Gustav Fechner, and Francis Galton claim that individual differences in people's cognitive abilities can be empirically measured.

1904 British psychologist Charles Spearman claims intelligence can be summed up in a single number.

1938 British psychologist L. L. Thurstone identifies seven independent factors that make up a person's "primary abilities" or intelligence.

AFTER
1969 Philip E. Vernon estimates that intelligence is 60 percent inborn.

1974 US psychologist Ellis Paul Torrance produces his own tests of creativity, which are most widely used today.

Although, in Europe, what makes up intelligence had been discussed since the time of ancient Greece, the first systematic method of measuring intelligence was not developed until 1905, when the French psychologist Alfred Binet was asked to identify children who might benefit from educational assistance. Together with researcher Theodore Simon, he created the "Binet–Simon Scale," which used memory, attention, and problem-solving tasks to measure and produce a number, or "quotient," that summarizes intellectual ability.

Questions of **memory** and simple **problem-solving** …

… can be answered using **convergent thinking**—the ability to come up with one "correct" answer.

This can be tested using **standardized intelligence (IQ) tests.**

Problems requiring **creative solutions** …

… can be solved using **divergent thinking**—exploring many possible avenues at once.

This requires a new form of testing that includes both **problem-solving and imagination**.

See also: Alfred Binet 50–53 ▪ Raymond Cattell 320–321 ▪ Hans J. Eysenck 322–327 ▪ William Stern 340 ▪ David Wechsler 342

Creative minds see even toothpicks as potentially having hundreds of uses. Guilford's "Alternative Uses Test" scores people on their ability to think of many original and widely assorted alternatives.

The average intelligence quotient (IQ) was set for convenience at 100, allowing psychologists to categorize people in relation to this score. In practice, around 95 percent of the general population score between 70 and 130, and the top 0.5 percent score over 145, the "genius" level.

Although the scale is still used for most IQ tests today, US psychologist J. P. Guilford believes it has fundamental flaws. Standard intelligence tests, he says, ignore creativity and assume that there is a "general intelligence" that can be represented by an IQ score.

Measuring creativity

By definition, creativity means there is more than one answer to any problem. It requires a different kind of thinking, which Guilford calls "divergent," since it goes in different directions and produces multiple solutions to a problem. In contrast, traditional IQ tests require thinking that ends up with a single answer: "convergent" thinking.

Guilford thought that creativity was measurable—it is indicated by the number of directions in which a person's thoughts travel. He devised a number of tests to quantify divergent thinking, including his 1967 "Alternative Uses Test," which asks participants to write as many uses as they can think of for: (a) a toothpick, (b) a brick, and (c) a paper clip. In his "Consequences Test," subjects were asked to imagine all the things that might possibly happen if all national and local laws were suddenly abolished. Guilford scored the answers on levels of four key components: originality, fluency, flexibility, and elaboration.

Guilford claims that intelligence is not made up of just one "general factor," but of three different groups of activities. "Operations" are the intellectual processes we use; there are six types of these, including memory, cognition, and evaluation. "Content" is the type of information or data involved—there are five of these, including visual and auditory content. "Products" are the results of applying operations to content, such as classes or relations, and there are six of these. The many ways in which we combine and use these different types mean there may be anything up to 180 (6 × 5 × 6) types of intelligence—more than 100 of these have already been verified.

The complexity of Guilford's theory and problems with testing mean that his tests are used less frequently than standard IQ tests, but his work has influenced research into intelligence and creativity. ■

J. P. Guilford

Joy Paul Guilford was born on a farm in Nebraska. Always markedly intelligent, he was the valedictorian of his high school class. His bachelor's degree in psychology was interrupted by a spell in the army as a private, but he went on to earn a PhD from Cornell University. In 1928, he returned to Nebraska as an associate professor, then took a position at the University of Southern California (USC) in 1940, remaining there—apart from a short secondment during World War II—until his retirement in 1967. Described as a devoted family man of enormous integrity and generosity, his shyness earned him the nickname "gray ghost" during his time in the army. An influential and prolific researcher, Guilford produced more than 25 books, 30 tests, and 300 articles.

Key works

1936 *Psychometric Methods*
1967 *The Nature of Human Intelligence*

The person who is capable of producing a large number of ideas per unit of time … has a greater chance of having significant ideas.
J. P. Guilford

DID ROBINSON CRUSOE LACK PERSONALITY TRAITS BEFORE THE ADVENT OF FRIDAY?

GORDON ALLPORT (1897–1967)

IN CONTEXT

APPROACH
Trait theory

BEFORE
2nd century BCE Galen classifies human temperament according to the four humors.

1890 In *Principles of Psychology*, William James makes an early attempt to define the self as having both an "I" (the knowing self) and a "me" (the experiencing self).

AFTER
1946 Raymond Cattell develops his 16PF (Personality Factors) questionnaire, based on Allport and Odbert's lexical hypothesis.

1970s Hans J. Eysenck creates the PEN (Psychoticism, Extraversion, Neurotisicm) personality questionnaire.

1993 American psychologist Dan P. McAdam demonstrates the idiographic method in his book *The Stories We Live By*.

Gordon Allport is sometimes referred to as one of the founding fathers of personality psychology, as he was the first psychologist of modern times to embark on a dedicated study of personality. Since the early work on the four temperaments by Hippocrates (c.400 BCE) and Galen (c.150 CE), there seems to have been no attempt to classify personality in any detail. In the 19th century, personality was barely mentioned in psychology, though there was much discussion of the self, or "ego."

In the early 20th century, the two predominant schools of psychology—psychoanalysis and behaviorism—were polar opposites in approach. Both were highly developed and influential schools that remain powerful (as well as enduringly controversial) to this day. Behaviorism, being interested only in how we acquire (or learn) our behavior, had nothing to say about personality; while psychoanalysis offered an in-depth approach, arguing for the existence of an unknowable unconscious that controls personality but reveals itself only fractionally and accidentally by slips of the tongue and in dream symbols.

People … are busy leading their lives into the future, whereas psychology, for the most part, is busy tracing them into the past.
Gordon Allport

The American psychologist Gordon Allport had fundamental problems with both of these approaches. He thought that behaviorism was wrong to discount the "person" doing the learning, because each person is unique and their perception is part of the process. He also considered psychoanalysis to be inadequate for explaining personality and behavior because it placed too much importance on a person's past, ignoring their current context and motivations. His view was

Personality is formed from …

… **cardinal traits** or "ruling passions," such as altruism. Not everyone has a cardinal trait, and those that do are often famous for it.

… **common traits**, such as honesty or aggression. In the absence of cardinal traits, personality is shaped by these traits.

… **secondary traits**, such as being nervous when meeting strangers or laughing at inappropriate moments. These traits are evoked by specific situations.

See also: Galen 18–19 ▪ William James 38–45 ▪ Sigmund Freud 92–99 ▪ Carl Rogers 130–137 ▪ Abraham Maslow 138–139 ▪ Martin Seligman 200–201 ▪ Paul Salkovskis 214–215 ▪ Raymond Cattell 320–321 ▪ Hans J. Eysenck 322–327 ▪ William Stern 340

affirmed when, as a young college graduate, he paid a visit to Sigmund Freud in Vienna. On first meeting, to make small talk, Allport told Freud of a small boy he had met on the train on the way, who was afraid of getting dirty and refused to sit near anyone dirty, despite his mother's encouragement. Perhaps, Allport suggested, the child had learned this dirt phobia from his mother, a neat and rather domineering woman. Freud then asked, "And was that little boy you?" Freud's reduction of this small observation of Allport's to some unconscious episode from his own childhood seemed, to Allport, dismissive of all his current motivations and intentions. Throughout his work, Allport emphasizes the present over the past, though later in his life he paid more attention to psychoanalysis as a supplement to other methods.

Allport argued for an approach to the study of human learning and personality that was reasoned, eclectic, and conceptually open-minded. He took some of what he believed from prevailing approaches, but his central belief is that the uniqueness of each individual and their personality is largely—but not exclusively—forged in human relationships.

Theory of personality

Allport's idea of personality is a complex amalgam of traits, human relationships, current context, and motivation. He identified two distinctly different approaches to the study of personality—the nomothetic and idiographic methods—both of which had been devised by the German philosophers Wilhelm Windelband and Wilhelm Dilthey, but had first been put into practice by Allport's university tutor, William Stern. The first method, the nomothetic, aims to be as objective and scientific as possible, and it is exemplified in the study of human intelligence. This involves obtaining test results from large populations of people, on personality traits such as extraversion and introversion. Results can be submitted to a sophisticated analysis, resulting in a number of general conclusions, such as the percentages of people who are extravert or introvert, or variations linked to age, gender, or geography. However, this method does not aim to comment in any way on traits at the individual level; it focuses on comparative comments and conclusions about a certain trait, rather than any particular person. This was the method that the behaviorist B. F. Skinner used for his observations of rat behavior.

The second method, the idiographic, stands in direct opposition to the nomothetic method; it studies one individual in breadth and depth, taking into account their biography, their personality traits, and their relationships, as well as how they are seen and experienced by others. This method is much closer to the psychoanalytic method with its focus on one person, one life.

Allport said that while the nomothetic method was a way of describing traits, it had little explanatory power; whereas the idiographic method, though unable to draw any general conclusions, could explain one person in illuminating detail. He was to use both methods, though his work in general is not known for its focus on empirical research; he was more of a theorist, almost a philosopher. Yet his very first paper, *Personality Traits: Their Classification and Measurement*, cowritten with his brother Floyd, was an excellent example of the nomothetic method. One of his last major pieces of work, the analysis of Jenny Masterson, was an extraordinarily detailed example of the idiographic method.

The lexical hypothesis

In his first study, Allport and his brother reported their research on personality traits. They asked the participants to complete a personality questionnaire, and to ask three people who knew them well to complete it too; this reflected the Allport brothers' view that personality is forged in relationship to others. They concluded from their results that there is a case for identifying traits, and for attempting to measure them. They also believed they had proven the possibility of developing a complete and sensitive instrument for the measurement of personality. »

Types exist not in people or in nature, but rather in the eye of the observer.
Gordon Allport

Allport and Odbert's lexical hypothesis rested on the idea that the most important and relevant personality differences are reflected by language; they identified 18,000 personality-describing words in English.

In 1936, Allport and his colleague H. S. Odbert proposed that individual differences that are most salient and socially relevant in people's lives eventually become expressed through language; and the more important the difference, the more likely it is to be expressed as a single word. This idea is known as the lexical hypothesis. The two researchers went on to study the most comprehensive dictionaries of the English language available at the time, to find 18,000 words that described personality. They narrowed this down to 4,500 adjectives that they considered to be observable and stable personality traits.

A man can be said to have a trait; but he cannot be said to have a type.
Gordon Allport

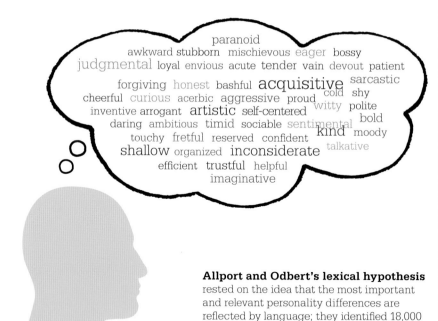

Cardinal traits

Based on a further analysis of his lexical study, Allport defined three distinct categories of traits: cardinal, common, and secondary. Cardinal traits are those that are fundamental to a person, governing their entire approach to life. Not everyone has a cardinal trait, according to Allport, but when they do, they may even be famous for them; in fact some people are so famous for them that their name becomes a byword for that trait, giving us terms such as Byronic, Calvinistic, and Machiavellian. On a less iconic scale, a person's cardinal trait might be something like "a fear of communism," where this is so central and important to someone that it guides and unifies their life in both conscious and unconscious ways; virtually every act is traceable to its influence.

In his later years, Allport considered a person's cardinal traits as contributing to the *proprium*: the essential drives, core needs, and desires of a person. This concept goes beyond the idea of temperament, and is more akin to a guiding purpose that will always press for expression. As an example of the *proprium*, Allport gave the Norwegian polar explorer Roald Amundsen, who had one dominant passion from the age of 15: he wanted to be a polar explorer. The obstacles to his ambition seemed insurmountable, and the temptation to relinquish his dreams was great, but the "propriate" striving persisted, and though he welcomed each success, it simply raised his level of aspiration. Having sailed the Northwest Passage, Amundsen embarked upon the project that led to his success in reaching the South Pole. Then, after years of planning and discouragement, he flew over the North Pole. His commitment never wavered, and he eventually died attempting to save the life of a less experienced explorer.

Less fundamental traits

In contrast to cardinal traits, common traits are general characteristics, such as honesty, that are found in most people. These are the building blocks that shape our behavior, but they are less fundamental than cardinal traits. Common traits, Allport said, develop largely in response to parental influences, and are a result of nurture. They are shared among many people within a culture but in varying degrees; aggressiveness, for instance, is a common trait that varies by degrees. According

Any theory that regards personality as stable, fixed, or invariable is wrong.
Gordon Allport

to Allport, most of us have personalities made up of five to ten of these traits at a level whereby they have become our "outstanding characteristics."

Over time, common traits may achieve "functional autonomy," by which Allport means that although we start doing something for one reason, we may carry on doing it for quite another. This is because our motives today are not continuously dependent on the past. We may start learning to draw, for instance, to compete in popularity with another child in class, but ultimately become more interested in perfecting the craft for its own sake. This means that how we think and act today is only indirectly affected by our past. Functional autonomy is also thought to explain obsessive and compulsive acts and thoughts: they may be manifestations of functionally autonomous traits, where someone has no idea why he is doing something, but can't stop himself from doing it.

Allport's third category of traits, known as secondary traits, exert much less influence on us than cardinal or common traits. They are only seen in certain circumstances, because they are determined by context or situation. For instance, we might say of someone "he gets very angry when tickled" or "she gets nervous on flights." These traits express preferences or attitudes that are open to change. In the absence of another person, secondary traits might be present but quite invisible. Added to the common and cardinal traits, they provide a complete picture of human complexity.

Traits and behavior

Allport was interested in how traits are forged in a person, and their connection with behavior. He suggested that a combination of internal and external forces influence how we behave. Certain internal forces, which he called "genotypes," govern how we retain information and use it to interact with the external world. At the same time, external forces, which he named "phenotypes," determine the way we accept our surroundings and how we let others influence our behavior. These two forces, he said, provide the groundwork for the creation of individual traits. »

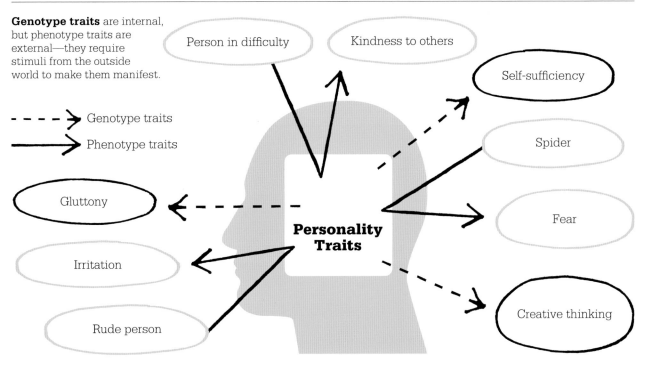

Genotype traits are internal, but phenotype traits are external—they require stimuli from the outside world to make them manifest.

Robinson Crusoe, Allport concluded, must always have had many distinctive personality traits, but some were only uncovered by new circumstances after he was shipwrecked and met Friday.

Applying these ideas to the story of Robinson Crusoe, Allport saw that, prior to his meeting with Friday, Crusoe's genotypes, or inner resources, along with some phenotype aspects, helped him to survive alone on a desert island. He had the resilience to overcome his initial despair, and fetched arms, tools, and other supplies from the ship before it sank. He built a fenced-in compound around a cave, and kept a calendar. He hunted, grew corn and rice, and learned to make pottery and raise goats, and he also adopted a parrot. He read the Bible and became religious. These activities demonstrated the expression of Crusoe's genotypical traits and resulting behaviors.

However, it was only with the arrival of Friday that other aspects of his phenotypic behaviors could find expression: he helped Friday to escape from his captors, he named him, and he had the patience and persistence to teach him to speak English and the capability to convert him to Christianity (although modern-day interpretations challenge whether Crusoe's treatment of Friday was truly beneficial). While Crusoe always had these personality traits, they remained unexpressed on the island until he formed a relationship with Friday. The idea is similar to a well-known philosophical puzzle: if a tree falls down in a forest, and there is nobody there, does it make a noise? For Allport, traits make behavior consistent; they are always there, even if no one is around to evoke them or witness them in action.

An idiographic study

After the publication of *Personality: A Psychological Interpretation* in 1937, Allport turned his attention to the topics of religion, prejudice, and ethics. But in 1965 he returned to the subject of personality by undertaking an idiographic study of the personality traits of Jenny Masterson, who lived from 1868 to 1937. During the last 11 years of her life, Jenny wrote 300 personal letters to a married couple with whom she was friendly. Allport used these letters for his analysis, asking 36 people to characterize Jenny's personality traits from her letters. Eight trait "clusters" encompassing 198 individual traits were relatively easy to identify, with broad agreement from all the people rating the documents. These traits were: quarrelsome–suspicious; self-centered; independent–autonomous; dramatic–intense; aesthetic–artistic; aggressive; cynical–morbid; and sentimental.

However, Allport concluded that this trait analysis of Jenny was somewhat inconclusive, and so he went on to use a number of other frameworks, including Freudian and Adlerian analysis. Assisted by his students Jeffrey Paige and Alfred Baldwin, he also applied "content analysis" to the material. This was a new form of computerized analysis, where the computer was programmed to count the number of times words or phrases occur that are related to a given topic or emotion. Allport was particularly impressed by this new method

Personality is far too complex a thing to be trussed up in a conceptual straight jacket.
Gordon Allport

because of its potential to analyze idiographic data, confirming his belief that the idiographic approach can identify subtleties of an individual character that trait questionnaires alone cannot reveal.

In 1966, Allport published a paper entitled *Traits Revisited* suggesting that the aim of personality study should not be the microanalysis of individual traits, but the study of the psychic organization of the whole person. He stated that his early writings about traits were written in an age of psychological innocence, although he maintained his belief that traits are a reasonable starting point for the description of personality.

Allport's influence

Allport's work forms the basis of many contemporary schools of thought, though he is rarely credited directly. Much of modern personality testing derives from the work of Raymond Cattell and Hans Eysenck, and both of these psychologists drew upon Allport's lexical study. Cattell's "16 Personality Factor Questionnaire," which is still used by psychologists today, uses 16 traits identified by Cattell through computer analysis of Allport and Odbert's original 4,500 adjectives.

Humanistic psychology, which forms the basis of most counseling and therapeutic practices, also relies heavily upon Allport's ideas, particularly his idiographic method and insistence upon the uniqueness of each and every person. Increased focus on the practitioner–client relationship as a vehicle for the expression and development of personality has its roots in Allport's assertion that personality is largely a function of relationships.

Allport was also one of the first to point out that even those psychological theories that attempt to explore positive human experience are based "largely upon the behavior of sick and anxious people or upon the antics of captive and desperate rats." He wondered why there were no theories based on the study of healthy human beings and those who strive to make life worth living. He pointed out that most studies are of criminals, not law-abiders; about fear, not courage; and focus on the blindness of humans rather than their vision. The burgeoning school of positive psychology, led by Martin Seligman, has taken up this idea and aims to develop a scientific psychology of positive experience.

By 1955, when Allport wrote *Becoming*, his thinking had developed further; he now saw human striving toward a higher level of consciousness and realization as the true motive of personality. The idea that "becoming" is the ultimate goal of human beings was also developed by the psychologists Carl Rogers and then Abraham Maslow, who renamed it "self-actualization." Although Allport's work is cited less often than other well-known figures, he had a profound and lasting influence on the field of psychology. ■

Allport urged psychologists to study personality traits and leave character to the province of philosophy.
Martin Seligman

Gordon Allport

Gordon Willard Allport was born in Montezuma, Indiana in 1897. The youngest of four sons, Allport was shy and studious as a child, but as a teenager he became editor of his school newspaper and ran his own printing business.

During World War I, Allport performed military duties, before winning a scholarship to Harvard University to study philosophy and economics. After graduating in 1919, he taught for a year in Türkiye, then went back to Harvard, where he gained his doctorate in psychology in 1922. He also studied with the Gestalt School in Germany, and at Cambridge University in England.

In 1924, Allport returned to Harvard to teach the first course in personality studies in the US. Apart from four years at Dartmouth College, New Hampshire, he remained at Harvard until his death from lung cancer, aged 70, in 1967.

Key works

1937 *Personality: A Psychological Interpretation*
1954 *The Nature of Prejudice*
1955 *Becoming*
1961 *Pattern and Growth in Personality*

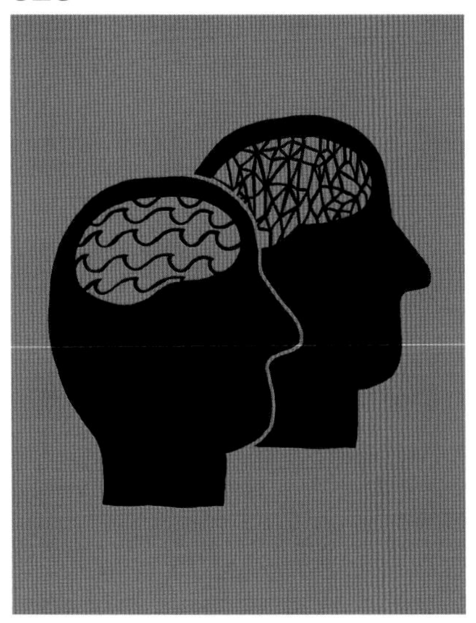

GENERAL INTELLIGENCE CONSISTS OF BOTH FLUID AND CRYSTALLIZED INTELLIGENCE

RAYMOND CATTELL (1905–1998)

IN CONTEXT

APPROACH
Intelligence theory

BEFORE
1900s Alfred Binet claims intelligence can be measured, and introduces the term "intelligence quotient" (IQ).

1904 Charles Spearman identifies "g" as an underlying property of intelligence.

1931 In *The Measurement of Intelligence,* Edward Thorndike says that there are three or four main types of intelligence.

AFTER
1950 J. P. Guilford claims that there are around 150 different types of intellectual ability.

1989 US psychologist John B. Carroll proposes a three-stratum psychometric model of intelligence, consisting of narrow abilities, broad abilities, and Charles Spearman's "g" factor.

Raymond Cattell, considered to be one of the dozen most eminent psychologists of the 20th century, contributed hugely to the study of human intelligence, motivation, and personality. His interest in intelligence was sparked early in his career when he was a student of Charles Spearman, the British psychologist who defined "g"—a single-factor, general intelligence that serves as the foundation for all learning.

In 1941, Cattell developed this concept further, defining two different types of intelligence that made up "g": fluid and crystallized intelligence. Fluid intelligence is a series of thinking or reasoning abilities that can be applied to any issue or "content." Sometimes described as the intelligence we use when we don't already know how to do something, it comes into play automatically in processes such as problem-solving and pattern recognition, and it is thought to be closely related to working memory capacity.

Cattell suggests fluid intelligence is genetically inherited, which may account for individual differences.

General underlying intelligence (g) is made up of two parts.

Fluid intelligence, which is the ability to think and reason abstractly, and to perceive relationships between things without prior practice or instruction.

Crystallized intelligence, which builds from past experiences and learnt facts, and amounts to judgement skills that accumulate as we age.

See also: Alfred Binet 50–53 ▪ J. P. Guilford 310–311 ▪ Hans Eysenck 322–327 ▪ William Stern 340 ▪ David Wechsler 342

It builds to a peak in young adulthood, then steadily declines, perhaps because of age-related changes in the brain. Brain injury can affect fluid intelligence, which suggests it is largely physiological.

Crystallized intelligence

As we use fluid intelligence for solving problems, we begin to develop stores of knowledge and working hypotheses about the world around us. This store of knowledge is our crystallized intelligence, described by Cattell as "the set of judgmental skills" gained from investing fluid intelligence in cultural activities. Vast differences in learning experiences occur because of factors such as social class, age, nationality, and historical era.

Crystallized intelligence includes skills such as verbal comprehension and numerical facility, because these abilities rely on knowledge already gained—such as the rules of grammar or addition, subtraction, and other mathematical concepts. This form of intelligence increases gradually over a lifetime and stays relatively stable until we are around 65 years old, when it begins to decline.

Cattell sees fluid and crystallized intelligence as fairly independent of each other, but reasons that having a higher fluid intelligence might lead to the broader and faster development of crystallized intelligence, depending on factors relating to personality and interests.

Noting that standard IQ tests tend to assess a combination of fluid and crystallized intelligence, Cattell developed tests to assess fluid intelligence in isolation. His culture-fair intelligence test, which uses nonverbal, multiple-choice questions based on shapes and patterns, requires no prior learning from the participants and can be used to test children and adults from any culture. ■

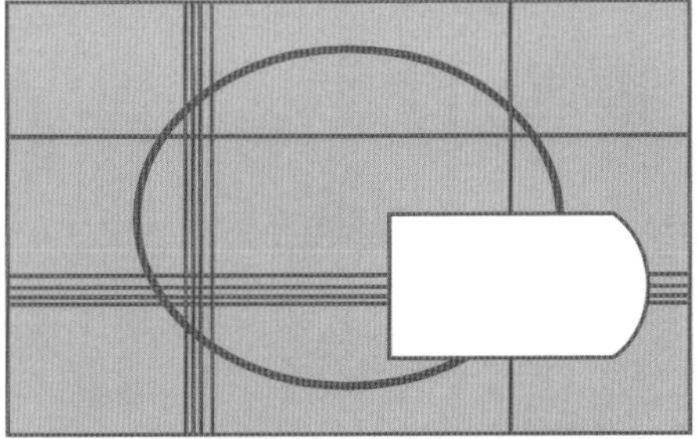

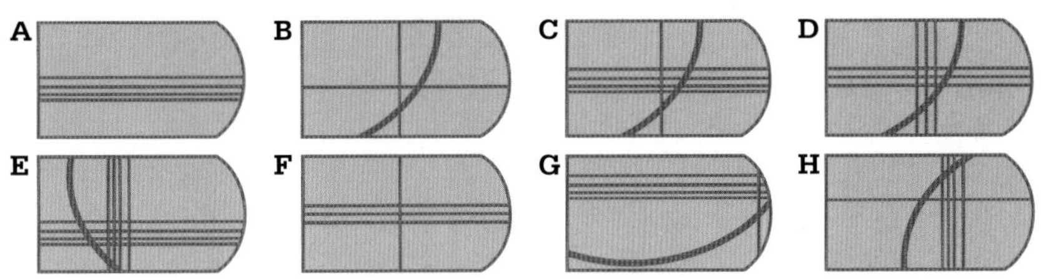

The culture-fair intelligence test was first presented by Cattell in 1940. It measures fluid intelligence through pattern-related problems that require reasoning ability but no prior learning or knowledge to solve.

Raymond Cattell

Born in Staffordshire, England, Raymond Bernard Cattell achieved a first-class degree in chemistry in 1924 before turning to psychology and receiving his doctorate in 1929. After teaching in London and Exeter universities, he ran the Leicester Child Guidance Clinic for five years before moving to the US in 1937. He lived and taught there until 1973, holding posts at Clark and Harvard universities, and the University of Illinois. Cattell married three times and moved to Honolulu as a professor at the University of Hawaii, spending the rest of his life there. In 1997, the American Psychological Association honored him with a Lifetime Achievement Award. However, his idea that nations should safeguard high, inherited intelligence through eugenics made this a controversial award, and led to critical attacks. Cattell defended himself and refused the award, but died of heart failure the following year.

Key works

1971 *Abilities*
1987 *Intelligence*

THERE IS AN ASSOCIATION BETWEEN INSANITY AND GENIUS

HANS J. EYSENCK (1916–1997)

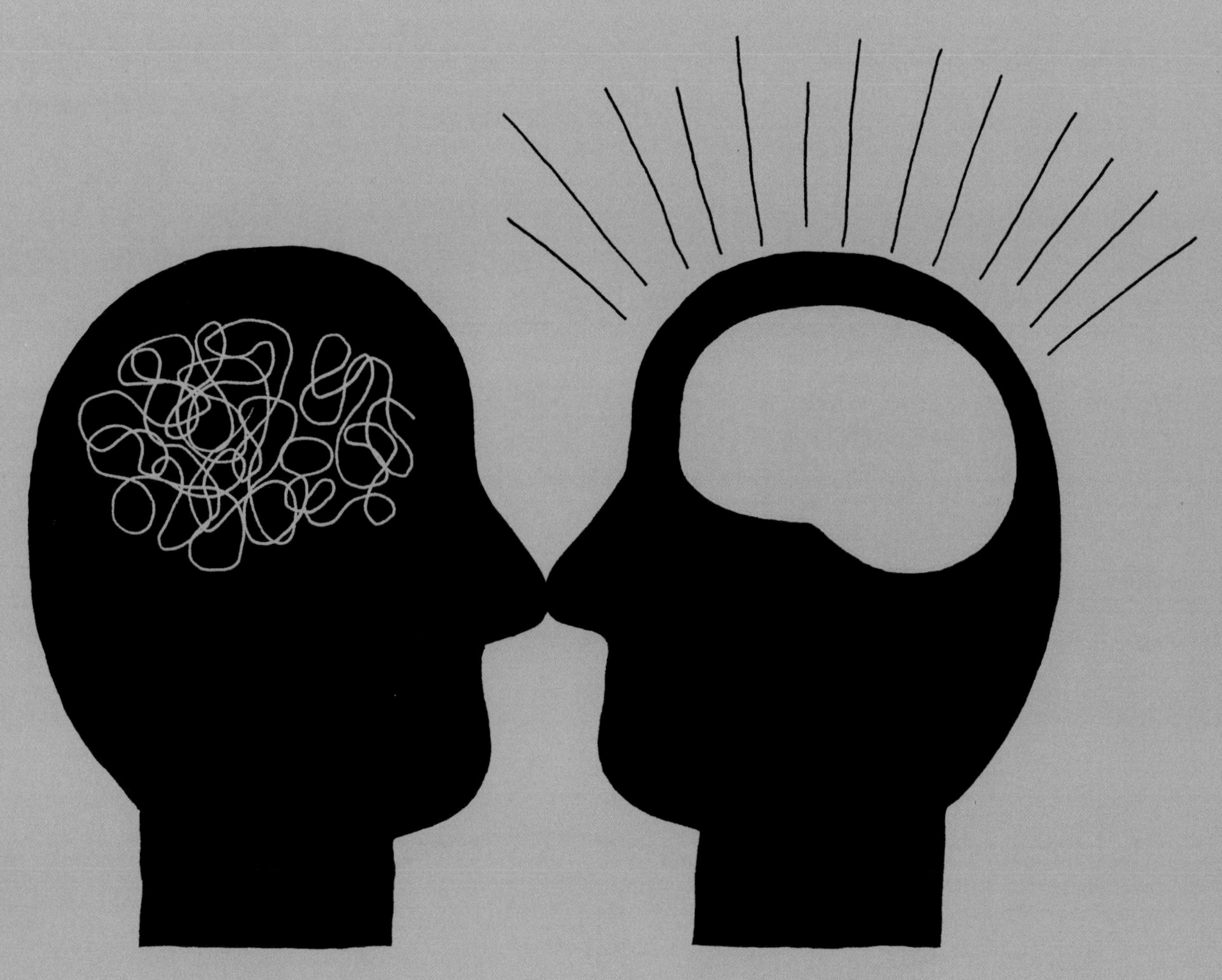

IN CONTEXT

APPROACH
Personality

BEFORE
1926 American psychologist Catharine Cox tests the intelligence and personalities of 300 geniuses and finds the average IQ to be 165+; key characteristics are tremendous persistence and motivation.

1956 J. P. Guilford develops the concept of divergent thinking to discuss creativity.

AFTER
2009 In *Genius 101: Creators, Leaders, and Prodigies,* American psychologist Dean Keith Simonton argues that geniuses are the result of good genes and good surroundings.

2009 Swedish psychologist Anders Ericsson attributes expert performance to 10,000 hours of practice.

Discussion about genius has been dominated for most of its history by the nature-versus-nurture debate: is a genius born or made? Prior to the early 1900s, ideas about genius were based largely on stories of people who were perceived as geniuses, such as Leonardo da Vinci and Beethoven. As early as Aristotle, creative genius and madness were seen as linked, and both assumed to be largely genetic in nature. In 1904, British psychologist Havelock Ellis's *A Study of British Genius,* reported controlled studies of both psychotic patients and creative people to establish a link between the two. Seventy years later the German psychologist Hans Eysenck reviewed the early evidence and concluded that it is not psychosis (full blown insanity) that is related to genius, but psychoticism, which he defined as an underlying disposition to develop psychotic symptoms.

There is a common genetic basis for great potential in creativity and for psychological deviation.
Hans J. Eysenck

Temperament and biology

Many psychologists have defined and measured personality traits, but Eysenck's interests focused on human temperament rather than the detailed characteristics that make up a whole person. He was a biologist, and like others before him, notably the ancient Greek physicians Hippocrates and Galen, he believed that physiological factors account for temperament. Hippocrates had suggested that personality type arises from an excess or deficit of a particular type of bodily fluids, known as humors. Galen expanded upon this idea to suggest there are four types of temperament: sanguine, choleric, phlegmatic, and melancholic.

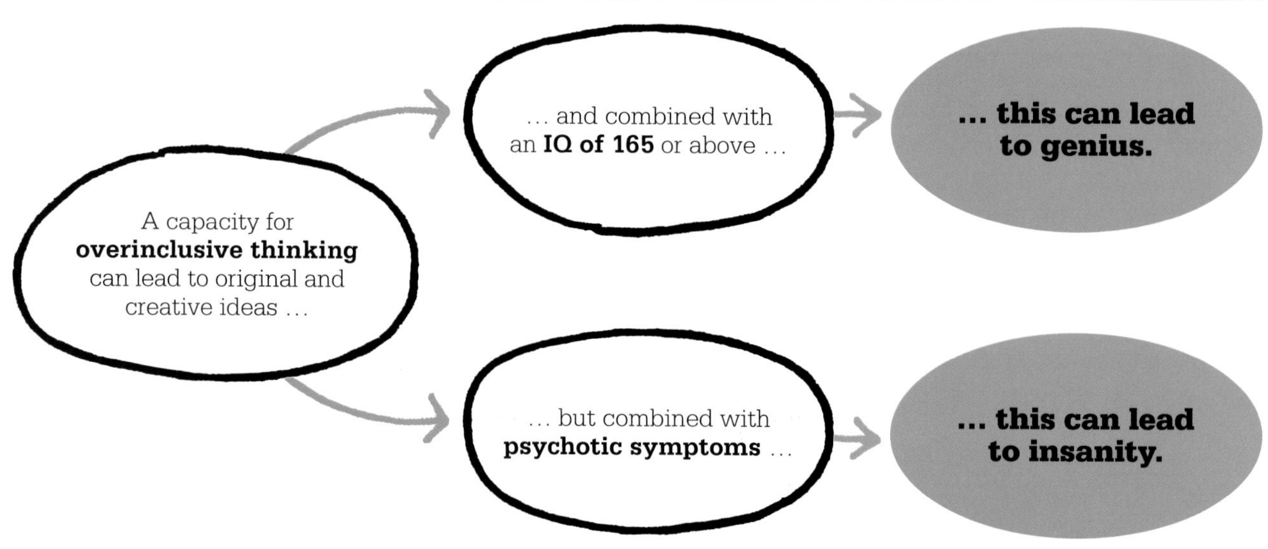
A capacity for **overinclusive thinking** can lead to original and creative ideas …
… and combined with an **IQ of 165** or above …
… this can lead to genius.
… but combined with **psychotic symptoms** …
… this can lead to insanity.

See also: Galen 18–19 ▪ Francis Galton 28–29 ▪ J. P. Guilford 310–311 ▪ Gordon Allport 312–319 ▪ Raymond Cattell 320–321 ▪ Walter Mischel 332–333 ▪ David Rosenhan 334–335

He claimed that sanguine people have an excess of blood, and are cheerful and optimistic. Those with a choleric temperament, stemming from an abundance of bile, are quick and hot-tempered. Phlegmatic individuals, with too much phlegm, are slow, lazy, and dull. Melancholics, who suffer from black bile, are sad, pessimistic, and depressed.

Galen's biological approach appealed to Eysenck, who considered temperament to be physiological and genetically determined. He proposed a measure of two dimensions, or overarching "superfactors" of personality, that encompass all the detailed traits: Neuroticism and Extraversion–Introversion, which he then mapped against Galen's four temperaments.

Eysenck's model of personality provides an overarching paradigm for defining temperament. Each of the superfactors (Extraversion and Neuroticism) is made up of lower-order habits, such as "lively." The two superfactors divide habits into four types that reflect Galen's four temperaments.

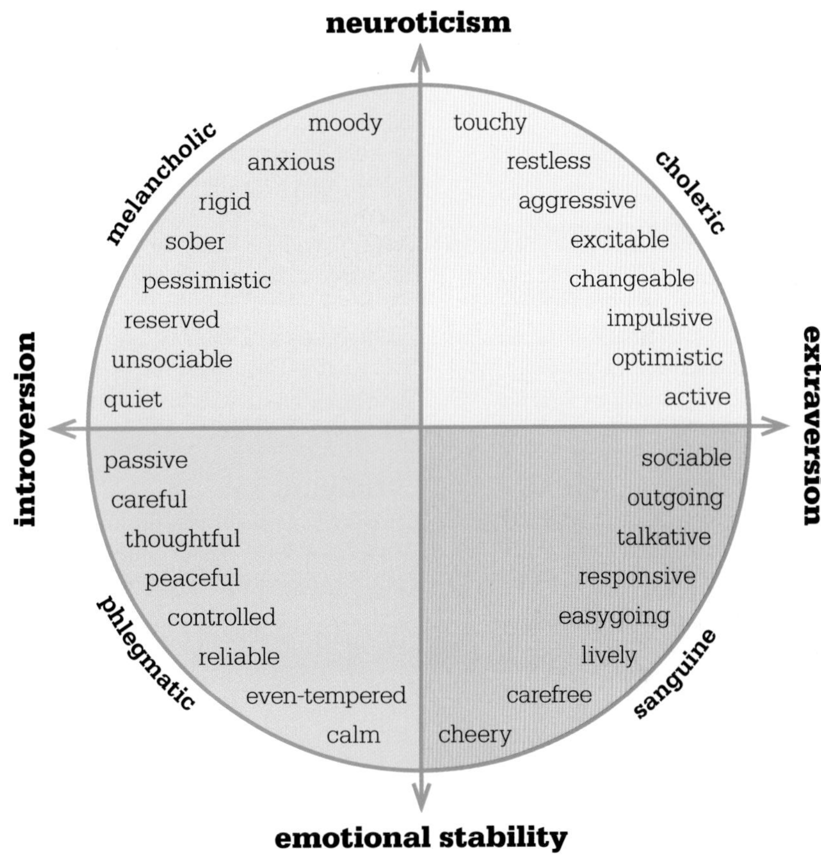

Eysenck's scales

"Neuroticism" was Eysenck's name for a personality dimension that ranges from emotionally calm and stable at one extreme, to nervous and easily upset at the other. He claimed that neurotics (at the less stable end of the spectrum) have a low activation threshold in terms of triggering the sympathetic nervous system, which is the part of the brain that activates the "fight or flight" response. People with this more responsive system are hyperactive in this regard, so they respond to even minor threats as though they are seriously dangerous, experiencing an increase in blood pressure and heart rate, sweating, and so on. They are also more likely to suffer from the various neurotic disorders. However, Eysenck was not suggesting that people who scored at the nervous end of this dimension are necessarily neurotic in practice, merely that they would be more likely to develop a variety of nervous disorders. Eysenck's second dimension of temperament was "Extraversion–Introversion." He used these terms very much as we use them to describe people around us: extraverts are outgoing and talkative, while introverts are shy and quiet. Eysenck claimed that variations in brain activity explain the difference: introverts are chronically overaroused and jittery, while extraverts are chronically underaroused and bored; so the brain must either wake itself up through seeking further excitement with other people (extraverts) or calm itself down through seeking peace and solitude (introverts).

Psychoticism

Eysenck tested his ideas on large groups of people, but realized there were some sections of society that he was missing; so he took his studies into mental institutions. »

Introverts are characterized by higher levels of activity than extraverts and so are chronically more cortically aroused than extraverts.
Hans J. Eysenck

Through this work, he identified a third dimension of temperament, which he labeled "psychoticism," a term that has largely replaced the word "insanity" in general use. In personality theory, this was quite a departure: most personality theorists were attempting to define and measure the normal (sane) personality. However, Eysenck said that, as with the neuroticism dimension, psychoticism ranges along a scale; his tests looked for the occurrence of personality traits commonly found among psychotics.

Eysenck found that a number of personality traits relate to each other to produce psychoticism; those who score highly on this scale are usually aggressive, egocentric, impersonal, impulsive, antisocial, unempathic, creative, and tough-minded. A high score on the scale does not mean a person is psychotic, and it is not inevitable that they will become so; they simply share characteristics with psychotic patients. In controlled studies, such as those by Norwegian psychologist Dan Olweus and his colleagues in 1980, the aggressive element of psychoticism has been related biologically to increased testosterone levels.

Studying genius

A clear psychological definition of creativity has proved slippery, but there is broad agreement that it involves originality and novelty, and is based on aspects of both intellectual ability and personality. In his paper, *Creativity and Personality: Suggestions for a Theory*, Eysenck aimed to throw some light on the nature of creativity and its relationship to intelligence, personality, and genius.

Genius is held to be the highest form of creativity, and it rests upon very high intelligence: an IQ score of at least 165 is considered to be a prerequisite. However, a high IQ is not enough on its own. Another relevant component of intelligence is the mental search process which we use to find solutions, by bringing together different ideas from memory to form new answers to problems. This mental scanning is guided by ideas of relevance: what past ideas and experiences do I have that are relevant to this problem? Each of us performs this differently, and it is an ability that is independent of our IQ. The ability runs along a scale, ranging from an expansive, overinclusive idea of what is relevant (seeing too many things as potential possibilities), to an overly narrow one (seeing few possibilities); at the center sits a more conventional sense of what might apply to any problem at hand.

Overinclusive thinking can be measured by word-association tests, which analyze two features: the number of responses to any given word, and the originality of responses. For example, when presented with the word "foot," those with a narrow range of responses are most likely to

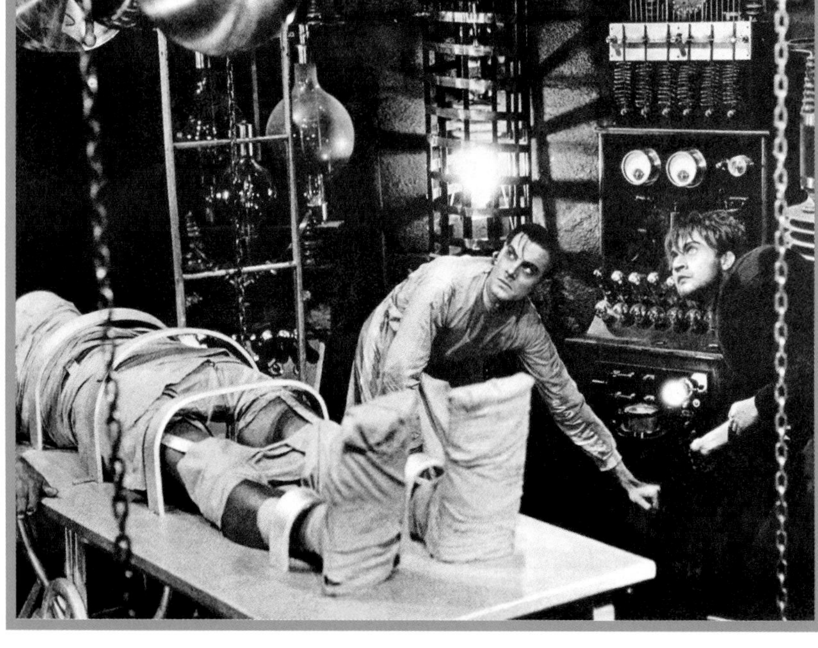

Professor Frankenstein creates a monster in Mary Shelley's novel, and exhibits classic psychotic symptoms: recklessness, disregard for conventions, and tough-mindedness.

Creative geniuses, such as the artist Vincent van Gogh, exhibit traits from Eysenck's psychoticism dimension, particularly overinclusive thinking, independence, and nonconformity.

respond with the word "shoe"; a slightly wider range of inclusive thinking might contain the words "hand" or "toe," while an over-inclusive person might generate words such as "soldier" or "sore." This kind of test makes it possible to measure people's creativity.

It is the element of overinclusive thinking that Eysenck demonstrated to be a common feature of both psychoticism and creativity. When overinclusive thinking and high IQ are present together, creative genius will result, because the combination generates creative and original ideas. This is the cognitive characteristic that lies at the base of creativity. When overinclusive thinking and psychotic symptoms are present together, psychosis, in varying degrees, may result.

Creativity and personality

Eysenck believed that creativity is a personality trait that provides the potential for creative achievement, but the realization of that potential lies in the character trait of psychoticism (in the absence of psychosis). The drive to translate the trait of creativity into achievement, for example by creating works of art, comes from aspects of the psychotic temperament, in particular the overinclusive thinking style. Eysenck was not suggesting a causal link between genius and insanity; while the two things have something in common—overinclusive thinking—this combines with other features of genius or insanity to lead to very different results.

Research into creativity faces a number of difficult challenges: with some researchers claiming that creativity can only be judged on what it produces. Eysenck felt unable to propose a fully developed theory of creativity, only a suggestion for one. As he said, "I am linking several fuzzy theories." His work ranged over many areas, though he is best known for his exploration into personality and intelligence. His PEN (Psychoticism, Extraversion, Neuroticism) model was hugely influential, and acted as the basis for much of the later research into personality traits. ■

Psychoticism in the absence of psychosis … is the vital element in translating the trait of creativity (originality) from potential to actual achievement.
Hans J. Eysenck

Hans J. Eysenck

Hans Jurgen Eysenck was born in Berlin, Germany, to artistic parents; his mother was a well-known film actress, and his Catholic father, Eduard, was a stage performer. His parents separated soon after his birth, and he was raised by his maternal grandmother. In 1934, he discovered that he could only study at Berlin University if he joined the Nazi party, so he traveled to England to study psychology at University College London.

He married in 1938 and after narrowly escaping internment as a German citizen during World War II, he completed a PhD, and took up work as a psychologist at an emergency hospital. He later founded and then headed the Institute of Psychiatry at the University of London. Eysenck married again in 1950, and became a British citizen in 1955. He was diagnosed with a brain tumor in 1996 and died in a London hospice in 1997.

Key works

1967 *The Biological Basis of Personality*
1976 *Psychoticism as a Dimension of Personality*
1983 *The Roots of Creativity*

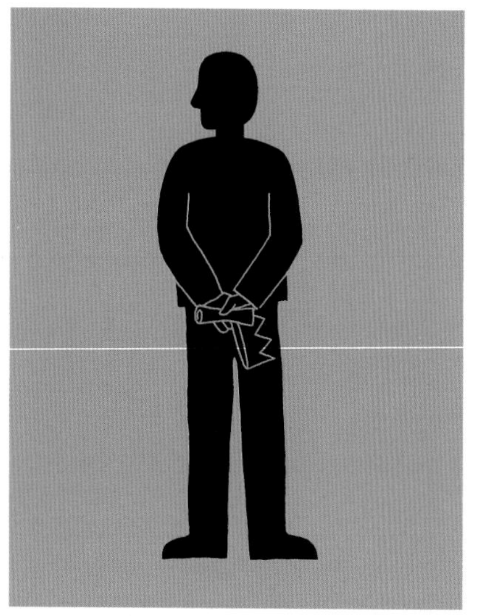

THREE KEY MOTIVATIONS DRIVE PERFORMANCE

DAVID C. McCLELLAND (1917–1998)

IN CONTEXT

APPROACH
Need theory

BEFORE

1938 American psychologist Henry Murray develops his theory of how personality is shaped by psychogenic needs.

1943 Abraham Maslow's *A Theory of Human Motivation* presents his hierarchy of needs.

1959 In *Motivation to Work*, US psychologist Frederick Herzberg states that achievement, rather than money, motivates people.

AFTER

1990 In *Flow: The Psychology of Optimal Experience*, Mihály Csíkszentmihályi discusses motivation for achievement.

2002 Martin Seligman explores motivation as the expression of character strengths.

2004 In *Leadership That Gets Results*, US psychologist Daniel Goleman applies McClelland's ideas to leadership in business.

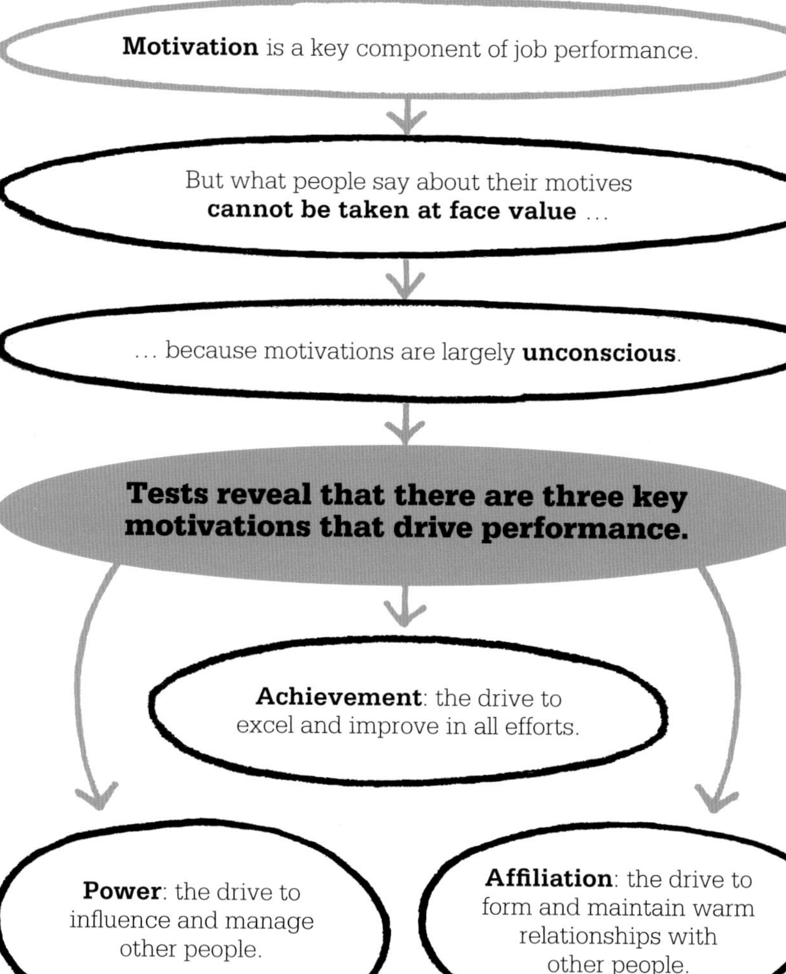

Motivation is a key component of job performance.
But what people say about their motives **cannot be taken at face value** …
… because motivations are largely **unconscious**.
Tests reveal that there are three key motivations that drive performance.
Achievement: the drive to excel and improve in all efforts.
Power: the drive to influence and manage other people.
Affiliation: the drive to form and maintain warm relationships with other people.

See also: Abraham Maslow 138–139 ▪ Mihály Csíkszentmihályi 198–199 ▪ Martin Seligman 200–201

In the 1960s and '70s, decisions about whether to employ someone or not were usually based on educational achievement, and the results of personality and IQ tests. David C. McClelland, however, suggested that people's motivations were the best predictor of success in the workplace. Through extensive research, he identified the three key motivations that he believed were responsible for job performance: the need for power, for achievement, and for affiliation. While everyone has all three motivations, he maintained that one would be dominant, shaping a person's performance in the workplace.

Three key needs

McClelland saw the need for power, or to have control over others, as the most important motivation for a good manager or leader. But this is only true as long as the need for power is on behalf of a company or an organization. Someone with a strong drive for personal power may make a poor team player.

High quality work, McClelland thought, stems from the need for achievement, which is therefore a far more accurate predictor of job success than intelligence. The drive to achieve, he believed, is what gives people a competitive edge, helping them to stretch for new goals and improve.

Lastly, McClelland claimed that the need for affiliation—to have good relationships with others—helps people to work well within a team. He also noted that people with a pronounced need for affiliation are unlikely to be successful managers.

McClelland pointed out that motivation stems from personality traits that are deeply embedded in the unconscious. We are not fully aware of our own motivations, he stated, so what we may say about our motives in job interviews or self-report questionnaires should not be taken at face value. He advocated using the Thematic Apperception Test (TAT), which psychologists Henry Murray and Christiana Morgan devised in the 1930s as a way of revealing aspects of the unconscious. Rarely used in a business setting, the test presents a series of pictures to the subject, who is then asked to develop a story based on them. The assumption is that the stories will be a projection of the subject's underlying abilities and motivations. McClelland went on to devise an innovative way of analyzing TAT responses to allow a comparison between the suitability of the different people who took the test to specific work-related roles.

McClelland's ideas revolutionized business recruitment, and although his intensive methods of assessing job applicants have lost some of their popularity, the basic principles endure. Motivation is now seen as critical to performance at work. ■

The Thematic Apperception Test was promoted by McClelland as a way of assessing job candidates. Telling a story based on a series of images was thought to uncover people's true motives.

David C. McClelland

David Clarence McClelland was born in Mount Vernon, New York. After graduating from Wesleyan University, Connecticut, and gaining an MA at the University of Missouri, he moved to Yale, where he completed his PhD in experimental psychology in 1941. He taught briefly at several universities, before accepting a position at Harvard in 1956. McClelland stayed there for 30 years, becoming Chairman of the Department of Social Relations.

In 1963, McClelland set up a business management consultancy, applying his theories to assist company executives in the assessment and training of staff. In 1987, Boston University made him a Distinguished Research Professor of Psychology, a position he held up to his death at the age of 80.

Key works

1953 *The Achievement Motive*
1961 *The Achieving Society*
1973 *Testing for Competence Rather Than for Intelligence*
1987 *Human Motivation*
1998 *Identifying Competencies with Behavioral-Event Interviews*

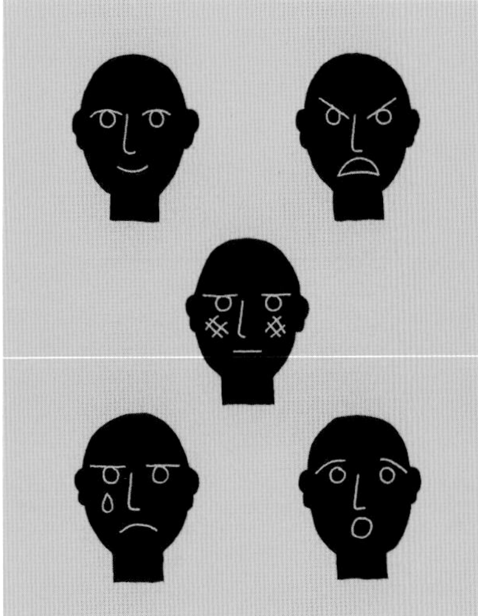

EMOTION IS AN ESSENTIALLY UNCONSCIOUS PROCESS

NICO FRIJDA (1927–2015)

IN CONTEXT

APPROACH
Psychology of emotion

BEFORE
1872 Biologist Charles Darwin publishes the first scientific study of human emotions in *The Expression of the Emotions in Man and Animals*.

Late 1800s William James and Danish physiologist Carl Lange propose the James–Lange theory of emotion: that emotions are the result of bodily changes, and not the cause of them.

1929 Physiologists Walter Cannon and Philip Bard say we experience physiological arousal and emotion at the same time, in the Cannon–Bard theory.

AFTER
1991 In *Emotion and Adaptation*, psychologist Richard Lazarus says a thought must precede any emotion or physiological arousal.

Our emotions and feelings are idiosyncratic; they seem to be purely subjective, and the mysticism surrounding them may explain why the psychology of emotion has advanced so slowly. But during the last 30 years, this situation has changed, as scientific findings regarding the "site" of emotions have led to renewed interest. Evolutionary psychologists have also posed questions. What is the purpose of emotions? How have they helped us survive and thrive?

Emotion is an essentially unconscious process.

Emotions are motivating forces, preparing us for action.

They are **spontaneous biological processes** that are out of our control.

They can be **understood by others** through spontaneous physical expression, such as laughter.

Feelings are how we interpret the emotions we experience.

We are **consciously aware** of our feelings and can make **decisions** based on them.

As we have control of our feelings, **others cannot guess** at our feelings through our behavior.

See also: William James 38–45 ▪ Albert Ellis 142–145 ▪ Gordon H. Bower 194–195 ▪ Charlotte Bühler 342 ▪ René Diatkine 344–45 ▪ Stanley Schachter 345

Nico Frijda's groundbreaking book, *The Laws of Emotion*, explores the substance and rules of emotions. He sees them as lying at the crossroads of biological and cognitive processes: some, such as fear, are biologically inherent or innate, and these basic emotions are the ones we share with other animals. Others arise in us in response to thoughts, so are clearly cognition-based. They may even—as in the case of indignation or humiliation—be shaped by culture.

Frijda makes clear distinctions between emotions and feelings. Emotions are beyond our control; they spontaneously arise and alert us to their presence by physical sensations, such as a tightening in the gut when we feel fear. For this reason he says that "emotion is an essentially unconscious process." Feelings, on the other hand, are our interpretations of whatever emotions we are experiencing, and have a more conscious element to them. When we feel something, we are able to have thoughts and make decisions about it. We are not suddenly hijacked by our feelings as we are by our emotions.

Action and thought

Frijda points out that emotions and feelings are also displayed differently. Emotions prepare us for action; in situations that induce fear, they are motivating forces that prepare the body to flee or stand and fight. Other people are able to understand, or at least guess at, our emotions from our behavior. Feelings, however, may or may not be consistent with behavior, because we can choose to behave in a way that hides them.

Frijda sees the basic emotions as an opportunity for greater self-awareness. They accompany a biological arousal that makes us notice them and become more aware of our feelings. This allows us to factor them into choices we make, and with honest reflection, to deepen self-awareness. But Frijda confines basic emotions to anger, joy, shame, sadness, and fear. Others, such as jealousy and guilt, do not have the same biological imperative.

Emotions, such as fear, Frijda says, are always "about something." They are spontaneous responses to changing circumstances, and reveal much about our relationship with our environment.

In defining and describing a very specific set of laws by which emotions operate, Frijda shows that they emerge, wax, and wane in a predictable way. Reason interprets them like a barometer, to ensure our mental well-being. "Our emotional selves and reasonable selves are not compartmentalized," Frijda says, "on the contrary, they are connected much more than they seem." ■

Nico Frijda

Nico Henri Frijda was born in Amsterdam to an academic Jewish family, and lived in hiding as a child to avoid the persecution of the Jews during World War II. He studied psychology at Gemeente Universiteit, Amsterdam, where he was awarded a PhD in 1956 for his thesis *Understanding Facial Expressions*. He attributes his initial interest in emotions to being in love, as a student, with "a very expressive girl."

From 1952 to 1955 Frijda worked as a clinical psychologist at the Dutch Army Neurosis Centre, before returning to research and teaching. For the next 10 years he was assistant professor at the University of Amsterdam, then professor in experimental and theoretical psychology.

Frijda held visiting posts in universities across Europe, including Paris, Italy, Germany, and Spain. He died on April 11, 2015, at the age of 87.

Key works

1986 *The Emotions*
2006 *The Laws of Emotion*
2011 *Emotion Regulation and Free Will*

BEHAVIOR WITHOUT ENVIRONMENTAL CUES WOULD BE ABSURDLY CHAOTIC

WALTER MISCHEL (1930–2018)

IN CONTEXT

APPROACH
Personality theory

BEFORE
c.400 BCE Ancient Greek physician Hippocrates suggests personality depends on the levels of the four humors in the body.

1946 Raymond Cattell begins developing his 16-factor model of personality.

1961 American psychologists Ernest Tupes and Raymond Christal propose the first "Big Five" personality-factor model.

AFTER
1975 Hans J. Eysenck's Personality Questionnaire identifies two biologically based, independent dimensions of personality.

1980 US psychologists Robert Hogan, Joyce Hogan, and Rodney Warrenfeltz develop comprehensive personality tests based on the "Big Five" model of personality.

Until the late 1960s, personality was most often described as a series of individual behavioral traits that were genetically inherited. Psychologists worked to define and measure these traits, because this was thought to be essential to understanding and reliably predicting a person's behavior. Raymond Cattell identified 16 different personality traits; Hans J. Eysenck suggested there were only three or four. In 1961, Ernest Tupes and Raymond Christal proposed that there are five major personality traits (the "Big Five"): openness, conscientiousness, extraversion, agreeableness, and neuroticism or emotional stability. Then, in 1968,

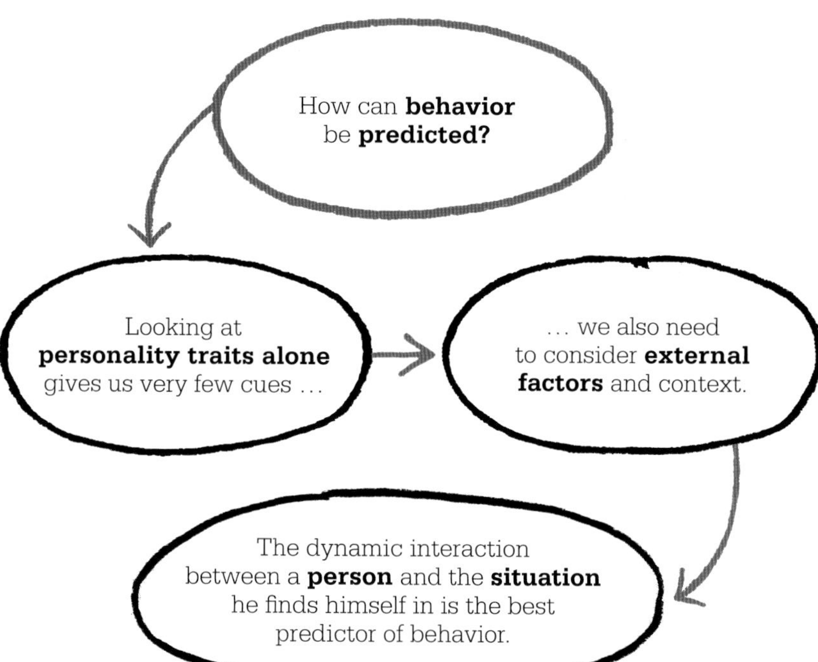

How can **behavior** be **predicted?**
Looking at **personality traits alone** gives us very few cues …
… we also need to consider **external factors** and context.
The dynamic interaction between a **person** and the **situation** he finds himself in is the best predictor of behavior.

See also: Galen 18–19 ▪ Gordon Allport 312–319 ▪ Raymond Cattell 320–321 ▪ Hans J. Eysenck 322–327

Walter Mischel shocked the world of personality theory when he proclaimed in *Personality and Assessment* that the classic personality test was almost worthless. He had reviewed a number of studies that tried to predict behavior from personality test scores, and found them to be accurate only 9 percent of the time.

External factors

Mischel drew attention to the part played by external factors, such as context, in determining behavior, believing that it was necessary to look at the dynamic interaction of people and the situation they find themselves in. Imagine how absurd it would be if people's behavior appeared to be independent of external factors. He proposed that an analysis of a person's behavior, in different situations, observed on numerous occasions, would provide clues to behavior patterns that would reveal a distinctive signature of personality, as opposed to a list of traits. Individual interpretation of a situation was also considered.

Later, Mischel explored habits of thinking, which might endure over time and across different situations.

What is a personality test really telling us about a person?
Walter Mischel

Resisting temptation, rather than succumbing to short-term gratification, often indicates a capacity for greater achievement in life, as Mischel's studies of behavior in young children revealed.

In his famous marshmallow experiments, aimed at testing willpower, four-year-old children were presented with a single marshmallow and told they could either eat it immediately, or wait 20 minutes and then have two. Some children were able to wait, others were not. Mischel monitored each child's progress into adolescence, and reported that those who had resisted temptation were better adjusted psychologically and more dependable; they did better at school, were more socially competent, and had greater self-esteem. Ability to delay gratification seemed to be a better predictor of future success than any previously measured trait.

Mischel's work led to a shift in the study of personality—from how personality predicts behavior to how behavior reveals personality. It also changed the way personality profiling is used in assessing job candidates. Tests that were once considered an accurate basis for staff recruitment are now seen as a guide, to be interpreted in the context of the situations that are likely to arise in doing a job. ■

Walter Mischel

Walter Mischel was born in Austria, but emigrated with his family to the US in 1938. He grew up in Brooklyn, New York, receiving his PhD in clinical psychology from Ohio State University in 1956. He then went on to teach at the Universities of Colorado, Harvard, and Stanford, moving in 1983 to Columbia University in New York City, where he was the Robert Johnston Niven Professor of Humane Letters.

Numerous honors were heaped on Mischel. These include the Distinguished Scientific Contribution Award as well as the Distinguished Scientist Award of the American Psychological Association, and the prestigious Grawemeyer Award in psychology in 2011. Mischel was also a prolific and talented artist.

Key works

1968 *Personality and Assessment*
1973 *Is Information About Individuals More Important Than Information About Situations?*
2003 *Introduction to Personality*

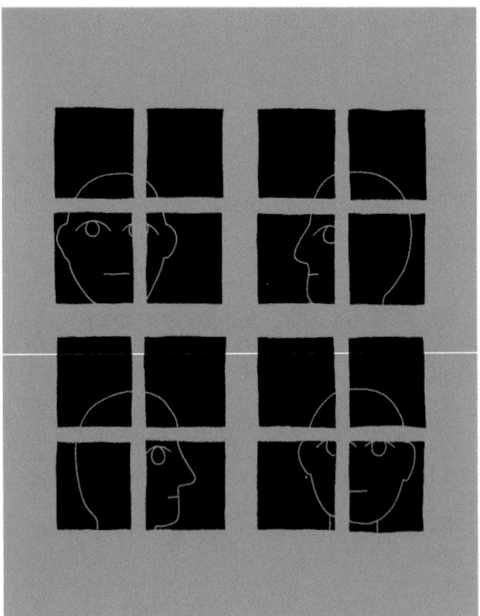

WE CANNOT DISTINGUISH THE SANE FROM THE INSANE IN PSYCHIATRIC HOSPITALS

DAVID ROSENHAN (1929–2012)

IN CONTEXT

APPROACH
Anti-psychiatry

BEFORE
1960 In *The Divided Self: An Existential Study in Sanity and Madness*, R. D. Laing emphasizes the family as a source of mental illness.

1961 Psychologists E. Zigler and L. Phillips demonstrate huge overlaps in the symptoms of different categories of psychiatric disorder.

1961 Hungarian-American psychiatrist Thomas Szasz publishes the controversial *The Myth of Mental Illness*.

1967 British psychiatrist David Cooper defines the anti-psychiatry movement in *Psychiatry and Anti-Psychiatry*.

AFTER
2008 Thomas Szasz publishes *Psychiatry: The Science of Lies*.

Psychiatrists say that mental disorders **can be accurately diagnosed through symptoms** that can be categorized into diseases.

So they should be able to **tell the difference** between the sane and the insane.

A first experiment showed that sane people can be judged insane.

A second experiment showed that people with genuine mental health disorders can be judged to be faking them.

We cannot distinguish the sane from the insane in psychiatric hospitals.

Psychiatric diagnoses are not objective, but exist only in the minds of the observers.

See also: Emil Kraepelin 31 ▪ R. D. Laing 150–151 ▪ Leon Festinger 166–169 ▪ Solomon Asch 228–231 ▪ Erving Goffman 232–233 ▪ Elliot Aronson 250–251 ▪ Thigpen & Cleckley 336–337

During the 1960s, psychiatry faced a vocal challenge to its fundamental beliefs by a number of experts known as the "anti-psychiatrists." This informal group of psychiatrists, psychologists, and welfare workers claimed that psychiatry is a medical model of mental health, yet there are no physical symptoms, and its treatment regimes largely ignore the patient's needs and behaviors.

In 1973, David Rosenhan carried out a field study in the US that explored the validity of psychiatric diagnosis and resulted in the dramatic conclusion that we cannot distinguish the sane from the insane in psychiatric hospitals.

In the first part of the study, Rosenhan assembled a group of eight sane people (including himself), made up of women and men of different occupations and ages, and designated them as pseudo-patients. They were briefed to make an attempt to be admitted as patients to different mental hospitals in five US states, first by telephoning the hospital to ask for an appointment. Later, at the admissions office, they were to complain of hearing an unfamiliar voice in their heads, which was unclear but used words such as "empty" and "thud." This suggested existential feelings of pointlessness. They were instructed to give false names and occupations, but otherwise true personal histories.

As a result, all the pseudo-patients were admitted to hospital with a diagnosis of schizophrenia, despite showing no symptoms of the disorder. Their hospital stays lasted an average of 19 days, during which time they behaved completely normally. They maintained journals of their experiences, surreptitiously at first but then openly, as it was never questioned. Demonstrating how even normal behavior might be interpreted as evidence of a psychiatric condition, Rosenhan found that a common comment in their medical notes was "patient engages in writing behavior."

The "patients" themselves described their experience in hospital as one of depersonalization and powerlessness. Their records showed that the average daily time they spent with medical staff was less than seven minutes. Although they were undetected by the hospital staff, other patients challenged their sanity, sometimes quite vigorously: "You're not crazy. You're a journalist checking up on the hospital."

Judging the insane sane

In the second part of Rosenhan's study, he falsely informed the staff at a teaching and research hospital (who were aware of the first study) that during the next three months, one or more pseudo-patients would try to be admitted to the hospital, and they were asked to rate each new patient on the likelihood of them being a pseudo-patient. Of 193 genuine new admissions, 41 were judged suspect by at least one member of staff, and 23 were flagged as possible pseudo-patients by at least one psychiatrist.

Rosenhan's work generated an explosion of controversy, and led many institutions to take steps to improve their care of patients. ■

David Rosenhan

David Rosenhan was born in the US in 1929. After gaining a BA in psychology from Yeshiva College, New York City, he moved to the city's Columbia University to study for his MA and PhD. He specialized in clinical and social psychology, and became an expert in legal trial tactics and decision-making. From 1957 to 1970, he taught at Swarthmore College, Princeton University, and Haverford College, then moved to Stanford, where he taught for nearly 30 years. He later became the university's Professor Emeritus of psychology and law. He was a fellow of the American Association for the Advancement of Science and was a visiting fellow at Oxford University. He founded the Trial Analysis Group and was a major advocate for the legal rights of mental health patients.

Key works

1968 *Foundations of Abnormal Psychology* (with Perry London)
1973 *On Being Sane in Insane Places*
1997 *Abnormality* (with Martin Seligman and Lisa Butler)

THE THREE FACES OF EVE

CORBETT H. THIGPEN (1919–1999) & HERVEY M. CLECKLEY (1903–1984)

IN CONTEXT

APPROACH
Mental disorders

BEFORE

1880s Pierre Janet describes MPD as multiple states of consciousness and coins the term "dissociation."

1887 French surgeon Eugene Azam documents the multiple personalities of Felida X.

1906 US physician Morton Prince reports Christine Beauchamp's case in *The Dissociation of Personality.*

AFTER

1970s US psychiatrist Cornelia Wilbur reports Sybil Isabel Dorsett's case and links MPD definitively with child abuse.

1980 The American Psychiatric Association publishes the third edition of the *Diagnostic and Statistical Manual of Mental Disorder,* legitimating MPD.

1994 MPD is renamed Dissociative Identity Disorder.

Multiple personality disorder (MPD, later known as dissociative identity disorder) is a mental condition in which an individual's personality appears to present as two or more distinct identities. MPD was first reported in 1791 by Eberhardt Gmelin; over the following 150 years, a further 100 clinical cases were documented. It was believed that the condition arose from childhood abuse, and could be cured by integrating the subpersonalities back into the main personality.

One of the most famous cases of multiple personality disorder is that of Eve White. Eve was referred to Thigpen and Cleckley in 1952, suffering from severe headaches and occasional blackouts. She was a neat, rather prim young woman aged 25, married, with a four-year-old daughter. Eve would remain in treatment for 14 months.

Eve described to the doctors a disturbing episode: she had bought some extravagant clothes she could not afford, yet had no memory of the purchase. As she recounted this, her

Eve White
Prim, reserved, timid, repressed, compulsive. No awareness of the other two personalities.

Eve Black
Wayward, harsh, irresponsible, shallow, hysterical. Aware of Eve White, but not of Jane.

Jane
Mature, boldly capable, interesting, compassionate. Aware of both Eves, but only from the point of her awakening.

See also: Pierre Janet 54–55 ▪ Timothy Leary 148 ▪ Milton Erickson 343

demeanor began to change. She looked confused, then the lines of her face altered. Her eyes widened, and she smiled provocatively. She spoke in a bright, flirtatious tone, requesting a cigarette, even though Eve did not smoke.

This was "Eve Black," a separate personality so distinct that she even suffered from a skin allergy to nylon that Eve White did not. Eve White was unaware of Eve Black, while the latter was wholly aware of the former, and was full of derision for her: "She's such a damn dope …."

Distinct personalities

Both personalities were submitted to extensive psychological testing. Eve White had a marginally higher IQ than Eve Black; both fell in the "bright, normal" category. Personality dynamics were explored using the Rorschach test (in which subjects report their perception of inkblots). There were dramatic differences: Eve Black showed a dominant hysterical tendency, and the ability to conform. Eve White showed "constriction, anxiety, and obsessive compulsive traits" and an inability to deal with her hostility.

'When I go out and get drunk,' Eve Black said, '*she* wakes up with the hangover.'
Thigpen & Cleckley

Eve's story was popularized in a book and a film, *The Three Faces of Eve*, which captured the public's imagination and made Eve's case the most famous example of Multiple Personality Disorder.

Eve's condition was believed to result from childhood abuse, so efforts were made to work back into her early childhood, using hypnosis to provoke the emergence of Eve Black. Eventually, an attempt was made to summon both personalities at once; Eve fell into a trance. She woke as a third personality: this was Jane, the third face of Eve—a more capable and interesting character than Eve White. She seemed to combine the assets of both Eves, without their weaknesses. While neither Eve was aware of Jane, she was aware of them both.

Jane appeared to be a balanced compromise between the two Eves, and she was nurtured as the personality with the best grasp of the complex dynamics of the three personalities: the two Eves were integrated into her character.

Full-blown cases of MPD such as Eve's are rare, but it is now thought that less pronounced cases are more common. The careful documentation of in-depth case studies like Eve's has resulted in diagnostic and treatment protocols that make MPD highly treatable. ■

Corbett H. Thigpen & Hervey M. Cleckley

Corbett H. Thigpen was born in Macon, Georgia. His childhood interest in amateur magic endured throughout his life, and he was inducted into the Southeastern Association of Magicians' Hall of Fame. Thigpen graduated from Mercer University in 1942, and from the Medical College of Georgia in 1945. He served in the US Army during World War II, then in 1948 he began his distinguished career as a psychiatrist in a private practice with Hervey M. Cleckley. For two decades, the pair taught in the departments of psychiatry and neurology at the Medical College of Georgia. Thigpen was known as "the professor who received a standing ovation after every lecture." He retired in 1987.

Hervey M. Cleckley was born in Augusta, Georgia. In 1924, he graduated from the University of Georgia, where he was also a keen sportsman. He won a Rhodes scholarship to Oxford University, graduating in 1926. He spent his entire career at Georgia Medical School, in a variety of positions, including that of founding chairman of the Department of Psychiatry and Health Behavior. In 1941, he wrote *The Mask of Sanity*, a seminal study of psychopaths.

Key works

1941 *The Mask of Sanity* (Cleckley)
1957 *The Three Faces of Eve* (Thigpen & Cleckley)

DIRECTO

RY

DIRECTORY

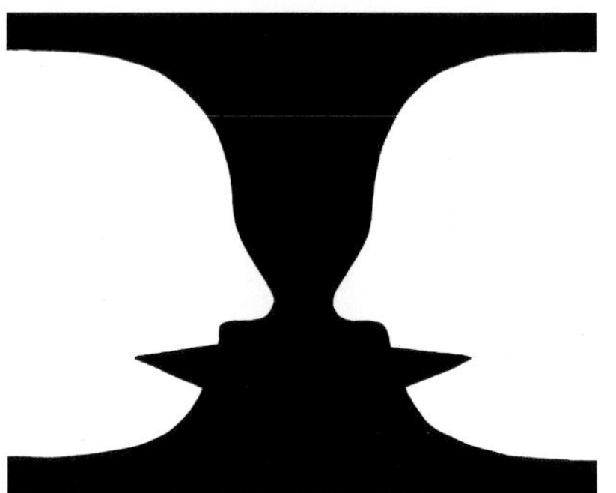

Investigation into the workings of the mind dates back to the earliest civilizations, although it was largely philosophical in nature rather than scientific in the modern sense. It was only with major advances in the biological sciences in the second half of the 19th century that a truly scientific analysis of our mental processes became possible. Psychology soon emerged as a distinct area of study in Europe and the US, where universities established major centers of research, attracting psychologists from around the world. At first, it was an almost exclusively male preserve, but the significant contribution made by female psychologists has become increasingly recognized. In addition to those already featured in this book, here are some of the many other key figures in the world of psychology.

JOHN DEWEY
1859–1952

American John Dewey greatly influenced the development of the science and philosophy of human thought in the first half of the 20th century. Although primarily a behaviorist psychologist, his application of the philosophy of pragmatism on society had a major impact on educational thinking and practice in the US.
See also: William James 38–45 ▪ G. Stanley Hall 46–47

W. H. R. RIVERS
1864–1922

William Halse Rivers Rivers was an English surgeon, neurologist, and psychiatrist who specialized in the relationship between the mind and the body. He published several key papers on neurological conditions, including hysteria. He is best known for his work on "shell shock" (post-traumatic stress disorder) and is also considered one of the founders of medical anthropology. The methods of cross-cultural analysis Rivers used on an expedition to the Torres Straits Pacific islands laid the foundations for future field study.
See also: Wilhelm Wundt 32–37 ▪ Hermann Ebbinghaus 48–49 ▪ Sigmund Freud 92–99

EDWARD B. TITCHENER
1867–1927

Englishman Edward Bradford Titchener studied experimental psychology, first at Oxford and then in Germany under Wilhelm Wundt. He moved to the US in 1892, where he became known as the founder of structural psychology, which breaks down the experiences of humanity and arranges them into elemental structures. As structural psychology is based on introspection, it was at odds with behaviorism, which was growing in popularity. By the 1920s, Titchener was fairly isolated in his beliefs, though he was still widely admired. He wrote several textbooks on psychology, including: *An Outline of Psychology* (1896), *Experimental Psychology* (1901–1905), and *A Textbook of Psychology* (1910).
See also: Wilhelm Wundt 32–37 ▪ William James 38–45 ▪ J. P. Guilford 310–311 ▪ Edwin Boring 342

WILLIAM & CLARA STERN
1871–1938/1877–1945

German husband and wife William and Clara Stern were key figures in the establishment of developmental psychology and co-authors of several important publications. The 1914 book *Psychology of Early Childhood* (published under William's name but acknowledging the contribution of Clara) was based on observations of their own three children over 18 years. Their method—"personalistic psychology"—explored the individual developmental path, combining applied, differential, genetic, and general psychology. Also a pioneer in forensic psychology, William developed intelligence quotient (IQ) tests to calculate a child's intelligence. A single-number score is awarded by dividing the "mental age" of the child by their "chronological age" and multiplying by 100.
See also: Alfred Binet 50–53 ▪ Jean Piaget 270–277

MARGARET FLOY WASHBURN
1871–1939

Born in New York City, Floy Washburn overcame the obstacles to women's education of the time to become the first female to receive a PhD in psychology (1894). In 1921, she became president of the American Psychological Association, and she pioneered the inclusion of women in psychology. Her book on animal behavior, *The Animal Mind: A Textbook of Comparative Psychology* (1908), was for many years the standard text on the subject.
See also: Edward Thorndike 62–65 ▪ Konrad Lorenz 77 ▪ B. F. Skinner 78–85

CHARLES SAMUEL MYERS
1873–1946

At Cambridge University, Myers studied experimental psychology under W. H. R. Rivers, and in 1912, he set up the Cambridge Laboratory of Experimental Psychology. During World War I, he treated soldiers for "shell shock" (a term he invented). After the war, he was a key figure in the development of occupational psychology. His books include *Mind and Work* (1920), *Industrial Psychology in Great Britain* (1926), and *In the Realm of Mind* (1937).
See also: Kurt Lewin 222–227 ▪ Solomon Asch 228–231 ▪ Raymond Cattell 320–321 ▪ W. H. R. Rivers 340

MAX WERTHEIMER
1880–1943

Together with Kurt Koffka and Wolfgang Köhler, Czech psychologist Max Wertheimer founded Gestalt psychology in the US in the 1930s. Gestalt built on existing theories of perceptual organization. Moving away from Wundt's molecularism, Wertheimer advocated the study of the whole, famously saying "the whole is more than the sum of its parts." He also devised Pragnanz, the idea that the mind processes visual information into the simplest forms of symmetry and shape.
See also: Abraham Maslow 138–139 ▪ Solomon Asch 228–231

ELTON MAYO
1880–1949

In the 1930s, while Professor of Industrial Management at Harvard, Australian Elton Mayo carried out his ground-breaking Hawthorne Experiments. Drawing on psychology, physiology, and anthropology, he studied the productivity and morale of six female workers as he made changes to their working conditions over a five-year period. The most surprising outcome was how the workers responded to the research itself. The Hawthorne Effect, as it is now known, is a change in human behavior that occurs when people know they are being studied. This discovery had a lasting impact on industrial ethics and relations and research methods in social science.
See also: Sigmund Freud 92–99 ▪ Carl Jung 102–107

HERMANN RORSCHACH
1884–1922

As a Swiss schoolboy, Rorschach was called "Klek" ("Inkblot") because he was always drawing. He later devised the inkblot test, whereby responses to specific blots may reveal emotional, character, and thought disorders. He died aged 37, a year after his "form interpretation test" *Psychodiagnostics* (1921) was published. Others later developed the test, but this gave rise to four different methods, each flawed. In 1993, American John Exner united them all in the Comprehensive System—one of the most enduring psychoanalytical experiments.
See also: Alfred Binet 50–53 ▪ Sigmund Freud 92–99 ▪ Carl Jung 102–107

CLARK L. HULL
1884–1952

American Clark Leonard Hull's early studies included psychometrics and hypnosis. He published *Aptitude Testing* (1929) and *Hypnosis and Suggestibility* (1933). Informed by his objective behaviorist approach, Hull's *Mathematico-Deductive Theory of Rote Learning* (1940) measured all behavior (including animal) by a single mathematical equation. He developed the theory in *Principles of Behavior* (1943), which examined the effects of reinforcement on the stimulus-response connection. His Global Theory of Behavior was one of the standard systems of psychological research at the time.
See also: Jean-Martin Charcot 30 ▪ Alfred Binet 50-53 ▪ Ivan Pavlov 60–61 ▪ Edward Thorndike 62–65

SABINA SPIELREIN
1885–1942

One of the first female psychoanalysts, Spielrein worked closely with both Carl Jung and Sigmund Freud and is known for introducing the idea of the death instinct, as well as her study of schizophrenia. She was

born in Rostov-on-Don, Russia, but following a mental breakdown aged 18, she went to Switzerland for treatment, where she was a patient of Carl Jung. Following her recovery, Spielrein assisted Jung (they later became more intimate) and studied psychiatry in Zurich. Her work brought her into contact with Freud, and later the developmental psychologist Jean Piaget in Vienna. She returned to Russia in 1923, but was murdered during the German invasion of Rostov-on-Don in 1942.
See also: Carl Jung 102–107 ▪ Sigmund Freud 92–99 ▪ Jean Piaget 270–277 ▪ Lev Vygotsky 278

TSURUKO HARAGUCHI
1886–1915

Frustrated by the lack of recognition of women's colleges and universities in Japan, Haraguchi graduated from the Japan Women's University in 1906 but could not be awarded a degree, so she moved to New York to study for her doctorate in psychology. Supervised by Edward Thorndike, she gained a PhD in 1912 for her experimental research into mental fatigue, becoming the first Japanese woman to attain a PhD in any field. She returned to Japan, where she died of tuberculosis aged only 29.
See also: Hermann Ebbinghaus 48–49 ▪ Edward Thorndike 62–65

EDWIN BORING
1886–1968

One of the most important figures in experimental psychology, Boring specialized in human sensory and perceptual systems. His interpretation of W. E. Hill's reversible old woman/young maid drawing led to it becoming known as the Boring Figure. At Harvard in the 1920s, Boring moved the psychology department away from psychiatry, turning it into a rigorously scientific school that unified structuralism and behaviorism. His first book, *A History of Experimental Psychology* (1929), was followed by *Sensation and Perception in the History of Experimental Psychology* (1942).
See also: Wilhelm Wundt 32–37 ▪ Edward B. Titchener 340

FREDERIC BARTLETT
1886–1969

Cambridge University's first Professor of Experimental Psychology (1931–1951), Bartlett is known for his memory experiments: participants were asked to read an unfamiliar, mythical story composed by Bartlett (such as *The War of the Ghosts*) before retelling it. Many added details that were not in the original story or changed meanings to fit their own specific culture. Bartlett concluded that they were not remembering, but rather reconstructing the text.
See also: Endel Tulving 186–191 ▪ Gordon H. Bower 194–195 ▪ W. H. R. Rivers 340

CHARLOTTE BÜHLER
1893–1974

German-born Bühler founded the Vienna Institute of Psychology in 1922 with her husband Karl. Her studies of childhood personality and cognitive development expanded to include adult life, too, proposing four stages of life rather than Jung's three: birth–15, 16–25, 26–45, and 46–65. Bühler found links between adult emotions and early childhood. Her "world test" is a therapeutic device that uses a set of numbered miniatures to reveal a child's inner emotional world. After publishing *From Birth to Maturity* (1935) and *From Childhood to Old Age* (1938), she moved to the US. In the 1960s, Bühler helped develop humanistic psychology.
See also: Carl Rogers 130–137 ▪ Abraham Maslow 138–139 ▪ Viktor Frankl 140 ▪ Gordon Allport 312–319

DAVID WECHSLER
1896–1981

During World War I, Wechsler, a Romanian-born American, worked as an army psychologist alongside Edward Thorndike and Charles Spearman, administering the Army Alpha Test for group intelligence. He later developed Binet's tests, adding nonverbal reasoning. Wechsler believed intelligence lies not only in the ability to think rationally, but also in the ability to act purposefully and to deal effectively with one's environment. In 1939, the Wechsler-Bellevue Intelligence Scale was published, followed a decade later by the Wechsler Intelligence Scale for Children (1949). The Wechsler Adult Intelligence Scale (1955) is still the most widely used intelligence test.
See also: Francis Galton 28–29 ▪ Alfred Binet 50–53 ▪ David C. McClelland 328–329

NANCY BAYLEY
1899–1994

Nancy Bayley, an eminent American child developmental psychologist, specialized in the measurement of motor and intellectual development. For her doctorate, she measured fear in children by analyzing the sympathetic nervous system via

moisture levels in sweat glands. Her Bayley Scales of Mental and Motor Development (1969) remains the worldwide standard measure of mental and physical development in infants from one to 42 months.
See also: Edwin Guthrie 74 ▪ Simon Baron-Cohen 347

MILTON ERICKSON
1901–1980

Nevada-born Erickson's trial-and-error observations of hypnosis over many years led him to become a world authority on hypnosis and trance. He is well known for his Ericksonian Handshake that induces a trance by confusing the mind with a moment of "behavioral void" as the flow of the handshake is interrupted. Considered the founder of hypnotherapy treatment, Erickson was also a major influence on the growth of family therapy; solution-focused therapy; systemic therapy; and a number of brief-therapy treatments, including NLP (neuro-linguistic programming).
See also: B. F. Skinner 78–85 ▪ Stanley Milgram 252–259

ALEXANDER LURIA
1902–1977

Born in Kazan, Russia, Luria studied at Moscow's Institute of Psychology. His work on reaction times and thought processes resulted in his "combined motor method" and the first ever lie-detector machine. He then specialized in neurology, making breakthroughs in brain damage, memory loss, perception, and aphasia (language disorders). The stories he told in books such as *The Man with a Shattered World: The History of a Brain Wound* (1972) helped popularize neurology.
See also: Sigmund Freud 92–99 ▪ B. F. Skinner 78–85 ▪ Noam Chomsky 302–305

DANIEL LAGACHE
1903–1972

French forensics and criminology expert Daniel Lagache was inspired to study experimental psychology, psychopathology, and phenomenology by the lectures of Georges Dumas. Expelled from the International Psychoanalytical Association in 1953 for his criticism of Sacha Nacht's medical authoritarianism, Lagache set up the breakaway French Society of Psychoanalysis with Jacques Lacan. A Freudian theorist, Lagache also popularized psychoanalysis among the general public, particularly by linking it with clinical experience. His key books included *Jealousy* (1947) and *Pathological Mourning* (1956).
See also: Jacques Lacan 122–123

ERNEST R. HILGARD
1904–2001

In the 1950s, Ernest Ropiequet "Jack" Hilgard and his wife Josephine collaborated on pioneering hypnosis studies at Stanford University, where they founded the Laboratory of Hypnosis Research in 1957. There, with André Muller Weitzenhoffer, Hilgard developed the *Stanford Hypnotic Susceptibility Scales* (1959). His controversial neodissociation theory and the "hidden-observer effect" (1977)—which asserts that under hypnosis, several subsystem states of consciousness are regulated by an executive control system—have stood the test of time, as have his books *Conditioning and Learning* (with D. G. Marquis, 1940) and *Introduction to Psychology* (1953).
See also: Ivan Pavlov 60–61 ▪ Leon Festinger 166–169 ▪ Eleanor E. Maccoby 292–293

GEORGE KELLY
1905–1967

Kelly made an important contribution to the psychology of personality through *The Psychology of Personal Constructs* (1955). His humanistic idea suggests that individuals make their own personalities through their cognitive appraisal of events. From this theory came the "role construct repertory test," which is used to research and diagnose the nature of personality. Valued in cognitive psychology and counseling, it is also used in organizational behavior and educational studies.
See also: Johann Friedrich Herbart 24–25 ▪ Carl Rogers 130–137 ▪ Ulric Neisser 345

MUZAFER SHERIF
1906–1988

Raised in Türkiye, Sherif gained his PhD in the US at Columbia with a dissertation on how social factors can influence perception. Published as *The Psychology of Social Norms* (1936), it became known as "the autokinetic effect" experiments. One of Sherif's legacies was combining successfully experimental methods in the laboratory and the field. He worked with his wife, Carolyn Wood Sherif, notably on the Robbers Cave Experiment (1954). In this, a number of boy campers were divided into two groups. Posing as a janitor, Sherif observed the origins of prejudice, conflict, and stereotype in social groups. His resulting Realistic

Conflict theory still underpins our understanding of group behavior. With Carl Havland, he also developed the Social Judgment theory (1961).
See also: Solomon Asch 228–231 ▪ Philip Zimbardo 260–261

NEAL MILLER
1909–2002

American psychologist Miller studied in Vienna under Anna Freud and Heinz Hartman. After reading K. M. Bykov's *The Cerebral Cortex and the Internal Organs* (1954), he set out to prove that internal organs and their functions could be manipulated at will. His work led to the treatment technique of Biofeedback, which aims to improve patients' conditions by training them to respond to signals from their own bodies.
See also: Anna Freud 111 ▪ Albert Bandura 294–299

ERIC BERNE
1910–1970

Canadian Eric Berne developed the theory of transactional analysis, which put verbal communication at the center of psychotherapy. The words of the first speaker, the Agent, were a Transaction Stimulus; the Respondent's reply was a Transaction Response. Every personality was split into alter-egos: child, adult, and parent; each stimulus and response was seen as playing one of these "parts." Exchanges were studied as an "I do something to you, and you do something back" transactional analysis. His *Games People Play* (1964) suggested that individuals' "games," or behavior patterns, can indicate hidden feelings or emotions.
See also: Erik Erikson 280–281 ▪ David C. McClelland 328–329

ROGER W. SPERRY
1913–1994

American neurobiologist Sperry's successful separation of the corpus callosum—the bundles of nerve fibers that transfer signals between left and right brain hemispheres—led to a dramatic breakthrough in the treatment of a certain kind of epilepsy. In 1981, with David Hubel and Torsten Wiesel, he was awarded the Nobel Prize for Physiology and Medicine for his work on his split-brain theory, which showed that the left and right hemispheres had separate specializations.
See also: William James 38–45 ▪ Simon Baron-Cohen 347

SERGE LEBOVICI
1915–2000

Lebovici was a French Freudian who specialized in adolescent, child, and infant development, especially the bonding process between baby and mother. He is credited with introducing child psychoanalysis to France. His many books include *Psychoanalysis in France* (1980) and *International Annals of Adolescent Psychiatry* (1988).
See also: Sigmund Freud 92–99 ▪ Anna Freud 111

BRENDA MILNER
1918–

Regarded as one of the founders of neuropsychology, Milner studied psychology at Cambridge University. When her postgraduate research was disrupted by the outbreak of World War II, she worked on tests for selection of aircrew. In 1944, she married neuroscientist Peter Milner and they moved to Canada, where she studied under Donald Hebb and gained her PhD in 1952 at McGill University. There, she became a pioneer in the study of memory and cognition, and she has continued her work past her 100th birthday.
See also: Karl Lashley 76 ▪ Donald Hebb 163

MILTON ROKEACH
1918–1988

Studying how religious belief affects values and attitudes, Polish-American social psychologist Rokeach saw values as core motivations and mental transformations of basic psychological needs. His theory of dogmatism examined the cognitive characteristics of closed- and open-mindedness (*The Open and Closed Mind*, 1960). Rokeach's Dogmatism Scale, an ideology- and content-free way to measure closed-mindedness, is still used, and the Rokeach Value Survey is viewed as one of the most effective ways of measuring beliefs and values in particular groups. In *The Great American Values Test*, Rokeach *et al* measured changes in opinions to prove that television could alter people's values.
See also: Leon Festinger 166–169 ▪ Solomon Asch 228–231 ▪ Albert Bandura 294–299

RENE DIATKINE
1918–1997

Diatkine, a French psychoanalyst and psychiatrist, was central to the development of dynamic psychiatry. He emphasized emotions and their underlying thought processes rather than observable behavior. Also very active in developing institutional mental health, he helped set up *The*

Association De Santé Mentale in 1958. His book on primal fantasies, *Precocious Psychoanalysis* (with Janine Simon, 1972), is a key work.
See also: Anna Freud 111 ▪ Jacques Lacan 122–123

PAUL MEEHL
1920–2003

The work of American Paul Meehl has had a lasting impact on mental health and research methodology. In *Clinical Versus Statistical Prediction: A Theoretical Analysis and a Review of the Evidence* (1954), he held that behavioral statistics were better examined via mathematical methods rather than clinical analysis. In 1962, he found a genetic link to schizophrenia, which until then had been attributed to poor parenting. In *The Determinism-Freedom and Mind-Body Problems* (with Herbert Feigl, 1974), he published his studies of determinism and free will focusing on quantum indeterminacy.
See also: B. F. Skinner 78–85 ▪ David Rosenhan 334–335

HAROLD H. KELLEY
1921–2003

American social psychologist Kelley gained his PhD under Kurt Lewin at the Massachusetts Institute of Technology. His first major work, *Communication and Persuasion* (with Hovland & Janis, 1953), split a communication into three parts: "who," "says what," and "to whom." Widely adopted, the idea changed the way people such as politicians presented themselves. Collaborating with John Thibaut, he wrote *The Social Psychology of Groups* (1959), followed by *Interpersonal Relations: A Theory of Interdependence* (1978).
See also: Leon Festinger 166–169 ▪ Kurt Lewin 222–227 ▪ Noam Chomsky 302–305

STANLEY SCHACHTER
1922–1997

New York–born Schachter is best known, with Jerome Singer, for the two-factor theory of emotion (the Schachter-Singer Theory). The pair showed that physical sensations are linked to emotions—for example, the way in which people experience increased heartbeat and muscle tension before feeling afraid—and that cognition is affected by an individual's physiological state.
See also: William James 38–45 ▪ Leon Festinger 166–169

HEINZ HECKHAUSEN
1926–1988

German psychologist Heckhausen was a world expert on motivational psychology. After a postdoctoral dissertation on hopes and fears of success and failure, his early work on childhood motivational development led to the Advanced Cognitive Model of Motivation (Heckhausen & Rheinberg, 1980). His book *Motivation and Action* (1980), co-authored with his psychologist daughter Jutta, has had a lasting influence.
See also: Zing-Yang Kuo 75 ▪ Albert Bandura 294–299 ▪ Simon Baron-Cohen 347

ANDRE GREEN
1927–2012

In the 1950s, Egyptian-born French psychoanalyst André Green became interested in communications theory and cybernetics as an intern for Jacques Lacan. He later became a harsh critic of Lacan who, he said, put too much emphasis on symbolic and structural form, invalidating his Freudian claims. In the late 1960s, Green returned to the Freudian roots of analysis with an exploration of the negative—most elegantly expressed in his paper *The Dead Mother* (1980), in which the mother is psychologically dead to the child, but, as she is still there, confuses and frightens him.
See also: Sigmund Freud 92–99 ▪ Donald Winnicott 118–121 ▪ Jacques Lacan 122–123 ▪ Françoise Dolto 287

ULRIC NEISSER
1928–2012

The best-known book by German-American Neisser is *Cognitive Psychology* (1967), which outlines a psychological approach focused on mental processes. He later criticized cognitive psychology, feeling that it had neglected the role of perception. He led the American Psychological Association task force "Intelligence, Knowns and Unknowns" in 1995, which explored intelligence testing. His papers were published as *The Rising Curve: Long-Term Gains in IQ and Related Measures* (1998).
See also: George Armitage Miller 170–173 ▪ Donald Broadbent 178–185

JEROME KAGAN
1929–2021

Kagan, a leading American figure in developmental psychology, believed that physiology had more influence on psychological characteristics than the environment. His work on the biological aspects of childhood development—apprehension and fear-revealed effects on self-

consciousness, morality, memory, and symbolism—laid foundations for research on the physiology of temperament. His work influenced studies of behavior in fields far beyond psychology, including crime, education, sociology, and politics.
See also: Sigmund Freud 92–99 ▪ Jean Piaget 270–277

MICHAEL RUTTER
1933–2021

British psychiatrist Michael Rutter changed our understanding of child development issues and behavior problems. In *Maternal Deprivation Reassessed* (1972), he rejected John Bowlby's selective attachment theory, showing that multiple attachments in childhood were normal. His later research revealed a split between deprivation (a loss of something) and privation (never having had something) and linked antisocial behavior to family discord rather than maternal deprivation.
See also: John Bowlby 282–285 ▪ Simon Baron-Cohen 347

ANNE TREISMAN
1935–2018

Graduating with degrees in French and psychology from Cambridge University, British psychologist Treisman gained a DPhil at Oxford University for her thesis on "Attention and speech." Working at Oxford for the Psycholinguistics Research Unit, she developed her Attenuation Theory, which built on the selective listening work of Donald Broadbent. With Garry Gelade, she published a paper on Feature Integration Theory. She moved to the US in 1986, where, with her second husband Daniel Kahneman, she ran the Attention Lab at the University of California, Berkeley, and later joined Princeton University's Psychology Department.
See also: Donald Broadbent 178–185 ▪ Daniel Kahneman 193 ▪ Chabris & Simons 216–217

RICHARD NISBETT
1941–

Best known for his influential paper "Telling more than we can know: Verbal reports on mental processes" (with T. D. Wilson), American social psychologist Nisbett is Director of the Culture and Cognition program at the University of Michigan, Ann Arbor. He studied under Stanley Schachter at Columbia University, and since gaining his doctorate has conducted research in the field of cognition. His books include *The Geography of Thought: How Asians and Westerners Think Differently … And Why* (2003) and *Intelligence and How to Get It: Why Schools and Cultures Count* (2009).
See also: Martin Seligman 200–201 ▪ Stanley Schachter 345

JOHN D. TEASDALE
1944–

British psychologist Teasdale explored cognitive approaches to depression. With Zindel Segal and Mark Williams, he developed Mindfulness-Based Cognitive Therapy (MBCT). This combines cognitive therapy with mindfulness and Eastern meditation techniques, asking patients with recurrent major depression to engage with negative thoughts intentionally rather than automatically and to observe them from a more detached perspective.
See also: Aaron Beck 174–177 ▪ Gordon H. Bower 194–195

FRIEDEMANN SCHULZ VON THUN
1944–

German psychologist Friedemann Schulz von Thun is famous for his Communication Model, published in the three-volume *To Talk With Each Other* (1981, 1989, 1998). Von Thun says there are four levels of communication in every part of a conversation: speaking factually; making a statement about ourselves; commenting on our relationship to the other person; or asking the other person to do something. He says that when people speak and listen on different levels, misunderstandings occur.
See also: B. F. Skinner 78–85 ▪ Kurt Lewin 222–227

SHELLEY TAYLOR
1946–

A prominent figure in the fields of social cognition, health psychology, and social neuroscience, American Shelley Taylor began her academic career at Harvard, after postgraduate study at Yale. At Harvard, she focused on social cognition but also became interested in what is now known as health psychology. As the Harvard medical school was far from the main campus, however, to follow up on this, she moved to the University of California, Los Angeles, where she is now a professor of psychology. She is best known for the book *Social Cognition* (co-authored with Susan Fiske in 1984) and for the development of her "tend and befriend" model of response to stress (especially in women) in contrast to the "fight-or-flight response."
See also: Daniel Kahneman 193 ▪ Richard Nisbett 346

VINDHYA UNDURTI
1955–

While studying at Andhra University for her PhD (1985), Indian feminist psychologist Undurti became involved with human rights activism and women's rights, particularly in India. Before joining the faculty of the Tata Institute of Social Sciences (TISS) in Hyderabad in 2010, her career included a Visiting Scholarship at Oxford University and a Fulbright Visiting Lecturer Fellowship. Now Professor of Psychology in the School of Gender Studies at TISS, her work is focused on the effects of strict gender roles and power structures on issues such as domestic abuse and women's mental health.
See also: Janet Taylor Spence 242 ▪ Eleanor Maccoby 292–293

SIMON BARON-COHEN
1958–

British clinical psychologist Simon Baron-Cohen is known for his interest in autism. He is the Director of the Autism Research Centre at Cambridge University, where he is professor of developmental psychopathology. In the 1980s, he developed the mindblindness theory of autism, and later the prenatal sex steroid theory for the condition. More recently, he has proposed a theory of empathizing–systemizing (E–S), contrasting the differences between typical "female" and "male" brains, arguing that autistic people are more likely to have extreme systematizing, "male" brains. Baron-Cohen also devised the autism-spectrum quotient, a means of measuring the signs of autism.
See also: Jerome Kagan 345–346 ▪ Michael Rutter 346

PATTI VALKENBURG
1958–

Dutch communication scientist Patti Valkenburg is a Distinguished Professor of Communication at the University of Amsterdam, with a special interest in the cognitive, emotional, and social effects of the media on young people in particular. Her research has been into all forms of media, but especially on social media, and the influence of violence, advertising, and pornography. In 2005, Valkenburg founded the Center for Research on Children, Adolescents, and the Media, based in Amsterdam University, bringing together researchers from the social and behavioral sciences. For her work in this field, she has been given an Advanced Investigator grant from the European Research Council and awarded the Spinoza Prize.
See also: Albert Bandura 294–299 ▪ Serge Moscovici 244–245

GIULIO TONONI
1960–

A key figure in the field of research into sleep and consciousness, Italian neuroscientist and psychiatrist Tononi studied at the Sant'Anna School of Advanced Studies in Pisa, and is now David P. White Chair in Sleep Medicine at the University of Wisconsin and a Distinguished Chair in Consciousness Science. In 2004, he proposed his Integrated Information Theory, an explanation of consciousness and different brain states and how these can be observed and measured using modern imaging techniques and computer models.
See also: William James 38–45 ▪ Colin Blakemore 211

PIA LAMBERTY
1984–

German social psychologist Pia Lamberty first studied literature and philosophy before joining the University of Cologne's Social Cognition Center as a research assistant in 2015. The following year, she went to the University of Mainz to research for a PhD on conspiracy ideologies, and in 2020 co-authored (with Katharina Nocun) a book on the causes of conspiracy theories titled *Fake Facts—Wie Verschwörungstheorien unser Denken bestimmen* (*Fake Facts—How Conspiracy Theories Influence Our Thinking*). Lamberty is also a co-founder and CEO of an extremism monitoring agency in Berlin, the Center for Monitoring, Analysis, and Strategy.
See also: Leon Festinger 166–169 ▪ Irving Janis 234–235

SARA ERREYGERS
1989–

Belgian clinical psychologist Sara Erreygers graduated in Primary Care Psychology at the University of Leuven in 2014, and was awarded her doctorate in Communication Sciences and Psychology at the universities of Antwerp and Leuven four years later for her research centered on the online social behavior of adolescents and the part that emotions play in it. She is now based in Antwerp at the Student Counseling and Study Advice Services, where she is continuing her research into the mental health of students at the university.
See also: Albert Bandura 294–299 ▪ Albert Nico Frijda 330–331

GLOSSARY

Anecdotal method The use of observational (often unscientific) reports as research data.

Archetypes In Carl Jung's theory, the inherited patterns or frameworks within the **collective unconscious** that act to organize our experiences. Archetypes often feature in myths and narratives.

Association *i)* A philosophical explanation for the formation of knowledge, stating that it results from the linking or association of simple ideas to form complex ideas. *ii)* A link between two psychological processes, formed as a result of their pairing in past experience.

Associationism An approach that claims that inborn or acquired neural links bind stimuli and responses together, resulting in distinct patterns of behavior.

Attachment An emotionally important relationship in which one individual seeks proximity to and derives security from the presence of another, particularly infants to parental figures.

Attention A collective term for the processes used in selective, focused perception.

Autism The informal term for autistic spectrum disorder (ASD)—a cluster of mental conditions that is characterized by difficulties with communication, interpretation of social interactions, recognition and regulation of emotions, and coping with change and anxiety.

Behavior modification The use of proven behavior change techniques to control or modify the behavior of individuals or groups.

Behaviorism A psychological approach that insists that only observable behavior should form the object of study, as this can be witnessed, described, and measured in objective terms.

Central traits In Gordon Allport's theory, the six or so main personality traits that are used to describe a person, such as "shy" or "good natured." These are the "building blocks" of personality.

Classical conditioning A type of learning in which a neutral stimulus acquires the capacity to trigger a particular response by becoming paired with an unconditional stimulus.

Cognitive To do with mental processes, such as perception, memory, or thinking.

Cognitive dissonance An inconsistency between beliefs or feelings, which leads to a state of tension.

Cognitive psychology A psychological approach that focuses on the mental processes involved in learning and knowing and how the mind actively organizes experiences.

Cognitive style The habitual way in which an individual processes information.

Collective unconscious In Carl Jung's theory, the deepest level of the psyche, which contains inherited psychic dispositions through the **archetypes**.

Conditioned response (CR) A particular response elicited by an initially neutral stimulus that has been paired with an **unconditioned stimulus**, which naturally provokes that response.

Conditioned stimulus (CS) In classical conditioning, a stimulus that comes to elicit a particular (conditioned) response by virtue of having been paired with an **unconditional stimulus**.

Contiguity The close occurrence of two ideas or events. This is thought to be necessary for **association**.

Control group Participants in an experiment who are not exposed to the manipulation of the researchers during an experiment.

Correlation A statistical term for the tendency of two data sets or variables to vary in a similar way in a certain set of circumstances. It is often mistaken for causation.

Crystallized intelligence The collected skills, cognitive abilities, and strategies acquired through the use of fluid intelligence. It is said to increase with age.

Defense mechanisms In psychoanalytic theory, mental reactions that occur to ward off anxiety by unconscious means.

Depression A mood disorder characterized by feelings of hopelessness and low self-worth, accompanied by apathy and loss of pleasure. In extreme cases, depression may impair normal functioning and can lead to thoughts of suicide.

Desensitize A process of weakening a strong response to an event or thing by repeated exposure to that stimulus.

Determinism The doctrine that all events, acts, and choices are determined by past events or previously existing causes.

Dichotic listening Listening to two different messages that are presented simultaneously, one to each ear.

Ego A psychoanalytic term for one of three elements of the human persona (see also **id**, **superego**). The ego is the rational aspect of personality that is in touch with the outer world and its requirements and is responsible for controlling the instincts.

Empiricism A philosophical and psychological approach that assigns the attribution of all knowledge to experience.

Encoding The processing of sensory information into memory.

Ethology The scientific study of animal behavior under natural conditions.

Extinction *i)* The elimination of something, especially a species. *ii)* The weakening of a strength of response in conditioned learning due to a lack of reinforcement.

Extraversion A personality type that focuses energy primarily toward the external world and other people (see also **introversion**).

False memory A recovered memory or pseudomemory of an event that did not take place. It is thought to arise through suggestion.

Family therapy A general term denoting therapies that treat a whole family rather than one person, on the assumption that problems lie in the interrelationships within the family system.

Field theory Kurt Lewin's model of human behavior, which uses the concept of force fields to explain the "life space" or field of social influences around an individual.

Fluid intelligence The ability to deal with totally new problems. It is said to decrease with age.

Free association A technique used in psychotherapy in which the patient says the first thing that comes to mind after any given word.

Freudian slip An act or word that is close but different to the one consciously intended and reflects unconscious motives or anxieties.

Functionalism A psychological approach that is concerned with investigating the adaptive functions of the mind in relation to its environment.

Fundamental attribution error The tendency to explain other people's behavior by reference to personality traits rather than external situational factors.

General intelligence ("g") As defined by Charles Spearman, a general factor of intelligence or ability determined through the correlation of scores on various mental tests; Spearman saw it as a measurement of mental energy, but others view it as an individual's abstract reasoning ability.

Gestalt psychology A holistic psychological approach that emphasizes the role of the organized "whole," as opposed to its parts, in mental processes such as perception.

Gestalt therapy A form of psychotherapy (unconnected with **Gestalt psychology**) developed by Fritz Perls in which clients are encouraged to be open and honest about their feelings in the present to resolve issues from the past.

Groupthink The phenomenon whereby, in decision-making, groups favor conformity rather than challenging the consensus.

Humanistic psychology A psychological approach that emphasizes the importance of free will and **self-actualization** in determining good mental health.

Hypnosis The induction of a temporary, trancelike state of heightened suggestibility.

Id A psychoanalytic term for one of three elements of the human persona (see also **ego**, **superego**). The id is the source of psychic energy and is allied with the instincts.

Imprinting In ethology, an innate system of rapid learning that takes place in animals immediately subsequent to birth. It commonly involves developing an attachment to a specific individual or object.

Inattentional blindness An inability to notice something right in front of one's eyes when one is paying attention to something else.

Individual differences All the psychological characteristics that are susceptible to variation between individuals, such as personality or intelligence.

Inferiority complex A condition suggested by Adlerian (after founder Alfred Adler) psychoanalysis that is said to develop when a person is unable to deal with real or imagined feelings of inferiority and becomes either belligerent or withdrawn.

Innate Inborn or present in an organism from birth; it may or may not be genetically inherited.

Instincts Natural drives or propensities. In psychoanalysis, these are the dynamic forces that motivate personality and behavior.

Intelligence quotient (IQ) An index of intelligence that allows people to be allocated comparative levels of intelligence. First suggested by William Stern, it is calculated by dividing an individual's mental age by their chronological age, then multiplying by 100.

Introspection The oldest method of psychology: self-observation—"looking (spection) within (intro)" one's own mind to examine and report on one's own inner state.

Introversion A personality type that focuses energy primarily toward its own internal thoughts and feelings (see also **extraversion**).

Just noticeable difference The smallest difference that can be detected by an individual between two physical stimuli.

Law of Effect Proposed by Edward Thorndike, this is the principle that, where several responses to an event are possible, those that lead to reward tend to become more strongly associated with the event, while those that lead to punishment become more weakly associated.

Materialism The doctrine that views only the physical realm as real and considers that mental phenomena are explicable through physical terms.

Mental age The age at which children of average ability can perform particular tasks, as indicated by levels of performance in standardized tests.

Mind-body problem The problem of defining the interaction of mental and physical events, first raised by René Descartes.

Negative reinforcement In instrumental or **operant conditioning**, the strengthening of a response through the removal of a negative stimulus.

Neuron A type of nerve cell involved in transmitting messages (as nerve impulses) between different parts of the brain.

Neuropsychology A sub-discipline of psychology and neurology that is concerned with the structure and function of the brain and studies the effects of brain disorders on behavior and cognition.

Nonsense syllables Syllables of three letters that do not form recognized words, first used by Hermann Ebbinghaus in a study of learning and memory.

Oedipus complex According to psychoanalytic theory, a developmental state that arises around the age of five, during which a boy experiences unconscious desire for his mother and the wish to replace or destroy his father.

Operant conditioning A form of conditioning in which the outcome depends upon an animal operating upon its environment, such as pressing a lever to obtain food.

Personality A person's stable and enduring mental and behavioral traits and characteristics, which incline them to behave in a relatively consistent way over time.

Phenomenology An approach to knowledge based on immediate experience as it occurs without any attempt to categorize it through preconceptions, assumptions, or interpretations.

Phobia An anxiety disorder characterized by intense and usually irrational fear.

Positive reinforcement A key concept in behaviorism, this is the process of increasing the probability of a response by immediately following the required response with a reward or positive stimulus.

Pragmatism The doctrine that sees ideas as rules for action. The idea's validity is measured by its practical consequences.

Psychoanalysis Sigmund Freud's set of theories and therapeutic methods, which explore the unconscious processes that influence human behavior.

Psychophysics The scientific study of the relations between mental and physical processes.

Psychosexual stages In psychoanalytic theory, the developmental stages of childhood, centering on zones of the body through which pleasure is derived.

Psychotherapy A collective term for all therapeutic treatments that use psychological rather than physical or physiological means.

Purposive behaviorism Edward Tolman's theory, which says all behavior is directed toward some ultimate goal.

Reality principle The set of rules in psychoanalysis that govern the ego and take account of the real world and its demands.

Reflex An automatic reaction to a stimulus.

Reinforcement In classical conditioning, the procedure that increases the likelihood of a response.

Replication Repetitions of research or an experiment in all details that lead to the same results. Replication is essential to establish validity of findings.

Repression In psychoanalytic theory, an ego-defense mechanism that pushes unacceptable thoughts, memories, or impulses beyond conscious awareness. Anna Freud also called it "motivated forgetting."

Retrieval Recovering information stored in the memory through a process of search and find.

Schizophrenia A group of severe mental illnesses (originally known as dementia praecox) that cause impairment in multiple areas of functioning. It is characterized by marked disturbance of thought, flat or inappropriate emotions, and distorted visions of reality.

Self-actualization The full development of one's potentialities and realization of one's potential. According to Abraham Maslow, this is the most advanced human need.

Shaping In behaviorism, shaping is the process of providing positive reinforcement for successive approximations of desired behavior.

Social learning A theory of learning based on observing the behavior of others and the consequences of those behaviors. Albert Bandura was the foremost proponent of this theory.

Stimulus Any object, event, situation, or factor in the environment that an individual can detect and respond to.

Stream of consciousness William James's description of consciousness as a continuous flowing process of thoughts.

Structuralism A psychological approach that investigates the structure of the mind.

Superego In psychoanalysis, the term for the part of the psyche that is derived from internalizing parental and societal values and standards. It is governed by moral restraints.

Trait theory The view that individual differences depend largely on underlying character attributes (traits) that remain essentially consistent across time and context.

Transference In psychoanalysis, the tendency for a patient to transfer emotional reactions from past relationships (particularly parental) onto the therapist.

Trial and error learning A theory of learning initially proposed by Edward Thorndike that claims learning occurs through the performance of several responses, with the repetition of those that produce desirable results.

Unconditional positive regard In Carl Rogers' client-centered therapy, the absolute acceptance of people purely because they are human beings.

Unconditioned response In **classical conditioning**, a reflexive (unconditioned, natural) response produced in response to a particular stimulus (e.g. moving a limb away from a painful stimulus).

Unconditioned stimulus In **classical conditioning**, a stimulus that elicits a reflexive (unconditioned, natural) response.

Unconscious In psychoanalysis, the part of the psyche that cannot be accessed by the conscious mind.

Validity The extent to which a test measures what it is supposed to measure.

Zeigarnik effect The tendency to recall incomplete or unfinished tasks more easily than completed ones.

INDEX

A

B

C

E

F

G

H

I

R

T

ACKNOWLEDGMENTS

For this edition, the publisher would like to thank Mrunali Sanjay Likhar for design assistance; Deepak Negi for picture research assistance; and Vijay Kandwal and Mohd Rizwan for DTP assistance. For their work on the first edition, the publisher thanks Shriya Parameswaran, Neha Sharma, Payal Rosalind Malik, Gadi Farfour, Helen Spencer, Steve Woosnam-Savage, and Paul Drislane for design assistance; Steve Setford for editorial assistance; and Stephanie Chilman for composing the Directory.

PICTURE CREDITS

The publisher would like to thank the following for their kind permission to reproduce their photographs:

(Key: a-above; b-below/bottom; c-centre; f-far; l-left; r-right; t-top)

19 The Bridgeman Art Library: Bibliothèque de la Faculté de Médecine, Paris / Archives Charmet (tr). **21 Corbis:** Bettmann (tr). **Getty Images:** Hulton Archive (bl). **23 akg-images:** Bibliothèque nationale (tc). **Alamy Images:** Tihon L1 (bl). **25 Getty Images:** Hulton Archive (tr). **27 akg-images:** Coll. Archiv f. Kunst & Geschichte (tl). **Corbis:** Bettmann (bl). **29 The Bridgeman Art Library:** Birmingham Museums and Art Gallery (bc). **Getty Images:** Hulton Archive (tr). **30 Getty Images:** Imagno / Hulton Archive (br). **35 Alamy Images:** Interfoto (br). **Corbis:** Visuals Unlimited (tc). **36 Corbis:** Bettmann (tr, tc). **37 Corbis:** Bettmann (bl). **40 Corbis:** (bl). **43 Corbis:** The Gallery Collection. **44 Corbis:** Underwood & Underwood (br). **45 Science Photo Library:** Chris Gallagher (tr). **47 Corbis:** Bettmann (tr). **49 Corbis:** Bettmann (bl); **Shutterstock.com:** Ground Picture (tr). **51 Science Photo Library:** US National Library of Medicine (tr). **52 Corbis:** Bettmann (bl). **55 Alamy Images:** Eddie Gerald (cr). **Lebrecht Music and Arts:** Rue des Archives / Varma (bl). **61 Corbis:** Bettmann (bl). **LawtonPhotos.com :** (tl). **65 Corbis:** Jose Luis Pelaez, Inc. (tl). **Science Photo Library:** Humanities and Social Sciences Library / New York Public Library (tr). **69 Corbis:** Underwood & Underwood (bl). **70 123RF.com:** Dolgachov (br). **71 The Advertising Archives:** (br). **73 Corbis:** Sandy Stockwell / Skyscan (cr). **Magnum Photos:** Wayne Miller (bl). **75 The Advertising Archives:** (cra). **77 Getty Images:** Nina Leen / Time & Life Pictures (br). **81 Getty Images:** Nina Leen / Time & Life Pictures (br). **82 Getty Images:** Joe Raedle (br). **83 Corbis:** Bettmann (tr). **84 Alamy Images:** Monashee Frantz (bl). **87 Alamy Stock Photo:** Lenar Nigmatullin (tr). **94 Getty Images:** Imagno / Hulton Archive / Sigmund Freud Privatstiftung (tr). **97 Alamy Images:** Bjanka Kadic (bl). **98 The Bridgeman Art Library:** Museum of Modern Art, New York / © Salvador Dali, Fundació Gala-Salvador Dalí, DACS, 2011. **99 Corbis:** Hulton-Deutsch Collection (tr). **101 Corbis:** Guo Dayue / Xinhua Press (tl). **Getty Images:** Imagno / Hulton Archive (tr). **105 Getty Images:** Imagno / Hulton Archive (br). **106 Getty Images:** Apic / Hulton Archive (bl). **107 akg-images:** Walt Disney Productions (tl). **Getty Images:** Imagno / Hulton Archive (tr). **108 Alamy Stock Photo:** GRANGER - Historical Picture Archive (cr). **109 Wellcome Images:** (bl). **116 Corbis:** Robert Wallis (tl). **117 Alamy Stock Photo:** 2checkingout (tl). **Science Photo Library:** National Library of Medicine (bl). **119 Getty Images:** Hulton Archive (tr). **120 Alamy Stock Photo:** Image Professionals GmbH (br). **121 Getty Images / iStock:** Prostock-Studio (tr). **123 Getty Images:** Ryan McVay (tl). **Lebrecht Music and Arts:** Rue des Archives / Collection Bourgeron (bl). **127 Corbis:** Michael Reynolds / EPA (tr). **129 Getty Images:** Leonard Mccombe / Time & Life Pictures (tr); Roger-Viollet (bl). **134 Corbis:** Pascal Deloche / Godong (tl). **135 Getty Images:** David Malan / Photographer's Choice (tr). **136 Corbis:** Roger Ressmeyer (bl). **137 Getty Images / iStock:** dmbaker (tl). **139 Corbis:** Ann Kaplan (tr). **144 Getty Images:** paul mansfield photography (tr). **147 Alamy Stock Photo:** Rick Laing (cla/Man). **Getty Images / iStock:** E+ / Izusek (ca/Girl); Ranta Images (cla); **Getty Images:** Westend61 (ca); **Corbis:** Larry Williams (tr/placator). **148 Getty Images:** Dennis Hallinan (b). **151 Corbis:** Allen Ginsberg (tr); Robbie Jack (bl). **153 Getty Images:** Miguel Medina / AFP (tr); Toru Yamanaka / AFP (tl). **155 Alamy Images:** Sigrid Olsson / PhotoAlto (cra). **161 TopFoto.co.uk:** Topham Picturepoint (tl, tr). **162 Getty Images / iStock:** E+ / Portra (cb). **165 Press Association Images:** (tr). **167 Science Photo Library:** Estate of Francis Bello (bl). **168 Alamy Stock Photo:** NASA Pictures (b). **169 Alamy Stock Photo:** Gado Images / Smith Collection (cb). **173 Corbis:** William Whitehurst (tl). **Jon Roemer:** (tr). **175 Beck Institute for Cognitive Behavior Therapy:** (tr). **176 Corbis:** Bettmann (br). **181 Alamy Images:** David O. Bailey (tl). **Science Photo Library:** Corbin O'Grady Studio (tr). **182 Corbis:** Carol Kohen (bl). **184 Getty Images / iStock:** E+ / AzmanL (b). **185 Dreamstime.com:** Natpol Rodbang (tr). **190 Getty Images / iStock:** Stockbyte / Comstock Images (tl); **Courtesy of Baycrest:** (bl). **192 Corbis:** Owaki/ Kulla (cra). **195 Alamy Stock Photo:** AlessandroBiascioli (tr). **197 Getty Images:** Steven Dewall / Redferns (bl). **199 Claremont Graduate University:** Photo by C. Sajgó (bl). **Corbis:** Charles Vlen / Bettmann (tl). **201 Getty Images:** Purestock (bc). **Positive Psychology Center, University of Pennsylvania. :** (tr). **204 Courtesy of UC Irvine:** (bl). **207 Getty Images / iStock:** IPGGutenbergUKLtd (bl). **210 Alamy Images:** Michele Burgess (cb). **211 Getty Images / iStock:** E+ / JaCZhou (cr). **212 Getty Images / iStock:** JTGrafix (cra).**214 Shutterstock.com:** Moviestore (bc). **215 University of Bath:** (tr). **217 Dreamstime.com:** Maksim Marchanka (bl). **225 Getty Images:** Chris Ryan / OJO Images (tr). **226 Corbis:** Moment / Cultura (bc). **227 Alamy Images:** Interfoto (bl). **Corbis:** K.J. Historical (tl). **229 Solomon Asch Center for Study of Ethnopolitical Conflict:** (tr). **231 Corbis:** Bettmann (bl). **233 American Sociological Association, www.asanet.org. :** Photo of Erving Goffman (bl). **Corbis:** Yi Lu (cr). **234 Alamy Stock Photo:** Wavebreakmedia Ltd PH87 (cr). **240 Corbis:** Claro Cortes / Hanoi, Vietnam (tl). **241 Corbis:** Hannes Hepp (bc). **Stanford News Service:** Linda A. Cicero (tr). **243 Corbis:** Walt Sisco / Bettmann (cr). **245 Corbis:** Sophie Bassouls / Sygma (bl). **247 The Bridgeman Art Library:** Musée national des arts et traditions populaires, Paris / Archives Charmet (tc). **William Glasser Inc. - www.wglasserbooks.com:** (tr). **249 Dreamstime.com:** Stanislav Vershinin (tl). **University of Waterloo:** Maurice Greene (bl). **251 Corbis:** Bettmann (bl). **255 Getty Images:** Apic / Hulton Archive (tr). **Alamy Stock Photo:**

INTERFOTO / Personalities (bl). **257 Getty Images:** Peter Stackpole / Time & Life Pictures (br). **258 Corbis:** Stapleton Collection (br). **259 Alamy Stock Photo:** Sipa US (tl). **261 Alamy Stock Photo:** Everett Collection Inc / © IFC Films (tl). **Philip G. Zimbardo, Professor Emeritus, Stanford University:** (tr). **263 Alamy Stock Photo:** Joseph Sibilsky (cr). **265 Universidad Centroamericana "José Simeón Cañas" (UCA), El Salvador:** (bl). **273 Corbis:** The Gallery Collection (tc). **275 Science Photo Library:** Bill Anderson (bl). **276 Corbis:** Bettmann (bl). **277 Alamy Images:** Thomas Cockrem (br). **279 Corbis:** Jerry Cooke (cr). **281 Corbis:** Ted Streshinsky (tr). **Getty Images:** Jose Luis Pelaez / Iconica (bc). **284 Corbis:** Hulton-Deutsch Collection (tr). **285 Richard Bowlby:** (bl). **Getty Images:** Lawrence Migdale (tr). **286 Science Photo Library:** Photo Researchers (cr). **289 Corbis:** Tim Page (tr). **290 Library Of Congress, Washington, D.C.:** Gordon Parks (cr). **291 Shutterstock.com:** Granger (tr). **293 Corbis:** Bob Thomas (tc). **Special Collections, Eric V. Hauser Memorial Library, Reed College, Portland, Oregon:** (bl). **297 Getty Images:** The Chronicle Collection / Jon Brenneis (cra). **298 Alamy Stock Photo:** Veronica Lorine (tr). **299 Alamy Stock Photo:** Associated Press / Carolyn Kaster (tr). **301 Corbis:** Bettmann (tr). **304 Corbis:** Christopher Felver (bl). **305 Corbis:** Frans Lanting (br); **Alamy Stock Photo:** Sally and Richard Greenhill (tl). **311 Getty Images:** Stan Munro / Barcroft Media (tl). **318 Getty Images:** MPI / Archive Photos (tl). **319 Corbis:** Bettmann (tr). **321 Courtesy of the University of Illinois Archives:** Image 0000950. Found in RS: 39/1/11, Box 12, Folder Raymond B. Cattell (bl). **326 Corbis:** Bettmann (bl). **327 Getty Images:** Universal History Archive/ Hulton Archive (tl). **Mary Evans Picture Library:** John Cutten (tr). **329 Harvard University :** Jane Reed / Harvard News Office (tr). **Science Photo Library:** Van D. Bucher (bc). **331 Getty Images:** Universal History Archive / Hulton Archive (tr). **Dolph Kohnstamm:** (bl). **333 Corbis:** Monalyn Gracia (tc). **Courtesy of University Archives, Columbia University in the City of New York. :** Joe Pineiro / Office of Public Affairs Negatives - Box 109 (tr). **335 Corbis:** Bettmann (bl). **337 The Kobal Collection:** 20th Century Fox (tc).

For more information see:
www.dkimages.co.uk

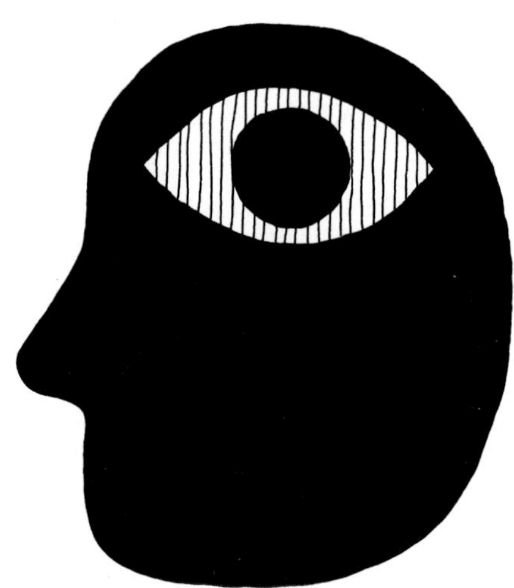